Introduction to Clinical Psychology

FIFTH EDITION

MICHAEL T. NIETZEL

University of Kentucky

DOUGLAS A. BERNSTEIN

University of Illinois

RICHARD MILICH

University of Kentucky

Prentice Hall
Upper Saddle River, New Jersey 07458

Library of Congress Cataloging-in-Publication Data

Nietzel, Michael T.

    Introduction to clinical psychology / Michael T. Nietzel, Douglas
A. Bernstein, Richard Milich. — 5th ed.

      p.   cm.

    Includes bibliographical references and index.

    ISBN 0-13-269549-9

    1. Clinical psychology. I. Bernstein, Douglas A. II. Milich,
Richard. III. Title.

      [DNLM: 1. Psychology, Clinical. WM 105 N677i 1998]

RC467.N54 1998

616.89—dc21

DNLM/DLC

for Library of Congress   97-29348

                                              CIP

Editor-in-chief: Nancy Roberts
Executive editor: Bill Webber
Editorial assistant: Tomsen Adams
Managing editor: Bonnie Biller
Production liason: Fran Russello
Project manager: Patty Donovan (Pine Tree Composition)
Prepress and manufacturing buyer: Lynn Pearlman
Cover director: Jayne Conte
Cover designer: Pat Wosczyk
Cover art: "Abstrakler Kopf" by Alexej Von Jawlensky
Director, image resource center: Lori Morris-Nantz
Photo research supervisor: Melinda Lee Reo
Image permission supervisor: Kay Dellosa
Photo researcher: Beth Boyd
Marketing manager: Michael Alread

This book was set in 10/12 Garamond Book by *Pine Tree Composition, Inc.,*
and was printed and bound by *Courier Companies, Inc.*
The cover was printed by *Phoenix Color Corp.*

© 1998, 1994, 1991, 1987 by Prentice-Hall, Inc.

Upper Saddle River, New Jersey 07458

Printed in the United States of America

10   9   8   7   6   5

ISBN: 0-13-269549-9

Prentice-Hall International (UK) Limited, *London*
Prentice-Hall of Australia Pty. Limited, *Sydney*
Prentice-Hall of Canada, Inc., *Toronto*
Prentice-Hall Hispanoamericana, S. A., *Mexico*
Prentice-Hall of India Private Limited, *New Delhi*
Prentice-Hall of Japan, Inc., *Tokyo*
Prentice-Hall Asia Pte. Ltd., *Singapore*
Editora Prentice-Hall do Brasil, Ltda., *Rio de Janeiro*

1956 Stanford Training Conference.

1958 Miami Training Conference.

Clinical Division of APA holds NIMH-sponsored conference about research on psychotherapy.

1959 The first psychotherapy benefit in a pre-paid insurance plan appears.

1965 Chicago Training Conference.

1968 Psy.D. training program begins at the University of Illinois, Urbana-Champaign.

Second edition of *Diagnostic and Statistical Manual (DSM-II)* published.

Committee on Health Insurance begins campaign to allow payment of clinical psychologists' services by health insurance plans without requiring medical supervision.

1969 California School of Professional Psychology founded.

APA begins publication of journal, *Professional Psychology.*

1970 Department of Defense health insurance program authorizes payment of clinical psychologists' services without medical referral.

Classes begin at California School of Professional Psychology, the first independent clinical psychology training program in the U.S.

1971 Council for the Advancement of Psycological Professions and Sciences, a political advocacy group for clinical psychology, is organized.

Journal of Child Clinical Psychology published.

1972 Menninger Conference on Postdoctoral Education in Clinical Psychology.

1973 Vail, Colorado, Training Conference.

1974 National Register of Health Service Providers in Psychology established.

Federal government allows payment for clinical psychologists' services to its empoyees without medical supervision or referral.

APA establishes *Standards for Providers of Psychological Services.*

First Interamerican Congress of Clinical Psychology held in Porto Alegre, Brazil.

1977 All fifty U.S. states have certification or licensing laws for clinical psychologists.

1980 Third edition of *Diagnostic and Statistical Manual (DSM-III)* published.

Smith, Glass, and Miller publish *The Benefits of Psychotherapy.*

Blue Shield health insurance companies in Virginia successfuly sued for refusing to pay for clinical psychologists' services to people covered by their plans.

1981 APA publishes its revised *Ethical Principles of Psychologists.*

1983 Joint Commission for the Accreditation of Hospitals allows clinical psychologists to become members of hospital medical staffs.

1987 *DSM-III-R* published.

Conference on graduate education in psychology, Salt Lake City, Utah.

1988 American Psychological Society formed.

1990 California Supreme Court affirms right of clinical psychologists to independently admit, diagnose, treat, and release mental patients without medical supervision.

1993 Commander John L. Sexton and Lt. Commander Morgan T. Sammons complete psychopharmacology program at Walter Reed Army Medical Center, becoming first psychologists legally permitted to perscribe psychoactive drugs.

1994 *DSM-IV* published.

Amendment to Social Security Act guarantees psychologists the right to independent practice and payment for hospital services under Medicare.

1995 APA task force of clinical psychologists publishes list of empirically validated psychological therapies and calls for students to be trained to use them.

1995 APA establishes new guidelines for the accreditation of programs in professional psychology, including clinical psychology. These guidelines reflect Shakow's original desire for flexible accreditation criteria.

1996 Dorothy W. Cantor becomes first president of APA to hold the Psy.D. degree rather than the Ph.D.

Contents

CHAPTER 2
Approaches to Clinical Psychology   36

CHAPTER 3
Assessment in Clinical Psychology   88

CHAPTER 4
Interviewing in Clinical Psychology   130

Preface

In the four earlier editions of this book, we tried to accomplish three goals. First, we wanted a book that, while appropriate for graduate students, was written especially with sophisticated undergraduates in mind. Many undergraduate psychology majors express an interest in clinical psychology without having a clear understanding of what the field involves and requires. An even larger number of nonmajors also wish to know more about clinical psychology. We felt that both groups of undergraduates would benefit from a thorough survey of the field which does not go into all the details typically found in "graduate study only" texts.

Second, we wanted to present a scholarly portrayal of the history of clinical psychology, its scope, functions, and future that reviewed a full range of theoretical perspectives. For this reason, we have not allowed our preference for cognitive-behavioral theories to limit our presentation. Instead, we present psychodynamic, phenomenological/experiential, interpersonal, and biological perspectives as well, and we have sought to do so in as neutral a manner as possible. We do champion the empirical research tradition of clinical psychology throughout the book because we believe it is a necessary and useful perspective for all clinicians to follow, regardless of their theoretical orientation.

Third, we wanted our book to be interesting and enjoyable to read. Because we like being clinical psychologists and because we enjoy teaching courses in the field, we tried to create a book that communicates our enthusiasm for its content.

Our goals for this fifth edition remain the same. However, in addition to the comprehensive updating of the content of all chapters, we have introduced some new material and reorganized our coverage of existing material somewhat. For example, we cover the latest developments in clinical diagnosis and assessment (DSM-IV, of course, and new versions of standard psychological tests). We have also strengthened our emphasis on the empirical foundations that we feel should support clinical practice, and we discuss a host of professional issues that have emerged in the last several years—including ethical standards for psychologists, the impact of new plans for funding mental health care, new forms of legal regulation over clinical psychology, proposals that would allow clinical psychologists to prescribe drugs, and the like. There is a new chapter on forensic psychology, and we now devote an entire chapter to health psychology. Finally, we have reorganized our coverage of clinical interventions into three chapters. The first offers an overview of these interventions—including individual, group, couples, and family psychotherapy, along with psychosocial rehabilitation, prevention, and community psychology programs. The second describes psychodynamic, behavioral, cognitive-behavioral, and phenomenological/experiential psychotherapy techniques, while the third covers the methods and results of research on the effectiveness of psychotherapy, psychosocial rehabilitation, and disorder-prevention.

ACKNOWLEDGMENTS

We want to thank several people for their valuable contributions to this book. Our colleagues, Dr. Stanley Badner, Adelphi University; Dr. Michael Levine, Kenyon College; Dr. Constance Dent, Kutztown University; and Dr. Louis Franzini, San Diego State University carefully read parts of the manuscript and offered many valuable suggestions for improving it. We also wish to express special appreciation to Dr. Wendy Heller for her careful updating of the chapter on neuropsychology.

Countless undergraduate and graduate students asked the questions, raised the issues, and argued the opposing positions that have found their way into the text; they are really the people who stimulated the creation of this book, and who continue to make us want to revise and update its content. We thank them all. We also want to thank Fran Russello, who coordinated production of the manuscript.

Finally, we owe our deepest appreciation to Diane Weidner and Shirley Jacobs for their invaluable assistance in coordinating the flow of chapter drafts and final manuscripts that had to find their way to and from Champaign, Illinois and Lexington, Kentucky, and on to Prentice Hall. We could not have done this new edition without you two, and we thank you very much.

MICHAEL T. NIETZEL

DOUGLAS A. BERNSTEIN

RICHARD MILICH

Chapter 1

Clinical Psychology: Definitions and History

For many years, psychology has been one of the most popular undergraduate majors at colleges and universities in the United States, and it will likely maintain this status for a long time to come (Clay, 1996; Wiggins, 1994). The latest available figures show that, in terms of the number of bachelor's degrees awarded, psychology ranks first among the arts and sciences and is second overall only to business administration (Murray, 1996). By 1993, more than 66,000 degrees were being awarded annually to undergraduate psychology majors, a figure reflecting an annual increase of about 5% per year since 1985 (U.S. Department of Education, 1995). At the graduate level, at least 3,000 Ph.D.s in psychology are awarded each year—more than in any other discipline at many universities—and by far the largest single group of psychology Ph.D.s (about 40% to 50%) are in clinical psychology (APA, 1995a).[1]

The particular appeal of clinical psychology is also reflected in the composition of the American Psychological Association (APA), the largest organization of psychologists in the United States. Of APA's more than 142,000 members, associates, and affiliates, about 44% list clinical psychology as their major field (APA, 1995b). It is no wonder, then, that of the 48 divisions within APA, the Division of Clinical Psychology is the largest.

---

[1]There is an average of twenty-three applications for each opening in clinical psychology graduate programs (Mayne, Norcross, & Sayette, 1994).

The prominence of clinical psychology is all the more remarkable when you consider that it is barely 100 years old and did not begin to grow rapidly until about fifty years ago. What defines the field of clinical psychology, and what is it that clinical psychologists do that makes so many people want to become one? There are no simple answers to these questions, but in this book we attempt to describe the field in a way that will allow you to draw your own conclusions. In the process, we examine the history, current status, and future of clinical psychology; its uniqueness and its overlap with other fields; the training and activities of its members; the factors that unite it; and the issues that threaten to divide it.

WHAT IS CLINICAL PSYCHOLOGY?

It is difficult to capture in a sentence or two the ever-expanding scope and ever-changing directions of clinical psychology. Thus, before offering any official definitions of the field, we will describe some of the characteristics that, taken together, roughly define the essential nature of clinical psychology.

First, as its name implies, clinical psychology is a subfield of the larger discipline of psychology. This means that, like all psychologists, clinical psychologists are interested in *behavior and mental processes*. Unlike some of their colleagues in other psychological subfields, however, clinicians are concerned almost entirely with *human*—rather than animal—behavior and mental processes.

Second, clinical psychologists conduct *research* on behavior and mental processes. Given their focus on humans, clinicians mainly study people, though they may do research on animals when practical or ethical concerns rule out working with people, and when they believe that studying animal behavior can lead to a better understanding of humans. Of course, psychologists in many other subfields also conduct research on human behavior and mental processes, so clinical psychologists' research activities do not make their subfield unique. Neither does the fact that clinicians seek to *apply* the knowledge gained from research to improve human welfare. Other specialties—such as educational, industrial/organizational, health, and engineering psychology—are also noted for their applied orientation.

A third important aspect of clinical psychology is its involvement in the *assessment* or *measurement* of the abilities and characteristics of individual human beings. Clinicians collect information that will be analyzed and interpreted to support conclusions about the person observed. While such information might be collected from many people as part of a clinical research project, it is more frequently employed by the clinician to understand one particular person. These assessment activities, however, do not set clinicians entirely apart, because other psychologists—especially those in the personality and industrial/organizational areas—administer and score various kinds of individual assessments.

A fourth characteristic of clinical psychology is the effort to *help* people who are psychologically distressed. Indeed, when members of the general public are asked what clinical psychologists do, they usually mention the treatment of mental disorders as a prominent activity. Still, providing therapy is not unique to clinical psychology:

Psychiatrists, family physicians, social workers, counselors, nurses, educators, and the clergy also intervene to alleviate psychological problems.

In summary, clinical psychology is a subarea of psychology whose members, like some other psychologists, generate research about human behavior, seek to apply the results of that research, and engage in individual assessment. And like the members of some other professions, clinical psychologists provide assistance to those who need help with psychological problems. So what distinguishes clinical psychology from the other branches of psychology? The most notable distinguishing feature has been called the *clinical attitude* or the *clinical approach* (Korchin, 1976), the tendency to combine knowledge from research on human behavior and mental processes with efforts at individual assessment in order to understand and help a particular person.

The clinical attitude sets clinicians apart from other psychologists who search for principles that apply to human behavior problems on a general, or *nomothetic*, level. Clinical psychologists are interested in research of this kind, but they also want to know how general principles shape lives, problems, and treatments on an individual, or *idiographic*, level. The clinical attitude is distinctive with respect to the helping professions outside psychology. The psychiatrists, social workers, and others who assist people in psychological distress work in fields that are not traditionally noted for research on—or systematic assessment of—the problems they seek to alleviate.

The clinical attitude can be most clearly seen when contrasted with the approach taken by psychologists in other subfields—and by professionals outside of psychology—in relation to a particular case. Suppose, for example, that upon admission to a mental hospital, a disheveled and confused man reports that space aliens are stealing his thoughts. In reading notes about this person, an experimental psychopathologist would probably be most interested in whether there are psychological and biological factors in the man's background that might support a certain theory about the cause of schizophrenia. Reading the same notes, a psychiatrist (a physician who specializes in psychological problems) might wonder whether the man should be given psychological, medical, or combined treatments. A clinical psychologist, however, would probably plan a strategy for further assessing the nature of the man's problem and, depending upon the outcome of the assessment process, develop an intervention for reducing his distress. Much of the research evidence that guides the clinical psychologist in these pursuits (and also aids other helping professions) may have come from the work of fellow clinical psychologists.

In other words, it is not the research, or the assessment, or the treatment, or any of the other activities described so far that makes clinical psychology unique. Rather, it is the clinical attitude which leads clinical psychologists to not only learn about behavior (particularly problematic behavior) but also to do something about it that is indigenous to clinical psychology (Wyatt, 1968). This emphasis on combining several functions *within a single field* is consistent with the "official" definition of clinical psychology adopted in 1991 by APA's Division of Clinical Psychology: "The field of Clinical Psychology involves research, teaching, and services relevant to the applications of principles, methods, and procedures for understanding, predicting, and alleviating intellectual, emotional, biological, psychological, social and behavioral maladjustment, disability and discomfort, applied to a wide range of client populations" (Resnick,

1991). A similar definition has been adopted by the Section on Clinical Psychology of the Canadian Psychological Association (Vallis & Howes, 1995). Thus, no *single* activity defines clinical psychology. Its uniqueness stems from the use of science and theory to guide specific interventions for persons experiencing adjustment problems or mental disorders.

CLINICAL PSYCHOLOGISTS AT WORK

Having outlined the nature of clinical psychology, let's consider in a little more detail some of the activities that clinical psychologists pursue, the variety of places in which they are employed, and the array of clients and problems on which they focus their attention. Not all clinicians are equally involved with all the functions, locations, clients, and problems we will describe, but our review should provide a better understanding of the wide range of options open to those who enter clinical psychology and, thus, of why the field remains so attractive to so many students.

The Activities of Clinical Psychologists

It is probably fair to say that 95% of all clinical psychologists spend their working lives engaged in some combination of six activities: *assessment, treatment, research, teaching, consultation*, and *administration*.

Assessment.   Assessment involves the collection of information about people: their behavior, problems, unique characteristics, abilities, and their intellectual functioning. This information may be used to diagnose problematic behavior, to guide a client toward an optimal vocational choice, to facilitate selection of job candidates, to describe a client's personality characteristics, to select treatment techniques, to guide legal decisions regarding the commitment of individuals to institutions, to provide a more complete picture of a client's problems, to screen potential participants in psychological research projects, to establish pretreatment baseline levels of behavior against which to measure posttreatment improvement, and for literally hundreds of other purposes. Most clinical assessment devices fall into one of three categories: *tests, interviews*, and *observations*.

Tests, interviews, and observations are not always distinct means of assessment. For example, a clinician might observe the nonverbal behavior of a client during a testing session or an interview to estimate the client's level of discomfort in social situations. Further, a test may be embedded in an interview, as when the client is asked to provide specific information whose accuracy provides clues to reality contact.

Various modes of assessment are combined in assessment *batteries* and *multiple assessment* strategies. Here, information necessary for the clinician's work is collected through a series of procedures, sometimes including a variety of tests. Often, a more elaborate combination of tests, interviews, and observations focuses not only on the client, but also on family, friends, and others in the client's life who can provide additional information.

Treatment.   Clinical psychologists offer treatments designed to help people better understand and solve distressing psychological problems. These interventions may be called psychotherapy, behavior modification, psychological counseling, or other names, depending upon the theoretical orientation of the clinician, and may involve an enormous range of specific treatment methods. More than 250 "brand name" therapies have been identified, and they literally run the gamut from A (Aikido) to Z (Zaraleya psychoenergetic technique) (Herink, 1980). Individual psychotherapy has long been the single most frequent activity of clinicians (e.g., Norcross, Prochaska, & Gallagher, 1989a,b), but psychologists may also treat two or more clients together in couple, family, or group therapy. Sometimes, two or more clinicians work in therapy teams to help their clients.

Treatment by a clinical psychologist may be conducted on an outpatient basis (i.e., the client lives in the community) or as one of the services offered to residents (inpatients) of mental health institutions. It may be as brief as one session or extend over several years. Treatment sessions may include client or therapist monologues, painstaking construction of new behavioral skills, episodes of intense emotional drama, or many other activities that range from the highly structured to the utterly spontaneous.

Treatment goals can range widely as well. They may be as limited as finding a specific solution to a particular problem, as ambitious as a complete analysis and reconstruction of a client's personality, or may fall somewhere between these extremes. And while most clinical psychologists design their treatments to reduce existing problems, we will see in chapter 7 that some focus instead on preventing psychological problems by altering the institutions, environmental stressors, or behavioral skills of people "at risk" for disorder (e.g., teenage parents) or of an entire community.

Therapy can be offered free of charge, for a fixed fee, as part of a pre-paid health care plan, or on a sliding scale that is adjusted in light of the client's ability to pay. The results of treatment are usually positive, though in some cases the change may be small, nonexistent, or even negative.

Research.   By training and by tradition, clinical psychologists are research oriented. This research activity makes clinicians stand out among other helping professions, and we believe that it is in this area that they make their greatest contribution. In the realm of psychotherapy, for example, theory and practice were once based mainly upon case study evidence, subjective impressions of treatment efficacy, and rather poorly designed research. This "prescientific" era (Paul, 1969a) in the history of psychotherapy research has now evolved into an "experimental" era in which the quality of research has improved greatly and the conclusions we can draw about the effects of therapy are much stronger (Lambert & Bergin, 1994). This development is due in large measure to the research of clinical psychologists.

The areas investigated by clinicians range widely, from neuropsychology, psychopharmacology and health psychology, to the causes of mental disorders in children and adults; from the diagnosis of those disorders to community interventions designed to prevent them, and from the evaluation of professional psychotherapy to the impact of nonprofessional helpers. A glance at a journal called *Psychological Abstracts,* which contains brief summaries of research in psychology, will document the diversity and intensity of clinical psychologists' involvement in research. Another journal, *Clinical Psychology Review*, includes longer reviews of topics germane to clinical psychology, while the *Journal of Consulting and Clinical Psychology, Psychological Assessment*, and the *Journal of Abnormal Psychology* publish many of the most influential research studies in clinical psychology.

Clinical research varies greatly with respect to its setting and scope. Some studies are conducted in the confines of a research laboratory, while others are conducted in the more natural, but less controllable, conditions prevailing in the world beyond the lab. Some projects are supported by governmental or private grants which pay for research assistants, clerical staff and other costs, but a great deal of clinical research is performed by investigators whose budgets are limited and who depend on volunteer help and their own ability to obtain space, equipment, and subjects.

Clinical psychology's tradition of research is reflected in graduate school admission criteria, which often emphasize applicants' grades in statistics or research methods over grades in abnormal psychology or personality theory, and which weigh applicants' research experience and publications at least as heavily as their clinical experiences (Mayne, Norcross, & Sayette, 1994; Purdy, Reinehr, & Swartz, 1989). And even though most clinical psychologists do not end up pursuing a research career—many never publish a single piece of research—most graduate programs in clinical psychology still include training in empirical research. Why? There are at least four reasons. First, it is important that all clinicians be able to critically evaluate published research so that they can determine which assessment procedures and therapeutic interventions are likely to be effective for their clients and which have not been empirically validated (Chambliss et al., 1995). Second, research training can help clinicians objectively evaluate the effectiveness of their own clinical work. Third, when psychologists who work in community mental health centers or other service agencies are asked to assist administrators in evaluating the effectiveness of the agency's programs, their research training can be very valuable. Finally, clinicians who work in academia must often supervise and evaluate research projects conducted by their students. In other words, the majority of clinical psychologists can assume that their research skills will be called upon sometime in their professional careers.

Teaching. A considerable portion of many clinical psychologists' time is spent in educational activities. Clinicians who hold full- or part-time academic positions teach graduate and undergraduate courses in areas such as personality, abnormal psychology, introductory clinical psychology, psychotherapy, behavior modification, interviewing, psychological testing, research design, and clinical assessment. They conduct specialized graduate seminars on advanced topics, and they supervise the work of graduate students who are learning assessment and therapy skills in practicum courses.

Supervising practica is a special kind of teaching which relies partly on empirical research evidence and partly on the instructor's clinical experience to enhance students' assessment and treatment skills. In most practica, each student sees one or more clients on a regular basis and, between sessions, meets with the supervisor to discuss the case (the client is aware of this arrangement, of course). Supervision may occur on an individual basis or may be part of a meeting with a small group of practicum students, all of whom keep what they hear strictly confidential. In teaching a practicum, the clinician must maintain a delicate balance between guiding students and allowing them enough independence to learn on their own. The therapist-in-training may feel stifled if supervision is too heavy-handed, but the supervisor cannot allow the student to make serious errors potentially detrimental to a client's welfare.

A good deal of clinical psychologists' teaching takes the form of research supervision. This kind of teaching begins when a student comes to the supervisor with a research topic and asks for advice and a list of relevant readings. In addition to providing the reading list, most research supervisors help the student frame appropriate research questions, apply basic principles of research design to address those questions, and introduce the student to the research skills relevant to the problem at hand. These tasks require considerable skill if the supervisor is to avoid giving so much direction that the student ends up merely assisting with the research rather than wrestling with and learning from the problems it presents.

Clinical psychologists also do a lot of teaching in the context of in-service (i.e., on-the-job) training of psychological, medical, or other interns, as well as social workers, nurses, institutional aides, ministers, police officers, suicide prevention personnel, prison guards, teachers, administrators, business executives, day-care workers, lawyers, probation officers, dentists, and many other groups whose vocational skills might be enhanced by increased psychological sophistication. Clinicians even teach while doing therapy—particularly if they adopt a behavioral approach in which treatment includes helping people learn more adaptive ways of behaving (see chapter 8).

Consultation.   Clinical psychologists often provide advice to organizations about a variety of problems. This activity, known as consultation, combines aspects of research, assessment, treatment, and teaching. Perhaps this is why some clinicians find consultation satisfying and lucrative enough that they engage in it full time. Organizations that benefit from consultants' expertise range in size and scope from one-person medical or law practices to huge government agencies and multinational corporations. The consultant may also work with neighborhood associations, walk-in treatment centers, and many other community-based organizations. Consultants perform many kinds of tasks, including education (e.g., familiarizing staff with research relevant to their work), advice (e.g., about cases or programs), direct service (e.g., assessment, treatment, and evaluation), and reduction of intraorganizational conflict (e.g., eliminating sources of trouble by altering personnel assignments).

When consulting is *case* oriented, the clinician focuses attention on a particular client or organizational problem and either deals with it directly or offers advice on how it might best be handled. When consultation is *program* or *administration* oriented, the focus is on those aspects of organizational function or structure that are causing trouble. For example, the consultant may suggest and develop new procedures for screening candidates for various jobs within an organization, set up criteria for identifying promotable personnel, or reduce staff turnover rates by increasing administrators' awareness of the psychological impact of their decisions on employees.

In some cases, responsibility for the solution to an organization's problem is transferred to the consultant, as when a mental health clinic signs a contract with a clinician who then conducts neuropsychological tests when new clients are suspected of having brain damage. More commonly, however, the responsibility for problem resolution remains with the organization served. A clinician may participate in decisions about which treatment would be of greatest benefit to a client, but if the client gets worse instead of better, the responsibility lies with the clinic, not the consultant.

Successful consultation is not easy. For one thing, outside consultants may be resented and resisted by staff who see them (and their recommendations) as a threat to their jobs. Further, interpersonal rivalries may cause staff members to distort information about a problem so as to shift blame away from themselves. Finally, consultants make great scapegoats; administrators often blame them when, for example, an unpopular change in the organization is made.

Administration. Many clinical psychologists find themselves engaged in the management or day-to-day running of organizations, even though they may hate paperwork, have little interest or expertise in the routine details of business and budgets, tire of conflicts among employees, are reluctant to deal with hiring and firing decisions, and dislike dealing with administrators. Clinicians may be asked to take on administrative jobs because of the sensitivity, interpersonal skills, research expertise, and organizational abilities associated with their field (Blouke, 1997). Some of these clinical skills can become administrative liabilities if they lead to overanalysis of problems and to conflicts between helping and managerial roles. Nevertheless, many clinicians find it satisfying to guide an organization toward reaching its goals and improving its services.

Examples of the administrative posts held by clinical psychologists include: head of a college or university psychology department, director of a graduate training program in clinical psychology, director of a student counseling center, head of a consulting firm or testing center, superintendent of a school system, chief psychologist at a hospital or clinic, director of a mental hospital, director of a community mental health center, manager of a government agency, and director of the psychology service at a Veterans Administration (VA) hospital.

Administration has become an increasingly popular professional activity for psychologists. Indeed, it may be the third most important job market for clinical psychologists, after direct clinical service and academic jobs. In one survey (Norcross, Prochaska & Gallagher, 1989a), clinicians reported spending an average of 16% of their time on administrative work.

Distribution of Clinical Functions

Though some clinical psychologists spend all of their time at one of the six functions we have described, most engage in two or more, and some perform all six. To many clinicians, the potential for distributing their time among several functions is one of the most attractive aspects of their field, and the data from several surveys conducted over the last thirty-five years provide some idea of the work pattern that results (see Table 1.1).

These surveys asked about clinical functions in different ways, making direct comparisons difficult, but some obvious trends appear. For one thing, clinicians spend

TABLE 1.1 Percentage of Clinicians Employed in Various Work Settings

Type	Kelly (1961) (N = 1,024)	Goldschmid et al. (1969) (N = 241)	Garfield & Kurtz (1976) (N = 855)	Stapp & Fulcher (1983) (N = 2,436)	Norcross, Prochaska, & Gallagher (1989b) (N = 579)
Academic	20%	17%	29%	17.9%	21%
Direct service[a]	50%	28%	35%	39.8%	30%
Research	c	c	c	c	c
Community agency	c	16%	b	d	c
Schools	3%	c	b	1.3%	c
Private practice	17%	28%	23.3%	31.1%	35%
Industry	3%	c	b	8.6%	c
Military	1.5%	c	b	c	c
Other	5.5%	11%	12.7%	c	10%

[a]Includes hospitals, clinics, medical schools, mental health centers, etc.

[b]Included under "other."

[c]Not included.

[d]Included under "direct service."

more time in various service activities than they do in research, and the majority of clinicians identify themselves primarily as practitioners rather than as researchers or academicians. (These data have caused concern in the field over what is feared to be the erosion of the traditionally strong research contributions of clinical psychologists.) Second, the percentage of clinicians engaged in full-time private practice doubled between 1960 and 1990; if we add to the private practice figure the 30% of clinicians employed in some kind of direct service agency, we see that by 1990 two-thirds of clinicians were working primarily in a health service provider role.

In the 1990s, however, the shape of clinical practice began to change, mainly as a result of health care reform and shifts in the payment methods for clinical services. We discuss these changes in more detail in Chapter 14, but it is relevant to highlight here the impact of *managed care*, an increasingly popular system of health care which has made it so difficult for clinical psychologists to function as solo private practitioners that, for the first time in the history of their field, the percentage of clinicians employed in traditional private practice settings has declined. Managed care systems have had this effect mainly because they use business principles, not just clinicians' judgments, to determine how much mental health treatment clients enrolled in the system may receive, and they place limits on the kinds of services for which they will pay. These systems also authorize payment only to their "approved providers," clinicians who are paid lower fees for their services than would be the case under clinician-controlled plans.

As clinical psychologists find it more difficult to make a living as solo practitioners with clients whose health care is paid for by managed care systems, more of them are joining the staffs of hospitals, medical clinics, and other general health care facilities (Groth-Marnet & Edkins, 1996), consulting with or joining the private practice of primary care physicians (Belar, 1995; Bray & Rogers, 1995), or offering clinical services through health maintenance organizations (HMOs), group practices, and specialty clinics. Too, the services that clinical psychologists offer are changing to better match those for which managed care systems will pay. They are doing less long-term therapy and testing and more brief psychotherapy and specialized treatment of childhood disorders, substance abuse problems, and difficulties associated with chronic medical illnesses (Johnstone et al., 1995; Nickelson, 1995; Norcross, Prochaska, & Gallagher, 1989a; Wiggins, 1994).

Clients and Their Problems

Within the limits imposed by their areas of expertise, clinical psychologists work on almost any kind of human behavioral problem. According to one survey of more than 6,500 clinicians, the most commonly treated problems are, in order of frequency: anxiety and depression, difficulties in interpersonal relationships, marital problems, school difficulties, psychosomatic and physical symptoms, job-related difficulties, alcoholism or other forms of drug abuse, psychoses, and mental retardation (VandenBos & Stapp, 1983). Requests for assessment and treatment services may come from the clients themselves, from the client's family, from a court or other legal agency, or from a hospital, school, or community service center. Because client complaints are often complex and frequently stem from a combination of biological, psychological, and social factors, the clinical psychologist—even the private practitioner—may not work alone. In many cases, clients are referred to another clinical psychologist, a psychiatrist, or a social worker for specialized testing, medication, or other services and, in some cases, clients may be served by an assessment and treatment team composed of experts from several helping professions.

Employment Settings for Clinical Psychologists

There was a time when most clinical psychologists worked in a single type of facility: child clinics or guidance centers. Today, however, the settings in which clinicians function are much more diverse. You will find clinical psychologists in college and university psychology departments, law schools, public and private medical and psychiatric hospitals, in city, county, and private mental health clinics, community mental health centers, student health and counseling centers, medical schools, the military, university psychological clinics, child treatment centers, public and private schools, institutions for the mentally retarded, police departments, prisons, juvenile offender facilities, business and industrial firms, probation departments, rehabilitation centers for the handicapped, nursing homes and other geriatric facilities, orphanages, alcoholism treatment centers, health maintenance organizations, and many other places. Further, as already noted, many clinicians are employed in full- or part-time private-practice positions, but, increasingly, as members of a group practice or behavioral health care network.

The dramatic growth of private practice in the 1980s (see Table 1.1) was caused in part by the satisfaction that private practitioners draw from independent work (Norcross & Prochaska, 1983) and also to a lower level of perceived stress compared to academic or mental health agency jobs (Boice & Myers, 1987; Raquepaw & Miller, 1989). The financial rewards were significant, too. According to an APA survey, the median 1995 salary of psychologists in independent practice ranged from $60,000 to $79,000, compared to a range of $36,000 to $60,000 for psychologists at various levels of academic seniority (Wicherski, Woerheide, & Kohout, 1996). Even when faculty salaries are adjusted to correct for their nine- to ten-month academic year, many academicians' annual salaries are still less than their practitioner colleagues. As managed care systems grow, however, these financial advantages are likely to erode, thus further accelerating recent trends away from solo private practice.

At Work With Three Clinical Psychologists

Having described clinical psychologists' functions, clients, and work settings, let's consider a few specific examples of how and where clinicians actually spend their time. Remember, though, that these examples are just the tip of the iceberg: As scientific discoveries continue, particularly in the areas of childhood psychopathology and treatment (Chapter 10), health psychology (Chapter 11), and neuropsychology (Chapter 12), clinicians will continue to expand the scope of their assessment and intervention techniques and the range of settings in which they perform their academic and service work (DeSantis & Walker, 1991). As we enter the twenty-first century, expect to see clinical psychologists devoting more of their expertise to ever more specialized services for substance abuse programs, forensic agencies, and medical facilities and to traditionally underserved groups such as the elderly, the poor, and members of ethnic minority groups. Clinicians will also find themselves increasingly called upon to guide policy decisions in the areas of health care, child care, education, and social services.

Dr. Sandy D'Angelo   I work in a hospital pediatrics department, where my clinical activities include: (1) delivering outpatient assessment and treatment services to children with behavioral and learning problems; (2) consulting with staff who serve children with craniofacial abnormalities, limb amputation, cerebral palsy, or other disabilities; (3) counseling teen parents and their children; (4) providing clinical assessments in an infant-toddler evaluation center; and (5) helping parents learn to manage infants and toddlers with behavior problems. In these roles, I often work with general pediatricians and with pulmonologists, cardiologists, nephrologists, surgeons, and other medical specialists.

My job is different every day. In the morning, I might assess the cognitive development of children displaying autism, violent temper tantrums, brain damage, or visual and hearing impairments. In the afternoon, I might assess suicide risk in a homeless seventeen year old, counsel an unwed teenage mother, and assist in hospitalizing a teen displaying severe mental disorder. On other days, I might help educate medical students and residents by leading a discussion, delivering a lecture, or conducting a case conference. I also devote a small portion of my time to working with other faculty on a research project on how children and their families cope with chronic illnesses.

The most appealing aspects of my position are the variety of services I am called on to perform, the wide range of childhood problems I see, the opportunity to work with professionals who view children's problems from different perspectives, and the chance to continue learning about childhood disorders and development.

Dr. Hector Machabanski   Practically all facets of clinical psychology are represented in my work, including direct clinical and community services, teaching, administration, and consultation. I am a faculty member at a school of professional psychology, where I teach courses in family therapy and culture and mental health. I also advise and mentor clinical graduate students and sit on various academic committees. In addition, I do accreditation site visits for the American Psychological Association, and I have served on the executive committee of national professional organizations. Finally, I offer workshops and presentations to hospital, mental health, and other professional groups, usually on topics related to culture and mental health. Other aspects of my teaching include speaking to community groups—including those in the Spanish-speaking community—on topics such as parenting, stress management, conflict resolution, and self-improvement.

My private practice focuses on delivering assessment and treatment services to culturally diverse clients—including children, adults, and families who are Spanish-speaking, bilingual, and who are immigrants—with a wide range of psychological concerns. I receive referrals from insurance companies, managed care organizations, private physicians, attorneys, and mental health professionals. Because I am a certified school psychologist as well as a clinical psychologist, my consulting activities involve schools as well as hospitals. I spend one day a week in the schools, meeting with parents, teachers, and administrators, observing and assessing children, and providing recommendations pertaining to individual children and group situations. Through employees under my supervision, I also provide psychological services to local Head Start programs. In addition, I offer *pro bono* services at an international center for torture survivors, providing psychotherapy for victims of torture from Latin America, working with attorneys on political asylum cases, and giving technical support to the administration.

The most appealing aspect of my work is my involvement in a broad range of services that constitute what clinical psychology is today. The diverse settings, populations, and problems that constitute my professional life are brought together by my interest in providing services to what have been underserved client populations.

Dr. Geoffrey Thorpe   I am a professor of psychology at a state university. My teaching, research, and service activities are quite diverse, and vary from day to day. I teach an undergraduate class in abnormal psychology three times a week, and I spend considerable time preparing lectures, study guides, and other course materials for use in class. My graduate teaching involves leading weekly three-hour seminars in which six graduate students and I discuss advanced topics covered in assigned readings. I also conduct live or videotaped observations of clinical psychology graduate students as they practice assessment and therapy methods in our training clinic, and then conduct weekly individual and group supervisory sessions with them.

My research activities involve exploring various aspects of behavior therapy. I meet for two hours each week with my staff of graduate and undergraduate research assistants to discuss current progress, plan new studies, and, sometimes, work on grant proposals.

Because I am the director of clinical training, I have significant administrative responsibilities. In this administrative role, I coordinate our doctoral program in clinical psychology, which includes chairing meetings of the clinical faculty, supervising the admissions process, establishing and overseeing off-campus practicum placements, organizing the doctoral qualifying exams, preparing students for their clinical internships, and insuring that our program meets APA accreditation standards. I perform service in the form of paid and unpaid consulting to community agencies, and as a reviewer for editors at scholarly journals and textbook publishing companies. I also maintain a part-time private practice in clinical psychology.

I find being a clinicial psychologist in an academic setting rewarding because, first, it offers me a variety of challenging roles that helps me avoid monotony and "burnout." In addition, the daily contact with colleagues and students creates a professional environment that inspires me to keep up with the latest developments in the exciting field of clinical psychology.

The way clinical psychologists spend their time is determined partly by their individual interests and expertise, partly by the demands of the work settings they choose, and partly by larger social factors. For example, a clinician could not work in a Veterans Administration hospital today if federal legislation had not been passed in the 1940s creating such hospitals. Similarly, much of the research conducted by clinical psychologists depends on grants from governmental agencies such as the National Institute of Mental Health, whose existence depends on continued congressional appropriations. Further, the clinical functions we have described are possible only because they are perceived by other professions—and the general public—as legitimate. If no one saw the clinician as capable of doing effective therapy, that function would soon disappear from the field.

In short, what clinicians do and where they do it has always depended—and always will depend—on the cultural values, prevailing attitudes, political climate, and pressing needs of the society in which they function. A look at the history of clinical psychology clearly shows the role played by these sociocultural factors in the development of the discipline.

THE ROOTS OF CLINICAL PSYCHOLOGY

Anyone born in the United States after World War II might assume that the field of clinical psychology has always existed. However, clinical psychology did not emerge as a discipline until the beginning of the twentieth century, and did not really begin to develop until World War II ended. Now, more than fifty years later, this child of the postwar era is experiencing a "midlife crisis" centering on several of the same issues that occupied its adolescence: How should clinical psychologists be trained? What is the role of science in the field? What are the best ways to ensure that clinicians offer high-quality services to the public?

The roots of clinical psychology extend back to periods before the field was ever named and to prewar years when it appeared only in embryonic form (Reisman, 1976; Resnick, 1997; Routh, 1994; Watson, 1953). Three sets of social and historical factors initially shaped the field and continue to influence it. These factors include (1) the use of scientific research methods in psychology, (2) the study of human individual differences, and (3) changes in how behavior disorders have been viewed and treated over the years.

The Research Tradition in Psychology

From its nineteenth-century beginnings in the psychophysics of Weber and Fechner, the experimental physiology of Helmholtz, and the work of the first "official" psychologist, Wilhelm Wundt, psychology sought to establish itself as a science that—like biology, physics, and other sciences—seeks knowledge through the application of empirical research methods. Even though the roots of psychology were partly in philosophy, and though many early psychologists were preoccupied with philosophical questions, the discipline was determined to study human behavior by conducting *research* that employed the two most powerful tools of science, observation and experimentation. Thus, the early history of psychology, which began in Wundt's psychological laboratory at the University at Leipzig in 1879, is primarily the history of *experimental* psychology (Boring, 1950).

By the time clinical psychology began to emerge, 17 years after the founding of Wundt's laboratory, the experimental research tradition in psychology was well established. Psychology laboratories had been set up at major universities in Europe and the United States, and early psychologists were experimenting on human behavior. The first clinicians had been trained as scientists in these laboratories, and thus tended to think about clinical problems in scientific terms and to use laboratory research methods in dealing with them. The research tradition they brought to their work took root and grew in the new field until clinical psychologists attained special recognition among the helping professions as experts in research.

The scientific orientation and the skill that forms the basis of clinicians' continuing reputation for research expertise also form the strongest link between clinical psychology and the larger discipline of psychology from which it grew. The question of whether this link should be maintained, intensified, or deemphasized in the training and daily activities of clinical psychologists continues to be one of the liveliest issues in the field. Nevertheless, the research tradition of experimental psychology undeniably shaped the development of clinical psychology. It provided a methodology for approaching clinical subject matter, engendered empirical evaluation of clinical functions, and, as a point of contention, keeps clinicians engaged in the healthy process of self-examination.

Attention to Individual Differences

Because clinical psychology deals with the individual, it could not appear as a discipline until differences among human beings began to be recognized and measured. There would be little impetus for learning about individuals in a world where everyone is thought to be about the same.

Differences among people have always been noticed and assessed. In his *Republic*, Plato pointed out that people should do work for which they are best suited; he suggested specifically that prospective soldiers be tested for military ability prior to their acceptance in the army. In the sixth century B.C., Pythagoras selected members of his brotherhood on the basis of facial characteristics, intelligence, and emotionality, and—4,000 years ago—prospective government employees in China were given individual ability tests prior to hiring (DuBois, 1970; McReynolds, 1975). It was not until the early 1800s, however, that the idea of paying systematic attention to subtle psychological differences really caught on. Until then, people were thought of as falling into a few categories such as male–female, good–evil, noble–commoner, sane–insane, wise–foolish.

The earliest developments in the scientific measurement of individual differences came in the fields of astronomy and anatomy. The astronomical story began in 1796, when Nevil Maskelyne was Astronomer Royal at the Greenwich (England) Observatory. He had an assistant named Kinnebrook, whose recordings of the moment at which various stars and planets crossed a certain point in the sky consistently differed from those of his boss by five- to eight-tenths of a second. Maskelyne assumed that his readings were correct and that Kinnebrook was in error. As a result, Kinnebrook lost his job.

This incident drew the attention of F. W. Bessel, an astronomer at the University of Konigsberg (Germany) observatory. Bessel wondered whether Kinnebrook's "error" might reflect something about the characteristics of various observers, and, over the next several years, he compared his own observations with those of other experienced astronomers. Bessel found that discrepancies appeared regularly and that the size of the differences depended upon the person with whom he compared notes. The differences associated with each observer became known as the "personal equation," because they allowed calculations to be corrected for personal characteristics. Bessel's work led to later research by psychologists on the speed of, and individual differences in, reaction time.

A second source of interest in individual differences stemmed from the early nineteenth-century work of anatomist Franz Gall and his pupil, Johann Spurzheim. As a child in Germany, Gall thought he saw a relationship between his schoolmates' mental characteristics and the shapes of their heads. This notion later led Gall to espouse *phrenology*, an alleged science based on the assumptions that (1) each area of the brain is associated with a different faculty or function (e.g., self-esteem, language, or reverence); (2) the better developed each of these areas is, the more strongly that faculty or function is manifested in behavior; and (3) the pattern of over- or underdevelopment of each faculty is reflected in corresponding bumps or depressions in the skull. Although the brain does play a major role in controlling behavior, and though some of its areas are associated with certain functions such as vision, movement, and language, Gall's specific claims were recognized—even by the scientists of his day—as spectacularly wrong.

Undeterred, Gall traveled throughout Europe measuring the bumps on people's heads. He began with prisoners and mental patients whose behavioral characteristics seemed well established (he thought the "acquisitiveness" bump was especially strong among pickpockets). Later, under Spurzheim's influence, a map of the brain's thirty-seven "powers" or "organs" was drawn, and phrenological measurements were made on more respectable segments of society. Many people actually paid to "have their head examined," after which they received a profile allegedly describing their mental makeup. Other efforts to relate people's physical characteristics to their mental or behavioral traits appeared in the late nineteenth-century work of Cesare Lombroso, an Italian psychiatrist whose theory of *physiognomy* correlated facial features with personality (Pettijohn, 1991).

Though World Wide Web sites dealing with phrenology and physiognomy exist, the two are no longer influential in scientific circles. Still, their orientation toward *systematically measuring* individuals' characteristics—and then drawing conclusions about those individuals—presaged the assessment function seen in clinical psychology today. The *methods* ultimately used in clinical assessment were quite different, however. They came not from measuring physical dimensions, but from systematically collecting *samples of behavior* from large groups of people as they responded to standard sets of stimuli. Such behavior samples were first used to make general statements about individual mental characteristics, but as statistical analyses became more sophisticated in the nineteenth century, they were used to establish group norms against which a person could be evaluated quantitatively. These behavior sampling procedures came to be called *mental tests* by 1890, but their story began some thirty years earlier.

In 1859 Charles Darwin published his momentous work, *Origin of Species*, in which he proposed two important ideas: that (1) variation of individual characteristics occurs within and between species (including humans), and (2) natural selection takes place in part on the basis of those characteristics. Darwin's cousin, Sir Francis Galton, was fascinated by these ideas, and he quickly applied Darwin's notions to the inheritance of individual differences—especially in mental abilities.

Galton designed tests aimed at measuring the relatively fixed capacities, structures, and functions he thought comprised the mind. Many of these tests focused on sensorimotor capacity. For example, Galton (1883) tried to distinguish high from low intelligence on the basis of individuals' ability to make fine discriminations between objects of differing weight and between varying intensities of heat, cold, and pain. He sought to measure individual differences in vividness of mental imagery; for this purpose, he invented the questionnaire. Galton's interests also extended to associative processes, so he developed the word association test to explore this phenomenon. Eventually, Galton set up a laboratory in London where, for a small fee, anyone could take a battery of tests and receive a copy of the results. This facility, the world's first *mental testing center*, was included in the health exhibition in the 1884 International Exhibition (an early World's Fair).

Galton's work began nearly twenty years before the official founding of psychology, but by the late 1880s, psychologists, too, were interested in measuring individual differences in mental functioning. The person usually credited with merging individual mental measurement with the new science of psychology is James McKeen Cattell, an American who completed his doctorate in Wundt's laboratory in Leipzig in 1886. Cattell's interest in the application of psychological methods to the study of individual differences, already evident in his doctoral dissertation on individual variation in reaction time, was intensified when he met Galton while lecturing at Cambridge University in 1887. In 1888, Cattell founded the third psychological laboratory in the United States (the first lab was set up by William James at Harvard in 1879; the second was established by G. Stanley Hall at Johns Hopkins in 1883). Cattell was one of the first psychologists to appreciate the practical uses of tests in the selection and diagnosis of people. This recognition of the applied potential of mental tests foreshadowed the emergence of clinical psychology.

Cattell's experience in Wundt's laboratory taught him that "psychology cannot attain the certainty and exactness of the physical sciences unless it rests on a foundation of experiment and measurement" (Dennis, 1948, p. 347). Consequently, one of his first tasks was to construct a standard battery of mental tests for use by researchers interested in individual differences. He chose ten tests that reflected the then-prevalent tendency to use sensorimotor functioning as an index of mental capacity, and he tested people's performance under varying conditions. He also collected less systematic

James McKeen Cattell (1860–1944). (From *Scientific Monthly*, 1929, *28*, 25. Reprinted by permission of the American Association for the Advancement of Science.)

information about people's dreams, diseases, preferences, recreational activities, and future plans (Shaffer & Lazarus, 1952).

Sensorimotor mental tests were adopted at universities, including Wisconsin, Clark, and Yale, but they were also criticized because of their low correlations with most other mental ability criteria (Sharp, 1899, cited in Reisman, 1976). By this time, however, an alternative approach to testing began to appear in several quarters. In 1891, Hugo Munsterberg, a psychologist at the University of Freiburg (Germany) who later came to Harvard, constructed a set of fourteen tests to assess children's mental abilities. These tests went beyond the Galton-Cattell tasks to measure more complex functions such as reading, classifying objects, and performing mathematical operations. The German psychiatrist Emil Kraepelin (originator of an early system for classifying mental disorders) also designed tests of complex mental functions such as memory and attention.

Finally, and most importantly, in 1895, Alfred Binet—the French lawyer and scientist who founded the first French psychology lab with Henri Beaunis—began to develop measures of complex mental ability in normal and defective children. Binet's involvement in this testing grew out of the recognition that retarded children (who had been distinguished as a diagnostic group only as late as 1838) might be helped if they could be identified and given special educational attention. In 1896, Binet and his colleague Victor Henri described a battery of tests that measured not just "simple part processes" such as space judgment, motor skills, muscular effort, and memory, but also comprehension, attention, suggestibility, aesthetic appreciation, and moral values.

Thus, by 1896 psychology was involved in measuring individual differences in mental functioning, and it hosted two overlapping approaches to the task: (1) the Galton-Cattell sensorimotor tests, aimed at assessing inherited, relatively fixed mental *structures*, and (2) the instruments of Binet and others, which emphasized complex mental *functions* which could be taught to some degree. Each of these approaches was important to the development of clinical psychology, the former because it fostered the appearance of the first psychological clinic and the latter because it provided a mental test which was to give the new field its first clear identity. Although early American psychologists came to rely on Binet's test, they embraced Galton's belief that intelligence was largely inherited.

The rest of this story must wait, however, until we examine a third major influence on clinical psychology: changing views of behavior disorder and its treatment.

Changing Conceptions of Behavior Disorder

From the beginning of recorded history, human beings have tried to explain behavior that is bizarre or apparently irrational. As the popularity of various theories has waxed and waned over the centuries, so too has the influence of various helping professions, including clinical psychology.

The earliest explanations of disordered behavior involved magical forces and supernatural agents. Persons who acted "crazy" were said to be possessed by demons or spirits, and treatment involved various forms of exorcism (including *trephining*, or boring small holes in the skull to provide evil spirits with an exit). In Greece before Hippocrates, these ideas appeared in revised form: Disordered behavior was attributed to the influence of one or more of the gods. Even in early monotheistic cultures, God was seen as a possible source of behavior problems. In the Old Testament, for example, we are told that "the Lord shall smite thee with madness, and blindness, and astonishment of heart" (Deuteronomy 28:28). Where supernatural approaches to behavior disorders were prevalent, philosophy and religion were dominant in explaining and dealing with them. (Though they are not prominent in Western cultures today, supernatural—and especially demonological—explanations remain influential in other cultures around the world and in some ethnic and religious subcultures in North America, too.)

Supernatural explanations of behavior disorders were still highly influential when, in about the fourth century B.C., the Greek physician Hippocrates suggested that these aberrations stem from natural causes. Hippocrates argued that behavior disorders, like other behaviors, are a function of the distribution of four bodily fluids, or humors: blood, black bile, yellow bile, and phlegm. This theory, generally acknowledged as the first medical model of disordered behavior, paved the way for the concept of *mental illness* and legitimized the involvement of the medical profession in its treatment. From Hippocrates until the fall of Rome in 476 A.D., physicians supported and reinforced a physical, or medical, model of behavior disorder.

In the Middle Ages, however, the medical model was swept away. The church became the primary social and legal institution in Europe, demonological explanations of behavior disorders regained prominence, and religious personnel again took over responsibility for dealing with all cases of deviance. Ever resourceful, many physicians soon became priests. The church began treating the "insane" by exorcising the spirits presumed to possess them. Here is part of a tenth-century invocation designed to alleviate hysteria, then believed to be a female-only disorder caused by a wandering uterus under demonic control.

O womb, womb, womb, cylindrical womb, red womb, white womb, fleshy womb, bleeding womb, large womb, neufredic womb, bloated womb, O demoniacal one! . . . I conjure thee, O womb, in the name of the Holy Trinity to come back to the place from which thou shouldst neither move nor turn away . . . and to return, without anger, to the place where the Lord has put thee originally. . . . I conjure thee not to harm that maid of God, N., not to occupy her head, throat, neck, chest, ears, teeth, eyes, nostrils, shoulderblades, arms, hands, heart, stomach, spleen, kidneys, back, sides, joints, navel, intestines, bladder, thighs, shins, heels, nails, but to lie down quietly in the place which God chose for thee, so that this maid of God, N., be restored to health. (Zilboorg & Henry, 1941, pp. 131–132).

Later, as the Church conducted inquisitions to identify heretics (nonbelievers) and others under the control of the devil, many people who would now be considered mentally ill were caught in the net. Physician-priests "diagnosed" suspected heretics by looking for signs of the devil (*stigmata diaboli*) on their skin, or by using sharp instruments to locate "dead spots," or local anesthesias (Spanos, 1978). After demonic possession was diagnosed (and it usually was), "treatment" consisted of torture to produce confessions of heresy, or burning at the stake.

These practices continued in varying forms in Europe—and in North America—until the eighteenth century, but long before they finally ended, the demonological model of disorder had come under scrutiny by physicians and scholars. Gradually, the treatment of deviant individuals took the form of confinement in newly established hospitals and asylums, such as London's St. Mary of Bethlehem (organized in 1547 and referred to by locals as "bedlam"). The hospital movement saved many lives, but it did not necessarily make them worth living. Even though many eighteenth-century scholars agreed that the insane were suffering from mental illness (not possession), the medical profession, which was now back in charge of the problem, had little to offer in the way of treatment. Feared and misunderstood by the general public—many undoubtedly still believed them to be possessed—the insane were little more than prisoners who lived under abominable conditions and received grossly inadequate care. Their doctors saw their mental illness as resulting from brain damage or—harking back to Hippocrates—an overabundance of blood. At St. Mary of Bethlehem, for example,

> A physician would visit once a year to prescribe treatment: bleeding of all patients in April, purges and "vomits" of surviving patients in May, and once again bleeding all patients in October. At smaller private institutions . . . a physician might visit once in ten years to prescribe a regime of treatment for the next decade. As a continuing feature of institutionalization, patients were chained to posts in dungeons, whipped, beaten, ridiculed, and fed only the coarsest of slops. (Reisman, 1976, p. 10)

Thanks to the efforts of European and North American reformers of the eighteenth and early-nineteenth centuries (Philippe Pinel, William Tuke, Benjamin Rush, and Eli Todd), more humane living conditions and treatments began to appear in mental institutions (see Figure 1.1). Pinel ushered in this era of *moral treatment* with the following comment: "It is my conviction that these mentally ill are intractable only because they are deprived of fresh air and liberty" (quoted in Ullmann & Krasner, 1975, p. 135). Thus began a new awareness of the possibility that mental patients could be helped, rather than simply hidden, and physicians retained the responsibility for helping them emerge from their confinement. The role of physicians in treating mental disorders was further solidified when, later in the nineteenth century, syphilis was identified as the cause of general paresis, a deteriorative brain syndrome that had once been treated as a form of insanity. Finding an organic cause for this mental disorder bolstered the view that *all* behavior disorders are organically based and that other disease entities awaited discovery. The notion that there could be "no twisted thought without a twisted molecule" (Gerard, 1956, quoted in Abood, 1960) hastened the decline of the moral treatment approach and triggered a "psychiatric revolution" in which doctors searched feverishly for organic causes of—and physical treatments for—all forms of mental illness (Zilboorg & Henry, 1941).

Ironically, this revolution also led to the idea that mental disorders might have *psychological* causes, too. In the mid-1800s a few French physicians, including Jean-Martin Charcot, Hippolyte Bernheim, and Pierre Janet, began studying what Franz Anton Mesmer had called "animal magnetism" and what James Braid, an English sur-

FIGURE 1.1 Tony Robert-Fleury's 1876 painting of Pinel freeing the insane from chains in the Bicêtre is one of the most famous artistic interpretations of the Moral Era's reformist and humanitarian spirit. (Photo reprinted by permission of Sander L. Gilman, John Wiley & Sons, Inc.)

geon, later termed "hypnotism." They found that hypnosis could alleviate certain behavior disorders, particularly hysteria (now known as conversion disorder) and speculated that, if mental illness is at least partly psychological, then psychological rather than medical treatment might be effective in dealing with it. Their work struck a responsive chord in a young Viennese neurologist named Sigmund Freud, who, by 1896, had already proposed the first stage of a theory in which behavior disorders were seen not as the result of organic problems, but as a consequence of the dynamic struggle of the human mind to satisfy instinctual (mainly sexual) desires while also coping with the rules and restrictions of the outside world. Freud's theory brought a less-than-ethusiastic reaction from his medical colleagues. One doctor called Freud's idea "a scientific fairy tale" (Krafft-Ebing, quoted in Reisman, 1976, p. 41). Nevertheless, the idea grew to become a comprehensive theory of the dynamic nature of behavior and behavior disorder, and it ultimately redirected the entire course of the mental health professions, including clinical psychology.

Freud's influence on clinical psychology was slight at first, partly because his theory was so controversial and partly because it dealt with mental illness, which was—in the late-nineteenth century—wholly within the province of the medical profession. Psychologists laid no claim to a treatment function at that time, but we shall see that the dynamic approaches to behavior pioneered by Freud and his followers shaped the activities of clinical psychologists in other areas and ultimately provided the foundation for their involvement in therapy.

THE BIRTH OF CLINICAL PSYCHOLOGY: 1896–1917

Our examination of the three main roots of clinical psychology shows that, by the end of the nineteenth century, the ground had been prepared for its appearance as a discipline. Psychology had emerged as a science, psychologists had started applying scientific methods to the study of individual differences, and Freud's dynamic approach to behavior disorder was about to open vast new areas of inquiry for psychologists interested in understanding deviance.

It was in this historical context that the first clinical psychologist appeared, an American named Lightner Witmer. Following his graduation from the University of Pennsylvania in 1888, Witmer worked on his Ph.D. in psychology with Wundt at the University of Leipzig. After completing his doctorate in 1892, Witmer was appointed director of the University of Pennsylvania psychology laboratory.

In March of 1896, a local schoolteacher named Margaret Maguire asked Witmer to help one of her students, "Charles Gilman," whom she described as a "chronic bad speller." Once a schoolteacher himself, Witmer "took the case," thus becoming the first

Lightner Witmer (1867–1956).
(Courtesy of George Eastman House.
Reproduced by permission.)

clinical psychologist and simultaneously beginning an enterprise that became the world's first psychological clinic (Routh, 1996). The willingness of a psychologist to work with a child's scholastic problems may not now seem significant enough to mark the founding of a profession, but remember that, until this point, psychology had dealt with people only to study their behavior in general, not to become concerned about them as individuals. Witmer's decision was as unusual then as would be an attempt by a modern astronomer to determine the "best" orbit for the moon in order to alter its path.

Witmer's approach was to assess Charles' problem and then arrange for appropriate remedial procedures. His assessment showed that Charles had a visual impairment, as well as reading and memory problems that Witmer termed "visual verbal amnesia." Today, these difficulties would probably be diagnosed as dyslexia, a learning disability. Witmer recommended intensive tutoring to help the boy recognize words without having to spell them first. This procedure successfully brought "Charles" to the point where he could read normally (McReynolds, 1987).

Not everything Witmer did was to be equally influential, but several aspects of his new clinic came to characterize subsequent clinical work for some time:

1. Most of his clients were children, a natural development since Witmer had been offering a course on child psychology, had published his first papers in the journal *Pediatrics*, and had attracted the attention of teachers concerned about their students.

2. His recommendations for helping clients were preceded by diagnostic assessment.

3. He did not work alone, but in a team approach which saw members of various professions consulting and collaborating on cases.

4. There was a clear emphasis on preventing future problems through early diagnosis and remediation.

5. He emphasized that clinical psychology should be built on the principles being discovered in scientific psychology as a whole.

In a talk at the 1896 meeting of the four-year-old American Psychological Association, Witmer described his new brand of psychology. His friend Joseph Collins recounted the scene as follows:

> [Witmer said] that clinical psychology is derived from the results of an examination of many human beings, one at a time, and that the analytic method of discriminating mental abilities and defects develops an ordered classification of observed behavior, by means of postanalytic generalizations. He put forth the claim that the psychological clinic is an institution for social and public service, for original research, and for the instruction of students in psychological orthogenics which includes vocational, educational, correctional, hygienic, industrial, and social guidance. The only reaction he got from his audience was a slight elevation of the eyebrows on the part of a few of the older members. (Quoted in Brotemarkle, 1947, p. 65)

This lead-balloon reception is understandable given the following four facts prevalent at the time:

> *One*, the majority of psychologists considered themselves scientists and probably did not regard the role described by Witmer as appropriate for them. *Two*, even if they had considered his suggestions admirable, few psychologists were prepared by training or experience to perform the functions he proposed. *Three*, they were not about to jeopardize their identification as scientists, which was tenuous enough in those early years, by plunging their profession into what they felt were premature applications. *Four*, aside from any prevalent skeptical and conservative attitude, Witmer had an unfortunate talent for antagonizing his colleagues. (Reisman, 1976, p. 46)

The responses to Witmer's talk provided the first clues that conflicts would arise between psychology as a science and psychology as an applied profession. As noted earlier, some of these conflicts are at least as active today as they were in 1896.

In spite of his colleagues' objections, Witmer continued his clinical work and expanded his clinic facility in order to handle the increasing caseload. At first, the clientele consisted mainly of "slow" or retarded children, but later, the clinic accepted children with speech disorders, sensory problems, and learning disabilities. Consistent with his orthogenic (preventive guidance) orientation, Witmer also worked with "normal" and intellectually superior children and provided guidance and advice to their parents and teachers.

In 1897, the new clinic began offering a four-week summer course in child psychology consisting of case presentations, instruction in diagnostic testing, and demonstrations of remedial techniques. By 1900, three children a day were being served by a clinic staff that had grown to eleven members and, in 1907, Witmer set up a residential school for training retarded children. That same year, he founded and edited the first clinical journal, *The Psychological Clinic*. By 1909, over 450 cases had been seen in Witmer's facilities. Under Witmer's influence, the University of Pennsylvania began offering formal courses in clinical psychology during the 1904–1905 academic year. Clinical psychology was on its way.

However, the influence of Witmer's clinic, school, journal, and training courses was limited. Witmer got clinical psychology rolling but he had little to do with steering it, mainly because he ignored most of the developments that would later become prominent in clinical psychology. For example, Witmer ignored Alfred Binet's new intelligence test, the Binet-Simon scale, when it was introduced in the United States. Like Binet's earlier tests, this instrument was designed to measure complex mental processes, not the fixed mental structures with which Witmer was concerned. In spite of Binet's warning that it did not provide a wholly objective measure of intelligence, the Binet-Simon test gained wide attention. Henry H. Goddard of the Vineland (New Jersey) Training School heard about it while in Europe in 1908 and brought the Binet-Simon scale to the United States for assessing the intelligence of "feebleminded" children in the clinic he had set up two years earlier. The popularity of Goddard's translation of the Binet-Simon scale and Lewis Terman's 1916 revision of it (known as the Stanford-Binet) grew so rapidly in the United States that they overshadowed all other tests of intelligence, including those used by Witmer. The Binet scales provided a focus for clinical psychology's assessment function which, until 1910, had been rather disorganized. All over the United States, new university psychological clinics (more than twenty of them by 1914) and institutions for the retarded began adopting the Binet approach while deemphasizing Witmer's "old-fashioned" methods.

Witmer also ignored the clinical assessment of adults, a service that other clinicians began to perform to help psychiatrists diagnose and plan treatment for brain damage and other problems. Indeed, after 1907, psychological examination of mental patients in some hospitals became routine. Similar assessments were done in prisons to assist staff members to identify disturbed convicts or plan rehabilitation programs.

Finally, Witmer did not join other clinicians in practicing psychotherapy or in adopting the Freudian approach to behavior disorder. Freud's approach became known to clinical psychology through association with psychiatry in mental hospitals and also through child-guidance clinics which, though often run by psychiatrists, routinely employed psychologists. The child-guidance movement in the United States was stimulated by the National Committee for Mental Hygiene, a group founded by a former mental patient, Clifford Beers, and supported by William James, a Harvard psychologist, and Adolf Meyer, the country's most prominent psychiatrist. With funds from philanthropist Henry Phipps, the committee (which ultimately became the National Association for Mental Health) worked to improve treatment of the mentally ill and to prevent psychological disorders.

The first child-guidance clinic was founded in Chicago in 1909 by an English-born psychiatrist named William Healy. Like Witmer, Healy worked with children, employed a team approach, and emphasized prevention, but otherwise his orientation was quite different. For one thing, instead of dealing mainly with learning disabilities or other educational difficulties, Healy focused on cases of child misbehavior that drew the attention of school authorities, the police, or the courts. Healy's clinic operated on the assumption that juvenile offenders suffered from mental illness that should be dealt with before it caused more serious problems. Second, the approach taken by the staff at Healy's Chicago clinic (first called the Juvenile Psychopathic Institute and later the Institute for Juvenile Research) was heavily influenced by Freud's psychodynamic theories.

This dynamic approach received a huge boost in popularity when, in the same year Healy opened his clinic, G. Stanley Hall, a psychologist, arranged for Sigmund Freud and two of his followers, Carl Jung and Sandor Ferenczi, to speak at the twentieth-anniversary celebration of Clark University in Worcester, Massachusetts. This event and the lectures associated with it "sold" psychoanalysis to American psychologists (though not to Witmer, who did not attend; Routh, 1996). Freud's theory was compatible with the psychologists' interest in the way the mind deals with its environment (the functionalism of William James and G. Stanley Hall) as opposed to what it is made of (the structuralism of Wundt). It also appealed to the emphasis on pragmatism in the United States.

As a result of this excitement over Freud, psychological and child-guidance clinics began to follow Healy's model, not Witmer's. This fact, coupled with the spreading use of Binet intelligence tests, left Witmer in the background of the clinical psychology he founded. He remained active, of course, but mainly with functions and clients that have since become more strongly associated with school psychology, vocational counseling, speech therapy, and remedial education than with clinical psychology (Fagan, 1996).

Once clinical psychology adopted the Binet-Simon scales, it became identified primarily with the testing of problematic children in clinics and guidance centers. This image led critics to argue that clinicians spent too much time diagnosing hopeless cases and that they were not sufficiently psychoanalytic in orientation. These criticisms had relatively little effect, however, because schools and other institutions that dealt with children were searching for clinical psychologists to do the testing which was fast becoming fashionable. As the need for clinicians' services slowly grew, so too did the field of clinical psychology during the years from 1910 to 1917. Clinicians gave established tests, constructed new ones, and conducted research on the reliability and validity of them all. Most of the new instruments were aimed at measuring intelligence, but a few focused on the assessment of personality through word associations or questionnaire items.

However, people who sought training in clinical psychology faced some real problems during this period. A few internships were available at places such as the Vineland Training School, and a few courses in intelligence testing and related subjects were taught here and there, but there were no formalized clinical training programs. Virtually anyone could claim the title of "clinical psychologist." APA offered little help in addressing clinical training needs because of its preoccupation with the scientific aspects of psychology. Indeed, its only official recognition of the problems of the new field was to pass a resolution in 1915 discouraging the use of mental tests by unqualified persons.

In December 1917, a group of disgruntled clinicians agreed that they could best advance the interests of their new profession by forming a separate organization, called the American Association of Clinical Psychologists (AACP). Their strategy was not successful, however, and, after the APA promised to give more consideration to professional issues and problems, the AACP rejoined the APA as its clinical section in 1919.

BETWEEN THE WARS: 1918–1941

When the United States entered World War I, large numbers of military recruits had to be classified in terms of intellectual prowess and psychological stability. No techniques existed to do this, so the Army asked Robert Yerkes (then APA president) to head a committee of assessment-oriented experimental psychologists who were to develop appropriate measures.[2] To measure mental abilities, the committee produced the Army Alpha and Army Beta intelligence tests (for group administration to literate or nonliterate adults, respectively), and to help detect behavior disorders, it recommended Robert Woodworth's Psychoneurotic Inventory (discreetly retitled "personal data sheet";

---

[2]The group included Henry Goddard of the Vineland School; Guy Whipple, publisher of a 1910 *Manual of Mental and Physical Tests;* and Lewis Terman, developer of the Stanford-Binet scales.

Yerkes, 1921, in Dennis, 1948). By 1918, psychologists had conducted evaluations of nearly 2 million men.

The role of clinical psychology in wartime assessment did not change some clinicians' focus on assessing children, but many began to find growing employment opportunities as testers in adult-oriented facilities as well. Clinicians were also using a wider variety of intelligence tests for children and adults and adding new measures of personality, interests, specific abilities, emotions, and traits. They developed many of these tests themselves, while adopting others from the psychoanalytically oriented psychiatrists of Europe. Some of the more familiar instruments of this period include Jung's Word Association Test (1919), the Rorschach Inkblot Test (1921), the Miller Analogies Test (1926), the Goodenough Draw-A-Man Test (1926), the Strong Vocational Interest Test (1927), the Thematic Apperception Test (TAT) (1935), the Bender-Gestalt Test (1938), and the Wechsler-Bellevue Intelligence Scale (1939).

In fact, so many psychological tests appeared (over 500 by 1940) that a *Mental Measurements Yearbook* was needed to catalog them (Buros, 1938). The development, administration, and evaluation of these instruments continued to stimulate clinicians' assessment and research functions. In 1921, Cattell formed the Psychological Corporation to sell tests and provide consultation and research services to business and industry. Clinical psychologists of this period also developed theories and conducted research on such topics as the nature of personality, the source of human intelligence (i.e., heredity or environment), the causes of behavior disorders, the uses of hypnosis, and the relationship between learning principles and deviance.

By the mid-1930s there were fifty psychological clinics and at least a dozen child-guidance clinics in the United States. Clinical psychologists in these settings "perceived themselves as dealing with educational, not psychiatric problems. But this distinction was growing increasingly difficult to maintain" (Reisman, 1976, pp. 176–177). Slowly, clinicians added a treatment function to their assessment, training, and research roles. By the late-1930s a few had even gone into private practice. For most clinicians of the day, this treatment function was a natural outgrowth of the diagnostic and remedial services they were already providing to children. It stemmed also from clinicians' growing use of personality tests—such as the Rorschach and the TAT. Discussing the results of these tests with therapists (psychiatrists) in a common clinical language brought clinical psychologists that much closer to the treatment role. They were motivated to enter that role because it expanded their professional identity beyond that of testing, allowed them to become involved with the "whole patient," and opened the door to better-paying, more responsible jobs.

Even though its settings, clients, and functions were expanding throughout the 1930s, clinical psychology was not yet a recognized profession. At the beginning of World War II, there were still no official training programs for clinicians. A few held Ph.D.s, some had M.A.s, most had B.A.s or less. To get a job as a clinical psychologist, all one needed was a few courses in testing, abnormal psychology, and child development, along with an "interest in people." University psychology departments were reluctant to develop graduate programs in clinical psychology because their faculties tended to question the appropriateness of "applied" psychology and to worry about the cost of clinical training. Nor was much help forthcoming from the APA. It had appointed committees on clinical training at various times during the 1920s and 1930s (and had even set up a short-lived clinical certification program), but its involvement was half-hearted. For example, in 1935 the APA Committee on Standards of Training in Clinical Psychology suggested that a Ph.D. plus one year of supervised experience was necessary to become a clinical psychologist, but after issuing its report the committee disbanded and little came of its efforts.

The discontent of clinical and other nonacademic psychologists erupted in 1937, and they again broke away from APA to form a separate organization, this time called the American Association of Applied Psychology (AAAP). It contained divisions of consulting, clinical, educational, and industrial psychology and remained independent for six years before rejoining APA.

By the end of the 1930s, all the ingredients for the modern field of clinical psychology had been assembled: its six functions (assessment, treatment, research, teaching, consultation, and administration) had appeared. Clinical psychology had expanded beyond its original clinics into hospitals, prisons, and other settings. Its practitioners worked with adults as well as children, and were motivated to stand on their own as a profession. Only the support of clinical psychology's parent discipline and the society it served was still needed. This support came as a result of World War II.

THE POSTWAR EXPLOSION

When the United States entered World War II, mass testing of the intelligence, ability, and personality of military personnel was again necessary and, as in World War I, a committee of psychologists was formed to help with the task. Because psychometric and clinical sophistication had increased greatly since the time of the Yerkes committee, this new group of psychologists produced a wider range of military-oriented tests, including the Army General Classification Test (a group intelligence instrument), a psychiatric screening questionnaire called the Personal Inventory, brief measures of intelligence, short forms of the Rorschach and the TAT, and several ability tests for selection of officers, pilots, and the like.[3]

The involvement of psychology in World War II was also far deeper than it had been in World War I. For example, about 1,500 psychologists (nearly 25% of those available) served in World War II. They were commissioned officers, just like physicians, and in 1944 alone, they gave over 60 million psychological tests to 20 million soldiers and civilians (Reisman, 1976). In addition to giving tests, psychologists conducted interviews, wrote psychological reports, and, because of the overwhelming caseload of psychological casualties, performed psychoanalytically oriented therapy. For those who had been clinicians before the war, military life meant an opportunity to consolidate and expand their clinical functions, but such individuals were in the minority.

---

[3]Some of the latter techniques included behavioral measures that required candidates to perform various tasks under frustrating or stressful conditions. Such "real-life" observation is now a popular clinical assessment strategy (see Chapter 6).

Most wartime psychologists came from academic settings. For them, the army's desperate need for applied psychological services meant taking on clinical responsibilities for the first time. These converted clinicians found they were able to handle their new jobs remarkably well.

By the end of the war, many clinicians were "hooked" on doing therapy with adults, and many former experimentalists became enamored of clinical functions. Military and civilian authorities, too, were impressed with psychologists' clinical skills, which brought psychologists increasing public attention and prestige. This awakening of interest in psychologists' clinical work might have come to nothing if there had not been so much of it to do. The war left over 40,000 people in Veterans Administration neuropsychiatric hospitals, and there were nowhere near enough clinical psychologists and psychiatrists to serve these patients adequately.

Where the APA and university psychology departments had vacillated over the education and roles of clinicians, the needs of the federal government prompted immediate action. A 1946 VA circular defined clinical psychology as a profession that engaged in diagnosis, treatment, and research relating to adult disorders; it described clinicians as holders of the Ph.D. More important, the VA said it needed 4,700 of these individuals to fill lucrative, high-prestige jobs and that it would help pay for clinical training. "This document, more than any other single thing, has served to guide the development of clinical psychology" (Hathaway (1958, p. 107). Here was the support clinical psychology had been waiting for. Early in 1946, the chief medical director of the VA met with representatives of major universities to ask them to start formal clinical training programs; by that fall, 200 graduate students became VA clinical trainees at twenty-two institutions (Peck & Ash, 1964). By 1951 the VA had become the largest single employer of psychologists in the United States.

Given their earlier misgivings, not all psychology departments that began clinical training programs after the war were enthusiastic about doing so. Faculty members sympathetic to clinical work saw government support as a boon, but those devoted to keeping psychology a "pure" science objected to professional training as an intrusion that was being performed only because the government (first through the VA and then the United States Public Health Service, USPHS) was willing to pay for it. David Shakow (1965) characterized this conflict as pitting the "virgins" against the "prostitutes." Whatever one calls it, the debate centered on the same "science versus profession" controversy that first appeared in 1896 and which continues today.

In any case, the VA and USPHS went ahead with their funding plans and turned to the APA for guidance about which university clinical programs merited federal support. In 1947, APA's Committee on Graduate and Professional Training provided a preliminary report on existing programs (Kelly, 1961). Later that year, a more extensive report came from David Shakow's Committee on Training in Clinical Psychology, which had been appointed by the APA to (1) recommend the content of clinical programs, (2) set up training standards to be followed by universities and internship facilities, and (3) report on current programs (Shakow, 1978). This "Shakow Report" was meant only to provide training guidelines, but since it was so intimately tied to the dispensation of federal money to individual students and whole departments, the "guidelines" were adopted as policy "and soon became the 'bible' of all departments of psychology desirous of having their programs evaluated and reported on favorably by the APA" (Kelly, 1961, p. 110). Shakow felt that this reaction prematurely froze the nature of clinical training, and that, if the guidelines had been less rigidly interpreted, the resulting programs might have been better.

Indeed, the Shakow Report laid the groundwork for later controversy over how clinicians should be trained, an issue that related directly to the science-profession problem. The recommendations in the report that have the greatest contemporary importance are these:

1. Clinical psychologists should be trained first as psychologists (i.e., as scientists) and second as practicing professionals.

2. Clinical training should be as rigorous as that given to nonclinicians and thus should consist of a four-year doctorate, including a year of supervised clinical internship experience.

3. Clinical training should focus on the "holy trinity" (assessment, research, and treatment) by offering courses in general psychology, psychodynamics, assessment techniques, research methods, and therapy (APA, 1947; Shakow, 1978).

Thus began "what later came to be recognized as something of an educational experiment: the training of persons both as scientists and as practitioners, not in a separate professional school [as is the case in medicine or law], but in the graduate schools of our universities" (Kelly, 1961, p. 112). This experiment continued with the support of the APA, the federal government, internship facilities, and universities. Two years after the Shakow report appeared, participants in a national conference on clinical training at Boulder, Colorado, formally adopted its recommendations. In addition, APA created an Education and Training Board to evaluate and publish lists of accredited doctoral-level clinical programs and internship settings.

The scientist-professional training package described in the Shakow Report and adopted at the Boulder Conference in 1949 came to be known as the "Boulder model"; it set the pattern for clinical training for the next twenty-five years. Nevertheless, not everyone in the field was enthusiastic about it, and though its official APA status was reaffirmed at subsequent training conferences in 1955, 1958, 1962, 1965, and 1973, discontent remained. In chapter 14, we consider the details of these conferences and the modifications of the Boulder model that have ensued. Suffice it to say here that psychologists committed to professional practice felt that the model emphasized research training at the expense of preparation for applied work, while more research-oriented psychologists failed to see the need for so much emphasis on application.

As debate continued over the appropriateness of the Boulder model, government support of its use in university-based clinical training programs fueled explosive growth in clinical psychology. In 1948, there were 22 APA-approved clinical training programs; there were 60 by 1962, 83 by 1973, more than 150 by 1993, and there are 187 today. Personality and intelligence assessment mushroomed following the introduction of tests like the Minnesota Multiphasic Personality Inventory (MMPI), new scoring procedures for projectives like the Rorshach, and new adult intelligence scales. Clinical psychologists' treatment roles, now recognized by the government and by the public, blossomed as well. Three times as many clinical psychologists engaged in therapy after the war as before it, and though many still treated children, the emphasis began to swing toward adult clients. As shown in Table 1.1, the clinician in private practice became more common as practitioners sought to pattern themselves after physicians.

Legal recognition of clinical psychology as a profession was growing as well. In the postwar years, states began passing laws providing for licensure or certification of qualified clinicians, and the APA set up an independent certification group to identify individuals who had attained particularly high levels of clinical experience and expertise. The APA also developed a code of ethics governing the behavior of all its members, but focusing on those engaged in applied activities. These and other aspects of clinical psychology as a profession are discussed more fully in Chapter 14.

Clinical research also expanded after World War II and produced some disturbingly negative conclusions on the usefulness of some personality tests (e.g., Magaret, 1952), the value of clinicians' diagnostic judgments when compared to statistically based decisions (Meehl, 1954), and the effectiveness of traditional (mainly Freudian) psychotherapy (Eysenck, 1952). This research created discontent with standard clinical assessment methods and motivated the development of many new approaches to treatment, including humanistic and behavioral varieties.

By the 1980s, almost everything that could have been said about clinical psychology before World War II had changed. The clinical psychologist before the war was primarily a diagnostician whose clients were children. After 1945 the functions, settings, and clients of clinical psychology expanded dramatically. Today's clinician enjoys a wider range of theoretical approaches and practical tools for assessing and altering human behavior.

CLINICAL PSYCHOLOGY IN THE TWENTY-FIRST CENTURY

The chronology on the inside front cover of this book shows that clinical psychology has advanced in spectacular fashion over the last 100 years, but neither its development nor its self-examination is complete. As clinical psychology enters the twenty-first century, it faces an unprecedented number of issues and challenges that promise to change almost every aspect of the field, including the way clinical students are trained, the services clinicians provide, the settings where they provide them, the manner by which they are paid, and the theories that guide their explanations and treatment of psychological disorders (Clarke-Kudless, 1996). Some of these issues and challenges— such as the scientist-practitioner distinction, the value of assessment and therapy, how to prevent psychological problems, and how best to serve the poor and other underserved populations—have been around for decades. Issues and challenges of more recent origin include whether clinicians should have the right to prescribe psychoactive drugs, the impact of health care reforms on private practice and the quality of clinical services, and the increasingly interdisciplinary and specialized nature of clinical work. We discuss all these factors in later chapters; here we highlight just a few.

The Challenges of Health Care Reform

For many decades, clinical psychology operated on a fee-for-service basis. That is, clients or their insurance companies reimbursed clinicians for whatever assessment or therapy services were provided. However, the last fifteen years have seen dramatic changes in the financing of the services provided by all health care professions, including clinical psychology. By far, the most important of these changes has been the introduction by insurance companies of *managed care*, a general strategy which, as mentioned earlier, controls health care costs by paying only for certain treatments, offered by specifically approved providers, for limited periods of time. In many managed care plans, the consumer pays a fixed annual fee, which is passed on to health care providers. If, in a given year, these providers offer fewer services than the prepaid plan anticipated, they stand to make a profit; if they must offer more services, they suffer a loss.

As a result of these economic forces, we anticipate a number of fundamental changes in the practice of clinical psychology in the twenty-first century, including (1) an emphasis on prevention, so that fewer clients will need extensive (and expensive) individual therapy, (2) a continuation of the post-1990 decline in the solo private practice of psychology as more clinicians join group practices in order to cut costs, (3) an increase in the use of brief therapies that emphasize problem-solving skills and rapid symptom reduction, (4) a demand that clinicians employ only those treatment methods that have been empirically demonstrated to be effective, whether or not they are the ones the clinicians normally use, (5) a larger role for clinicians trained at B.A. or M.A. levels, because they tend to be paid less than doctoral personnel, (6) more involvement of clinicians with clients suffering from cancer, cardiovascular diseases, diabetes, and other health problems associated with or complicated by psychological factors, and (7) more intense calls for clinical psychologists to receive the training needed to prescribe cost-effective psychoactive drugs (Cullen & Newman, 1997; Cummings, 1995; Murray, 1996).

Trends Toward Integrated Theories and Interdisciplinary Work

In the next chapter, we will see that clinicians are influenced by several specific *psychological* theories of personality and psychopathology, but it is also the case that many of these theories are becoming increasingly multidisciplinary. That is, clinicians are becoming increasingly aware that mental disorders can often best be understood and treated by focusing on a combination of biological, sociocultural, and psychological factors. In particular, the increasing prominence of biological factors in these theories is rapidly changing how clinical psychologists are trained and how they think about mental disorders. As scientists continue making new discoveries in behavioral genetics, as neuroimaging studies of the living brain become more sophisticated, and as the biochemistry of behavior becomes better understood, we suspect that assessments, explanations, and treatments of many mental disorders will take a pronounced biological turn. Indeed, almost every major mental disorder has now been linked to interactions of various biological vulnerabilities and psychological processes, and these *diathesis-stress* theories are generally proving much more powerful than the single-variable explanations of the past. Clinicians of the twenty-first century will need training in, and an appreciation of, the neurosciences if clinical psychology is to continue as a psychological science.

Specialization of Clinical Activity

In the past, the ideal training for clinical psychologists included a core of knowledge about scientific methods and psychopathology, along with courses in and practical experience with valid assessment and treatment strategies. This "core curriculum" model has come under increasing challenge, mainly because clinical psychologists are now working in many specialized areas that demand specialized training not included in traditional graduate programs. Increasingly, this training is provided through post-doctoral traineeships in which clinicians work under expert supervision for a year or two in a designated specialty area. Several of these specializations are described in later chapters; in fact, most of the revisions we have made to this book over the past two decades have been designed to keep up with this "specializing" of clinical psychology. Consistent with trends in psychology in general, many of the developing clinical specialties reflect a biological orientation; neuropsychology, health psychology or behavioral medicine, and pediatric psychology are prominent examples. Forensic psychology is another specialization that will expand the definition of clinical psychology in the twenty-first century. In short, it is unclear today whether, as that century passes, clinical psychology will be one large field or several smaller ones.

The Scientist-Practitioner Issue

In contemporary clinical psychology, there are—to use William James's famous distinction—"tough-minded" clinicians who insist that clinical work should be based on scientifically verified findings and that clinical training should be grounded in basic psychological theory and rigorous research. There are also "tender-minded" clinicians who believe that wisdom can be distilled from many sources, including research, clinical experience, and personal intuitions, and that scientific methods may not capture the subtleties of human behavior and are therefore an insufficient base for clinical practice. Although many clinicians try to stake out a middle ground that allows them to be both empirical *and* intuitive, the fact is that the gulf between tender- and tough-minded clinicians is often wide and reflects fundamental differences in the way they are trained, the types of clinical services they provide, and the sort of evidence they consider convincing. In fact, the extent to which clinicians endorse tough- or tender-minded beliefs predicts their positions on many of the major controversies facing clinicians today— such as whether memories of childhood trauma can be repressed and then accurately recalled years later, whether specific types of psychotherapy are effective, and even whether certain mental disorders are real (Hasemann, Nietzel, & Golding, 1996).

Can clinicians be tough-minded without being cold-hearted? Can they be critical enough to scrutinize faddish ideas and fuzzy thinking without being so skeptical that they reject all new ideas whose worth is simply hard to prove? Finding just the right

balance between close-minded skepticism and uncritical acceptance of anything that
"feels" right is an elusive goal, not only in clinical training, but also in the daily activities
of clinicians already in the field. These clinicians continue to ask how they can be
scientifically-minded psychologists who wait for carefully validated evidence before diagnosing a condition or proceeding with a treatment and, at the same time, function as
"front-line" practitioners who try to help distressed people with complex problems
about which little knowledge may be available.

Some observers feel that the scientific and professional roles are basically incompatible, and that a psychologist must choose one or the other. Accordingly, some clinical students become intuitive practitioners to whom *data* is a nasty word, while others
work as full-time researchers in hopes of generating empirical findings that will some-
day make all clinical practice scientific. Another indication of the conflict between
academic psychologists and practitioners is seen in their preferences for the type of
professional organization that best represents their respective views. In 1988, the
American Psychological Society (APS) was formed by a group of psychologists who
wanted an organization that is more scientifically-oriented than what, in their eyes, the
APA had become. Although some research-oriented clinicians belong to both APA and
APS, most full-time practitioners appear to prefer APA over APS as their professional
"home."

If the past is any indication of the future, the scientist-professional debate will
continue well into the twenty-first century. Unfortunately, the debate has polarized
clinical psychology. It threatens to isolate practitioners from research that may be useful in applied work, and it may keep researchers in laboratory settings that are so artificial that their results apply only to other laboratories or to situations where the most interesting and important clinical problems may not appear. The cumulative result of this
polarization could be a reduction in the mutual stimulation between clinic and laboratory that we, and many others in the field, consider vital to the future of clinical psychology (Bootzin, 1996; Strupp, 1989).

In our view, clinical psychology will advance and prosper as a profession and a
scholarly field only to the degree that it remains firmly grounded in the foundations of
science. We recognize that science can be defined in several ways (Gergen, 1985), but
for our purposes in this book the essential feature of a scientific clinical psychology is
that clinicians evaluate the validity of their theories, the effectiveness of their techniques, and the impact of their practice with public, replicable, and well-controlled empirical research methods. The clearest call for building a scientific clinical psychology
has been sounded in Richard McFall's (1991) "Manifesto for a Science of Clinical Psychology." McFall's manifesto has been echoed by other clinical psychologists (Chambliss et al., 1995; Sechrest, 1992) and consists of the following three principles:

1. Scientific clinical psychology is the only legitimate and acceptable form of clinical
   psychology.
2. Psychological services should not be delivered to the public (except under strict
   experimental control) until they meet four criteria: the service is described
   clearly, its claimed benefits are stated explicitly, its effects are validated scientifically, and its positive effects are shown to outweigh its possible negative effects.

3. The primary and overriding objective of doctoral training programs in clinical psychology must be to produce the most competent clinical scientists possible.

As the size and stature of clinical psychology have grown, the field has become more tolerant of divergent ideas about clinical training, professional roles, and basic issues like the development of human problems and the means through which they can best be alleviated. Throughout this book we review the most important of these contrasting ideas and illustrate their importance for clinical psychologists. We have tried to describe the various models and methods of clinical psychology fairly, but we also intend the book to reflect our conviction that these models and methods are best judged against the scientific standards suggested by McFall's manifesto.

CHAPTER SUMMARY

Clinical psychology, the largest single subfield within the larger discipline of psychology, involves six main functions: assessment, treatment, research, teaching, consultation, and administration. In carrying out these functions, clinicians are distinguished from other psychologists, and other helping professions, by their clinical attitude: the tendency to use the results of research on human behavior in general to assess, understand, and assist particular individuals. They deal with a wide range of clients from all age groups and focus on an even wider range of behavior problems, from anxiety, depression, and psychoses, to occupational stress, mental retardation, and difficulties at school. Clinical psychologists are employed in many different settings, from university psychology departments and medical clinics to community mental health centers and prisons. Many are self-employed private practitioners.

Clinical psychology began in 1896, when Lightner Witmer agreed to assess and treat a child with problems at school. His efforts in this regard, and his establishment of the world's first psychological clinic, were not supported by most other psychologists (who saw these professional activities as falling outside the realm of scientific psychology), but the assessment and treatment functions of clinical psychology grew over the next 100 years, spurred by the need for psychological testing and treatment services in schools, military recruitment centers, and hospitals that cared for veterans, especially the psychological casualties of World War II. After that war, the prestige, activities, and training programs for clinical psychologists experienced explosive growth. Today, clinical psychology is a well-established field whose members engage in an ever-expanding range of research and services while continuing to address a number of persistent issues (such as the scientist-practitioner distinction) and to face challenges posed by health care reform and other social changes.

Chapter 2

Approaches to Clinical Psychology

To fully appreciate the characteristics and dimensions of an object, one must examine it from several angles; this is why sculpture is often displayed where the viewer can walk around it. Events are also subject to multiple interpretations, depending on one's focus of attention and point of view. For example, when psychology professors ask students to recall a staged classroom event—a "disgruntled former student" bursting in to berate the professor, for example—there is inevitable variability in observers' reports of what happened and what the intruder looked like.

Listening to differing accounts of the same occurrence from varying points of view can be confusing. It can also be illuminating in the sense that, as with a statue, one is allowed to examine all the angles. And though the "truth" about an event, relationship, or person may not necessarily be revealed, there is at least the assurance that potentially important material has not been overlooked. Clinical psychologists often follow a similar strategy by gathering assessment information not just from a client, but from the client's family, teachers, and peers.

Similarly, the field of clinical psychology can be most fully understood when examined from several different perspectives, each of which emphasizes some of its aspects over others. Each of these perspectives, or *approaches*, tries to explain how behavior develops and becomes problematic, and each influences the assessment, treatment, and research activities of those who adopt a particular approach. For example, suppose there were an approach to clinical psychology which sees behavior as caused by what people eat. Clinicians taking this approach would probably make predictions about how diet affects human development (e.g., "Mushy foods produce mushy thinking and uncoordinated behavior."). They would also generate hypotheses about how diet is related to mental disorder (e.g., excess carbohydrate intake causes anxiety; too little fiber creates obsessive rituals). They would develop specialized measurement procedures to assess clients' eating patterns and to monitor the nutritional components of each meal. Their treatments would probably focus on changing clients' eating habits; merely talking about a client's problems would be regarded as a waste of time. Finally, their research would probably evaluate procedures for measuring and altering food intake, as well as test the validity of causal links between diet and disorder.

Though diet is important in many aspects of life, the thinking and activities of most clinicians today are influenced mainly by some combination of the *psychodynamic, behavioral, phenomenological*, and *interpersonal* approaches to clinical psychology. In this chapter, we review the assumptions and implications of these approaches.

THE PROS AND CONS OF TAKING A SPECIFIC APPROACH

The various approaches to clinical psychology help clinicians organize their thinking about behavior, guide their clinical decisions and interventions, and communicate with colleagues in a common language. Specific approaches also impose order on, and suggest relationships among, vast amounts of complex material.

For example, human behavior can be examined on several levels, from the interactions among brain cells to the interactions among people, or even among nations or cultures. Clinicians must decide which aspects of behavior deserve special attention, which kinds of assessment data will be of greatest value for a given purpose, which treatment techniques merit exploration, and which research targets are likely to be most fruitful. A clinician's approach guides these decisions, thereby helping bring order to what may otherwise be conceptual and procedural chaos.

Each specific approach tends to attract followers whose commitment to it ranges from healthy skepticism to fanatic zeal. However, the usefulness of these approaches must be evaluated on dimensions other than how intuitively appealing they are or how many adherents they claim. In scientific terms, the best approaches to clinical psychology are those whose implications and hypotheses can be rigorously investigated in a wide range of contexts. To be of greatest value to clinical psychologists, an approach should include a complete and testable account of the development, maintenance, and alteration of both problematic and nonproblematic human behavior. Approaches that meet these requirements are open to experimental evaluation, and they will stand or fall as the data accumulate.

Ironically, a specific approach to clinical psychology can act not only as a compass and guide, but also as a set of blinders. Some clinicians, for example, allow their favorite approach to so completely organize their thinking about behavior and behavior disorder that they become rigid and closed to new and potentially valuable ideas associated with other approaches. In short, their views become not just organized, but fossilized in a way that makes objective evaluation and subsequent modification of professional practices unlikely. Clinicians who become overly dependent on a specific approach may continue to perform in strict accordance with its tenets even when empirical evidence suggests that change is in order. In other words, taking a consistent perspective can evolve from an asset to a liability if it produces such a narrow focus that other points of view are overlooked. Finally, an approach is like a region of the world that develops its own dialect. That dialect eases communication among those who share it, but it can obstruct discussions with those who do not. Often, the exchange of ideas between persons espousing different approaches to clinical psychology is hampered by this kind of language barrier. Both parties think they are speaking clearly and comprehensibly when, in fact, their specialized terms and meanings keep them from fully understanding each other. We have heard heated theoretical arguments of this type that ended when the participants finally realized that, in many ways, they agreed with one another!

Fortunately, most problems associated with taking a specific approach to clinical psychology can be reduced by (1) avoiding the overzealous commitment to it that fosters conceptual rigidity, behavioral inflexibility, and semantic narrowness, and (2) evaluating that approach according to rigorous scientific methods, and revising the approach when the data demand it. This is not to say that systematic use of a particular approach is not important; quite the opposite. However, understanding and appreciating other points of view can act as insurance against a narrow-mindedness that could be detrimental to clinicians and clients alike. We hope that the material in this chapter will help you remain open-minded. If you are already acquainted with psychodynamic, behavioral, phenomenological, and interpersonal theories of personality, some of the chapter may be familiar, but we also go beyond abstract theory to outline the assessment and treatment implications that flow from each approach and how they are likely to be applied to individual cases. In subsequent chapters, we will consider in more detail the specific tactics that translate these strategies into action.

One final point: None of the models discussed in this chapter is a single, unitary entity. Each is made up of variations on a basic theme; thus, to characterize adequately each model, we must describe several of these variations.

THE PSYCHODYNAMIC APPROACH

The psychodynamic model is rooted in the writings of Sigmund Freud, but it has broadened to include the ideas of those who revised and challenged many of Freud's concepts. The model is based upon the following assumptions:

1. Human behavior is determined by impulses, desires, motives, and conflicts that are *intrapsychic* (within the mind) and often out of awareness.
2. Intrapsychic factors cause both normal and abnormal behaviors. Thus, just as disabling anxiety might be attributed to unresolved conflicts or unmet needs, a

person's outgoing style might be seen as reflecting inner fears of worthlessness or a hidden desire to be more popular than a sibling.

3. The foundations for behavior are set down in childhood through satisfaction or frustration of basic needs and impulses. Because of their central role in these needs, early relationships with family, peers, and authority figures are given special attention.

4. Clinical assessment, treatment, and research should emphasize the subtle aspects of intrapsychic activity which, though often hidden from direct observation, must be uncovered if behavior is to be understood and behavior problems are to be alleviated.

Freudian Psychoanalysis

Freud's psychodynamic theory, known as *psychoanalysis*, was founded on a few basic principles. One of these is *psychic determinism*, the notion that behavior can be caused by psychological factors that are hidden from outside observers and the behaving individual as well. From this perspective, almost all behaviors (even "accidents") are seen as meaningful because they provide clues to hidden conflicts and motivations (Freud, 1901). Thus, reading the word *breast* when the text says *beast*, forgetting a relative's name, or losing a borrowed book might all be interpreted as expressing feelings or impulses that may not appear in awareness. Freud called *unconscious* the part of mental functioning that is out of awareness and not readily accessible to it.

Another of Freud's basic postulates was that human behavior is derived from the constant struggle between the individual's desire to satisfy inborn sexual and aggressive instincts and the need to respect the rules and realities imposed by the outside world. He saw each individual facing a lifelong search for ways of expressing instinctual urges without incurring punishment or other negative consequences. To Freud, then, the human mind is an arena where what the person *wants* to do (instinct) must be reconciled with the controlling requirements of what *can* or *should* be done (reason and morality). Suppose, for example, a mother tells her seven-year-old boy to stop playing video games. If he then eats sixteen oatmeal raisin cookies and throws up on her, a psychoanalyst might see the boy's behavior as the expression of aggressive impulses that is sufficiently well-disguised to avoid punishment.

Mental Structure.   In Freud's system, unconscious instincts make up the *id*, which is present at birth and contains all the psychic energy—or *libido*—available to motivate behavior. Id seeks to gratify its desires without delay, and therefore it is said to operate on the *pleasure principle* (i.e., "If it feels good, do it!"). As the newborn grows and the outside world imposes more limitations on direct id gratification, the *ego* begins to organize as an outgrowth of id around the age of one year and begins to find safe outlets for expression of instincts. It was our seven-year-old's ego, for example, that engineered the revenge wreaked upon his mother. Since ego adjusts to external demands, it operates on the *reality principle* (i.e., "If you are going to do it, at least do it quietly"). A third mental agency, *superego*, is another result of the socializing influence of reality. It contains all the teachings of family and culture regarding ethics, morals, and values, and according to Freud, these teachings are internalized to become the "ego ideal," or how one would like to be. Superego also contains the conscience, which seeks to promote perfect, conforming, and socially acceptable behavior usually opposed by id.

Mechanisms of Defense. Freud's three-part mental structure is constantly embroiled in anxiety-provoking internal conflicts. The ego attempts to keep these conflicts and their discomfort from reaching consciousness by employing a variety of *defense mechanisms*, usually at an unconscious level. One of the most common—and for Freud, the most prototypic of these mechanisms—is *repression*, where ego simply holds an unacceptable thought, feeling, or impulse out of consciousness. Repression has also been called *motivated forgetting*. For example, an individual whose hatred toward a parent is not consciously experienced may repress that hatred (when a person is aware of an impulse and *consciously* denies its existence, the process is called *suppression*).

In spite of constant efforts at repression, undesirable urges—much like an inflated balloon held under water—may sometimes threaten to surface. To guard against this, the ego employs additional unconscious defenses, such as *reaction formation*, in which the person thinks and acts exactly opposite to the unconscious impulse. Thus, a son who hates his father may express unbounded love and concern for him. If the defense mechanism called *projection* is used, the son may attribute negative feelings to others and accuse them of mistreating *their* fathers. A defense mechanism called *displacement* allows some expression of id impulses, but it aims them at safer targets, such as co-workers or others who may be father figures. Thus, the son may harshly criticize an older colleague instead of his father.

Though they may be at least temporarily successful, defense mechanisms waste a lot of psychic energy, and, under stress, they may fail, thus forcing the troubled person to fall back, or *regress*, to levels of behavior characteristic of earlier, less mature stages of development. The depth of regression in a given case is partly a function of the individual's history of psychosexual development.

Developmental Stages. Freud postulated that children pass through several psychosexual stages of development, each named for the part of the body most associated with pleasure at the time. The first year or so is called the oral stage, because eating, sucking, biting, and other oral activities are the predominant sources of pleasure. If, because of premature or delayed weaning, oral needs are frustrated or overindulged, the child may fail to pass through the oral stage without clinging to, or becoming *fixated* on, behavioral patterns associated with it. Adults who depend inordinately upon oral behavioral patterns such as smoking or overeating may be seen as orally fixated. Freud felt that the stronger an individual's fixation at a given psychosexual stage, the more behaviors typical of that stage would be shown at a later point and the more likely it would be that regression to that level would occur under stress. A person who becomes excessively dependent or depressed when dependency needs are not met are sometimes viewed by Freudians as having regressed to the oral stage.

The second year or so is called the *anal* stage, because Freud saw the anus and the stimuli associated with eliminating and withholding feces as the important sources of pleasure at that point. The significant feature of this period is toilet training, in which there is a clash of wills between parents and children. Anal fixation is thought to result from overly strict or overly permissive practices in this area. Adults who are either stingy, obstinate, highly organized, and overconcerned with cleanliness, or who are sloppy, disorganized, and especially generous with money might be seen as fixated at the anal stage.

The child enters Freud's *phallic* stage at about age three or four, as the genitals become the primary source of pleasure. He theorized that during the phallic stage young boys begin to have sexual desires for their mothers and to want to do away with their fathers' competition. This situation was labeled *Oedipal* because it recapitulates the plot of the Greek tragedy *Oedipus Rex*. Because the boy fears punishment for his incestuous and murderous desires, Oedipal conflicts are normally resolved by repressing sexual desires toward the mother, *identifying* with the father, and ultimately finding an appropriate female sex partner.

Although Freud emphasized male psychosexual development, he did discuss a female Oedipus complex—he rejected the term *Electra complex*, used by some of his students—in which a little girl suffers *penis envy* and a sense of inferiority because she believes she has already been "castrated" for desiring her father. She ultimately sublimates these feelings by substituting a desire to have a baby for a desire to have a penis, thus identifying with her mother. (As you might imagine, these views have not made Freud a popular figure among feminists.) Freud believed that successful resolution of conflicts in the phallic stage was crucial to healthy psychological development and that fixation at the phallic stage is responsible for many adult interpersonal behaviors, including rebellion, aggression, and sexual practices such as homosexuality, exhibitionism, and fetishism.

Freud believed a dormant or *latency* period follows the phallic stage. During latency, id impulses recede and the reality principle becomes a stronger force in the child's life, allowing the child to focus on developing social and academic skills. The latency period extends until adolescence, when the individual's physical maturity ushers in the *genital* period. In this final stage—which lasts throughout the adult years—pleasure is again focused on the genital area, but if all has gone well in earlier stages, sexual interest is directed not just toward the self-satisfaction characteristic of the phallic period, but toward establishment of a stable, long-term relationship in which the needs of another are valued and considered.

Other Psychodynamic Approaches

Some of Freud's followers created variations on his psychodynamic approach. These variations were stimulated by several factors, including (a) dissatisfaction with the central role Freud gave to unconscious instincts in motivation, (b) increased recognition of the influence of social and cultural variables on human behavior, (c) recognition of the role of *conscious* aspects of personality, and (d) belief that personality development does not end in childhood (Liebert & Spiegler 1990).

For example, some of the less radical variations on psychoanalysis see ego as a positive, creative, coping mechanism, not just the "referee" in intrapsychic conflicts. In these versions (e.g., Hartmann, 1939), the ego is seen as having independent energy and growth potential that is not tied up in unconscious defensive functions. Another important revision of psychoanalysis was presented by Erik H. Erikson, an American psychologist who emphasized social factors in human development. Erikson (1959, 1963) outlined a sequence of eight psychosocial stages that is oriented toward people's social, rather than intrapsychic, activities. As shown in Table 2.1, a social crisis is either successfully handled or left partly unresolved at each stage.

Other psychodynamic theorists rejected rather than revised certain aspects of psychoanalysis. For example, Alfred Adler, one of Freud's original followers, developed a brand of psychoanalysis known as *individual psychology*, in which the most important psychological factor in human behavior and development is inferiority, not instinct. Adler also emphasized the family as a whole, not just the Oedipal situation. He proposed a theory about the effects of birth order on personality which is still debated today (Sulloway, 1996). Noting that each person begins life in a helpless and inferior position, Adler suggested that subsequent behavior represents a compensatory "striving for superiority" (first within the family, then in the larger social world). The particular ways each individual seeks superiority comprise a *style of life*. Adaptive lifestyles are characterized by cooperation, social interest, courage, and common sense. Maladaptive styles are reflected in extreme competitiveness or dependency, lack of concern for

TABLE 2.1   Erikson's Eight Stages or Crises and Associated Emerging Traits

Stage	Age	Successful Resolution Leads to:	Unsuccessful Resolution Leads to:
I. Trust vs. Mistrust (Oral)*	Birth–1 yr.	Hope	Fear
II. Autonomy vs. Shame and Doubt (Anal)*	1–3 yr.	Willpower	Self-doubt
III. Initiative vs. Guilt (Phallic)*	4–5 yr.	Purpose	Unworthiness
IV. Industry vs. Inferiority (Latency)*	6–11 yr.	Competency	Incompetency
V. Ego Identity vs. Role Confusion	12–20 yr.	Fidelity	Uncertainty
VI. Intimacy vs. Isolation	20–24 yr.	Love	Promiscuity
VII. Generativity vs. Stagnation	25–65 yr.	Care	Selfishness
VIII. Ego Integrity vs. Despair	65 yr.–death	Wisdom	Meaninglessness and despair

*Roughly corresponding Freudian stage.

SOURCE: E. J. Phares. *Introduction to Personality,* 2nd ed. Glenview, IL: Scott, Foresman and Company, 1988, p. 123.

others, and distortion of reality. Adler believed that maladaptive lifestyles and behavioral problems are caused by misconceptions the individual has about the world. Thus, if a little boy discovers that he can control others (and thus attain feelings of superiority) by asking for their assistance in everything from dressing to eating, he might eventually develop the misconception that he is a "special case" and that he cannot deal with the world on his own. The person whose lifestyle evolves from such a mistaken idea might appear frightened, sick, or handicapped in ways that demand special attention and consideration from others (Mosak & Dreikurs, 1973).

Revisions and reformulations of Freud's ideas by Carl Jung, Karen Horney, Erich Fromm, and Harry Stack Sullivan have also contributed to the psychodynamic approach to clinical psychology (see Munroe, 1955). More recently, *object relations* theorists such as Donald Winnicott (1965) and W. R. D. Fairbairn (1952) replaced most of Freud's ideas with very different explanations of how early experiences affect personality and mental disorder. Closely aligned with object relations theory are the views of Otto Kernberg (1976) and Heinz Kohut (1977), both of whom stressed that adult personality is based on the nature of very early interactions between infants and their caregivers. We discuss object relations theories further in chapter 8.

Evaluation of Freud's Psychodynamic Model

Sigmund Freud presented the most comprehensive and revolutionary theory of behavior ever articulated. He introduced concepts that captured the imagination of psychiatry, psychology, and other helping professions, not to mention literature, religion, sociology, and anthropology. The intensive study of a single individual, the one-to-one assessment or treatment session, the view that overt behavior is systematically related to identifiable psychological causes, the possibility that individuals' behavior may be influenced by factors of which they are unaware, the effects of childhood experience on adult behavior, the symbolic significance of overt behavior, the importance of conflict and anxiety, and other factors emphasized by many types of clinicians are directly traceable to Freud.

Today, however, Freud's approach is under increasingly harsh criticism on several grounds:

1. Basic psychodynamic concepts—such as projection, unconscious motivation, and repression—are seen as too vague to be measured and tested scientifically (e.g., Crews, 1996). Indeed, attempts to empirically investigate psychoanalytic constructs (e.g., Epstein, 1994; Silverman & Weinberger, 1985) have been faulted for methodological and conceptual problems (e.g, Brand, 1995). A related critique is that the psychoanalytic view is not easily influenced by contradictory data. For example, hostile behavior can be evidence for unconscious feelings of hostility, but so too can friendly behavior—if it is seen as a reaction formation.

2. Freud's approach did not evolve out of systematic research but out of his clinical experiences with a small number of upper-class patients living in Vienna in the late 1800s. Questions have been raised about whether these case reports might have been biased, or, in some instances, even falsified, to suit Freud's pet theories

(e.g., Esterson, 1993; MacMillan, 1991) and about how well Freud's ideas apply to people from other socioeconomic and cultural backgrounds (Landrine & Klonoff, 1992). Freud's biased views about women have also caused many male and female feminists to reject his account of human development (Chesler, 1972).

3. The reliability and validity of techniques designed to measure Freudian personality constructs appear weak (Smith & Dumont, 1995; Wood, Nezworski, & Stejskal, 1996; see Chapter 5), and the effectiveness of psychoanalytic treatment has been questioned (see Chapter 9).

4. Psychoanalytic explanations of behavior are seen as placing too much emphasis on sexual and aggressive instincts and not enough on people's inherent growth potential, learning experiences, and sociocultural background.

5. Freud's emphasis on childhood causes of adult behavior neglects the role of more immediate situational influences on behavior. This aspect of classic psychoanalysis led many neo-Freudians to stress the importance of factors that stretch across the life span, an emphasis that the other approaches to clinical psychology share.

THE BEHAVIORAL APPROACH

Instead of emphasizing intrapsychic conflicts, instincts, or unconscious motivation in the development and alteration of human behavior, the behavioral approach focuses directly on that behavior and its relationship to the environmental and personal conditions that affect it. The basic assumption of this approach is that behavior is primarily influenced by *learning*, which takes place in a *social context*.

Clinicians who take a behavioral approach tend to attribute individual differences in behavior to people's unique learning histories, not to traits, personality characteristics, or "mental illness." Thus, a student who benefited in the past from cheating may cheat again to earn a high grade, while an individual rewarded in the past for diligent study may be less likely to behave dishonestly. More general cultural factors are also seen as a part of people's learning histories. Upon receiving a failing grade on a vital exam, some students' cultural values may prompt so much shame as to engender a suicide attempt; for others, the failure may evoke a culturally traditional desire for revenge.

The behavioral approach sees similarities among people as resulting from the commonalities in rules, values, and learning histories shared by most people in the same culture. Thus, students' attentiveness during a lecture would not be seen as a collective manifestation of some intrapsychic process, but rather as a group fulfillment of the socially learned student role, which appears in certain academic situations for specified periods of time.

The same principles of learning that account for behavioral differences and similarities *among* individuals are also employed to explain consistencies and discrepancies *within* individuals. Behaviorists view behavioral consistency (which other approaches refer to as "personality") as stemming from generalized learning, stable cognitive abilities, and/or similarities across stimulus situations. For example, a person may appear calm under most circumstances if calmness has been rewarded over a period of years in a wide range of social situations. The behavioral approach explains *inconsistencies* and other unpredictable human phenomena in terms of *behavioral specificity*. Walter Mischel (1971, p. 86) summarized this point well:

> Consider a woman who seems hostile and fiercely independent some of the time but passive, dependent, and feminine on other occasions. . . . Which one of these two patterns reflects the woman that she really is? Is one pattern in the service of the other, or might both be in the service of a third motive? . . . Social behavior theory suggests that it is possible for the lady to be *all* of these—a hostile, fiercely independent, passive, dependent, feminine, aggressive, warm, castrating person all in one. . . . Of course which of these she is at any particular moment would not be random and capricious; it would depend on discriminative stimuli—who she is with, when, how, and much, much more. But each of these aspects of her self may be a quite genuine and real aspect of her total being.

The three main versions of the behavioral approach—operant learning, respondent learning, and cognitive-behavioral—differ on certain specifics, but share a common set of assumptions:

1. Measurable behavior is seen as the subject matter of clinical psychology. *Measurable* does not always mean "overt." The behaviorally oriented clinician may be interested in behaviors ranging from the objective and obvious (amount of time spent in conversation) to the subtle and covert (clarity of visualization, content of thoughts). Almost any behavior can be the target of the behavioral approach as long as it can be reliably measured.

2. While genetic and biological factors provide the foundation from which behavior develops, environmental factors are especially important influences. Thus, it is assumed that genes influence a person's general behavioral tendencies, which learning experiences then shape into more specific patterns.

3. Empirical research methods are the best way to learn about the assessment, development, and modification of behavior. The behavioral approach to clinical psychology has led the way in operationalizing and experimentally investigating psychopathology and psychotherapy.

4. Clinical assessment and treatment should be guided by the results of empirical research. The behavioral approach encourages practitioners to scrutinize the empirical evidence about an assessment or treatment procedure before deciding to adopt it and to proceed with caution in areas where little empirical evidence is available.

5. The same principles of learning determine both problematic and nonproblematic behaviors. Therefore, clinical assessment should be designed to determine how a client's current difficulties were learned and how they are being maintained so that more adaptive, individually tailored learning can be arranged. In working with a kindergarten child's fear of school, for example, the behaviorally oriented clinician's treatment would not be based on "standard procedures" for dealing with children diagnosed as phobic, but would depend instead on what the

assessment data have to say about what is causing the problem. In other words, treatment and assessment should be integrated.

Three versions of the behavioral approach differ primarily in terms of whether they emphasize operant conditioning, classical conditioning, or social/cognitive factors in learning.

Operant Learning

The operant version of the behavioral approach reflects the ideas of B. F. Skinner. Skinner argued that learned relationships between environmental stimuli and overt behavior—especially the relationships between behavior and its antecedents and consequences—can fully explain the development, maintenance, and alteration of human behavior. Skinner's methods are called *functional analysis* because they focus on describing and explaining functional relationships among stimuli, responses, and consequences.

Thus, rather than assuming that human behavior reflects various motives or needs (e.g., aggressive behavior indicates needs for dominance), the Skinnerian clinician looks at the relationship between aggressive behavior and its consequences. If a client's aggressive behavior has been rewarded, at least part of the time, no further explanation in terms of internal need is necessary; the client has simply learned to behave aggres-

B. F. Skinner (1904–1990). Photo from Ken Heyman/Blackstar.

sively. Similarly, a mental hospital resident who spends the day staring into space and is incontinent need not be considered "mentally ill." Instead, these behaviors can be thought of as learned responses prompted by environmental factors and maintained by the reinforcement of "crazy" behavior provided by society and especially by the hospital (Ullmann & Krasner, 1975).

Classical Conditioning

Another version of the behavioral approach is exemplified by the writings of Joseph Wolpe (1958, 1982) and Hans Eysenck (1982). They focus on the applications of *classical*, or *respondent* conditioning principles (Hull, 1943; Pavlov, 1927) to understanding and eliminating human distress, particularly anxiety. While not denying the importance of operant reinforcement and punishment in shaping behavior, behaviorists who emphasize classical conditioning emphasize the association of conditioned and unconditioned stimuli. For example, a man who fearfully avoids social events may do so not only because of past humiliations or other negative experiences (i.e., operant conditioning), but also because the discomfort from those experiences has, through classical conditioning, become so *associated* with parties that he may experience anxiety upon receiving a party invitation.

Social Learning (Cognitive-Behavioral) Theories

The views of Skinner, Wolpe, Eysenck, and others who focus on overt behaviors as the targets of clinical assessment and treatment have been quite influential, but some behaviorists see these views as incomplete. Accordingly, *social-learning* and *cognitive-behavioral* theorists have added an emphasis on the role of cognitive (i.e., thought) processes in the development, maintenance, and modification of behavior Two of the most prominent representatives of the social-learning point of view are Albert Bandura and Walter Mischel, who have studied and described how social influence and cognitive activity contribute to learning (Bandura, 1986; Mischel, 1993).

A major feature of Bandura's theory is its attention to *observational learning* or *vicarious cognitive processes*. In his view, behavior develops not only directly through operant and classical conditioning, but also *indirectly* (vicariously) through observation and cognitive representations of the world. For example, Bandura highlighted the fact that humans can acquire new behaviors without obvious reinforcement or practice, but rather by observing another individual, or *model*, engage in the behavior. In one illustrative experiment, preschoolers who had observed a model behaving aggressively toward an inflatable "Bobo" doll later tended to match the models' behavior, while those who had seen a passive model tended to be nonaggressive (Bandura, Ross & Ross, 1963). According to Bandura, the effects of vicarious processes can be as substantial as the effects of direct learning.

Bandura also sees cognitive variables playing a role in behavior disorders. Consider the man mentioned earlier who feared social situations. Bandura would point out that his discomfort stems not only from negative social experiences and environmental stimuli associated with them, but also from anxiety-provoking thoughts about social situations (e.g., "I will make a fool of myself" or "I'm no good at making friends") that serve to support continued avoidance. Bandura believes that people's expectancies about what they can and cannot do in given situations—their sense of *self-efficacy* (Bandura, 1986)—exerts an enormous influence over how they actually behave. The higher the level of self-efficacy, he says, the better their performance will be.

Bandura (1982) proposes that people's emotional life is largely determined by the combined influence of their self-efficacy and outcome judgments. For example, people who are low in self-efficacy are likely to feel *apathy* if they also believe that no one can control any life events, *anxiety* if they feel unable to control life's dangers, and *depression* if they believe that *other people's* actions, but not theirs, bring about desired outcomes. People who have high self-efficacy are likely to be resentful if they also see the world as unresponsive to their efforts, but self-assured if they see their efforts as bringing good outcomes.

Table 2.2 summarizes five cognitive factors, or *person variables*, that Mischel (1986) sees as important to understanding human behavior from a social-learning point of view. Other cognitive-behavioral theorists have drawn attention to several additional factors, including how people evaluate and explain their own behavior and how they believe that events in the world should unfold (Abramson, Seligman & Teasdale, 1978; Beck, 1976; Ellis, 1962). These additional factors have proven especially useful in dealing with depression and anxiety disorders.

For example, according to Aaron Beck (1976), people's cognitive evaluations, or *appraisals*, of their own behavior precede and influence their emotional reactions to events. Thus, individuals who continually evaluate their performance as inadequate are likely to interpret compliments as evidence that others are merely being polite. Thus, they gain no pleasure from positive reinforcement, may tend to see themselves as worthless and inadequate and are thus predisposed to depressive thoughts. According to Beck, these thoughts can eventually become so automatic that they influence future emotional reactions without conscious awareness. The goal of Beck's cognitive-behavioral therapy is to make these automatic thoughts conscious, so the individual can logically appraise their merit (see Chapter 8).

TABLE 2.2   Summary of Cognitive Social Learning Person Variables

1. *Competencies:* Ability to construct (generate) particular cognitions and behaviors. Related to measures of IQ, social and cognitive (mental) maturity and competence, ego development, social-intellectual achievements and skills. Refers to what the person knows and can do.

2. *Encoding Strategies and Personal Constructs:* Units for categorizing events, people, and the self.

3. *Expectancies:* Behavior-outcome and stimulus-outcome relations in particular situations; self-efficacy or confidence that one can perform the necessary behavior.

4. *Subjective Values:* Motivating and arousing stimuli, incentives, and aversions.

5. *Self-Regulatory Systems and Plans:* Rules and self-reactions for performance and for the organization of complex behavior sequences.

SOURCE: Mischel (1986)

Habitual explanations, or *attributions*, about the causes of events—including one's own behavior—can also have important emotional consequences. These attributions tend to vary along three dimensions: *internality*—whether people see the cause of an event as due to something about themselves or something about the environment; *stability*—whether they see the cause as persisting or temporary; and *globalness*—whether they see the cause as specific to a given situation or as operating in all situations. For example, explaining poor performance on a test by blaming it on test difficulty exemplifies an external, unstable, and specific attribution. Saying "I am just plain stupid" would reflect an internal, stable, and global attribution. Individuals who make internal, stable, and global attributions for failure experiences are especially likely to experience depressive symptoms (Seligman et al., 1979, 1984).

Albert Ellis's (1962, 1993) cognitive-behavioral theory focuses not only on the role of people's expectancies, appraisals, and attributions, but also on how specific irrational and self-defeating long-term beliefs can produce psychological distress. These irrational beliefs often include "should" statements ("Everyone should like me.") and unrealistically high standards ("I must be perfect.") that doom people to failure or disappointment. Ellis's rational-emotive therapy attacks such beliefs until the client realizes they are counterproductive and abandons them (see Chapter 8).

Evaluation of the Behavioral Approach

Since its beginnings in the late 1950s, the behavioral approach has enjoyed enthusiastic support from an increasing number of adherents who value its scientific view of human behavior, its operationally defined concepts, its application of laboratory-based learning principles to clinical problems, and its commitment to empirical evaluation of assessment and treatment. In short, the behavioral approach is seen as the best approach to applying psychology *as a science of behavior* in the clinical field. Nevertheless, critics fault this approach on several counts:

1. It is seen by some as reducing humans to a set of acquired responses derived from a mechanistic relationship with the environment. Even its cognitive-behavioral versions appear to pay less attention than other approaches do to subjective experiences and to genetic, physiological, and other non-learning-based influences on behavior.

2. Learning principles might explain phobias and other relatively simple stimulus-response relationships, but may not adequately deal with more complex, internal processes. "Likening human to animal behavior, and focusing on visible behavior rather than inner states, minimizes precisely those values, feelings, fantasies, and motives which most distinguish and trouble human life" (Korchin, 1976, p. 349).

3. The learning principles on which the behavioral approach is based are still a matter of debate among learning theorists and, even if all these principles were agreed upon, there is the question of whether their animal-laboratory origins allow them to be applied meaningfully to human beings.

4. The behavioral approach is not as uniquely scientific or as clearly validated as its proponents might wish. Many of its assessment and treatment procedures are based more on clinical experience than experimental research, and where research evidence is available, it is often not unequivocally supportive of learning-based techniques (see Chapter 9).

THE PHENOMENOLOGICAL APPROACH

So far we have considered approaches to clinical psychology in which human behavior is viewed as primarily influenced by (a) instincts and intrapsychic conflicts, or (b) the environment and cognitive factors. The phenomenological approach rejects many assumptions of both psychodynamic and behavioral clinicians, asserting instead that the behavior of each human being at any given moment is determined primarily by that person's unique *perception of the world*.

Consider two college students on the first day of class. While one of them is enthralled by the professor, the other stomps out and drops the course. Phenomenologists attribute such divergent reactions as reflecting different perceptions of the same professor. Clinicians who take a phenomenological approach tend to share the following assumptions:

1. Human beings are active, thinking people who are individually responsible for what they do and fully capable of making choices about their behavior. In fairness, it should be pointed out that psychodynamic and cognitive-behavioral clinicians also see people in this way, but their approaches tend to look at the *processes* underlying self-discipline, decision making, and other uniquely human characteristics rather than to focus on those characteristics themselves.

2. No one can understand another person's behavior without perceiving the world through that person's eyes. In line with this notion, the phenomenological approach assumes that all human activity is comprehensible *when viewed within the social context, and from the point of view, of the person being observed*. Thus, a violent woman would not be seen as expressing id impulses or displaying reinforced behavior, but as behaving in line with her perception of those around her at the time.

The phenomenological approach evolved partly as a reaction against Freud that began when Adler rejected instincts as the basis of behavior and emphasized people's perceptions and growth potential. Emphasis on individual perceptions of reality was also prompted by Heidegger, Kierkegaard, Sartre, and other existentialist philosophers who asserted that the meaning and value of life are not intrinsic, but are constructed by the perceiver. Thus, people are not attractive or ugly; these qualities are assigned when someone else reacts to them, and there is a different "reality" in the eye of each beholder. This focus on individual views of reality was sharpened by a group of German psychologists—known as the gestalt school (e.g., Koffka, 1935; Köhler, 1925)—who

FIGURE 2.1 What is "Reality"? Your shifting perceptions of this fixed stimulus allow you to see it as either a young woman in a feathered hat or an old woman in a shawl.

noted there are many cases in which a person's subjective perception goes beyond the stimuli that are "objectively" there and in which the "same" object may be interpreted in different ways (see Figure 2.1).

In North America, clinicians who adopt a phenomenological approach tend to assume that each person possesses a potential for growth that gives impetus to most behavior. They see people as basically good and as striving naturally toward creativity, love, and other positive goals (for this reason, their approach is often called *humanistic*). In their clinical work, the emphasis is not on gathering assessment data about a client's past or trying to solve specific behavioral problems, but on facilitating clients' personal growth and choice in the "here and now."[1]

Kelly's Personal Construct Theory

George Kelly (1955) developed a theory based on the fundamental assumption that human behavior is determined by *personal constructs*, or ways of anticipating the world. Kelly believed individuals act in accord with their unique set of expectations about the consequences of behavior (note the similarity to Bandura) and that people's

---

[1]Another phenomenological approach popular in Europe has been called "philosophically grounded phenomenology" (Fischer 1989). Based on the writings of Edmund Husserl (1969), Martin Heidegger (1968), and other European philosophers, this approach is devoted to the qualitative study of human knowledge and human consciousness. While philosophically grounded phenomenologists may adopt a humanistic perspective as practicing therapists, their theoretical approach to psychology differs from the humanistic wing of phenomenology in several ways. Unlike the humanistic tradition, they do not concentrate on conscious experience alone, do not deny the importance of exploring the past, and do not assume that all behavior is rational or that all human beings are basically good.

constructs about life comprise their reality and guide their behavior. For example, a person who sees knives as potentially dangerous would exercise caution when handling them. Because caution reflects an accurate anticipation of the consequences of carelessness and does avoid accidents, the construct "sharp knives are dangerous" is *validated*. In Kelly's view, the major goal of human beings is not to satisfy their instincts or maximize their rewards but to validate their personal constructs, and thus to make sense of the world as they perceive it. Like scientists who revel in discovering why and when a phenomenon occurs, people seek to understand and predict the phenomena in their lives.

Kelly's theory says that disordered behavior results when a person develops inaccurate, oversimplified, or otherwise faulty constructs about social experiences. Much as a scientist will make incorrect predictions from faulty constructs, people are likely to behave inappropriately if their personal constructs do not allow them to anticipate and comprehend daily events. Thus, a man who construes everything in life as either "good" or "bad" is going to have problems, because not all events and people can be classified this way without distorting them. He may decide that all college students, political activists, and foreigners are bad, and that all children, doctors, and clergy are good, but he will be wrong—at least part of the time. He will also be seen by others as close-minded, prejudiced, and a poor judge of character. His interpersonal relationships are likely to be stormy.

Rogers's Self-Actualization Theory

The prolific writings of Carl Rogers (1942, 1951, 1961, 1970) have made his name practically synonymous with the phenomenological approach to clinical psychology in North America. Rogers assumed that people have an innate motive toward growth, which he called *self-actualization*: "the directional trend which is evident in all organic and human life—the urge to expand, extend, develop, mature—the tendency to express and activate all the capacities of the organism" (Rogers, 1961, p. 351). Rogers saw all human behavior—from basic food-seeking to artistic creativity, from normal conversation to bizarre delusions—as a reflection of the individual's efforts at self-actualization in a uniquely perceived world.

In Rogers's view, these efforts begin at birth. As the developing child begins to differentiate between the self and the rest of the world, there is a growing awareness of this self—a recognition of the "I" or "me." According to Rogers, all of a person's experiences, including "self" experiences, are evaluated as positive or negative, depending on whether they are consistent or inconsistent with the child's self-actualizing tendency. However, these evaluations are not made on the basis of direct or *organismic* feelings alone, as when a child evaluates the taste of candy as positive. They are also influenced by the judgments of other people. Thus, a young boy may end up negatively evaluating the experience of fondling his genitals (even though the direct feelings are positive) because his parents tell him that he is a bad boy to do so.

These socializing influences help integrate the developing individual into society, especially when the judgments of others coincide with organismic feelings. For example, if a child practices reading and experiences both positive direct feelings upon gaining competence and positive regard from a parent for doing so, the result will be a positively evaluated self-experience ("I like to read"). Here, the self-experience is congruent with the organismic experience and the child is able to reconcile behavior ("I read a lot") and its evaluation ("I enjoy reading").

Rogers noted, however, that most people value the positive regard of others so highly that they will seek it even if it means thinking and acting in ways that are *incongruent* with organismic experience and the self-actualizing motive. This tendency is encouraged by what Rogers called *conditions of worth*—circumstances in which one receives positive regard from others (and, ultimately, from the self) only for certain approved behaviors, attitudes, and beliefs. Conditions of worth are usually first created by parents, family, and other societal agents, but they are later maintained internally by the individual (note the similarity to Freud's concept of superego). People who face extreme or excessive conditions of worth are likely to be uncomfortable. If they behave primarily to please others, it may be at the expense of personal growth, as in the case of a woman who tries to fulfill the culturally encouraged role of working mother despite genuine desires to be a full-time homemaker. On the other hand, people who display authentic feelings and behaviors that are discrepant with conditions of worth risk loss of the positive regard of others and the self.

Rogers believed that to reduce discomfort stemming from such incongruity, individuals may distort reality in problematic ways. For example, a man whose parents set up conditions of worth in which crying was discouraged and stoic "masculinity" was praised may assert that "anyone who cries is weak." This statement may represent a distortion of his true feelings, however. Rogers believed that the greater the discrepancy between the individual's real feelings and the individual's socially-influenced self-concept, the more severe will be the problematic behavior that results. Thus, if admitting failure in social dating would be somewhat discrepant with a young man's self-concept, he might simply become "too busy" to ask anyone for a date. But suppose the discrepancy is more extreme, as in a man whose self-concept casts him as self-sufficient and career-oriented when he really wants to enjoy quiet mediocrity. If this man were passed over for promotion or got a poor performance rating, his responses might be quite inappropriate. Instead of recognizing that his lack of success stems from lack of genuine interest in his work, he may claim that others are out to get him. Concerns over persecution may grow to the point that he trusts no one and sees conspiracies on every side. Ultimately, his behavior may become so troublesome as to require hospitalization.

Rogers believed that these problems can be avoided. "If an individual should experience only unconditional positive regard, then no conditions of worth would develop, self-regard would never be at variance with organismic evaluation, and the individual would continue to be psychologically adjusted, and would be fully functioning" (Rogers, 1959, p. 224). Even if these optimal conditions have not existed in the past, they may help in the present. Accordingly, Rogers developed a therapeutic approach that employs unconditional positive regard and other factors to help troubled people reduce incongruity without having to distort reality (see Chapter 8).

Maslow and Humanistic Psychology

Abraham Maslow's (1954, 1962, 1971) version of the phenomenological approach has also been influential in North America. In founding the movement known as humanistic psychology, Maslow emphasized that which is positive and creative about human beings. Like Rogers, Maslow saw people as capable of (and needing) self-actualization, but he suggested that failure to realize one's full potential is caused not by incongruity between self-experience and organismic experience, but by the presence of unmet needs.

Maslow believed that those needs form a hierarchy starting with basic requirements (like food and water) and moving to higher-level requisites like safety, security, love, belonging, self-esteem, and, finally, self-actualization. Satisfaction of needs at one level, he said, is unlikely until needs at lower levels have been met. Thus, a person will not be concerned with the need for love and belonging when there is uncertainty over where that person's next meal is coming from. Maslow pointed out that most people in Western cultures seek to meet needs below the self-actualization level, and are thus oriented toward what they lack—usually things relating to security, love, belonging, and self-esteem. These *deficiency motivated* people's incompletely satisfied needs often lead them to engage in mindless buying, vicious competitiveness, and other problematic need-seeking behaviors. Only in rare cases, said Maslow, are all lower-order needs satisfied, thus freeing the person to seek full self-actualization. These fortunate few have what Maslow called *growth motivation*, which allows them to focus on what they can *be*, not on what they do not *have*. Momentary experiential high points, or *peak experiences*, at which full self-actualization is reached, are common in these individuals and represent the best that is within all of us. Maslow's approach to therapy focused on helping people overcome the obstacles blocking their natural growth, happiness, and fulfillment.

Fritz Perls and Gestalt Psychology

Yet another phenomenological view was provided by Freidrich S. (Fritz) Perls, a European psychiatrist who first expressed dissatisfaction with traditional Freudian theory in a 1947 book, *Ego, Hunger and Aggression: A Revision of Freud's Theory and Method*. Perls felt that Freud overemphasized sexual instincts and ignored what he called *hunger*: an instinct or tendency toward self-preservation and self-actualization. Like Freud, Perls saw the ego as facilitating people's growth and self-preservation by mediating conflicts between internal needs and environmental pressures. However, he thought of ego not as a psychic structure, but as a *process* whose goal is the reduction of tension between the person and the environment.

As this process takes place, the person grows psychologically, finding new ways to take environmental demands into account while meeting internal needs. Perls said that this growth depends on the person remaining acutely *aware* of these internal needs and environmental demands. However, if people organize their attention and perceptions so as to avoid focusing on unpleasant demands, unmet needs, or distressing conflicts, their awareness can become fragmented or distorted. When this happens, growth stops and problems start. For example, a person with strong sexual desires who grows up in a family where such feelings are considered "immoral" may find certain distortions of awareness to be temporarily helpful, but ultimately problematic. These distortions may involve denial of sexual feelings or perceptions that exaggerate peer pressures for sexual promiscuity. More severe distortions can result in more serious problems. If a person is unable to consciously acknowledge hostile feelings toward others, for example, the result might be a perception of other people as hostile (a form of projection) and intense anxiety about being away from home. This person may selectively attend to the ordinary risks that surround us all and, "because the world is so dangerous," refuse to leave home. Perls's treatment approach, called *gestalt therapy*, aims at restarting growth by reestablishing aware processes (see Chapter 8).

Evaluation of the Phenomenological Model

The phenomenological approach to clinical psychology has a strong intrinsic appeal. It gives a central role to each person's experience, it emphasizes each person's uniqueness, and it celebrates those human characteristics that make our species special. Finally, humanistic phenomenologists' optimistic approach focuses on the potential of human life and on each individual's capability to grow toward maximum personal fulfillment.

Still, the phenomenological approach seen in North American clinical psychology has its share of detractors. Critics say that:

1. Humanistic phenomenology is too concerned with immediate conscious experience and does not pay sufficient attention to unconscious motivation, reinforcement contingencies, situational influences, and biological factors.

2. The approach does not deal adequately with the *development* of human behavior. Postulating an innate tendency toward actualization can account for development, but does not explain its processes. Saying that a child develops because of an actualizing tendency is like saying that a person eats because of hunger; this may be true, but it says little about what hunger is or how it influences behavior. More generally, though phenomenological theories provide excellent descriptions of human behavior, they are not focused on the scientific exploration of its causes. To suggest that people act as they do because of their unique perceptions of reality may be personally satisfying, but not very informative in terms of understanding the variables that promote, maintain, and alter human behavior.

3. Phenomenological concepts are vague and difficult to comprehend, let alone investigate. When human beings are described as "a momentary precipitation at the vortex of a transient eddy of energy in the enormous and incomprehensible sea of energy we call the universe" (Kempler, 1973, p. 225), it becomes difficult to generate testable hypotheses about their behavior. Although phenomenologists have been chided for being unscientific, it may be more accurate to describe them as pursuing an approach to science that violates Western traditions. Their research methods are more qualitative than quantitative, and they approach psychology as a human science, not as a natural science.

4. The clinical applicability of the phenomenological approach is limited to those segments of the population whose intellectual and cultural background is compatible with its introspective nature. Further, the range of problems addressed by the approach is limited. Phenomenological notions may be of great subjective value to the person struggling with a crisis of identity or values, but these notions (like the tenets of most other approaches) may not be very useful in situations where human distress results from unmet needs near the bottom of Maslow's hierarchy—needs for food, decent housing, and a job, for example.

INTERPERSONAL PERSPECTIVES

There are several interpersonal theories of human behavior, though most textbooks on personality theory, abnormal psychology, psychopathology, and clinical psychology pay scant attention to them. This neglect stems partly from the fact that the major approaches to clinical psychology, especially the behavioral and psychoanalytic, have absorbed so many principles from interpersonal theories that there is no single, distinctly interpersonal approach to psychological assessment, disorder, and treatment. Further, most early interpersonal theorists, such as Harry Stack Sullivan, were not prolific writers, and did not try to popularize their views, attract followers, or build a clinical movement. Finally, unlike the three dominant approaches to clinical psychology we have reviewed, interpersonal theories have not traditionally been associated with explaining or treating specific forms of psychopathology, such as hysterical symptoms, phobias, or existential crises.

Nevertheless, we believe that interpersonal theories offer a perspective whose influence on clinical psychology now matches that of the approaches emphasized in most textbooks. In this section, we summarize two major interpersonal theories and consider their implications for clinical psychology. [More detailed coverage of this material is provided by Anchin and Kiesler (1982), Carson (1969), Kiesler (1983), and Wiggins (1982).]

Harry Stack Sullivan's Interpersonal Theory

Although he is often described as a neo-Freudian, American psychiatrist Harry Stack Sullivan (1892–1949) developed a personality theory and treatment approach that was much different from other revisionists of Freud. Believing that personality consists of "the relatively enduring pattern of recurrent interpersonal situations which characterize a human life" (Sullivan, 1953, pp. 110–111), he sought to understand personality as it was revealed in the pattern of what a person did with others, said to others, and believed about others. Sullivan also saw psychological disorders as stemming from interpersonal relationships that have become so taxing, cumbersome, or frustrating that constructive, or "normal" interactions with others are not possible. Sullivan believed that individuals overcome these problems by becoming aware of their interpersonal relations and understanding them in a way that is consistent with the views of others.

In Sullivan's view, the development of personality begins with biological and acquired needs that require infants to interact repeatedly with caregivers, especially the mother. Out of these interactions, the infant experiences the caregiver's moods through what Sullivan called "empathy." An infant feels fear or joy, for example, through empathy with mother's anxious or happy moods. Similarly, through a primitive form of understanding that Sullivan called the "prototaxic" mode of experience, the infant comes to associate the caregiver's approval or disapproval with two different "personifications" (a personification is our mental image, or organized understanding, of a person which—even if inaccurate—guides our subsequent behavior toward that person). A "good mother" personification grows from satisfying, pleasurable experiences the infant has in mother's presence; the "bad mother" image develops from experiencing anxiety in her presence. Gradually, the infant also develops a personification of "me," which is the beginning of the self. This personification is based on what Sullivan called "reflected appraisals"; infants gain an early sense of self based on the way significant others in their world behave toward them. It is as if others' reactions to us provide a kind of mirror in which we see ourselves. The major aspects of the self that are established in these early years consists of (1) a "good me," the result of reflected appraisals conveying tenderness and acceptance of positive feelings, (2) a "bad me," the outcome of anxiety and reflected disapproval from others, and (3) the "not me," the result of such intense anxiety or panic that the person feels that the associated experience is not really happening.

The self develops to preserve the child's feelings of security in an interpersonal world where feelings of anxiety are the major threat. The self functions like a benevolent authority figure who guides the development of personality, tries to maintain security with other people, seeks prestige, and protects against anxiety and threats to self-esteem. This is accomplished by several psychological processes, including selective inattention (ignoring upsetting information about oneself), dissociation (a more extreme form of denial in which information is banished from awareness), sublimation (substituting an acceptable activity for one less socially approved), and obsessionalism (a preoccupation with details that distract oneself and others from sources of anxiety). If anxiety becomes too severe, these maneuvers can become so extreme or so rigid that disturbed interpersonal relationships result.

Like Freud, Sullivan saw personality developing in a series of stages. However, where Freud emphasized the psychosexual qualities of these developmental periods, Sullivan concentrated on the major interpersonal issues typical of each stage. Sullivan's first stage is *infancy*, extending from birth to the development of meaningful speech at around the age of fifteen to eighteen months. During this period, babies gradually shift from primitive prototaxic understandings to "parataxic" thought which allows them to associate events that occur close together in time. While more sophisticated than the prototaxic mode, parataxic thought is impulsive, highly idiosyncratic, and based on hunches; it is not much more advanced than superstitious or stereotyped thinking.

In *childhood*, an era extending from the end of infancy to about the age of four, thought and language develop further. The child begins to engage in greater amounts of "syntaxic" thinking, which requires the use of consensually understood language and other symbols. These skills are essential for communicating effectively with other people. Children also begin to experience punishment more frequently in this stage, as their parents attempt to train them to behave in certain ways. At the same time, the child begins to learn how to use language to manipulate parents. What parent hasn't been dissuaded from following through on a threatened punishment by their child's plaintive "I'm sorry," followed by the promise that "I'll never do it again"? Language also makes it possible for children to play "pretend," acting as if they were a grown-up and imitating adult behaviors.

In the *juvenile* era, lasting from about four to ten years of age, people learn to co-operate and compete with peers. Rejection is a painful experience of the juvenile era, and juveniles will go to great lengths to avoid it. Strong identification with a close-knit group of schoolmates is commonly observed.

The *preadolescent* era, which lasts from about the age of ten until puberty, is important because its main interpersonal task is learning how to be psychologically intimate with another person. Such relationships usually involve a friend, whom Sullivan termed a "chum." A chum is central to a later capacity for closeness because he or she serves as the first peer to whom we divulge our secrets and disclose our fears. And, through the chum's self-disclosure, we realize that other people also have fears, fantasies, doubts, preoccupations, and other characteristics that we once thought were ours alone.

In *early adolescence*, ushered in by the onset of puberty, the person becomes more driven by lustful urges. Ideally, the adolescent will be able to integrate lustful needs with a desire for psychological intimacy with a partner. By *late adolescence*, the person uses increasing syntaxic understanding to enter into a range of satisfying sexual and nonsexual interpersonal relationships.

To the extent that people's behavioral options are restricted during development because of inaccurate personifications or extensive anxiety, they will be unable to participate fully in satisfying interpersonal relationships. Sullivan (1953) believed that when two people engage each other interpersonally, the goal is to achieve satisfaction under conditions of maintained security for both individuals. In relationships that work well, the parties usually negotiate these complementary needs so smoothly that they remain largely unaware of why they interact easily. Smooth transactions occur, for example, when both parties share a friendly attitude toward each other or when a dominant person interacts with someone who is typically submissive. However, if one person approaches interpersonal situations with anxiety and inordinately strong needs for security (developed during an interpersonally troubled infancy, childhood, and adolescence), that person will almost inevitably frustrate relationships to the point that they are either fraught with feelings of desperation and unhappiness by both parties or are simply terminated.

Timothy Leary's Interpersonal Circle

A major system for organizing interpersonal behavior was developed by Timothy Leary and his associates at the Kaiser Foundation in Oakland, California. As described in his 1957 book, *Interpersonal Diagnosis of Personality*, Leary's system organizes different styles of interpersonal behavior around a circle, called a circumplex. As shown in

Figure 2.2, the vertical axis of the circumplex runs along a dimension from dominance to submission, while the horizontal axis connects the polar opposites of love and hate. Each of eight sections, or octants, described around the perimeter of the circle represents differing blends of power (dominance-submission) and affiliation (love-hate) in interpersonal behavior. The first word of each octant's label (e.g., aggressive) describes a mild form of the interpersonal behavior represented in that slice of the circle; the second word (e.g., sadistic) refers to an extreme form of the behavior. In addition, the intensity of interpersonal behavior increases as one moves from the center of the circle to the perimeter. For example, "manage, direct, lead" becomes, in its extreme form, "dominate, boss, order."

The sectors of the circumplex that are closer to each other are assumed to be more positively correlated with each other. Thus, cooperative-overconventional behavior should correlate more highly with docile-dependent behavior than it would with self-effacing-masochistic behavior. Further, sectors lying directly opposite each other

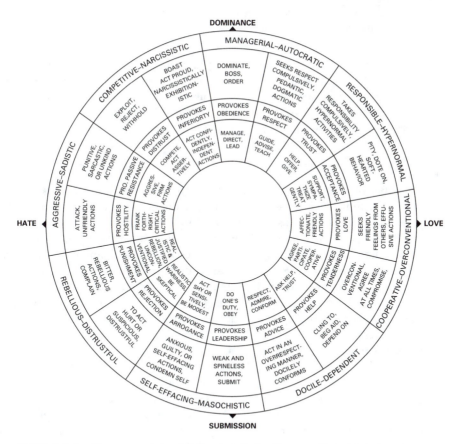

FIGURE 2.2 The Interpersonal Behavior Circle (Source: Timothy Leary, *Interpersonal Diagnosis of Personality—A Functional Theory and Methodology for Personality Evaluation,* copyright 1957 The Ronald Press Company, New York.)

on the circle (e.g., aggressive-sadistic and cooperative-overconventional) should be strongly negatively correlated. Empirical research conducted on Leary's system and others similar to it (Wiggins, 1982) has supported this circular ordering of interpersonal styles, although certain octants are not as well understood or described as others.

Leary's system and other circular models suggest that a person can "pull" certain behaviors from others by deploying a typical interpersonal style. Robert Carson (1969) observed that this "pull" is Leary's way of describing Sullivan's idea that people develop unique interpersonal styles to protect security and prevent anxiety in their interactions:

> The purpose of interpersonal behavior ... is to induce from the other person behavior that is complementary to the behavior proffered. It is assumed that this induced, complementary behavior has current utility for the person inducing it, in the sense that it maximizes ... momentary security. Leary suggests that we learn how to "train" others to respond to us in security-maintaining ways ... and that each of the eight categories of interpersonal behavior may be viewed as a distinct set of learned operations for prompting desired behavior from others (Carson, 1969, p. 112).

Are certain "pulls" or combinations of interpersonal actions and reactions more common than others? In general, the rule of *complementarity* predicts the following interpersonal matches: Along the dominance-submission axis, dominant behavior is reciprocated by submissiveness and vice versa; along the love-hate dimension, there is correspondence—with love inviting love and hate evoking hate.

Using Interpersonal Theory in Clinical Psychology

A number of clinical psychologists have argued that mental disorders can be conceived of as rigid and extreme patterns of interpersonal behaviors (e.g., Kiesler, 1986a). Interpersonal theories seem especially useful for explaining *personality disorders*, which are lifelong patterns of inflexible and maladaptive behavior and thought that cause substantial difficulties in a person's social or occupational life and may lead to unhappiness and distress (American Psychiatric Association 1994). Examples include antisocial personality disorder (which involves irresponsible, often repetitively unlawful, behavior about which the person feels no remorse), dependent personality disorder (characterized by inability to make even simple decisions without lots of advice and reassurance from others), and schizoid personality disorder (typified by indifference to social relationships and a constricted range of emotional feeling and expression).

As these examples illustrate, many personality disorders involve interpersonal behaviors that are extreme versions of various octants around Leary's interpersonal circle (Kiesler, 1986a; Widiger & Frances, 1985; Wiggins & Pincus, 1989). Antisocial personality disorder, for example, can be seen as pathologically intense displays of the hateful and dominant behaviors found in the upper left section of the circle. Dependent personalities appear to "live" in the docile-dependent octant, where they show extremely clingy submissiveness. In schizoid personality disorder, there is an extension of the introverted aloofness found in the lower left portion of the circle (Soldz et al., 1993).

Interpersonal theories have also influenced clinicians' thinking about other mental disorders, including depression. As depressed people develop feelings of inferiority and powerlessness, they often look to others for help and support. Others typically respond to these requests with suggestions and advice which inadvertently reinforce the depressed person's feelings of inadequacy and lead to even more demanding dependence. Irritated and frustrated, these well-intentioned advisors begin to avoid or berate the depressed person, thus deepening the depression (Coyne, 1976; Horowitz & Vitkus, 1986). This analysis fits nicely with cognitive-behavioral views of depression. Indeed, some authors are so convinced of the value of interpersonal theories for understanding abnormal behavior, that they have recommended abandonment of the traditional diagnostic methods described in Chapter 3 in favor of a system in which behavioral disorders would be described almost exclusively in interpersonal terms (Benjamin, 1980; 1993).

Interpersonal theories have also led to suggestions about how therapists should respond to their clients' habitual interpersonal maneuvers. Interpersonal theory suggests, for example, that clients continue malaladaptive behavior because they "pull" behaviors from others that justify and reinforce those maladaptive behaviors. If this is the case, it might be a good idea for therapists to adopt a stance that defeats their clients' usual interpersonal gambits and promotes different, and more adaptive alternatives. For example, the hostile dominance of an antisocial client typically "pulls" hostile submissiveness from others. However, if the therapist acts in a *friendly*, dominant manner, this might swing the client around the interpersonal circle toward friendly submissiveness. Psychodynamic, behavioral, and phenomenological therapists have all incorporated various interpersonal strategies into their treatment methods (see chapter 8).

BIOLOGICAL INFLUENCES ON CLINICAL PSYCHOLOGY

Various approaches to clinical psychology traditionally emphasize *psychological* variables such as unconscious conflicts, learned associations, and self-actualizing tendencies, but research in neuroscience, experimental psychopathology, behavioral genetics, and related areas has made today's clinicians increasingly aware that the behavioral and mental processes they study and treat rest on a foundation provided by each person's biological makeup. This makeup includes genetically inherited characteristics as well as the activity of the brain and other organs and systems that underlie all kinds of behavior, both normal and abnormal (Bernstein et al., 1997). Some researchers and practitioners in clinical psychology pay more attention to biological influences than others, but few would disagree that disordered behavior can be most fully understood by taking biological as well as psychological factors into account. In fact, the growing recognition of biological factors in shaping human behavior suggests that there may eventually be a full-fledged biological approach to clinical psychology.

To take but one example, the role of genetics in personality is being explored in research like the Minnesota Study of Twins Reared Apart (Bouchard, 1984; Tellegan et al., 1988). This study and others have compared the personality similarities of identical versus nonidentical twin pairs and show that an average of about 50 percent of the differences in most personality characteristics is caused by genetic influence (McCart-ney, Harris & Bernieri, 1990; Tellegen et al., 1988).

Clinical psychologists' growing appreciation and acceptance of biological factors in psychopathology stem in part from the results of research showing clear genetic, anatomical, or neurochemical contributions to certain mental disorders (Nietzel et al., 1998). Clinicians also recognize that finding biological contributions to disorders does not automatically negate the value of psychological treatments. Thus, even if a child's hyperactivity is traced to a neurological defect, a solution might be provided by cognitive-behavioral therapy instead of, or in addition to, drugs. Clinicians are also be-coming more interested in biological causes of mental disorders because it appears that those factors can sometimes be modified by psychological interventions. You will see in Chapter 11, for example, that researchers in health psychology are finding that the mind and body affect each other in ways that we are just beginning to understand. In short, recognizing the importance of biological variables in psychopathology does not render traditional approaches to clinical psychology irrelevant; indeed, it deepens and expands their range of inquiry.

The Role of Biological Factors in Psychopathology

Biological factors can influence mental disorders in various ways. Sometimes, the influ-ence is *direct*, as when alcohol or other drugs cause intoxication, when degeneration of neurons in certain areas of the brain causes Alzheimer's disease, and when genetic abnormalities cause particular forms of mental retardation. Other disorders can result from more than one cause, only some of which involve biological factors. Such *multi-ple pathways* to disorder are suspected in the appearance of various subtypes of de-pressive disorders, anxiety disorders, schizophrenia, and personality disorders. How-ever, clinical researchers today are focusing special attention on the *diathesis-stress* view of psychopathology, in which biological factors are seen as one of three causal components.

The first, known as a *diathesis*, is the presence of some kind of biological de-fect—usually a biochemical or anatomical problem in the brain, the autonomic nervous system, or the endocrine system. This defect or set of defects is often inherited, but can also result from physical trauma, infection, or other disease processes.

Second, the diathesis may create a *vulnerability* to developing a psychological disorder. People who carry certain diatheses are said to be "at risk" or "predisposed" to developing the disorders with which those diatheses have been associated.

The third causal component is the presence of *pathogenic (disease-causing) stressors*. If at-risk persons are exposed to such stressors, their predisposition for disor-der may actually evolve into disorder. However, if those same at-risk individuals en-counter less stressful environmental experiences, their predisposition may never ex-press itself as a clinically significant disturbance.

Biological Factors in Schizophrenia

The diathesis-stress perspective has been applied to several disorders, including anxiety disorders, depressive disorders, and schizophrenia, a severe form of psychopathology that affects about 3 million people in the United States alone (DiLalla & Gottesman, 1995; Fowles, 1992; Gottesman, 1991). Schizophrenia is actually a group of disorders whose differing combinations of symptoms have been classified into five somewhat overlapping subtypes: disorganized, catatonic, paranoid, undifferentiated, and residual. At some point, virtually all schizophrenics display disordered thought processes and hallucinations, but they may also show other kinds of disturbances, such as lack of motivation, reduced or inappropriate emotion, social withdrawal, delusions (false beliefs), bizarre movement rituals, confusion about personal identity, and deterioration in personal hygiene (Nietzel et al., 1998).

There is still no definitive answer to the question, "What causes schizophrenia?", but two biological factors—genetics and brain abnormalities—may play a role in the appearance of this distressing disorder.

The Genetics of Schizophrenia. It has been known for some time that schizophrenia tends to run in families (Gottesman, 1991). One study found, for example, that 16% of the children of schizophrenic mothers—compared to only 2% of those of nonschizophrenic mothers—developed schizophrenia themselves (Parnas et al., 1993). The incidence of schizophrenia in children with two schizophrenic parents is about 35% (Rosenthal, 1970). Even if they are adopted by nonschizophrenic families, the children of schizophrenic parents are ten times more likely to develop schizophrenia than are adopted children whose biological parents were not schizophrenic (Kety et al., 1994). Numerous twin studies, too, support the role of genetics in schizophrenia. Schizophrenia is more likely to appear in both members of identical, or *monozygotic*, twin pairs (who share identical genes) than in nonidentical, or *dizygotic*, pairs (who share no more genes than any other two siblings). Thus, for people who have an identical twin who is schizophrenic, the risk of developing schizophrenia themselves is about 46%, but it is only about 14% if they have a nonidentical twin who is schizophrenic (Gottesman & Shields, 1982).

Schizophrenia and the Brain. Numerous brain imaging studies have shown that some schizophrenics have less tissue in thalamic regions, prefrontal cortex, and some subcortical areas than do nonschizophrenics (Andreasen et al., 1994). These brain areas are related to emotional expression, thinking, and information processing— functions which are disordered in schizophrenia.

Researchers are also investigating abnormalities in brain chemistry—especially in areas that use the neurotransmitter dopamine—that might play a role in schizophrenia. Drugs that stimulate dopamine activity can intensify schizophrenic symptoms, and can even create schizophrenia-like symptoms in normal people. Further, drugs that block the brain's dopamine receptors often reduce schizophrenics' hallucinations, disordered thinking, and other symptoms. Accordingly, some investigators initially speculated that schizophrenia results from an excess of dopamine. This theory is probably too simple, however. Research now suggests, for example, that excess dopamine may be related to the appearance of some schizophrenic symptoms—such as hallucinations and delusions—while abnormally low dopamine may be associated with social withdrawal symptoms (Cohen & Servan-Schreiber, 1992; Davis et al., 1991). Or schizophrenia might be related to *dysregulation* of dopamine mechanisms in several interconnected regions of the brain (Breier et al., 1993).

The Vulnerability Model of Schizophrenia

Research on genetics and the brain suggests that biological factors play an important role in schizophrenia but it also shows that these factors do not tell the whole causal story. For example, the fact that schizophrenia appears in about half of people whose identical twin displays schizophrenia means that about 50% of identical siblings do *not* become schizophrenic (McGue, 1992). Other, nongenetic, factors must be at work, too. Similarly, while some schizophrenics show abnormal brain anatomy, many do not and some normal people do. Finally, the relationship between neurotransmitters and schizophrenia is very complex; excess dopamine, for example, is not always associated with schizophrenia, or with all of its symptoms.

Accordingly, the diathesis-stress view has been employed in the construction of a *vulnerability model* of schizophrenia which includes and integrates biological, psychological, and environmental causes (Cornblatt & Erlenmeyer-Kimling, 1985; Zubin & Spring, 1977). This model suggests that (1) vulnerability to schizophrenia is mainly biological, (2) different people have differing degrees of vulnerability, (3) vulnerability is transmitted partly through genetics and partly through neurodevelopmental abnormalities associated with prenatal risk factors, birth complications, and other problems (Barr, Mednick & Munk-Jorgensen, 1990; DiLalla & Gottesman, 1995; Susser & Lin, 1992; Tyrka et al., 1995), and (4) psychological components, such as exposure to poor parenting or inadequate coping skills, may play a role in whether schizophrenia appears—and in how severe it will be.

As shown in Figure 2.3, many different blendings of vulnerability and stress can lead to schizophrenia. And, in accordance with the diathesis-stress perspective, people vulnerable to schizophrenia will be especially likely to actually display it *if* they are exposed to environmental demands, family conflicts, and other stressors that elicit and maintain schizophrenic patterns of thought and action. Those same stressors would not be expected to lead to schizophrenia in people who are less vulnerable to it.

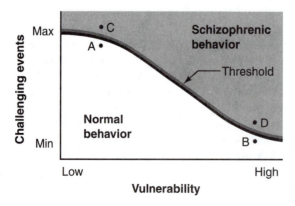

FIGURE 2.3 The Vulnerability Model of Schizophrenia. According to this model, a strong predisposition for schizophrenia and little environmental stress (point D), a weak predisposition and a lot of stress (point C), or any other sufficiently potent combination can lead a person to cross the threshold into schizophrenia.

Numerous textbooks on abnormal psychology provide more detailed coverage of biological factors in mental disorders, and of the use of diathesis-stress perspectives in explanatory theories (e.g., Nietzel et al., 1998).

CLINICAL APPROACHES IN ACTION

Having described the main approaches to clinical psychology, and the interpersonal and biological theories that have influenced them, it is time to examine how they affect the day to day assessment, treatment, and research activities of clinical psychologists.

Perhaps the best way to do this is to consider the clinical strategies that would be employed by adherents of each approach in relation to a hypothetical case. Reading real clinicians' descriptions of their strategies will give you an idea of how the principles and assumptions of each general approach act as a guide to dealing with the problems of a specific troubled person. In addition, reading discussions of the same person by clinicians who take different approaches will highlight an important point about those approaches: Human behavior does not have to appear in any particular form in order to be dealt with by a particular approach, nor does any particular approach have a monopoly on describing and explaining certain kinds of behavior. Any pattern of behavior can be dealt with by any approach.

We asked several clinicians to read a case report on "Mr. B." and to describe (1) their initial reaction, (2) the assessment strategy they would use to learn more about the client, (3) their hypotheses about the cause of his problems, (4) the potential impact of further assessment data, and (5) an outline of their plan for treating the client. Most of these clinicians represent the psychodynamic, behavioral, or phenomenological approaches, but one takes the interpersonal perspective described earlier as being related to all three. Here is the case they read, and the responses they gave.

The Case of Mr. B.

Mr. B is a fifty-eight-year-old business executive at a national computer company. He grew up in a working-class family, the oldest of three brothers. He was an average student throughout his school years and though he never gave his parents any trouble, he also remembers "never having much fun." As a child, he was pampered by his parents and teased by his peers for being a "momma's boy." He was somewhat overweight as a teenager and always felt slighted by other boys who were more interested in and successful at sports. Mr. B. married his high-school girlfriend while both were attending the same college. They have been married for thirty-five years and have two grown children. In addition to his salary of about $150,000 per year, Mr. B. has reaped large profits from rental properties and other business ventures.

Mr. B. tends to judge himself and others in terms of material wealth and physical appearance. He is always fishing for compliments, sometimes to the point of annoying people, and while he is hypersensitive to criticism by others, he is also hypercritical *of* others. Mr. B. has always tried to win his children's affection with money and other gifts, but his relationship with them remains rather distant. He feels he has "bought" a say in how they live their lives, but they tend to reject his advice as unwelcome interference. His constant lament is "I work my butt off, and nobody seems to notice."

Mr. B. has felt restless and unhappy for the past two years, and has been "constantly nervous" for the last year or so. His stomach is "always upset," and he often "can't catch my breath." A medical examination revealed that Mr. B. has Crohn's disease, a potentially dangerous intestinal disorder. Some of the numerous physicians he has consulted have prescribed anti-anxiety or antidepressant medications, but the side effects always cause Mr. B. to stop taking them. At the moment, he feels so agitated that he can't sit still, can't concentrate at work, and has trouble remembering things. Recently, he drove home from work and left his briefcase on the ground in the office parking lot. The quality of his work has also begun to decline. He doesn't fall asleep until 3 A.M. most nights because his mind is "spinning" with worry about work and marital problems.

He describes his marriage as "extremely tense and uncomfortable"; he and his wife avoid each other as much as possible. Though he reports being sexually "impotent" with his wife—a problem that caused them to "just give up" trying to have sex—he has maintained a sexual affair with a co-worker for over a year. He feels that the deceptions involved in hiding this relationship from everyone are beginning to take a toll on him. Mr. B. is also worried because his company is "downsizing" its work force. Other mid-level executives have been fired recently, and Mr. B. is sure it is just a matter of time before he gets his pink slip. He is convinced that, at his age, no one else will hire him. Increasingly, when he thinks about the future, Mr. B. feels depressed and desperate. In fact, he becomes so obsessed that he will die an early death that he sometimes wonders if he just shouldn't kill himself and put an end to his insecurity and fear.

A Psychoanalytic Approach to Mr. B: Dr. Thomas A. Widiger[2]

1. Initial Reaction   My initial impression is that Mr. B is suffering from a generalized anxiety disorder with clinically significant narcissistic personality traits. A careful, systematic assessment might indicate the presence of a mood disorder, but what is most significant is that Mr. B's anxiety and dysphoria are due in part to, and are occurring in the context of, quite significant narcissistic pathology.

There are a number of overt indicators of a narcissistic personality disorder, including Mr. B's excessive need for admiration (e.g., "always fishing for compliments"), preoccupation with success and status (e.g., judging himself and others by superficial indicators of value, such as wealth, occupational success, and physical appearance), hypersensitivity to criticism, derogatory and disdainful attitude toward others (hypercritical), and lack of empathy (e.g., distant relationship with children and wife). Dysphoria is in fact not uncommon during this period of life in persons with narcissistic conflicts. It is not unusual for persons with narcissistic personality disorder to avoid its complications, pain, and suffering for substantial periods, as long as their narcissistic insecurity continues to be fed (or avoided) by occupational success or social popularity. However, the illusions are often crushed in middle age by accumulating effects of occupa-

---

[2]Professor, Department of Psychology, University of Kentucky.

tional stagnation, failed relationships, and declining physical health. Mr. B appears to have been hit on all three fronts. His facade of what he has valued or worked for in life is now crumbling, and he lacks sufficient personal security and social support to overcome the injuries.

2. Assessment Strategy I would first obtain a more detailed life history, with particular attention to his experiences in childhood and the course of his relationships and symptoms over time. I would like to hear Mr. B describe his life in his own words, and assess his motivation for treatment, particularly his capacity for and receptivity to self-criticism, change, and insight.

I might also administer psychological tests to alert me to areas of conflict, symptomatology, and dysfunction that I have missed, as well as to provide a possible confirmation of the formulation that I have proposed. The Thematic Apperception Test (TAT) [see chapter 5] would be particularly useful to assess interpersonal dynamic issues. His responses to the TAT stimuli might also indicate his disposition toward and receptivity to self-reflection.

Mr. B's overt suggestion of suicidal ideation should be carefully assessed and closely monitored. I do not currently consider Mr. B to be a serious suicide risk. However, I am concerned about the future potential for suicide, particularly if he were in fact to lose his job, marriage, and health.

3. Causal Hypotheses Feelings of self-esteem and security are due in large part to the experience of having been loved, valued, encouraged, and supported by the significant persons of one's life. How one feels about oneself is, for the most part, a reflection of how one was appreciated, valued, or loved by one's parents. In more technical terms, persons introject their parents' view of them as their own self-concept.

Narcissistic conflicts are usually a reflection of a conflicted or contingent parental love. Ideally, parents would provide an unconditional positive regard. Children would be valued for their own sake, developing thereby a strong, confident, and resilient self-image and self-esteem. However, the love provided by many parents is ambivalent, conflicted, or inconsistent. As a result, children become comparably uncertain, ambivalent, or insecure in how they feel about themselves.

Mr. B does not describe his parents as being indifferent, ambivalent, or inconsistent in their affection and love for him. However, we also know very little about his childhood. We do know that it was a time of "never having much fun" and this does suggest that it was not a normal, happy, or satisfying childhood. What is childhood to a child other than a time for having fun? It is quite revealing that Mr. B characterizes it otherwise. In addition, Mr. B indicates that "he never gave his parents any trouble." This was not a child who felt comfortable simply being himself.

Mr. B suggests that he was "pampered" by his parents, to the point that others characterized him as a "momma's boy." This does not suggest an indifferent or ambivalent attachment, but it does suggest a pathological relationship, one in which they, or perhaps especially she, related to him more for their (or her) own needs than for his best interests or personal development. He probably did receive substantial attention and overt affection, at least from his mother, but apparently at the cost of not being any trouble and never having any fun. It was a love contingent on something; it was not an unconditional positive regard. We also know that he felt inadequate as a male, and was apparently unsuccessful in traditional masculine activities. This does suggest that he did not spend a significant amount of time bonding with his father (or his father also felt comparable inadequacies).

Life as an adult for a narcissistic person is often a continued search for symbolic representations of a sense of worth, value, and meaning. This preoccupation with su-perficial symbols is usually unfulfilling, as it is only symbolic of what one really wants but cannot obtain. As Mr. B states in "his constant lament, 'I work my butt off, and no-body seems to notice.'" "Nobody" is his parents. They never really did "notice" and never will.

Narcissistic persons will often extend and exacerbate their conflicts by re-creating the pathology within their adult relationships. They will seek others who will value and admire them primarily for their achievements and will fail to obtain any truly intimate or meaningful relationships. They are usually impaired in their ability to value, appreciate, or love others. Acknowledging the worth or meaning of others would only make them susceptible to acknowledging the absence of such a relationship with the persons who, for the longest and most significant period of time, meant the most to them.

Mr. B married his high-school girlfriend, and has been married for 35 years, but it does not appear to have been a mutually satisfying relationship. He has had at least one extramarital affair, he has been sexually impotent with his wife, and they "avoid each other as much as possible." His relationship with his children does not appear to be much better. "Mr. B has always tried to win his children's affection with money and other gifts." He is unable, or is at least substantially impaired, in his ability to obtain their affection through his own affection for them. "His relationship with them remains rather distant." They probably recognize, at least to some extent, that any effort to re-late to him in a meaningful way, to need him as a sincerely intimate and involved fa-ther, would be disappointing. "He feels he has 'bought' a say in how they live their lives, but they tend to reject his advice as unwelcome interference." Emotionally, they have left him behind, in a manner perhaps comparable to his wife.

Many narcissistic persons could simply abandon their spouses, children, and friends, as long as they continue to be successful at work. As long as there are achieve-ments to be made, and other persons who will admire them, they are able to avoid the emptiness of their personal lives. However, at some point the achievements may wane, and the emptiness can become apparent. Mr. B has apparently placed considerable im-portance on his occupational success for his sense of self-worth, but he is now "sure it is just a matter of time before he gets his pink slip." He is failing at that by which he be-lieves he is valued by others. He could not hope to win back his wife, his children, or his mistress, if he is a failure at work. Mr. B laments that others have failed to notice how hard he has tried and despairs at how inadequate he has become in the effort. A person who had developed substantively meaningful attachments to others could weather the storm of an occupational setback. His wife and children would still love him. Mr. B, however, has failed to establish their emotional investment and support, and he will be left with nothing if his career and health fail him.

The impending sense of loss has become so severe that he is unable to evaluate accurately his chances of occupational and physical survival. "He is convinced that, at his age, no one else will hire him" and that he may even "die an early death." Hypochondriacal concerns are common in persons with a narcissistic personality disorder. Narcissistic persons often have difficulty downplaying the meaning of minor ailments. What is only a minor symptom to others is of major importance to them. Their worth is that which is superficial, as beneath the surface there really is very little. If the surface wealth and health are peeled away, they will have little left to sustain them.

Crohn's disease is not, of course, trivial or insignificant. It is a potentially dangerous intestinal disorder. However, it need not be lethal. It does not mean that life is over. Mr. B, however, has become "so obsessed that he will die an early death that he sometimes wonders if he just shouldn't kill himself and put an end to his insecurity and fear."

4. Potential Influence of Further Assessment Data   We currently know very little about Mr. B's childhood. My psychodynamic speculations could be entirely wrong, although I am confident that the roots of his current difficulties in his marriage, in his relationships with his children, and in his inability to withstand the stress of the setbacks to his health and career, can be traced to issues and conflicts that developed over time within his relationship with his parents.

I would be particularly interested in learning more about his relationship with his father. There are allusions to conflicts regarding an inadequate masculine identity, but we know very little about how this father and son related to one another. Some theorists suggest that narcissism is derived in part through an overevaluation of the child by one or both parents. There is a reference to pampering, but I believe this was an infantalization conveying a low self-esteem rather than an idealization contributing to feelings of excessive self-importance and arrogance. Nowhere in the description of Mr. B are there indications of a cocky, self-assured arrogance, although I suspect that Mr. B was very self-assured, self-absorbed, and perhaps even arrogant when the narcissistic illusion was being maintained by his occupational success, his mistress, and the facade of a successful family life.

5. General Treatment Plan   Personality disorders are among the most difficult to treat, as many of the problematic traits, beliefs, values, and attitudes are ego-syntonic (i.e., feel normal). Narcissistic persons can be especially difficult to treat because the need for psychotherapy is itself an injury to self-esteem. To be in treatment is to acknowledge a character flaw, an inadequacy, a failure. They often feel terribly ashamed and embarrassed at being so apparently inadequate and needing the help of others.

The treatment of Mr. B should initially be supportive and nonthreatening. He might convey the impression that he needs to be considered as a particularly special, unique, or important client, and this defensive, face-saving illusion would not be questioned in the early stages of treatment. He will also need to be reassured that he will once again become "captain of his universe," although his ultimate success in life will come when he no longer wants to be.

It is unlikely that Mr. B would stay in treatment if he did not experience immediate improvement. However, psychodynamic treatment would ultimately require Mr. B's willingness to uncover, acknowledge, and address additional stressors from his past, and he does not currently appear to have the emotional strength or resilience to do this work. Uncovering therapy might also have to wait until his concentration, sleep, and mood returned to a more normal level. Cognitive-behavioral techniques and pharmacologic interventions would be particularly helpful in this respect. Mr. B has currently refused pharmacotherapy because of his experience of its side effects, but the basis for this refusal is likely to be irrational and could itself be an early focus of treatment. It is possible that he perceives medication as a further sign of personal inadequacy, or he has an exaggerated fear of the meaning of the side effects.

Ironically, it is possible that once Mr. B experienced sufficient relief from his dysphoria he would lose the motivation for a more thorough, exploratory psychodynamic treatment. Ideally, he would recognize that a patching of his feelings of self-confidence and self-control would provide only a temporary solution. He needs to discover the true extent and source of his insecurities if he is to overcome his vulnerabilities and make a lasting and meaningful change in his life with his wife, his children, and his friends.

I would be nondirective within the sessions, allowing Mr. B to govern the focus and pace. This does not imply a passive acceptance of resistance to change, but a respect for the limits on his readiness and receptivity to change. I would encourage Mr. B to discuss and reflect on his problems, attempting to discover how they developed, how they are being maintained, and what needs to change. He would be instructed to say whatever came to his mind, freely associating to his thoughts and fantasies. I would respond by reflecting and clarifying his thoughts, feelings, and associations to highlight what I believe are the most important issues upon which to focus his attention. Interpretations would focus on the thematic relationships among Mr. B's associations, dreams, clinical symptoms, current relationships, and childhood history. Interpretations would be offered in a nonthreatening and suggesting manner, always encouraging him to offer his own insights and interpretations, as the most compelling insights will be the ones he reaches himself.

A good prognostic sign is the apparent guilt Mr. B experienced over his affair. "The deceptions involved in hiding this relationship from everyone are beginning to take a toll." Mr. B was not empathic enough to avoid deceiving his wife and children for a significant period of time, but he does, at least to some extent, recognize cognitively and appreciate emotionally that there is something wrong in what he has been doing within his marriage. In more severe forms of narcissistic pathology, the person would fail to have any feelings of empathy, doubt, or guilt, providing instead some form of rationalization to justify deceit, exploitation, and/or mistreatment. Mr. B has opened the door to some extent for questioning himself; perhaps he would be willing and able to reflect more broadly on his life and his relationships.

A Behavioral Approach to Mr. B: Dr. Edward Craighead and Dr. Linda Wilcoxon Craighead[3]

1. Initial Reaction   During the first four weeks the therapist would meet twice each week with Mr. B; thereafter, he would be seen once per week until he is substantially improved, which usually takes twelve to sixteen weeks for individuals with prob-

---

[3]Professor and Associate Professor, respectively, Department of Psychology, University of Colorado.

lems similar to his. The initial sessions would focus on gathering additional information from Mr. B about the nature of his various problems. In addition, the first two sessions would be used to begin to establish an alliance with Mr. B. The first session would begin with a discussion of confidentiality and a few brief statements about the therapist's background and experience, and a brief overview of the model of therapy (i.e., that cognitive-behavior therapy focuses on identifying current problems and working with the client to arrive at possible solutions to those problems). Mr. B would then be asked to describe his problems as he sees them, beginning with the most urgent. If the discussion does not include Mr. B's suicidal ideation, this topic would be brought up near the end of the first session in order to allow the therapist to determine if any specific precautions or contracts regarding self-harm are warranted.

2. Assessment Strategy   The second session would continue the discussion of problems as Mr. B sees them. Because Mr. B has been diagnosed with Crohn's disease, he would be referred to a gastroenterologist to determine the seriousness of the disorder and how much it is interacting with his psychological problems.

During the second week of therapy, the therapist would conduct the relevant portions (e.g., anxiety and mood disorders) of the Structured Clinical Interview for DSM-IV Axis I Disorders (SCID) [see chapter 4]. Based on the information in the case report of Mr. B, the preliminary diagnosis is generalized anxiety disorder, major depression, and dysthymia. Mr. B may very well meet criteria for one or more Axis II disorders (narcissistic personality disorder and obsessive-compulsive personality disorder are most likely), but a formal interview such as the International Personality Disorders Examination will be administered only if the patterns of behavior associated with Axis II type problems interfere with therapy. Although cognitive-behavioral therapists avoided making formal diagnoses during the 1960s and 1970s, we have come to realize there may be considerable clinical value to conducting such a formal overview of clients' problems. In addition, the current system of mental health services delivery necessitates obtaining diagnostic information to allow for a diagnosis in DSM-IV terms.

In addition to the interviews and the SCID, the therapist would rate the client after each session on a clinical rating scale for the symptoms of anxiety and depression (e.g., the Hamilton Anxiety Rating Scale, the Hamilton Depression Rating Scale, or the Montgomery-Asburg Depression Rating Scale). In an effort to conduct efficient assessment and minimize Mr. B's expenses, the therapist would ask him to complete the following self-report scales: Beck Depression Inventory-II; Attributional Style Questionnaire (assesses client's view of causality for positive and negative events); Dysfunctional Attitudes Scale (measures perfectionism and need for social approval); and Dyadic Adjustment Scale (measures marital satisfaction) which would also be completed by his wife if she would be willing to do so. The BDI-II, ASQ, DAS (cognitive), and DAS (marital) would be given to Mr. B after the first session, and he would be asked to return them at the second session; his wife would be asked to mail her completed copy of the DAS (marital) to the therapist.

The BDI-II would also be administered to Mr. B once each week for weeks one to six and once every other week for the remainder of the therapy sessions; this instrument gives the therapist a quick overview of Mr. B's level of depression, and it serves as a measure of change over time. One of the cardinal features of cognitive-behavior therapy is that the therapist evaluates the effectiveness of the therapy on an ongoing basis. The other scales provide information to the therapist and client about how his cognitive styles compare to those of other individuals his age, and they give the therapist a good idea of which cognitive patterns are most clearly associated with Mr. B's anxiety and depression. Although it is obvious that Mr. B is not very happily married, the information on the Dyadic Adjustment Scale will provide detailed information about the level of discord in his marriage as well as his wife's view of their problems.

After the first three to five assessment sessions (assuming there are no immediate crises), the therapist would offer a summary of Mr. B's clinical problems, along with formal diagnoses and a treatment plan. The treatment plan would include the rationale for each component of the proposed treatment and how each therapeutic intervention will address Mr. B's problems. (For present purposes, it is assumed that Mr. B is not imminently suicidal and that, while his stress may be aggravating his Crohn's disease, and vice versa, the treatment of the Crohn's disease and his mental health problems will not have a major impact on each other.)

3. Causal Hypotheses   Mr. B meets the criteria for *Generalized Anxiety Disorder* (GAD): he worries on a regular basis, and he finds it difficult to control the worrying; he worries about several aspects of his life; he is distressed by his level of anxiety and worry; and he is restless, has difficulty concentrating, is forgetful, tense, and has difficulty getting to sleep. He also suffers from *Major Depressive Disorder* (MDD), which has been present for several months and is causing him great distress. Indicators of depression include his being "down" almost every day, a loss of pleasure in many aspects of his life, his initial insomnia, problems concentrating, poor memory, and suicidal ideation. Because of the chronicity of several symptoms, Mr. B also meets criteria for *Dysthymia*: his dysphoric symptoms have persisted for two years, and his depressed mood is present for more days than not; he also experiences initial insomnia, low self-esteem, poor concentration, and a sense of hopelessness. Although Mr. B meets criteria for Axis II Personality Disorders of narcissistic and obsessive-compulsive types, the problems associated with these disorders overlap substantially with the problems associated with the Axis I diagnoses, so Axis II diagnoses will not be discussed here except to point out the persistence of some of his interpersonal difficulties. Finally, Mr. B also suffers from both parent-child and from partner relational problems. In DSM parlance, these disorders will initially be diagnosed on Axis IV, but if they become the major focus of treatment (marital discord is likely to need treatment), then each may be considered as a major Axis I problem.

Based on what is known from the case report, it appears that Mr. B's various disorders have been brought about by independent causes which interact in certain ways.

Mr. B's high need for approval appears to stem from lack of acceptance as a child, both within the context of his family and with his peers. He seldom received positive social feedback as a child and adolescent, and, although not much is known about his college experiences, it seems likely that the absence of social approval continued during that period of his life. Also, his parents were not good role models for the expression of affection and approval. Consequently, it seems that he has never developed the ability to understand and express the feelings that are essential to long-standing and meaningful relationships. There are several indications of his poor social functioning in that he constantly seeks approval from others, is lonely and close to no one, and has difficulty communicating, which has taken its toll on his thirty-five-year marriage (e.g., the lack of positive feeling and affection—"distance"—is probably fundamental to the lack of a satisfying sexual relationship with his wife). The social issues likely also play a role in the development of his ongoing affair. For example, the lack of interpersonal and sexual satisfaction in the marital relationship may have contributed to his search outside the marriage for approval both socially and sexually. The affair helps to meet his high need for approval (the sexual gratification in addition to being immediately re-inforcing also serves to support a self-view that he is okay). Even though the affair has been ongoing for a year it seems that it is happening in the context of a fairly comfort-able but superficial (distant?) relationship. His excessive need for approval stems from both the lack of good social skills and a fundamental belief (schema) that he is a good person only if other individuals approve of him. Undoubtedly, his almost continuous worry about the possibility of his ongoing affair's being discovered and the anticipated resulting social disapproval contribute to his stress.

In the work area, Mr. B also has excessively high standards regarding his perfor-mance and financial success. He tends to evaluate everyone, including himself, on the level of material success. This seems to be important in a symbolic as well as literal way. For example, he tries to "buy" the approval and affection of his children, even though they are adults, and his view of his own adequacy appears to be connected to his attainment of financial success. His view of himself as successful is now being threatened by the possibility of his being given a "pink slip." Even though the firing of his colleagues resulted from "downsizing," Mr. B can only think about his own firing as a sign of failure. Mr. B's early life experiences probably began a process in which he de-veloped and maintained a "schema" or belief of inadequacy that is being activated by the stress of impending job loss *and* the stress of his thought patterns associated with that possibility. In other words, his "self-talk" is creating a crisis about the work situation.

4. Potential Influence of Further Assessment Data   It is important to sort out Mr. B's presenting problems, fit them into their proper domains, and try to deter-mine their causes. It is important to determine causes because there are alternative so-lutions to the various problems, and the intervention strategy chosen will be partially determined by the clinician's conceptualization of those causes. For example, there are effective sex therapy strategies for treating Mr. B's ineffective sexual behavior with his wife, but it would be inappropriate to implement those strategies in the context of his poor marital relationship. In other words, his inability to perform sexually with his wife would be viewed as being caused by the relationship rather than Mr. B's physical inabil-ity to perform sexually. (Also, he is able to perform in the context of his affair.) This does not mean that a therapist must always figure out exactly what caused a problem in order to help the client change, but the more valid the clinician's understanding of the cause, the more effective the treatment is likely to be. For this reason, the therapist would continue to collect assessment data and revise the treatment plan in ways the data indicate are necessary.

5. General Treatment Plan   The relative urgency of Mr. B's problems will be a major factor determining the sequencing of the treatment plan, and that information will be obtained from the assessments conducted during the first three to five sessions. The following treatment plan is based on what is known of Mr. B at this point in time; the order of treatment strategies and the use of possible alternatives would depend on additional assessment information.

The absence of most of the major biological symptoms of GAD or MDD as well as Mr. B's prior failure to respond to anti-anxiety or antidepressant medications, suggests that cognitive-behavioral therapy (CBT) should begin without an initial referral to a psychiatrist for possible drug treatment. The main environmental problem that is a candidate for change is his marital discord (he has not yet been fired, so his worry about the "pink slip" may be a cognitive distortion). His cognitive problems appear related mainly to his distorted negative self-statements regarding social situations and work as well as his fundamental schemata regarding his inadequacy as a person. His behavioral problems include poor communication skills, lack of positive assertion, and general lack of social skills. Within a CBT model, change of emotions is achieved indirectly, in other words, through change in other domains such as cognitive restructuring, biological change (e.g., relaxation), and behavioral change. It will be important for Mr. B. to adopt this view—that his emotional states are a function of his behavioral and cognitive patterns.

The therapist would begin treatment by teaching Mr. B progressive muscle relaxation. The reason for beginning with relaxation training (or a comparable procedure such as biofeedback or a form of meditation), is that it should help reduce his stress during the day, and most importantly, he can use the relaxation to prevent his insomnia. Clients also often become more expressive about their problems during therapy as they become more relaxed.

Cognitive restructuring would be undertaken so Mr. B can learn to talk differently to himself and, ultimately, to change his fundamental views of himself as inadequate. His negative cognitive style, particularly in regard to work, is viewed as a major aspect of his stress. Mr. B would first be taught to monitor his strong feelings (both good and bad), to record the situations in which they occur, and then to record the thoughts he had in those situations. The major purpose of this type of three-column (situations-thoughts-feelings) monitoring is to allow Mr. B to see that his feelings are caused by his thoughts both at work and socially. Since Mr. B. is catastrophizing about the work situation and, in particular, distorting the situation regarding his being fired (he is talking to himself as if it had already happened), the first attempts at cognitive change would focus on work. A particular area of emphasis will be to get Mr. B to see how his high standards for social approval result in his feeling negative toward himself, even when he receives a "normal" level of positive feedback from others. Once Mr. B develops a clear understanding of the role of thoughts in relation to feelings, he will be taught to substitute alternative thoughts for the self-defeating thoughts characteristic of GAD and MDD. Then, he would continue monitoring using five columns (situations-thoughts-feelings-alternative thoughts-new feelings). It typically takes four to six sessions of monitoring for clients to become proficient at developing alternative adaptive thoughts in stressful situations. (Since clients need to have firsthand experience with this method of changing feelings in order to believe that this process works, do not be surprised if, at about this point, you are saying to yourself, "that would never work for me, my feelings are too strong, and they are independent of my thought processes." Monitoring and changing cognitions are not easy to learn, even with the help of a good clinician, but it does seem to work for most people.)

The next step in CBT would focus on helping Mr. B develop an understanding of how his automatic thoughts are related to his fundamental beliefs or schemata of inadequacy and social rejection. This would be accomplished through a variety of hypothesis testing and cognitive challenging procedures. Mr. B would come to see that the stressors he is currently facing are activating fundamental questions about his self-sufficiency and self-efficacy, and he would learn new ways of thinking about himself (both at the level of self-statements and at the more fundamental beliefs level).

CBT would then focus on helping Mr. B change several of his behaviors, particularly in the social area. Many of Mr. B's problems are due to his lack of skill in adaptively interacting with others. Behavioral change therapy would include teaching him positive assertions skills—such as how to give and receive compliments and how to express positive feelings toward others. Improving specific communication skills with co-workers would be addressed (communications skills would also be a major component of marital therapy) General social skills training including such matters as over-self-disclosure, appropriate approval-seeking behavior, tone of voice, smiling, etc., would also be a part of therapy.

Two other major issues would still need to be addressed—the extramarital affair (a behavioral problem) and the marital discord (an environmental problem). These may have already been touched on during assessment or therapy sessions, but once cognitive and behavioral procedures have reduced Mr. B's anxiety and depression (it usually takes about six to eight weeks until clients with GAD and MDD start to feel considerably better), the therapist would initiate discussion of the affair and the marital relationship. Regarding the affair, Mr. B first would have to decide if he wants to continue it, knowing that it may be discovered. This issue would be discussed within the context of his value system, since the guilt associated with the affair appears to be coming from his behaving inconsistently with that value system. The discord in the marriage would also be discussed, and alternative ways of addressing it would be developed. Mr. B has to make some very difficult decisions, which he has probably avoided; individuals with MDD typically have a difficult time making decisions. In Mr. B's case this difficulty may have been complicated by fear regarding his career.

If Mr. B decided he wants to stay in the marriage, and if his wife were willing to participate, they would be referred to a cognitive-behavioral marital therapist. Since there are many individual problems which Mr. B must address, including the loss associated with terminating the affair or the difficulty in dealing with two relationships (depending on his choice), he would be continued in individual CBT until these stresses are relieved and his GAD and MDD have improved. If Mr. B stayed in his marriage, and if he and his wife and adult children were interested in doing so, it could also be valuable for them to have a few sessions of family therapy. This intervention would focus on the new ways of living that Mr. B has developed over the course of therapy and how the family members could develop more positive and meaningful relationships with one another.

The therapist would consider *termination* of individual therapy at the point that Mr. B reports significant reduction of his presenting problems (i.e., falling asleep within thirty minutes most nights, few somatic complaints other than those associated with the Crohn's disease, substantially less anxiety and dysphoria, and improved performance at work). At that time, Mr. B should also understand how his longstanding family and marital difficulties and his affair contributed to his depression, and he would have made some decisions about how to resolve those ongoing concerns. Therapy would be likely to have helped him clarify how he contributed to his problems and the necessity of taking an active role in creating a life that will be more satisfying for him. Within the CBT approach, the goal is to help the client resolve the presenting problems and learn skills so that he is better equipped to deal with new problems in living as they arise. It is likely that Mr. B would demonstrate significant changes in the specific interpersonal behaviors that were contributing to distress and unhappiness in his relationships (through increased assertion and better communication), but he should also be more aware of his cognitive patterns and the ways in which he is most vulnerable to new stressors.

Therapy would be decreased from once a week, to every other week, to monthly in order to ease the transition as Mr. B takes more responsibility for making changes. This tapering of therapy sessions is likely to increase his confidence that he can handle any new problems that might arise. The therapist would express confidence that Mr. B will be able to handle new problems, but will also remain available as a consultant if he needs future assistance, either for a few sessions just to get back on track or to restart therapy should there be a significant return of symptoms.

An Existential-Phenomenological Approach to Mr. B:
Dr. Constance T. Fischer[4]

1. Initial Reaction My initial impressions took form as the case reverberated with my experience of prior clients, with other aspects of my own life, with theoretical writings, with traditional and qualitative research, and with diagnostic literature. These perspectives sensitized me to Mr. B's situation, but I did not impose any of them as a single best explanation. In terms of the prevailing diagnostic system (DSM IV), Mr. B's current state meets the criteria for dysthymic disorder and for generalized anxiety disorder. His longstanding efforts to be beyond criticism probably meet criteria for narcissistic personality disorder. These classifications coalesce much of Mr. B's reported struggles, and they remind us of additional features that may turn out to pertain to Mr. B. My point of departure into such classifications and my point of return from that framework is Mr. B's life. I ask myself how the "disorders" point back to a disordering of his life—a disruption of a personal world that used to make sense and used to support his goals, values, and

---

[4]Professor, Department of Psychology, Duquesne University.

actions. What has changed for Mr. B? Who was he trying to be? Where was he going? What were his assumptions about life? What purpose does his behavior now serve?

The following initial impressions will serve as a useful starting point for exploration with Mr. B, but they might be modified through use of tests and through discussions with him and his family. It seems likely that Mr. B grew up extraordinarily attuned to the danger of being criticized. I wonder if his reports of never giving his parents any trouble, and of never having had much fun reflect a lonely life, one in which he worried about sustaining what pampering he received, and in which he tried to solidify his place within his family. He must have been keenly sensitive to being teased by his peers for his chubbiness, for being a mama's boy, for being only an average student, and for not quite fitting in. Marrying a high school girlfriend while in college may have served to avoid risking himself with other women. By his late-50s however, through "working his butt off," he had built a stronghold of income, business position, and investments that announced to himself and others that he was indeed accomplished and worthy, and safe from criticism. In getting there, with his central concern being his own safety, he likely did not develop much empathy in relation to his children or to other people. Perhaps his bastion is barren. The case example does not report satisfying interpersonal involvement. And now, suddenly, he is under siege: He is acutely anxious and despairing at the prospect of being "downsized."

2. Assessment Strategy   Before meeting with Mr. B, I would review my initial impressions and conjectures so that I could revise them as I came to know Mr. B more directly. I would not be looking for proof of my impression nor for causes of his condition, but rather for a revised, refined, and deepened understanding of what that condition is, especially in terms of how Mr. B participated in bringing it about and how he is living it now. In my meeting with him, I would try to assess how viable his prior life course might still be, and how I and others might help him revise his assumptions, goals, and ways of going about being the person he has strived to be.

Our starting point would be Mr. B's own story, which would be our common ground for collaborative exploration. We would try to make sense of his life in its own terms, using his language and themes. Perhaps I would affirm that he must feel terribly disoriented, as though the ground had shifted under him, leaving him and his accomplishments to crumble. I would ask if I was on track in assuming that he must be wondering whether he had overreached, whether he was only average after all. We would try to make sense of when and how he had begun to fall apart, as well as of what options he could now conceive.

The purpose of assessment, beyond understanding the person's circumstance, is to identify viable interventions and points at which he or she might opt for alternative, more satisfying routes. I would hope that during the assessment process, Mr. B would rediscover that he does participate in directing his life. In this way, transformation is initiated prior to, and sometimes instead of, counseling or psychotherapy. To underline his responsibility, and possibilities I speak in past and in future tense, and in verbs and adverbs rather than constructs, and I ask for instances when the person has made other choices. For example, if Mr. B says, "I've been told that I have this tendency toward self-aggrandizement," I might reply, "It does seem that up to now you have often thought more about looking good than about the other person's well-being. But you also told me that you have tried to make arrangements for your secretary to be transferred if your unit is closed. Tell me what you already know about the circumstances in which you have empathized with another person's situation and have helped out even though you didn't get any credit." We might then go on to look at instances of what may have been meant by self-aggrandizement, and at how Mr. B. now imagines he could bypass such excesses and still feel good about himself.

I would want to conduct part of the assessment in Mr. B's home, where I could see more of his life, observe him interacting with his wife, and perhaps engage her in the assessment. More of his actual life would therefore be available to both of us. I might use psychological tests, for three main purposes. First, patterns and specific responses might surprise me and allow me to consider additional perspectives. For example, the MMPI-2 [see chapter 5] might suggest that Mr. B. has been much more outgoing than I had imagined. Second, Mr. B would make discoveries of his own, perhaps realizing as he tells a story for a TAT card, that just as he wants to have control over the characters, so he has wanted to direct his family's ways of relating to him. Third, test data would provide concrete instances of our general discussions, which we could then explore collaboratively as we developed understandings of Mr. B's life journey, crisis, and options.

3. Causal Hypotheses   In my effort to understand Mr. B's disordered life situation, I would not look for "the cause of his problem," but rather try to appreciate how he has his own "life journey" and how he engages that situation now. By "situation," I include interpersonal, biological, physical, cultural, historical features. Once we have understood this development holistically, and in ways that promote viable change, we have successfully accounted for Mr. B's situation. The *existential* aspect of this approach is its attention to Mr. B's co-authoring of his life—his purposes, choices, and responsibility for the meaning of his life across his life course, even though none of us can ever clearly foresee all options and consequences. Moreover, neurophysiology, culture, developmental events, and so on, also co-author our lives.

In order to explore Mr. B's journey from his parental home to his present crisis, I might remark that he must feel betrayed by life, which suddenly no longer honored his hard work, production, and control. I also might say that he must feel that events had left him with no way to continue his past into the future. Depending on his responses, I might pursue with him the idea that his acute anxiety, depression, and resulting memory problems were all parts of an understandable life crisis.

We probably would meet several times, affording Mr. B time to experience and reflect on the issues we raised. As we went further, I might suggest that even without the likelihood of being fired, he had probably already been wondering what all his work and control had been for if it not only did not buy him a say in his children's lives but resulted in their distancing themselves from him. I might mention that the name "introjective depression" is sometimes given to the experience of failure in having been work-oriented rather than person-oriented as one pursed one's parents' values. I would also say that (phenomenological) research has indicated that sometimes depression is largely despair—holding one's self accountable for not living up to one's core values, perhaps for example, his not having let his children know that they were as special to him as he was to his parents, and perhaps that his office affair had betrayed his wife.

I would ask whether he had discovered that he could be a different person with the woman at work, and whether he had discovered new personal potential. If this seemed to be at least partially the case, we would explore whether he now felt guilty, and how that played into his current emotional state and his impotence at home. If instead he replied in essence that his lover provided him with adoration and unconditional sympathy, and if his concerns about deceiving his wife were not evidence of growth beyond self-centeredness but were only fears of being caught, then I would be less hopeful that his crisis might serve as a developmental transformation point.

In any case, we would wonder together about the extent to which his pain and anguish at least served to gain family sympathy, and perhaps as an excuse for the affair.

4. Potential Influence of Further Assessment Data   While developing the preceding understandings, I would have assessed the following, each of which is important for advising Mr. B and his family: (a) danger of suicide; (b) whether Mr. B experienced full-fledged panic attacks; (c) appropriateness of a referral to a psychiatrist for evaluation for possible re-instatement of medication for depression and anxiety/panic; (d) whether the memory problems were related to neurological conditions beyond anxiety or panic; (e) whether his "obsession" with death is an instance of a general obsessive coping style; and (f) how his siblings and children are faring, how they and his wife relate to Mr. B. A Rorschach test and Wechsler subtest [see Chapter 5] would help me estimate how far Mr. B has fallen from his earlier levels of functioning and what his current strengths are.

Perspectives offered by Mrs. B and the children, including descriptions of the influence of the B's parents on their lives and marriage, would affect my understandings and suggestions. Upon receiving legal releases, I might check with Mr. B's superiors for their views of his performance and future.

5. General Treatment Plan   Our assessment sessions were meant to lead to change: We assessed Mr. B's current situation *and* his readiness to understand it in revised ways and to consider moving on in modified ways and directions. We already would have made some sense together of how his controlling style in conjunction with circumstances beyond his control contributed to specific features of his Crohn's disease, anxiety, and depression. We also would have assessed his employment and retirement options. Further sessions would continue this process, inviting Mr. B to comprehend his interpersonal world still more fully, to own his missteps and losses even while recovering the useful aspects of his style, values, and accomplishments, and to expand them into a less restrictive existence. As he reported his efforts to try himself out in slightly revised ways, he would discover that although his old ways were an appropriate solution early in his life, they were by now no longer useful or necessary. Concurrently, Mr. B would rediscover lost desires and would dare to pursue them.

I would repeatedly affirm Mr. B's experience of being personally "downsized," and of having experienced multiple criticisms and losses. His legitimate worth, past productivity, and personal ambitions would be affirmed even as his interpersonal shortcomings were also acknowledged. A therapist would do well to gently and honestly apprise Mr. B of moments when he or she felt dismissed *or* affirmed by him, and of what that was like. He would be reminded that no one can always control outcomes, that we must all plan and accommodate. In the context of his life stage and crisis, Mr. B likely would gradually acknowledge that he, as all of us, is both special and not so special, and yet no more at risk than most of us. Nevertheless, I would guess that Mr. B for the rest of his life would remain in many instances more self-centered than others would wish.

Working with Mr. B in the company of any willing family members would enhance recovery and growth through building shared understandings. In addition, Mr. B would discover that his worth is not just in being right and materially productive, but also in the quality of his relationships. He would come to appreciate more consistently the inevitability of diverse viewpoints and the wisdom of respecting both diversity and ambiguity.

Along the way I would no doubt witness episodes of angry blame toward myself and others as Mr. B protested breaches of his (unilateral) contract with the world: that if he produced material evidence of his worth and rightness, he would be respected by everyone. The course of recovery and growth would at first appear chaotic, and would require many difficult decisions on Mr. B's part. Nevertheless, he would find that he is not helpless, that he can pick up and continue on a modified course, engaging in productive activities. Indeed he would find that his crisis, for all its pain, has occasioned new possibilities.

An Interpersonal Perspective on Mr. B:
Dr. Todd F. Van Denburg[5]

1. Initial Reaction Interpersonal treatment of Mr. B would focus on the apparent lack of security and intimacy he experiences in his relationships. The symptoms associated with the ostensible diagnosis of generalized anxiety disorder would not be targeted initially in treatment. Instead, their significance within the client's central interpersonal maladaptive patterns and his maladaptive sense of self would be assessed throughout the course of therapy. I expect that treatment of his basic interpersonal problems will begin to relieve Mr. B's emotional and cognitive symptoms. However, an immediate and continuing priority would be the close monitoring of Mr. B's suicidal thoughts.

The data suggest that Mr. B has significant features of a narcissistic personality disorder which, in turn, suggests a preliminary baseline profile translation onto a version of the interpersonal circle at the *competitive*, *dominant*, and *assured* categories (see Figure 2.4). However, this hypothesized preferred interpersonal profile of Mr. B would require validation through further interpersonal assessment.

2. Assessment Strategy A basic assumption of interpersonal therapy is that the client's central problems reside in maladaptive transaction cycles (MTC) with significant others, including the therapist. The therapist must identify the specific compo-

[5]Assistant Professor, Department of Psychology, Transylvania University.

FIGURE 2.4 Kiesler's Version of Leary's Interpersonal Circle. Donald Kiesler (1983) revised the original arrangement shown in Figure 2.2, using somewhat different labels. We include the newer version here so that Dr. Van Denburg's clinical conception of Mr. B. can be more easily visualized.

nents of this repetitious, self-defeating maladaptive pattern: the client's covert experience (e.g., "I work my butt off, and nobody seems to notice"), overt actions (e.g., his attempts to elicit compliments while criticizing others), the covert experience of others in reaction to the client (e.g., Mr. B's children experience him as controlling and interfering), and the overt reactions of significant others (e.g., his family's rejection of him) which in turn, confirm the client's maladaptive covert experience of himself and others. The client's specific MTC needs to be the central target of psychotherapy; the therapist attempts to help the client understand and disrupt the maladaptive vicious cycle at any or all of these four MTC components (Kiesler, 1996; Van Denburg & Kiesler, 1996).

The interpersonal circle helps the therapist identify the specific content present in the four causally linked components of the client's MTC. The circle both guides interpersonal diagnosis and permits formulation of interpersonal interventions with a particular client. A repertoire of interpersonal measures, with multiple applications, is available to locate and describe a client's interpersonal behavior at specific segments of the circle.

I would concentrate on determining Mr. B's predominant interactional patterns with significant others in his life. I would use the Check List of Interpersonal Transactions-Revised (CLOIT-R) (Kiesler, 1987a), the Impact Message Inventory (IMI) (Kiesler, 1987b; Kiesler et al., 1985), and the Inventory of Interpersonal Problems (IIP) (Horowitz et al., 1988). I would use three sources of assessment: (a) Mr. B himself (who would be asked to describe his own typical, desired, and dreaded interpersonal behavior on three separate CLOIT-Rs, and to characterize his interpersonal problems on the IIP); (b) Mr. B's wife and children (who would rate Mr. B's interpersonal behavior on the CLOIT-R and report their covert experiences of him on the IMI); and (c) my own CLOIT-R ratings of Mr. B's actions with me and my report—via the IMI—of the impacts I experience with him. The results would be circle profiles of Mr. B's interpersonal behavior with his spouse, his children, and his therapist—as well as his perceptions of his own typical, dreaded, and desired interpersonal behavior patterns and of his interpersonal problems.

As his interpersonal behavior appears rigid across relationships, it is likely that his significant others' ratings of Mr. B's interpersonal functioning would show a high degree of consistency and generality. Since clients are often unaware of the negative impacts their interpersonal styles have on others, I would also expect that there would be important discrepancies between Mr. B's characterizations of himself and those coming from others. For example, Mr. B's significant others may view his enacting of behaviors from the competitive, dominant, and assured segments of the interpersonal circle as shrewd, dictatorial, and egotistical, while Mr. B may see them as industrious, decisive, and self-reliant. Others are also more likely than Mr. B himself to see him behaving in a hostile-dominant manner.

3. Causal Hypotheses   Mr. B's most prototypical self-definition (Sullivan's "self-personification") seems to be that he is hard-working, ambitious, in control, fiscally successful, and generally knows what is best. In general, in interpersonal therapy, it is assumed that individuals' sense of self and interactional tendencies develop in order to gain acceptance and security and to avoid anxiety in relationships. Although there is not enough detailed information about his developmental history to speculate specifically about how his sense of self and interactional tendencies were formed, some tentative hypotheses may be made concerning the formulation of his self-system.

The contradiction between being described as "pampered" by his parents and remembering "never having much fun" as a child points to his having internalized a stance of entitlement, yet not believing others will readily and easily provide him what he wants. In other words, Mr. B is not comfortable experiencing, acknowledging, or expressing dependency needs. Several manifestations of this conflict include attempting to elicit compliments, being sensitive to criticisms, possessing empathic deficits, and in general, maintaining a superficial stance in his relationships—as illustrated by judging himself and others by physical appearances and financial status. The outcome of this internalization process likely currently operates outside of awareness. When significant others behave toward him in unassured, submissive, and deferent ways that complement his preferred interpersonal baseline, Mr. B's psychological equilibrium is maintained. When this is not the case, however, his personification (schema) of others seems to be that they are being *hostile* (resisting advice), *detached* (not initiating contact), and *inhibited* (not expressing positive emotions for him). At these times, Mr. B reacts by being hostile, cold, and mistrusting.

His physical problems, his estrangement from his family, and his perceived tenuous job status seem to be challenging Mr. B's lifelong self-definition. His recent behavior is producing major dissonance in relation to his self-conception and, in turn, lowering his self-esteem. Anxious, depressed, and desperate, he has lost the success of his job performance. Instead of being in control and receiving accolades for his performance, he feels impotent; instead of thanking him for the money and gifts he has provided, his children become more distant; instead of experiencing intimacy with his wife, he has engaged in an affair—probably in an attempt to bolster his flagging self-esteem. However, Mr. B is blind to the automatic process through which his own rigid and extreme controlling stance with significant others eventually *actually evoke and reinforce* these behaviors. Unsuccessful in changing other people's reactions, he intensifies his maladaptive pattern ("transactional escalation"), becomes increasingly disparaging of others, and develops symptoms of an anxiety disorder.

4. Potential Influence of Further Assessment Data   In assisting Mr. B to tell and explore the story of his life and problems I would be especially attentive to those interpersonal situations I hypothesize to be problematic. First, I would explore more fully his relationships with his parents, siblings, and peers during his childhood and adolescence to help him, and me, to understand the roots of his maladaptive transactional cycle. Also, I would want to understand how he and his wife have become so distant from one another and try to understand the functions that his affair is serving. Further, I would want to assess the nature of Mr. B's relationships with his co-workers and friends. Finally, I would carefully monitor his suicidal thinking, especially during periods of heightened stress, both within and outside of therapy sessions.

5. General Treatment Plan   Because of the apparent intensification of Mr. B's symptoms, I would initially arrange to see him twice a week. The goal of therapy would be to help Mr. B increase the experience, frequency, and intensity of interpersonal actions that represent segments on the interpersonal circle opposite to those that currently underlie his rigid and extreme maladaptive interpersonal behavior. Those opposite segments are *unassured* (relies on others for support, humble, etc.), *submissive* (accepts advice, agrees to others' wishes, etc.), and *deferential* (compliments others, content, etc.)

Especially in early therapy sessions, I would expect that Mr. B's interpersonal behavior will evoke or "pull" from me covert and overt responses that are complementary to his behavior. Thus, I would be likely to enact unassured, submissive, and deferential behaviors, and in the process inadvertently reinforce and confirm his maladaptive interpersonal approach to living. For example, I might find myself letting him dominate our conversations, tacitly agreeing that his wife and children are ungrateful, and complimenting him on his financial success. And I would soon experience the negative impacts reported by others who interact with Mr. B.

To disengage myself from the responses Mr. B pulls from me, and to help him become aware of what he is doing, I would begin to detect and label the complementary engagements (thoughts, feelings, action tendencies, images, etc.) being evoked during our sessions. This disengagement process would permit me to discontinue my complementary responses and to begin applying interventions (clarifications, reflection of feelings surrounding areas of conflict). My goal would be to help Mr. B experience the cognitive and emotional ambiguity that results when his preferred maladaptive style does not produce its expected effects.

During the middle and later stages of therapy, I would emphasize interpersonal feedback in the form of "therapeutic metacommunication" (Kiesler, 1996; Kiesler & Van Denburg, 1993) in which I would disclose to Mr. B my perceptions of and reactions to his interpersonal actions. My disclosures would focus on the four components of the maladaptive transaction cycle: my covert experiences (impacts), my overt reactions and any discrepancies or incongruities I notice, Mr. B's covert experience (as I infer them to be), and Mr. B's overt maladaptive pattern as it occurs in our sessions, and elsewhere. For example, I might say to Mr. B "I'm trying to figure out why it is that at those times you seem most upset, you are the least willing to allow me to try to help you. It is as if you expect me to somehow humiliate you for feeling vulnerable," or "When I would not join you in criticizing your children for being ungrateful brats, you looked like you felt resentful and angry at me. This made me feel that if I don't agree with you one hundred percent of the time, that I am of no use to you. I wonder if your children ever have a similar reaction?" Together, we would continue to validate these components until the regularity of their appearance with me, and with his family, are indisputably obvious.[6]

As a crucial first step in discovering more adaptive interpersonal alternatives—in this case, unassured, submissive, deferent behaviors—Mr. B and I would seek to "etch in marble" the vicious MTC that represents his central problem in living with his significant others. In the pretermination stage of therapy, we would focus on helping Mr. B display alternative interpersonal behaviors with me. Ideally, he will see that his fears about expressing his dependency needs are unfounded and he will experience relief and a heightened security and intimacy in our relationship. We would then explore ways for Mr. B to interact with his family that are more likely to create intimacy than the heavyhanded strategies he had been using. Finally, we would assess the status of his anxiety symptoms, discuss what future interpersonal situations are likely to trigger anxiety, and design strategies for coping adaptively with these circumstances.

There are similarities among the conceptualizations of Mr. B's case offered by these clinicians. They all note Mr. B's interpersonal difficulties, his rigid personality style, and his depressive mood. However, it is also evident that the type of therapeutic experience Mr. B would have depends on whose office door he enters. These therapists reveal dramatic differences in the ways they conceptualize Mr. B's difficulties, the types of assessment data they would gather, the issues they would focus on in therapy, and the way they would conduct the interventions. For example, the behavioral approach focuses on the present-day nature of Mr. B's depression and interpersonal problems, whereas the psychodynamic approach downplays these symptoms and attempts to uncover unresolved conflicts from childhood. Similarly, the various therapeutic descriptions differ in how directive, confrontive, or nondirective the therapist would be with Mr. B. The diversity of these four presentations demonstrates that the approach to clinical psychology that clinicians take influences all aspects of their work.

CHOOSING AN APPROACH TO CLINICAL PSYCHOLOGY

How do clinicians choose their approach to clinical psychology? There are no universally agreed-upon criteria available to guide the choice; even the advice offered at the beginning of this chapter about the value of scientifically testable approaches is based on the authors' personal biases, which, though shared by many, are biases nonetheless. Freudians might suggest that unconscious motivation influences clinicians' choices, behaviorists might argue that we tend to choose the approach modeled for us by our mentors, while phenomenologists might seek the answer in the perceived congruity between a particular approach and the self-concepts of its adherents. Perhaps the

---

[6]Prior to implementing metacommunication, it is important for the client to have some understanding of where maladaptive transaction cycles come from. I try to help clients see that behaviors that cause interpersonal problems today may have once functioned to avoid anxiety and maintain feelings of security.

choice is made on the basis of "cognitive style" (Kaplan, 1964), emotional and personality characteristics (L'Abate, 1969), world view (Andrews, 1989), or just plain "personal preference" (Zubin, 1969).

The truth is that no one really knows exactly *why* particular clinicians choose particular approaches, but we do know *what* approaches they choose. Among clinicians expressing a specific choice, Freudians and neo-Freudians appear to be somewhat less numerous than phenomenologists and behaviorists or cognitive-behaviorists (Conway, 1988; Smith, 1982). In recent years, cognitive and cognitive-behavioral approaches have become more popular (Milan, Montgomery & Rogers, 1994). Behavioral and cognitive-behavioral models appear to be especially attractive to scientist-practitioners (Zook & Walton, 1989). However, the largest single group of clinical psychologists is made up of those who have not made a clear choice among the various approaches (Milan, Montgomery & Rogers, 1994). These people tend, instead, to adopt those aspects of two or more approaches that they find personally satisfying (Zook & Walton, 1989).

To those who value openmindedness, flexibility, and moderation above systematic consistency, this solution to the choice-of-approach problem is called *eclecticism*. To those who emphasize the value of an integrated and unitary point of view, eclectics are merely confused individuals destined to spin their intellectual wheels for lack of theoretical traction. Whatever the case, the ranks of the eclectic or the confused have grown in clinical psychology. Indeed, the spirit of current times seems to favor a search for commonalities among various approaches, not evidence of their differences (Callaghan, 1996; Kimble, 1989; Staats, 1991).

CLINICAL APPROACHES AT WORK

Q.: How and to what extent do various approaches to clinical psychology affect your daily work?

DR. SANDY D'ANGELO: My daily work is most influenced by the behavioral approach and the biological perspective. Much of my clinical case load involves young children with behavioral problems; I typically use a behavioral approach when working with parents to identify target behaviors, analyze contingencies affecting behavior, and help parents restructure their interactions with children. The biological perspective is also extremely important because I work with many children who have congenital syndromes, neurological disorders, learning disabilities, and behavioral or learning problems associated with low birth weight or *in utero* exposure to alcohol, drugs, or prescription medications.

DR. HECTOR MACHABANSKI: I find that all the major approaches to clinical psychology have something to contribute to the individualized treatment plans that I develop for my clients.

DR. GEOFFREY THORPE: My own approach is behavioral, but in teaching a graduate seminar in psychotherapy I cover all the major approaches. It is my responsibility as a teacher to present all views fairly, even when they differ from my own. Being familiar with all approaches is also helpful in my clinical work, where I need to communicate effectively with colleagues who use different psychotherapy approaches. The biological perspective is of particular importance to me because I must often communicate with psychiatrists and family physicians about matters relating to medications that these professionals may have prescribed for my clients.

CHAPTER SUMMARY

Each of several theoretical approaches to clinical psychology emphasizes different explanations of how behavior develops and becomes problematic, and each influences the assessment, treatment, and research activities of clinicians who adopt a particular approach.

The psychodynamic approach is based on Sigmund Freud's psychoanalysis, which sees both normal and abnormal behavior as determined by intrapsychic processes—and conflicts among id, ego, and superego—that have roots in infancy. These conflicts revolve around the expression of sexual and aggressive instincts while heeding society's rules. Defense mechanisms employed by the ego keep us largely unaware of these conflicts, but their nature, severity, and outcome are seen in overt behavior. Revisions of Freud's theories by Adler and others tend to de-emphasize instincts and the unconscious and focus instead on the adaptive role of the ego, and on the importance of sociocultural rather than intrapsychic processes in shaping behavior and behavior disorders.

The behavioral approach focuses on measurable behavior, not inferred personality constructs, and assumes that that behavior is primarily influenced by learning experiences, especially those occuring in a social context. This approach emphasizes the principles of operant learning, classical conditioning, and the cognitive-behavioral processes—such as observation, expectations, and other "person variables"—that influence both.

The phenomenological approach sees behavior as determined primarily by unique perceptions of the world, as experienced by humans who are responsible for themselves and capable of changing themselves. Kelly, Rogers, Maslow, Perls, and other clinicians taking this approach try to see the world through their clients' eyes and help them reach self-actualization by encouraging their awareness of genuine feelings, wishes, and goals.

From the interpersonal perspective of Sullivan, personality is revealed in the recurrent patterns of social interactions that develop in infancy, childhood, and adolescence as people work to protect their security and self-esteem. Sullivan said that psychological disorders occur when these interpersonal relationships become dysfunctional and that becoming aware of problematic interpersonal patterns is the first step to changing them. Leary developed a system for organizing various styles of interpersonal behavior around a circle, or circumplex.

Research in neuroscience and other areas has made clinicians from all approaches aware of the important role played by genetics, the nervous system, and other biological factors in behavior and behavior disorders. The value of integrating psychological and biological factors can be seen in diathesis-stress explanations of various forms of mental disorder.

Though some approaches to clinical psychology are more popular than others, none has a monopoly on describing and explaining behavior; many clinicians adopt elements of more than one of them in their daily work.

Chapter 3

Assessment in Clinical Psychology

Dictionaries define *assessment* as an estimate of value or worth. A real estate assessor, for example, looks at a house and estimates its value. Assessment does not take place in isolation, however; it is a process leading to a goal. The value assigned to a house will be used to establish its market value or the property tax to be paid on it. For our purposes, then, assessment can be defined as *the process of collecting information to be used as the basis for informed decisions by the assessor or by those to whom results are communicated*.

Almost everyone engages in some type of assessment at one time or another. For example, whether we realize it or not, we collect, process, and interpret information about the background, attitudes, behaviors, and characteristics of the people we meet. Then, in light of our experiences, expectations, and sociocultural frame of reference, we form impressions that guide social decisions that prompt us to seek out some people and avoid others. When accurate social assessment data are processed efficiently and without too much bias, our decisions are likely to be good ones. Thus, our ability to see beyond someone's tough talk to appreciate the sensitive person behind it can mark us as a good judge of character and a source of good advice about people.

However, our social judgments and decisions are prone to errors caused by problems in data collection, data processing, or both. For example, it is easy to jump to false conclusions about another person on the basis of inadequate information ("As soon as he said he hated ballet, I knew I wasn't going to like him."), unrepresentative behavior (someone in a foul mood seldom leaves a good impression), stereotypes ("Her accent really turned me off."), and personal biases ("I love people who wear sweaters like that!").

Clinical psychologists collect and process assessment information that is more formal and systematic than that available to nonprofessionals, but because they are still human beings, the quality of their judgments and decisions about clients can be threatened by the same sources of bias and error that affect everyone else. This fact is of special concern because, unlike most people, the consequences of bias or error in clinical assessment can be more dramatic and enduring than merely spending time with a boring companion. In this chapter, we consider what clinical psychologists—as fallible humans possessed of no unique powers of perception or judgment—have learned about the challenge of clinical assessment and how they have attempted to meet that challenge.

THE CLINICAL ASSESSMENT PROCESS

Clinical assessment has been described in various ways (Tallent, 1992), but all of them portray it as a process of gathering information to solve a problem and recognize that, to be most effective, assessment activities should be organized in a sequence of systematic, logically related steps (see Figure 3.1).

At each step, clinicians are confronted by important questions and daunting challenges. With respect to planning and data collection, for example, how much information about a person is "enough"? Which kinds of data will be most valuable? How can inaccurate information be detected and eliminated? Where should information be sought? The data-processing step raises questions such as: How should assessment data be combined? How can the assessor minimize bias when interpreting data? Might a computer process assessment data more competently than a human being? And with respect to communicating assessment data: Who should be given access to assessment results, and for what purposes? How will assessment affect those who are assessed? How can people be protected from misuse or abuse of assessment information? We will examine these and many other clinical assessment issues in the following sections.

Planning for Assessment

Two related questions must be answered before clinical assessment can begin (McReynolds, 1975): What do we want to know, and how should we find out about it? Replies to both questions tend to be dictated by what factors clinicians see as most important in shaping human behavior and mental processes. As we saw in Chapter 2, different sets of factors are emphasized by different theoretical approaches to clinical psychology. So, depending on the approach or approaches adopted, a clinician's

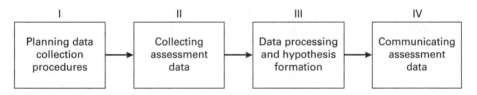

FIGURE 3.1　A schematic view of the clinical assessment process.

assessment efforts might focus on a client's personality dynamics and traits, learning history and current environmental factors, interpersonal interaction patterns, perceptions of self and reality, or genetic background and physiology.

Even with guidance from one's theoretical approach, the particulars of exactly what to look for, and how, can still vary enormously in each case, making it a challenge to plan, organize, and implement an efficient and useful assessment strategy. To illustrate the problem, consider the sheer number of things that can be asked about a person at several interrelated levels, from biological functioning to relationships with other people (see Table 3.1). The enormous diversity of possible assessment data means that we can never learn all there is to know about a client. Even if total knowledge were possible, it would not be a practical goal. Fully exploring every assessment level for a given client would be extremely expensive and time consuming, and though it would surely turn up a lot of important information, the process would also reveal much that is trivial, redundant, or outdated.

The Case Study Guide

The clinician's plans for exploring particular levels form a rough outline of the assessment task. Ideally, this outline, or *case study guide*, will be broad enough to provide a

TABLE 3.1   Levels of Assessment and Some Representative Data From Each

Assessment level	Type of Data
1. Somatic	Blood type, RH factor, autonomic stress response pattern, kidney and liver function, genetic characteristics, basal metabolism, visual acuity, diseases
2. Physical	Height, weight, sex, eye color, hair color, body type
3. Demographic	Name, age, address, telephone number, occupation, education, income, marital status, number of children
4. Overt behavioral	Reading speed, eye-hand coordination, frequency of arguments with other people, conversational skill, interpersonal assertiveness, occupational competence, smoking habits
5. Cognitive/intellectual	Response to intelligence test items, reports on thoughts, performance on tests of information processing or cognitive complexity, response to tests of reality perception and structuring
6. Emotional/affective	Reports of feelings, responses to tests measuring mood states, physiological responsiveness
7. Environmental	Location and characteristics of housing; number and description of cohabitants; job requirements and characteristics; physical and behavioral characteristics of family, friends, and co-workers; nature of specific cultural or subcultural standards and traditions; general economic conditions; geographical location

general overview of the client, yet focused enough to allow coverage of all the more specific questions that the clinician wishes to address. Table 3.2 presents a comprehensive and theoretically neutral example of a case study guide. Notice that it is sufficiently problem-oriented to be used with clients seeking help, while also reminding the assessor to consider broader and less problematic aspects of a person's life.

TABLE 3.2 A Case Study Guide

1. *Identifying data,* including name, sex, occupation, income (of self or family), marital status, address, date and place of birth, religion, education, cultural identity.

2. *Reason for coming* to the agency, expectations for service.

3. *Present and recent situation,* including dwelling place, principal settings, daily round of activities, number and kind of life changes over several months, impending changes.

4. *Family constellation* (family of orientation) including descriptions of parents, siblings, other significant family figures, and respondent's role growing up.

5. *Early recollections,* descriptions of earliest clear happenings and the situation surrounding them.

6. *Birth and development,* including age of walking and talking, problems compared with other children, view of effects of early experiences.

7. *Health and physical condition,* including childhood and later diseases and injuries, current prescribed medications, current use of unprescribed drugs, cigarettes, or alcohol, comparison of own body with others, habits of eating and exercising.

8. *Eduction and training,* including subjects of special interest and achievement, out-of-school learning, areas of difficulty and pride, any cultural problems.

9. *Work record,* including reasons for changing jobs, attitudes toward work.

10. *Recreation, interests, and pleasures,* including volunteer work, reading, respondent's view of adequacy of self-expression and pleasures.

11. *Sexual development,* covering first awareness, kinds of sexual activities, and a view of adequacy of current sexual expressions.

12. *Marital and family data,* covering major events and what led to them, and comparison of present family with family of origin, ethnic or cultural factors.

13. *Social supports, communication network, and social interests,* including people talked with most frequently, people available for various kinds of help, amount and quality of interactions, sense of contribution to others and interest in community.

14. *Self-description,* including strengths, weaknesses, ability to use imagery, creativity, values, and ideas.

15. *Choices and turning points in life,* a review of the respondent's most important decisions and changes, including the single most important happening.

16. *Personal goals and view of the future,* including what the subject would like to see happen next year and in 5 or 10 years, and what is necessary for these events to happen, realism in time orientation, ability to set priorities.

17. Any further material the respondent may see as omitted from the history.

(From N. D. Sundberg, 1977, *Assessment of Persons,* pp. 97–98, Reprinted by permission of Prentice-Hall, Inc., Englewood Cliffs, New Jersey.)

Case study guides tied to a particular theoretical approach to clinical psychology encourage the clinician to pursue questions and levels emphasized by that approach. Thus, psychodynamically oriented outlines (e.g., Korchin, 1976) tend to include questions about unconscious motives and fantasies, ego functions, early developmental periods, and character structure. Cognitive-behavioral case study outlines (e.g., Kanfer & Saslow, 1969) focus on clients' skills, habitual thought patterns, and the stimuli that precede and follow problematic behaviors. Phenomenologically-oriented clinicians are less likely to follow a set assessment outline; indeed, they are likely to see assessment as a collaborative process in which they seek to understand with each client how that client perceives the world (Fischer, 1989).

Factors Guiding Assessment Choices

Clinicians' choices about how much attention should be devoted to each assessment level, what questions to ask at each level, and what assessment techniques to employ are guided not only by their theoretical approach, but also by research on the reliability and validity of the interviews, tests, observations, and life records that serve as the main sources of assessment data in clinical psychology. Indeed, reliability and validity are the primary criteria by which any assessment instrument should be judged.

Reliability. *Reliability* refers to consistency in or agreement among assessment data. It can be evaluated in several ways. If the results of repeated measurements of the same client are very similar, the assessment procedures are said to have high *test–retest* reliability. Another way to evaluate reliability is to examine internal consistency. If data from one part of an assessment—such as odd-numbered test items—are similar to other parts—such as the even-numbered items—that assessment is said to be *internally consistent*. This dimension has sometimes been called *split-half* reliability. Finally, *interrater* reliability is measured by comparing the conclusions drawn by different clinicians using a particular assessment system to diagnose, rate, or observe the same client. The more they agree, the higher the interrater reliability.

Validity. The *validity* of an assessment method reflects the degree to which it measures what it is supposed to measure. Like reliability, validity can be evaluated in several ways. The *content* validity of an assessment method is determined by how well it taps all the relevant dimensions of its target. An interview-based assessment of depression that includes questions about sad feelings, but not about their duration or cause would have low content validity. *Predictive* validity is measured by evaluating how well an assessment forecasts events—violent behavior or suicide attempts, for example. When two assessment devices agree about the measurement of the same quality, they are said to have *concurrent* validity. Predictive and concurrent validity are subtypes of *criterion* validity, which measures how strongly an assessment result correlates with important independent criteria of interest.

Finally, there is *construct* validity (Cronbach & Meehl, 1955). To oversimplify somewhat, an assessment device has good construct validity when its results are shown to be systematically related to the construct it is supposed to be measuring. Psychologists evaluate construct validity by determining whether a test or other assessment method yields results that make sense in light of some theory about human behavior and mental processes. For example, scores on a measure of anxiety should increase under circumstances thought to increase anxiety (e.g., facing major surgery). If no change occurs, the measure's construct validity is suspect. Fully evaluating construct validity requires numerous studies and an elaborate set of statistical analyses (Campbell & Fiske, 1959).

After reviewing these separate aspects of validity, Samuel Messick (1995) has suggested that construct validity can and should be viewed in a way that incorporates all of them, and more. To him, the *unified validity* of any assessment method should be evaluated not only in terms of content, predictive, and concurrent validity, but also in terms of how well the method taps into the mental characteristics and processes of interest, whether the construct to be measured has guided the development and scoring of the method, and whether using the method results in decisions about people that are unbiased and beneficial to them in the short-run and the long-run.

While validity is related to reliability—an assessment device cannot be any more valid than it is reliable—high reliability is no guarantee of high validity. Consider a situation in which fifty people use their eyes to assess the gender of a man skilled in female impersonation. All fifty observers might agree on their judgment that the man is a female, but they would all be wrong. Here is a case in which visual assessment had high interrater reliability, but very poor criterion validity.

Clinician-Specific Factors. Clinicians' assessment choices are also influenced by personal experiences and preferences. Clinical psychologists may tend to use, or avoid, particular assessment methods simply because those methods were either emphasized or criticized by faculty in their graduate training program. Similarly, those who find certain measurement tactics tedious or unrewarding tend to seek answers to assessment questions through other procedures with which they are more comfortable. These personal factors help explain why some assessment methods continue to be used by some clinicians even when research evidence fails to support their reliability or validity.

Bandwidth-Fidelity Issues. Clinicians' assessment choices are further guided by their attempts to resolve the "bandwidth-fidelity" dilemma (Shannon & Weaver, 1949). Just as greater bandwidth is associated with lower fidelity in broadcasting, clinicians have found that—given limited time and resources—the more extensively they explore a client's behavior, the less intensive each aspect of that exploration becomes (and vice versa). The breadth of an assessment device is thus referred to as its *bandwidth* and the intensity or exhaustiveness of the device as its *fidelity* (Cronbach & Gleser, 1965). If, during a two-hour interview, for example, a clinician tries to cover a long list of questions, the result would be superficial information about a wide range of topics (broad bandwidth, low fidelity). If the time is spent exploring the client's early childhood memories, the result would be a lot of detailed information about only one part of the client's life (narrow bandwidth, high fidelity).

Accordingly, clinicians must seek assessment strategies and measurement tools that result in an optimum balance of bandwidth and fidelity. The choices they make are dictated not only by the time and resources available, but by the goals of their assessment enterprise. The questions, levels of inquiry, and assessment techniques that will be useful in identifying stress-resistant executives differ substantially from those that will help detect brain damage in a four-year-old child.

THE GOALS OF CLINICAL ASSESSMENT

The major goals of clinical assessment fall into three general categories: *diagnostic classification, description*, and *prediction*. Each of these goals may be sought in relation to one client or as part of clinical research projects in which assessment is conducted with groups of people.

Diagnostic Classification

Once clinical psychologists began working with adult clients during and after World War I, they came under the influence of medical personnel, particularly psychiatrists. As a result, they were often asked to perform clinical assessments for the purpose of diagnosing mental disorders in psychiatric patients—a process variously referred to as diagnostic classification, psychodiagnosis, differential diagnosis, or diagnostic labeling.

Accurate psychodiagnosis is important for several reasons. First, proper treatment decisions often depend on knowing what, exactly, is wrong with a client (Vermande, van den Bercken, & De Bruyn, 1996). Second, research into the causes of psychological disorders requires reliable and valid identification of disorders and accurate differentiation of one disorder from another. Finally, classification allows clinicians to efficiently communicate with one another about disorders in a professional "shorthand" (Sartorius et al., 1996).

During the late 1930s and early 1940s, assessment for the purpose of diagnostic classification played an increasingly prominent role in clinicians' work with clients as well as in their research activities. For example, they conducted numerous studies of whether particular test responses—called *pathognomonic signs*—indicated the presence of particular mental disorders. Today, diagnostic classification remains a significant part of clinical research and practice, especially among clinicians who work in psychiatric or other medically oriented settings.

Diagnostic Systems: DSM-IV. Though various systems for classifying mental disorders had been used since the early 1900s, classification of mental disorders became more formalized in 1952, when the American Psychiatric Association published its first official classification system, the *Diagnostic and Statistical Manual of Mental Disorders*. This system, known as DSM-I, remained in use until 1968, when—to make the DSM more similar to the World Health Organization's (WHO) International Classification of Diseases (ICD)—it was replaced by DSM-II.

DSM-I and DSM-II provided a uniform terminology for describing and diagnosing abnormal behavior, but they offered no clear rules to guide mental health professionals' diagnostic decisions. Some diagnoses were to be made when unconscious processes or other theory-based causes were inferred, others depended on seeing certain clusters of symptoms, and some depended on a mixture of criteria. With many disorders so vaguely defined, it was no wonder that interrater reliability tended to be low (e.g., Little & Shneidman, 1959; Schmidt & Fonda, 1956). Low reliability, in turn, insured low validity for many diagnoses. For example, diagnostic labels did not predict the course of disorders the way a valid classification should. Furthermore, these early editions of DSM focused almost exclusively on giving clients a single diagnosis and they failed to consider client background factors such as medical problems, psychosocial stress, and cultural influences—all of which can influence the severity and prognosis of disorders.

Obviously, DSM needed further improvement. Accordingly, DSM-III appeared in 1980, followed in 1987 by a revised version called DSM-III-R. It was hoped that these new systems would be more reliable because they provided more systematic rules for reaching diagnostic decisions. Beginning with DSM-III, clinicians were given a set of *operational criteria* for assigning each diagnostic label. These criteria—which referred mainly to specific symptoms and symptom durations, not inferred causes—were increased in number and specificity in DSM-III-R. Clients were now to be diagnosed with a particular disorder only if they met a preestablished number of criteria from the full list of criteria associated with that disorder. Because a client need not meet *every* criterion for a disorder to be diagnosed with it, clients with similar, but not identical, sets of symptoms may receive the same label—much as physical resemblance among relatives identifies them as members of the same family. There is evidence that the introduction of operational criteria improved the reliability of psychiatric diagnoses (APA, 1980; Grove, 1987).

Efforts to improve the validity of DSM included development of a *multiaxial* structure for DSM-III and DSM-III-R. This structure allowed clients to be described along five dimensions, or axes, which, together, provide a more complete picture of clients' problems and the factors affecting them. Any of sixteen major mental disorders displayed could be listed on Axis I, while various developmental problems and personality disorders could appear on Axis II. Placing these latter difficulties on a separate axis was designed to ensure that they are not overlooked when an Axis I disorder is present. Axis III provided a place to list physical disorders or conditions that might be related to a person's mental disorder, while Axis IV provided a six-point scale for rating the severity of recent psychosocial stressors that may have contributed to an Axis I or II disorder. Axis V listed the clinician's rating of the person's psychological, social, and occupational functioning during the past year.

In spite of the improvements they contained, DSM-III and DSM-III-R were criticized because some of their diagnostic criteria were still too vague and open to biased use, because Axes II, IV, and V had measurement deficiencies, and because too little emphasis was placed on the construct validity of diagnoses (Bellack & Hersen, 1988; Kaplan, 1983; McReynolds, 1989; Millon & Klerman, 1986; Nathan, 1987; Vaillant, 1984). So in 1988, only a year after DSM-III-R appeared, the American Psychiatric Association established a task force to begin work on DSM-IV. The rush to develop a new edition of DSM was spurred not only by criticisms of the existing one, but also by WHO's plan to publish the tenth edition of its ICD in 1993.[1] Further impetus for DSM-IV came from a desire to increase the empirical foundation of diagnostic practices. DSM-III and DSM-III-R were to have reflected the latest research on diagnoses, but this goal was not fully realized, partly because too few adequate diagnostic studies were available and because no specific guidelines had been established for translating research findings into specific diagnostic criteria. As a result, final decisions about diagnostic criteria often reflected experts' best clinical judgments rather than available empirical findings (Widiger et al., 1991). Because neither DSM-III nor DSM-III-R documented the rationale or empirical support for the diagnostic criteria they established, it was difficult to critically evaluate the validity of these classification systems.

DSM-IV planners sought to rectify these problems by organizing numerous experts into thirteen *work groups*, each of which followed a three-step procedure for studying a different set of disorders and how best to diagnose them (Widiger et al., 1991). Each group first reviewed all the clinical and empirical literature relevant to a given disorder and used their findings to guide initial suggestions for changes in diagnostic criteria for that disorder. Next, each group obtained and analyzed relevant but unpublished data that might shed light on the effects of using these revised diagnostic criteria. Finally, *focused field trials* were conducted to resolve specific diagnostic controversies and to examine the reliability and validity of proposed DSM-IV criteria by asking clinicians to use them in clinical settings with real clients.

To reduce the possible effects of group members' biases in reaching final decisions, those decisions—and the process used to reach them—were reviewed by as many as 100 independent advisers (Frances et al., 1989).

Today, DSM-IV is the standard diagnostic classification system used by clinical psychologists and other mental health professionals in North America (see Table 3.3). It retains the multiaxial structure of DSM-III-R, and, as before, an Axis I disorder can be assigned only if the person meets a preset minimum number of criteria from a longer list of symptoms.

To be diagnosed with schizophrenia, for example, a person must display two of the following five symptoms for at least one month: delusions, hallucinations, disorganized speech, grossly disorganized or catatonic behavior, and lack of emotion or extreme apathy. In addition, the person must show marked deterioration in a major area of functioning such as work, interpersonal relations, or self-care. There must also be continuous signs of disturbance for at least six months, including one month during which symptoms from the first list of five are present. Finally, other conditions that might account for all these problems must be ruled out. And, as before, DSM-IV would

---

[1]United States treaty obligations require the United States to maintain classification systems consistent with those of the WHO. DSM-IV was coordinated with ICD-10, but in spite of efforts being made to develop international guidelines for their use (Sartorius, et al., 1996) several differences in the two systems persist, both in terms of specific diagnostic criteria and overall orientation (Frances, Pincus, & Widiger, 1996).

TABLE 3.3 Classification of Mental Disorders Using DSM–IV

DSM–IV retains the multiaxial system of classification and diagnosis first introduced in DSM–III, with some modifications in the earlier terminology and rating schemes used on the various axes.
Axis I: Major Mental Disorders

1. Disorders Usually First Diagnosed in Infancy, Childhood, or Adolescence (e.g., hyperactivity, severe conduct problems)
2. Delirium, Dementia, Amnestic and Other Cognitive Disorders (problems caused by deterioration of the brain due to aging, drugs, or disease)
3. Mental Disorders Due to a General Medical Condition Not Elsewhere Classified
4. Substance-Related Disorders (problems caused by alcohol, cocaine, or other drugs)
5. Schizophrenia and Other Psychotic Disorders (severe abnormalities in thinking, perception, emotion, motivation, or movement; often accompanied by hallucinations and/or delusions)
6. Mood Disorders (disturbances in mood, especially severe depression, overexcitement, or alternating periods of both)
7. Anxiety Disorders (e.g., specific or general fears, panic attacks, physical or mental rituals to control anxiety)
8. Somatoform Disorders (e.g., blindness, deafness, or paralysis that have no physical cause; preoccupation with physical health or illness)
9. Factitious Disorders (faking disorder for psychological reasons)
10. Dissociative Disorders (e.g., memory loss or identity fragmentation caused by psychological factors)
11. Sexual and Gender Identity Disorders (unsatisfactory sexual interactions, arousal prompted by problematic stimuli, or identification with the opposite gender)
12. Eating Disorders (self-starvation or binge eating followed by self-induced vomiting)
13. Sleep Disorders (severe problems caused by sleeping too little or too much)
14. Impulse Control Disorders Not Elsewhere Classified (e.g., compulsive gambling, stealing, or fire-setting)
15. Adjustment Disorders (failure to adjust to divorce or other stressors)
16. Other Disorders That May Be a Focus of Clinical Attention (e.g., noncompliance with treatment, problems caused by medication, or effects of physical or sexual abuse)

Axis II: Here, the diagnostician can list various forms of mental retardation and various personality disorders, such as paranoid, antisocial, narcissistic, avoidant, and dependent.

place clients into one of five schizophrenia subtypes (paranoid, disorganized, catatonic, undifferentiated, or residual), depending upon their current condition and which symptoms are most prominent. The diagnosis would be further embellished by indications of whether the disorder is continuous or occurs in episodes, and by information on Axes II, III, IV, and V.

The DSM-IV diagnosis of Mr. B, whose case was addressed in detail in chapter 2, might look like this:

Axis I: Generalized Anxiety Disorder

Axis II: Narcissistic Personality Disorder

Axis III: Crohn's Disease

Axis IV: Occupational problems (note that the six-point severity scale used in DSM-III-R is replaced in DSM-IV with named stressors)

Axis V: Global assessment of functioning: 45 [on a scale from 100 (superior functioning) down to 1 (indicating very poor functioning)]

Despite the goal of basing DSM-IV diagnostic criteria on a firm foundation of research findings, some critics argue that lack of empirical evidence forced too much reliance on expert consensus (Spitzer, 1991). Others object to the disease model of psychopathology inherent in DSM-IV, and to its implication that disorders are either present or absent (Carson, 1991; Millon, 1991): if individuals meet a certain number of criteria, they are said to "have" a disorder, while if they do not reach the cutoff they do not "have" it. These critics argue that psychological disorders can be present in varying degrees. Behaviorally oriented clinicians are particularly concerned that DSM-IV classification ignores the context in which "symptoms" occur, thus providing no basis for understanding the meaning or purpose that the same behavior might have in different social circumstances (Follette, 1996). By failing to promote such an understanding, they argue, DSM-IV has done little to promote progress in discovering the psychological and social causes of many kinds of behavioral problems (Follette & Houts, 1996). So although DSM-IV pays more attention to overt behavior than earlier versions did, behavioral theorists see its failure to analyze behavior in relation to antecedents and consequences as one of its biggest failings (Wulfert, Greenway, & Dougher, 1996). Finally, Robert Carson (1991) suggested that in the development of DSM-IV too much attention was devoted to diagnostic reliability, and not enough to diagnostic validity. Simplifying diagnostic criteria, he said, tends to raise interrater reliability, but doing so can cause us to lose sight of the core features or implications of disorders.

It is no wonder that the diagnostic classification enterprise continues to be a hotbed of controversy. After all, it attempts to reliably differentiate a wide variety of complex, socioculturally defined disorders caused by multiple (often unknown) factors using a relatively small set of shorthand labels organized in a way that will help clinicians' make the best possible decisions about their clients. No diagnostic system is likely to ever accomplish all these goals, but the DSM is likely to remain influential because (1) the medical tradition of diagnosis emphasizes identification of discrete disorders, and (2) clinicians find categorical systems relatively easy to use.

Description

As clinical psychology developed an identity independent of psychiatry after World War II, some changes in its assessment goals appeared. Merely giving and interpreting psychological tests in order to assign diagnostic labels became increasingly distasteful to clinicians who were interested in conducting broader assessments that produced a fuller understanding and more elaborate descriptions of clients (see Watson, 1951).

The desire to go beyond diagnostic classification was based partly on clinical psychologists' burgeoning self-confidence, but also on their growing conviction that people cannot be understood simply on the basis of an interview or a test. Interest in knowing more about the *content* of clients' behavior was supplemented by a desire to consider its social, cultural, and physical *context*. The result was a movement among clinical psychologists toward assessments that more fully describe people's personalities by looking at *person–environment interactions*. This movement got its earliest impetus from the extensive batteries of interviews, tests, and observational methods developed in the 1930s and 1940s by Henry Murray at the Harvard Psychological Clinic and David Rapaport at the Menninger Clinic, which were designed to assess "normal" people as well as those with psychological problems (Murray, 1938; Rapaport, Gill, & Schafer, 1945). These comprehensive batteries were unusual in that they measured not only internal (psychological) determinants of behavior, but external (situational) factors, too (Wiggins, 1973).

The desire to describe people instead of classify them was further stimulated during the 1960s by research that revealed reliability and validity problems in the DSM. It was at this time, too, that the stigma associated with being given a diagnostic label began to be more clearly recognized (e.g., Goffman, 1961; Szasz, 1960). As the popularity of the psychiatric/psychodynamic approach on which diagnostic classification had been based waned, other more descriptive alternatives were proposed. Some involved assigning clients to *descriptive categories* on the basis of whatever factors the clinician's approach suggests are important—motivation, intrapsychic functions, test responses, conditionability, subjective experience, relationship patterns, needs, or behavioral excesses and deficits (Adams, Doster, & Calhoun, 1977; Mahrer, 1970; McLemore & Benjamin, 1979). More recently, some clinicians have suggested describing disorders in terms of a small number of personality dimensions (Widiger et al., 1987). In this *dimensional* approach, discrete diagnostic labels would be replaced by a profile of each client's extraversion, openness to experience, conscientiousness, emotional stability, agreeableness, and other traits measured by modern personality tests. Though appealing, this approach is hampered by the fact that theorists have been unable to agree on the nature or number of dimensions necessary to adequately describe psychopathology (Millon, 1991).

Despite such problems, description-oriented assessment makes it easier for clinicians to pay attention to clients' assets and adaptive functions, not just to their weaknesses and problems. Accordingly, descriptive assessment data are used to provide pretreatment measures of clients' behavior, to guide treatment planning, and to evaluate changes in behavior after treatment. They also are valuable in clinical research. For example, in an investigation of the relative value of two treatments for depression, assessments that *describe* clients' posttreatment behaviors (e.g., absenteeism, self-reported sadness, and depression test scores) are of greater value than diagnostic labels (e.g., depressive versus nondepressive).

Unfortunately, the movement toward description is unlikely to dominate clinical assessment, especially in inpatient psychiatric settings and other managed care facilities (see chapter 1). As skyrocketing health care costs have increased economic pressures to limit hospital stays and to concentrate on short-term treatments, comprehensive battery-based patient evaluations are becoming too time consuming and expensive. Further, they are not sufficiently focused on reaching a discrete diagnosis that can be associated with a particular treatment plan. Today, many clinicians are asked to limit their assessments to initial screening of patients, rapid measurement of symptoms, differential diagnosis of disorders, and recommendations for treatment (Fox, 1995; Miller, 1996). In response to these demands, more clinicians than ever before are using the computerized testing services and structured interviews described in chapters 4 and 5.

Prediction

The third goal of clinical assessment is to make predictions about human behavior. For example, clinicians are sometimes asked by businesses, government agencies, police and fire departments, and the military to help them select people who are most likely to perform well in certain jobs. In such cases, the clinician must first collect or examine descriptive assessment data on which to base predictions and selections.

A classic example of how descriptive and predictive assessment can overlap was provided by Henry Murray's use of specialized tests, interviews, and observations to select soldiers who would be the most successful spies, saboteurs, and other behind-enemy-lines operatives during World War II (Office of Strategic Services, 1948). As described in chapter 6, Murray's assessment program was so comprehensive that it took several days to complete and measured everything from intelligence to ability at planning murder.

Similar, though less extensive, prediction-oriented clinical assessment programs also appeared in large-scale postwar screening programs designed to select civilian and military employees (Institute of Personality Assessment and Research, 1970), graduate students in clinical psychology and psychiatry (Holt & Luborsky, 1958; Kelly & Fiske, 1951), and Peace Corps volunteers (Colmen, Kaplan, & Boulger, 1964). Because such assessment programs influence decisions affecting large numbers of people, they must be evaluated not only for their predictive validity, but also for their impact on the people being assessed and on the organizations that utilize them. One must be concerned with (1) the number of correct selections ("hits") prompted by particular assessment procedures, (2) the cost of correct decisions in terms of money, time, and effort, and (3) the costs of errors ("misses") that result when inappropriate candidates are chosen or appropriate ones are rejected.

Predicting Dangerousness. These concerns become especially harrowing when clinical predictions involve life and death situations, such as "Will Client X attempt suicide?" or "Is Client Y going to hurt someone if released from a mental hospital?" How accurate are such predictions? When, as often happens, clinicians must make "yes" or "no" judgments, and when the person's behavior can be clearly judged as "dangerous" or "not dangerous," for example, then the accuracy of clinical predictions can be evaluated in terms of the pattern of four possible outcomes. If the clinician predicts dangerousness and the person indeed behaves dangerously, the outcome is called a *true positive*. If the clinician predicts that there is no danger, and the person does not behave dangerously, we have a *true negative* outcome. If the clinician predicts no danger, but the person does act dangerously, a *false negative* outcome occurs. Finally, when dangerous behavior is predicted, but the person commits no dangerous act, we call it a *false positive*.

In fact, clinical psychologists find it difficult to accurately predict dangerousness (Monahan, 1988; Borum, 1996). One reason for this problem is that the *base rate*, or frequency with which dangerous acts are committed in any group of people, is usually very low. The following example shows why this is important. Assume that a clinician is 80% accurate in predicting homicidal behavior. Assume also that the base rate for homicide in the population the clinician examines is 10 murders per 10,000 people. As indicated in Table 3.4, the clinician would correctly predict who 8 of the 10 murderers would be. However, these 8 true positives must be viewed in light of 1,998 false positive cases in which the clinician predicted homicides that did not occur.

In this example, then, the clinician's *positive predictive power* to identify murderers would be woefully low (less than 1% of predicted murderers would actually kill someone), while the accuracy of predicting *non*dangerousness, called *negative predictive power*, would be greater than 99.9%. To maximize true positives, then, the clinician could predict that *no one* will commit a murder, a prediction that would be correct 99.9% of the time. However, all the errors would be false negatives, and society usually believes that such mistakes (i.e., predicting that dangerous people are safe) are more serious than false positives. To err on the side of caution, clinicians tend to over-predict dangerousness, but they try to minimize false positives by following certain guidelines (e.g., Gardner et al., 1996). For example, they try to focus their assessments

TABLE 3.4 Measuring the Accuracy of Clinical Predictions of Dangerousness

Clinician's Prediction	Ultimate Outcome	
	Homicide	*No Homicide*
Homicide	8 (True positives)	1,998 (False positives)
No homicide	2 (False negatives)	7,992 (True negatives)

on the most important risk factors for future violence: a history of violent behavior and current substance abuse or psychotic delusions (Zabow & Cohen, 1993). They also try to learn as much as possible about the person's environment, keeping in mind that, among people with a history of violent behavior, those at highest risk for future dangerousness tend to live in violence-filled areas. Finally, they analyze the accuracy of their predictions so that they can learn from their errors. Using these guidelines has indeed improved clinicians' accuracy in predicting dangerousness (Gardner et al., 1996).

COLLECTING ASSESSMENT DATA

So far we have looked at ways clinicians answer the first question about assessment: "What do we want to know?" Now it is time to answer the second question: "How should we find out about it?"

Sources of Assessment Data

As noted earlier, clinical psychologists collect assessment data from four main sources: interviews, tests, observations, and life records. The first three of these sources are so central to clinical assessment that we offer detailed coverage of each in the next three chapters. In this chapter, we merely touch on their strengths and weaknesses and consider how the data arising from them are integrated into assessment reports.

Interviews.   George Kelly (1958, p. 330) said, "If you don't know what is going on in a person's mind, ask him; he may tell you." The simple truth of this statement is one reason why the interview is the most basic and widely employed source of clinical assessment data. It is popular for other reasons as well. For one thing, interviews mimic ordinary social interaction, thus providing a way of collecting simultaneous samples of a person's verbal and nonverbal behavior. Second, interviews require no special equipment and can take place almost anywhere. Third, the interview is highly flexible. Except when research purposes prescribe interview content, the clinician is free to direct the inquiry to whatever topics and issues might help the assessment process.

What about the quality of interview data? Donald Peterson (1968, p. 13) noted that the interview is ". . . another form of data whose reliability, validity, and decisional utility must be subjected to the same kinds of scrutiny required for other modes of data collection." As we will see in the next chapter, interview data can be distorted by interviewer characteristics and questions, by client characteristics, including memory skills and frankness, and by the circumstances under which the interview takes place.

Tests.   Like interviews, tests provide a sample of behavior, but the stimuli to which the client responds on a test are more standardized than in most interviews. A test exposes each client to the same stimuli under the same circumstances. Tests can be easy, economical, and conveniently administered (in some cases, a mental health professional need not be present). Further, the test's standardized form helps eliminate bias that might otherwise influence an assessor's inquiries. Responses to most tests can be translated into *scores*, thus making quantitative summaries of a client's behavior possible.[2] In this way, test data facilitate communication between professionals about a client. Finally, test data allow the clinician to compare a client's behavior with that of thousands of others who have taken the same test.

The use of these reference scores, or *norms*, allows the clinician to establish a frame of reference for interpreting the meaning of a given client's test score. Assume, for instance, that during a word-association test, the first thing that pops into a client's mind when the tester says "house" is "pantyhose." If the clinician had never heard this association before, she might interpret it as unusual, perhaps even indicative of a psychological problem. But if the tester has access to a book containing the associations of 12,000 subjects to the word "house," she might discover that "pantyhose" is a popular response and thus not worthy of concern. (This is not what she would discover, by the way.)

However, tests are not magical devices that always reveal the "truth" about people. Like interviews, they must be evaluated in terms of reliability and validity and, like other assessment techniques, they are sometimes found wanting. As described in Chapter 5, anything that is not standard about test stimuli, including the tester, the client, or the testing situation, can threaten the value of test data.

Observations. The old adage that "actions speak louder than words" supports many clinicians' desire to supplement interviews or tests with direct observation of clients' behavior in situations of interest. The goal of observation is to go beyond what clients *say* to find out what they *do*.

An example of the value of observational data was provided by R. T. LaPiere during the 1930s, a time when many people in the United States expressed anti-Chinese sentiment. LaPiere (1934) took several long automobile trips with a Chinese couple and he took notes on their treatment at 250 hotels and restaurants. Only once were they denied service, and LaPiere rated their service as above average in 40% of the restaurants they visited. However, when LaPiere later wrote to all these hotels and restaurants to ask if they would accept Chinese guests, more than 90% of the 128 owners who responded said that they would not. Here, observational data provided different and perhaps more accurate views of anti-Chinese prejudice than did self-reports.

Indeed, many consider observation the most valid form of clinical assessment because it is so direct and capable of circumventing problems of memory, motivation, response style, and situational bias that can reduce the value of interviews and tests. Teachers' self-reports about the amount of attention paid to male and female students, for example, might be affected by self-perceptions, memory retrieval errors, or a desire to avoid appearing sexist. Analysis of a videotapes of actual classroom behavior, however, would get around these biasing factors.

---

[2]Certain aspects of interview and observational data can be handled in this way as well, but may involve more cumbersome procedures.

A second advantage of observation is its *relevance* to behaviors of greatest clinical interest. A child's aggressiveness, for example, can be observed as it occurs on the playground, where the problem has been most acute. A related advantage is that observation can assess behavior in its social context. Knowing that a mental hospital patient appears most depressed following a visit from family members may be more valuable to a therapist than an affirmative response to the query, "Are you ever depressed?" Finally, observations allow for description of behavior in specific terms and in great detail. For example, a person's sexual arousal in response to particular stimuli might be defined in terms of penile volume or vaginal blood flow, both of which can be objectively measured with special monitoring equipment. Observations can also quantify psychotic behavior by recording the frequency of explicitly defined actions (e.g., Paul & Lentz, 1977).

In spite of its advantages, observational assessment is not problem free. As described in Chapter 6, the reliability and validity of observational data can be threatened by observer error or bias, inadvertent observer influences on behavior under observation, and specific situational factors.

Life Records.   As they pass through life, people leave a paper trail consisting of school, work, police, medical, and financial records, letters and diaries, photographs, awards, and the like. Much can be learned about a person through these life records, and because this approach to assessment does not require the client to make any further responses (as do interviews, tests, and observations), there is little chance that memory, motivation, response style, or situational factors can distort the data obtained. Thus, a ten-minute review of a person's high school transcript may provide more specific and accurate academic information than a one-hour interview focused on questions such as "How did you do in school?" Similarly, diaries written during significant periods in a client's life can reveal feelings, wishes, actions, and situational details that might be lost or distorted by imperfect recall during an interview.

By summarizing a lot of information about a client's thinking and behavior over a long period of time and across a range of situations, life records provide an inexpensive way for clinicians to understand their clients better. They act like a wide-angle camera lens that brings into view material that might otherwise be missed. Wide-angle lenses produce distortion, however, and life records can do the same. For one thing, they tend to be superficial and often incomplete. Records may show that a person was divorced in 1995, but they may say nothing about why, or how the person felt about it.

The Value of Multiple Assessment Sources

Clinical psychologists seldom rely on a single source of assessment data as they create a working image of a client. Instead, they use multiple assessment channels to cross-validate information. Thus, hospital records may reveal that a patient has been there for twenty years, thus correcting the patient's self-reported estimate of six months. Indeed, the whole story of a client's problems is seldom clear until multiple assessment sources are tapped. One study showed, for example, that college students who described themselves as socially unassertive were observed to be capable of assertiveness, given the right conditions (Nietzel & Bernstein, 1976). It often takes multiple sources of assessment to separate those who *cannot* engage in certain behaviors from those who *do not* engage in them.

Another benefit of using multiple assessment sources appears when the clinician evaluates the effects of treatment. Suppose a couple enters therapy because they are considering divorce and then, three months later, they do divorce. If the only outcome assessment employed in this case were "marital happiness," as expressed during interviews, the treatment might be seen as having worsened marital distress. However, observations, third-person reports, and life records might show that one or both partners find their newly divorced status liberating and that they are developing new interests and abilities. These changes might not be obvious in an interview if the clients feel guilty about divorce, or if they fear appearing callous. Similarly, a young man whose therapy has helped him stand up for his rights may report improved self-esteem and comfort in social situations, but he might fail to mention the he has become too pushy and aggressive. Observational assessment might reveal this potentially problematic situation.

PROCESSING ASSESSMENT DATA

After assessment data are collected, the clinician must determine what those data mean. If the information is to be useful in reaching the clinician's assessment goals, it will have to be transformed from raw form into interpretations and conclusions. For example, it is important to know that a young child cries at high intensities for certain lengths of time each evening when placed in its crib. It is also important to know that after the crying continues for varying periods, someone enters the baby's room to provide comfort. However, these data mean little in psychological terms until the clinician translates them into meaningful statements about the infant's behavior and interprets what psychological processes are involved. This crucial part of assessment is often referred to as data *processing* or *clinical judgment*.

The processing task is formidable because a degree of *inference* is involved, and inference requires a mental leap from known data to what is assumed to be true on the basis of those data. In general, as the leap from data to assumption gets longer, inference becomes more vulnerable to error.

Consider this: A young boy is sitting on a lawn cutting an earthworm in half. It would be easy to infer from this observational data that the child is cruel and aggressive and that he might become dangerous later in life. These inferences would be off the mark, however, for "what the observer could not see . . . was what the boy—who happened to have few friends—thought as he cut the worm in half: 'There! Now you will have someone to play with'" (Goldfried & Sprafkin, 1974, p. 305). In short, elaborate inference—especially when based on minimal data—can be dangerous.

The only way to eliminate inference error is to eliminate inference, but doing so would also eliminate the meaning of most assessment data. Indeed, it is virtually impossible for human beings to avoid inferences, even in relation to the simplest stimuli. For

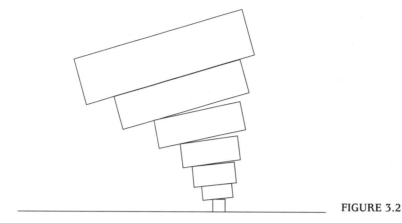

FIGURE 3.2

example, the raw sensory information coming to your eyes from Figure 3.2 could be described as a series of increasingly large rectangles arranged from right to left at differing angles on the page. However, it is difficult to avoid inferring that it is a stack of blocks about to fall over. The main questions about clinicians' processing of assessment data do not revolve about *whether* inferences will be drawn, but about *what kinds* of inferences to draw, *how* clinicians go about drawing them, how *accurate* they are, and how inference error can be minimized.

Levels and Types of Clinical Inference

Clinicians' judgments or inferences can be characterized in terms of their *goal*, their underlying *theoretical approach* to clinical psychology, and their *level of abstraction*. An inference might serve the goal of classification ("the client suffers from an anxiety disorder"), description ("his symptoms worsen in the presence of women"), or prediction ("he will benefit from cognitive-behavioral therapy").

The impact of a clinician's theoretical approach can be seen in the differing inferences that might be drawn about a client's suicide attempt. A cognitive-behavioral clinician might infer that the attempt reflected a habitual pattern of pessimistic thinking about a lost reinforcer. A psychodynamic assessor might see it as stemming from conflicted identification with a parent who had abandoned the client at an early age. To a phenomenological clinician, the attempt might be seen as reflecting the client's perception that there was no other way to deal with the world.

Inferences can vary widely in their level of abstraction, from cautious, low-level inferences that do not stray far from the original data to bolder statements that go well beyond the data on the basis of the assessor's theoretical approach, personal experience, or even intuitive hunch. At the lowest inference level, assessment data are taken at face value, as when a test score determines whether a student is admitted to graduate school. At higher inference levels, statements go somewhat beyond what assessment data actually say. For example, behavior revealed through tests, interviews, observations, and records might be interpreted as characteristic of the person and then used to justify trait labels such as *anxious, depressed, hostile,* or *agreeable*. At the highest level of abstraction, assessment data are processed more elaborately to form an overall picture of the client. Ideally, the person's "whole story" is reconstructed, and any mental disorders are viewed in light of this panorama. It is at this level, where clinical judgment ventures furthest from the original data, that clinicians depend most on their theories and experience to guide their inferences.

Three Views of Assessment Data

Clinicians tend to view assessment information in three main ways: as samples, correlates, or signs (Goodenough, 1949; Wiggins, 1973). Consider the following raw assessment data: A person took sixteen sleeping pills before going to bed at a hotel last night, but was saved after being discovered by a housekeeper and rushed to a hospital.

If this incident is seen as a *sample* of the client's behavior, the following judgments might result:

1. The client has access to potentially lethal medication.
2. The client did not wish to be saved because no one knew about the suicide attempt before it occurred.
3. Under similar circumstances, the client may attempt suicide again.

Notice that viewing the client's behavior as a sample results in low-level inferences. The suicide attempt is seen as an *example* of what the client is capable of doing under certain circumstances. No effort is made to infer *why* the individual tried suicide; more assessment would be required before specific causal statements would be justified.

The same incident could be viewed as a *correlate* of other aspects of the client's life. Even though no further information is available about the client, knowledge of similar cases might guide the following inferences:

1. The client is likely to be a middle-aged male who is single or divorced and lives alone.
2. The client is, or has recently been, depressed.
3. The client has little emotional support from family or friends.

Here, higher-level inferences are based on a combination of (1) facts about the client's behavior, and (2) the clinician's knowledge of what tends to correlate with that behavior. These inferences go beyond the original data with the support of empirically demonstrated relationships among variables such as suicide, age, gender, marital status, social support, and depression. In general, the stronger the known relationships between variables, the more accurate the inferences will be.

This correlate-oriented, or *psychometric*, approach is not tied to any theoretical approach. Any kind of quantifiable assessment data—tests of ego strength, reinforcer preferences, personality traits, perceptions of others—can be dealt with as correlates.

Accordingly, the psychometric view of assessment data processing links individual–oriented clinical psychology to the broader field of research on general personality theory.

Finally, the suicide attempt might be viewed as a *sign* of other, less obvious client characteristics. A sign-oriented view might result in inferences like these:

1. The client's aggressive impulses have been turned against the self.
2. The client's behavior reflects intrapsychic conflicts.
3. The pill-taking represents an unconscious cry for help.

These inferences go well beyond the information at hand, using assessment data as signs that can be interpreted by a particular theory of behavior—in this case, psychodynamic theory. Indeed, the relationship between sign and inference may stem solely from theoretical speculation.

Approaches, Views, and Levels

Levels of inference, views of assessment data, and theoretical approaches are interrelated. When assessment information is viewed primarily as a behavior sample, inference is likely to be minimal and the guiding theory will probably be behavioral. Viewing assessment data as signs usually results in higher levels of inference, often guided by a psychodynamic or phenomenological approach. In between, where assessment data are viewed as *correlates*, inferences tend to be at low to moderate levels, and there is more emphasis on statistical analyses of relationships among variables representing a range of theories.

As shown in the right-hand column of Table 3.5, assessment data processing may be based on formal statistical procedures or informal, subjective means. The informal approach usually involves looking at assessment data as signs, while the formal approach typically sees such data as correlates.[3] The informal, subjective, inferential approach is a reflection of Freud and his influence on clinical psychology. The formal, objective, statistical approach reflects the traditions of experimental psychology and the work of Galton, Cattell, Binet, and other psychometrically-oriented pioneers mentioned in Chapter 1. In the next section, we examine the ways clinicians have followed both traditions as they draw inferences about assessment data.

The Process of Clinical Inference

The mass media have long cast clinical psychologists as sign-oriented users of the informal approach to clinical inference who can astutely translate obscure signs into accurate statements about a person's past, present, or future. For example, a 1949 film called *The Dark Past* is the story of how a psychologist saves himself and his family

---

[3]There are many exceptions to this rule of thumb; clinicians often use informal procedures even when they view data as correlates. In dealing with attempted suicides, for example, clinicians are likely to *mentally* correlate information about a client with everything that they know about suicidal people. This task is difficult and fraught with errors, as we shall see later.

TABLE 3.5   Three Views of Assessment Data

Data Seen as	Level of Inference	Underlying Theory	Source of Data	Typical Data-Processing Procedures
Sign	High	Psychoanalytic or phenomenological	Interviews, tests, observations, life records	Informal; based on subjective judgments about assessment data
Sample	Low	Behavioral	Interviews, tests, observations, life records	Formal and informal; based on subjective judgments and functional analysis of client behavior
Correlate	Low to moderate	Various theories	Interviews, tests observations, life records	Formal; based on statistical analysis of assessment data

from death at the hands of an escaped killer named "Mad Dog" by getting the villain to talk about his life, his dreams, and his paralyzed hand. Guided by psychoanalytic theory, the clinician uses these assessment data to draw the correct inference: As a child, Mad Dog was responsible for his hated father's death and his crippled hand and murderous ways are symptoms of unconscious conflicts about it. (As a bonus, the paralysis disappears as soon as Mad Dog hears this interpretation.)

Clinical Intuition.   To a limited extent, such long-shot inferences have their counterparts in fact. In a famous example, psychoanalyst Theodore Reik describes his interview with a young woman who was upset about the breakup of her romance with a medical doctor:

> After a few sentences about the uneventful day, the patient fell into a long silence. She assured me that nothing was in her thoughts. Silence from me. After many minutes she complained about a toothache. She told me that she had been to the dentist yesterday. He had given her an injection and then had pulled a wisdom tooth. The spot was hurting again. New and longer silence. She pointed to my bookcase in the corner and said, "There's a book standing on its head." Without the slightest hesitation and in a reproachful voice I said, "But why did you not tell me that you had had an abortion?" The patient jumped up and looked at me as if I were a ghost. Nobody knew or could know that her lover, the physician, had performed an abortion on her.... (Reik, 1948, pp. 263–264)

Reik (1948) suggests that his correct inference from the data presented by the client (the toothache, the injection, the extraction, the pain, the book "on its head") was based partly on an intuitive gift. It has long been supposed that many clinical psychologists possess this same gift which, along with their experiences and guiding theories, makes them better than other people at drawing high-level inferences from assessment data.

Although certain individuals do seem better than others at correctly interpreting assessment data, this ability is not unique to clinicians. Further, empirical research does not support the idea that clinicians have special inferential capabilities. Donald Peterson made this point forcefully thirty years ago: "The idea that clinicians have or can develop some special kinds of antennae with which they can detect otherwise subliminal interpersonal stimuli and read from these the intrapsychic condition of another person is a myth which ought to be demolished." (Peterson, 1968, p. 105)

In fact, when an informal approach to assessment data processing is used, clinical psychologists are not significantly better than nonclinicians at making judgments, and do not make more accurate judgments than could be obtained through formal, statistical procedures. Let's first review research comparing the inference abilities of clinicians and others and then look at data comparing the quality of inferences based on formal versus informal procedures.

The Clinician as Inference Expert.   A classic example of research on the clinician's alleged special inference abilities is provided by a study in which people were asked to infer the presence of brain damage on the basis of clients' responses to a psychological test widely used for such purposes (Goldberg, 1959). Half of the thirty clients actually had organic damage; the other half did not. The test results were judged by four Ph.D. clinical psychologists with four to nine years of experience with the test, ten master's-level psychology trainees who had used the test for one to four years, and eight secretaries with no psychology background or experience with the test. The inference to be drawn in this study was simply "organic" or "not organic," so the probability of being correct by chance in any given case was 50%. However, Table 3.6 shows that only one of the four Ph.D. clinicians did better than chance. Indeed, they were no better than their students or their secretaries. More recent studies have obtained similar results (e.g., Gardner et al., 1996).

Other research shows that clinical psychologists also have no special memory capacity or other information-processing abilities. For example, numerous studies suggest that having larger amounts of assessment information may increase clinicians' *confidence* about their inferences, but it does not necessarily improve the accuracy of those inferences (Einhorn & Hogarth, 1978; Garb, 1984; Kleinmuntz, 1984; Rock et al., 1987). Some studies do show that trained clinicians can be more accurate judges than

TABLE 3.6   Inference Accuracy of Three Types of Judges

Group	N	% Correct	% Exceeding Chance
Psychology staff	4	65	25
Psychology trainees	22	70	60
Secretaries	8	67	62
Total	22	68	54

SOURCE: After Goldberg, 1959.

laypersons when they use well-validated psychological tests (Garb, 1992), but this advantage is neither large nor frequent, and many other studies find no superiority for trained clinicians' judgments. Why don't clinicians make better clinical judgments than other people, even after years of training and experience?

One explanation may relate to the manner in which clinical judgment has been studied. This *ecological* argument says that, by setting up test situations that do not reflect the way clinicians actually practice, researchers put them at an unfair disadvantage (e.g., Rock et al., 1987). For example, researchers often ask clinicians to make predictions about criteria such as school grades that are not part of their normal practice and for which they have no training. Further, research protocols often require clinicians to use assessment devices that they may not normally use in their day-to-day work.

A more substantive explanation of inaccuracies in clinical judgments is that clinicians are prone to the same cognitive habits and biases that can lead to error in anyone's information processing (MacDonald, 1996). For example, there are limits on how much data any human can perceive, hold in memory, and mentally combine, so people develop cognitive habits, called *heuristics*, that serve as shortcuts in drawing conclusions and making judgments (Garb, 1996; Tversky & Kahneman, 1974). These mental rules of thumb save time, but they can also cause errors, including errors in inferences based on clinical assessment data (Faust & Ziskin, 1988).

Like the first impressions all people form, clinicians tend to display an *anchoring bias* in which they establish their views of a client more on the basis of the first few pieces of assessment information than on any subsequent information (Tutin, 1993). Anchoring bias can also influence clinicians to let assessment information coming from certain sources (e.g., a parent's report of a child's behavior) outweigh any other information they receive (McCoy, 1976). If anchoring bias combines with *confirmation bias*—the tendency to interpret new information in line with existing beliefs—the clinician may ignore contradictory evidence or even distort it to fit initial impressions (Strohmer & Shivy, 1994). Clinicians' judgments may also rely too heavily on experiences that are recent enough or remarkable enough to make them especially available to recall. This *availability bias* can lead to judgment errors if what one recalls from highly memorable cases does not apply in the current case, and if it causes potentially important, but less memorable, information to be neglected (Garb, 1996). Availability bias can even create *illusory correlations* (Chapman & Chapman, 1967). Just as one vivid example can lead some people to falsely believe that it rains every time they wash their cars, memorable clinical "folklore" can influence clinicians to draw false inferences from assessment data (Krol, DeBruyn, & van den Bercken, 1995; Lewis, 1991). Thus, some clinicians see paranoid tendencies in clients who draw large eyes on figure-drawing tests—even though there is no firm empirical evidence to support this association (Golding & Rorer, 1972). Like other people, clinicians tend to remember their successes more clearly than their failures and so may remain wedded to incorrect inference tendencies (or invalid assessment methods) simply because they *think* of them as valid (Garb, 1989).

Various personal biases can also distort inferences (Rabinowitz, 1993). For example, clinicians' theoretical approach to clinical psychology can give them specific preconceptions about what behaviors to expect from clients and what those behaviors mean (Shoham-Salomon, 1985). Further, some clinicians may more readily infer the presence of disorder, or certain kinds of disorder, in males versus females, or in people of a particular age, health status, or ethnic group (Atkinson et al., 1996; Coontz, Lidz, & Mulvey, 1994; James & Haley, 1995). The results of empirical research on the prevalence of such bias is mixed. In one study of gender bias (Ford & Widiger, 1989), for example, psychologists were asked to diagnose a case report with clear signs of either antisocial personality disorder (APD; usually seen in males) or histrionic personality disorder (HPD; usually seen in females). Some of the psychologists in each group were told that the client was female, others were told the client was male. The inference errors made by both male and female psychologists showed gender bias in that they were significantly more likely to miss the APD diagnosis if they thought the client was female and significantly more likely to miss the HPD diagnosis if they thought the client was male. Though other studies have failed to find a robust overall bias in clinical judgments based on gender (e.g., Lopez, Smith, & Wolkenstein, 1993; Tomlinson-Clarke & Camilli, 1995), socioeconomic class, or ethnic minority status (Atkinson, et al., 1996; Tomlinson-Clarke & Cheatham, 1993), individual clinicians must always guard against such bias (Lopez, 1989; Malgady, 1996).

Finally, as mentioned earlier, the accuracy of clinical judgments will suffer if clinicians ignore the base rates of events they are trying to predict (Faust & Ziskin, 1988). Unfortunately, clinicians seldom have accurate knowledge of these base rates or do not pay sufficient attention to them.

In short, there is "little empirical evidence that justifies the granting of 'expert' status to the clinician on the basis of . . . training, experience, or information processing ability" (Wiggins, 1981). As we shall see later, however, efforts have been made to train clinicians to avoid some of the more common sources of inference errors. Further, there *are* clinicians whose inference accuracy appears superior to that of their colleagues and intelligent laypersons. Does this superiority reflect a stable ability, or is it more sporadic, depending on the client, situation, and judgment task involved? The answer is not clear; a person's inference ability may be a joint function of general skill as it interacts with situational variables (Bieri et al., 1966).

Inference by Formal Versus Informal Procedures. The sobering body of research that tarnished the image of clinicians as experts who consistently draw accurate inferences from assessment signs was prompted by research on another question about their inference ability. Many investigators had wondered whether inferences based on clinicians' informal (i.e., subjective) interpretation of assessment data—either as signs or correlates of client characteristics—were any more accurate than inferences based upon formal, statistical data processing in which clinicians play no role. Clinicians have traditionally been divided on this question. Those who favor the informal, "clinical" approach see it as meaningful, organized, rich, deep, and genuine, while critics characterize it as mystical, vague, unscientific, sloppy, and muddleheaded. Proponents of formal, "statistical" inference praise it as objective, reliable, precise, and empirical; opponents label it artificial, trivial, superficial, and rigid.

When clinicians interpret assessment data informally, make recommendations based on these interpretations, and do research on such activities, it is usually because they believe that they, or most members of their profession, at least, are good at these things. Thus it came as a shock when Paul Meehl's 1954 review of twenty studies comparing formal versus informal inference methods found that, in all but one case, the accuracy of the statistical approach equaled or surpassed that of the clinical approach. Later, even the sole exception to this surprising conclusion was called a tie, and, as additional research became available, the superiority of the statistical method of prediction was more firmly established (Dawes, Faust, & Meehl, 1989; Meehl, 1957, 1965; see Table 3.7).

In the years since Meehl's review, at least eighteen published responses appeared, most of which pointed out methodological defects in some of the studies that could have biased results in favor of statistical procedures. The ecological validity of the research was also questioned; many felt that the variables being predicted (e.g., grades) were not like those typically dealt with by practicing clinicians, while others suggested that the clinicians in several studies were handicapped by inadequate or unfamiliar information about clients and about what they were supposed to predict (Holt, 1958, 1978). Frederick C. Thorne (1972, p. 44) put it this way: "The question must not be what naive judges do with inappropriate tasks under questionable conditions of comparability with actual clinical situations, but what the most sophisticated judges can do with appropriate methods under ideal conditions."

TABLE 3.7   Summary of Outcomes of Studies Comparing Clinical vs. Statistical Predictive Inference

| | | | Outcome | | |
| | Number of | | --- | --- | --- |
Source	Studies Reviewed	Variables Predicted	Clinical Better	Statistical Better	Tie
Meehl (1954)	20	Success in school or military; recidivism or parole violation; recovery from psychosis	1[a]	11	8
Meehl (1957)	27	Same as above, plus personality description; therapy outcome	0	17	10
Meehl (1965)	51	Same as above, plus response to shock treatment; diagnosis label; job success and satisfaction; medical diagnosis	1[b]	33	17

[a]Later called a tie.
[b]Later called a tie by Goldberg (1968)
SOURCE: After Wiggins, 1973.

Still, the furor over Meehl's conclusions could not negate the fact that inference based on subjective, clinical methods is not as accurate as it was once assumed to be (Dawes, 1994). This apparently discouraging conclusion is not without positive aspects, however. Meehl's reviews, along with other reports on the limitations on clinicians' information-processing capabilities, focused research on those limitations and stimulated improvements in both formal and informal inference (Kleinmuntz, 1984; Wiggins, 1981).

Improving Informal Inference. Thorne suggested that "clinicians must become much more critical of the types of judgments they attempt to make, the selection of cues upon which judgments are based, and their modes of collecting and combining data" (1972, p. 44). Work in these areas began in the 1960s as researchers attempted to analyze the logic of inference (Sarbin, Taft, & Bailey, 1960), relate it to social and physical judgment processes and errors (Bieri et al., 1966; Hunt & Jones, 1962), analyze the nature and influence of specific cues used by clinicians (Goldberg, 1968; Hoffman, 1960), optimize the amount of assessment data to be processed (Bartlett & Green, 1966), and identify the conditions under which inference can be most reliable and valid (Watley, 1968). These efforts continue today (e.g., Garb & Schramke, 1996; Sleek, 1996; Todd, 1996).

Unfortunately, the results of most efforts to help clinicians avoid the common pitfalls that beset clinical judgment have been disappointing. Experienced clinicians still tend to do no better at personality assessment than inexperienced clinicians or graduate students (Garb, 1989). Clinicians with training in specific assessment areas perform better than laypersons, but the size of their advantage is surprisingly small. Informing clinicians about their biases is also not very helpful, although there may be benefits from having clinicians keep a written record of the biases they show and the mistakes they make (Dawes, 1986).

Even though the accuracy of clinical inference can be improved over levels previously reported (Kahneman & Tversky, 1979), it is not clear that the amount of improvement justifies the extra effort. Even the most superior human judges operating under optimal conditions are variable enough in their accuracy to raise questions about their suitability for the data-processing task. Consider, for example, a study which tried to specify the rules by which the very best clinical judges draw inferences from a particular personality test. In this study, a recognized expert at drawing inferences from the test was asked to "think aloud" while interpreting the test scores of 126 people (Kleinmuntz, 1963). The decision rules that emerged for designating these people as "adjusted" or "maladjusted" were then used to write a computer program that would formalize the process of interpreting the test. The study showed that an expert clinician's inference rules can be objectified and taught, but that the best "student" may not be a human. The computer used the rules so perfectly and consistently with each new set of test scores that—in line with earlier data on formal versus informal inference—it did better at interpreting subsequent test scores than the clinician who had "taught" it (Kleinmuntz, 1969).

Improving Formal Inference. The performance of formal inference procedures has provided the impetus for efforts to elaborate and improve techniques for the statistical processing of assessment data. Though it may seem that this type of research might put clinicians out of a job, one of its by-products has been to map out the assessment tasks at which clinicians can be most effective.

For one thing, Meehl (1954) and other researchers (e.g., Sawyer, 1966) have distinguished between the clinical psychologist's role in data *processing* versus data *collection*. They highlighted the fact that, just as data processing can be formal or informal, collection of assessment data can be done mechanically (with objective tests and life records) or subjectively (through unstructured interviews and informal observations). Thus, as shown in Table 3.8, many combinations of formal and informal procedures are possible in a given assessment enterprise. When the studies reviewed by Meehl are reexamined with the collection–processing distinction in mind, it becomes clear that while clinicians' subjective methods may be inferior to statistical methods for *processing* assessment data, their uniquely human abilities at *collecting* data and reporting judgments can make vital contributions to the assessment process (Sawyer,

TABLE 3.8   Some Combinations of Formal and Informal Procedures for the Collection and Processing of Assessment Data

Data-Collection Procedure	Data-Processing Procedure	Example
1. Formal	Formal	Psychological test scores processed by computer according to a statistical formula which predicts potential for behavior problems
2. Formal	Informal	Psychological test scores interpreted by clinician based on experience, theory, and hunches to establish psychiatric diagnosis
3. Informal	Formal	Clinician's subjective judgments (based on an interview) converted into quantitative ratings, which are then processed by a computer or statistical formula to describe client's personality
4. Informal	Informal	Subjective impressions and judgments (from interviews, projective tests, etc.) interpreted subjectively to decide whether client needs to be hospitalized
5. Formal and Informal	Formal	Psychological test scores and clinician's subjective impressions and judgments all fed into computer, which used complex formula to describe client or make predictions about behavior
6. Formal and Informal	Informal	Psychological test scores and clinician's subjective impressions and judgments all scanned and interpreted by clinician to decide whether client is capable of standing trial for a crime.

1966). Indeed, the most accurate clinical inferences are likely to be based on the formal, statistical processing of data collected by *both* mechanical and subjective techniques—for example, by objective tests *and* clinical interviews (Sawyer, 1966). ". . . The clinician may be able to contribute most not by direct prediction, but rather by providing, in objective form, judgments to be combined mechanically" (Sawyer, 1966, p. 193).

This research confirms a role for clinicians in the assessment process. They may not be very accurate *combiners* of assessment data, but they can be an unsurpassed *source* of data (Anastasi, 1988). Clinicians can use their interviewing skills to obtain information from clients that might not otherwise be available. Guided by their theoretical approach, they can develop hypotheses about what aspects of clients' lives warrant further exploration, and they provide a stimulus that elicits a sample of how clients respond in a social situation. Though disagreement remains over exactly what assessment questions and roles clinicians should handle, the following conclusion still seems to apply: "Clinicians need not view themselves as second-rate IBM machines unless they choose to engage in activities that are more appropriately performed by such machines. In the realm of clinical observation and hypothesis formation, the IBM machine will never be more than a second-rate clinician" (Wiggins, 1973).

With this conclusion in mind, many clinicians and researchers now tend to focus on upgrading observational and other data-collection skills to optimize their value in the clinical assessment process. For example, clinical "intuition" has been recast as skill in observing a client's verbal and nonverbal behavior. Viewed this way, "intuition" can be developed, practiced, and improved (see Arkes, 1981; Dawes, 1986).

At the same time, other investigators are studying the accuracy of statistical, usually computer-based, data-processing methods. Some of these methods are thoroughly mechanical and empirical, as when a client's test scores are interpreted according to formulae derived from statistical relationships between other clients' test scores and behavior (see example 1 in Table 3.8). Here, the computer takes the client's test profile and "looks up" the characteristics of other people with similar profiles. Developing this type of purely actuarial program is expensive because it requires a storehouse of data from thousands of clients.

When, as is usually the case, there are too few data on the relationship between assessment results and client characteristics to create a good statistical formula for drawing inferences, hybrid systems of formal data processing have evolved. As in the Kleinmuntz (1963) study, such systems use a computer to interpret assessment data, not through an empirically derived formula, but through decision rules distilled from clinicians' experiences and beliefs. This process of "automating clinical lore" (Wiggins, 1973) has resulted in systems that can generate *computerized narrative interpretations* of the results of more than 100 psychological tests. As shown in Table 3.9, these interpretations can be remarkably detailed, but the programs that generate them vary considerably in sophistication and quality. Many have been developed with the logic pioneered by Benjamin Kleinmuntz (1963), but not all have been adequately concerned with assessing reliability and validity (Matarazzo, 1983a; 1986).

Critics have also noted the following additional limitations and problems associated with computerized assessment:

TABLE 3.9   A Computerized Narrative Interpretation of the Marital Satisfaction Inventory

A carefully developed computerized interpretation system is available for use with the 280-item, 11-scale Marital Satisfaction Inventory (MSI; Snyder, 1981). Here are excerpts from a computer's report on Mr. and Mrs. D., a couple who had just entered marital therapy (Snyder, Lachar, & Wills, 1988). Each spouse took the MSI independently, but the report combines their results.

Global Marital Affect

Both spouses openly acknowledge serious difficulties in their marriage and dissatisfaction with their spouse; they may have a tendency to emphasize marital conflict to the exclusion of acknowledging more positive aspects of their relationship. Relationship problems are likely to be of long duration and generalized across different areas of the marriage. Persons with similar profiles describe their marriage as a major source of disappointment. Determination of specific steps either spouse has taken toward separation or divorce would be prudent.

Spousal Communication

Both spouses express dissatisfaction with the amount of affection shown by their partner, although the wife reports somewhat less distress in this regard. Women with similar scores often feel emotionally distant from their husbands, and may feel unappreciated or misunderstood. In comparison, the husband describes extensive dissatisfaction with the quality of affective communication in the marriage. Men with similar scores typically describe their wives as emotionally distant and uncaring. Both the husband and wife describe difficulties in resolving disagreements. although the husband's dissatisfaction in this regard is somewhat less than his wife's. When differences arise, there may be a notable shift toward more negative forms of interaction including reciprocity of negative affect, failure to acknowledge each other's view, or attribution of negative intentions to the partner's behavior. There may exist a long accumulation of unresolved differences, such that even minor disagreements precipitate major arguments. Each partner is likely to regard the other as being entrenched in their own position and unresponsive to legitimate concerns or complaints.

Specific Areas of Interaction

Overall, the husband and wife have evaluated specific dimensions of spousal interaction in a somewhat different manner. This divergence in spouses' views of the marriage may hinder their collaboration in rank-ordering relationship concerns and identifying therapeutic goals. Both respondents indicate dissatisfaction with their sexual relationship, although the wife reports somewhat less distress in this area. Disagreements regarding the frequency or variety of sexual behaviors may be frequent; it is somewhat unlikely that sexual difficulties evolve exclusively from more general marital distress, and specific interventions in this area may be warranted.

Concerns Regarding Children

The husband and wife both indicate significant conflict rearing childrearing issues, although the husband reports somewhat less distress in this respect. Conflicts around division of child care responsibilities are likely, and spouses may experience frequent disagreements regarding discipline and their children's privileges and responsibilities. The couple could likely benefit from interventions aimed at clarifying their respective expectations for their children's behavior and identifying each spouse's responsibilities for various childrearing tasks. Given the respondents' somewhat different perceptions in this area, a careful assessment should be conducted of possible alliances of one or more children with one parent against the other; an in-depth evaluation of one or more children may be warranted.

TABLE 3.9   A Computerized Narrative Interpretation of the Marital Satisfaction Inventory (*Continued*)

Role Orientation and Family History

The husband and wife differ sharply in their role orientations, with the husband expressing a more traditional view toward marital and parental roles. The husband may prefer a traditional division of household and childrearing responsibilities, with his assuming the role as primary wage-earner and the wife investing herself more fully in her role as wife and mother at home. In contrast, the wife describes a fairly nontraditional view of marital and parental roles. She is likely to prefer a more flexible division of household and childrearing tasks, with both spouses pursuing independent careers and sharing equally in decision making and in housework and child care responsibilities at home. Given their different attitudes in this domain, the potential for marital role conflict merits further examination. Finally, both respondents report a history of moderate distress within their families of origin. Maladaptive relationship patterns in both families of origin should be carefully examined to determine the extent to which they generalize to the couple's own marriage.

SOURCE: Reprinted from Volume 14, Number 4, of the *Journal of Marital and Family Therapy*, Copyright 1988, American Association for Marriage and Family Therapy. Reprinted with permission.

1. Actuarial techniques can be applied only where adequately developed, fully standardized assessment devices, inference norms, and formulae are available. Although the number of actuarial assessment systems is increasing, many clinicians still do not use them, preferring instead to rely on their personal judgments and predictions.

2. New discoveries about behavior are less likely to occur if clinicians become less involved in assessment data processing.

3. Relegation of clinicians to a data-collection role decreases the chances of future improvement of human data-processing skills (Matarazzo, 1986).

4. Excluding the clinician from the data-processing role reduces the probability that rare behavioral events and relationships will be noticed, because actuarial tables and statistical formulae may not be sensitive to them.

5. Certain kinds of assessment may be more appropriately dealt with by informal means. For example, specific, "bounded" questions (Will this person be likely to abuse children?) may most adequately be answered by formal data processing, while more general "unbounded" concerns (What is this person like?) seem best handled through informal means (Levy, 1963).

6. Computerized testing may make it easier for poorly trained testers to provide impressive-sounding assessment reports that they may not fully understand and are not prepared to use in the most appropriate way.

7. Computerized narratives usually focus on only one plausible interpretation of test results rather than considering and evaluating the merits of the several possible interpretations that a more complete assessment battery almost always suggests (Matarazzo, 1986).

As criticisms like these focused attention on crucial computerized assessment issues, several steps were taken to improve and regulate computer-based testing and interpretation. There is now a special set of guidelines pertaining to computer testing (APA, 1986), the APA's *Standards for Educational and Psychological Testing* (APA, 1985) includes several provisions about computerized testing, the journal called *Computers in Human Behavior* includes a section on computer software used to interpret psychological tests, and numerous journal articles on the pros and cons of computerized psychological assessment have appeared (e.g., Fowler, 1985).

One point that some critics of computer-based test interpretation appear to miss is that many of their criticisms apply at least as well to the assessment reports of human clinicians. A core problem in clinical assessment is the lack of validation research on all kinds of assessment reports, whether computer generated or prepared by people (Ben-Porath & Butcher, 1991).

The Behavioral Approach to Assessment

Clinical psychologists have traditionally been concerned with formal and informal processing of assessment data that are viewed as signs or correlates. In that tradition, assessment information is interpreted in terms of psychological traits or intrapsychic dynamics, and the clinician's goal is to predict something about the client or to describe the client's personality. Clinical psychologists who adopt a behavioral approach tend not to adopt these guidelines. Their main criticisms and alternative formulations can be summarized as follows:

1. The use of assessment data as *signs* of personality traits involves too much inference. Behaviorists do not see personality traits, psychological dispositions, or personality dynamics as the most useful concepts for learning about people. In their view, dispositional constructs have limited utility for describing people, predicting their behavior, or evaluating behavior change programs.

   Many behaviorists argue that part of the reason for clinicians' poor data-processing skills is that they use vague trait concepts to reach inferences that stray too far from initial assessment information. When clinicians do not share common definitions for terms like *anxiety, aggression*, and *ego*, the reliability and validity of clinical judgments are likely to be low (Goldfried, 1995). Trait concepts are seen by behavioral assessors as adding confusing and ultimately superfluous labels to behavior that does not need them. As noted earlier, the behavioral approach treats assessment data as samples of client capabilities, not evidence for personality traits or dynamic states.

2. Trait concepts often isolate people's behavior from the environment in which it occurs. Since behavior is learned in a social context, one cannot describe or predict that behavior accurately unless situational factors are taken into account: A person who displays dominance on a psychological test may behave quite differently toward a supervisor at work.

   Accordingly, behavioral assessment includes collecting information about (a) client capabilities, (b) characteristics of the physical and social environment in which behavior occurs, and (c) the nature of *client–environment interactions*. The person–situation orientation in the behavioral view of assessment has emphasized *interactionism* or the *reciprocal relationship* between people and the situations which they create and to which they respond (Bandura, 1978; Mischel, 1984).

3. Traditional clinical assessment practices promote separation between data collection and data use. Too often, assessment information is processed into descriptions or predictions that are sufficiently irrelevant to planning or evaluating treatment that they may actually be ignored (Dailey, 1953; Meehl, 1960).

From the behavioral perspective, clinical assessment must be tied to efforts at modifying behavior (Haynes, 1993). Toward this end, clients, situations, and client–situation interactions are described along dimensions that are as precise and data based as possible, have direct implications for treatment planning, and can be monitored during and after treatment. Rather than merely describing a child's problem in trait-oriented terms such as *aggressiveness* or *hyperactivity*, behavioral assessment would focus on the *frequencies, durations*, or *intensities* with which specific acts (e.g., striking others) occur, the settings in which they occur, and the environmental factors that appear to elicit and reinforce them. The acronym *SORC*, for Stimulus-Organism-Response-Consequence, captures the variables that a thorough behavioral assessment must consider (Goldfried & Sprafkin, 1974). The spirit of interactionism is suggested by this system's attention to environmental (the C and S components) and organismic (the O component) control of important responses (R). Behaviorists also study extended sequences, or *chains*, of interaction in an attempt to understand the nature of, and problems in, the complex and reciprocal influences that occur as people interact in couples or other social situations (Gottman & Roy, 1990).

In general, questions asked during behavioral assessment are not oriented toward *why* people behave in a particular way, but *what* they do, and *when, where*, and *under what circumstances* they do it. When behavior is described in this fashion, tactics for changing behavior tend to follow directly from assessment. If assessment suggests that Sam's high-frequency whining in the classroom is reinforced by teacher attention, a program to terminate reward of the maladaptive behavior and plan reinforcement of more appropriate behaviors might be instituted. As that program begins, its effect on the variables identified in the initial assessment would be observed and used as a guide for continuing, altering, or terminating the intervention.

In recent years, behavioral and more traditional approaches to assessment have begun to recognize each other's strengths (Haynes & Uchigakiuchi, 1993). For their part, behaviorists increasingly stress the need to demonstrate rather than presume that their assessment methods meet the classic psychometric criteria of reliability and validity. And where they once avoided considering client personality characteristics, behaviorists are now more willing to recognize and assess "person variables" that give stability and unity to behavior across situations (Mischel, 1986, 1993). At the same time, those engaged in trait assessment and psychiatric diagnosis have embraced some behavioral recommendations. One example of the influence of behavioral assessment principles on traditional diagnostic practices is seen in the specific, criterion-based decision-making structure used in DSM-IV.

The behavioral approach to assessment is not without its critics, however. Many clinicians see objective assessment of overt behaviors in relation to specific environmental situations as too narrow and inadequate for tapping the various personality dimensions stressed in their own approaches. Other critiques center on the fact that, compared to traditional personality tests, for example, many behavioral assessment instruments are still in a rather primitive stage of development in terms of standardization norms. Still others note that, like other clinicians, those using behavioral assessments usually do so without benefit of statistical inference formulae and thus depend on their own subjective judgments in interpreting the data they collect. Also, though behavioral assessment provides excellent descriptions of behavior that can be used to guide treatment planning, it has not resolved the question of what behaviors constitute a problem and who sets up the definitions (Morganstern, 1988). Finally, behavioral assessment has not yet reached a level of sophistication that allows for a reliable, empirically determined choice of specific treatment techniques, especially in complex cases. (For more on the theory, practice, and problems of behavioral assessment, see Bellack & Hersen, 1988; Ciminero, Calhoun, & Adams, 1986).

Phenomenology and Assessment

Many objections raised by behavioral theorists to traditional assessment procedures relate to the belief that people should not be examined apart from their physical and social environment and burdened with labels that focus on problems and weaknesses to the exclusion of assets and strengths. In this respect, the behavioral and phenomenological approaches to assessment are in accord. However, phenomenologically-oriented clinicians have suggested assessment alternatives that differ substantially from those of the behavioral approach (e.g., Fischer & Fischer, 1983). Some of them have argued against assessment on the grounds that such procedures are dehumanizing, take responsibility away from clients, and threaten the quality of clinician–client relations (Rogers, 1951). Advocates of this position may be unwilling even to review existing assessment data and inferences made about a client by others because they assume that all the information necessary will emerge during interviews with the client (see Chapters 4 and 8).

Other phenomenologists raise the possibility that assessment data *collected* through traditional means such as personality tests can be useful if they are *processed* in line with humanistic principles (Fischer, 1989). For example, test results can be viewed as clues to how a client looks at the world, and conducting those tests can provide opportunities for the clinician and client to build their relationship (Dana & Leech, 1974; Fischer, 1985). Phenomenologists who feel that traditional assessment devices do not facilitate the growth of clinician–client relationships have developed specialized instruments that they believe do the job better. These tests include the Personal Orientation Inventory (Shostrom, 1968) and the Purpose-in-Life Test (Crumbaugh, 1968).

COMMUNICATING ASSESSMENT DATA

The organized presentation of assessment results is called an *assessment report*. If assessment results are to have maximal value, they must be presented in reports that are *clear*, *relevant* to assessment goals, and *useful* to the intended consumer. Accordingly, clinicians must guard against problems that can make reports vague, irrelevant, and useless.

Report Clarity

The first criterion for an assessment report is clarity. Without this basic attribute, relevance and usefulness cannot even be evaluated. Lack of clarity in psychological reports is troublesome because misinterpretation of a report can lead to misguided decisions. Here is a case in point:

> A young girl, mentally defective, was seen for testing by the psychologist, who reported to the social agency that the girl's test performance indicated moderate success and happiness for her in "doing things with her hands." Three months later, however, the social agency reported to the psychologist that the girl was not responding well. Although the social agency had followed the psychologist's recommendation, the girl was neither happy nor successful "doing things with her hands." When the psychologist inquired what kinds of things, specifically, the girl had been given to do he was told "We gave her music lessons—on the saxophone." (Hammond & Allen, 1953, p. v)

A related problem exists when the assessor uses jargon that may be meaningless to the reader. Consider the following excerpt from a report on a thirty-six-year-old man:

> Test results emphasize a basically characterological problem with currently hysteroid defenses. Impairment of his ability to make adequate use of independent and creative fantasy, associated with emotional lability and naivete, are characteristic of him.... Due to markedly passive-aggressive character make-up, in which the infantile dependency needs are continually warring with his hostile tendencies, it is not difficult to understand this current conflict over sexual expression. (Mischel, 1968, p. 105)

The writer may understand the client, but will the reader understand the writer? Anyone not well versed in psychoanalytic terminology would find such a report mystifying. Professionals may not even agree on the meaning of the terms employed. Factors such as excessive length (or cryptic brevity), excessively technical information (statistics or esoteric test scores), and lack of coherent organization also contribute to lack of clarity in assessment reports (Olive, 1972; Tallent & Reiss, 1959).

Relevance to Goals

The second requirement of a valuable assessment report is that it be relevant to the goal that prompted the assessment in the first place. If that goal was to classify the client's behavior, information relevant to classification should be highlighted. If description of the client's current psychological assets and liabilities was the purpose, the report should contain those descriptions. If predictions about a client are requested, these should appear, unless the clinician believes that no sound basis exists for making them.

These simple, self-evident prescriptions are sometimes lost, especially when explicit assessment goals are never stated. Although far less common today than in the past, clinicians may still be asked for "psychologicals" (usually a standard test battery and interview) without being told why assessment is being done. Under such circumstances, the chances of writing a relevant report are minimal. Unfortunately, there are other cases in which a report's lack of relevance is due mainly to the clinician's failure to keep established objectives in mind.

Usefulness of Reports

Finally, one must ask if an assessment report is useful. Does the information it contains add anything important to what we already know about the client? Reports that present clear, relevant information that is already available through other sources may appear useful, but have little real value. Such reports tend to be written when the assessor has either failed to collect new information or has not made useful statements about new data. In the former case, the clinician may have employed techniques that have low *incremental validity* (Sechrest, 1963). For example, a clinician may use psychological tests to conclude that a client has strong hostile tendencies, but if police records show that the client repeatedly has been arrested for assault, this conclusion doesn't add much to the clinical picture. In other instances, the assessor's report may have limited usefulness because it says nothing beyond what would be expected on the basis of base rate information, past experience, and common sense.

Consider the following edited version of a report written entirely on the basis of two pieces of information: (1) The client is a new admission to a Veterans Administration hospital, and (2) the case was to be discussed at a convention session entitled "A Case Study of Schizophrenia." The report said:

> This veteran approached the testing situation with some reluctance. He was cooperative with the clinician, but mildly evasive on some of the material. Both the tests and the past history suggest considerable inadequacy in interpersonal relations, particularly with members of his family. It is doubtful whether he has ever had very many close relationships with anyone.... He has never been able to sink his roots deeply. He is immature, egocentric, and irritable, and often he misperceives the good intentions of the people around him.... He tends to be basically passive and dependent, though there are occasional periods of resistance and rebellion against others.... Vocationally, his adjustment has been very poor. Mostly he has drifted from one job to another. His interests are shallow and he tends to have poor motivation for his work. Also he has had a hard time keeping his jobs because of difficulty in getting along with fellow employees. Although he has had some relations with women, his sex life has been unsatisfactory to him. At present, he is mildly depressed.... His intelligence is close to average, but he is functioning below his potential.... Test results and case history ... suggest the diagnosis of schizophrenic reaction, chronic undifferentiated type. Prognosis for response to treatment appears to be poor. (Sundberg, Tyler, & Taplin, 1973, pp. 577-579)

In generating this impressive, but utterly generic report the clinician relied heavily on knowledge of VA hospital residents and familiarity with hospital procedures. For example, since the case was to be discussed at a meeting on schizophrenia, and since schizophrenic diagnoses are common for VA residents, it was easy to surmise the correct diagnosis. Also, because it fits the "average" VA resident, the report was likely to be at least partially accurate. This bogus document exemplifies a feature of assessment reports that reduces their usefulness: overgenerality, or the tendency to write in terms that are so ambiguous they can be true of almost anyone. Documents laden with overly general statements have been dubbed "Barnum Reports" (in honor of P.T. Barnum's maxim that there is a sucker born every minute), "Aunt Fanny Reports" (because the statements could be true of "my aunt Fanny"), or "Madison Avenue Reports" (given that they "sell" well) (Klopfer, 1983; Meehl, 1956; Tallent, 1992). Such overly general material has the dual disadvantages of spuriously increasing a report's impressiveness while actually decreasing its usefulness.

Organizing Assessment Data

While there is no universally "right" way to organize assessment data, several guidelines are worth noting. First, the criteria of clarity, relevance, and usefulness may be more easily achieved by using an outline organized around the issues that the clinician's theoretical approach suggests are most important to the goals of assessment. Here we present sample outlines representing three approaches to clinical psychology. [For more detailed discussions of the techniques and problems associated with writing clinical assessment reports, see Sattler (1988) and Tallent (1976, 1992).]

A Psychodynamic Outline.   This outline is an edited version of one used to report the clinical assessment of a young man in trouble with the law for gambling and assault (Tallent, 1976, pp. 121–122):

I. Conflicts
   A. Self-perception
   B. Goals
   C. Frustrations
   D. Interpersonal relations
   E. Perception of environment
   F. Drives, dynamics
   G. Emotional cathexes
   H. Emotional controls
II. Social stimulus value
   A. Cognitive skills
   B. Conative factors
   C. Goals
   D. Social role
III. Cognitive functioning
   A. Deficit
   B. Psychopathology

IV. Defenses
   A. Denial
   B. Interpersonal tactics
   C. Fantasy

A Phenomenological Report.   In line with their subjective approach and tendency to avoid formal assessment, phenomenologically oriented clinicians are more likely to follow general frameworks rather than detailed outlines:

   I. Client from own point of view
   II. Client as reflected in tests
   III. Client as seen by assessor

A Cognitive-Behavioral Outline.   Here is an assessment outline representative of the cognitive-behavioral approach (Pomeranz & Goldfried, 1970):

   I. Description of client's physical appearance and behavior during assessment
   II. Presenting problems
      A. Nature of problems
      B. Historical background of problems
      C. Current situational determinants of problems
      D. Relevant organismic variables
         1. Physiological states
         2. Effects of medication
         3. Cognitive determinants of problems
      E. Dimensions of problems
         1. Duration
         2. Pervasiveness
         3. Frequency
         4. Magnitude
      F. Consequences of problems
         1. Positive
         2. Negative
   III. Other problems (observed by assessor but not stated by client)
   IV. Personal assets
   V. Targets for change
   VI. Recommended treatments
   VII. Client motivation for treatment
   VIII. Prognosis
   IX. Priority for treatment
   X. Client expectancies
      A. About solving specific problems
      B. About treatment enterprise in general
   XI. Other comments

Table 3.10 illustrates how an assessment outline—in this case, a cognitive-behavioral outline—is translated into an assessment report.

A Note on Ethics

The collection, processing, and communication of assessment data require that clinicians have access to sensitive information that the client might not ordinarily reveal. This places a heavy responsibility on the assessor to use and report this privileged information in a fashion that safeguards the client's welfare and dignity and shows concern for (1) how psychological assessment data are being used, (2) who may have access to confidential material, and (3) the possibility that improper or irresponsible interpretation of assessment information will have negative consequences for clients.

TABLE 3.10   An Assessment Report Based on a Cognitive-Behavioral Outline

Behavior During Interview and Physical Description

James is a clean-shaven, long-haired young man who appeared for the intake interview in well-coordinated college garb: jeans, wide belt, open shirt, and sandals. He came across as shy and soft-spoken, with occasional minor speech blocks. Although uneasy during most of the session, he nonetheless spoke freely and candidly.

Presenting Problem:

A. *Nature of problem:* Anxiety in public speaking situations, and other situations in which he is being evaluated by others.

B. *Historical setting events:* James was born in France, and arrived in this country seven years ago, at which time he experienced both a social and language problem. His social contacts had been minimal until he entered college, at which time a socially aggressive friend of his helped him to break out of his shell. James describes his father as being an overly critical and perfectionistic person who would, on occasion, rip up his homework if it fell short of the mark. The client's mother is pictured as a controlling, overly affectionate person who was always showing concern about his welfare. His younger brother, who has always been a good student, was continually thrown up to James by his parents as being far better than he.

C. *Current situational determinants:* Interaction with his parents, examinations, family gatherings, participation in classes, initial social contact.

D. *Relevant organismic variables:* The client appears to be approaching a number of situations with certain irrational expectations, primarily unrealistic strivings of perfection and an overwhelming desire to receive approval from others. He is not taking any medication at this time.

E. *Dimensions of problem:* The client's social and evaluative anxiety are long-standing and occur in a wide variety of day-to-day situations.

F. *Consequences of problem:* His chronic level of anxiety resulted in an ulcer operation at the age of 15. In addition, he has developed a skin rash on his hands and arms, apparently from excessive perspiration. He reports that his nervousness at one time caused him to stutter, but this appears to be less a problem in more recent years. His anxiety in examination situations has typically interfered with his ability to perform well.

Other Problems:

A. *Assertiveness:* Although obviously a shy and timid individual, James said that lack of assertiveness is no longer a problem with him. At one time in the past, his friends would take

With these concerns in mind, clinicians must first be sure their inquiries do not comprise an unauthorized invasion of a client's privacy (see Bongar, 1988, for suggestions on how to maintain privacy when using computers in assessment). Next, care should be taken to assure that assessment goals are not socially or culturally biased so that certain clients (e.g., members of ethnic or racial minorities) are placed at a disadvantage (Malgady, 1996). For example, some psychological tests are alleged to be inappropriate for use with minority groups, leading to court decisions prohibiting their use for educational placement and other purposes (see Lambert, 1981 for discussion of the landmark *Larry P. v. Wilson Riles* case in California). Finally, clinicians must wrestle with the problem of who may have access to assessment data if they do not maintain sole control over them. When test scores, conclusions, predictions, and other information are communicated in a report, they may be misused by persons who see the report but are not qualified to interpret it. In such cases, not only is the client's privacy

---

TABLE 3.10 An Assessment Report Based on a Cognitive-Behavioral Outline (*Continued*)

advantage of him, but he claims that this is no longer the case. This should be followed up further, as it is unclear what he means by assertiveness.

   B. *Forgetfulness:* The client reports that he frequently misses appointments, misplaces items, locks himself out of his room, and generally is absent-minded.

Personal Assets:
The client is fairly bright and comes across as a warm, friendly, and sensitive individual.

Targets for Modification:
Unrealistic self-statements in social-evaluative situations; possibly behavioral deficits associated with unassertiveness; and forgetfulness.

Recommended Treatment:
It appears that relaxation training would be a good way to begin, especially in light of the client's high level of anxiety. Following this, the treatment should move along the lines of rational restructuring, and possibly behavior rehearsal. It is unclear as yet what would be the best strategy for dealing with forgetfulness.

Motivation for Treatment:
High.

Prognosis:
Very good.

Priority for Treatment:
High.

Expectancies:
On occasion, especially when going out on a date with a female, James would take half a sleeping pill to calm himself down,. He wants to get away from this, and feels what he needs is to learn to cope with his anxieties by himself. It would appear that he will be very receptive to whatever treatment plan we finally decide on, especially if the emphasis is on self-control of anxiety.

Other Comments:
Considering the brief time available between now and the end of the semester, between-session homework assignments should be emphasized as playing a particularly important role in the behavior change process.

From *Clinical Behavior Therapy* by M. R. Goldfried and G. C. Davison. Copyright © 1976 by Holt, Rinehart and Winston. Reprinted by permission of Holt, Rinehart and Winston.

invaded, but the assessment may harm the client. Minimizing these problems is a major concern of public officials, government agencies, citizens groups, and private individuals. Some of them advocate elimination of all psychological assessment (especially testing), while others urge safeguards to protect clients from assessment abuses. The latter option has been adopted by the American Psychological Association, whose *Ethical Principles of Psychologists and Code of Conduct* (APA, 1992), *General Guidelines for Providers of Psychological Services* (APA, 1987), and *Standards for Educational and Psychological Testing* (APA, 1985) contain extensive guidelines for assessors to follow as they go about the sensitive task of learning about their clients. These guidelines reflect federal legislation, including the Equal Employment Opportunity Act (part of the Civil Rights Act of 1964), which prohibits discriminatory use of tests that have "adverse impact" on the selection of minority group job candidates, and the Civil Rights Act of 1991 which bans adjustment of test scores on the basis of race, color, religion, sex, or national origin (Sackett & Wilk, 1994). The guidelines must also be implemented in accordance with the regulations of the Individuals with Disabilities Education Act and the Americans with Disabilities Act. Ethical problems and standards associated with clinical psychology will be considered in greater detail in Chapter 14.

CLINICAL ASSESSMENT AT WORK

Q.: How and why is the general idea of clinical assessment important to your work?

DR. SANDY D'ANGELO: Assessment is always the first component of treatment or consultation, whether it is conducted by standardized testing methods, observation, interview, or review of history.

DR. HECTOR MACHABANSKI: Clinical assessment is an activity that permeates all aspects of my work. Whether it is in the context of a long-term therapy relationship or a one-time psychological assessment or consultation, clinical assessment is vital to my efforts to understand clients and monitor the effectiveness of my interventions with them.

DR. GEOFFREY THORPE: To me, clinical assessment is inseparable from psychotherapy, whatever therapeutic approach one uses. Assessment is essential not only for characterizing clients' problems and formulating a treatment plan, but also for evaluating progress. In the part of my clinical practice that involves conducting court-ordered evaluations, I use specialized forms of clinical assessment to shape my opinions about criminal defendants' competency to stand trial, their criminal responsibility, and related matters.

CHAPTER SUMMARY

Clinical assessment is the process of collecting information to be used as the basis for informed decisions by the assessor or by those to whom results are communicated. A combination of interviews, tests, observations, and life records serves as the main sources of assessment data in clinical psychology. The clinical assessment process includes four stages: planning, collecting, processing, and communicating assessment data. The methods and levels of inquiry in assessment tend to follow a case study guide that is shaped by the clinician's goals, theoretical approach, personal preferences, and time constraints. Selection of assessment methods is also guided by research on their reliability (consistency) and validity (ability to measure what they are supposed to measure).

The goals of clinical assessment tend to involve diagnostic classification, description, and prediction. Diagnostic classification normally employs DSM-IV. Description involves broader assessments of clients' personalities by looking at person–environment interactions. Predictions often involve personnel selection, but sometimes focus on a client's potential for violence or suicide.

Unfortunately, clinicians have no unique intuitive power or special information-processing capacity, so the quality of their judgments and decisions about clients can be threatened by the same cognitive biases and errors that affect all human beings. Indeed, research on clinical judgment suggests that, in many situations, clinicians can make their greatest contribution to assessment as collectors of information that is then processed by computer-based statistical formulae.

Instead of using assessment data as signs or correlates, behaviorally-oriented clinicians see them as samples of the specific stimuli, skills, consequences, and cognitive tendencies that account for a client's behavior. Advocates of the phenomenological approach view assessment data as clues to how a client looks at the world, and they use the assessment process as an opportunity to build a relationship with the client.

The results of clinical assessment are presented in an organized assessment report which should be clear, relevant to assessment goals, and useful to the intended consumer. These reports usually reflect the theoretical approach taken by each clinician.

Chapter 4

Interviewing in Clinical Psychology

The interview is the most widely employed tool in clinical psychology. It is a major component of clinical assessment and also plays a prominent role in psychological treatment. Indeed, much of what we have to say in this chapter about assessment interviews also applies to treatment interviews because treatment usually begins in—and is based on—the relationship established through the assessment process.

Good interviewing techniques are described in a number of sources (e.g., Cormier & Cormier, 1991; Fine & Glasser, 1996; Pedersen & Ivey, 1993; Rogers, 1995; Shipley & Wood, 1996), but learning how to use these techniques effectively takes more than reading (Bogels, 1994). Clinicians must also engage in carefully supervised practice as part of their professional training. Accordingly, this chapter does not attempt to teach you how to interview; it offers instead an introduction to the interview as an assessment data source.

WHAT IS AN INTERVIEW?

In simplest terms, an interview is a conversation with a purpose or goal (Matarazzo, 1965). Consider the following interchange between Alan and Bruce:

ALAN: How did you spend the weekend?

BRUCE: It was pretty quiet. I slept in on Saturday and then watched a football game in the afternoon. That night, my wife's brother came over with their eight-year-old boy. We sat around and talked most of the night. Drank a lot of beer.

A: Were you home on Sunday, too?

B: Most of it. I didn't feel too great so I just took it easy. Later I watched the Packers game on TV, and then my wife and I went out for dinner. We had a flat tire on the way home and I ruined a perfectly good shirt while I was putting on the spare.

If Alan were Bruce's co-worker and this interaction took place on the way to the office Monday morning, it would simply be a conversation like the billions of others that occur every day. But this same exchange could have been part of an interview in which Alan (a clinician) is gathering information about Bruce and his lifestyle. The distinction between social conversations and interviews is based not so much on content as on whether they serve a particular purpose.

CLINICAL INTERVIEW SITUATIONS

The fact that interviews resemble other forms of conversation makes them a natural source of clinical information about clients, an easy means of communicating with them, and a convenient context for attempting to help them. Interviews are flexible, relatively inexpensive, and, perhaps most important, provide the clinician with simultaneous samples of clients' verbal and nonverbal behavior. These advantages make the interview useful in a variety of clinical situations.

Intake Interviews

The most common type of clinical interview occurs when a client first comes to the clinician because of some problem in living. These *intake* interviews are designed mainly to establish the nature of the problem. Information gathered in this situation may also help the clinician decide whether the client has come to the right place. The interviewer must answer questions such as, Can I work with this person? Is this problem within my area of expertise? and Will this person likely benefit from treatment? (e.g., Couch, 1995; Safran, et al., 1993). If, on the basis of one or more intake interviews, the answer to such questions is no, the clinician will refer the client to another professional or agency for alternative services. If further contact is seen as desirable, assessment or treatment sessions are scheduled. Most clinicians conduct their own intake interviews, but in some agencies and group practices, social workers or other personnel perform this function.

The intake interview is often critically important to successful treatment because almost half the clients who attend an intake interview fail to return for scheduled treatment (Baekeland & Lundwall, 1975; Morton, 1995). One variable that appears to affect this pattern is clients' perception of their intake interviewer. Clients are more likely to return for subsequent treatment after talking to an interviewer who treats them with warm friendliness as opposed to businesslike professionalism (Kokotovic & Tracey, 1987; Tryon, 1990).

Problem Identification Interviews

The decision to accept or refer a client on the basis of intake information rests, in part, on the nature of that client's problems. For this reason, intake interviews are also aimed at *problem identification*. In clinical situations where a decision to work with the client has already been made, an interview may focus entirely on identification or elaboration of the client's problems. Often, the interviewer is asked for a *classification* or *diagnosis* of the problem in the form of a DSM-IV Axis I label (e.g., Major Depressive Disorder), along with associated descriptions on the other four axes. If not required to provide diagnostic labels, behaviorally- and phenomenologically-oriented clinicians may use problem-identification interviews to develop broader descriptions of clients and the environmental context in which their behavior occurs (see chapter 3).

Problem identification interviews (sometimes also called *psychiatric* interviews) may also lay the groundwork for subsequent therapy efforts by establishing a productive working relationship and organizing the clinician's hypotheses about the origins and development of the client's problems (Siassi, 1984). Originally patterned after the question-and-answer format of medical history taking, problem-identification interviews are often structured according to a sequence of important topics suggested by the case study outlines described in chapter 3. In fact, many psychiatric interviews include a *mental status examination*, a planned sequence of questions designed to assess a client's mental functioning in a number of important areas (see Table 4.1). The mental status examination is analogous to the physical exam that makes up part of the assessment of medical problems.

Interviews designed to *classify* client problems are most common in mental hospitals and other facilities where a diagnosis is required. Similar interviews may also occur when psychologists serve as diagnostic consultants to psychiatrists, courts, schools, or others interested in such questions as, Is Mr. P. competent to stand trial?, Is Mrs. L. psychotic?, Is Jimmy G. mentally retarded? Interviews focused on *describing* clients and their problems in more comprehensive terms usually occur in the context of the full-scale clinical exploration that precedes treatment by a mental health professional.

Orientation Interviews

People receiving psychological assessment or treatment often do not know what to expect, let alone what is expected of them. This is especially true if they have had no previous contact with mental health professionals. To make these new experiences less mysterious and more comfortable, many clinicians conduct special interviews (or reserve segments of interviews) to acquaint the client with the assessment, treatment, or research procedures to come (Prochaska & Norcross, 1994).

Such *orientation* interviews are beneficial in at least two ways. First, because the client is encouraged to ask questions and make comments, misconceptions that might obstruct subsequent treatment progress can be discussed and corrected. Thus, clients

---

TABLE 4.1 The Mental Status Examination (MSE)

Here is a typical MSE topic outline (Siassi, 1984), followed by a short excerpt from an MSE interview:

I. General appearance and behavior—client's level of activity, reaction to interviewer, grooming and clothing are assessed.

II. Speech and thought—Is client's speech coherent and understandable? Are delusions present?

III. Consciousness—Is the sensorium clear or clouded?

IV. Mood and affect—Is client depressed, anxious, restless? Is affect appropriate to situation?

V. Perception—Does client experience hallucinations, depersonalization?

VI. Obsessions and compulsions—amount and quality of these behaviors are noted.

VII. Orientation—Is client aware of correct time, place, and personal identity?

VIII. Memory—What is condition of short- and long-term memory?

IX. Attention and concentration—Asking client to count backwards by 7's is a common strategy.

X. Fund of general information—Questions like "Who is the President?" or "What are some big cities in the U.S.?" are asked.

XI. Intelligence—estimated from educational achievement, reasoning ability, and fund of information.

XII. Insight and judgment—Does patient understand probable outcomes of behavior?

XIII. Higher intellectual functioning—What is the quality of patient's form of thinking? Is patient able to deal with abstraction?

CLINICIAN: Good morning. What is your name?

CLIENT: Randolph S.

CLINICIAN: Well, Mr. S, I would like to ask you some questions this morning. Is that all right?

CLIENT: Fine.

CLINICIAN: How long have you been here?

CLIENT: Since yesterday morning.

CLINICIAN: Why are you here?

CLIENT: I don't know. I think my wife called the police and here I am.

CLINICIAN: Well, what did you do to make her call the police?

CLIENT: I don't know.

CLINICIAN: What day is today?

CLIENT: Tuesday, the twelfth.

CLINICIAN: What year is it?

CLIENT: 1997.

CLINICIAN: What city are we in?

CLIENT: Chicago.

CLINICIAN: Who is the mayor of Chicago?

---

are more likely to speak freely once an orientation interview assures them that the clinician will hold the content of their sessions in confidence. Orientation interviews can also help clients understand upcoming assessment and treatment procedures and what their roles in these procedures will be (Couch, 1995). Thus, the clinician might point out that the clients who benefit most from treatment are those who are candid, cooperative, serious, and willing to work to solve their problems. Good orientation interviews, then, can help focus clinicians' efforts on those clients who are most willing to be full partners in the assessment or treatment enterprise.

Termination Interviews

A different kind of orienting interview occurs when it is time to terminate a clinical relationship. For example, people who have just completed a series of assessment sessions involving extensive interviews, tests, and observations are understandably anxious to know "what the doctor found," how the information will be used, and who will have access to it. These concerns are particularly acute when the assessor has acted as consultant to a school or a court. A *termination* interview can help alleviate clients' anxiety about the assessment enterprise by explaining the procedures and protections involved in transmission of privileged information, and providing a summary and interpretation of the assessment results.

Termination interviews following clinical research are called *debriefing*, and include an explanation of the project in which the person has participated and a discussion of the procedures employed in it. Debriefings permit participants to ask questions and make comments about their research experiences. In accordance with the standards for ethical research established by the APA and other organizations, debriefing of participants is aimed at assuring that the research experience has done no harm and that the participant feels comfortable about it (APA, 1992; see chapter 14). Debriefing interviews can also benefit the clinical researcher by helping to clarify how participants perceived the experiment and whether factors outside the experimenter's control affected participants' behavior (Orne, 1962).

Termination interviews also occur at the completion of psychological treatment. Many loose ends need to be tied up. There is gratitude to be expressed and accepted, reminders to be given about the handling of future problems, plans to be made for follow-up contacts, and reassurance given to clients about their ability to go it alone. Treatment termination interviews help make the transition from treatment to posttreatment as smooth and productive as possible.

Crisis Interviews

When a person's problems are intense and pressing, and when normal problem-solving skills prove inadequate to deal with the situation, that person is said to be in a crisis. When people in crisis appear at clinical facilities or call a hotline, suicide prevention center, or other agency, interviewers do not have the luxury of scheduling a series of assessment and treatment sessions. Instead, they conduct *crisis* interviews in which they attempt to provide support, collect assessment data, and provide help, all in a very short time (Somers-Flanagan & Somers-Flanagan, 1995).

The interviewer must deal with the client in a calm and accepting fashion, ask relevant questions ("Have you ever tried to kill yourself?" "What kinds of pills do you have in the house?"), and work on the immediate problem directly or by putting the client in touch with other services. One or two well-handled interviews during a crisis may be the beginning and the end of contact with a client whose need for assistance was temporary and situation-specific. For others, the crisis interview leads to subsequent assessment and treatment sessions.

Observational Interviews

As already noted, interviews provide an opportunity to observe particular client behaviors, such as how the person deals with stressful, ambiguous, or conflict-laden situations. This sort of interview will be more thoroughly described in Chapter 6.

INTERVIEW STRUCTURE

The most fundamental feature of clinical interviews is their *structure*: the degree to which the interviewer determines the content and course of the conversation. At one end of the structure continuum are *nondirective* interviews, in which the clinician does as little as possible to interfere with the natural flow of the client's speech and choice of topics. At the other end are *structured* interviews, which involve a carefully planned question-and-answer format (see Table 4.1). In between are many blends, usually referred to as *guided* or *semistructured* interviews.

Some examples should make the structure dimension clearer. Consider first this segment from a nondirective intake interview.

CLINICIAN: [Your relative] didn't go into much detail about what you wanted to talk about, so I wonder if you'd just start in at whatever you want to start in with, and tell me what kind of nervousness you have.

CLIENT: Well, it's, uh, I think if I were to put it in, in a few words, it seems to be a, a, a complete lack of self-confidence in, and an extreme degree of self-consciousness. Now, I have always been a very self-conscious person. I mean every, just about, since I was probably fourteen years old the first I remember of it. But for a long time I've realized that I was sort of using people as crutches. I mean I, a lot of things I felt I couldn't do myself I did all right if someone was along.

CLINICIAN: Um-hm.

CLIENT: And it's just progressed to the point where I'm actually using the four walls of the house as an escape from reality. I mean I don't, I don't care to go out. I, I certainly can't go out alone. . . . It's sort of a vicious circle. I find out I can't do it, and then I'm sure the next time I can't do it.

CLINICIAN: Um-hm.

CLIENT: And it just gets progressively worse. I think the first that I ever noticed it . . . (Wallen, 1956, p. 146)

The client continued a narrative about the onset and duration of her problems, her occupation and marriage, her father's death, and other topics. Notice that the clinician hardly says a word, although as we shall see, there are things he could have done to nondirectively encourage the client to talk had it been necessary.

Compare this nondirective approach to both the structured interview in Table 4.1 and in the following semistructured interview, in which an organized set of topics is explored in a way that gives the interviewer flexibility in wording questions, interpreting answers, and guiding decisions about what to address next.

> CLINICIAN: You say that you are very jealous a lot of the time and this upsets you a great deal.
>
> CLIENT: Well, I know it's stupid for me to feel that way, but I am hurt when I even *think* of Mike with another woman.
>
> CLINICIAN: You don't want to feel jealous but you do.
>
> CLIENT: I know that's not the way a "liberated" woman should be.
>
> CLINICIAN: What is your idea of how a liberated woman should feel?
>
> CLIENT: I don't know. In many ways I feel I have changed so much in the last year. I really don't believe you have the right to own another person—and yet, when it happens to me, I feel really hurt. I'm such a hypocrite.
>
> CLINICIAN: You're unhappy because you are not responding the way you really would like to?
>
> CLIENT: I'm not the person I want to be.
>
> CLINICIAN: So there's really "double jeopardy." When Mike is with someone else, it really hurts you. And, when you feel jealous, you get down on yourself for being that way.
>
> CLIENT: Yes, I guess I lose both ways. (Morganstern & Tevlin, 1981, p. 86)

Notice the nondirective and structured features in this excerpt; the interviewer encouraged the client to express herself freely, but also placed limits on the topic by asking a specific question.

While some clinicians consistently adopt a structured or nondirective approach, most adjust interview structure in light of circumstances and assessment goals. For example, by their nature, crises demand more structure than might be desirable during a routine intake interview. Structure may also change during an interview; many problem-identification interviews begin in a nondirective way and become more structured as the interview continues.

Structure also depends on the theoretical orientation and personal preferences of the interviewer. In general, phenomenological clinicians tend to establish the least interview structure. Freudians usually provide more, while cognitive-behavioral clinicians are likely to be the most verbally active and directive.

Trends Toward Structure

In recent years, new structured and semistructured interviews have proliferated for use in a variety of situations (Rogers, 1995). The popularity of these new interview formats stems partly from the fact that they provide a systematic way of reliably measuring many of the specific criteria used in making psychiatric diagnoses via *DSM-IV* or international classification systems (Robins, 1995). Structured interviews have also proven valuable in clinical research, where they help select participants who have the specific characteristics or problems the researcher is seeking (e.g., Kendler & Roy, 1995). In addition, structured interviews have become almost indispensable in *epidemiology*, the study of how disorders and other behavior patterns are distributed in the population and of the factors that affect this distribution (Wittchen, 1994; Loranger, 1992).

In structured and semistructured interviews, the interviewer asks specific questions phrased in a standardized fashion and presented in a pre-established order. Consistent rules are also provided for scoring the clients' answers or for using additional probes to elicit scorable responses. Thus, while structured interviews do not outlaw open-ended questions or prohibit interviewers from formulating their own questions to clarify ambiguous responses, they do provide detailed rules (sometimes called "decision trees" or "branching rules") that tell the interviewer what to do in certain situations (e.g., "if the respondent answers 'no' skip to question 32; if the respondent answers 'yes' inquire as to how many times it happened and continue to the next question"). Table 4.2 shows that many of today's most widely-used structured interviews were designed to help clinicians arrive at psychiatric diagnoses by asking questions relevant to specific DSM diagnostic criteria. Some pages from a structured interviewing form based on DSM-III-R criteria are presented in Table 4.3 (for more detailed coverage of structured interviews, see Rogers, 1995).

The increasing use of structured interviews parallels other trends in the history of clinical assessment. We saw in Chapter 3, for example, that using formal, statistical rules for *combining* assessment data is consistently more effective than clinicians' subjective judgments. Structured interviews are designed to make the data *collection* process more consistent by replacing or at least controlling clinicians' judgment via formal decision rules. (Indeed, the fact that questions on structured interviews function like individual items on objective tests of personality may help explain why the results of these tests correlate more highly with structured than with unstructured interview data.) The increasing popularity of objective over projective tests in clinical assessment (discussed in Chapter 5) is another example of the trend toward increased structure in data collection methods.

Structured interviews offer several major advantages, including improved reliability of assessment, a standard format that allows interviews to be conducted systematically by professional clinicians, trained nonprofessionals, or even computers (First et al., 1995; Pilkonis et al., 1995; Reich et al., 1995; Wittchen et al., 1995), and assurance that the interview will be long enough and comprehensive enough to reach assessment goals. At the same time, however, clinicians who are overdependent on structured interviews run the risk of becoming so "protocol bound," that they miss important information that the interview protocol did not explore (Ruegg et al., 1992). Further, the routine nature of structured interviews can alienate clients if the clinician fails to establish *rapport*, the harmonious and comfortable working relationship that helps ensure clients' motivation and cooperation (Rosenthal, 1989). Finally, structured interviews—like all other interviews—depend heavily on the memory, candor, and descriptive abilities of respondents. So while the reliability of clients' reports (or of different clinicians' inferences from those reports) might be excellent, the validity or meaning of structured interview data can be threatened if the client misunderstands

TABLE 4.2   **Structured Interviews Frequently Used in Clinical Psychology**

Name of Interview	Reference	Purpose
The Schedule for Affective Disorders & Schizophrenia (SADS)	Endicott & Spitzer (1978)	Differential diagnosis of more than twenty categories of mental disorder.
Diagnostic Interview Schedule (DIS)	Robins et al. (1981)	Used by nonprofessionals in large-scale epidemiological studies of mental disorder.
Structured Clinical Interview for DSM-IV (SCID)	Spitzer et al. (1990)	Broad-scale differential diagnoses tied to DSM-IV criteria.
Diagnostic Interview Schedule for Children, Revised (DISC-R)	Shaffer et al. (1993)	Parallel formats for children and parents for making differential diagnoses of childhood disorders.
Anxiety Disorders Interview Schedule-Revised (ADIS-R)	DiNardo & Barlow (1988)	Differential diagnoses among anxiety disorders.
Personality Disorder Interview-IV	Widiger, et al. (1995)	Differential diagnoses among DSM-IV Personality Disorders.
Schedules for Clinical Assessment in Neuropsychiatry (SCAN)	World Health Organization (1994)	Used in national and international studies of the epidemiology of mental disorders; also used in individual diagnoses.
Interdisciplinary Fitness Interview (IF)	Golding, Roesch, & Schreiber (1984)	Evaluation of competence to stand trial.
Rogers Criminal Responsibility Assessment Scale (RCRAS)	Rogers, Wasyliw, & Cavanaugh (1984)	Assess criminal responsibility against specific legal criteria.
Structured Interview of Reported Symptoms (SIRS)	Rogers et al. (1991)	Assess malingering in clinical populations.
Cambridge Cognitive Examination (CAMDEX)	Roth et al. (1986)	Assess cognitive dysfunctions such as memory loss and language problems.

questions, is not motivated to answer truthfully, or can't recall relevant information. We will return to issues of interview reliability and validity later.

STAGES IN THE INTERVIEW

No one has developed a single "right" way to conduct an interview, but certain strategies have proven valuable in practice and have thus been adopted by skilled clinicians representing every theoretical approach (Goldfried, 1980). In the following

TABLE 4.3 Excerpt from the Structured Clinical Interview for *DSM-III-R* (SCID)

Designed to help clinicians make rapid, valid *DSM-III-R* diagnoses, the SCID is organized into several different modules. Each module is devoted to a major class of disturbance, such as mood disorders, anxiety disorders, or adjustment disorders. An advantage of this organization is that the SCID can be customized for specific research purposes by including only those modules relevant to the study. The excerpt below comes from a portion of the Mood Disor-

ders module addressed to the question of whether the patient has ever experienced a major depressive episode. In the left-hand column are the structured questions of the interview; notice that some of them are open ended, some call for a yes-no answer. In the middle column are the *DSM-III-R* criteria relevant to the interview questions. These are the criteria that interviewers (known as "SCID-ers") must judge, using the right-hand column ratings.

PAST MAJOR DEPRESSIVE SYNDROME	MDS CRITERIA						
IF NOT CURRENTLY DEPRESSED: Have you <u>ever</u> had a period when you were feeling depressed or down most of the day nearly every day? (What was that like?)	A. At least 5 of the following symptoms have each been present during the same two-week period (and represent a change from previous functioning); at least one of the symptoms was either (1) depressed mood, or (2) loss of interest or pleasure.					* * * * * * * * *	
IF CURRENTLY DEPRESSED BUT FAILED TO MEET FULL CRITERIA, SCREEN FOR PAST MDS: Has there ever been <u>another</u> time when you were depressed and had even more of the problems [SXS] that I just asked you about? IF YES: When was that? How long did it last? (As long as two weeks?)	(1) depressed mood most of the day, nearly every day, as indicated either by subjective account or observation by others	?	1	2	3		33
IF PAST DEPRESSED MOOD: During that time, were you a lot less interested in most things or unable to enjoy the things you used to enjoy? (What was that like?) IF NO PAST DEPRESSED MOOD: What about a time	(2) markedly diminished interest or pleasure in all, or almost all, activities most of the day, nearly every day (as indicated either by subjective account or observation by others of apathy most of the time)	?	1	2	3	* * * * * * * *	34

IF NEITHER ITEM (1) NOR (2) IS CODED "3," GO TO *CURRENT MANIC SYNDROME,* A. 10

?=inadequate information 1=absent or false 2=subthreshold 3=threshold or true

TABLE 4.3   Excerpt from the Structured Clinical Interview for DSM-III-R (SCID) (*Continued*)

---

when you were a lot less interested in most things or unable to enjoy the things you used to enjoy? (What was that like?)						
IF YES: When was that? Was it nearly every day? How long did it last? (As long as two weeks?)						
Have you had more than one time like that?						
IF MORE THAN ONE: Which time was the worst?	NOTE: DO NOT INCLUDE SXS THAT ARE CLEARLY DUE TO A PHYSICAL CONDITION, MOOD-INCONGRUENT DELUSIONS OR HALLUCINATIONS, INCOHERENCE OR MARKEDLOOSENING OF ASSOCIATIONS, OR- SIMPLY PRDROMAL OR RESIDUAL SYMPTOMS OF SCHIZOPHRENIA.					* * * *
FOCUS ON THE WORST EPISODE THAT THE SUBJECT CAN REMEMBER						
During that time . . .						
. . did you lose or gain any weight? (How much?) (Were you trying to lose weight?) IF NO: How was your appetite? (What about compared to your usual appetite?) (Did you have to force yourself to eat?) (Eat [less/more] than usual?) (Was that nearly every day?)	(3) significant weight loss or weight gain when not dieting (e.g., more than 5 % of body weight in a month) or decrease or increase in appetite nearly every day	?	1	2	3	35

?=inadequate information	1=absent or false	2=subthreshold	3=threshold or true

TABLE 4.3   Excerpt from the Structured Clinical Interview for DSM-III-R (SCID) *(Continued)*

. . how were you sleeping? (Trouble falling asleep, waking frequently, trouble staying asleep, waking too early, OR sleeping too much? How many hours a night compared to usual? Was that nearly every night?)	(4) insomnia or hypersomnia nearly every day	?	1	2	3	36
. . were you so fidgety or restless that you were unable to sit still? (Was it so bad that other people noticed it? Was that nearly every day?) IF NO: What about the opposite — talking or moving more slowly than is normal for you? (Was it so bad that other people noticed it? Was that nearly every day?)	(5) psychomotor agitation or retardation nearly every day (observable by others and not merely subjective feelings of restlessness or slowed down)	?	1	2	3	37
. . what was your energy like? (Tired all the time? Nearly every day?)	(6) fatigue or loss of energy nearly every day	?	1	2	3	38
. . how did you feel about yourself? (Worthless?) (Nearly every day?) IF NO: What about feeling guilty about things you had done or not done? (Nearly every day?)	(7) feelings of worthlessness or excessive or inappropriate guilt (which may be delusional) nearly every day (not merely self-reproach or guilt about being sick) NOTE: CODE "1" OR "2" FOR LOW SELF-ESTEEM BUT NOT WORTHLESSNESS	?	1	2	3	39
During that time . . .						
. . did you have trouble thinking or concentrating? (Nearly every day?) IF NO: Was it hard to make decisions about everyday things? (Nearly every day?)	(8) diminished ability to think or concentrate, or indecisiveness, nearly every day (either by subjective account or as observed by others)	?	1	2	3	40

?=inadequate information	1=absent or false	2=subthreshold	3=threshold or true

TABLE 4.3   Excerpt from the Structured Clinical Interview for DSM-III-R (SCID). (*Continued*)

		?	1	2	3		
. . were things so bad that you were thinking a lot about death or that you would be better off dead? What about thinking of hurting yourself? IF YES: Did you do anything to hurt yourself?	(9) recurrent thoughts of death (not just fear of dying), recurrent suicidal ideation without a specific plan, or a suicide attempt or a specific plan for committing suicide NOTE: CODE "1" FOR SELF-MUTILATION W/O SUICIDAL INTENT	?	1	2	3	* * * *	41
	AT LEAST FIVE OF THE ABOVE SXS [A(1-9)] ARE CODED "3" AND AT LEAST ONE OF THESE IS ITEM (1) or (2)		1		3		42

IF NOT ALREADY ASKED: Has there been any other time when you were (depressed/OWN EQUIVALANT) and had even more of the symptoms that I just asked you about?

   IF NO: GO TO "CURRENT MANIC SYNDROME,* A. 10.

   IF YES: RETURN TO "PAST MAJOR DEPRESSIVE SYNDROME,* A. 5, AND INQUIRE ABOUT WORST EPISODE.

?=inadequate information	1=absent or false	2=subthreshold	3=threshold or true

Source: R. L. Spitzer, J. B. Williams, M. Gibbon, and M. B. First, *Instruction Manual for the Structured Clinical Interview for DSM-III-R (SCID, 6/1/88 Revision).* Biometrics Research Department, New York State Psychiatric Institute, 722 W. 168th St., New York, NY 10032.

sections, we examine the interview techniques commonly employed by clinical psychologists.

Interviews can be characterized as having a beginning, a middle, and an end. These three stages are most obvious in intake or problem-identification interviews, which usually begin with efforts at making the client comfortable and ready to speak freely (Stage 1), continue into a central information-gathering stage (Stage 2), and end with summary statements, client questions, and, if appropriate, plans for additional assessment sessions (Stage 3). As the client gets to know the clinician in those sessions, Stage 1 tends to be shorter while Stage 2 grows longer. Similarly, Stage 3 may be brief until the final assessment interview, when it may take up most of the time available.

Treatment interviews follow a different three-stage format. A session may begin with the client's report on thoughts and events since the last meeting, continue with whatever treatment procedures are being employed, then conclude with a summary of current progress, plans for the next meeting, and/or "homework" assignments.

Interviews relating to crises, orientation, and termination may not be organized around a beginning–middle–end framework, but the three-stage model offers a convenient guide for our discussion of "typical" clinical interviews.

Stage 1: Beginning the Interview

It is important that clinicians handle the first few minutes of initial interviews carefully. This early stage is important because clients may not be ready to talk candidly about personal matters yet, preferring instead to take a wait-and-see approach in which they carefully control what they say, and don't say. If this reserved attitude prevails throughout the interview, the clinician is unlikely to gather very much valuable assessment information.

Accordingly, most clinicians see establishing rapport as their main task during the first part of initial interviews. Rapport can be built in several ways, many of which involve common sense and courtesy. A client's anxiety and uncertainty can be eased by demystifying the interview. A warm smile, a friendly greeting, and a handshake are excellent beginnings to an interview. "Small talk" about the weather or difficulty in finding the office also ease the client's transition into the interview but should not go on so long that the interview loses its distinctive quality.

Although interviews can occur anywhere, certain settings are especially conducive to building rapport for most clients. Except for clients whose cultural background might cause such surroundings to be threatening, interviews are best conducted in a comfortable, private office. This is because most people find it easier to relax when they can be physically comfortable. Also, privacy makes it easier to assure the client of the interview's confidential nature.

Several other office characteristics can aid rapport. A reassuring equality is established when two people sit a few feet apart on similar chairs of equal height. If the clinician sits in a massive, high-backed chair behind a huge desk placed six feet from the client's smaller, lower seat, rapport may be impaired. A desk cleared of other work, along with precautions to hold phone calls and prevent other intrusions, makes it clear that the clinician is fully attentive and sincerely interested in what the client has to say. The list of rapport-building techniques could be extended almost indefinitely; the point is that from the beginning, the clinician should try to create a warm, comfortable environment and a relationship that encourages the client to speak freely and honestly about whatever topics are relevant to the interview.

Skilled clinicians can establish remarkable rapport during the first stage of an initial interview, but even for them, the process continues into the second and third stages and into subsequent sessions as well. Like other social relationships, the one between client and clinician takes time to grow. Once that relationship takes root, the initial interview can move into its second, or information-gathering, stage.

Stage 2: The Middle of the Interview

Transition to the middle of an initial interview should be as smooth as possible. The ways in which the clinician accomplishes this transition illustrate a number of important interview tactics.

Nondirective Techniques.   In most cases, interviewers begin the second stage with nondirective, *open-ended* questions. Common examples are: "So what brings you here today?" or "Would you like to tell me something about the problems you referred to on the phone?" A major advantage of this approach is that it allows clients to begin in their own way. An open-ended invitation to talk allows the client to ease into painful or embarrassing topics without feeling coerced.[1] This relatively nonstressful way of beginning can also aid rapport because it lets clients know that the clinician is willing to listen to whatever they have to say.

Contrast the open-ended questions just mentioned with more "binding" questions like: "You said on the phone there is a sex problem in your marriage. Is it yours or your wife's?" Openings of this type focus the conversation on topics that may be too threatening to address for the moment. An interview whose second stage employs binding questions can degenerate into a question-and-answer session in which the client may feel put-upon, misunderstood, and frustrated. As noted earlier, clinicians using structured interview formats must guard against this situation.

Open-ended questions are used whenever the clinician wishes to prompt clients to speak while exerting as little influence as possible over what they say. Classic remarks like "Tell me a bit more about that" and "How did you feel about that?" exemplify a nondirective strategy. This strategy is supplemented by tactics designed to help clients express themselves fully and to enhance rapport by communicating the clinician's understanding and acceptance. The most general of these tactics is called *active listening*, which involves responding to the client's speech in ways that indicate under-

---

[1]Clients often begin with a "ticket of admission" problem which may not be the one of greatest concern to them. The real reason for the client's visit may appear only after varying amounts of diversionary conversation.

standing and encourage further elaboration. Active listening was represented in the clinician's "mm-hmms" in the nondirective interview excerpt presented earlier. Other signs of active listening include comments such as "I see," "I'm with you," or "Right."

A related nondirective strategy is called *paraphrasing*, in which clinicians restate what their clients say in order to (1) show that they are listening closely, and (2) give the client a chance to correct the remark if it was misinterpreted. Carl Rogers called this strategy *reflection* and emphasized the importance of not only restating content, but also highlighting client feelings. Consider these examples.

A:

CLIENT: Sometimes I get so mad at my husband, I could kill him.
CLINICIAN: You would just like to get rid of him altogether.

B:

CLIENT: Sometimes I get so mad at my husband, I could kill him.
CLINICIAN: He really upsets you sometimes.

Notice that, in example A, the clinician merely reworded the client's remark. In example B, the *feeling* contained in the remark was reflected. Most clients respond to paraphrasing by continuing to talk, usually along the same lines as before, often in greater detail. Paraphrasing often is preferable to direct questioning because such questioning tends to change or restrict the conversation, as illustrated in the following interactions.

A:

CLIENT: What it comes down to is that life just doesn't seem worth living sometimes.
CLINICIAN: Sometimes it all just seems to be too much.
CLIENT: Yeah, and I don't know what to do when I feel that way. I don't really think I want to die, not really. But I also dread the thought of another day starting. For example. . . .

B:

CLIENT: What it comes down to is that life just doesn't seem worth living sometimes.
CLINICIAN: How often do you feel that way?
CLIENT: Oh, off and on.

There is a place for questions like the one in example B, but unless the clinician knows enough about the general scope of a problem to start pinpointing specifics, interrupting with such questions is likely to limit, and even distort, the assessment picture. Clients who are immediately hit with direct queries may conclude that they should wait for the next question rather than spontaneously tell their story. For many clients, this experience can be frustrating and damaging to rapport.

Paraphrasing can also be helpful when the clinician is confused about what a client has said. Consider the following:

> CLIENT: I told my husband that I didn't want to live with him anymore so he said "fine" and left. Well, when I got back, I found out that the son of a bitch kept all our furniture!

Most clinicians would have a hard time deciphering the sequence of events described here, but if they say "What?", the client might be put off or assume that the clinician is a dunce. Instead, a combination of paraphrase and request for clarification serves nicely:

> CLINICIAN: OK, let's see if I've got this straight. You told your husband you didn't want to live with him, so *he* left. You later came back to your house from somewhere else and found he had taken the furniture?

Ideally, the client will either confirm this interpretation or fill in the missing pieces. If not, the clinician may wish to use more direct questioning.

Directive Techniques

Most interviewers supplement nondirective tactics with more directive questions whose form, wording, and content are often the result of careful (though often on-the-spot) planning. Consider the following illustrative questions:

A. Do you feel better or worse when your husband is out of town?
B. How do you feel when your husband is out of town?

Example A offers a clear, but possibly irrelevant, two-choice situation. This is a "Do you walk to work or carry your lunch?" question, for which the most valid answer may be "Neither." Some clients are not assertive enough in an interview to ignore the choice, so they settle for one unsatisfactory response or the other. Unless there is a special reason for offering clients only a few response alternatives, skilled interviewers ask direct questions in a form—such as in example B, above—that gets at specific information, but also leaves clients free to choose their own words.

Experienced clinicians also avoid asking questions that suggest their own answers. Notice the implications contained in this query: "You've suffered with this problem a long time?" Such questions communicate what the interviewer expects to hear, and some clients will oblige by biasing their response. "How long have you had this problem?" is a better alternative. Similarly, inquiries based on unwarranted assumptions should be avoided. Notice the hidden assumption in the example: "How bad is your insomnia when you are depressed?" If the client tends to oversleep when feeling low, this question cannot be answered without contradicting the clinician. A careful interviewer might explore the sleep topic with the following question: "You said you are often depressed. What changes in yourself do you notice during those times?"

Combining Interview Tactics

Because interviews can be flexible, clinicians are usually free to combine the tactics we have described. They may facilitate the client's speech with open-ended requests, paraphrasing, prompts, and other active listening techniques, and then use more directive questions to "zoom in" on topics of special importance. However, directive procedures do not take over completely as interviews progress. They continue to be mixed with less directive tactics. An example of this blending is provided by the concept of *repeated scanning and focusing*, in which interviewers first scan a topic nondirectively, then focus on it in more directive fashion:

> CLINICIAN: You mentioned that your family is back East. Could you tell me something about them?
>
> CLIENT: There's not much to tell. There's Dad, Mom, and the twins. They all seem to like it back there so I guess they'll stay forever.
>
> CLINICIAN: What else can you say about them?
>
> CLIENT: Well, Dad is a retired high school principal. Mom used to be strictly a housewife but, since us kids have grown, she's been working part time.
>
> CLINICIAN: How did you get along with your folks when you lived at home?
>
> CLIENT: Really fine. I've always thought they were great people and that's probably why they had so little trouble with me. Of course, now and then there would be a problem, but not often.
>
> CLINICIAN: What kinds of problems were there?

The interviewer might go on to explore several specific issues about the client's relationship with both parents, then move on to another topic, again beginning with scanning procedures and later moving on to more direct questions.

Clinicians who emphasize rapport and other relationship factors tend to conduct interviews heavily weighted toward the nondirective side. Behavioral interviewers also emphasize a good client–clinician relationship, but mainly as the context for assessing specific information. Their tactics tend to be more directive (Goldfried & Davison, 1994; Spiegler & Guevremont, 1993).

Stage 3: Closing the Interview

The last stage of an interview can provide valuable assessment data as well as an opportunity to enhance rapport. The interviewer may initiate the third stage with a statement like this:

> We have been covering some very valuable information here and I appreciate your willingness to tell me about it. I know our session hasn't been easy for you. Since we're running out of time for today, I thought we could look back over what we've covered and then give you a chance to ask *me* some questions.

The clinician accomplishes several things here. First, the impending conclusion of the interview is signaled. Second, the client is praised for cooperativeness and reassured that the clinician recognized how stressful the interview has been. Third, the suggested plan for the final minutes invites the client to ask questions or make comments that may be important, but had not been put into words.

The clinician's recap of the session summarizes interview content and checks that nothing important was misunderstood. Comments from the client during this stage can be enlightening, especially when they disclose misconceptions or information gaps. This part of the interview (especially when it ends a first contact) becomes a miniature version of the termination interview described earlier. It usually concludes with leave-taking rituals ("It was good of you to come") and, when appropriate, confirmation of plans for future contact with the interviewer or another professional.

Sometimes, the last stage of an interview evokes clinically significant behavior or information. For example: "Oh gosh, look at the time. I have to hurry to my lawyer's office or I won't be able to find out until Monday whether I get custody of my son." Some clients wait until the end of the interview to reveal this kind of information because they want the clinician to know about it, but they had not yet been ready to discuss it. Others might just let such information slip out because the interview "feels" over and they let down the defenses they had been using earlier. Some simply don't want the interview to end. For these reasons, the clinician devotes as much attention to the final stage of the interview as to the stages that precede it.

COMMUNICATION IN THE INTERVIEW

A sensitive combination of nondirective and directive interview procedures is necessary for effective rapport building and fruitful information gathering, but there are other factors that contribute significantly to the quality of an interview. Chief among these is the clarity of communication between interviewer and interviewee. Clinicians' skill at posing good questions, encouraging the client to talk, or making smooth transitions between topics may be of little value if they do not understand what the client is saying and vice versa.

The fundamental problem in interview communication—as in all human communication—is to accurately encode, transmit, and decode messages. Speakers must encode what they want to convey into transmittable messages made up of words and gestures which listeners must receive and decode (interpret) within their personal and cultural frame of reference. Lapses in both verbal and nonverbal communication can occur at many points in this process. To take just the simplest of examples, giving the "thumbs up" sign signals approval to people in the United States, but it says "up yours" in Australia.

Clinicians attempt to avoid the much more subtle communication problems that can plague interviews by maximizing the clarity of the messages they send to their clients and by clarifying the meaning of the messages received from them. Let's consider an example of poor clinical communication and then look at some ways to reduce the likelihood of such communication breakdowns. In the following hypothetical exchange, the speakers' thoughts are in parentheses:

CLINICIAN: (I wonder what his teenage social life was like.) Tell me a little about the friends you had in high school.

CLIENT: (I had dozens of social acquaintances, but only one person who was a really close friend.) There was just one, a guy named Mike.

CLINICIAN: (So he was pretty much of a loner.) How did you feel about that?

CLIENT: (It was fine. I had a great time, went to lots of parties, had lots of dates, but knew I could always depend on Mike to talk with about really personal things.) I enjoyed it. Mike and I got along really well.

CLINICIAN: (Not only was he a social isolate, he claims to have liked it that way. I wonder if he is being honest with himself about that.) Did you ever wish you had more friends?

CLIENT: (For crying out loud, he makes it sound like it's a crime to have one really close friend. I think we've talked enough about this.) No.

Verbal Communication

In the preceding illustration, the clinician used *friend* to refer to casual as well as intimate acquaintances. Because this word had a different meaning for the client, it led to misunderstanding. The conversation could have gone on in this fruitless way for quite a while before the interviewer and the client straightened out their communication problem.

Although the client and clinician may technically be speaking the same language and thus assume they understand one another, the interviewer must be aware that educational, social, ethnic, cultural, economic, and religious factors can impair communication (Yutrzenka, 1995). Unless the clinician takes the client's background and frame of reference into account, and asks for clarification when verbal referents are unclear, the interview will suffer. Consider this example:

CLIENT: When I'm in such heavy situations, I just get real uptight.

CLINICIAN: What makes you uptight?

CLIENT: Well, the whole thing. Everybody kind of hanging out and running around. I can't seem to get it together with anybody, so I guess I freak out.

CLINICIAN: And then what happens?

CLIENT: I usually go home and go to sleep. But I'm usually pretty bummed out.

CLINICIAN: Are you saying that you don't fit in with these people and that's what makes you feel bummed out?

CLIENT: Well, I don't know. These are my friends, I guess—but it never seems to work out. (Morganstern & Tevlin, 1981, p. 91)

Do these two people understand each other? We do not know for sure, and as long as the interview goes on this way, neither will they. Obviously, the clinician needs to ask the client to clarify some terms:

> CLIENT: When I'm in such heavy situations, I just get real uptight. . . .
>
> CLINICIAN: When you say that you're uptight in these situations, what does that mean to you?
>
> CLIENT: Well, uptight, you know. Tense.
>
> CLINICIAN: You mean your muscles get tense?
>
> CLIENT: My neck gets very sore—and I get a headache lots of times.
>
> CLINICIAN: What else happens?
>
> CLIENT: Well, either because of my neck or my headache, I start sweating a lot.
>
> CLINICIAN: When you say you're uptight you are really experiencing it physically. What are you thinking when this happens?
>
> CLIENT: I'm thinking, man you are really paranoid. You just can't relax in any situation. You really are a loser. And then I want to get out of there fast. . . . (Morganstern & Tevlin, 1981, p. 91)

Clients can become as confused as clinicians, but if they are reluctant to appear stupid or to question a person in authority they may not reveal their dilemma. Some evidence on this point comes from a study conducted in a medical setting by Korsch and Negrete (1972). Their data showed that communication from doctors to patients' mothers in a pediatric clinic was obstructed by the use of medical terms and that client confusion and dissatisfaction often resulted. For example, a "lumbar puncture" (spinal tap) was sometimes assumed to be an operation for draining the child's lungs; "incubation period" was interpreted by one mother as the time during which her child had to be kept in bed.

Circumventing such problems in clinical interviews can be facilitated by attention to certain guidelines. Skilled interviewers avoid jargon, ask questions in a straightforward way ("What experiences have you had with masturbation?" not "Do you ever touch yourself?"), and request feedback from their client ("Is all this making sense to you?"). They also try to assure that their verbal behavior conveys patience, concern, and acceptance. Expressing impatience or being judgmental are not usually desirable.

Nonverbal Communication

As in all human communication, a constant stream of nonverbal behavior accompanies the clients' and interviewers' verbal behavior. Indeed, the nonverbal communication channel usually remains open even when the verbal channel shuts down. Perceptive individuals throughout history have understood the truth of this statement. King Solomon, for example, noted that "He winketh with his eyes, he speaketh with his feet, he teacheth with his fingers" (Proverbs 6:13). Freud (1905) summarized the point well: "He that has eyes to see and ears to hear may convince himself that no mortal can keep a secret. If his lips are silent, he chatters with his fingertips; betrayal oozes out of him at every pore" (pp. 77-78). Since both members of an interview dyad are sending and receiving nonverbal messages, clinicians must not only be sensitive to incoming signals, but also to those they transmit.

Here are some aspects of clients' nonverbal communication that tend to be of greatest interest to clinicians during interviews:

1. Physical appearance—height, weight, grooming, style and condition of clothing, unusual characteristics, muscular development, hairstyle
2. Movements—gestures; repetitive arm, hand, head, leg, or foot motions; tics or other apparently involuntary movements; pacing; handling of cigarettes, matches, or other objects
3. Posture—slouching, rigidity, crossed or uncrossed arms or legs, head in hands
4. Eye contact—constant, fleeting, none
5. Facial expressions—smiles, frowns, grimaces, raised eyebrows
6. Emotional arousal—tears, wet eyes, sweating, dryness of lips, frequent swallowing, blushing or paling, voice or hand tremor, rapid respiration, frequent shifts in body position, startle reactions, inappropriate laughter
7. Speech variables—tone of voice, speed, slurring, lisp, stuttering, blocking, accent, clarity, style, sudden shifts or omissions

In addition to noting nonverbal client behaviors, clinicians also look for inconsistencies between the verbal and nonverbal channels. The statement "I feel pretty good today" will be viewed differently if the client is on the verge of tears than if a happy smile is evident.

Interviewers also try to coordinate their own verbal and nonverbal behavior so as to convey unambiguous messages to their clients. A client will perceive the message to "take your time" in talking about a sensitive topic as more genuine if the clinician says it slowly and quietly than if it is blurted out after glancing at the clock. Similarly, friendly eye contact, some head nodding, an occasional smile, and an attentive posture lets the client know that the interviewer is listening closely. Overdoing it may backfire, however. A plastered-on smile, a continuously knitted brow, sidelong glances, and other theatrics are more likely to convey interviewer anxiety or inexperience than concern.

Observation of nonverbal behavior begins when the client and clinician meet and continues until they part. Clinicians differ, however, as to what their clients' nonverbal behavior means. Interviewers committed to a sign-oriented approach draw higher-level inferences from nonverbal behaviors than those adopting a sample-oriented stance. For example, a behaviorist's interpretation of increased respiration, perspiration, and fidgeting while a client talks about sex would probably be that emotional arousal is associated with that topic. Psychodynamic interviewers may infer more, postulating perhaps that nonverbal behaviors (e.g., twirling a ring on a finger) are symbolic representations of sexual activity or other unconscious impulses. Alfred Adler interpreted where a client chose to sit: "One moves toward the desk; that is favorable. Another moves away; that is unfavorable" (Adler, 1933). Whatever they might infer from it, most clinicians believe that nonverbal behavior serves as a powerful communication channel and a valuable source of interview data.

RESEARCH ON THE INTERVIEW

In addition to concerns about nonverbal communication and the other aspects of interviewing that we have covered in this chapter, clinicians face many other interview-related challenges. Dealing with silences, how to address the client, the pros and cons of note taking, handling personal questions from clients, and confronting a client's inconsistencies are just a few of these. (If you are interested in a more detailed exploration of interviewing issues and techniques, consult the sources listed at the beginning of this chapter.) Clinicians must also remain aware of empirical research on the value of interviews as a source of assessment data and a format for therapy.

Social Interaction and Influence in the Interview

Until 1942, when Carl Rogers published the first transcripts from phonographic recordings of therapy interviews, the exact nature of clinical interactions had been unknown.[2] Research on the clinical interview grew rapidly thereafter. At first it focused on such issues as the effects of audio recording and the accuracy of clinicians' summaries versus electrical recordings of the same interview (Covner, 1944; Snyder, 1945). After it was established that recording devices were not disruptive and provided the most complete account of an interview, research expanded in several new directions.

Descriptive Research. One of these new directions involved efforts to describe relationships between interview characteristics—such as warmth and empathy—and outcome variables such as rapport-building and therapy effectiveness. Some studies focused on differences in interview tactics used by Rogerians and non-Rogerians (Porter, 1943; Seeman, 1949; Strupp, 1960), while others tried to define interview variables such as client resistance (Snyder, 1953). Still other investigators performed detailed analyses of the content of conversations as a means of better understanding the interview process (Auld & Murray, 1955). One team of researchers devoted years to the content analysis of the first five minutes of a single interview (Pittenger, Hockett, & Danehy, 1960).

In an attempt to better define interview concepts such as *empathy, transference,* and *insight,* researchers also sought to describe interviews in terms of noncontent variables. Using specialized equipment, they recorded information about clients' and interviewers' physiological arousal during interviews (Greenblatt, 1959) and about the stability, idiosyncrasies, and equilibrium of their speech, and about the length of their silences (Lennard & Bernstein, 1960; Saslow & Matarazzo, 1959).

Experimental Research. The research of the 1940s and 1950s generated large amounts of data about the interview and highlighted its complexity as a social event. One aspect of this complexity was revealed by experiments confirming that interviews are not only data-gathering contexts, but *social influence* situations as well.

---

[2]Rogers's recordings were considered scandalous at the time because tradition ruled out all but narrative case reports. The fact that he was a psychologist (not a psychiatrist) doing therapy with adults made Rogers's revelations even more distasteful to those not yet accustomed to the expanding roles of postwar clinicians.

Those experiments were stimulated in large measure by B.F. Skinner's (1948, 1957) assertion that, like other forms of behavior, verbal behavior during interviews can be modified by its consequences. Dozens of *verbal conditioning* studies soon appeared, showing that everything from the use of plural nouns to reports of life events, expression of feelings, self-evaluations, and delusional speech can be increased or decreased depending on how the interviewer responds to the client (Greenspoon, 1962; Kanfer, 1968; Salzinger, 1959). Ultimately, clinicians lost interest in the effects of verbal conditioning on interviewing after several investigators showed that contingency-based changes in clients' verbal behavior occurred only when clients were aware of clinicians' efforts to influence them—and when they were willing to comply (e.g., Dulany, 1968).

Other research found that clinicians could also systematically influence noncontent variables in the interview. For example, the duration of interviewees' speech tends to increase when interviewers nod their heads or say "mm-hmm" while listening (Kanfer & McBrearty, 1962; Matarazzo, 1965). When interviewers first increased, then decreased, the duration of their own utterances over three parts of a conversation, interviewees did the same. When the interviewer's speech duration first decreased, then increased, interviewees again followed suit (Matarazzo et al., 1963).

However, this *synchrony* phenomenon does not always appear (Matarazzo et al., 1968). And in therapy situations, the synchrony-producing influence of clinician upon client may be moderated, or even reversed, by the client's influence on the clinician. Thus, the duration of a therapist's utterances may increase with quiet clients and decrease with those who are more talkative (Lennard & Bernstein, 1960). Social status can also affect interview interactions. In one laboratory study, synchrony occurred when students were interviewed by fellow students, but it disappeared when they were interviewed by high-status professionals (Pope et al., 1974).

Research on social interaction and influence not only shows that interviews that can be affected by interviewer, client, relationship, and situational factors, it also helped sensitize clinicians to the potential influence of these factors in their own assessment interviews. So while skilled interviewers today use verbal reinforcement to encourage their clients to talk about or elaborate on particular topics, they are also aware that interview data can be biased if they reinforce only those aspects of client speech consistent with their expectations or beliefs about a client.

Reliability and Validity of Interview Data

Client, interviewer, and situational factors may also affect the degree to which clients give the same information on different occasions or to different interviewers (reliability) and the degree to which that information is accurate (validity). The impact of these factors is of special interest to researchers trying to establish the value and understand the limits of interview data.

Reliability.   Some researchers have studied interview reliability by looking at the degree to which different judges agree on the *inferences* (ratings, diagnoses, or personality trait descriptions) they draw from conversations with the same client (DiNardo et al., 1993; Ferro et al., 1995). However, this approach confounds the reliability of what the client said with the quality of the interviewer's inference system. If a client tells two clinicians the same thing and they draw different conclusions from it, it may be the interviewers' inference system, not the interview, that is unreliable. If a client gives *different* answers to the same questions by different interviewers, their discrepant inferences may be caused by unreliability in the interview format itself. One strategy for isolating the reliability of interviewers' judgments is to have several clinicians view videotaped interviews and then make ratings or draw other inferences from the tapes. This approach has been widely used to establish the reliability of clinicians' judgments about DSM-IV diagnoses (Widiger et al., 1991), clients' progress in therapy (Goins, Strauss, & Martin, 1995), the severity of Alzheimer's disease (Boothby, Mann, & Barker, 1995), the credibility of children's reports of sexual abuse (Anson, Golding, & Gully, 1993), and the like (Derksen, Hummelen, & Bouwens, 1994).

To study the reliability of interview data, researchers examine the consistency of clients' responses across repeated interview occasions by the same or different interviewers. As you might expect, test–retest reliability tends to be highest when adult clients are asked for innocuous information such as age and other demographic data and when the interval between interviews is short (e.g., Ross et al., 1995). Lower reliability coefficients tend to appear when test–retest intervals are long, when clients are young children, and when interviewers explore sensitive topics such as illegal drug use, sexual practices, or traumatic experiences (Fallon & Schwab-Stone, 1994; Schwab-Stone, Fallon, & Briggs, 1994; Weiss et al., 1995). Unstructured interviews, too, generally tend to be associated with lower levels of reliability (e.g., Rogers, 1995; Ruegg et al., 1990; Steiner et al., 1995). Overall, however, the test–retest reliability of structured interviews tends to be +.70 or higher, even when the most sensitive information is requested for diagnostic or other purposes (e.g., Cohen & Vinson, 1995; Grant et al., 1995; Segal, Hersen, & Van Hasselt, 1994).

Validity.   In 1968, Walter Mischel cited evidence that what people say they will do is a better predictor of future behavior than test scores are. Mischel's data reflect a view held by many clinicians today, namely that the validity, or accuracy, of interview data is superior to that of any other assessment source.

Clinicians' faith in the validity of structured interviews, in particular, is reflected in the fact that the results of such interviews are often used as criteria for evaluating psychological tests or other assessment methods. Thus, the validity of a test for depression, for example, will be seen as supported if clients' scores on the test correlate strongly with what they say about depression during a structured interview (Rogers, 1995). As noted earlier, structured interviews have also become the most widely accepted procedure for gathering epidemiological data on the prevalence of various mental disorders and for identifying research participants who display particular forms of disorder (e.g., Kendler & Roy, 1995; Lewis et al., 1992; Robins & Regier, 1991).

While there is evidence to support the validity of interview data in general, and structured interviews in particular, it is also important to remember that the accuracy of interview responses can be affected by a number of factors. For example, the phrasing of questions in unstructured interviews can be important. A client's responses to

"Tell me something about your marital problems" will probably be more accurate and less distorted by defensiveness than if the interviewer asked "Why can't you get along with your spouse?" (e.g. Thomas, 1973). Evidence also exists that responses to clinical and survey research interviews may be more accurate when people feel comfortable with the interviewer, a factor that may be enhanced when the two of them share the same gender, ethnicity, and native language (Axin, 1991; Grantham, 1973; Kane & Macauley, 1993; Sue et al. 1991; Webster, 1996; Ying, 1989). Other aspects of a person's emotional state can also affect response accuracy. For example, mothers' reports about their children's behavior are significantly influenced by the mothers' emotional adjustment, in particular by feelings of depression (Webster-Stratton, 1988).

Interview validity can also be threatened if clients misremember or purposely distort information. The probability of error or distortion increases when clients are mentally retarded (e.g., Heal & Sigelman, 1995), suffer from various brain disorders (e.g., West, Bondy, & Hutchinson, 1991), or would prefer not to reveal the truth about their behavior problems, drug use, sexual behavior, criminal activity, or previous hospitalizations (e.g., Morrison et al., 1995; Williams, 1994). At the other extreme, clients motivated to appear mentally disturbed may give inaccurate interview responses aimed at creating the appearance of a mental disorder. Concern about such *malingering* led to the creation of special interview methods aimed at detecting it (Rogers, Gillis, Dickens, & Bagby, 1991; see Table 4.2). In short, the desire to present oneself in a particular light to a mental health professional—called "impression-management" (Braginsky, Braginsky, & Ring, 1969)—can undermine the validity of interview data.

Interviewer Error and Bias

Reliable and valid interview data are of little value if they are distorted by the interviewer. Therefore, evaluation of the interview as a source of assessment data must consider its susceptibility to error or bias in the interviewer's processing of what clients say.

Some errors are accidental, as when the volume of incoming information overwhelms the interviewer's memory capacity and results in the loss or distortion of information. This problem can be minimized by the use of audio- or videotaping equipment. There have also been cases in which erroneous information appears because of an interviewer's misguided desire to "do a good job." For example, a person hired to conduct structured interviews was quoted as saying: "One of the questions asked for five reasons why parents had put their child in an institution. I found most people can't think of five reasons. I didn't want [the boss] to think I was goofing off, so I always filled in all five" (Schwitzgebel & Kolb, 1974).

More worrisome is the possibility that personal biases might affect interviewers' perceptions and color their inferences and conclusions about what clients say during interviews. The role of such biases was noted nearly seventy years ago in a study showing that social workers' judgments of why skid-row bums had become destitute were related to the interviewers' personal agendas, not just to what respondents said (Rice, 1929). Thus, an anti-alcohol interviewer saw drinking as the cause of poverty in 62% of the cases, while a socialist interviewer concluded that interviewees' plights stemmed from capitalist-generated economic conditions. Similarly, as discussed in chapter 2, psychoanalysts and behavior therapists tend to draw different causal conclusions about the behavior problems clients describe during interviews (Plous & Zimbardo, 1986). Indeed, interview-based psychodiagnoses, job interview decisions, and the outcome of medical school admissions interviews may all be prejudiced by information that interviewers receive about interviewees prior to the interview (Dipboye, Stramler, & Fontenelle, 1984; Shaw et al., 1995; Temerlin, 1968).

Other biases or preconceptions about client characteristics can also affect interviewers' interpretations of interview data. In one large-scale study, for example, medical and mental health professionals were more likely to diagnose depression in female rather than male clients, whether or not these clients' interview responses met standard criteria for defining depressive disorders (Potts, Burnam, & Wells, 1991). Other studies conducted in mental health, employment, and other settings have shown that interviewers' judgments, evaluations, and conclusions can also be affected by clients' ethnicity (Singer & Eder, 1989; Tomlinson & Cheatham, 1989). These effects are not always large or significant, however (e.g., Garb, 1995; Williams, 1988; Williams & Heikes, 1993), and they can be further reduced through the use of structured interviews that provide clear rules about what to infer from particular interview responses. In one study, for example, gender bias was not evident when clinical judgments were based on the Diagnostic Interview Schedule described in Table 4.2 (Potts, Burnam, & Wells, 1991). Computer-based interviewing can also help reduce the impact of interviewer preconceptions (Rodgers, 1987), as can training programs that sensitize interviewers to the potential effects of personal biases (Brown, 1990; Sinacore-Guinn, 1995).

To sum up, research on the interview as an assessment tool does not justify a single, all-encompassing conclusion. As one distinguished researcher put it, "The interview has been used in so many different ways for various purposes, by individuals with varying skills, that it is a difficult matter to make a final judgment concerning its values" (Garfield, 1974, p. 90). The skill of the interviewer is very important, but the exact nature of what "skill" means is still not clear. Although the interview will continue to occupy a primary assessment role in clinical psychology, it must also remain the object of research. Any tendency to view interviews as primarily an art form practiced by gifted

Miss Peach by Mell Lazarus. (Courtesy of Mell Lazarus and News America Syndicate.)

clinicians and therefore exempt from scientifically rigorous examinations of reliability and validity will ultimately result in the loss of the interview's utility as an important assessment tool.

INTERVIEWING AT WORK

Q.: How and why is interviewing important in your work?

DR. SANDY D'ANGELO: When I first meet with newly referred children and families, I must collect a large amount of information quickly so that I can conceptualize the child's difficulty and begin forming recommendations for intervention. These initial assessments typically include a semistructured interview designed for our clinic which describes current behavior and concerns and elicits history in the following areas: family; pregnancy, birth, and development; medical; education; and daily routine.

DR. HECTOR MACHABANSKI: Interviewing is important to me because in almost all aspects of my clinical work I interact with people who are sources of information about clients—whether they are the clients themselves, members of clients' families, those who made the referral, or others. The basic elements of interviewing are involved in all these interactions.

DR. GEOFFREY THORPE: Interviewing is the most common technique used in clinical assessment, and I use it in virtually every clinical situation. Because the interview is highly flexible and versatile, it can be adapted to many purposes. My colleagues and I even use interviewing as part of our admissions process with prospective clinical psychology graduate students.

CHAPTER SUMMARY

The interview is the most widely employed tool in clinical psychology for assessment and therapy. Interviews are defined as conversations with a purpose, and, in clinical situations, these purposes include client intake, problem identification, orientation, termination, crisis intervention, and observation.

In nondirective interviews, the clinician interferes as little as possible with the client's speech, while structured interviews present planned inquiries in a fixed sequence. Semistructured interviews fall between these extremes. Structured and semistructured interviews are growing in popularity and are now widely used for making psychiatric diagnoses, selecting participants for research, and collecting epidemiological data.

Most interviews have a beginning, a middle, and an end. Intake and problem-identification interviews, for example, usually begin with efforts at making the client comfortable, enter an information-gathering middle stage, and end with a summary and discussion. Conducting each phase of an interview, and moving smoothly from one to the next requires a combination of common sense, active listening skills, well-phrased questions, and tact. If interviews are to have maximum value, communication between client and interviewer must be as clear as possible in both verbal and nonverbal channels.

Research on interviews reveals that they are complex social interactions whose content and outcome can be affected by a multitude of client, interviewer, and situational factors. For example, clients' responses can be influenced by interviewers' behavior, and vice versa. So while the reliability of interviews, especially structured interviews, is generally good, it can depend on the age of the client, what topics are being explored, and other variables. The validity of interview data can depend on how questions are phrased, the client's comfort with the interviewer, emotional state, memory skills, and motivation. Reliability and validity can both be threatened by interviewer errors or biases, especially those relating to preconceived views of clients with particular characteristics. Eliminating such errors and biases is a major challenge for clinicians.

Chapter 5

Testing in Clinical Psychology

As described in chapter 1, the history of clinical psychology is intimately related to the development and use of psychological tests. And though clinicians now perform many functions in addition to testing, tests remain an important part of clinical research and practice. In this chapter, we consider the nature of psychological tests, how they are constructed, and the research on their value as assessment tools.

WHAT IS A TEST?

A test is a systematic procedure for observing and describing a person's behavior in a standard situation (Cronbach, 1970). Tests present a set of planned stimuli (inkblots or true–false questions, for example) and ask the client to respond to them in some way. The client's reactions become the test's results or scores, to be used as samples, signs, or correlates in the clinician's assessment strategy. Test data may lead to conservative, situation-specific statements ("The client appeared disoriented during testing and was correct on 15 out of 60 items.") or to sweeping, high-level inferences ("The client's ego boundaries are so ill defined as to make adequate functioning outside an institution very unlikely."). Most commonly, test results guide inferences that are between these extremes.

Tests are like highly structured interviews in that they ask clients to respond to specific assessment stimuli presented in a predetermined sequence. They also share characteristics with observational assessments by providing an opportunity for the clinician to watch the client in the test situation. In some ways, however, tests are distinct from all other assessment techniques. For example:

1. A test can be administered in a nonsocial context in which observational assessment does not supplement test data.

2. Usually, a client's test responses can be quantitatively compared to statistical *norms* established by the responses of hundreds or thousands of other people who have taken the same test under *standardized* conditions. Standardization—in which all respondents take the test under similar physical circumstances and all scoring is done using uniform methods—is designed to insure that differences in testing methods do not influence test results.

3. Tests can be administered in groups as well as individually. The SAT and other college entrance examinations provide examples of how tests are used to assess large numbers of people at the same time.

WHAT DO TESTS MEASURE?

The thousands of psychological tests used today are administered to infants, children, adolescents, adults, senior citizens, students, soldiers, mental patients, office workers, prisoners, and every other imaginable group (Kramer & Conoley, 1995). Some of these tests pose direct, specific questions ("Do you ever feel discouraged?"), while others ask for general reactions to less distinct stimuli ("Tell me what you see in this drawing."). Some are presented in paper-and-pencil form, some are given orally. Some require verbal skills ("What is a chicken?"), some ask the client to perform various tasks ("Please trace the correct path through this puzzle maze"), and still others include both kinds of items.

Despite their enormous variety, many tests have similar purposes and can be grouped into four general categories based on whether they seek to measure (1) *intellectual functioning*, (2) *personality characteristics*, (3) *attitudes, interests, preferences*, and *values*, or (4) *ability*. The tests most commonly used by clinical psychologists in the U.S. and elsewhere are those of intellectual functioning and personality (Archer et al., 1991; Chan & Lee, 1995; Miller, 1991; Piotrowski & Keller, 1989). This pattern results not only because these variables are especially relevant to most clinicians' treatment and research activities, but also because other people expect clinicians to offer advice on such things.

One reason for the proliferation of tests is that testers are forever hoping to measure clinical constructs in ever more reliable, valid, and sophisticated ways. For example, one clinician may feel that a popular anxiety test does not really "get at" anxiety very well, and so the clinician creates a new, improved instrument. Other psychologists might be dissatisfied with both tests and soon come up with yet other devices. This sequence is especially noticeable in personality testing, but it is evident in other test categories as well. Another factor responsible for the increasing array of tests is that testers' interests are becoming more specific, thus prompting the development of special-purpose tests. In intelligence testing, for example, instruments are available for use with infants, the physically handicapped, and persons not fluent in English or from specific cultural backgrounds. Similarly, surveys of general preferences or interests can now be followed up with special-purpose tests aimed at assessing the way adolescents spend leisure time or the things children find rewarding.

There are so many psychological tests available that it takes special publications to list them all and review their reliability, validity, and utility. The best known and most authoritative of these is the *Mental Measurements Yearbook*, first published in 1938 (Buros, 1938), and updated frequently; the latest edition appeared in 1995 (Kramer & Conoley, 1995).

TEST CONSTRUCTION PROCEDURES

The seemingly odd items on some psychological tests, especially on certain personality tests, lead many people to ask "How do psychologists come up with these things?" The answer is that they usually construct their tests using *analytic* or *empirical* approaches, though they sometimes use a *sequential system* approach which combines the two (Burisch, 1984).[1]

Psychologists using the analytic approach begin by asking, "What are the qualities I want to measure?", "How do I define these qualities?", and "What kind of test and test items would make sense for assessing these qualities?" They then proceed to build a test that answers the last question. In short, the analytic approach is a deductive approach to test construction. In its simplest form, it relies on creating content validity by designing tests that include items tapping all aspects of some domain. A more comprehensive analytic approach involves deriving test items from a theory of the characteristics to be measured.

To illustrate the simplest analytic approach, suppose a clinician wants to use it to develop a test for reliably and accurately identifying adult humans as male or female. The first step would be to ask what kinds of test items are likely to be answered differently by members of the two sexes. The choice of items, then, will be shaped by what the clinician's knowledge, experience, and favorite theories say is different about males and females. If the clinician chooses to focus on variations in physical characteristics, and prefers a true–false format, the test might contain items such as:

1. I was born with a prostate gland.
2. I was born with a uterus.
3. I was born with a penis.
4. I was born with a vagina.

---

[1]Anastasi (1988) describes factor analytic methods as a fourth approach to test development.

Suppose, however, that the clinician believes that physical characteristics are only surface indicators of sex and that to get at "real" sex differences, a test should tap unconscious processes associated with masculinity and femininity. Such a test might search for unconscious themes by asking clients to fill in incomplete sentences such as:

1. A dependent person is _____.
2. Strength is _____.
3. The trouble with most men is _____.
4. Most women are _____.
5. I like to _____.

In either case, items on an analytically constructed test will strongly reflect the tester's theory of what aspects of some concepts should be tested, and how.

The main alternative to analytic test construction is the empirical approach. Here, instead of deciding ahead of time what test content should be used to measure a particular target, the tester lets the content "choose itself." Thus, in building a sex test, the clinician would amass a large number of self-report test items, performance tasks, or inkblots, and then administer all of them to a large group of people who have *already been identified* as males or females using a chromosome analysis or other biological measure. The clinician would then examine the entire group's responses to all these testing materials to see which items, tasks, or other stimuli were consistently answered differently by men and women.

Any test stimuli that differentiated the sexes would be used to create the initial version of the sex test, *regardless of whether they have any obvious relationship to sex differences*. Thus, if only males answered "true" to items like "My nose runs a lot," "Coffee makes me sleepy," or "My shoes are too tight," those items would be made part of the developing test. The reasons *why* such items separate males from females might become the subject of further theoretical research, but for practical purposes testers are usually willing to employ an empirically constructed test in spite of the fact that the conceptual relevance of its individual items cannot be explained clearly. *This* is why some tests contain such apparently odd items.

Several factors affect test developers' choice of analytic or empirical procedures. The analytic approach can be faster and less expensive because it does not require initial administration of many items to many people in order to settle on those that will comprise the test. These features make analytic procedures attractive to clinicians who do not have access to a large pool of test material and willing subjects or who are forced by circumstances to develop a test on short notice. Analytic procedures also tend to be favored by clinicians evaluating a particular theory. Suppose that theory suggests that people differ in terms of "geekiness," but that no test is available to measure it. To explore the geekiness dimension of personality, the researcher will need a test that taps what the theory says geekiness is and that uses methods consistent with what the theory says about how it should be measured. Development of a Geek Test would thus likely proceed on analytic grounds.

Clinicians who are less concerned with theoretical notions and who have time and other resources available often find the empirical approach more desirable, especially when attempting to make specific predictions about people. If the tester's task is to identify individuals likely to graduate from law school, for example, it makes sense to find out if students who graduate respond to any test items in a way that is reliably different from those who fail or drop out.

The sequential system approach to test construction combines aspects of the analytic and empirical techniques. For example, testers who choose initial test items analytically may then examine results statistically to determine which item responses are, and are not, correlated with one another. Groups of correlated items are then identified as *scales*, which are thought to be relatively pure measures of certain dimensions of personality, mental ability, or the like (Maloney & Ward, 1976). If administration of the new instrument reveals that certain items or scales are especially good at discriminating between target groups (e.g., successful versus unsuccessful students), those items and scales are more likely to be retained in the test than are items with little discriminative power. The sequential system approach is also valuable to those wishing to construct a test using empirical procedures, but who don't want to include hundreds or thousands of items in the initial research trial. The decision about which items to try is usually made on analytic grounds; some items are selected from existing tests, while others are those the clinician believes "ought" to be evaluated.

Regardless of how a test is constructed initially, its value as an assessment instrument ultimately must be established through empirical research on its reliability and validity (see Chapter 3). Later we shall look at how various tests have fared when scrutinized by such research. For now, let's consider prominent examples of tests designed to assess (1) intellectual functioning, (2) ability, (3) attitudes, interests, preferences, and values, and (4) personality. We begin our exploration of psychological tests with measures of intelligence, because, as noted in Chapter 1, the early history of clinical psychology is essentially the early history of intelligence tests.

TESTS OF INTELLECTUAL FUNCTIONING

While everyone would agree that intelligence is a good thing to have, there is far less consensus about what intelligence actually *is* (Sternberg & Detterman, 1986). This state of affairs has generated the half-joking suggestion among clinicians that "intelligence is whatever intelligence tests measure." Indeed, the developers of most intelligence tests have initially proceeded on analytical grounds; each of the more than 200 assessment instruments they have produced reflects its creator's theoretical views about the essential nature of intelligence and about how best to measure intellectual functioning.

A description of those theories is beyond the scope of this chapter (see Neisser et al., 1996 for a succinct review), but it is worth noting that various researchers employing a mental testing, or *psychometric* approach to intelligence have described it as a *general* characteristic (called *g*), as a set of up to 150 *specific* intellectual functions (called *s*'s) such as word fluency, reasoning, and memory, or as some hierarchical combination of the two (Carroll, 1993). Debate and empirical research about the nature of intelligence remains active, but the practical relevance of whether intelligence is *g*, a set of *s*'s, or something else is limited by the fact that none of the major intelligence tests in wide use today reflects the *g* or *s* approach clearly enough to provide definitive validation of one theory or another (Kaufman & Harrison, 1991). Nor do those tests measure all aspects of what might be considered intelligence (Neisser et al., 1996). They are, however, the main methods clinicians have available for assessing certain kinds of mental abilities.

The Binet Scales

Alfred Binet was not the first person to develop a measure of intelligence, but his original test and the revisions based on it have been among the most influential means of assessing the mental ability of children. In its earliest form (1905), Binet's test consisted of thirty questions and tasks, including things like unwrapping a piece of candy, following a moving object with the eyes, comparing objects of differing weights, repeating numbers or sentences from memory, and recognizing familiar objects. The child's test score was simply the number of items passed.

Beginning with a 1908 revision, the tasks in Binet's test were *age graded*, which means that the items were arranged so that younger children were expected to pass the earlier ones, while older children were expected to pass later ones. Binet and his collaborator, Theodore Simon, observed the test behavior of about 200 children and suggested, for example, that three-year-olds ought to be able to identify their eyes, nose, and mouth, repeat a two-digit number and a six-syllable sentence, and give their last name. At seven years, success at finding missing parts of drawings, copying simple geometric figures, and identifying denominations of coins was expected. Items to be passed at the eleventh-year level included criticism of absurd sentences, definition of abstract concepts, and rearranging words to form a sentence. A child's *mental age* was the highest age level at which *all* test items were passed (plus credit for any correct responses at higher levels).

The 1908 scale, which covered ages three to thirteen, was brought to the United States by Henry Goddard. Though popular, the Binet-Simon test had several shortcomings. Some users were dissatisfied because the test emphasized children's verbal skills more than their capacity for judgment. Others felt that the test was too easy at lower age levels and too difficult at the upper end. Binet attempted to correct some of these problems in a 1911 revision of his test, but a far more influential version was written in 1916 by Lewis Terman, a Stanford University psychologist.

Terman believed that expressing a child's intelligence in terms of "mental age" was imprecise and left too much room for misinterpretation: "If a child's mental age equalled his chronological age, he was considered 'regular' (average) in intelligence; if his mental age was higher, he was 'advanced'; if his mental age was lower, he was 'retarded'" (Reisman, 1976). Terman's edition of the Binet-Simon was called the Stanford-Binet; it soon became the most popular intelligence test among clinical psychologists in the United States. The Stanford-Binet was standardized on a larger sample (1,400 European-Americans) and across a wider age range (three to sixteen) than had been used for Binet's 1911 revision. Terman also adopted an idea suggested in 1912 by

German psychologist William Stern for representing numerically the relationship between mental and chronological age: Stanford-Binet results were expressed as the *intelligence quotient* (or IQ) that results when mental age (MA) is divided by chronological age (CA) and multiplied by 100. Thus, a six-year-old whose score on the Stanford-Binet yielded a mental age of eight would have an IQ of 133 [(8 ÷ 6) × 100].

Terman suggested that various IQ ranges be given labels such as "average," "feeble-minded," and "genius." Today, the following categories are used: "very superior," "superior," "high average," "average," "low average," "borderline," and "mentally retarded." Similar systems are used to classify persons at the lower end of the IQ scale as "mildly," "moderately," "severely," or "profoundly" retarded. The original intent of such labels was to provide a shorthand summary of a person's score relative to others of the same age. However, IQ scores and the labels associated with them are often overemphasized and misused, especially by those unfamiliar with their meaning. This unfortunate tendency is one reason why, as we shall see later, the use of IQ data for diagnostic, academic, or occupational decision-making is so controversial.

Terman and his colleague, Maud Merrill, revised the Stanford-Binet in 1937, 1960, and again in 1973. The 1973 edition retained the same content as the 1960 edition but used larger standardization samples consisting of 2,100 children representing more diverse socioeconomic, geographical, ethnic, and cultural subgroups. In addition to being more representative, the norms provided by this sample showed a substantial increase in IQ estimates for children of all ages. This improvement has been attributed to several influences, including the effects of greater literacy among parents, improvements in nutrition, the educational effects of mass media, and the fact that children stay in school longer now than they did in the 1930s (Flynn, 1984; Neisser et al., 1996).

Beginning with the 1960 edition of the Stanford-Binet, the MA/CA × 100 formula for computing IQ was replaced by IQ tables in which the formula's results are corrected in light of the mean and variance in IQs at each age level in the standardization sample. Thus, if a 6-year-old girl earns a mental age score of 9 (which is not only high relative to her chronological age, but also higher than most 6-year-olds in the standardization population), she would receive an IQ of 156 rather than the 150 that would have resulted from simply calculating MA/CA × 100. Such "corrected" scores were arrived at by setting up IQ tables in which the mean IQ at each age level is 100, with a standard deviation of 16. These *deviation IQ* scores represents the degree of deviation from the average of any age group. Thus, an IQ of 100 is average for any age; 116 would be one standard deviation above average, and 84 would be one standard deviation below average.

In spite of its widespread use with children, the Stanford-Binet continued to be criticized for its emphasis upon verbal aspects of intelligence, its outdated item content, and its reliance on one score rather than a pattern of different cognitive strengths and weaknesses.

The Fourth Edition of the Stanford-Binet. Published in 1986, the *Stanford-Binet Intelligence Scale: Fourth Edition* (Thorndike, Hagen, & Sattler, 1986) differs in many respects from earlier versions of the test. It is still an individually administered test, and it retains many of the same kinds of items as in earlier editions, but the organization and content have dramatically changed. Unlike previous editions, which grouped items according to age levels, items in the fourth edition are grouped into fifteen subtests (some examples are described in Table 5.1). Within each subtest, the items are arranged in increasing order of difficulty and their results are organized to assess four major areas of intellectual functioning: verbal reasoning, abstract/visual reasoning, quantitative reasoning, and short-term memory.

Because the fifteen subtests can be given in varying combinations, the latest edition of the Stanford-Binet is more flexible than previous versions, and it is more useful as a diagnostic tool for the assessment of cognitive strengths and weaknesses in individuals aged two to adult. The choice of which tests to give and at what level of difficulty to begin each depends on the purpose of the evaluation, the client's age (not all of the tests are appropriate for children of certain ages), and initial test results that help guide the examiner to the correct entry level for individual tests. Typically, examiners administer between eight and thirteen subtests, although a quick screening battery of four tests (vocabulary, bead memory, quantitative, and pattern analysis) is recommended when testing must be completed in less than forty minutes.

A *Standard Age Score*, or SAS, is determined for each subtest by using tables that convert raw scores to normalized standard scores with a mean of 50 and a standard deviation of 8 for each age group. For example, an SAS of 58 would be one standard deviation above the mean for children of a given age and would place a child at the 84th percentile—meaning that 58 is better than 84% of the child's age mates. The tables can also be used to calculate composite SAS scores for each of the four content areas and for any combination of them. These area and composite scores are also normalized standard scores, and because their means are 100 and their standard deviations are 16, they can be expressed in the same units as the deviation IQ scores used in earlier versions of the test.

Research on the fourth edition of the Stanford-Binet suggests that it has very high internal consistency and test–retest reliability (generally, above .90). In addition, its scores correlate highly with other measures of intelligence and discriminate among

The Stanford-Binet being administered to a young child.

TABLE 5.1   A Sampling of Subtest Items Similar to Those Included in the Fourth Edition of the Stanford-Binet

Vocabulary: Define words like train, wrench, letter, error, and encourage.

Comprehension: Answer questions like, "Why should people brush their teeth?" "Why should people be quiet in a library?" "What is one advantage and one disadvantage of living in a small town instead of a big city?"

Absurdities: Identify the mistakes or "silly" aspects of pictures in which, for example, a man is shown using the wrong end of a rake or a girl is shown putting a piece of clothing on incorrectly.

Copying: Arrange a set of blocks to match different designs; draw designs like those shown in pictures.

Memory for Objects: Choose the right order in which a series of pictures were presented.

Number Series: Determine which numbers come next in a series of numbers such as the following—32, 26, 20, 14, _____, _____.

Verbal Relations: Indicate how three objects or words are alike but different from a fourth. For example, how are dog, cat, horse alike but different from boy.

Bead Memory: Arrange different colored and shaped beads to match pictures of the beads organized in different layouts.

As shown at the bottom of the table, performance on each of fifteen subtests is seen to reflect one of four areas of intellectual functioning.

samples of gifted, retarded, and learning disabled children (Anastasi & Urbina, 1997; Barrett & Depinet, 1991). However, though the fourth edition of the Stanford-Binet was designed to yield separate scores for four different cognitive abilities, it appears to measure only two basic abilities in young children—verbal reasoning and nonverbal intelligence. For children older than six years, a third ability—memory—emerges as an important component on the test (Laurent, Swerdlik, & Ryburn, 1992).

The Wechsler Scales

In the 1930s, David Wechsler, chief psychologist at New York's Bellevue Psychiatric Hospital, began developing an intelligence test specifically for adults. The result of his efforts, the Wechsler-Bellevue (W-B) Intelligence Scale, was published in 1939. This test differed in several ways from the Stanford-Binet, even though some W-B tasks were borrowed or adapted from it. First, the W-B was aimed at adults, aged seventeen and older. Second, the W-B was a *point* scale in which the client receives credit for each correct answer. With this method, IQ does not reflect the relationship between mental age and chronological age, but a comparison of points earned by the client to those earned by persons of equal age in the standardization sample.

Like the latest version of the Stanford-Binet, Wechsler-Bellevue items were arranged in groups or *subtests* based on similarity. Each subtest contained increasingly difficult items. For example, on the digit-span subtest, the client was asked to repeat numbers, starting with three digits and progressing to nine digits. The score on this subtest was determined by the maximum number of digits the client could repeat without error. The W-B contained six *verbal* subtests (information, comprehension, arithmetic, similarities, digit span, and vocabulary) and five *performance* subtests (digit symbol, picture completion, block design, picture arrangement, and object assembly).

The W-B had some deficiencies, however, the most serious of which was an inadequate standardization sample (1,700 caucasian New Yorkers aged seven to seventy). Accordingly, in 1955 Wechsler revised his test and restandardized it on a more ethnically diverse and representative sample of more than 2,000 individuals (aged sixteen to seventy-four) living in all parts of the United States. This revision was called the Wechsler Adult Intelligence Scale, or WAIS, and it soon became the most popular adult intelligence test in the United States. Like the W-B, the WAIS contained six verbal and five performance subtests, allowing computation of a client's Verbal IQ, Performance IQ, and Full-Scale IQ (which combines the other two). The latest revision, known as the WAIS-R, was published in 1981. It was restandardized on a sample of 1,880 U.S. adults whose age, ethnicity, and other demographic characteristics reflected 1970 census data (Wechsler, 1981). Some examples of the types of items included on the WAIS-R are presented in Table 5.2.

The structure of the WAIS-R allows not only for the computation of IQ scores, but also for the analysis of patterns of subtest scores (Kaufman, 1990). Some clinicians use WAIS-R subtest variability, or "scatter," to help them reach clinical diagnoses, to assess the possibility of brain damage, or to describe impulsivity or other personality characteristics (e.g., Ryan, Paolo, & Smith, 1992).

After publication of the W-B, Wechsler's interest in extending the point-scale test format to children resulted in the Wechsler Intelligence Scale for Children (WISC). Appearing in 1949, the WISC was made up of twelve subtests (six verbal, six performance) of which only ten were usually administered. The subtests were similar to those of the W-B, but easier. The WISC was standardized on 2,200 European-American children from all parts of the United States, but because they ranged in age from five to fifteen, the WISC was not useful for the very young. The Wechsler Preschool and Primary Scale of Intelligence (WPPSI) was developed later, but still only reached the four-year-old level (Wechsler, 1967). A revision of this test (WPPSI-R) lowers the age limit to three years. In 1974, a new version of the WISC was published. Called the WISC-R, it includes six verbal and six performance subtests; again, only five of each are usually administered. The content of the WISC-R items was changed to make it more representative of current social and cultural values, and the entire test was standardized on a new sample of 2,200 ethnically diverse children from varying socioeconomic levels and geographical locations.

The latest version of the WISC, the WISC-III, was published in 1991 (Wechsler, 1991). Although it retains the basic structure and format of its predecessors, scoring of the WISC-III is based on new norms collected on 2,200 children, ranging in age from six to sixteen and representative of 1988 U.S. census data. New items were added to replace WISC-R items that were outdated, culturally unfair, too easy, or too difficult. In addition, a new subtest called Symbol Search was added as a supplementary test that can be substituted for the Coding subtest.

The WISC-III Manual (Wechsler, 1991) presents unusually thorough data about the test's reliability and validity, and additional research on the interpretation of WISC-III scores is in progress. WISC-III scores are extremely stable over time and show very

TABLE 5.2   Items of the Type Included in the Wechsler Adult Intelligence Scale-Revised (WAIS-R)

	(WAIS-R)
Information:	What does bread come from?
	What did Shakespeare do?
	What is the capital of France?
	What is the malleus malleficarum?
Comprehension:	What should you do with a wallet found in the street?
	Why do foreign cars cost more than domestic cars?
	What does "the squeaky wheel gets the grease" mean?
Arithmetic:	If you have four apples and give two away, how many do you have left?
	If four people can finish a job in six days, how many people would it take to do the job in two days?
Similarities:	Identify similar aspects of pairs like: hammer-screwdriver, portrait-short story, dog-flower.
Digit Symbol:	Copy designs that are associated with different numbers as quickly as possible.
Digit Span:	Repeat in forward and reverse order: two- to nine-digit numbers.
Vocabulary:	Define: chair, dime, lunch, paragraph, valley, asylum, modal, cutaneous.
Picture Completion:	Find missing objects in increasingly complex pictures.
Block Design:	Arrange blocks to match increasingly complex standard patterns.
Picture Arrangement:	Place increasing number of pictures together to make increasingly complex stories.
Object Assembly:	Arrange parts of puzzles to form recognizable objects (e.g., dog, flower, person).

high correlations with the WISC-R, as well as appropriately strong correlations with criteria such as school grades, achievement test scores, and neuropsychological performance. In addition to Full Scale, Verbal, and Performance IQ scores, the WISC-III can be interpreted in terms of four other factors: Verbal Comprehension and Perceptual Organization (which are similar, but not identical to, Verbal and Performance IQ, respectively), Freedom from Distractibility (emphasizing memory and attention), and Processing Speed.

Other Intelligence Tests

Another intelligence test that has gained popularity in recent years is the Kaufman Assessment Battery for Children (K-ABC) (Kaufman & Kaufman, 1983). Suitable for children two-and-a-half to twelve-and-a-half years of age, the K-ABC was based on research and theory in cognitive psychology and neuropsychology. It defines intelligence as the ability to solve new problems (an ability sometimes referred to as *fluid intelligence*) rather than knowledge of facts (which has been termed *crystallized intelligence*). The standardization sample for the K-ABC was closely matched to the U.S. census on several demographic factors, and its psychometric qualities are excellent. In addition, several studies show that the K-ABC can be used to assess and study neuropsychological problems in children (Kaufman & Harrison, 1991). A brief version called the Kaufman Brief Intelligence Test (K-BIT) (Kaufman & Kaufman, 1991) and an adult version, the Kaufman Adolescent and Adult Intelligence Test (KAIT), are also available (Kaufman & Kaufman, 1993).

Another relatively new intelligence test is the 1989 revision of the Woodcock-Johnson Psycho-Educational Battery (Woodcock & Johnson, 1977, 1989). Although usually administered to children, this test can also be used with adults. A special feature of the Woodcock-Johnson is that its twenty-seven subtests cover cognitive ability, academic achievement, and individual interests. Scoring is more complex than for most other intelligence tests, and there is some evidence that the separate ability and achievement subtests are not as clearly differentiated as intended (Kaufman & Harrison, 1991).

Several other intelligence tests in use today assess intelligence without emphasis on verbal or vocalization skills. The Peabody Picture Vocabulary Test-Revised, the Porteus Maze Test, the Leiter International Performance Scale, and the Raven's Progressive Matrices, for example, allow clinicians to assess intellectual functioning in clients who are very young or have other characteristics that impair their ability at verbal tasks. These tests also provide a backup in cases where the clinician suspects that a client's performance on a standard IQ test may have been hampered by anxiety, verbal deficits, cultural disadvantages, or other situational factors.

Further information about these and other intelligence tests for individual and group administration to adults and children is available from numerous sources (e.g., Anastasi & Urbina, 1997; Goldstein & Hersen, 1990; Kaufman, 1994; Kramer & Conoley, 1995; Vane & Motta, 1990).

ABILITY TESTS

Intelligence is one aspect of mental ability, and intelligence tests can be viewed as general mental ability instruments. However, there are a number of other tests designed to measure more specific mental abilities. These include *aptitude* and *achievement* tests. Aptitude tests are designed to predict success in an occupation or an educational program. They measure the accumulated effects of many different educational and living experiences and attempt to forecast future performance on the basis of these effects. The Scholastic Aptitude Test (SAT), used to predict high school students' potential for college-level work, is an example familiar to most undergraduates.

Achievement tests measure proficiency at certain tasks; that is, they measure how much people know or how well they can perform. The Wide Range Achievement Test (WRAT-3) is a well-known example (Wilkinson, 1993). Though achievement tests mea-

sure the effects of a more uniform set of learning or training experiences than do aptitude tests, many psychologists argue that intelligence, aptitude, and achievement tests
are more alike than they are different in that they all attempt to measure "developed
abilities" (Reschly, 1990). While the Wide Range Achievement Test remains the most
popular of these achievement tests, three more sophisticated alternatives have now
been developed and may find increased use by clinicians: the achievement subtests of
the Woodcock-Johnson test mentioned earlier, the Kaufman Test of Educational
Achievement (K-TEA) (Kaufman & Kaufman, 1985), and the Wechsler Individual
Achievement Test (WIAT), which was introduced in 1992. The more specific the ability or aptitude tested, the less familiar the test is likely to be (see Kramer & Conoley,
1995). If you have never heard of the Seashore Measures of Musical Talents or the
Crawford Small Parts Dexterity Test, it is probably because you have never had occasion to be tested on these very specialized abilities. Such ability testing is more often
done by personnel officers and educational, vocational, and guidance counselors than
by clinical psychologists.

Clinicians' interest in ability testing is usually related to assessment of specific
cognitive capabilities or deficits. Though clinicians may draw inferences about specific
cognitive abilities, deficits, or even brain damage from the pattern of subtest scores on
the WAIS-R or the WISC-III, they may also utilize a variety of special-purpose tests,
some of which emphasize perception and memory. For example, the Benton Visual Retention Test (Benton, 1974), the Bender Visual Motor Gestalt (or Bender-Gestalt), (Bender, 1938) and the Memory-for-Designs Test (Graham & Kendall, 1960) ask the client to
copy or draw from memory geometric figures or other designs. Other tests in this category assess the client's ability to form concepts and engage in other types of abstract
thinking. The use of tests to detect brain damage or deterioration is known as neuropsychological assessment and is described in more detail in Chapter 12.

TESTS OF ATTITUDES, INTERESTS, PREFERENCES, AND VALUES

Clinical psychologists often find it useful to assess a person's attitudes, interests, preferences, and values. For example, before beginning to work with a distressed couple, the
clinician may wish to get some idea about each spouse's attitudes about marriage. Similarly, it may be instructive for the clinician to know that the interests of a client who
is in severe conflict about entering the medical profession are utterly unlike those of
successful physicians. Finally, assessment of attitudes, interests, preferences, and values
can encourage clients to engage in their own self-exploration with respect to career
decisions (Holland, 1996). We do not have room to describe all the many tests available
to assess these dimensions (see Anastasi & Urbina, 1997 for a review), but some of
the more commonly used tests in this category include the Strong-Campbell Interest
Inventory (Hansen & Campbell, 1985), the Kuder Occupational Interest Survey
(Zytowski, 1985), the Career Assessment Inventory (Johansson, 1982), the Self-
Directed Search (Holland, 1994), and the Career Attitudes and Strategies Inventory
(Holland & Gottfredson, 1994). These are paper-and-pencil tests designed to assess
clients' preferences for various pursuits, occupations, academic subjects, recreational

activities, and people. Many of these tests result in an interest profile that can be compared with composite profiles gathered from members of occupational groups such as biologists, engineers, army officers, carpenters, police, ministers, accountants, salespeople, lawyers, etc. The Self-Directed Search is notable for attempting to predict job satisfaction, stability, and productivity by looking at how well clients' scores on six personality-related dimensions (realistic, investigative, artistic, social, enterprising, and conventional) match up with the demands and opportunities associated with various job environments (Gottfredson & Holland, 1989; Holland, 1996).

Generalized life orientations can be assessed via the Allport-Vernon-Lindzey Study of Values (Allport, Vernon, & Lindzey, 1970), a paper-and-pencil test that asks the client to choose among alternatives about things like use of leisure time, interest in various news items, and the importance of various activities. The resulting profile of values shows the relative strength of six basic interests: theoretical ("intellectual"), economic, aesthetic, social, political, and religious. More phenomenologically oriented general value assessments include the Purpose-in-Life Test (Crumbaugh, 1968) and the Personal Orientation Inventory (Knapp, 1976; Shostrom, 1968).

There are many tests designed to assess more specific interests and preferences (Hansen, 1984). For example, the behavioral model of clinical psychology has generated several tests aimed at illuminating client preferences and attitudes as a prelude to treatment. Among the most prominent of these is the Reinforcement Survey Schedule (Cautela & Kastenbaum, 1967), a list of situations and activities that the client rates in terms of their desirability. The Pleasant Events Schedule (MacPhillamy & Lewinsohn, 1976) provides an example of a behaviorally oriented preference assessment.

PERSONALITY TESTS

People's attitudes, interests, preferences, and values can be seen as one aspect of their personalities, but the tests described in the previous section are not meant to be personality tests. In this section, we consider prominent examples of psychological tests that *have* been designed specifically to assess various aspects of personality.

Personality can be defined as the pattern of behavioral and psychological characteristics by which a person can be compared and contrasted with other people. When studying personality, then, clinicians seek ways to describe and understand consistencies and inconsistencies in a given person, and also how people in general tend to resemble and differ from one another. Guided by their theoretical approaches, some clinicians see personality as an organized collection of traits, while others see it in terms of dynamic relationships among intrapsychic forces, recurring patterns of learned behavior, or perceptions of the world. This theory-driven variation in how clinicians think about personality is reflected in a wide range of methods through which they have attempted to assess it. Indeed, more psychological tests are devoted to personality assessment than to any other clinical target.

There are two major types of personality tests: *objective* and *projective*. Objective tests present relatively clear, specific stimuli such as questions ("Have you ever wanted to run away from home?"), statements ("I am never depressed.") or concepts ("Myself" or "Large dogs") to which the client responds with direct answers, choices, or ratings. Most objective personality tests are of the paper-and-pencil variety and can be scored arithmetically, often by computers, much like the multiple-choice or true-false tests used in many college classes. Some objective tests focus on one aspect of personality such as anxiety, dependency, or ego strength, while others provide a comprehensive overview of many personality dimensions.

Projective tests grew out of the psychodynamic approach to clinical psychology, especially from the idea that people use unconscious defense mechanisms to protect themselves from anxiety or guilt arising from unacceptable impulses and wishes. Broadening Freud's notion that people "project," or attribute to others, the unacceptable aspects of their own personality, it was suggested that there is a "tendency of people to be influenced in the cognitive mediation of perceptual inputs by their needs, interests, and overall psychological organization" (Frank, 1939, quoted in Exner, 1976, p. 61). In other words, the *projective hypothesis* states that each individual's personality will determine, in part at least, the way she or he interprets things. Tests that encourage clients to display this tendency are called "projective methods" (Frank, 1939). Clients taking these tests are usually asked to respond to ambiguous or unstructured stimuli (such as inkblots, drawings, or incomplete sentences), and their responses are interpreted as a reflection of both conscious and unconscious aspects of their personality structure and dynamics.

Objective Personality Tests

The first objective personality test developed by a psychologist was the Personal Data Sheet used during World War I to screen soldiers with psychological problems (Woodworth, 1920). It asked for yes or no answers to questions such as "Did you have a happy childhood?" "Does it make you uneasy to cross a bridge?" These items were selected because they reflected problems and symptoms reported at least twice as often by previously diagnosed "neurotics" as by "normals." No item was retained in the test if more than 25% of a normal sample answered it in an unfavorable manner. Item selection procedures such as these were a prelude to later, more sophisticated empirical test construction procedures (Butcher & Keller, 1984).

The MMPI.   Among the hundreds of objective personality measures that have appeared since the Personal Data Sheet, the most influential and widely used is the Minnesota Multiphasic Personality Inventory (MMPI). This test was developed during the late 1930s at the University of Minnesota by Starke Hathaway (a psychologist) and J. C. McKinley (a psychiatrist) as an aid to psychiatric diagnosis of clinical patients. The MMPI was one of the first personality tests to be constructed empirically. Hathaway and McKinley took about 1,000 items from older personality tests and other sources and converted them into statements to which clients could respond "true," "false," or "cannot say." More than half of these items were then presented to thousands of normal people as well as to people already diagnosed with psychiatric disorders.

Certain response patterns appeared. When compared to normals, members of various diagnostic groups showed statistically different responses to many items. For example, a particular group of items tended to be answered in the same way by depressed persons, while another group of items was answered in a particular way by persons diagnosed as schizophrenic. Eight of these item groups, or *scales*, were identified as discriminating between normal and abnormal individuals and as being associated with a certain diagnostic category. Later, two additional scales were identified as being responded to differently by males and females and by shy, introverted college students. Thus, there are 10 *clinical scales* on the MMPI; their titles and a sample item[2] from each are presented in Table 5.3.

Also included in the MMPI are four *validity scales*. These are groups of items designed to help detect various test-taking attitudes or response distortions. The *cannot say*, or *?*, scale is the number of items that the respondent does not answer. An elevated *?* scale can be attributed to reading problems, uncooperativeness, failure to understand items, or defensiveness. The *L*, or *lie*, scale consists of statements which, if answered honestly, reveal mildly negative characteristics (such as the fact that the respondent does not keep up with world news every day). The assumption behind the L scale is that clients who deny trivial negative behaviors or thoughts, will probably not be honest about more serious problems covered by other items. The *F*, or *frequency*, scale contains items rarely endorsed by normal people, but which are not associated with any particular diagnosed group. A high F score is interpreted as indicating carelessness in responding, a purposeful attempt to exaggerate symptoms, a very severe disorder, or some related factor. The *K*, or *correction*, scale is designed to detect a client's tendency to be overly defensive or overly disclosing about problems. A high K score is taken as evidence that the client is downplaying the severity of his or her problems; a low K score suggests that problems are being overstated. In either case, the K scale is used as a guide for "correcting" scores on five of the clinical scales.

People's responses to the 567 items on the MMPI are converted into clinical and validity scale scores. Originally, scores on the clinical scales were taken literally; people with high depression or schizophrenia scores, for example, were diagnosed as depressive or schizophrenic. It soon became obvious, however, that elevation of a particular scale did not always mean that the individual belongs in the associated diagnostic category. Recognition of this problem led to the practice of calling the clinical scales by number (1 to 10) rather than by name, and also to plotting all scale scores on a graph and analyzing the resulting profile, not just the highest score.

Clinicians conduct these profile analyses by comparing a client's MMPI scores with those of other clients. This can be done *clinically* by recalling previous clients' patterns, or *statistically* by reference to books containing sample profiles and the characteristics of the people who produced them (e.g., Butcher & Williams, 1992; Dahlstrom, Lachar, & Dahlstrom, 1986; Dahlstrom, Welsh, & Dahlstrom, 1972; Graham, 1990). The MMPI can also be scored by computers using either statistical formulae or

---

[2]To avoid biasing the responses of readers who might take the MMPI at some point, only items *of the type* found on the test are presented here. The MMPI has been widely parodied in "tests" such as the "Maryland Malpractice and Pandering Inventory," whose items include: "I used to tease vegetables" and "The sight of blood no longer excites me."

TABLE 5.3   MMPI Scales and Simulated Items

Validity (or Test-Taking Attitude) Scales

? (Cannot Say) Number of items left unanswered.

L (Lie) Fifteen items of overly good self-report, such as "I smile at everyone I meet." (answered True)

F (Frequency or Infrequency) Sixty items answered in the scored direction by 10% or less of normals, such as "There is an international plot against me." (True)

K (Correction) Thirty items reflecting defensiveness in admitting to problems, such as "I feel bad when others criticize me." (False)

Clinical Scales

1 or **Hs** (Hypochondriasis). Thirty-two items derived from patients showing abnormal concern with bodily functions, such as "I have chest pains several times a week." (True)

2 or **D** (Depression) Fifty-seven items derived from patients showing extreme pessimism, feelings of hopelessness, and slowing of thought and action, such as "I usually feel that life is interesting and worthwhile." (False)

3 or **Hy** (Conversion Hysteria) Sixty items from neurotic patients using physical or mental symptoms as a way of unconsciously avoiding difficult conflicts and responsibilities, such as "My heart frequently pounds so hard I can feel it." (True)

4 or **Pd** (Psychopathic Deviate) Fifty items from patients who show a repeated and flagrant disregard for social customs, an emotional shallowness, and an inability to learn from punishing experiences, such as "My activities and interests are often criticized by others." (True)

5 or **Mf** (Masculinity-Femininity) Fifty-six items from patients showing homoeroticism and items differentiating between men and woman, such as "I like to arrange flowers." (True, scored for femininity)

6 or **Pa** (Paranoia) Forty items from patients showing abnormal suspiciousness and delusions of grandeur or persecution, such as "There are evil people trying to influence my mind. (True)

7 or **Pt** (Psychasthenia) Forty-eight items based on neurotic patients showing obsessions, compulsions, abnormal fears, and guilt and indecisiveness, such as "I save nearly everything I buy, even after I have no use for it." (True)

8 or **Sc** (Schizophrenia) Seventy-eight items from patients showing bizarre or unusual thoughts or behavior, who are often withdrawn and experiencing delusions and hallucinations, such as "Things around me do not seem real" (True) and "It makes me uncomfortable to have people close to me." (True)

9 or **Ma** (Hypomania) Forty-six items from patients characterized by emotional excitement, overactivity, and flight of ideas, such as "At times I feel very 'high' or very 'low' for no apparent reason." (True)

0 or **Si** (Social Introversion) Sixty-nine items from persons showing shyness, little interest in people, and insecurity, such as "I have the time of my life at parties." (False)

SOURCE: Adapted from Norman Sundberg, *Assessment of Persons,* © 1977, p. 183. (Reprinted by permission of Prentice-Hall, Inc., Englewood Cliffs, New Jersey.)

automated clinical lore (Butcher, 1987; see Chapter 3) to match a current client's profile with those in large databases.

Though widely used (it has even been translated into American Sign Language; Brauer, 1993), the original MMPI was eventually widely criticized for its outdated and unrepresentative standardization sample, for deficiencies in its coverage of some aspects of mental disorders, for its antiquated items, and for the unreliability of some of its scales (Dahlstrom, 1992). Accordingly, an extensive revision of the MMPI began in 1982. The revision effort focused on gathering new normative data from randomly selected samples of normal adults and adolescents in seven U.S. states, as well as from several clinical populations. The 2,600 people included in the restandardization sample represented the 1980 U.S. census figures in terms of age, marital status, and ethnic group membership. Also, 154 items were evaluated for possible addition to the test. Some were reworded examples of existing items, but most were new items intended to provide better coverage of topics and problems not covered in the original item pool.

The revised test, called the *MMPI-2* (Butcher, et al., 1989) was made available for general clinical use in 1989. Among the major new developments contained in the MMPI-2, three are especially important:

1. There are fifteen new *content scales* which allow supplementary assessment of personality factors not previously measurable with the basic clinical scales (see Table 5.4).

2. Some new validity scales have been added to supplement the ?, L, F, and K scales. Two of these new scales, abbreviated VRIN and TRIN, are designed to identify people whose test responses were inconsistent or careless.

3. Scoring has been changed to equalize the clinical significance of similar scores on different scales. In the original MMPI, similar scores on different scales signified different levels of disturbance (Tellegen & Ben-Porath, 1992). In addition, the definition of a clinically significant score elevation has been lowered from 70 or higher on the MMPI to 65 or higher on the MMPI-2.

Interpretation of the MMPI-2 is similar to that of the original version, although changes in the wording and ordering of the items, along with the addition of new items, is designed to allow better assessment in areas such as substance abuse and certain personality patterns. A sample MMPI-2 profile is presented in Figure 5.1.

The MMPI-2 is probably the most popular objective personality test in clinical use today (Dahlstrom, 1992). It has spawned thousands of research reports and more than 400 related tests and scales, many of which go beyond the test's original diagnostic purposes. For example, MMPI items have been grouped into scales designed to measure such specific aspects of personality as ego strength, anxiety, dependency, dominance, social status, and prejudice. These new scales have been used in conjunction with the full MMPI-2, or as separate tests. Shortened versions of the MMPI have also been developed. Called the "Mini-Mult" or "Midi-Mult," these abbreviated editions are less comprehensive and designed for quick classification and screening purposes (Stevens & Reilly, 1980).

TABLE 5.4   The MMPI-2 Content Scales

Among the changes appearing in the MMPI-2 are 15 new content scales. The developers of these new scales began by defining clinically relevant areas of personality that were not measured specifically enough by the MMPI. They then used sequential test construction procedures to create groups of items that clinical judgment and statistical analyses suggested would tap these areas. The names and targets of these new scales are as follows:

Scale Name	Description of Content
Anxiety	Measures symptoms of anxiety, including tension, physical complaints, sleep problems, worry, and/or concentration.
Fears	Assesses the presence of many specific fears such as fear of the dark, fire, leaving home, etc.
Obsessiveness	High scores on this scale indicate people who have trouble making decisions and ruminate excessively. They may also show some compulsive behaviors.
Depression	Measures symptoms of depression including sad mood, hopelessness, suicidal concerns, and despair.
Health Concerns	Measures frequent complaints about health, covering several different body systems, High scorers worry a lot about their health.
Bizarre Mentation	Persons who score high on this scale may show psychotic thinking. They may recognize that their thoughts are strange and peculiar.
Anger	Measures problems with controlling anger. High scorers on this scale report being irritable, grouchy, impatient, hotheaded, and stubborn.
Cynicism	High scorers on this scale see hidden, negative motives behind the acts of others. They are frequently distrustful of people.
Antisocial Practices	Measures a tendency toward mistrust as well as a pattern of such problem behaviors and antisocial practices as being in trouble with the law, stealing, or shoplifting.
Type A	High scorers on this scale are hard-driving, fast-moving individuals who are absorbed in their work and frequently become impatient, irritable, and annoyed.
Low Self-Esteem	Persons who score high on this scale hold low opinions of themselves. They feel that they are not liked by others and that they are not important.
Social Discomfort	Measures a tendency to be very uneasy around others and to prefer to be alone. High scorers feel shy and dislike group activities.
Family Problems	Assesses family discord. High scorers describe their families as quarrelsome, unpleasant, and lacking in love.
Work Interference	A high score on this scale indicates behaviors and attitudes likely to lead to poor work performance. The problems include low self-confidence, concentration problems, and difficulties in making decisions.
Negative Treatment	Measures the tendency to hold negative attitudes toward doctors and mental-health treatment. Persons scoring high on this scale are not comfortable discussing their problems with others.

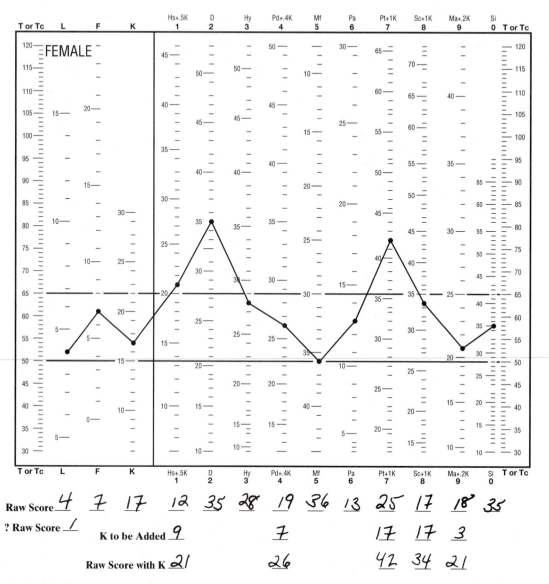

FIGURE 5.1   An MMPI-2 profile. (Minnesota Multiphasic Personality Inventory-2, Copyright © by THE REGENTS OF THE UNIVERSITY OF MINNESOTA 1942, 1943 [renewed 1970], 1989. This Profile Form 1989.)

The CPI.   The California Psychological Inventory is another prominent example of a broad-range, empirically constructed, objective personality test. It was introduced in 1957, and revised in 1987 with updated content and reworded items (Gough, 1987). In contrast to the MMPI, the CPI was developed specifically for assessing personality in the "normal" population. About half of its 462 true–false items come from the MMPI, but CPI items are grouped into more diverse and positively oriented scales including sociability, self-acceptance, responsibility, dominance, self-control, and others. There are also three validity scales that serve essentially the same purpose as those on the MMPI. The CPI's strengths include the representativeness of its standardization sample (13,000 males and females from all socioeconomic categories and all parts of the United States) and its relatively high reliability. The test has been used to predict delinquency, parole outcome, academic grades, and the likelihood of dropping out of high school (Anastasi & Urbina, 1997). Computerized scoring and interpretation services are available.

The PRF, MCMI-II, and MBTI. Other objective personality inventories that deserve mention here are the Personality Research Form (PRF), the Millon Clinical Multiaxial Inventory (MCMI-II), and the Myers-Briggs Type Indicator (MBTI). The PRF (Jackson, 1984) is one of the best examples of the sequential system approach to test construction. Its items were selected on theoretical grounds (using Henry Murray's 1938 book, *Explorations in Personality*, as a guide), combined into scales on empirical grounds, and then empirically validated against external criteria. In addition, the PRF was constructed to minimize response biases that can distort test results. It comes in five different forms, the most comprehensive of which contains 440 true–false items combined into twenty-two independent scales, and is generally used with normal rather than clinical populations (MacLennan, 1992).

The MCMI-II, a 175-item test first published in 1982 and revised five years later (Millon, 1987a), was also constructed using a combination of analytic and empirical methods. It reflects Millon's unique theory of personality (Millon, 1981) and was designed to coordinate its interpretations with the diagnostic criteria of the DSM (Craig, 1993).

The Myers-Briggs Type Indicator (Myers & Briggs, 1943), an analytically derived test based on Jung's personality-type classification system, has become quite popular in nonclinical settings for describing and matching people who work or live together (Bayne, 1995).

Objective Tests Based on Factor Analysis. For much of the 20th century, psychologists have tried to determine the minimum number of traits or characteristics necessary for an adequate description of human personality. One approach to this problem has been to examine how much different traits overlap with one another. *Factor analysis* is a mathematical procedure that helps reduce the complexity of many different traits by grouping them into clusters or factors based on the pattern of correlations between the different traits.

For example, Raymond B. Cattell used factor analysis to identify sixteen basic factors in personality, and created the Sixteen Personality Factors Questionnaire, or 16PF, to measure them in particular individuals (Cattell, Eber, & Tatsuoka, 1970, 1992). Hans Eysenck's factor-analytic methods led him to three basic personality factors—Psychoticism, Introversion-Extraversion, and Emotionality-Stability—and to develop the Eysenck Personality Questionnaire (Eysenck & Eysenck, 1975) to measure them. Factor-analytic methods also guided Auge Tellegen (1982) in the development of the

Multidimensional Personality Questionnaire (MPQ), a 300-item personality inventory that measures three factors called Positive Emotionality, Negative Emotionality, and Constraint.

Many factor analyses have resulted in a five-factor system for describing and assessing personality. These "big five" factors include (1) *neuroticism* (a tendency to feel anxious, angry, and depressed in many situations), (2) *extraversion* (a tendency to be assertive, active, and to prefer to be with other people), (3) *openness* (a quality indicating active imagination, curiosity, and receptiveness to many experiences), (4) *agreeableness* (an orientation toward positive, sympathetic, helpful interactions with others), and (5) *conscientiousness* (a tendency to be reliable and persistent in pursuing goals). The NEO Personality Inventory (NEO-PI; Costa & McCrae, 1985) was designed to assess these five factors (NEO refers to Neuroticism, Extraversion, and Openness). Its latest revision, called the NEO-PI-R (Costa & McCrae, 1992a) consists of 243 items that measure the "big five" dimensions as well as six specific facets of each (see Table 5.5). The NEO-PI-R was developed as a comprehensive measure of normal adult personality, but its authors suggest that it can also be used to diagnose psychological disorders, predict progress in psychotherapy, and select optimal forms of treatment for some clients (Costa & McCrae, 1992b). This suggestion has been challenged by clinicians who are not convinced that instruments like the NEO-PI-R add any clinically useful information beyond that provided by tests like the MMPI-2 (Ben-Porath & Waller, 1992).

Behavioral Tests. In accordance with their view of personality as a pattern of learned behavior, proponents of the behavioral approach to clinical psychology have

TABLE 5.5   Facets of Major Personality Dimensions Measured by the NEO-PI-R

Extraversion	Neuroticism	Conscientiousness
Warmth	Anxiety	Competence
Gregariousness	Angry Hostility	Order
Assertiveness	Depression	Dutifulness
Activity	Self-Consciousness	Achievement Striving
Excitement Seeking	Impulsiveness	Self-Discipline
Positive Emotions	Vulnerability	Deliberation

Openness to Experience	Agreeableness	
Fantasy	Trust	
Aesthetics	Straightforwardness	
Feelings	Altruism	
Actions	Compliance	
Ideas	Modesty	
Values	Tendermindedness	

SOURCE: Based on Costa and McCrae (1992a).

constructed objective tests which, unlike those described so far, gather *behavior samples* from which only minimal inferences are drawn. These tests tend to be short and analytically constructed.

One of the earliest and most frequently employed behavioral "personality tests" is the Fear Survey Schedule (FSS). It is simply a list of objects, persons, and situations that the client rates in terms of fearsomeness (see Table 5.6). Differing versions of this test contain from 50 to 122 items and use 1-to-5 or 1-to-7 scales for the fear ratings (e.g., Geer, 1965; Lawlis, 1971; Wolpe & Lang, 1969). The current version, FSS-III, is used to assess the prevalence of various fears in the general population, to identify persons with specific fears, and to measure progress in fear-reduction treatment. The FSS-III has been translated into several languages (Abdel, 1994; Johnsen & Hugdahl, 1990) and there are special written and illustrated versions available for use with normal and retarded children (Fleisig, 1993; Gullone & King, 1992; Ramirez & Kratchowill, 1990).

Other behavioral tests of anxiety include the State-Trait Anxiety Inventory (Spielberger et al, 1983), the Social Avoidance and Distress Scale (Watson & Friend, 1969), the Social Phobia and Anxiety Inventory (SPAI) (Turner et al., 1989), and the PTSD Symptom Scale—Self-Report (PSS-SR) (Foa et al., 1993). Behaviorally oriented clinicians have also developed tests that assess other clinical targets (Ciminero, Calhoun, & Adams, 1986; Mash and Terdal, 1988). These tests include the Beck Depression Inventory (Beck et al., 1961), the Multiple Affect Adjective Checklist (Zuckerman & Lubin, 1965), the Bulimia Test-Revised (BULIT-R) (Thelen et al., 1991), the Expanded Attributional Style Questionnaire (Peterson & Villanova, 1988), and The Maudsley Obsessional-Compulsive Inventory (Hodgson & Rachman, 1977).

Projective Personality Tests

Projective assessment goes back to the 1400s, when Leonardo da Vinci is said to have selected his pupils partly on the basis of the creativity they displayed while attempting to find shapes and patterns in ambiguous forms (Piotrowski, 1972). In the late 1800s Binet adapted a parlor game called "Blotto" to assess "passive imagination" by asking

TABLE 5.6   Sample Items From a Fear Survey Schedule

1. Snakes	6. Arguing with parents	11. Being alone
2. Death of a loved one	7. Hypodermic needles	12. Heights
3. Seeing a fight	8. Swimming alone	13. Closed places
4. Being a passenger in a car	9. Making mistakes	14. Cemeteries
5. Failing a test	10. Strange dogs	15. Roller coasters

On Fear Survey Schedules, persons are asked to rate how much fear they feel in response to items like those above on a 1-to-5 or 1-to-7 scale.

Source: Geer, 1965.

children to tell what they saw in inkblots (Exner, 1976). Sir Frances Galton constructed a word association test in 1879, and Carl Jung was using a similar test for clinical assessment by 1910. These informal projective techniques evolved into projective *tests* when their content was standardized such that each client was exposed to the same stimuli in the same way.

Most projective tests can be characterized as follows (Lindzey, 1961):

1. They are designed to be sensitive to unconscious personality dimensions.[3]
2. They permit clients a broad range of responses.
3. They are designed to measure many different aspects of personality.
4. They leave clients unaware, or at least unsure, of the specific meaning of their responses. [This can be helpful when clients might be upset by direct questions about sensitive material; Babiker, (1993).]
5. They generate a large amount of complex assessment data.
6. They employ relatively ambiguous stimuli.
7. They can be interpreted to provide an integrated picture of the client's personality as a whole.
8. They are capable of evoking fantasy material from the client.
9. They have no right or wrong answers.

We have space here to consider only a few of the most prominent projective personality tests, but much more detailed coverage of the full range of such tests is available in standard references (e.g., Exner, 1993; Kramer & Conoley, 1995; Sundberg, 1977).

The Rorschach Inkblot Test.   One of the most widely known and frequently employed projective tests of personality is the *Rorschach Inkblot Test*, a set of ten colored and black-and-white inkblots created by Swiss psychiatrist Hermann Rorschach between 1911 and 1921. At that time, many researchers in Europe and North America already employed inkblots to assess fantasy, imagination, and perception, but it was Rorschach who first attempted to use such stimuli for diagnosis and personality assessment.

Rorschach began with geometric figures cut from colored paper and later switched to inkblots, partly as a result of having read about an inkblot test of fantasy developed by a Polish medical student named Hens. The book in which Rorschach described his test and its interpretation was rejected by seven publishers; an eighth agreed to print it only if he would cut five of his original fifteen inkblots. When the book finally appeared (Rorschach, 1921), the few copies sold were not well received.

---

[3]It has been suggested that objective intelligence tests, too, can provide projective clues to personality: "The best answer to the question, 'why does the state require people to get a license in order to get married?' is that it is for purposes of record keeping. However, if a subject says, 'To prevent the scourge of VD from being inflicted on unsuspecting women,' then the answer . . . conveys something about the peculiar interests of the respondent." (Exner, 1976, pp. 66–67).

European test experts such as William Stern "denounced it as faulty, arbitrary, artificial, and incapable . . . of understanding human personality. . . ." (Reisman, 1976).

The Rorschach would have had an early demise if David Levy, an American psychiatrist studying in Switzerland in 1921, had not brought a copy of the test back to the United States and, in 1927, instructed a psychology trainee named Samuel Beck in its use. Beck published the first North American report involving the Rorschach, and, in 1937, he provided a standardized procedure for administering and scoring the test. Another scoring manual appeared that same year (Klopfer & Kelley, 1937), and the Rorschach was on its way to popularity among North American psychologists who, until then, had no global test of personality available to them. The growing clinical use of the test was paralleled by an explosion of research on its reliability, validity, scoring, and interpretation.

The test itself is simple. The client is shown ten cards, one at a time. Each presents an inkblot similar to that shown in Figure 5.2 and the client is asked what she or he sees or what the blot could be. The tester records all responses verbatim and takes notes about response times, how the card was held (e.g., upside down, sideways) as responses occurred, noticeable emotional reactions, and other behaviors. Next, the tester conducts an *inquiry* or systematic questioning of the client about the characteristics of each blot that prompted the responses.

Initial reactions to the blots and the comments made during the inquiry are then coded, using a special scoring system. Scoring involves the location, determinants, content, and popularity of the responses. *Location* refers to the area of the blot to which the client responds: the whole blot, a common detail, an unusual detail, white space, or some combination of these are location responses. The *determinants* of the

FIGURE 5.2 Inkblot similar to those used in the Rorschach. (From Norman D. Sundberg. *Assessment of Persons,* © 1977, p. 207. Reprinted by permission of Prentice-Hall, Inc., Englewood Cliffs, New Jersey.)

response refer to the characteristic of the blot that influenced a response; they include form, color, shading, and "movement." While there is no movement in the blot itself, the respondent's perception of the blot as a moving object is scored in this category. *Content* refers to the subject matter perceived in the blot. Content might include human figures, parts of human figures, animal figures, animal details, anatomical features, inanimate objects, art, clothing, clouds, blood, X-rays, sexual objects, and symbols. *Popularity* is scored on the basis of how often various responses have been made by previous respondents.

Assume that a client responded to Figure 5.2 by saying, "It looks like a bat" and during subsequent inquiry noted that "I saw the whole blot as a bat because it is black and is just sort of bat shaped." Using one of the available scoring systems, these responses would probably be coded as "WFC′ + AP," where W indicates that the whole blot was used (location); F means that the blot's form (F) was the main determinant of the response; and C′ means that achromatic color was also involved. The + shows that the form described corresponded well to the actual form of the blot; A means that there was animal content in the response; and P indicates that "bat" is a popular response to this particular card.

The fact that responses could be coded somewhat differently by different scoring systems, and that each system tends to be used somewhat differently by individual clinicians, led John Exner (1974, 1993) to propose what he called a Comprehensive System for scoring and interpreting the Rorschach via seven coding categories. Though now quite popular, the Comprehensive System has not eliminated variance in coding Rorschach responses (Wood, Nezworski, & Stejskal, 1996). Nor has it eliminated clinician subjectivity in drawing inferences about Rorschach results. Those inferences can be based on normative data about the popularity of particular responses, and even on computer-based systems for interpreting clinician-coded responses (Cohen, Swerdlik, & Smith, 1992; Fowler, 1985), but for the most part, clinicians tend to rely on subjective judgments based on their personal experience with the test and on general interpretive guidelines. For example:

> Using the whole blot suggests integration and organization; many small details indicate compulsiveness and over-control, and the use of white space suggests oppositional and negativistic tendencies. The presence of much poor form, uncommon responses, and confused thinking suggests a psychotic condition. Responsiveness to color is supposed to represent emotionality, and in the absence of good form, it suggests uncontrolled emotions and impulsivity. Responses mentioning human movement indicate imagination, intelligence, and a vivid inner life.... Content also has much potential for interpretation.... Knives, guns, mutilated bodies, and angry interactions suggest strong hostility. (Sundberg, 1977, p. 208)

Using the Comprehensive System, the clinician also looks for recurring patterns of responses across cards, and certain test statistics contained in a "structural summary" are interpreted. The overall number of responses (called *productivity*), the frequency of responses in certain categories, and more than twenty response percentages, ratios, and relationships between and among categories are seen as significant (Exner, 1993).

For example, because most people tend to use form more often than color in determining their responses, a high proportion of color-dominated determinants may be taken as evidence of weak emotional control. The client's overt behavior while responding to Rorschach cards is also interpreted by the clinician. Evidence of tension, enjoyment, or confusion; attempts to impress the examiner; and other behavioral cues are an important part of Rorschach interpretation (e.g., Goldfried, Stricker, & Weiner, 1971).

There are a number of variants on the Rorschach, the most notable of which are mainly new sets of blots. With the possible exception of the Holtzman Inkblot Test (Holtzman et al, 1961), none of these procedures has approached the popularity of the Rorschach.

The Thematic Apperception Test. The Thematic Apperception Test (TAT) consists of thirty drawings of people, objects, and landscapes (see Figure 5.3). In most clinical applications, about ten of these cards (one of them blank) are administered; the subset chosen is determined by the client's age and sex and by the clinician's interests. A separate set of cards depicting African-Americans is also available. The examiner shows each picture and asks the client to make up a story about it, including what led up to the scene, what is now happening, and what is going to happen. The client is encouraged to say what the people in the drawings are thinking and feeling. For the blank card, the respondent is asked to imagine a drawing, describe it, and then construct a story about it. The TAT was designed in 1935 by Christiana D. Morgan and Henry Murray at the Harvard Psychological Clinic (Murray, 1938, 1943). It was based on the projective hypothesis and the assumption that, in telling a story, the client's needs and conflicts will be reflected in one of the story's characters (Lindzey, 1952).

Analysis of the TAT can focus upon both the *content* and the *structure* of TAT stories. Content refers to *what* clients describe: the people, the feelings, the events, the outcomes. Structure refers to *how* clients tell their stories: their logic, organization, and use of language, the appearance of speech dysfluencies, the misunderstanding of instructions or stimuli in the drawings, and obvious emotional arousal. The original interpretive scheme (Morgan & Murray, 1935) takes a "hero-oriented" approach in which responses are seen as reflecting the *needs* (e.g., for achievement, aggression, affiliation) and *presses* (perceived environmental influences such as criticism, affection, or physical danger) associated with the story's main character (with whom the client often identifies). The frequency and intensity of each need and press are scored on a 1-to-5 scale, and the themes and outcomes of each story are noted as well.

As with the Rorschach, however, there is more than one way to score and interpret clients' TAT responses. In fact, there are at least twenty systems available (Harrison, 1965). Those that use elaborate quantitative procedures for scoring TAT stories helped create TAT response norms to which clinicians can compare their clients' responses (Vane, 1981). Others make little use of formal scoring procedures (Henry, 1956), while still others combine preliminary quantitative analysis with subjective interpretation of the resulting numbers (Bellak, 1986).

Most clinicians seem to prefer TAT scoring systems that are relatively unstructured. As with the Rorschach, they tend to employ TAT response norms and formal scoring criteria only as general guides as they develop an idiosyncratic combination of

FIGURE 5.3 Drawing of the type included in the TAT. (Reprinted by permission of the publisher from Henry A. Murray, *Thematic Apperception Test,* Cambridge, MA: Harvard University Press, copyright © 1943 by the president and fellows of Harvard College, © 1971 by Henry A. Murray.)

principles derived from psychodynamic theory and their own clinical experience (Sundberg, 1977). This tendency is illustrated by a TAT user's working notes about the following story told by a twenty-five-year-old single man in response to a TAT card showing a young boy looking at a violin resting on a table in front of him:

This child is sick in bed. He has been given sheet music to study, but instead of the music, he has come across a novel that interests him more than the music. It is probably an adventure story. He evidently does not fear the chance that his parents will find him thusly occupied as he seems quite at ease. He seems to be quite a studious type and perhaps regrets missing school, but he seems quite occupied with the adventure in the story. Adventure has something to do with ocean or water. He is not too happy, though not too sad. His eyes are somewhat blank—coincidence of reading a book without any eyes or knowing what is in the book without reading it. He disregards the music and falls asleep reading the book.

Here are some of the clinician's notes: "On the basis of this story alone, I feel certain that there is a schizophrenic process present, even though not necessarily a pure schizophrenia. Slightly pretentious, facade tone, helped along with basic fact of perverse refusal to acknowledge presence of violin, strongly suggests that he *does* see violin but consciously thinks that he's being 'clever' or 'original,' or is out-tricking the examiner (whom he might see as trying to trick him) by ignoring it or seeing it as a book. That he is aware of it on some level is suggested by the fact that the basic theme, p Parental Imposed Task →n Auto Resis, passive Aggression, comes through. Consistent also is statement at the end: he *disregards* the music. Not a psychopath trying to act smart—too schizzy.

"*Sick in bed as a child* may be an autobiographical theme. He's almost certainly 'sick' (that is, psychotic) now, and so that may be enough explanation for it. But most psychotics don't [see the card this way]; therefore it becomes plausible that he may have had long illnesses as a child, cutting him off from other kids, and → to fantasy escape—dreams of travel and adventure. Sentence 3 may also describe his overt behavior: nonchalant, seemingly 'at ease,' really frightened underneath. Above are almost all hypotheses, to be confirmed or excluded by later stories. *Strong passivity* throughout—especially in outcome. Also suggestion of *flight* and *avoidance* of very passive sort—drastic enough to include denial of threatening aspects of reality. *Nothing holds* his interest long—not even adventure novel. Hero soon withdraws into his *own* fantasy, to conviction of knowing what's in book without reading it even though 'took a chance' to read it, and finally withdraws into sleep" (Holt, 1978, pp. 166–167).

Other projective tests similar to the TAT include the Rosenzweig Picture-Frustration Study (Rosenzweig, 1949), which presents twenty-four cartoons showing one person frustrating another in some way (e.g., "I'm not going to invite you to my party."). The client's task is to say what the frustrated person's response would be. The cards of the Children's Apperception Test (CAT) (Bellak, 1992) depict animal characters rather than human beings; those of the Roberts Apperception Test for Children (RATC) (McArthur & Roberts, 1982) show children interacting with adults and other children. Scores on several RATC scales are derived by comparing children's responses to norms collected on 200 well-adjusted children.

Incomplete Sentence Tests. As their name implies, these tests ask clients to complete incomplete sentences. The projective assumption is that how the client finishes the sentences reflect important personality characteristics. Originally used as a measure of intellect in the nineteenth century (Reisman, 1976), incomplete sentences began to be widely employed as projective stimuli in the 1940s; they are now the most frequently used of all projective tests (Watkins et al., 1995).

The most popular version of sentence completion tests is the Rotter Incomplete Sentences Blank (Rotter & Rafferty, 1950). It contains forty sentence stems such as "I like … ," "My father … ," "I secretly … " The client's response to each stem is compared to norms provided in the test manual and is then rated on a seven-point scale of adjustment–maladjustment based on how much they deviate from those norms. Finally, ratings for all the sentences are summed to provide an overall adjustment score. These relatively objective scoring procedures are primarily associated with Rotter's test and a few other research-oriented sentence-completion instruments aimed at assessing specific aspects of personality (Lanyon & Lanyon, 1980).

The Draw-a-Person Test. Another projective test whose name describes its nature is the Draw-a-Person Test, or DAP (Machover, 1949). The client's drawings of a person—and sometimes also of a family, a mother, the self, and so on—serve as the basis for the clinician's inferences about various aspects of the client's personality. These inferences are guided by projective assumptions that the inclusion, exclusion, and characteristics of each body part, along with the placement, symmetry, organization, size, and other features of the drawing, are indicative of the client's self-image, conflicts, and perceptions of the world (Machover, 1949; see Figure 5.4).

Other projective drawing tests include the House-Tree-Person Test (HTP), which asks clients to draw each of those objects and then discuss them in an extended inter-

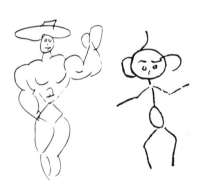

Beneath the obvious attempts at an impressive figure of masculine prowess, there are more subtle trends of the opposite: of inadequacy and inconsequentiality. The muscles of the drawn figure have been inflated beyond the hard and sinewy, into a puffy softness as if it is a figure made of balloons; the legs taper down to insubstantiality and, finally, absent feet, and an incongruous hat is placed on the boxer making comical his lifting of one gloved hand in victory. . . On the one hand, emblematic of his defenses, his drawn achromatic person is the "twenty-year-old" boxer with muscles flexed and a weight-lifter's build. Beside this inflated image, however, on the crayon drawing of a person—which, due to the impact of color, tends to tap the relatively deeper levels of personality (Hammer, 1958)–he offers now only a "six-year-old boy" who then looks even more like an infant than a child: with one curlicue hair sticking up and the suggestion of diapers on (. . . shown here in black and white). The ears are rather ludicrous in their standing away from the head and, all in all, the total projection in this drawing is that of an infantile, laughable entity, rather than the impressive he-man he overstated on the achromatic version of a person. Beneath his attempts to demonstrate rugged masculinity (which may have culminated into the offense with which he is charged), the patient experiences himself as actuallly a little child, dependent and needing care, protection, and affection.

FIGURE 5.4 Interpretaton of a DAP drawing. This drawing was made by an eighteen-year-old male who had been caught stealing a television set. (Reprinted from Emanuel Hammer, "Projective Drawing," in A. I. Rabin, ed., *Projective Techniques in Personality Assessment*, pp. 375–376. opyright © 1968 by Springer Publishing Company, Inc., New York. Used by permission.)

view (Buck, 1948), and the Bender-Gestalt Test. The latter is a figure-copying test described earlier as measuring certain aspects of mental ability, but some clinicians see errors and distortions in the copied figures as indicators of a client's personality.

THE STATUS OF TESTING IN CLINICAL PSYCHOLOGY

Although new psychological tests are introduced every year (see Anastasi & Urbina, 1997; Kramer & Conoley, 1995; Goldstein & Hersen, 1990; and the *Journal of Personality Assessment*), clinicians tend to use those with which they are most familiar. For this reason, even though test usage differs across clinical settings (counseling centers versus VA hospitals, for example) (Lubin, et al., 1985), overall preferences for psychological tests—in North America and elsewhere—have remained surprisingly stable over the past fifty years. As shown in Table 5.7, the most popular tests are "the old reliables": the

TABLE 5.7   Testing's Top Ten

Test	Sundberg (1961)[a]	Lubin, Wallis, & Paine (1971)[b]	Lubin, Larsen, & Matarazzo (1984)[c]	Sweeney, Clarkin, & Fitzgibbon (1987)[d]	Watkins et al. (1995)[e]
WAIS	6	1	1	4[f]	1
MMPI	7.5	6	2	2	2
Bender-Gestalt Visual Motor Test	4	3.5	3	5	6
Rorschach	1	2	4	1	5
TAT	2.5	3.5	5	3	4
WISC	10	7	6	4[f]	9
Peabody Picture Vocabulary Test	—	13	7.5	—	12
Sentence Completion Tests (All Kinds)	13.5	8.5	7.5	7	3
House-Tree-Person Test	12	9	9	6	7
Draw-A-Person Test	2.5	5	10	6	7

[a]Ranking of 185 respondents mentioning some use of test.
[b]Ranking of 251 respondents mentioning some use of test.
[c]Ranking of 221 respondents mentioning some use of test.
[d]Ranking of 107 Directors of Association of Psychology Internship Centers.
[e]Ranking of 410 to 412 respondents mentioning some use of test.
[f]Reported for WAIS and WISC combined.

MMPI, the Wechsler Scales, the Rorschach, and the TAT (Borum & Grisso, 1995; Chan & Lee, 1995; Piotrowski & Keller, 1992; Sharpley & Pain, 1988; Watkins et al., 1995).

In contrast, the role of *testing* as an activity in clinical psychology has undergone large shifts in popularity. Beginning in the 1930s and continuing through the mid-1960s, tests were touted as semi-magical pathways to the "truth" about intelligence, personality, and ability (Reisman, 1976). During those years, clinical psychology students were trained intensively in the use of tests. One prominent clinician noted that "it is hard to conceive . . . of anyone in the field of clinical psychology reaching the postdoctoral level without being thoroughly well-versed in the Rorschach" (Harrower, 1965, p. 398).

From the late 1960s through the 1970s, however, testing lost much of its appeal and was deemphasized as a training goal and professional activity for clinicians. The decline of testing during this time was brought about by several factors. For one thing, as behavioral approaches gained influence in clinical psychology, there was a corresponding shift away from traditional diagnostic assessment, including the tests used for that purpose. Further, many clinicians did not like the "tester" role, which they saw as subservient to psychiatry and potentially damaging to relationships with clients. Finally, clinical psychologists, the public, the government, and clients were becoming increasingly critical of the whole testing enterprise. These concerns stemmed from (1) unflattering results from research on the reliability and validity of many tests; (2) awareness of the susceptibility of tests to various biases; (3) recognition that tests, particularly those assessing intelligence, may place members of certain minority groups at a disadvantage; (4) fear that the testing process may invade respondents' privacy; and (5) worry that tests are too easily misused or misinterpreted.

Psychometric Properties of Tests

A fundamental criticism of psychological tests has been that they do not do their job very well; that is, they are unreliable, invalid, or both. While it is unfair to say that this is true about all tests under all circumstances, research on their psychometric properties has often been unfavorable. This research is too voluminous to be described on a test-by-test basis, but can be summarized as follows.

Reliability.   In general, the reliability of psychological tests tends to be adequate, but not uniformly so. Test–retest reliability coefficients for the MMPI and MMPI-2 scales range from .60 to .90, for example (Pope, Butcher, & Seelen, 1993). Parallel form, test–retest, and split-half reliabilities are commonly .80 to .96 for major intelligence tests. Similarly, aptitude and ability tests such as the GRE, the Miller Analogies Test (MAT), the Medical College Admission Test (MCAT), and the Law School Admission Test (LSAT) display reliability coefficients ranging from .71 to .97. Tests of interests and values have produced reliabilities from the .70s to the low .90s.

Determining the reliability of projective tests is more problematic because split-half, parallel form, and test–retest coefficients often do not make sense with such instruments (see Atkinson, 1981). This is partly because, compared to the true–false choices or ratings flowing from objective tests, projective test responses are more difficult to translate into numerical scores. Further, the scoring of projective tests has traditionally been far more subjective than for objective tests. Guidelines came from experts, who, after administering hundreds of projective tests, summarized their experience into numerous rules of thumb for scoring and interpreting various responses. Low interrater reliabilities for the Rorschach, the TAT, and other projective tests were common (Anastasi & Urbina, 1997; Vane, 1981), but did they reflect unreliable tests or inconsistent scoring methods? To help answer this question, clinicians developed more objective scoring systems for some of the most popular projective tests, such as the Rorschach (Exner, 1986, 1993).

Projective test advocates now point to the relatively high levels of agreement shown by different clinicians using similar scoring systems. Interrater and intrarater reliability coefficients for the Rorschach, for example, have been found to average above .80 (Exner, 1996; Parker, Hanson, & Hunsley, 1988). While these figures are comparable to those for the WAIS and MMPI, critics note that the way they are calculated gives an overestimate of the Rorschach's reliability (Wood, Nezworski, & Stejskal, 1996).

Validity. Overall, the validity of psychological tests has been less impressive than their reliability. To a certain extent, this *must* be the case because the principles of mathematics dictate that no test's validity can be higher than its reliability. Still, for most tests the size of the discrepancy between reliability and validity is too great. In general, the closer a test's content or tasks are to the content or tasks being assessed (i.e., the criterion), the higher the validity will be.

For example, aptitude and ability tests that ask respondents to provide information or perform tasks directly related to academic skills are consistently among the most valid tests available. The major intelligence tests are next in terms of relative validity. These tests, especially their verbal sections, correlate with academic performance, specific skills (such as reading and arithmetic), and teacher ratings in the .17 to .75 range. When intelligence tests are used to draw inferences about a client's psychiatric disorder or personality characteristics, however, validity has been disappointing (Boone, 1993; Williams, Voelker, & Ricciardi, 1995), just as it has when IQ tests are used to predict job performance, socioeconomic status, or other important social outcomes (Neisser et al., 1996). True, IQ scores are correlated with such measures, but not as strongly as has sometimes been claimed.

Because their content is often remote from the criteria they aim to describe or predict, personality tests have been among the less valid assessment instruments. There are several other reasons for this pattern. Faking and distortion are usually more common in personality assessment than in intelligence testing. Temporary fluctuations in emotion and other personality-relevant behavior is also likely, posing problems for reliability and validity of personality assessment. There are also many theoretical reasons for the limited validity of personality tests. For example, the criteria these tests try to describe or predict are themselves often vague, multidimensional, and variable, depending upon situational and other factors. In addition, different people may have different interpretations of the meaning of personality test items ("I enjoy people.") or response alternatives ("often" or "rarely"). Galton recognized this problem when he invented the questionnaire: "There is hardly any more difficult task than that of framing questions which are not likely to be misunderstood, which admit of easy reply, and which cover the ground of inquiry" (Galton, 1883, p. 279). Finally, the question of whether to use test responses as samples or signs is still not resolved.

Still, the validity of objective personality tests is superior to that of projective tests (Anastasi & Urbina, 1997). For example, despite a host of problems involving its outdated and limited norms, its development for a now obsolete diagnostic system, and its high intercorrelations between scales (Helmes & Reddon, 1993), the MMPI has proven to be a remarkably useful instrument for many different assessment purposes. Its predictive and concurrent validity coefficients are generally in the .30 to .50 range (Dahlstrom, Welsh, & Dahlstrom, 1975; Parker et al., 1988; Pope, Butcher, & Seelen, 1993). The validity of projective tests tends to suffer by comparison, leading most researchers to avoid using them in the study of personality. As shown in Table 5.7, however, many clinicians continue using them. Later, we discuss why this is the case.

Distortion of Test Scores

Tests are designed to collect assessment data under standard conditions. When those conditions are not standard, test scores may be distorted in ways that can mislead clinicians. A multitude of factors can alter the outcome of all types of tests. A classic example is provided by a study in which college men who had just seen photographs of nude females gave more sex-related responses to the TAT when it was administered by a young, informally dressed male graduate student than when given by a man who was older and more formal (Mussen & Scodel, 1955).

Clients' motivation can also influence their test responses. In one study, for example, mental hospital residents took a true–false psychological test after hearing either that it was an index of mental illness on which "true" responses indicated pathology or that it measured self-insight and that "true" responses were associated with readiness to leave the hospital (Braginsky, Grosse, & Ring, 1966). Scores on the "mental-illness" test were higher for those who wished to stay in the hospital than for those who wanted to leave. The "self-insight" description was associated with the opposite pattern: Patients wishing to leave scored higher than those wanting to stay. Motivational effects have also appeared on employee integrity tests (Alliger, Lillienfeld, & Mitchell 1996), IQ tests (Engleman, 1974), and objective and projective personality tests (Barrick & Mount, 1996; Stewart & Patterson, 1973).

On some tests, the structure of the items and response alternatives may influence results. Suppose a tester wants to know how parents feel about allowing their children to display aggression toward them. The tester may write an item that says "No child should be permitted to strike a parent" and ask the client to agree or disagree. In order to decide whether to agree or disagree, however, the client must mentally construct the item's opposite, such as "A child should be encouraged to strike a parent." Because each respondent is likely to construct different mental opposites the *psychological* content of the test may vary from client to client.

The circumstances under which a test is given—anything from temperature extremes and outside noise to crowding and the presence of a stranger—can also affect its results if they act as stressors (Plante, Goldfarb, & Wadley, 1993). In one case, for example, a child's scores on repeated IQ tests went from 68 to 120 and back to 79 depending on whether or not a particular adult was in the testing room (Handler, 1974). Establishing trust can thus become an important element maximizing the validity of certain kinds of tests (e.g., Grossarth, Eysenck, & Boyle, 1995).

Another source of distortion in test results is the fact that some clients tend to respond in particular ways to most items, regardless of what the items are. This tendency has been called response *set* (Cronbach, 1946), response *style* (Jackson & Messick, 1958), and response *bias* (Berg, 1955). For example, clients exhibiting a *social desirability* bias will respond to test items in ways that are most socially acceptable, whether or not those responses reflect their true feelings or impulses (Edwards, 1957; Rychtarik, Tarnowski, & St. Lawrence, 1989). Clients have also been suspected of *acquiescent* response styles (Jackson & Messick, 1961), in which they tend to agree with virtually any self-descriptive test item. Defensive, deviant, and exaggerated styles have also been postulated (e.g., Isenhart & Silversmith, 1996). The significance of response styles in determining test scores has been hotly debated, partly because it is unclear whether response tendencies represent stable client characteristics (McCrae & Costa, 1983) or temporary behaviors dictated and reinforced by the testing circumstances (Linehan & Nielsen, 1983). Whatever the case, the client's point of view while taking a test cannot be ignored when evaluating a test.

Other client variables may also be important determinants of test responses. For example, clients whose cultural background leaves them unfamiliar with the concepts and vocabulary of middle-class America may perform poorly on psychological tests whose items reflect those concepts and words (Herrnstein & Murray, 1994). The influence of one's cultural and ethnic background on intelligence test scores is of particular concern, especially to members of certain minority groups in the United States (Laosa, 1996). As noted earlier, one approach to this problem has been to develop intelligence tests that are not strongly influenced by culture-specific experiences or particular verbal skills. Unfortunately, "culture-fair" tests may be influenced just as much as, or more than, standard tests by cultural and environmental factors (Samuda, 1975), and their validity tends to be lower (Humphreys, 1988). Another approach has been to "correct" for ethnic differences in test scores by adjusting those scores on the basis of norms associated with various ethnic groups. This practice, known as *subgroup norming*, enjoys some popularity among social scientists, but it was banned by the Civil Rights Act of 1991 (Gottfredson, 1994; Sackett & Wilk, 1994).

It has been suggested that instead of trying to *remove* all cultural effects from IQ tests, we should *examine* the differential performance of various groups in order to identify those who are most in need of corrective educational programs (Krull & Pierce, 1995). As Anne Anastasi (1988) put it:

> Tests are designed to show what an individual can do at a given point in time. They cannot tell us *why* he performs as he does. To answer that question, we need to investigate his background, motivations, and other pertinent circumstances. Nor can tests tell how able a culturally or educationally disadvantaged child might have been if she had been reared in a more favorable environment. Moreover, tests cannot compensate for cultural deprivation by eliminating its effect from their scores. On the contrary, tests should reveal such effects,

so that appropriate remedial steps can be taken. To conceal the effects of cultural disadvantages by rejecting tests or by trying to devise tests that are insensitive to such effects can only retard progress toward a genuine solution of social problems. Such reactions toward tests are equivalent to breaking a thermometer because it registers a body temperature of 101°. Test scores should be used constructively: by the individual in enhancing self-understanding and personal development and in educational and vocational planning; by teachers in improving instruction and in adjusting instructional content to individual needs; and by employers in achieving a better match between persons and jobs, recognizing that persons can be trained and jobs can be redesigned. (p. 66)

Others have made a related suggestion for reducing irrelevant cultural effects: When specific predictions are desired, use instruments that sample as directly as possible the particular behaviors and skills of interest. When this is done, the opportunity for extraneous characteristics to distort performance is greatly reduced. The sources of test-score bias discussed here barely scratch the surface of the problem, which is discussed at far greater length in numerous sources (e.g., Anastasi & Urbina, 1997).

Abuse of Tests

Like all assessment procedures, tests involve entry by the clinician into the privacy of clients' thoughts and behaviors. The extent to which such entry is desirable or even legal is a matter of debate and litigation. Many observers contend that there are too many tests and too much testing. They argue that testing is irrelevant, inaccurate, and too easily misused. Overdependence on IQ scores by ill-informed test consumers and misinterpretation of personality tests by clinicians provide two examples (Anastasi, 1992; Clark & Abeles, 1994).

During the mid-1960s, the U.S. Congress conducted hearings on psychological testing, particularly as it was being used in educational and vocational selection. These inquiries were prompted in part by serious, knowledgeable test critics and also by the appearance of nonexpert books with sensational titles like *The Brain Watchers* (Gross, 1962), *The Tyranny of Testing* (Hoffman, 1962), and *They've Got Your Number* (Wernick, 1956). The concern over privacy and other issues produced restrictions on testing in certain settings (Cohen et al., 1992; Reschly, 1984). For example, personality tests have been eliminated from routine selection procedures for federal employees. IQ tests are restricted in some school systems, and the Civil Rights Act of 1991 prohibits their use in hiring decisions if they result in bias against minorities.

The American Psychological Association is sensitive to these issues and has urged its members to reduce the possibility of abuse in the testing field by adhering to its *Standards for Educational and Psychological Tests* (APA, 1985), which were recently supplemented by a *Statement on Test-Taker Rights and Responsibilities* (Roberts, 1996). In addition, the *Uniform Guidelines on Employee Selection Procedure* was developed by the Equal Employment Opportunity Commission (EEOC) to regulate the use of tests and other methods as selection techniques. These documents reflect the argument that, when developed, evaluated, administered, interpreted, and published with due regard for scientific principles and the rights and welfare of clients, psychological tests can positively contribute to society (Robertson & Eyde, 1993). More extensive discussions of the pros and cons of testing are available in a variety of sources (e.g., Anastasi & Urbina, 1997; Kaplan & Saccuzzo, 1993; Neisser et al., 1996).

Testing Today

One might anticipate that the many problems associated with testing would make clinicians wary of using tests as a source of assessment data. This does not appear to be the case, however. Testing is still an active enterprise in North America and elsewhere (Chan & Lee, 1995; Piotrowski & Keller, 1992), in spite of the fact that (1) many managed health care plans provide limited support for the pretreatment psychological testing that was once routine for clinicians, and (2) structured interviews are becoming a popular alternative diagnostic tool (see Chapter 4). Why has psychological testing remained so much a part of clinical psychology? For one thing, focusing attention on the shortcomings of tests and the testing process provided the impetus for efforts to improve both (Glaser & Bond, 1981). The fruits of these efforts began to appear by the mid-1980s, as reflected in the following five trends (Lanyon, 1984):

1. The mutual influence of behavioral and traditional testing approaches on one another improved several areas of assessment. This collaboration is best revealed in the evolution of DSM's behaviorally-based rules for making psychiatric diagnoses. Clinicians are also now less apologetic about their role in diagnostic classification because the system is more reliable than ever.

2. Assessment procedures are more specifically related to the criteria they attempt to describe or predict. Giving a broad-based personality inventory such as the MMPI and then attempting, after the fact, to make sense out of whatever correlations emerge is giving way to the use of focused tests designed on the basis of theory and prior findings to illuminate specific constructs or clinical conditions. Assessing cognitive functioning in depressed persons (Ilsley, Moffoot, & O'Carroll, 1995), information processing as a component of intelligence (Kaufman, 1990), and specific symptoms of schizophrenia (Cuesta & Peralta, 1995) are prime examples of this development.

3. Greater attention is being given to psychometrically-sound evaluation of children and adolescents. Prominent examples include the MMPI-A, a special form of the MMPI for adolescents (Butcher et al., 1992); the Personality Inventory for Children (PIC) (Wirt et al., 1984), which is completed by parents and provides clinically useful descriptions of the behavior and problems of children between ages three to sixteen (a self-report version called Personality Inventory for Youth is now available as well; Lacher & Gruber, 1993); the Millon Adolescent Personality Inventory (MAPI) (Millon, Green, & Meagher, 1982), which provides information on twenty scales particularly relevant for clients aged thirteen to nineteen; and the Child Behavior Problem Checklist (CBCL) (Achenbach & Edelbrock, 1991), a widely used and researched test, completed by parents, which compares children against norms on several different dimensions of potentially problematic behavior.

4. There is increasing interest in developing well-constructed tests for the assessment of specific clinical targets such as marital distress (Jones et al., 1995; Snyder, 1981), eating disorders (Thelen, Mintz, & Boman, 1996), and social support and coping resources (Cohen et al., 1985; Folkman & Lazarus, 1988).

5. There is more careful theorizing about the nature and structure of intelligence, mental abilities, attitudes, and personality, leading in turn to broader conceptualizations of the *construct validity* of psychological tests. As noted in Chapter 3, construct validity refers to the ability of an instrument to measure a psychological quality in ways related to a theory of the quality in question. Construct validation of a test never stops; it is a continuing process of elaborating and testing theories about what a construct actually means (Messick, 1995). An unwavering commitment to construct validation not only enhances test development, it also promotes a better understanding of fundamental psychological phenomena such as intelligence and personality.

A second reason for clinicians' continued involvement in testing is that the availability of improved tests sustains a demand for it, especially in educational, industrial, and medical settings. Clinicians' testing activities can be profitable, and the ready availability of computer-based test scoring and interpretation has made the assessment task easier and more efficient. Indeed, most clinicians' strong personal interest in at least one specific type of testing has prompted many of them to develop a testing specialty within their professional practice.

Finally, as ordinary mortals, clinical psychologists tend to form habits that are hard to break. Graduate training tends to set patterns of assessment practices to which clinical psychologists become personally attached. In other words, clinicians tend to do what they were taught to do and tend to continue doing so because it is what they have always done. Fair enough, but why don't they at least abandon tests such as the Myers-Briggs, the DAP, and the TAT, whose validity appears weakest (Boyle, 1995; Keiser & Prather, 1990; Smith & Dumont, 1995)? Part of the answer is that many clinicians pay more attention to data that supports these tests than to damaging evidence about their validity. Indeed, they may view negative research findings about a test as irrelevant to that test's *clinical* value (Masling, 1992). One observer put it this way: "Published indexes of validity . . . are but rough guides, for the psychologist must reach his own judgments of clinical validity and meaningfulness in each particular case" (Tallent, 1976, p. 14).

Indeed, certain clinicians are, for reasons not clearly understood, able to draw remarkably accurate inferences from test data. Almost every practitioner knows of at least one MMPI or Rorschach "ace" whose reputation shores up general confidence in particular tests. Most clinical psychologists are themselves reinforced for using even the least scientifically-supported tests by the fact that, now and then, they make their own insightful inferences on the basis of test data. Clinicians remain loyal to projective tests, in particular, because they believe that—regardless of what research results show—these measures offer special information about clients. They may also find them useful for building rapport with clients (especially children) and for confirming what they might already suspect about a client on the basis of other assessment data.

These cognitive and practical factors, in combination with the traditional view of clinical psychologists as test experts and the societal demand for testing services, make the continued popularity of psychological testing more comprehensible. And after all, when important decisions about people must be made, a psychological test with even modest proof of validity will usually be accepted for use because it promises at least some increase in the accuracy of those decisions. Thus, though more stringent standards and limitations regarding the use of tests in many spheres appear likely, testing will probably continue to be a major activity of clinical psychologists.

TESTING AT WORK

Q.: How and why is psychological testing important in your work?

DR. SANDY D'ANGELO: Approximately 60% of my clinical time is devoted to assessment of children. These assessments vary from interdisciplinary team evaluations of young children with developmental delay to assessments for learning disabilities and mental retardation to assessment of emotional problems. Most children can complete standardized testing with instruments such as the Wechsler Intelligence Scale for Children-III, the Bayley Scales of Infant Development, and the Woodcock-Johnson Tests of Achievement. Older children can complete self-report measures such as the Minnesota Multiphasic Personality Inventory for Adolescents.

DR. HECTOR MACHABANSKI: Psychological testing is important in my work because, as a licensed clinical psychologist and a certified school psychologist, I am frequently asked to conduct psychological evaluations. My psychological testing work typically revolves around referrals from schools, attorneys, or medical personnel.

DR. GEOFFREY THORPE: Formal psychometric testing is important in providing objective information about clients. I mainly use validated self-report instruments such as the MMPI-2 and the Millon (MCMI-III) in my forensic evaluations because these inventories provide information untainted by my own impressions and expectations. When my own independent observations converge with the MMPI-2 profile, for example, I place greater faith in the results of the assessment.

CHAPTER SUMMARY

Psychological testing is an important part of clinical assessment research and practice. A test is a systematic procedure for observing and describing behavior in a standard situation. Test responses can be used as samples, signs, or correlates in drawing inferences about clients.

Most psychological tests are designed to measure intellectual functioning; ability; attitudes, interests, preferences, and values; or personality. They are usually constructed either analytically (on the basis of what a theory says they should contain) or empirically (on the basis of research on which items tap dimensions of interest). The sequential system approach combines aspects of both methods. Regardless of how a test is constructed, it must be evaluated in terms of its reliability and validity.

Prominent tests of intellectual functioning (whose results are usually expressed as IQ scores) include the Stanford-Binet (4th edition), and the Wechsler Scales (e.g., WAIS-R, WISC-III). The Scholastic Aptitude Test (SAT) and the Wide Range Achievement Test (WRAT) exemplify general ability tests in use today; others, such as the Bender-Gestalt, test more specific abilities. Attitudes, interests, preferences, and values are typically measured through tests such as the Strong-Campbell Interest Inventory, the Self-Directed Search, the Allport-Vernon-Lindzey Study of Values, and the Reinforcement Survey Schedule. Tests of personality can be objective or projective. The Minnesota Multiphasic Personality Inventory (MMPI-2), the California Psychological Inventory (CPI), the Personality Research Form (PRF), the Sixteen Personality Factor Questionnaire (16PF), and the NEO Personality Inventory (NEO-PI) are examples of the objective type. The Rorschach, the Thematic Apperception Test (TAT), sentence completion tests, and the Draw-a-Person (DAP) test are projective instruments.

Although the tests listed above have remained very popular around the world over the past fifty years, testing itself came under heavy criticism during the 1970s because of concerns about the reliability and validity of tests, about factors that distort their results and interpretation, and about their potential for misuse. Today, the reliability of many tests, especially those of intellectual functioning, is adequate, and while the validity of many tests (particularly projective personality tests) remains marginal, the testing enterprise continues because tests can be useful and because clinical traditions and societal demands make it difficult to abandon this activity. Standards published by the APA and the federal government are designed to assure that tests are used with due regard for scientific principles and the rights and welfare of clients.

Chapter 6

Observation in Clinical Psychology

Observation of the behavior of other people is a fundamental aspect of modern clinical assessment, but it is hardly a new idea. Because there was overt behavior long before there was language, observation was probably the first source of human assessment data. In prehistoric times, for example, those who survived were surely those who learned to judge the intentions of others on the basis of their actions (e.g., an offer of food; a raised club), and the importance of observation did not diminish as language developed. In ancient Greek and Chinese civilizations, conclusions about an individual were sometimes based on physical and behavioral characteristics. In the Western world, the practice of interpreting physical features and behaviors came to be called *physiognomy* (McReynolds, 1975). Homer provides an early illustration in his *Iliad*:

> There is nothing like an ambush for bringing a man's worth to light and picking out the cowards from the brave. A coward changes color all the time; he cannot sit still for nervousness, but squats down, first on one heel, then on the other.... But the brave man never changes color at all and is not unduly perturbed from the moment when he takes his seat in ambush with the rest. (Translation by Rieu, 1950; quoted in McReynolds, 1975, p. 488)

Pythagoras, Hippocrates, Plato, Aristotle, and Galen elaborated on the relationship between overt behavior and personality characteristics. The Bible, too, contains references to assessment via behavioral observation. In order to help Gideon defeat the Midianites with the smallest possible force, God tells how to identify the most able soldiers:

> And the Lord said unto Gideon, The people are yet too many; bring them down unto the water, and I will try them for thee there.... So he brought down the people into the water; and the Lord said unto Gideon, Everyone that lappeth of the water with his tongue ... him shalt thou set by himself; likewise everyone that boweth down upon his knees to drink. And the number of them that lapped, putting their hand to their mouth, were three hundred men; but all the rest of the people bowed down upon their knees to drink water. And the Lord said unto Gideon, By the three hundred men that lapped will I save you, and deliver the Midianites into thine hand.... (Judges 7:4–7)

Obviously, the best warriors were those who remained alert to danger, even when drinking. Thus, the foundations of observational assessment, content analysis of speech, gesture and movement analysis, and research on the relationship between facial expressions and emotion were laid down centuries ago. Like the test and the interview, clinical observation is the modern form of an old tradition (Ben-Porath & Butcher, 1991).

The more importance clinicians attach to observational data, the more systematic they are likely to be in gathering and analyzing those data. At one end of the spectrum are informal, anecdotal accounts of client behaviors occurring during tests or interviews. An example of this informal observation is contained in this excerpt from a Stanford-Binet IQ test report on a twelve-year-old boy:

> John's principal difficulties were on tests requiring precise operations, as in the use of numbers. With such tests he became insecure and often seemed confused with slips of memory and errors in simple calculations. He asked to have instructions repeated, was dependent on the examiner, and easily discouraged. Although cooperative and anxious to do well, it was extremely hard for him to master a task (such as "memory span") in which he was required to be exact by fixed standards. (Jones, 1943, p. 91)

Clinicians who place greater emphasis on overt behavior improved on such casual observation methods in at least two ways. First, they developed more accurate and systematic methods for observing and quantifying behavior. Second, they demonstrated the feasibility of collecting observational data in situations beyond the testing or interview room. Together, these developments make it possible for clinicians and researchers to observe scientifically a wide range of human behavior in a multitude of settings.

In this chapter, we describe and evaluate some of the observational systems and techniques now in use. The goals of these observational assessment systems are to (1) collect information that is not available in any other way, and/or (2) supplement other data as part of a multiple-assessment approach. For example, if a teacher and a pupil give different reports of why they fail to get along ("He's a brat." "She's mean."), a less-biased picture of the relationship will probably emerge from observations by neutral parties of relevant classroom interactions. In other instances, knowing what a person can or will do is so important that only observation can suffice. Thus, knowing that a mentally disturbed person feels better and wishes to leave the hospital may be less valuable than observing that person's ability to hold a job, use the bus system, and meet other demands of everyday life.

BENEFITS AND METHODS OF OBSERVATIONAL ASSESSMENT

Collecting observational data is a difficult, time-consuming, and expensive procedure, and the problems associated with this type of assessment discourage many clinicians from attempting to do it (Foster, Bell-Dolan, & Burge, 1988). Despite these obstacles, proponents of observational assessment argue that its benefits more than outweigh its difficulties and they offer several reasons why observation is necessary if clinicians are to obtain a complete picture of their clients' functioning.

Supplementing Self-Reports

For one thing, as noted in Chapters 4 and 5, self-reports gathered via interviews and some tests may be inaccurate. It is very difficult for most people to provide objective and dispassionate reports on their own behavior, especially in relation to highly charged emotional events. It is questionable, for example, that a distressed couple can accurately and objectively describe their own behavior, especially behavior that occurs during arguments. Observational data are likely to provide much more valid information about these crucial events (Gottman & Levenson, 1992).

In some cases, clients purposely distort their self-reports, usually by offering an overly positive portrayal of their behavior. Such distortions are particularly common in the self-reports of participants in smoking, drug, or alcohol treatment programs, which is the main reason why such reports are often supplemented by family members' observations or by biological measures that can detect target substances. Intentional distortions on personality tests such as the MMPI-2 are so widely recognized that special methods have been devised to detect it when clients do not respond honestly (Berry, Baer, & Harris, 1991; see Chapter 5).

Even when clients try to give accurate reports, perceptual biases and expectations can easily cause them to misinterpret or misremember events (Dawes, 1986). Thus, parents who report that their child engages in "constant" temper tantrums are often surprised to learn that such tantrums actually occur an average of twice a day. If the tantrums are intense and upsetting enough to color the parents' perceptions, a clinician who gathers no observational data might get a distorted view of the target problem.

Highlighting Situational Determinants of Behavior

Much of traditional assessment is guided by the assumption that responses to interviews and tests are adequate for understanding clients' personalities and problems because these responses reflect traits that control behavior across differing situations and relatively long time periods. For clinicians adopting this view, a client's overt behavior provides, at most, supplementary clues to personality traits and dynamics. Others give approximately equal weight to observable behavior, interviews, and tests as they draw inferences about underlying personality characteristics or mental disorders but, in both cases, observations are seen as *signs* of more fundamental, unobservable constructs. In contrast, clinicians who take a behavioral or cognitive-behavioral view tend to regard observational data as *samples* of behavior that help them understand important *person-situation interactions* rather than draw inferences about hypothesized personality characteristics or problems.

These nontraditional clinicians do not necessarily deny that traits or person variables help account for behavior (Mischel, 1993), but they argue that clinical assessment must also explore the role played by the larger context in which behavior occurs (Follette, 1996). Observational assessments allow the clinician to determine the circumstances under which problematic behaviors are most likely to occur, what situational stimuli tend to trigger the behaviors, and what reinforcing consequences in the situation serve to maintain the unwanted actions (Patterson, 1982). Traditional tests and interviews are not designed to accomplish this kind of functional analysis (Cairns & Green, 1979).

Minimizing Inference

Conducting observation-driven functional analyses allows clinicians to avoid the relatively high levels of inference associated with sign-oriented testing and interviewing approaches. While the highest levels of inference—and the lowest levels of validity—are found in relation to projective test interpretation, some degree of inference is found in virtually any kind of clinical assessment. Even clinicians who employ systematic observational assessments realize that it is difficult, if not impossible, to eliminate all clinical inference, and they also know that a certain amount of inference may be justified at times. However, in the tradition of Sergeant Friday on the old *Dragnet* television series, observational procedures are designed to collect "just the facts," thereby minimizing the likelihood of drawing unsubstantiated inferences about clients. Of course, deciding which facts are the most important ones to observe still requires a considerable degree of clinical inference and judgment. Using observational data, clinicians can develop hypotheses about the causes or maintenance factors in behavior problems by looking at the specific antecedents and consequences surrounding those problems; they do not have to infer what the problems mean about the client.

Enhancing Ecological Validity

Advocates of observational assessment argue that it can provide the clearest possible picture of people and their problems because observations can occur in the physical and social environments where clients actually live their lives. Not only are these observations likely to be *ecologically valid*, they often provide situational details that help clinicians design treatment programs that can be most easily implemented in the home, school, or work environments where clients function every day. This custom-tailoring of interventions may increase the chances for treatment success.

Approaches to Observational Assessment

The appeal of observational assessment is that it provides a first-hand look at behaviors of clinical interest and yields many clues about the causes and treatment of those behaviors. What, exactly, does it entail?

Observational methods have been defined as "the *selection, provocation, recording*, and *encoding* of ... behaviors" (Weick, 1968; italics added). This definition highlights the fundamental elements of nearly every type of observational system. The observer first *selects* people, classes of behavior, events, situations, or time periods to be the focus of attention. Second, a decision is made about whether to *provoke* (i.e., artificially bring about) behaviors and situations of interest or to wait for them to happen on their own. Third, plans are made to *record* observations using observer memory, record sheets, audio- or videotape, physiological monitoring systems, timers, counters, or other means. Finally, a system for *encoding* raw observations into usable form must be developed. Encoding is often the most difficult aspect of any observational procedure.

Differing assessment goals, unique client populations, specific environmental limitations, and other factors result in many approaches to clinical observation. The clearest way to organize this array is in terms of the observational *settings* employed. At one extreme is *naturalistic* observation, where the assessor looks at behavior as it occurs in its natural context (e.g., at home or school). *Controlled*, or *experimental*, observation lies at the other extreme, as the clinician or researcher sets up a special situation in which to observe behavior. Between these extremes are approaches that blend elements of both to handle specific assessment needs, thus creating many subtypes of both naturalistic and controlled observation. In some assessment situations, observers may be *participants* who are visible to the clients being watched and who may even interact with them (as when parents record their child's behavior). *Nonparticipant* observers are not visible, although in most cases the clients are aware that observation is taking place.

To present a reasonably complete picture of clinical observation, we describe naturalistic and controlled observational systems that focus on several kinds of behavior. The examples we have chosen will illustrate the use of (1) participant and nonparticipant observers; (2) human, mechanical/electronic, and combined recording procedures; and (3) informal and formal encoding systems that deal with behavior as samples and signs. More comprehensive coverage of this material is available in a number of sources (e.g., Bellack & Hersen, 1988; Ciminero, Calhoun, & Adams, 1986; Haynes, 1990).

NATURALISTIC OBSERVATION

Watching clients behave spontaneously in a natural setting such as their homes has several obvious advantages. Natural settings provide a background that is realistic and relevant for understanding the client's behavior and the factors influencing that behavior. Additionally, naturalistic observation can be done in ways that are subtle enough to provide a picture of behavior that is not distorted by client self-consciousness or motivation to convey a particular impression.

The classic case of naturalistic observation is the anthropological field study in which a scientist joins a tribe, subculture, or other social organization to observe its characteristics and the behavior of its members (e.g., Mead, 1928; Williams, 1967).

In such cases the observer is a participant in every sense of the term, and observations are usually recorded in anecdotal notes which later appear as a detailed account called an *ethnography*.

In psychology, the work of Roger G. Barker provides an example of naturalistic observation whose intensity approaches anthropological proportions. In an effort to understand the ecology of human behavior, Barker and his colleagues observed as much of it as possible to capture the richness and details of its relationship to the environment. This involved participant (but noninteractive) observation of children on a continuous basis from morning until night as they went about a normal day's activities in their hometown (Barker & Wright, 1951, 1955). No attempt was made to select particular behaviors, situations, or events for special attention. Observations were recorded in notebooks as narrative "day records" (see Figure 6.1) and later encoded as "behavioral episodes." When episodes involved other people, they were treated as signs representing "nurturance," "resistance," "appeal," "submission," "aggression," "avoidance," etc. Notice the amount of observer inference involved in the day records (e.g., "He looked briefly at me *as if wondering what I thought*").

The data generated by these procedures are staggering. For example, one eight-year-old girl had 969 behavioral episodes involving 571 objects in the course of a single day. Barker was aware that this full-scale ecological approach produced too much information, and he suggested more practical alternatives, including periodic rather than continuous observation. In current practice, most assessors collect their observational data intermittently, focusing on those aspects of behavior and person–situation interactions that are of special theoretical or practical importance (Haynes, 1984).

5:39
Raymond tilted the crate from side to side in a calm, rhythmical way.

Clifford's feet were endangered again. Steward came over and very protectively led Clifford out of the way. [Observer's opinion.]

Raymond slowly descended to the ground inside the crate.

When Stewart came back around the crate, Raymond reached out at him, and growled very gutturally, and said, "I'm a big gorilla." Growling very ferociously, he stamped around the "cage" with his arms hanging loosely.

He reached out with slow, gross movements.

Raymond reached toward Clifford but didn't really try to catch him. Then he grabbed Stewart by the shirt.

Imitating a very fierce gorilla, he pulled Stewart toward the crate.

Stewart was passive and allowed himself to be pulled in. He said, "Why don't you let go of me?" He spoke disgustedly and yet not disparagingly. Raymond released his grasp and ceased imitating a gorilla.

He tilted the crate so that he could crawl out of the open end. As he crawled out, he lost control of the crate and it fell over on its side with the open end perpendicular to the ground.

Stewart said, "Well, how did you get out?"

Raymond said self-consciously, "I fell out," and forced a laugh.

He looked briefly at me as if wondering what I thought.

SOURCE: Barker and Wright (1951).

FIGURE 6.1   Excerpt from a day record.

Psychologists interested in child development, for example, have devised observational systems aimed at categories of behavior thought to be indicative of physical, cognitive, and social functioning (e.g., Bayley, 1965; Piaget, 1947). Other psychologists have developed observational tools to code the complex interplay of people's behaviors in pairs or groups (e.g., Gottman, 1979; Santoyo, 1996; Roberts et al., 1991).

Naturalistic observation has been used to infer personality characteristics (Santostefano, 1962), intelligence (Lambert, Cox, & Hartsough, 1970), social goals (Brown, Odom, & Holcombe, 1996), and cognitive development (Schweinhart et al., 1993), but its primary focus has been on assessing the nature of, and changes in, problems that clinicians are asked to solve—everything from eating disorders, intrusive thoughts, maladaptive social interactions, and psychotic behavior to community problems such as classroom violence and littering (Haynes, 1990).

In its early forms, naturalistic clinical observation required observers to make decisions and draw inferences about what certain behaviors mean and which behaviors should or should not be recorded. As a result, the interobserver reliability of naturalistic observation suffered (see Figure 6.2). Lee Cronbach (1960, p. 535) summarized the problem well: "Observers interpret what they see. When they make an interpretation, they tend to overlook facts which do not fit the interpretation, and they may even invent facts needed to complete the event as interpreted." Attempts to improve anecdotal accounts in naturalistic clinical observation have taken many forms. To reduce unsystematic reporting of client behaviors, most modern observation schemes focus the observer's attention on specific behaviors. The frequency and intensity of these behaviors are then recorded on a checklist or rating scale. The observers are also trained to use these methods consistently so that interobserver reliability is as high as possible.

Another approach to naturalistic observation is to inspect the by-products of behavior. For example, analysis of school grades, arrest records, and court files have been used to evaluate the treatment of delinquent youth and adult offenders (Davidson et al., 1987; Rice, 1997), and changes in academic grade point averages have served as indices of improvement in test anxiety (Allen, 1971). Life records, also called *institutional* or *product-of-behavior* measures (Haynes, 1990; Maisto & Maisto, 1983), are actually part of a broader observational approach, called *nonreactive* or *unobtrusive* measurement, that clinical psychologists and other behavioral scientists use to learn about people's behavior without altering it in the process (see Webb et al., 1966).

In clinical research, unobtrusive measures may be used to test theories about the causes of behavior problems. One research team, for example, was interested in the hypothesis that social isolation early in life, and particularly during adolescence, was related to a later diagnosis of schizophrenia (Barthell & Holmes, 1968). As a partial test of this hypothesis, they inspected the high school yearbooks of people labeled "schizophrenic" or "neurotic" and compared the activities listed for these individuals with nonlabeled students from the same schools. A similar use of life records is illustrated by research that relates factors such as age, marital status, employment history, and education to the development of schizophrenia and to chances for its improvement. Another creative use of unobtrusive measures in identifying the precursors of

Observer A: (2) Robert reads word by word, using finger to follow place. (4) Observes girl in box with much preoccupation. (5) During singing, he in general doesn't participate too actively. Interest is part of time centered elsewhere. Appears to respond most actively to sections of song involving action. Has tendency for seemingly meaningless movement. Twitching of fingers, aimless thrusts of arms.

Observer B: (2) Looked at camera upon entering (seemed perplexed and interested). Smiled at camera. (2) Reads (with apparent interest and with a fair degree of facility). (3) Active in roughhouse play with girls. (4) Upon being kicked (unintentionally) by one girl he responded (angrily). (5) Talked with girl sitting next to him between singing periods. Participated in singing. (At times appeared enthusiastic). Didn't always sing with others. (6) Participated in a dispute in a game with others (appeared to stand up for his own rights). Aggressive behavior toward another boy. Turned pockets inside out while talking to teacher and other students. (7) Put on overshoes without assistance. Climbed to top of ladder rungs. Tired to get rung which was occupied by a girl but since she didn't give in, contented himself with another place.

Observer C: (1) Smiles into camera (curious). When group break up, he makes nervous gestures, throws arm out into air. (2) Attention to reading lesson. Reads with serious look on his face, has to use line marker. (3) Chases girls, teases. (4) Girl kicks when he puts hand on her leg. Robert makes face at her. (5) Singing. Sits with mouth open, knocks knees together, scratches leg, puts fingers in mouth (seems to have several nervous habits, though not emotionally overwrought or self-conscious). (6) In a dispute over parchesi, he stands up for his rights. (7) Short dispute because he wants rung on jungle gym.

Observer D: (2) Uses guide to follow words, reads slowly, fairly forced and with careful formation of sounds (perhaps unsure of self and fearful of mistakes). (3) Perhaps slightly aggressive as evidenced by pushing younger child to side when moving from a position to another. Plays with other children with obvious enjoyment, smiles, runs, seems especially associated with girls. This is noticeable in games and in seating in singing. (5) Takes little interest in singing, fidgets, moves hands and legs (perhaps shy and nervous). Seems in song to be unfamiliar with words of main part, and shows disinterest by fidgeting and twisting around. Not until chorus is reached does he pick up interest. His special friend seems to be a particular girl, as he is always seated by her.

SOURCE: Excerpts from pages 534–535 from *Essentials of Psychological Testing* 5th Ed. by Lee J. Cronbach. Copyright 1949. © 1984 by Harper & Row, Publishers, Inc. Copyright © 1960, 1970, 1990 by Lee J. Cronbach.

FIGURE 6.2 Four observations of the same client. Notice the differing images and inferences generated by four observers who watched a ten-minute film, *This Is Robert*, which showed a boy in classroom and playground situations. (The observers were told to use parentheses to indicate inferences or interpretation. The numbers used refer to scenes in the film and were inserted to aid comparison.)

schizophrenia is seen in a study which took advantage of the fact that many families today make videotapes of their children as they grow (Walker et al., 1993). In this study, trained observers analyzed childhood videotapes of individuals who later became schizophrenic, as well as of their same-sex siblings who did not. The results revealed that, long before they were diagnosed, the schizophrenics-to-be showed significantly more negative facial expressions than the other children (some of the differences appeared before the children were four years old).

Unobtrusive measures are not problem free, however. For one thing, in comparison to simply asking clients to report on their behavior, they are harder to collect. In addition, data from unobtrusive observations may not generalize well to situations that differ from those in which the measures were taken. Accordingly, some researchers have experimented with embedding unobtrusive measures in a computer-assisted instruction program that asks clients about selected topics at the same time as it delivers instructional material. This approach has been found to result in data that correlate well with self-report measures (Meier & Wick, 1991).

In the following sections, we consider a set of naturalistic observation systems that, while not entirely unobtrusive, do allow for recording the frequency, intensity, duration, or form of specific categories of behaviors by persons who are both familiar to clients and in a position to observe them in a minimally intrusive way.

Hospital Observations

The Inpatient Multidimensional Psychiatric Scales, or IMPS (Lorr, McNair, & Klett, 1966), is an excellent example of a hospital observation system that can be used by ward staff. The IMPS contains seventy-five items which are either rated by the observer on five- or nine-point scales or responded to with a yes or no (see Figure 6.3). These data are translated into scores on dimensions such as excitement, hostile belligerence, paranoid projection, grandiose expansiveness, disorientation, and conceptual disorganization. The scores can then be plotted as a profile describing the observed client. More recent examples of such systems include the Routine Assessment of Patient Progress, or RAPP (Ehmann et al., 1995).

Other hospital observation systems not only specify the targets to be recorded, but also reduce the observer/coder inferences required by having observers record a client's behavior as it occurs. When such observations are made at regular intervals (e.g., once per hour), the process is called *time sampling*. When only certain activities are observed (e.g., social interactions or aggressive episodes), the method is called *event sampling*. These techniques are often combined, as when observations are made once per minute during meals or on other occasions.

One of the first low-inference observation systems to be used with hospital inpatients was the Behavioral Study Form, or BSF (Schaefer & Martin, 1975). Developed at Patton State Hospital in California, the BSF requires ward staff (usually nurses) to record specific behaviors occurring during observations that take place approximately

Compared to the normal person, to what degree does/is the client:

1. Exhibit an attitude of superiority
2. Ramble off the topic discussed
3. Assume bizarre positions
4. Unrestrained in showing feelings

5. Blame others for difficulty
6. Believe he has unusual abilities or talents
7. Believe people are against him
8. Make unusual facial grimaces

FIGURE 6.3 Sample items from the Inpatient Multidimensional Psychiatric Scales (IMPS).

every thirty minutes (see Figure 6.4). At each observation point, the nurse records a "mutually exclusive" behavior (which defines the client's general activity) and any other behavior that accompanies that activity. The client's location and other relevant facts are also noted.

The Behavioral Study Form served as the basis for more elaborate observation systems now being used in psychiatric hospitals. The most sophisticated and well-

Watch Especially for:

19- *head in hands, HH*
18- *Working-assigned*
16- *Talking to others*

GENERAL CODE

Mutually Exclusive Behaviors
1. Walking   4. Sitting
2. Running   5. Lying down
3. Standing

Concomitant Behaviors
6   Drinking
7   Eating–meals
7a Eating–other than meals
8   Grooming (describe)
9   Group meeting
10 Medication
11 Reading
12 Receiving pay
13 Rocking
14 Pacing
15 Smoking
16 Talking to others
17 T V
18 Working–assigned
19 Other

Location
A Dining room
B Hall of lounge
C Sleeping quarters
D Lavatory
E Outside

Patient *Susan R.*

Admission

Followup:

① 2   3   4   5   6   7   8   9

Date: *August 24, 1967*

Time	Code		Location
0630	3-8		D
0700	3-6		B
0730	4-15		B
0800	3-10		A
0830	4-18		A
0900	3-18		A
0930			
1000	4-19 HH		B
1030	4-19 HH		B
1100	3-19 Buying item		B
1130	3-18		A
1200	4-7		A
1230	3-16 (Employer)		B
1300	4-11		A
1330	4-9		A
1400	4-9		A
1430	4-9		A
1500	Unavailable		
1530	1		E
1600	3-11		A
1630	3-18		A
1700	3-18		A
1730	4		D
1800	4-16		E
1830	3		C
1900	3-16		C
1930	3-17		B
2000	3-11		A
2030	2-19 (screaming)		B
2100	5		C

FIGURE 6.4   The Behavioral Study Form (BSF). Here is the coding system and a sample record from the BSF. Each observation target is clearly defined during observer training, thus increasing the likelihood that different observers will use the system reliably. (H. H. Schaefer and P. L. Martin, *Behavioral Therapy,* 2nd ed. © 1975 by McGraw-Hill Book Company, New York. Reprinted by permission.)

researched of these is the Time-Sample Behavioral Checklist (TSBC) (Paul & Lentz, 1977; Paul & Licht, 1987), which was developed to allow trained observers to assess a large number of behaviors displayed by psychiatric inpatients. The TSBC provides measurement of clinically significant behavior in great detail (any of sixty-nine behaviors can be coded for a two-second focus on one patient) and with great regularity (each patient is observed at least once during every waking hour, seven days a week). These data can then be converted into several TSBC index scores that describe the overall nature of a patient's behavior. For example, the TSBC Total Inappropriate Behavior Index measures twenty-four inappropriate, or "crazy" actions, while the Total Appropriate Behavior Index provides a summary of twenty-seven appropriate, or "normal" behaviors. Figure 6.5 illustrates how other TSBC indices were used to compare the effects of social-learning versus milieu therapy in two hospital treatment programs.

Barker-style ethological observations have also been used in hospital, school, and home settings by clinicians interested in a detailed view of children's behavior problems (Dunlap, Koegel, & O'Neill, 1985). Rather than attempting to observe all aspects of the client's behavior, however, these clinicians tend to focus on certain subcategories, such as social behavior. They then concentrate on analyzing the long-term functional relationships between these behaviors and the stimuli that precede and follow them. Researchers using this approach have found, for example, that autistic children are more likely to engage in hand flapping or other bizarre motor behaviors when new people or objects are introduced into their environment (Hutt & Hutt, 1968).

School Observations

The desire to observe children's behavior for clinical purposes has spawned a number of systems for use in schools, playgrounds, and similar settings (Ollendick & Greene, 1990). In the tradition of early experimental sociologists (e.g., Dawe, 1934), recording and coding systems designed by Sidney Bijou (Bijou, Peterson, & Ault, 1968) and Daniel O'Leary (O'Leary & Becker, 1967) use symbols to represent the behavior of children and the adults around them during time-sample observations (see Figure 6.6). Like other observation systems of this type, the data gathered can be summarized in quantitative form. In this case, percentages can be calculated to summarize how much time a child spends on-task, out-of-seat, or talking to other children. Classroom observation may focus on a single child and those with whom the child interacts, or an observer can sequentially attend to and assess the behavior of several target children or even of a whole class (Milich & Fitzgerald, 1985).

Home Observations

Observational assessment procedures are also available to measure clinically relevant behaviors in clients' homes. As was the case in other areas, early home-based clinical observations allowed much inference and rather unsystematic target selection (e.g., Ackerman, 1958). More reliable home observation systems have now evolved. One of the first of these was designed by Gerald Patterson (Patterson et al., 1969) for use in the homes of conduct-disordered children. After obtaining consent to do so, Patterson

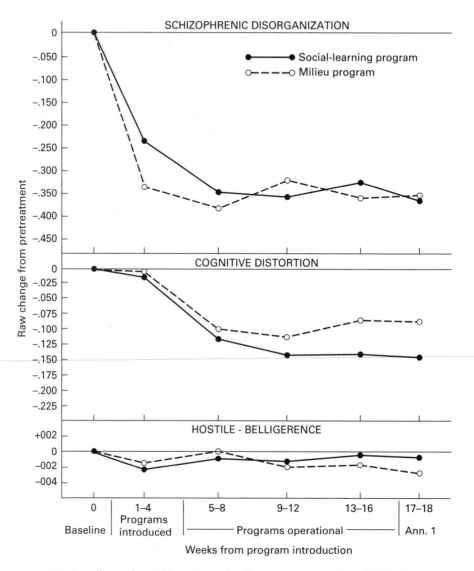

FIGURE 6.5 Effects of social-learning and milieu programs on three TSBC dimensions. These graphs compare patients in each treatment group on Schizophrenic Disorganization (bizarre behaviors such as rocking and staring), Cognitive Distortion (bizarre verbal behaviors, including incoherent speech), and Hostile-Belligerence (screaming, cursing, and other aggressive behaviors). (After G. Paul and R. Lentz, *Psychological Treatment of Chronic Mental Patients,* published by Harvard University Press, 1977. Reprinted by permission.)

places trained observers in the client's living area for an hour or two on each of several days, usually just before dinner. The observers avoid interacting with the family and concentrate on using Patterson's Family Interaction Coding System to record the behavior of one member at a time as well as the family member with whom the person interacted. It is thus possible to record the target child's inappropriate behavior as well

Symbol	Definition
	First Row **(Social Contacts)** *S* verbalizes to himself. Any verbalization during which he does not look at an adult or child or does not use an adult's or child's name. Does not apply to group situation.
	S verbalizes to adult. *S* must look at adult while verbalizing or use adult's name.
	S verbalizes to child. *S* must look at child while verbalizing or use child's name. If in a group situation, any verbalization is recorded as verbalization to a child.
S	Child verbalizes to *S*. Child must look at *S* while verbalizing or use *S*'s name.
△	Adult verbalizes to *S*. Adult must look at *S* while verbalizing or use *S*'s name.
S	Adult gives general instruction to class or asks question of class, or makes general statement. Includes storytelling.
	S touches adult. Physical contact with adult.
	S touches child with part of body or object. Physical contact with child.
V	Adult touches *S*. Physical contact with adult.
T	Child touches *S* with part of body or object. Physical contact with child.

Symbol	Definition
▪	**Second Row** **(Sustained Activity)** *Sustained activity in art.* S must be sitting in the chair, facing the material and responding to the material or teacher within the 10-sec interval. Responding to the material includes using pencil, paint brush, chalk, crayons, string, scissors or paste or any implement on paper, or working with clay with hands on clay or hands on implement which is used with clay, or folding or tearing paper. Responding to the teacher includes following a command made by an adult to make a specific response. The behavior must be completed (child sitting in his chair again) within two minutes.
▪	*Sustained activity in storytime.* S must be sitting, facing the material, or following a command given by the teacher or assistant. If the S initiates a verbalization to a peer, do not record sustained activity in the 10-sec interval.
▪	*Sustained activity in show-and-tell.* S must be sitting, facing the material, or following a command given by the teacher. If the S initiates a verbalization to a peer, do not record sustained activity in that 10-sec interval.
▪	*Sustained activity in reading.* S must be sitting in the chair, facing the material and responding to the material or the teacher within the 10-sec interval.
▪	*Sustained activity in writing.* S must be sitting in the chair, facing the material and responding to the material or the teacher within the 10-sec interval. Responding to the material includes using the pencil (making a mark), or holding the paper or folder. Responding to the teacher includes responding verbally to a cue given by the teacher.
▪	*Sustained activity in arithmetic.* S must be sitting in the chair, facing the material and responding to the material or the teacher within the 10-sec interval. Responding to the material or teacher includes using the pencil or eraser or holding the paper or folder or responding verbally to cue.
	Sustained activity did not occur in interval.

FIGURE 6.6 Part of a symbol-coding system for observation of children. Here are the symbols (and their definitions) developed for use in an observational study of nursery school children (Bijou, Peterson, & Ault, 1968).

as the antecedents and consequences of this behavior (Patterson, 1982). Each type of behavior observed (talking, crying, hitting, laughing, ignoring) is summarized by one of twenty-nine symbols similar in nature to those in Figure 6.6 (see Reid, 1978). Other home observation systems are available as well (see McIntyre et al., 1983), some of which have been used not only to assess individual clients but to gather data on how certain parental behaviors contribute to children's maladjustment (e.g, Forehand et al., 1986). Recently, structural equation modeling and other complex mathematical procedures have been applied to the analysis of data flowing from these systems (e.g. Melby et al., 1995).

More complex recording and encoding systems are usually needed when the goal is to observe adult interactions at home. For example, in a study of social skills in depressed clients (Lewinsohn & Shaffer, 1971), the system used to encode time-sampled observations of family interactions at mealtimes categorized verbal behavior as self-initiated *actions* (questions, comments, requests for information, complaints) or positive and negative *reactions* to the behavior of others (approval, laughter, criticism, disagreement). These dimensions were then used to examine differences between depressed and nondepressed persons (e.g., Johnson & Jacob, 1997; Libet & Lewinsohn, 1973) as well as changes in depressed behavior as a function of treatment.

John Gottman (1979) developed a complex coding system for the assessment of couple interactions called the Couples Interaction Coding System (CISS, pronounced "kiss"). CISS categorizes each client statement in terms of its (1) *content*, (2) *affect*, and (3) *context*. Two aspects of Gottman's work merit special mention. The first involves his use of sequential, or *time-series*, analysis of the observational data (Gottman, Markman, & Notarius, 1977). This technique allows the assessor to look not only at the influence of one person on the other at a given point (as when a wife insults her husband or vice versa), but also at the influence of previous interactions on later ones. Negative "spirals" and other long-term social sequences can be discovered more easily with this technique than with procedures that merely present "percent of time spent" summaries. Clinicians can use such observations to calculate the *conditional probability* of a behavior—the likelihood that a behavior (such as criticism) will occur given the prior occurrence of another behavior or event (such as an insult). The second notable feature of Gottman's observational system is its use in the study of emotion in couple interaction. In addition to developing a coding system devoted to the study of emotions in marital interactions (known as the Specific Affect Coding System; Gottman & Krokoff, 1989), Gottman and his colleagues have studied how couples' overt interactions are linked to physiological indicators of emotion such as heart rate and skin conductance. One finding from this research is that during emotional conflicts, couples tend to reciprocate each other's reactions, not only behaviorally, but physiologically as well (Levenson & Gottman, 1983).

Observations by Insiders

The naturalistic observation systems we have described so far employ specially trained personnel as participant or nonparticipant observers. Because some researchers question whether these outsiders can do their job without inadvertently influencing the behavior they are to watch, some observations are conducted by persons who are part of the client's day-to-day world. The IMPS data collected by nurses or other ward staff, is an example of such a system. Similarly, observation of children in classrooms and at home has been accomplished by teachers, parents, and even other children who have been trained to collect and record data on specific behaviors (e.g., Lyman, 1984).

The use of insiders as observers of adult behavior for clinical purposes is less common, but not unknown. For example, in helping clients quit smoking, a clinician may ask for corroborative reports of success or failure from family members or friends (e.g., Mermelstein, Lichtenstein, & McIntyre, 1983). Such reports may also be solicited as part of the assessment of alcoholism (e.g., Foy, Nunn, & Rychtarik, 1984), sexual activity (e.g., Rosen & Kopel, 1977), marital violence (Jouriles & O'Leary, 1985), and other adult behaviors (Margolin, Michelli, & Jacobson, 1988).

Self-Observation

Although insiders usually have a less-obstructed view of a client's behavior than an outside observer would, no one spends as much time with the client as the client. In many clinical and research settings, therefore, clients are asked to observe and record their own behavior using a procedure called *self-monitoring*. Though usually done by adults, self-monitoring can be done successfully by children as well.

Self-monitoring requires clients to record the frequency, duration, or intensity of events such as exercise, headaches, pleasant thoughts, hair pulling, giving or receiving praise, pain, and so on. Figure 6.7 illustrates a self-monitoring diary of smoking behavior; similar diaries detailing the antecedents, consequences, and other behavioral specifics are commonly used in research on eating habits (Brownell, 1981), stress (Lutgendorf et al., 1997), sleep problems (Miller & DiPilato, 1983), anxiety disorders (Cooper & Clum, 1989), and health promoting behaviors (Rodrique, 1996).

Unfortunately, self-monitoring can be *reactive*, meaning that the mere act of self-observation might alter the observed behavior. Further, the effects of reactivity are difficult to predict; self-monitoring sometimes increases and sometimes decreases the rate of observed behavior (Kanfer & Gaelick, 1986; Nelson, 1977).

Aids to Naturalistic Observation

Because human vision, hearing, and memory are limited in their ability to detect, discriminate, and retain information about events occurring in the environment, mechanical and/or electronic devices are often used to assist observers in their assessment tasks. For example, mechanical devices are sometimes used in self-monitoring, especially when frequency measures are of primary concern. Clients might be asked to press a hand-held counter each time a target behavior occurs, later transferring daily totals to a summary sheet. Some of these counters are commercially available, others are designed especially for clinical assessment purposes.

Precise monitoring of the duration of target responses can be accomplished by timers. In some cases, an electric clock can be turned into a cumulative timer by having the client set it to 12 o'clock, plug it in each time some targeted activity begins (studying,

Name_____   Date_____

Time	Intensity of craving*	Was cigarette smoked? (✔)	Place	With whom	Mood
1.					
2.					
3.					
4.					
5.					
6.					
7.					
8.					
9.					
10.					
11.					
12.					
13.					
14.					
15.					
16.					
17.					
18.					
19.					
20.					

*indicate the intensity of your craving on a scale of 1 to 5: 1 = no perceptible craving; 2 = slight craving; 3 = moderate craving; 4 = fairly strong craving; 5 = intense craving.

Total number of cigarettes smoked_____

FIGURE 6.7   A self-monitoring diary for recording smoking behavior. Note that space is provided on this diary form for noting the time at which each cigarette is lit as well as for information about the physical and social setting and the mood that preceded smoking. (From O. F. Pomerleau & C. S. Pomerleau, *Break the Smoking Habit,* © Research Press, Champaign, Illinois, 1977. Reprinted by permission.)

exercising, or sleeping), and unplug it each time the activity stops. The time on the clock face at the end of the day thus displays the total duration of the target behavior for that day. Specially designed stopwatches that record time automatically can be used in the same way (Hoelscher, Lichstein, & Rosenthal, 1986). A continuous record of behavior can be provided by mechanical devices (usually a combination of switches and counters) that are connected directly to the client. Such systems have been used to measure physical activity, which is a variable of interest with depressed, hyperactive, and other clients (see Milich, Loney, & Landau, 1982).

Electronic data collection devices also play a role in naturalistic observation procedures. Audio- and video-tape recorders can gather larger amounts of continuous data than would be possible using human observers. Notebook computers allow efficient on-the-spot data entry (e.g., Greenwood et al., 1994). Tiny microphones and pocket-size transmitters allow wireless audio recordings of clients' verbal behavior in naturalistic settings. Miniaturized wireless telemetric devices that detect and transmit data about physiological functioning have also made it possible to analyze heart rate and other clinically relevant variables in clients who are living freely in the environment (Rugh, Gable, & Lemke, 1986).

CONTROLLED OBSERVATION

The major appeal of naturalistic observation is that it yields large samples of spontaneous client behavior occurring under circumstances of greatest relevance and interest to the clinician. The assets of naturalistic observation can become liabilities, however, especially when observation targets occur infrequently. Suppose, for example, that the clinician wants to observe a client's response to stress. Using naturalistic procedures, the client's behavior would have to be continuously monitored in all settings where stressful events might occur. However, there is no guarantee that the client will actually encounter clinically relevant stress in a given situation, so much time and effort could be wasted.

Further, as its name implies, naturalistic observation usually takes place in an uncontrolled environment, so even if a stressor occurs, unanticipated events can interfere with the assessment: The client may move out of the observer's line of vision or might get help from someone else in dealing with the stressor. How would the client have reacted without help? The assessor would not know unless the same situation recurs when the client is alone and under observation. The fact that the situation of interest may not soon recur points to another limitation of naturalistic observation: Repeated assessment of a client's reaction to low-probability events is difficult. This problem is important because comparison of the behavior of many people under identical conditions is a cornerstone of many experimental designs and assessment approaches.

One way of getting around some of the difficulties associated with naturalistic observation is to set up special circumstances under which clients can be observed as they react to planned, standardized events. This approach is usually called *controlled observation* because it allows clinicians to maintain control over the assessment stimuli in much the same way as they do when giving the psychological tests described in Chapter 5. Controlled observations are also referred to as *situation tests, analogue assessments*, and *contrived observations*.

Like early naturalistic observations, the first controlled observations involved a great deal of observer inference. For example, one group of researchers set up a frustration situation by first allowing nursery school children to play with highly desirable toys in a fenced area, then locking the youngsters outside the fence (Barker, Dembo, & Lewin, 1941). The varying reactions to frustration displayed by each child were interpreted as evidence of maturity, constructiveness, regression, and other characteristics. Earlier, Hartshorne and May (1928) studied honesty by observing children in situations where they could steal money without fear of being detected (see Hinshaw, Simmel, & Heller, 1995, for an updated application of this procedure).

During World War II, military psychologists devised controlled observations for assessing personality traits as well as behavioral capabilities. In the Operational Stress Test, for example, would-be pilots were asked to manipulate the controls of an aircraft flight simulator. The candidates did not know that the tester was purposely trying to frustrate them by giving increasingly complicated instructions accompanied by negative feedback (e.g., "You're making too many errors"; Melton, 1947). During the test, the assessor rated the candidate's reaction to criticism and stress, and these ratings supplemented objective data on skill with the simulator.

Traits of initiative, dominance, cooperation, and group leadership were inferred from observational assessments developed by the staff of the Office of Strategic Services (OSS; later to become the CIA) to help select espionage agents and other special personnel. One example was a construction test, in which a candidate was assigned to build a five-foot cube-shaped frame out of large wooden poles and blocks resembling a giant Tinker Toy® set. Because the test was supposed to measure the candidate's organizational and leadership ability, he was given two "assistants" (actually, psychologists) who called themselves Buster and Kippy.

> Kippy acted in a passive, sluggish manner. He did nothing at all unless specifically ordered to, but stood around, often getting in the way.... Buster, on the other hand, ... was aggressive, forward in offering impractical suggestions, ready to express dissatisfaction, and quick to criticize what he suspected were the candidate's weakest points.... It was their function to present the candidate with as many obstructions and annoyances as possible in ten minutes. As it turned out, they succeeded in frustrating the candidates so thoroughly that the construction was never ... completed in the allotted time. (OSS, 1948, p. 103)[1]

Since World War II, milder versions of the OSS situational tests have been used for personnel selection. In current clinical and research settings, controlled observations take many forms. In some cases, the "control" consists of asking clients (usually couples, families, or parent-child pairs) to come to a clinic or laboratory and have a discussion, attempt to solve a problem, or just talk while under observation by TV cameras, tape recorders, or human coders (e.g., Hahlweg, Revenstorf, & Schindler, 1984; Johnson & Jacob, 1997). In other instances, clients are presented with a structured task or situation designed to elicit behaviors of relevance to clinical assessment (e.g., Humphrey, Apple, & Kirschenbaum, 1986).

Role-Playing Tests

Psychologists sometimes create make-believe situations in which the client is asked to *role-play* his or her typical behavior. Role playing has been advocated by clinicians for many years (e.g., Borgatta, 1955) and serves as the cornerstone for several group, psychodynamic, and phenomenological treatments (e.g., Moreno, 1946; Perls, 1969).

---

[1]The fact that Kippy and Buster were Army privates and often got to torment high-ranking officers "set an untouchable record for job satisfaction among psychologists" (Cronbach, 1960, p. 568).

However, it was not until the late 1960s that role playing became part of systematic clinical assessment. Its most common use in controlled observation has been in the assessment of social competency, self-expression, and assertiveness.

Sometimes the procedures are simple and structured, as in the Situation Test (ST), which was developed to explore social skills in heterosexual college males (Rehm & Marston, 1968). In the ST, the client sits with a young woman and listens to tape-recorded descriptions of scenes to be role played. The woman (an assistant to the clinician) then reads a question or statement such as "What would you like to do now?" or "I thought that was a lousy movie," and the client is asked to respond as if the situation were real. In another observational assessment, clients were asked to role-play their responses to interpersonal situations such as the following: "You have been seeing this man/woman for about four months. He/she has been very demanding on you and he/she gets extremely jealous when he/she sees you just talking to another man/woman. He/she says he/she doesn't want to lose you but you want to end this relationship. So you say. . . ." (Nelson et al., 1985).

Role-playing tests have become a standard ingredient in the observational assessment of children's social and safety skills (Harbeck, Peterson, & Starr, 1992), parent–child interactions (Jouriles & Farris, 1992), depressive behavior (Bellack, Hersen, & Himmelhoch, 1983), and the social competence and conversational skills of socially anxious or chronically mentally ill persons (Bellack et al., 1990; Dilk & Bond, 1996; Turner, Beidel, & Long, 1992). In most role-plays, the clients' responses are videotaped and then rated by observers on any of dozens of criteria such as appropriateness of content, level of positive and refusal assertiveness, anxiety, latency to respond, response duration, speech dysfluencies, posture, eye contact, gaze, hand gestures, head movements, and voice volume.

A number of variables influence the way people respond to role-playing assessments. Instructions to behave as one naturally would versus instructions to behave as an assertive person would have been shown to produce very different behavior (Kazdin, Esveldt-Dawson, & Matson, 1983; Rodriguez, Nietzel, & Berzins, 1980; Wallace et al., 1992). The content of the scenes used in role plays (Nelson et al., 1985), their level of difficulty (Kolotkin, 1980), the responses of the experimenter to the client (Kirchner & Draguns, 1979), and the social impact of role-played behavior (Kern, Cavell, & Beck, 1985) also influence performance. As investigators have learned about the impact of these and other variables, they have modified role-playing methods to make them more realistic and more diagnostic of the specific problems of individual clients. For example, the Extended Interaction Test assesses the generality and robustness of clients' assertiveness skills by presenting a tape-recorded antagonist who makes a series of gradually escalating unreasonable requests and demands (McFall & Lillesand, 1971). Here is an excerpt from the Extended Interaction Test:

NARRATOR: You are feeling really pressed for study time because you have an exam on Friday afternoon. Now, you are studying at your desk, when a close friend comes in and says, "Hi, Guess what. My parents just called and offered to pay for a plane ticket so I can fly home this weekend. Great, huh!? The only problem is, I'll have to skip my Friday morning class, and I hate to miss out on those notes; I'm barely making it in there as it is. Look, I know you aren't in that class, but it'd really be a big help if you'd go to the class Friday and take notes for me so I could go home. Would you do that for me?"

If subject refuses, the tape continues:

"I guess it is kinda crazy to expect you to do it, but, gee, I've got so many things to do if I'm gonna get ready to leave, and I don't want to waste the time asking around. Come on, will you do it for me this once?"

If subject refuses, the tape continues:

"Look, what're friends for if they don't help each other out of a bind? I'd do it for you if you asked. What do you say, will you?"

If subject refuses, the tape continues:

"But I was *counting on you* to do it. I'd hate to have to call my folks back and tell them I'm not coming. Can't you spare just *one* hour to help me out?"

If subject refuses, the tape continues (sarcastically):

"Now look, I don't want to *impose* on your *precious* time. Just tell me. Will you do it or do I have to call my folks back?"

Presumably, a person who withstands repeated requests is more assertive than one who gives in after an initial refusal. The Extended Interaction Test provides but one example of assessing the generality of client behavior through controlled observation. Some administer various role-play items to measure the range of situations in which a client is skilled or assertive (e.g., Edelstein & Eisler, 1976), while others attempt to observe the client in naturalistic settings (e.g., Kazdin, Matson, & Esveldt-Dawson, 1984). Because the first strategy may not be realistic and because the second is difficult to arrange, a third approach, called the *staged naturalistic event* is sometimes used. The idea here is to look at behavior in a controlled setting that appears naturalistic to the client (Gottman & Markman, 1978). For example, unobtrusive role-playing tests have been used to measure social skills in psychiatric inpatients (Goldsmith & McFall, 1975). In these tests, the client is asked to meet and carry on a conversation with a stranger (actually an assistant to the clinician) who has been instructed to confront the client with three "critical moments": not catching the client's name, responding to a lunch invitation with an excuse that left open the possibility of lunch at another time, and saying "Tell me about yourself" at the first convenient pause in the conversation. Similar contrived situations have been used in other psychiatric settings (Holmes, Hansen, & St. Lawrence, 1984), with children (Saywitz & Snyder, 1996), and with college students (Kern, 1982).

Of course, observations involving deception and possible invasion of privacy must be set up with care and with regard for clients' welfare and dignity. Proponents of unobtrusive controlled observation try to avoid its potential dangers and point out that its value may be limited to measuring specific behaviors (such as refusal) rather than more complex interactive social skills.

Performance Measures

In most of the controlled observations described in the previous section, the client is asked to act as if an event were taking place. In other controlled observational assessments, however, clients actually face a clinically relevant situation. Controlled observations of performance have focused on behaviors such as eating, drinking, or smoking. For example, the eating style (amount, speed, preferences) of normal or obese individuals has been recorded during a meal or snack in a controlled setting (Spiegel, Wadden, & Foster, 1991). Alcoholic and nonalcoholic drinkers have been observed in specially constructed cocktail lounges or living rooms located in hospitals (Collins, Parks, & Marlatt, 1985; see Figure 6.8). The details of cigarette use (puff rate, depth of inhalation, number of puffs) have been scrutinized in volunteers smoking in simulated social settings (Ossip-Klein et al., 1983).

Physiological Measures. Other performance tests measure physiological activity—such as heart rate, respiration, blood pressure, galvanic skin response, muscle tension, and brain waves—that appears in relation to various stimuli. An early example was provided by a study of forehead muscle tension in a headache patient as she watched a film about headaches (Malmo, Shagass, & Davis, 1950). In recent years,

FIGURE 6.8 Simulated bar in a hospital setting. (Courtesy of G. Alan Marlatt. Reprinted by permission.)

clinical psychologists have increased their use of such physiological measures because (1) they have become much more involved in studying insomnia, headache, chronic pain, sexual dysfunctions, gastrointestinal disorders, diabetes, and other disorders that have clear physiological components; and (2) assessment of physiological responses becomes crucial in evaluating treatments for several of these disorders.

Physiological measures are also important in the assessment of sexual arousal, particularly arousal in response to socially inappropriate stimuli. In one such performance assessment system, male subjects listen to or watch tapes that present various types of erotic behavior involving appropriate and inappropriate sexual stimuli. While the tape is playing, a strain gauge attached to the subject's penis records changes in its circumference. Greater erectile responses to the taped material are assumed to signal higher levels of sexual arousal. Several studies have shown rapists have equal or greater arousal to rape stimuli than to scenes of consenting sexual activity (Hall, 1990). In contrast, nonrapists usually show less sexual excitation in response to rape scenes. Similar procedures have been used in the diagnosis of pedophilia (Freund & Watson, 1991) and in the identification of child molesters (Haywood, Grossman, & Cavanaugh, 1990). Unfortunately, the expected patterns of arousal are not found consistently enough to ensure that physiological measures are valid measures of deviant sexual arousal (see Figure 6.9).

Assessment of the physiology of fear in controlled settings has also occupied many clinical researchers. A classic example was Gordon Paul's (1966) use of measures of heart rate and sweating taken just before giving a talk to help identify speech-anxious clients. These measures were repeated following various anxiety-reduction treatments to aid in the evaluation of their effects (see also Nietzel, Bernstein, & Russell, 1988). Researchers are finding that measures of physiological arousal can accurately reflect other emotional states as well. In one study, for example, measures of physiology collected as undergraduates wrote essays about positive, then negative, experiences changed as the content of the essays changed (Hughes, Uhlmann, & Pennebaker, 1994). With increased interest in the role of psychological factors in health and illness (see Chapter 11), the use of physiological recording devices in clinical assessment probably will continue to increase as well. This is especially likely now that many companies are able to market relatively inexpensive, portable recording devices.

Having ever more precise measurements of the physiological responses that occur while clients experience fear, anger, or other intense emotions is helping psychologists to better understand emotional behavior and emotional disorders (Lang, 1995). For example, better physiological measures have led to new theories of and treatments for such serious problems as posttraumatic stress disorder.

Behavioral Avoidance Tests (BATs). Another popular performance measure in controlled observation is the behavioral avoidance test, or BAT, which is designed to assess overt anxiety in relation to specific objects and situations. In BATs, clients are confronted with a stimulus they fear while observers record the type and degree of avoidance displayed. Informal BATs were conducted with children as early as the 1920s (e.g., Jones, 1924a, b), but it was not until the early 1960s that systematic avoidance-testing procedures became a common form of controlled observational assessment.

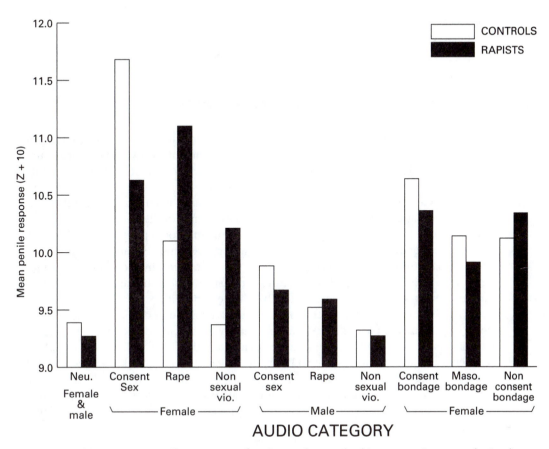

FIGURE 6.9 Average penile responses of rapists and control subjects to various sexual stimuli.

In a study of systematic desensitization (see Chapter 8) for snake phobia, Peter Lang and David Lazovik (1963) asked clients to enter a room containing a harmless caged snake and to approach, touch, and pick up the animal. Observers gave the clients avoidance scores based on whether they were able to look at, touch, or hold the snake. Many other fear stimuli, including rats, spiders, cockroaches, and dogs have been used in other versions of the BAT, and the "look-touch-hold" coding system for scoring responses has been replaced by more sophisticated measures. These include recording how close the client is able to come to the fear target, maximum amount of interaction achieved, length of time between entering the test room and making physical contact with the target, overt anxiety behaviors during the test, and changes in physiological arousal (heart rate, respiration, galvanic skin response). Usually, clients are asked to approach the feared target, but occasionally BATs are set up to measure how long clients can look at a frightening stimulus or how close they will allow that stimulus to approach them.

Controlled performance tests have also been developed to assess fear of certain *situations*. Paul's (1966) use of contrived speeches to assess public speaking anxiety was an early example of this type of assessment. Others include asking people who fear heights to climb fire escapes (Emmelkamp & Felten, 1985) or observing dental phobics as they wait for and receive dental treatment (Getka & Glass, 1992).

EVALUATION OF OBSERVATIONAL ASSESSMENT

As noted in Chapter 3, direct observation of behavior can help avoid many inference problems that reduce the reliability and validity of some interview and test procedures. Behaviorally oriented clinicians, the most enthusiastic proponents of observational assessment, have argued that this approach provides the most accurate and relevant source of clinical assessment data. Observations have even been likened to photographs in that they are thought to provide a clear and dispassionate view of human behavior. But just as a photograph is the combined product of the content of the scene, the equipment used, the photographer's techniques, and the developing process, data from observational procedures are influenced by factors other than the behavior of clients. Some of these factors can distort observational assessment, meaning that observations are not automatically reliable and valid.

To illustrate, consider a situation in which a clinician decides to include observational procedures as part of an assessment battery for a distressed couple. A controlled situation is set up in which the couple is videotaped as they talk about one of their problems and attempt to resolve it. Later, the videotape is scored by trained observers using a coding system. A summary of the couple's behavior would result, and it might be inferred that the tape conveyed a representative sample of how the members of the pair relate to one another. This observational procedure is direct and apparently objective, but is it reliable and valid?

Reliability in Observational Assessment

The first question to ask about observational data is, "Are they reliable?" To what extent do observers arrive at the same ratings or conclusions about the behavior they see? If interobserver agreement is low, such that our couple's interaction was scored in different ways by different individuals, one cannot place much confidence in the observation, or in the summary flowing from it. The assessor would either have to believe one particular observer or come up with some average of all the observers' data. Neither alternative is attractive because (1) there is usually an inadequate basis for trusting one observer above others, and (2) averages of widely discrepant scores represent a mathematical but not a behavioral reality (the *average* scores from unreliable observers probably does not reflect the client's *actual* behavior).

Fortunately, the interobserver reliability of modern clinical observation systems that use trained observers is usually very high; coefficients in excess of .80 and .90 are not uncommon (Paul & Lentz, 1977; Ward & Naster, 1991; Zuardi, Loureiro, & Rodrigues, 1995). When clients observe their own behavior through self-monitoring, agreement between their data and those of external observers is sometimes in the .90s (Kazdin, 1974). Although such impressive figures do not always appear, when they do occur it is usually because the clinical assessor has avoided some of the pitfalls, caused by the following factors, that can threaten the reliability of observational data (see Cone & Foster, 1982).

Task Complexity.   If observers must make many difficult discriminations in recording, coding, or rating behavior, reliability will probably be lower than if fewer, easier judgments are required (Mash & McElwee, 1974). In the case of our couple, the clinician would be more likely to obtain reliable observations using a fifteen-category rather than a one-hundred-category coding system. Observation will also be more reliable if clients do not engage in a large number of short-duration responses in quick succession.

Knowledge of Reliability Checks.   Another factor affecting reliability is the observers' knowledge that their agreement is being monitored. When people are first trained to use an observation system, they usually work hard during practice sessions and pay close attention to the task, partly because they are being evaluated. Later, when "real" data are being collected, the observers may become careless if they think no one is checking their reliability (Romanczyk et al., 1973; Taplin & Reid, 1973). The same can be said for clients who self-monitor their behavior (Lipinski et al., 1975). Of course, observers' knowledge that they are being checked can have other effects, too; for example, they might deliberately or inadvertently collaborate, thus producing misleadingly high levels of interobserver agreement (see Foster, Bell-Dolan, & Burge, 1988). The best protection against this threat to reliability is unobtrusive or random checking of performance. Thus, our clinician should tell the observers that their agreement about the couple's behavior will be checked from time to time but that they will not be told when.

Observer Training.   If the observers of our couple are told to record laughter in their coding system but are not given a definition of laughter, one observer might count belly laughs but not giggles, while another might include everything from smiles to violent guffaws. Obviously, when observers define for themselves what is meant by specific coding category labels or by global constructs such as "hostile" or "happy," the reliability of observational data tends to drop dramatically.

Yet, as already noted, high reliability coefficients do not always mean that an observation system is being used properly, because reliability estimates can be artificially inflated (Harris & Lahey, 1982; Cone & Foster, 1982). For one thing, observers sometimes cheat, especially when they want to please their employer and when they are unsupervised. Cheating usually takes the form of altering scores to enhance agreement. Obviously, our clinician should supervise the coding of the couple's behavior and arrange for reliability coefficients to be calculated by someone other than the observers.

Another situation in which high reliabilities may be misleading is when there is *observer drift* (O'Leary & Kent, 1973). When observers work together in unchanging pairs or groups, they tend to form their own well-agreed-upon version of the rating system so that, over time, each pair or group "drifts" away from the others. Within each pair or group, reliability may be very high, but if new pairings are made or if between-pair reliabilities are calculated, interobserver agreement may be much lower. This problem can be combated by constantly rotating membership in observer pairs and/or periodic retraining of all observers.

Interpreting Reliability Figures.   Another question arises when high reliability figures are encountered: How were they calculated? For example, suppose that our clinician reported interobserver agreement as 95%. Depending on how this figure was calculated, it could either mean there was strong agreement about what the observers *saw* or about what they did *not* see. If agreement is registered only when two observers record the occurrence of the same behavior at the same time, 95% would be impressive indeed. However, if agreement also means that each of two observers did *not* record the occurrence of a particular behavior that seldom occurs, the agreement percentage could be inflated by the low base rate of that behavior. Agreeing about the nonoccurrence of a behavior that happens rarely is not a useful indicator of reliability.

Several mathematical procedures are available to control or correct problems of this type, but they are not used uniformly enough to warrant unequivocal faith in the reliability figures cited in observational assessment literature. So while interobserver agreement in clinical observation can be high, interpretation of what various reliability figures mean depends on how they were calculated (Lagenbucher, Labouvie, & Morganstern, 1996; Suen, Ary, & Covalt, 1990).

Validity of Observational Assessment

The next questions to ask about observational procedures are those concerning validity: Are these procedures measuring what they are supposed to measure, and how well are they doing it? At first glance, observation of behavior would appear to rank highest in validity among all clinical assessment approaches. Instead of hearing about behavior in interviews or speculating about behavior through tests, the clinician using observation can watch the "real thing."

To a certain extent, however, the directness or face validity of clinical observation has led to a deemphasis on measuring its validity in traditional terms (Cone, 1988). After all, if we *observe* aggression in our married couple, are we not *assessing* aggression, and is that not enough to establish the validity of our technique? The answer is yes only if we can show that (1) the behaviors coded (e.g., raised voices) constitute a satisfactory definition of aggression, (2) the data faithfully reflect the nature and degree of aggression occurring during observation, and (3) the clients' behaviors while under observation accurately represent their behavior in related, but unobserved, situations.

When numerous nonparticipant observers repeatedly report that a child engages in violent, unprovoked attacks on siblings and peers at home and in school, and when these data agree in detail with the reports of parents and teachers, the validity of the observational data seems well established. Still, there are a number of factors that can threaten the validity of observation.

Defining Observation Targets. A fundamental requirement for establishing the validity of observational assessment is clarifying the target to be measured. When clinicians set out to develop an observation system for assertion, for example, they typically use what we referred to in Chapter 5 as an analytical approach. Thus, instructions to observers about what aspects of behavior to look for and code, and how these targets are defined, reflect the assessor's view of what constitutes assertiveness. One clinician might assess assertiveness by observing clients' ability to refuse unreasonable requests, while another might focus on the direct expression of positive affect. This problem of definition may never be resolved to everyone's satisfaction, but evaluating the validity of an observational system begins with questions about what behavioral features are being coded.

Another way to assess the validity of observation is to ask to what extent the resulting data correlate as expected with other criteria. For example, does the ability to refuse unreasonable requests occur more often in people judged to be assertive by their peers? If the observation system is targeting an important part of a phenomenon of interest, meaningful relationships of this type should emerge (Foster et al., 1988). Clinicians who assume that such relationships exist, but don't measure them, run the risk of collecting samples of behavior whose validity is minimal beyond the confines of the clinicians' idiosyncratic target definitions.

This problem has been given surprisingly little attention by users of observational assessment, partly because, as already noted, the validity of observation appears so obvious. Still, one series of studies explored the relationship between certain categories of a Behavioral Coding System (BCS) and other variables (Jones, Reid, & Patterson, 1975). The results showed that children who had been previously identified as aggressive were, in fact, aggressive when observed through the BCS.

Other researchers have tried to get around target-definition problems by designing their observation systems using empirical rather than analytical methods. So instead of deciding ahead of time what particular behaviors reflect anxiety, for example, the assessor might code virtually all client behavior that occurs during observation. These overt behavioral data are then correlated with other information (e.g., client self-reports, physiological measures, and third-party accounts) about the client's responses to the observed situation and to other relevant situations. If a pattern of overt behavior, such as trembling and freezing, is strongly associated with high scores on other measures also designed to assess anxiety, that behavior pattern can be referred to as "anxious" with greater confidence than if the assessor had simply decreed that trembling and freezing indicate anxiety. If, in addition, the anxious behavior increases under circumstances that are known to be stressful, or if it changes for the better following some form of treatment, evidence for the validity of the observational system becomes stronger. This empirical approach has been used to develop an observation system for measuring patients' fear while in a dental office (Kleinknecht & Bernstein, 1978).

A more sophisticated strategy for building validity into an observation system is embodied in Goldfried and D'Zurilla's (1969) *behavior-analytic* model. Here, the assessor first carefully explores the construct to be measured and then custom tailors observations to that construct. An example of an observation system based on this strategy is the Taxonomy of Problematic Social Situations for Children, or TOPS (Dodge, McClaskey, & Feldman, 1985). Researchers first asked teachers and psychologists to describe social situations in which peer problems might occur for school children. The resulting sixty-four situations were then classified into one of eight categories by undergraduate assistants. The categories involved activities such as responding to failures, attempting to join a peer group, being rejected or excluded by a peer group, and the like. Next, teachers were asked to use the TOPS to rate a group of children who frequently suffered rejection from peers as well as a group who enjoyed good peer relationships. At the same time, thirty-nine clinic-referred children with a history of rejection and thirty-four socially adjusted children were asked to role-play responses to a subsample of representative situations from the TOPS. Results showed that socially rejected children were less competent in several social situations, whether measured by teacher ratings or role-play assessments. Other behavior-analytic approaches to assessment have been used to observe and treat social-skill deficits in juvenile delinquents (Gaffney & McFall, 1981), violent men (Holtzworth-Munroe, 1992), and rapists (Lipton, McDonel, & McFall, 1987).

Observer Effects.   No matter how reliable observers are, they must also be accurate about what they see if their data are to be valid. Clinicians and researchers must attend to several issues relating to observer accuracy. First, there is the problem of observer error. Just as interviewers sometimes remember certain client responses more accurately than others, observers can also make mistakes.

Second, the quality of observational data can also be compromised by observer *bias* (Harris & Lahey, 1982). Observers sometimes see things that are not objectively there, partly because, as the Gestalt school of psychology emphasized, there is a tendency in human perceptual systems to "complete" or "close" incomplete stimulus patterns. Thus, an observer might *see* a child raise a hand toward another child, but *record* the behavior as "striking" rather than "hand raising." There are many similar examples in other situations; one radiologist assumed that a button appearing on an X-ray was on the patient's vest when, in fact, it was lodged in the patient's throat (Johnson, 1953). "Our assumptions define and limit what we see, i.e., we tend to see things in such a way that they will fit in with our assumptions even if this involves distortion or omission" (Johnson, 1953, p. 79). In this case, the error arose because "buttons occur more frequently on vests than in throats" (Rosenthal, 1966, p. 6).

The effects of bias are stronger when observers are asked to make broad, general ratings about behavior after getting information about what to expect (e.g., Martell & Willis, 1993). In one study of this phenomenon, psychiatrists, psychologists, and graduate students listened to a taped interview in which an actor portrayed a well-adjusted man (Temerlin, 1968). When they listened under neutral conditions, 57% of the observers rated the man as "healthy," while 43% called him "neurotic." No one thought he was psychotic. However, ratings were biased if the tape was described as either that of a "perfectly healthy man" or a person who "looks neurotic but actually is psychotic." In the healthy-bias condition, 100% of the listeners rated the man as "healthy," but in the psychotic-bias condition, an average of nearly 30% diagnosed the man "psychotic," and over 60% called him "neurotic."

In another study involving global descriptions based on observations, eight pairs of observers watched a child in a nursery school (Rapp, 1965, cited by Johnson & Bolstad, 1973). One member of each pair was told that the client was feeling "under par," while the other was told the child was feeling "above par." In seven of the eight pairs, the observers' descriptions differed significantly and corresponded with their induced expectations. It is important to note, however, that (1) when specific, well-defined behavioral coding systems rather than global ratings are used, observers are much less vulnerable to the effects of externally imposed bias (Foster et al., 1988); and (2) some better-designed studies have failed to replicate the effects of bias on observation (Cone & Foster, 1982).

Reactivity of Observation.   In addition to worrying about observer bias, clinicians using observational assessment must be concerned about *reactivity*: Clients may react to being observed by intentionally or unintentionally altering the behaviors that are of greatest clinical interest. This problem parallels the issues of response bias and impression management discussed in relation to interviews and tests in Chapters 4 and 5. To appreciate the problem of reactivity, simply turn on a tape recorder or video camera at a social gathering. Noticeable changes in people's behavior usually occur immediately and last either until the device is switched off or the novelty wears off. Awareness of the reactivity of clinical observation has a long history (Covner, 1942), but the magnitude of the problem is still unclear.

Some psychologists claim that observational procedures have only a minimal and short-term reactive influence on subjects, after which their behavior regains its natural spontaneity. One research team found that the amount of appropriate behavior by retarded adult women did not change when they were watched by a visible observer versus a hidden video camera (Mercatoris & Craighead, 1974). The majority of other studies, however, suggest stronger reactivity effects (e.g., Baum, Forehand, & Zegiob, 1979; Cone & Foster, 1982; Harris & Lahey, 1982). For example, increases in mothers' play, positive verbal statements, and other behaviors appeared when mother–child interactions were overtly as opposed to covertly observed (Zegiob, Arnold, & Forehand (1975).

As already noted, even self-monitoring can be reactive. For example, smoking usually decreases when smokers record each cigarette they light (Nelson, 1977). In fact, because self-monitoring can produce beneficial changes in recorded behavior, it has been used—with inconsistent results—as a part of therapy programs for habit control, hair-pulling, suicidal thinking, and improved study skills (Allen, 1996; Clum & Curtin, 1993; Mouton & Stanley, 1996; Murtada & Haccoun, 1996). In short, it is not easy for clinicians to draw firm conclusions about whether and to what extent awareness of observations will alter clients' behavior. "There seems little reason to doubt that the presence of an observer may, in fact, affect the behavior of those he observes. But the number of factors determining the magnitude and direction of behavior change may be so great that manifest reactivity is scattered and almost completely unpredictable" (Kent & Foster, 1977, p. 289). To be on the safe side, then, it would appear that clinicians should observe clients as unobtrusively as possible (using two-way mirrors and hidden video cameras), or at least schedule assessment sessions that are long enough to give clients ample time to become used to being observed (Haynes & Horn, 1982).

Representativeness of Observed Behavior.   Even after reactive effects have disappeared, observed behavior may not provide a *representative* or *ecologically valid* (Brunswick, 1947) picture of the client. There is a certain irony to this criticism, because it implies that observations fail to meet the main goal for which they were designed. However, the problem arises because the high cost of observations often limits the number of occasions on which they are made. Therefore, any idiosyncratic events that may arise on those occasions can undermine the validity of the observation. For example, the client might have a hangover on the day of an observation, or there may have been a recent death in the family. Any number of factors can result in temporary patterns of depressed, euphoric, or hyperactive behavior that are atypical of the client.

Further, the observation situation itself can exert an influence on client behavior through social cues, or *demand characteristics* (Orne, 1962), that suggest what actions are, or are not, appropriate and expected. Thus, if a clinician observes a couple in a setting that contains strong social cues about how the clients should behave (e.g., "We would like to measure just how much fighting you two actually do."), the observation may reveal a degree of conflict that is unusually high for that couple. In such a case, the clinician will have learned more about the effects of the situation than about the couple's typical interaction style.

Problems of situational bias occur most often in controlled settings, because the client must go to some identified location to be observed and is thus aware of the purpose of assessment. Further, specific instructions about the observation are usually given to orient clients and to help them recognize when assessment begins and ends. The social and situational cues in such observational assessments can alter client behavior radically. In one study, for example, male college-student volunteers were asked to undergo a period of isolation in a small, well-lit room (Orne & Schiebe, 1964). For half the subjects, the room was described as a sensory deprivation chamber, the experimenter wore a white coat, conducted a medical history interview, asked the subject to sign a medical release form, and displayed an "emergency tray" of drugs and equipment that were part of the "precautionary measures" in the laboratory. He also mentioned that release from the chamber was possible by pressing an emergency alarm if "the situation becomes difficult," and that a physician was available "if you should feel upset." The rest of the subjects were told they were in a control group; there was no white coat, medical interview, "emergency tray," "emergency alarm," or attending physician. Once in the isolation room, control subjects appeared relaxed and comfortable. They rested or slept, worked on various time-filling tasks, and said little. "Sensory deprivation" subjects, on the other hand, were restless, slept very little, expressed discomfort or feelings of disorientation, and "gave an impression of almost being tortured" (Orne & Schiebe, 1964, p. 11).

Similar situational effects operate in the assessment of social skills, fears, and other clinical targets. For example, in a study designed to measure assertiveness, college students were asked to respond to tape-recorded social situations similar to those described earlier (Nietzel & Bernstein, 1976). The assertiveness of their responses was scored on a five-point scale. All subjects heard the tape twice, under either the same or differing demand situations. The "low-demand" situation asked subjects for their "natural reactions," but in the "high-demand" situation they were told to be "as assertive as you think the most assertive and forceful person could be." The results are summa-

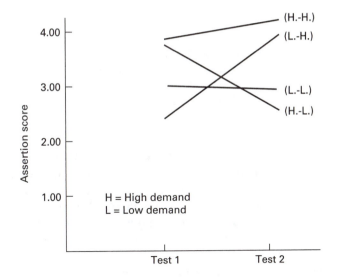

FIGURE 6.10 Situational effects on observed assertiveness. (Nietzel & Bernstein, 1976).

rized in Figure 6.10. Obviously, these instructions not only had an initial effect, but were capable of significantly altering subjects' behavior from test to test.

Other research on observational anxiety assessment has shown that the instructions given, the presence or absence of an experimenter, the characteristics of the physical setting, and other situational variables influence the amount of fear clients display during BATs (e.g., Bernstein, 1973; Bernstein & Nietzel, 1977). Similarly, the behavior of children during at-home observations can be influenced to look "good" or "bad," depending upon what their parents think the assessor wants to see (Johnson & Lobitz, 1974). Demand characteristics may also influence the symptoms of mental disorder observed in psychotherapy. Some researchers believe, for example, that the dramatic changes in clients' behavior and emotion seen in cases of dissociative identity disorder (formerly multiple personality disorder) may be a response to cues coming from therapists during treatment sessions (Spanos, 1994).

Various strategies have been suggested to minimize situational bias in observational assessment (Bernstein & Nietzel, 1977; Borkovec & O'Brien, 1976), but the problem cannot be entirely eliminated. As long as the stimuli present when the client's behavior is being observed differ from those present when the client is not being observed, we cannot be sure that the behavior displayed during formal observation will generalize to other situations. The best clinicians can do is minimize any cues that might influence client behavior. Utterly naturalistic or unobtrusive observation is theoretically possible, but often not practical. Accordingly, clinicians will continue to rely on contrived, analogue observations to assess some behavioral targets.

A Final Word

Like interviews and tests, observation is not a perfect clinical assessment tool. Nevertheless, it has advantages that make it a valuable source of data. Perhaps the biggest challenge facing clinicians is to translate often cumbersome, expensive, and time-consuming procedures into a practical approach for collecting observational data that are both reliable and valid. In addition, the clinician or researcher must use observation in a way that minimizes the influence of the various distorting factors we have discussed, so that the data generated can have maximum value in an overall assessment plan.

OBSERVATION AT WORK

Q.: How and why is observational assessment important in your work?

Dr. Sandy D'Angelo: A number of children are unable to complete standardized testing because they do not comprehend the instructions or they have behavioral problems that interfere with cooperation. For these children, observational methods, informal assessment during play, and history are the primary sources of information. Observational assessment is also important in tracking progress toward behavioral goals during treatment.

Dr. Hector Machabanski: Observational assessment is important to the work that I do in the schools and with families. In order to gather valid data about a child's functioning, it is essential that I conduct observational assessments in settings relevant to the child's life. In working with families, observational assessment is important in learning about family communication patterns.

Dr. Geoffrey Thorpe: As a behavior therapist, I use observational assessment frequently in my clinical work, but the most structured assessments are reserved for research investigations. For example, observers assess how long a client with agoraphobia can stay in a crowded shopping mall, or rate hesitations and extraneous movements in people with public speaking fears as they give a test speech.

CHAPTER SUMMARY

The goals of observational assessment systems are to collect information about clients that is not available in other ways. Observational methods provide a valuable supplement to test and interview data that may provide even more reliable and valid information. By providing behavior samples, they also allow clinicians to better understand person–situation interactions while minimizing the need to draw inferences about clients' actions. Observation can be conducted in naturalistic or controlled settings (or some blend of the two) by participant or nonparticipant observers who make use of devices ranging from notebooks and timers to video cameras and wireless telemetry. Sometimes, clients are asked to observe and record their own behavior, a procedure called self-monitoring.

Naturalistic observation systems have been developed for use in hospitals, schools, and homes. These systems have the advantage of realism and relevance, but they are expensive and time-consuming, and may be affected by uncontrollable situational factors. To minimize these problems, clinicians often use controlled observations—special circumstances under which clients can be observed as they react to standardized events—including role-played social interactions and performance tests of smoking, eating, drinking, or dealing with a feared object or situation. During controlled observation, clinicians may monitor clients' physiological as well as overt responses.

While observation gets around some of the inference problems that reduce the reliability and validity of many interview and test procedures, it is not a perfect assessment tool. For one thing, data from observational assessments can be influenced by factors other than the behavior of clients. The reliability and validity of observational data depend on the careful training and constant monitoring of observers, precise definition of observation targets, and efforts to guard against the effects of observer bias, reactivity in the observation process, and situational influences such as demand characteristics that might create unrepresentative samples of client behaviors.

Chapter 7

Clinical Interventions: An Overview

People are always trying to change other people's behavior. Politicians work for voters' votes. Advertisers persuade consumers to buy their products. Parents encourage children to abide by their wishes. In fact, almost every human interaction involves an attempt by one party to influence another. Of special interest in this book, of course, is the influence exerted by clinical psychologists in their efforts to help troubled people.

When a clinician acts in a professional capacity to influence clients, the activity is called *clinical intervention* because it constitutes a deliberate attempt to change behavior or social circumstances in a desirable direction. Clinical intervention can take many forms, including *psychotherapy, psychosocial rehabilitation,* and *prevention*. Our description of clinical intervention spans three chapters, beginning here with an overview of psychotherapy, the form of intervention most traditionally associated with clinical psychology. We pay special attention to the common features of most therapeutic approaches, the core assumptions shared by most psychotherapists, and the various modes or formats (individual, group, couples, and family) in which psychotherapy can be offered. (In this chapter, too, we outline the rehabilitative and prevention-oriented interventions that psychologists have developed as part of a movement known as *community psychology*.) In Chapter 8, we provide a more detailed description of the methods associated with the psychodynamic, behavioral, and phenomenological approaches to psychotherapy and, in Chapter 9, we consider the results of research on the effectiveness of various forms of psychotherapy, prevention, and other forms of clinical intervention.

WHAT IS PSYCHOTHERAPY?

The literal translation of *psychotherapy* is "treatment of the psyche." While this is not a sufficient definition, it does suggest something about the fundamental elements that define psychotherapy.

The Participants

To speak of "treating psyches" suggests that minds or personalities are in distress. In some clients, the disturbance is so great that day-to-day functioning is impaired, there is a risk of suicide or harm to others, and hospitalization may be necessary. In others, the disturbance may be less extreme, but still very upsetting. An unhappy marriage, a lack of self-confidence, a nagging fear, an identity crisis, depression, sexual problems, and insomnia are just a few of the problems that motivate people to enter psychotherapy. The common essential feature is that the person's usual coping strategies—such as utilizing the support of friends and family or taking a vacation—are no longer sufficient to deal with the problems. These individuals are suffering and/or have become disturbed enough that they seek, or need, the help of a professional. When that point is reached, the first participant in psychotherapy—the *client*—is identified.

The second participant is the *therapist*. By special training and experience, the therapist is prepared to help clients overcome the disturbance that requires treatment. Therapists should possess skills that enable them to understand clients' problems and then to interact with clients in a way that helps them alleviate, or at least cope more effectively with, those with problems.

In addition to advanced training, psychotherapists are expected to possess personal characteristics that contribute to therapy. The ability to listen and to convey a sense of understanding and sensitivity without being judgmental is one important therapist quality. Another vital attribute is the ability to warmly support troubled clients while, at the same time, reminding them of their capacity and responsibility for making beneficial changes in their lives. Clinicians often summarize these qualities as *genuineness, empathy,* and *unconditional positive regard.* They are called *Rogerian qualities* because Carl Rogers claimed that they are the necessary and sufficient conditions for bringing about therapeutic change.

Clinical psychologists are but one of many types of professionals who provide psychotherapy services. People seeking or requiring these services may receive them from psychiatrists, counseling psychologists, psychiatric social workers, psychiatric nurses, family counselors, and pastoral counselors. Not surprisingly, though, most people do not immediately approach mental health professionals for help with their problems. They are more likely to first consult one of a variety of nonprofessional caregivers, including friends, physicians, ministers, teachers, police officers, lawyers, family members, and neighbors. Emory Cowen (1982) studied four groups of these "natural caregivers"—hairdressers, divorce lawyers, bartenders, and industrial supervisors—and found that some of the helping strategies they used resembled professionals' techniques (e.g., proposing alternative solutions). In short, just as psychotherapy is not the exclusive province of clinical psychologists, efforts to help people change are not restricted to the mental health professions alone.

The Therapeutic Relationship

What makes professional psychotherapy unique is not its cast of characters, but the special relationship that develops between therapist and client. What are the characteristics of this relationship? First, it is one in which both parties are aware of why they are meeting and of certain rules and goals associated with their interaction. The relationship should be a voluntary one initiated by the client and accepted by the therapist.[1]

Psychotherapy often begins with a therapeutic contract that specifies the goals of treatment, the procedures to be employed, the potential risks, and the rights and responsibilities of client and therapist. In many instances the contract is negotiated informally, with both parties providing information about what they expect therapy to accomplish. In other instances, the contract takes the form of a signed document. In either case, contracts are designed to help the therapeutic relationship become one in which clients are active decision makers, not passive recipients of help (Blau, 1988).

Although the therapist may be friendly and sympathetic, the therapeutic relationship involves more than compassion. Therapy sometimes requires the clinician to be an objective assessor of clients' problems and at other times to be an insistent coach who helps clients overcome their reluctance to look at and deal with those problems. Therapists give psychological support even as they challenge clients to give up old ways of thinking and behaving in exchange for new, more adaptive alternatives.

The intensity of the therapeutic relationship may tempt the therapist to discard a professional orientation toward clients in favor of more spontaneous reactions, including pity, frustration, hostility, boredom, or sexual attraction. Most therapists try to stay alert to the way in which their personal needs intrude upon therapy. A desire to detect and neutralize these needs in the therapy situation is a major reason why some therapists undergo therapy themselves. The ethical obligations of psychologists, discussed more fully in Chapter 14, require them to avoid any romantic involvement with their clients.

The therapist attempts to form an attentive relationship with the client without losing sight of the fact that the relationship must advance the client's efforts to change. Thus, the therapeutic relationship requires a "balance of attachment and detachment" (Korchin, 1976). With some clients, a therapeutic relationship develops easily; with others, the "capacity for collaboration" is lacking and therapy suffers as a result (Strupp & Hadley, 1979).

The relationship between client and therapist imposes several commitments on the therapist's part that function to insulate the relationship from the influence of out-

---

[1]This is the ideal arrangement, but in many cases the client enters therapy not as a voluntary participant, but because a parent, judge, employer, spouse, or other family member becomes distressed by the client's behavior and compels the individual to seek help.

side forces. Confidentiality is the most essential of these commitments. The therapist protects the client's privacy and does not reveal information that the client shares in therapy.[2] In addition, therapists are obligated to regard the welfare of their clients as their main priority. With very few exceptions, the therapist's actions must be directed by a singular concern: What is best for my client?

How can a therapist best nurture the therapeutic bond? What client qualities tend to promote a positive alliance with a therapist? Extensive research on these questions suggests that, in general, therapeutic relationships flourish when both parties are capable of bringing three elements to the situation (Orlinsky & Howard, 1986): *role investment* (the personal effort both parties commit to therapy), *empathic resonance* (the degree to which both parties are "on the same wavelength"), and *mutual affirmation* (the extent to which both parties care for each other's well-being).

Hans Strupp (1989) provides the following eloquent recipe for therapists' contributions to the therapeutic relationship:

> Patients reasonably expect a therapist to be human—keenly attentive, interested, caring, respectful, and empathic. His or her manner should be natural and unstudied; there should be a willingness to respond to patients' questions and concerns; a therapist should never criticize, never diminish the patient's self-esteem and self-worth, and should leave no doubt about his or her commitment and willingness to help. There may be occasions when reassurance and even advice are appropriate. The patient should never feel that he or she is "just another patient." The therapeutic relationship should be experienced as a "real" relationship rather than an artificial or contrived one. This should be possible even though its "professional" aspects are observed. A good therapist should obviously refrain from fueling power struggles or reciprocating angry provocations. The therapist's language should be simple, straightforward, and understandable. The patient should feel that the therapist understands his or her feelings, at least a good part of the time. (p. 723)

Varying Views of the Therapeutic Relationship. All therapists attribute considerable importance to the therapeutic relationship and work carefully to establish a good one. In general, therapists of all theoretical stripes believe that a helping alliance between client and therapist is formed when the therapist responds with consistent empathy to the needs of the client. When an accepting atmosphere is provided by the therapist, the client will be able to feel securely attached to another person (perhaps in a manner not previously experienced), will have a model for clear interpersonal communication, and will feel strong enough to attempt new solutions to old personal problems. Beyond these general goals, proponents of the main approaches to clinical psychology described in Chapter 2 tend to hold differing views of the ideal therapeutic relationship and the role it plays in therapy.

Phenomenologically oriented therapists regard the therapeutic relationship as the essential element in therapy. Carl Rogers, the founder of client-centered therapy, took the position that the client–therapist relationship is the crucible in which all the

---

[2] There are some exceptions to this rule. See Chapter 14 for a fuller discussion of situations that compel the psychologist to break confidentiality.

necessary and sufficient ingredients for therapeutic change were generated. According to Rogers (1951, pp. 172-173), "the words—of either client or [therapist]—are seen as having minimal importance compared with the present emotional relationship which exists between the two."

In *classical psychoanalysis*, the therapeutic relationship is seen as a vehicle through which clients can begin to see how their present behavior is determined by experiences in earlier periods of life. Psychoanalysts speak of the *transference relationship,* or simply *transference* to refer to the fact that, after a period of therapy, the client begins to attach to the therapist the friendly, hostile, or ambivalent attitudes and feelings the client formerly felt in relation to parents or other significant figures from the past. As a consequence, the original conflicts of early familial relationships are repeated—and can be examined—in the therapy relationship. To encourage transference, the analyst remains passive, detached, and far less spontaneous than is the case in Rogerian therapy, for example. The following advice from Freud reveals his view of the therapeutic relationship: "I cannot recommend my colleagues emphatically enough to take as a model in psychoanalytic treatment the surgeon who puts aside all his own feelings, including that of human sympathy, and concentrates his mind on one single purpose, that of performing the operation as skillfully as possible (Freud, 1912, p. 121).

Contemporary psychodynamic therapists, however, tend to take a more humanistic view of the client–therapist relationship than Freud did (e.g., Kohut, 1971). They recommend that the analyst not be so detached or neutral about the client's human needs that the client comes to lose faith in the analyst as a helper. They see the therapeutic relationship as offering clients a second chance to correct interpersonal problems that linger from the past.

Interpersonal therapists regard the therapeutic relationship as the means by which the client can learn alternative styles of interacting with other people that are more productive and satisfying than the narrow, selfish security maneuvers in which the client is entrenched. This view requires the therapist to actively assess and evoke specific types of interpersonal behavior, react to it in prescribed ways, and monitor the effects of his or her own interpersonal style on clients. Because of these requirements, interpersonal therapists tend to take a more provocative, strategic approach to the therapeutic relationship than do other therapists.

Most *behavioral* and *cognitive-behavioral* therapists tend to view the therapy relationship as an important but not sufficient condition of therapy (Sweet, 1984). It is seen as a useful context in which more specific behavior-change techniques are introduced. Alan Goldstein (1973, p. 221) put it this way: "In most cases, it is required that an atmosphere of trust be established if any therapeutic intervention is to be effective. This usually is accomplished quickly by the therapist through his establishing that (1) he understands and accepts the patient, (2) that the two of them are working together, (3) and that the therapist has at his disposal the means to be of help in the direction desired by the patient." Other behavioral therapists, however, believe that the therapeutic relationship plays a larger role; they see it as the crucial element in bringing about beneficial change because it gives the therapist the opportunity to model new skills and reinforce specific changes in the client's behavior (Follette, Naugle, & Callaghan,

1996). In their view, providing contingent reinforcement of clients' appropriate behavior as it occurs in the therapeutic relationship is one of the most powerful intervention tools therapists have (Kohlenberg & Tsai, 1991).

THE TECHNIQUES OF PSYCHOTHERAPY

There are dozens of psychotherapeutic techniques. Every system of psychotherapy has its preferred procedures, and every therapist has a unique style of employing those procedures. The therapist's methods are usually based on some formal theory of personality and psychopathology in general and the client's problem in particular (see Chapter 2). Although therapists remain flexible, their therapeutic methods are also usually guided by personal preferences and the general principles which they believe underlie effective treatment. These general principles should be grounded in empirical research, though many therapists do employ methods whose effectiveness is not well supported (see Chapter 9).

Psychotherapeutic approaches differ in the extent to which their underlying theories of personality and disorder are related to specific techniques. For example, complex psychoanalytic theories of personality are not very specific about what procedures should be used in applying them to a given case, while many behavioral and cognitive-behavioral theories specify in great detail the procedures to employ in treatment.

Treatment approaches also vary in terms of the changes they are designed to produce (Andrews, 1989; Messer & Winokur, 1980). (Refer again to the case of Mr. B. in Chapter 2.) Behavioral therapists are likely to deal directly with the problem as the client initially presents it (along with other difficulties that might contribute to the primary complaint). For example, a mother who reports depression and fears that she will kill her children might be assigned a variety of "homework assignments" involving her relationship with her husband, disciplinary methods for her children, or the development of new, out-of-the-house activities for herself. By contrast, a psychoanalyst would explore the presumed underlying causes of the mother's depression; therapy might be aimed at helping the woman understand how her current symptoms relate to feelings of inadequacy as a mother because of failure to meet her own mother's rigid and unrealistic standards. Finally, a phenomenological therapist might deal with the problem by helping the mother discover her potential for creating alternatives that would free her from the one-dimensional life in which she now feels trapped.

These theory-driven differences notwithstanding, several common factors are found in most therapeutic approaches. One of these, as already noted, is the use of the therapeutic relationship in the client's best interests. The others are described in the following sections.

Fostering Insight

Insight into psychological problems was a chief objective for Freud, who described it as "re-education in overcoming internal resistances" (Freud, 1904, p. 73). While Freud was interested in a particular type of insight—analysis of unconscious influences—most therapists aim for insight in the general sense of greater self-knowledge. Clients are expected to benefit from learning why they behave in certain ways, because such knowledge is presumed to contribute to the development of new behavior. The psychotherapist's rationale for fostering a client's insight is like the well-known justification for studying history: to know the errors of the past in order to avoid repeating them.

Therapists of all theoretical persuasions seek to promote self-examination and self-knowledge in their clients, though they may go about it in differing ways. Some clinicians focus on a specific type of content; dream analysis would be an example. Others try promoting insight by asking their clients to examine the implications of certain behaviors (e.g., "What relationship do you see between your troubles with your boss and the dislike you express for your father?"). Behavioral therapists stress the importance of helping the client understand how behavior is functionally related to past learning and current environmental factors.

A common technique for developing insight is for the therapist to *interpret* the client's behavior. The purpose of interpretation is not to convince clients that the therapist is right about the significance of some event, but to motivate clients to carefully examine their own behavior and draw new conclusions about its meaning. Although interpretation remains a main technique for many psychotherapists, some clinicians caution against the dangers of interpretations that are too confrontive or challenging (Strupp, 1989). Particularly when working with very disturbed clients, therapists who minimize their use of interpretation in favor of being actively supportive, emotionally soothing, and directly reassuring tend to achieve the best outcomes (Jones, Cumming, & Horowitz, 1988). Conversely, less-disturbed clients benefit more from therapy experiences in which the therapist interprets connections between their behavior in therapy and their relationships outside of therapy (Jones et al., 1988).

Reducing Emotional Discomfort

Clients sometimes come to a therapist in such emotional anguish that it is difficult for them to participate actively in therapy. In such instances, the therapist will try to reduce the client's distress enough to allow the person to begin working on the problem. Therapists do not strive to eliminate all discomfort; in so doing, they might also eliminate the client's motivation for working toward more lasting change. The challenge is to diminish extreme distress without sapping the client's desire to deal with enduring problems.

A common method for reducing client discomfort is to use the therapeutic relationship to boost the client's emotional strength. Clients gain emotional stability and renewed confidence by knowing that the therapist is a personal ally, a buffer against the onslaughts of a hostile world. Some therapists offer direct reassurances such as "I know things seem hopeless right now, but I think you will be able to make some important changes in your life."

Encouraging Catharsis

Clients are usually encouraged to express emotions freely in the protective presence of the therapist. This technique is known as *catharsis,* and it involves the release of pent-up emotions that the client has not acknowledged for a long time, if ever. The therapist encourages the client to give voice to those emotions, believing that through their release they will be eased. At the least, catharsis may help the client become less frightened of certain emotions.

Although therapists have always been concerned with their clients' emotional experiences, empirical research on the value of emotion-focused techniques has been slow to accumulate. Recent research points to the value of emotion-focused interventions in at least five areas (Greenberg & Safran, 1989): (1) synthesizing or getting in touch with emotions so they can be understood and expressed in acceptable, even constructive ways; (2) intensifying certain emotions, often through nonverbal, expressive methods, so they can instigate useful behavior; (3) restructuring emotions by giving new information that allows emotions to be modified in desired directions; (4) evoking emotions so that thoughts and behaviors strongly and specifically bound up with these emotions can be reexamined; and (5) directly modifying those emotions that have become so maladaptive that the client's functioning is impaired.

Providing New Information

Psychotherapy is often educational. The therapist provides new information to correct gaps or distortions in a client's knowledge. Certain areas of adjustment are plagued by misinformation, sexual functioning being a notable example. Some therapists offer direct advice to their clients, adopting a teacherlike role. Others suggest reading material about a topic, a process known as *bibliotherapy* (Marx, et al., 1992). Still others rely on less direct methods—a shrug of the shoulder or a skeptical facial expression—to suggest to clients that there are other ways of perceiving the world. New information gives clients an added perspective on their problems that makes them seem less unusual as well as more solvable.

Assigning Extratherapy Tasks

Therapists often ask clients to perform tasks outside of therapy for the purpose of encouraging the transfer of positive changes to the "real world." Behavioral and cognitive-behavioral therapists are enthusiastic advocates of homework assignments, believing them to be an effective way to promote the generalization of new skills learned in the therapist's office (Nietzel, Guthrie, & Susman, 1991).

Developing Faith, Hope, and Expectations for Change

Of all the procedures common to all systems of therapy, raising clients' faith, hope, and expectations for change is the ingredient most frequently mentioned as a crucial contributor to therapeutic improvement. The curative power of faith is not restricted to psychotherapy. It has been said, for example, that the history of medical treatment is largely the history of the placebo effect (Shapiro, 1971). Some therapy techniques may be particularly potent in raising expectations and creating placebo effects because they appear dramatic or high-tech or because they tap into ingrained cultural norms associated with the best ways to achieve personal change.

Clinicians are so accustomed to thinking about placebo effects in psychotherapy that many attribute much of the success of psychotherapy not to specific techniques, but to the ability of those techniques to generate clients' expectancy for improvement. Recognizing placebo effects in psychotherapy does not eliminate the importance of the specific techniques that distinguish one therapeutic approach from another. It does mean, however, that one important element (some might say the *most* important element) of any effective therapy is that it causes clients to believe that positive changes are attainable (Orlinsky, Grawe, & Parks, 1994).

Part art and part science, psychotherapy profits from the mystique that surrounds both fields. Clients often begin psychotherapy with the belief that they are about to engage in a unique, powerful experience conducted by an expert who can work miracles. The perceived potency of psychotherapy is further enhanced by the fact that clients usually enter it after having fretted for a long time about whether they really need treatment. By the time this internal debate is resolved, the client has a large emotional investment in making the most of a treatment that is regarded with a mixture of fear, hope, and relief.

For their part, therapists encourage clients' faith in the power of psychotherapy by providing assurance that they understand the problem and that, with hard work and commitment by both partners in the therapy relationship, desired changes are possible. The client's perception that "I have been heard and understood and can be helped" can be as important as the soothing effect that physicians create by displaying calm confidence in the face of a patient's mysterious physical symptoms. Most therapists bolster this perception by offering a theory-based *rationale* for why psychotherapy will be effective.

Having structured therapy to increase the client's motivation and expectations for success, the therapist attempts to ensure that the client actually does experience some success as soon as possible. This success might be minor at first—a limited insight after a simple interpretation by the therapist or the successful completion of a not-too-difficult homework assignment. Whatever the means, the objective is to bring about the kind of change the client expects. The cumulative impact of many small changes in the initial stages of therapy helps reinforce clients' confidence that they can control their lives and that their problems are understandable and solvable. Ideally, despair begins to be replaced by a growing feeling of capability as the client glimpses the possibility of a new self-image. As more positive expectancies are confirmed, they grow and, as clients believe that more meaningful changes can be attained, they pursue them with even greater determination which, in turn, makes further success more likely (Howard et al., 1993). All the while, the therapist enhances the client's self-esteem by pointing out that the changes are the result of the client's own efforts (Bandura, 1982).

Some Conclusions

Our discussion reveals that the answer to the question "What is psychotherapy?" must emphasize the following attributes:

1. Psychotherapy consists of a relationship between at least two participants, one of whom has special training and expertise in handling psychological problems and one of whom is experiencing a problem in adjustment and has entered the relationship to alleviate this problem.

2. The psychotherapeutic relationship is a nurturant but purposeful alliance in which varying methods of a psychological nature are employed to bring about the changes desired by the client.

3. These methods are based on some theory regarding psychological problems in general and the specific complaint of the client in particular.

4. Regardless of theoretical preferences, most therapists employ several of the following techniques: development of a productive therapeutic relationship, fostering insight, reducing emotional discomfort, encouraging catharsis, providing new information, assigning extra-therapy tasks, and raising clients' expectancy for change.

The Effects of Psychotherapy

An enormous amount of research has been devoted to measuring the *outcome* of psychotherapy and to understanding the *process* through which therapy works. We discuss this research in more detail in Chapter 9, but the short version of the story is that (1) most forms of therapy usually help most clients (Lambert & Bergin, 1994; Smith, Glass, & Miller, 1980), and (2) the benefits of all forms of treatment probably depend on a few core elements (Orlinsky, Grawe, & Parks, 1994). The most important of these elements appears to be the establishment of a strong therapeutic alliance or relationship in which clients feel supported, accepted, and therefore more capable of changing for the better.

Openness and self-relatedness are the two client characteristics most strongly associated with successful therapy. Clients who display these qualities tend to be open-minded and flexible, to listen carefully to therapists, and to use what they hear in constructive ways. When therapists can form a good therapeutic relationship with such clients, the therapeutic techniques described in this section have the greatest chance of being successful.

Alternative Modes of Intervention

So far, we have described the best-known and most widely used mode of clinical intervention: individual, or one-to-one, psychotherapy. There are several other modes, as well. Some of them—such as group therapy, marital or couples therapy, and family therapy—employ techniques similar to those used in individual psychotherapy and may be derived from the same theories that guide individual treatment. Other modes of intervention—such as psychosocial rehabilitation and primary prevention—bear almost no resemblance to psychotherapy. They rely on different techniques, embrace different assumptions about mental disorders, and may pursue different goals.

Each of these alternative intervention modes tend to be more *social-* than *psycho-*therapy in the sense that they seek, in varying degrees, to deal with how other people contribute to or are affected by disturbed behavior. Couples therapy addresses these issues through understanding and changing interactions in an intimate dyad. Family therapy focuses on how forces within a family affect the functioning of each of its members. Group therapy seeks changes in the way individuals tend to interact in a wide

TABLE 7.1 Socially-Oriented Clinical Intervention Modes	
Intervention Mode	**Emphasis**
Couples Therapy	Help couples in intimate relationships to improve problem-solving and communication skills.
Family Therapy	Change harmful family interaction patterns so that the family system functions better.
Group Therapy	Understand and alleviate disturbances in interpersonal relationships, as revealed in a group setting.
Psychosocial Rehabilitation	Improve clients' abilities to cope with mental disordrs, to limit resulting impairments, and to live in the community.
Prevention	Head off the appearance of mental disorders by counteracting risk factors and strengthening protective factors.

range of interpersonal relationships. Psychosocial rehabilitation aims to help people displaying mental disorders cope with the occupational, economic, family, and environmental effects of those disorders. Finally, prevention programs attempt to modify social, economic, and environmental factors that lead to dysfunction among vulnerable populations or to strengthen positive qualities that can protect individuals from developing disorders (see Table 7.1).

GROUP THERAPY

Group therapy is more than the simultaneous treatment of several individuals. First practiced at the turn of the twentieth century in Boston by Joseph Pratt, and later stimulated by the shortage of professional personnel around the time of World War II, group therapy has progressed to the point that it is now regarded as a valuable intervention in its own right (Klein, 1983).

Every major approach to clinical psychology offers group treatment. There are analytic groups, client-centered and gestalt groups, and behavioral groups. Groups are also popular with many nonprofessional self-help organizations (Gottlieb & Peters, 1991). Weight-control groups, assertiveness groups, consciousness-raising groups, and Alcoholics Anonymous are common examples. Accordingly, it is difficult to provide a complete and general account of group therapy, *per se*. What we can say, however, is that most group therapists emphasize the importance of interpersonal relationships and assume that personal maladjustment involves difficulties in those relationships. Further, as in the case of individual psychotherapy, most group therapies share a set of common features, some of which resemble those found in one-to-one treatment, but most of which are unique to groups. We summarize these features below; a fuller discussion is contained in standard references on group therapy (e.g., Bednar & Kaul, 1994; Yalom, 1985).

Sharing New Information

New information is imparted from two sources in groups: The group leader may offer advice, and advice also comes from other members of the group who share their experiences. The multiple perspectives of the group constitute a richer store of information than would usually be the case with a single therapist. The impact of all this information is magnified by its *consensuality*: While it might be tempting to discount feedback from a therapist, it is more difficult to dismiss as biased or inaccurate the similar opinions of eight or ten group members. In numbers there is strength, especially when the numbers all agree.

Instilling Hope

As with individual psychotherapy, confidence in the therapist and an expectancy that treatment can be helpful are important features of the group mode. The hopes of new group members can be buoyed not only by optimistic therapist comments, but also by special features of groups that increase the positive expectancies of their members. One of these features is the opportunity for group members to observe improvement in others. So even if some clients are impatient about their own slow pace of improvement, seeing positive changes in others may lead to the recognition that progress will eventually come; this may sustain faith in the group.

Universality

By showing that everyone struggles with problems in living, therapy groups help their members learn that they are not alone in their fears, low moods, or other difficulties. This discovery is important because many people are secretive about their problems, which restricts their ability to find out that they are not unique. As group members share their problems they derive comfort from knowing "there are others like me." Learning about the universality of one's problems also soothes anxiety about "going crazy" or "losing control."

Altruism

Groups give clients a chance to discover that they can help other people. Just as group therapy produces new insights into interpersonal weaknesses, it confirms the presence of interpersonal strengths. In addition to being clients, group therapy members serve as therapists for one another. Clinicians refer to the positive emotions that follow altruistic behavior as "feelings of self-worth," an outcome that is promoted by effective group therapy.

Interpersonal Learning

When a group first forms, the interpersonal contacts between members are usually hesitant and guarded, but as group members come to know one another, their contacts become more spontaneous and direct. A properly conducted therapy group is an ideal setting to learn new interpersonal skills. It presents repeated opportunities to practice fundamental social skills with various types of people and with immediate feedback on performance. Groups also contain numerous models for imitative learning, one of the most efficient ways to learn new behaviors.

Recapitulation of the Primary Family

Some group therapists regard the therapy group as a "reincarnation" of clients' primary families. This *family reenactment* is thought to be a curative factor because it allows clients to deal with those early family experiences that still impair their current functioning. Recapitulation of the family is group therapy's counterpart to the transference relationship in individual psychodynamic therapy.

Group Cohesiveness

Cohesiveness is the "attractiveness of a group for its members" (Frank, 1957). Members of cohesive groups are accepting of one another; they are willing to listen to and be influenced by the group. They participate in the group readily, feel secure in it, and are relatively immune to outside disruption of the group's progress. Cohesive groups also permit the expression of hostility, provided such conflicts do not violate the norms of the group. Attendance is reliable in cohesive groups, and premature termination of treatment is not usually a problem (Yalom, 1985).

Cohesiveness is often regarded as the most important factor underlying the beneficial effects of group therapy, partly because it enhances the development of other curative factors (Yalom, 1985). The *acceptance* that members receive from the group may counteract their own feelings of worthlessness. The *public esteem* of the group serves as a reference point that increases members' own *self-esteem* because groups tend to evaluate individual members more favorably than the individuals evaluate themselves. Group members, in turn, will try to change in order to confirm the group's impression. This effect is something like a *group-fulfilling prophecy,* where members are motivated not to let down the group. Behaviors that a client once thought were impossible may be accomplished because of the group's supportive demand that they at least be attempted.

The Practice of Group Therapy

Therapy groups usually consist of six to twelve members. If a group is too small, the advantages of universality and cohesiveness may be jeopardized. With larger groups, feedback may become too mechanical and superficial. There may also be less sensitive exploration of others' viewpoints. Another problem with larger groups is that "isolates" (members who make infrequent contributions) are more likely.

Initial assessment of candidates for a therapy group is often not as structured as it might be in individual psychotherapy, though many group therapists do seek to exclude brain-damaged individuals or those who are paranoid, hypochondriacal, suicidal, extremely narcissistic, sociopathic, drug or alcohol addicted, or psychotic. Group leaders tend to disagree on whether groups should be *homogeneous,* consisting of members who are similar in age, sex, and type of problem, or *heterogeneous,* in which there is a mix of client types. Heterogeneous groups are easier to form. They also have the advantage of exposing members to a wider range of people and perspectives. The major advantage of homogeneous groups is that they facilitate a direct focus on the common problem that motivated each member to enter treatment.

Some groups, like old soldiers, never die; they just add new members as old ones depart. Other groups meet for only a specified number of sessions. These groups may be open to new members, but more often they continue only with the initial participants.

Group meetings are typically longer—usually lasting about two hours—than sessions of individual psychotherapy, mainly because it takes more time for, say, eight clients to talk things over. It also tends to take more time for a group to reach a meaningful level of dialogue. Especially lengthy sessions are a defining characteristic of *marathon* groups, whose meetings may last from six to forty-eight hours or more. The rationale for marathon groups is that as people get tired, they also become less defensive. As social facades erode, people are assumed to be more willing to express their true feelings. (There is little, if any, empirical evidence to support these ideas; in fact, one might just as reasonably suggest that fatigue reduces motivation and makes one more hostile toward other members of the group.)

Regardless of session length, group therapists must walk a fine line between exerting too much control over the group and allowing it to lose its focus. The effective group therapist is a "first among equals" who is responsible for keeping the group on course, steering the group in constructive directions and preventing individual members from getting lost or becoming disruptive along the way.

An Example of Group Therapy

Here is a brief description of the fifth session of therapy for a group of five women and three men, all in their late-twenties and thirties and all unmarried or separated. The cognitive-behavioral orientation of the group's therapist is evident in that the members are asked to concentrate on helping each other improve their coping skills and interpersonal relationships (Rose & LeCroy, 1991).

> As the group settled into places on the floor or on chairs, the therapist welcomed them and asked each member to review what he or she had done throughout the week to complete the assignment of the previous week. One at a time, members described their social achievements, their success in coping with anxiety, and the frequency with which they used the relaxation exercise. Several also related unusually stressful situations they had experienced during the week.
>
> After each had summarized her or his experiences, amid a great deal of praise and support from group members for achievements, Delores volunteered to describe in some detail her situation in which her ever-present feelings of helplessness were intensified. Her supervisor at her office, she stated, was always giving her instructions on the least little thing. "It was as if she thought I was stupid and, frankly, I'm beginning to believe it." The other members inquired as to the nature of her job, which was quite complicated. They noted that she did receive good feedback from her peers, who often consulted with her with various problems. She also noted that in a previous job no one gave her more than

the briefest instructions, and she did fine. Charles wondered whether she couldn't conclude that there was a problem between her and her supervisor and not with her as a person. There was just no evidence that she was dumb in any way; in fact, she appeared to be uniquely qualified to do the job. The others agreed.

Delores said she guessed they were right, but she didn't know what to do about it, and it was making her miserable. She had thought about quitting, but it was in other ways a good job; and besides, she added, "good jobs were hard to get these days."

After careful questioning by the other clients in order to have a clear picture of what was going on, they then provided her with a number of strategies she could employ to deal with the situation and suggested what she could specifically say to herself and to her supervisor. She evaluated and selected several from among these for practice in the group.

MARITAL THERAPY

In *marital therapy*, also known as *couples therapy*, the client is the marriage or other intimate relationship. This treatment mode is also described as conjoint therapy, which means that both members of the couple see the same therapist(s) within the same sessions. In contrast to individual psychotherapy, the focus of marital therapy is usually the couple's *disturbed relationship*, not disturbed individuals who happen to be in a relationship. Indeed, the need for marital therapy usually arises out of the conflicting expectations and needs of the couple. A wife who was initially attracted to her husband because of his dashing charm and playboy image might now find that these qualities threaten the emotional security she wants from their relationship. A husband might come to feel that what he once admired as spunkiness in his wife now challenges his need to dominate the marriage. Intimate relationships are frequently beset by problems in the areas of sexual satisfaction, personal autonomy, dominance–submission, responsibility for child rearing, communication, intimacy, money management, fidelity, and the expression of disagreement and hostility.

Couples therapy can be the main intervention when relationship difficulties are the primary treatment target, or it can be combined with other methods designed to address other problems. For example, when depression, alcoholism, or severe anxiety disorders affect the quality, and even the existence, of a client's marriage or intimate relationship, some mental health experts recommend couples therapy—or at least the involvement of the client's partner—in the treatment of these disorders (Jacobson, Holtzworth-Monroe, & Schmaling, 1989). Some couples even obtain therapy to help them end a marriage or long-term relationship with a minimum of conflict. Such *separation counseling* is often desirable when questions about child-custody must be resolved.

The goals and techniques of marital therapy depend partly on which of these conflicts is the most pressing for a given couple and partly on the theoretical orientation of the therapist. For example, a behaviorally-oriented marital therapist would be likely to help with a couple's communication problems by teaching the partners to replace hostile, unconstructive criticism with comments that clearly express feelings and directly convey requests for the behaviors that each wants from the other. To bring about quick changes in a troubled relationship, *behavioral exchange* contracts may be established. Using such agreements, whenever one partner does something on the other's "wish list" (e.g., listening without interrupting), the other partner will reciprocate by doing something that is desired by the first partner (e.g., paying a compliment).

Cognitive-behavioral marital therapists work to help couples change the way they think about their relationship and modify the attributions they make about each other (Baucom et al., 1989; Bradbury & Fincham, 1990). When couples are preoccupied with deciding who is to blame for their relationship problems, and especially when each member begins to attribute dishonorable motives to everything the other one says or does, it becomes almost impossible for the couple to even work on, let alone solve, their problems. Accordingly, the cognitive-behavioral therapist may teach each member of the couple to recognize, for example, that the other member's anger may reflect anxiety about the future of the relationship, not necessarily an effort to end it.

Marital therapists who adopt a more phenomenological approach may focus on restoring the emotional bond and sense of intimacy the couple once enjoyed. Thus, the goal of *emotionally focused* couples therapy is to help partners become more comfortable expressing and accepting each others' emotional needs (Greenberg & Johnson, 1988). To reach this goal, the therapist may use techniques that allow each partner to get in touch with and resolve, or at least disarm, the lingering resentments or other emotional problems that always seem to be surfacing in their relationship.

Psychodynamically-oriented couples therapy is also designed to help partners understand and resolve areas of conflict, but here it is assumed that the problems may be unconscious. Accordingly, the partners work to understand that the actions of each that cause unhappiness for the other may (unconsciously) arise out of unresolved conflicts experienced in their families of origin or may stem from unmet emotional needs that impair their ability to handle intimacy. The partners may also come to realize that the *pairing* of these individual characteristics may tend to bring out the worst in each other. Following such insights, the partners are helped to work through the emotional meaning of their problems, and to work on conscious efforts to solve them.

Regardless of theoretical orientation, however, most marital therapists tend to emphasize *problem solving*. The touchstone of problem solving is teaching the couple how to communicate and negotiate more effectively with each other. Among the multiple tasks involved in building better communication are teaching the couple to accept mutual responsibility for working on problems, maintaining focus on current relationship problems rather than old grudges, fostering expression of preferences rather than demands for obedience, and negotiating compromises to problems the couple decide cannot be solved.

The following brief excerpt from a couples therapy session illustrates an attempt by the therapist (T) to help a wife (W) learn new ways of communicating some of her negative feelings to her husband:

> T: I do think that what Pete is saying is an important point. There are things that are going to be different about you and each of you is going to think the things you do maybe make more sense than the other person's, and that's probably

going to be pretty much of a reality. You're not going to be able to change all those. You may not be able to change very many of them. And everybody is different. They have their own predilections to do things a certain way and again what's coming through from you is sort of like damning those and saying those are wrong; they're silly, they don't make sense, I don't understand them or whatever. You may not understand them but they are a reality of each of you. That's something you have to learn how to deal with in some way. Otherwise, you . . . the reason I'm stressing this is I think it plays a large part in your criticalness.

W: Well, I do find it difficult to cater to, I guess that's the word, cater to some idiosyncrasies that I find or think are totally foolish. I am intolerant. I am, and I find it very difficult. I find it almost impossible to do it agreeably and without coming on as "Oh, you're ridiculous."

T: I guess what would be helpful would be if you could come on honestly enough to say "I don't like them" or "It doesn't sit well with me" without having to add the additional value judgment of whether they're foolish or ridiculous or whatever. That's the part that hurts. It's when you damn him because of these things—that's gonna hurt. I'm sure from Pete's point of view they make sense for his total economy of functioning. There's some sense to why he does things the way he does, just as there is for why you do things the way you do. It's not that they're foolish. They make sense in terms of where you are, what you're struggling with, and what's the best way you can deal with right now. I'm not trying to say that means you have to like them, but when you come across and say "It's ridiculous or foolish"—that's the part that makes it hurt.

W: Well, tell me again how to say it, because I find it hard to say anything except "That's really stupid—that's silly." I know you said it a minute ago but I lost it.

T: Well, anytime you can say it in terms of how it affects you and say with it, like "It's hard—I find it hard to take," that doesn't say "I find you're an ass for wanting to do that such and such a way. It's just that, I find it hard to take—I get upset in this circumstance" or whatever. Stay with what your feelings are rather than trying to evaluate Pete. (Ables & Brandsma, 1977, pp. 92-94)

FAMILY THERAPY

Just as marital therapy is aimed at changing a *couple's* relationship, family therapy is a mode of treatment aimed at changing patterns of *family* interaction so as to correct family disturbances (Gurman, Kniskern, & Pinsof, 1986). And like couples therapy, family therapy arose from observations that problems seen in individual psychotherapy clients have social contexts and social consequences. It was observed, for example, that clients who showed great improvement during individual therapy while hospitalized often relapsed when they returned to their families. This observation, along with other clinical insights and research, led to several early theories of psychopathology that emphasized the family environment and parent–child interactions as causes of mal-adaptive behavior (Bateson et al., 1956; Lidz & Lidz, 1949; Sullivan, 1953).

The basic concepts underlying family therapy differ from those of individual psychotherapy. In particular, family therapy is grounded in systems theory (von Bertalanffy, 1968), which emphasizes three principles. The first is *circular causality*, meaning that events are interrelated and mutually dependent rather than fixed in a simple cause–effect sequence. Thus, no one member of a family is the cause of another's problems; the behavior of each member depends to some degree on each of the others. The second principle is that of *ecology*, which says that systems can only be understood as integrated patterns, not as collections of component parts. In a family system, a change in the behavior of one member will radiate to affect all the others. The third principle of systems theory is *subjectivity*, which means that there are no objective views of events, only subjective perceptions filtered by the experiences of perceivers within a system. In other words, family members each have their own perception of family events.

Family therapy often begins with a focus on one family member who is having problems. Typically, this *identified client* is a male child (often of adolescent age) whom the parents label as having an unmanageable behavior problem, or a teenage girl who displays an eating disorder. Soon, however, the therapist will try to reframe the identified problems in terms of disturbed family processes or faulty family communication, to encourage all family members to examine their own contributions to the problem, and to consider positive changes that each member can make. As in marital therapy, a common goal of family therapy is improved communications, because disturbed families often rely on coercion as their major means of communication (Patterson, 1982). The message from both parents and children is, "Do what I want or you'll be sorry."

Family therapists operating from a *behavioral* point of view try to teach family members alternative, noncoercive ways of communicating their needs. They teach parents to be firm and consistent in their child-discipline practices, encourage each family member to communicate clearly with one another, educate family members in behavior-exchange principles, discourage blaming of the identified client for all family problems, and help all members of the family to consider whether or not their expectations of other members are reasonable.

Another influential approach is called *strategic*, or *structural* family therapy (Minuchin, 1974; Satir, 1967). Here, the therapist seeks to reframe the main problems of the identified client as a disturbed family process rather than as an individual problem. The goal is to minimize the blame being directed at a person who has become a convenient family scapegoat. For example, the therapist might suggest that an adolescent son's aggressive and defiant behavior may be a sign of teenage insecurity or a plea for more attention from his father. The structural family therapist also helps families communicate more clearly and directly. In many distressed families, emotional messages are so disguised or distorted that family members frequently talk *at* rather than *to* each other. Often they assume they can "read each others' minds," as when a daughter accuses her mother of "never believing anything I say" or when a father accuses his son of "never caring about anyone but yourself."

Virginia Satir (1967), a well-known practitioner of family therapy, offered the following example of how the family therapist tries to help parents and children communicate better with one another. In the first example, the therapist helps a parent understand her son and receive feedback from him.

MOTHER: His pleasure is doing things he knows will get me up in the air. Every minute he's in the house . . . constantly.

THERAPIST: There's no pleasure to that, my dear.

MOTHER: Well, there is to him.

THERAPIST: No, you can't see his thoughts. You can't get inside his skin. All you can talk about is what you see and hear. You can say it looks as though it's for pleasure.

MOTHER: All right. Well, it looks as though, and that's just what it looks like constantly.

THERAPIST: He could be trying to keep your attention, you know. It is very important to Johnny what Mother thinks.

The therapist also helps the child express frustration and anger and specify situations which precipitate anger:

THERAPIST: Do you kind of get mad at Daddy when he gets mad at you?

SON: Yeah, and sometimes he gets real mad and pinches my ear.

THERAPIST: He pinches your ear. Do you feel like hitting him back?

SON: Yeah, I get real mad sometimes.

THERAPIST: So what keeps you from hitting him?

SON: Well he's, uh, he's bigger than me. (pp. 151–152)

Recently, structural family therapy has been adapted to take into account cultural factors that might interfere with the treatment of families from certain ethnic groups. For example, José Szapocznik and his colleagues in Miami, Florida commonly encountered problems in providing family-based drug abuse treatment to adolescents from Hispanic, largely Cuban, backgrounds (Szapocznik et al., 1986). To get these families into treatment, and to keep them coming back, Szapocznik evaluated a set of "family engagement" procedures designed to counter four forms of resistance (Szapocznik et al., 1990): (1) refusal by the adolescent to enter treatment, (2) mothers' ambivalence about entering their families into treatment, (3) fathers' disengagement from their families, and (4) family members' concerns about disclosing secrets to strangers.

In his evaluation study, Szapocznik randomly assigned families to receive either a standard invitation to begin treatment or an experimental program which used structural family techniques to overcome the family's initial resistance to therapy. Results indicated that the experimental engagement technique was highly successful; 93% of families receiving the culturally sensitive engagement methods began treatment compared to 42% of the standard-invitation families. Further, families receiving the structured engagement method were three times more likely to complete treatment than were families in the control condition.

PSYCHOSOCIAL REHABILITATION AND PREVENTION

Despite the dominant status of individual, group, couples, and family psychotherapy, not all psychologists believe that these are the best modes of intervention for psychological problems. To produce truly meaningful improvements in people's lives, these critics say, psychologists must employ intervention strategies based on an *ecological perspective* on behavior disorder (Rappaport, 1977). This means looking at the causes of disorder not just in terms of biological and psychological factors, but in terms of the *interactions* between individuals and the economic, social, and physical aspects of their environment. Taking an ecological perspective means developing interventions designed to maximize the "fit" between individuals and specific environments that are likely to promote their adjustment. Examples of these interventions—which include efforts at psychosocial rehabilitation and prevention of mental disorders—are described in the next two sections.

Psychosocial Rehabilitation

The effectiveness of antipsychotic medications has allowed an increasing number of severely mentally ill people to be discharged from public mental institutions into local communities in recent decades. This trend was encouraged by the community psychology movement of the 1960s (described later), which presented evidence that severely mentally ill people could receive more beneficial (and less expensive) care as outpatients at neighborhood mental health centers (Kiesler & Sibulkin, 1987). Accordingly, the number of mental patients confined in public mental hospitals has declined from approximately 550,000 in 1955 to only 100,000 in 1992 (Lamb, 1992). This *deinstitutionalization* process should have been a great success for the field of mental health, but for many former mental patients, release did not improve the quality of their lives, at least not on a permanent basis (Moscarelli & Capri, 1992). Sadly, thousands of them have simply "fallen through the cracks" and are not receiving any kind of regular treatment. Many have drifted into unemployment and homelessness, often becoming the unwanted responsibility of police and the criminal justice system.

Obviously, these severely mentally ill people are unlikely to enter individual or group psychotherapy and, even if pushed into it by family members, may not benefit much. An alterative intervention called *psychosocial rehabilitation* teaches patients displaying schizophrenia, major mood disorders, or other severe mental disorders how to cope better with the effects of these problems, and especially how to prevent or lessen the crises that often threaten their ability to function in society. In other words, rather than trying to cure serious mental disorders, psychosocial rehabilitation helps patients normalize their lives, compensate for their impairments, and achieve the highest possible quality of life in the community (Hunter, 1995).

A goal of psychosocial rehabilitation is *empowerment* (Rappaport, 1981; 1987), the development of a belief among formerly dependent and powerless people that they can master and control their lives. Empowerment requires both an adequate understanding of the environment and skills for living effectively in it. It also includes the abilities to maintain stable housing and engage in regular, meaningful employment. Thus, psychosocial rehabilitation programs are designed to teach formerly hospitalized mental patients the basic competencies they need to live successfully and independently in the community (Stroul, 1993). These programs typically include four components.

The first is the effort to help patients understand their disorder so that they can cope with it more effectively. For example, Assertive Community Treatment (ACT)—a multicomponent program developed in Madison, Wisconsin in the late 1960s—uses mental health teams to teach patients how to recognize the early warning signs of psychological deterioration in time to avoid high-risk situations and obtain social support to avert a crisis. When patients and their families are able to detect specific symptoms, such as insomnia or auditory hallucinations, that precede psychotic "breaks" and lead to hospitalization or arrest, they can call on treatment staff for help in managing the situation (Herz & Melville, 1980).

Psychosocial rehabilitation programs also help patients learn community living skills such as making change, using public transportation, obtaining medical care, buying groceries, cooking meals, and most important, interacting with other people. Patients are helped to understand how their symptoms may affect others. They will be told, for example, that it is frightening to the average person on the street to see someone who is disheveled or is talking back to hallucinated voices. When patients understand onlookers' reactions, they can more easily learn to ignore them. Note that the goal here is not to eliminate the symptoms of mental disorder, but to cope better with its consequences.

A third component of most psychosocial rehabilitation programs is case management, in which a staff person helps the client obtain services related to employment, housing, nutrition, transportation, recreation, medical care, and finances.

Finally, psychosocial rehabilitation promotes treatment efforts by maintaining a coalition among mental health professionals, family members, and patients. Often, treatment occurs in self-help groups. Organizations such as GROW and Recovery, Inc. have demonstrated that severely mentally ill people are capable of providing mutual support and effective crisis intervention services (Galanter, 1988; Rappaport et al., 1985).

Preventive Interventions

Using principles borrowed from the field of public health, Gerald Caplan (1964) described three levels at which mental health problems can be prevented.

Tertiary prevention seeks to lessen the severity of disorder and to reduce its short-term and long-term consequences. Psychosocial rehabilitation falls in this category because it seeks to minimize the severity and reduce the adverse consequences of being mentally ill. *Secondary prevention* involves interventions for people who are at risk for developing a disorder. Effective secondary prevention requires knowledge of how risk factors culminate in specific disorders. It also usually requires assessment methods that reliably and validly detect the initial signs of a disorder so that attempts can be made to intervene at the earliest possible point. *Primary prevention* involves eliminating disorders by either modifying environments or strengthening individuals so that they are not susceptible to disorder in the first place. Primary prevention programs seek one of two main goals: *counteracting risk factors* and *reinforcing protective factors* (Coie et al., 1993).[3] There are five basic methods through which these primary prevention programs seek to accomplish their goals.

Encouraging Secure Attachments and Reducing Family Violence. One method is to help parents and their children form the kind of warm, nurturant, and secure early attachments that tend to be associated with mental health as the children grow. (Insecure or disrupted attachments are one of the earliest and most pernicious risk factors for many mental disorders; Nietzel et al., 1998). Why don't healthy attachments form naturally? For one thing, some parents do not understand the importance of such attachments or may believe that if they are too responsive their baby will be "spoiled." In other cases, substance abuse or depression might leave parents unable to care properly for a child. Severe poverty can also make it difficult for parents to properly nurture children. Various types of preventive interventions can be devised to deal with these and other sources of attachment problems and, if applied early enough, can reduce the harm they might otherwise have done.

Related primary prevention programs are aimed at the reduction of family violence. The fact that at least 1 million children a year are victims of physical or sexual abuse or severe neglect—and that 3 to 4 million households may be the site of other forms of family violence every year (Gelles & Straus, 1988)—is tragic enough on its own, but there is also evidence that children reared in violent homes are more likely to become aggressive, abusive, or criminal adults themselves (Ollendick, 1996).

Teaching Cognitive and Social Skills. A second approach to primary prevention of mental disorder involves teaching children and adolescents the cognitive and interpersonal skills crucial to later development and adjustment. For example, children lacking in such skills tend to display, as early as kindergarten, a pattern of behavior that elevates their risk for later delinquency (Farrington, 1991). A core element of this pattern is impulsivity, which is manifested in refusing to wait one's turn, being disrespectful and defiant toward teachers, and constantly interrupting others. In other words, these children have trouble regulating their behavior so as to abide by rules and accommodate other people. However, there is evidence that if these children can be taught to control their impulses (Kendall & Braswell, 1985), to use effective problem-solving strategies (Spivack & Shure, 1974), and to respond nonaggressively to provocation and teasing by peers (Dodge, McClaskey, & Feldman, 1985), they can avoid developing the academic and social problems that are common in the backgrounds of conduct-disordered youngsters (Ollendick, 1996).

---

[3]More recently (Mrazek & Haggerty, 1994), prevention has been described as being *indicated* (focusing on persons showing the early signs of disorder), *selective* (aimed at persons who are at heightened risk to develop a disorder), or *universal* (intended to improve the functioning of the general population.

One program called the Montreal Longitudinal Experimental Study was designed to teach social skills to a group of inner-city boys, averaging seven years of age, whose classroom disruptiveness placed them at serious risk for delinquency. They were randomly assigned to either (1) two years in a multicomponent treatment consisting of child-rearing training for their parents and social skill training for them, (2) two years of frequent psychological assessments and referral for treatment at a mental health center, if requested by their parents, or (3) no contact. After the initial two years, all three groups were followed for several more years to determine how each was doing in school and how often they were engaging in delinquent behavior (Tremblay et al., 1995). The boys who received multicomponent treatment were more likely to be in a classroom appropriate to their age than were boys in either of the two control groups. However, this difference had disappeared by the middle of high school, at about age fifteen. Boys in the treatment group reported significantly lower rates of delinquent behavior up to age fifteen, but they did not differ from the control boys in the number of times they had actually been arrested. And in spite of the parent-training component of the treatment program, boys in that program did not report any lasting differences in their parents' disciplinary practices. The effects of this multi-component program were modest, at best, so it will be important to determine if "booster sessions" in early adolescence can increase its impact.

Changing Environments.   A third approach to primary prevention entails making environments more supportive of adaptive behavior. Prime targets for such "re-engineering" are settings—such as homes, schools, neighborhoods, and the criminal justice system—that powerfully shape human development. For example, programs such as Head Start that expand preschool opportunities and increase the commitment of parents and children to academic success have been shown to decrease antisocial behavior in the long-run, even though this was not their original goal (Schweinhart, Barnes, & Weikhart, 1993; Zigler, Taussig, & Black, 1992). Programs that help children and adolescents adjust to the transition from elementary to middle school or from middle school to high school have also been found to prevent school dropout and antisocial behavior in school (Olweus, 1995; Seidman et al., 1994).

Enhancing Stress-Coping Skills.   A fourth approach to primary prevention takes the form of reducing environmental stressors and/or helping people cope more effectively with the stressors they must endure. In either case, harmful mental and physical stress reactions are likely to decrease, along with the incidence of the disorders associated with them.

For example, increasing the availability of affordable housing can reduce the frequency of household moves, a major stressor for poor families that has been linked to psychological maladjustment. Further, strengthening or creating social support for the elderly, for immigrants, and for other people facing social isolation can help protect against future problems (Felner, Farber, & Primavera, 1983). Problems might also be prevented by helping the millions of people who face ethnic prejudice every day develop new strategies for coping with unfair employment and housing practices, verbal abuse, and social rejection. Thus, some minority children who anticipate discrimination at school tend to devalue and withdraw from academic activities, but interventions designed to prevent this counterproductive coping strategy could improve these youngsters' academic performance, bolster their self-esteem, and keep them on the path to success (Basic Behavioral Science Task Force of the National Advisory Mental Health Council, 1996).

   Promoting Empowerment. Finally, there are primary prevention programs designed to empower the powerless, to help those for whom old age, poverty, homelessness, ethnic minority status, physical disability, or other factors have left them without the ability or confidence to take control of their lives. Many psychologists believe that the disproportionately high levels of mental disorder seen in these groups is largely caused by the psychological and physical problems that often accompany their chronic sense of *dis*empowerment. Accordingly, prevention programs or social changes that help people gain a sense of control can be expected to decrease their risk for developing mental disorders. There is already some evidence that empowering minority parents to influence school policies or empowering neighborhoods to control crime can have long-term mental health benefits (Comer, 1987).

COMMUNITY PSYCHOLOGY

Interventions aimed at psychosocial rehabilitation and prevention have been stimulated largely by work in the field of community psychology. In the remainder of this chapter we describe the history, principles, and current status of this field.

What Is Community Psychology?

Community psychology seeks to apply psychological principles to (1) understanding individual and social problems, (2) preventing behavioral dysfunction, and (3) creating lasting social change. All of these efforts are based on the ecological perspective described earlier, which says that human behavior develops out of interactions between people and all aspects of their environment—physical, social, political, and economic. Accordingly, community psychologists argue that alleviating individual and social problems requires that we make changes in *both environmental settings and individual competencies*. Along with their emphasis on environmental factors in disorder, community psychologists also focus on the plight of the urban and rural poor and other groups whose problems have (1) tended to be underserved by traditional systems for psychotherapy service delivery and (2) appear more social than psychological and thus require social rather than individual change.

The History of Community Psychology

In the 1950s and 1960s, an array of influences came together to accelerate the development of community psychology. Some of these influences appeared within psychology itself, while others were associated with the extensive social and political changes taking place throughout North America during this period.

Prominent factors within psychology included (1) disenchantment with a clinical psychology that was then dominated by psychodynamic approaches to psychopathology (Rappaport, 1977); (2) skepticism about the reliability and validity of psychological diagnosis of disorders (Rosenhan, 1973) and about the benefits of traditional psychotherapy (Eysenck, 1952, 1966; see Chapter 9); (3) prophecies of shortages of mental health professionals to deliver individual treatment (Albee, 1959); and (4) dissatisfaction with the training models and role expectations for clinical psychologists (Korman, 1974; Peterson, 1968; see Chapters 1 and 14).

At the same time, the United States was in turmoil over the civil rights movement, black separatist ideology, urban crises, the war on poverty, and protests against the Vietnam War. These upheavals helped stimulate the growth of community psychology because they prompted many psychologists to broaden their conceptions of what the helping professions should do in the interest of social change. The roots of community psychology are also found in the 1961 report of the Joint Commission on Mental Health and Illness, which recommended the construction of multiservice comprehensive care centers to serve the mental health needs of local communities. This report led to passage in 1962 of the Community Mental Health Centers Act, which provided funds for the construction of a network of comprehensive mental health centers that could cover service areas of not less than 75,000 nor more than 200,000 people. In 1965, legislation was passed that provided grants to pay the personnel to be employed in these "comp care" centers.

The official "birth" of community psychology came in the spring of the same year when about thirty psychologists, many employed in community mental health centers,

"Yes, what is it? I'm very busy . . . ."

The community psychology movement suggested new ways of delivering mental health services to all those who need it. This is not one of them. (© 1972, Punch/Rothco)

met in Swampscott, Massachusetts and issued a call for community psychologists who would be "change agents, social system analysts, consultants in community affairs, and students generally of the whole man in relation to all his environments" (Bennett, 1965, p. 833). The Swampscott conference participants stressed three principles for the new field. First, community psychology was not to be limited to combating mental illness; it should work for "community well-being" and "furthering normal development" (Bennett, 1965). Second, community psychology should promote community growth through planned social action and the scientific method. Finally, community psychology must be broader than the *community mental health* movement's efforts to deliver traditional mental health services in community settings.

Today, community psychology is in its fourth decade. It boasts its own division within the American Psychological Association and there are several journals—including *The American Journal of Community Psychology, The Community Mental Health Journal,* and *The Journal of Community Psychology*—devoted to reporting the research and accomplishments of its members. Their work has also been surveyed and evaluated in numerous textbooks (e.g., Glenwick & Jason, 1980; Heller et al., 1984; Rappaport, 1977; Seidman, 1983; Tolan et al., 1991). The training of community psychologists has also become an important activity of graduate psychology programs. In 1962 there was one program offering an M.A. or Ph.D. in community psychology and community mental health. By the late 1980s, about 100 U.S. graduate programs in the United States offered training in community psychology (Elias, Dalton, & Godin, 1987), a number that has remained reasonably stable throughout the 1990s (Suarez-Balcazar, Durlak, & Smith, 1994).

Principles and Methods of Community Psychology

We have already seen that community psychology takes an ecological perspective on mental disorder and that it emphasizes the importance of primary, as well as secondary and tertiary prevention programs. Let's now consider some of the other principles and methods associated with community psychology that help differentiate it from clinical psychology.

Social-System Change. In accordance with their ecological approach, community psychologists are often more interested in promoting *social-system-level changes,* than *person-oriented changes.* Social-system changes are intended to make the social institutions in our lives more growth-enhancing. Changes in social systems can occur at a low level, as when one schoolteacher begins using a reward system to increase class participation. Social changes also can occur at a higher level, as when a group of parents, dissatisfied with the quality of public education, begins its own alternative school. This is not to say that community psychologists avoid person-oriented interventions, but their preference is for social-system changes because these changes present the greatest opportunity to bring about important improvements for large numbers of people.

Promoting a "Psychological Sense of Community". Community psychologists are also concerned with strengthening the ability of a community to plan and implement its own changes. To make this more likely, they work at promoting a "psychological sense of community," the sense that one is " . . . part of a readily available, mutually supportive network of relationships upon which one could depend and as a result of which one did not experience sustained feelings of loneliness that impel one to actions or to adopting a style of living masking anxiety and setting the stage for later and more destructive anguish." (Sarason, 1974, p. 351).

Community psychologists try to foster this sense of community by developing people's strengths rather than focusing on their weaknesses. They encourage collective action by people with common needs or interests and they seek to help these coalitions maintain their commitment to mutual problem solving. This goal involves the development of collective power mobilized for the purpose of specific reforms, a strategy described earlier as empowerment (Rappaport, 1981).

Expansion of Professional Roles.   Clinical psychologists usually offer *direct services* to clients who, because they have some psychological complaint, are willing to pay for them. In contrast, community psychologists emphasize *indirect services* that have no particular target client, but which are expected to achieve benefits because the social-system changes they produce radiate to intended target groups. Thus, *consultation* with educational, social, political, and other community agencies and groups is a common activity for the community psychologist (O'Neill & Trickett, 1982).

Another example of expanding roles for community psychologists is seen in their preparation of *nonprofessionals* for behavior-change functions that had previously been reserved for professionals. These nonprofessionals then act as child care workers, mental health workers, peer counselors, abortion counselors, and in many other roles. The nonprofessional movement creates meaningful careers for people wishing to help, offers help for troubled people from individuals with whom they share a cultural heritage, and provides an important new source of personnel capable of delivering needed mental health services. Many of these helpers are known as *indigenous nonprofessionals* because they are drawn from the very groups that will receive their services. Indeed, their cultural rootedness in the to-be-served group is one of their fundamental assets. Community psychologists also train clients' relatives (Guerney, 1969), peers (Harris & Sherman, 1973), teachers (Meyers, 1975), and friends (Sulzer, 1965) to initiate behavior-change programs or to maintain programs that were introduced during a professional intervention.

Community psychologists also tend to support the goals of *self-help* groups, whose members assist one another by exchanging information, providing social support, and discussing mutual problems (Backer & Richardson, 1989; Jacobs & Goodman, 1989). The number of Americans—about 6 to 7 million—who belong to such groups (Jacobs & Goodman, 1989) rivals the number of clients in formal psychotherapy. Most self-help groups fall into one of five subtypes (Powell, 1987). *Habit disturbance* groups such as Alcoholics Anonymous and Gamblers Anonymous focus on a specific behavior-change goal. *General-purpose* groups address a wide range of difficulties such as dealing with the death of a child (Compassionate Friends) or helping psychiatric patients cope with crises (GROW; Recovery, Inc.). *Lifestyle organizations* support individuals—such as single parents (Parents Without Partners) or the elderly (Gray Panthers)—who feel their interests are underserved by society. *Significant-other* organizations provide advocacy, education, support, and partnership for relatives of disturbed persons; examples include Gam-Anon (relatives of compulsive gamblers) and Al-Anon (relatives of alcoholics). Finally, *physical handicap organizations* such as Mended Hearts and the Cerebral Palsy Association provide support to heart surgery or cerebral palsy patients.

Use of Activism.

Social activism refers to the use of *power* to accomplish social reform. This power may be economic, it may be political, or it may be the coercive power of civil disobedience. Power can be manipulated through publicity, and it is for this reason that community psychologists cultivate media contacts to spread their influence. Finally, power resides in positions of leadership. Accordingly, some community psychologists seek employment where they have access to the formation of social policy—on urban planning teams, as consultants to city councils, as advisors to legislators, as directors of citizen's advocate groups, or heads of social-service agencies.

Social action has been considered both an essential contribution and an unnecessary evil in community psychology. Advocates of activist tactics claim that professionals' willingness to provoke, agitate, and confront accounts for a large measure of their effectiveness in promoting change. Opponents of professional social action argue that such activity is incompatible with the objective empiricism that is the scientist's defining characteristic.

Use of Research as a Form of Intervention.

George Fairweather, a psychologist at Michigan State University, coined the phrase *experimental social innovation* to describe research which, after demonstrating the value of a new community psychology program, can be used to support that program's implementation. Research as intervention is also exemplified by what is called *dissemination research.* This is experimentation designed to evaluate alternative methods of implementing programs that initial studies have shown to be successful. In the course of finding the most effective means of persuading other communities to adopt a given program, that program is, by necessity, adopted.

The best example of dissemination research is Fairweather's experimental project on the effectiveness of various approaches to persuading mental hospitals to adopt an outpatient "lodge program" designed as a form of supported housing and employment for chronic mental patients (Fairweather, Sanders, & Tornatzky, 1974). The research investigated which techniques were most effective in activating the lodge program once a decision had been made to adopt it and explored the procedures used in spreading the lodge approach to other mental health programs (Fairweather, 1980).

Some Final Comments on Community Psychology

Despite its innovativeness and obvious good intentions, community psychology has evoked a number of concerns. One fear is that community programs, particularly those aimed at prevention, may threaten people's privacy, individual freedom, and other rights to live their lives the way they please (Halleck, 1969). This fear is probably exaggerated, mainly because Americans are notably resistant to controls and coercion. Our mistrust of undue regulation from any source, whether political, military, or medical, has been effective protection against excessively intrusive control. At present, this quality appears sufficiently strong to prevent abuses by even the most zealous community psychologist.

Other critics fear that community psychology's emphasis on prevention will distract professionals from offering the intensive treatment severely disturbed clients require (Lamb & Zusman, 1981). This outcome, too, appears unlikely, since professional mental health fields suffered from an insufficiency of professional personnel long before community psychology came along.

Finally, there is uncertainty about exactly who in a community decides the goals of community interventions. Is it the psychologist, the recipients of the program, the majority of the community, or only influential leaders? Community psychologists assure us that the aims of their interventions are directed by the people they serve (Zax & Specter, 1974), but the notion of community participation is a complex ideal made all the more difficult by the frequent value conflicts between community residents and professional psychologists.

CLINICAL INTERVENTION AT WORK

Q.: How and why is psychotherapy important in your work? What modes of therapy (individual, group, family, couples, rehabilitative, and preventive) are most important for you, and why?

DR. SANDY D'ANGELO: Psychotherapy is only a small portion of my clinical work. These cases consist primarily of female children or adolescents treated for depression or behavioral and emotional reactions to loss or trauma. These problems lend themselves to individual treatment with adjunct family or parent counseling.

DR. HECTOR MACHABANSKI: I provide psychotherapy services as part of my work as a private practitioner and as a consultant to a pediatric department of an urban hospital. The modes of therapy most important to me are individual, couples, and family therapy. The choice of mode depends on the type of presenting problems and what the research literature says about the best approaches to these problems.

DR. GEOFFREY THORPE: Much of my clinical practice is devoted to psychotherapy. I chiefly use behavioral and cognitive therapy methods with individual clients, but I also often work with couples on relationships or sexual difficulties.

CHAPTER SUMMARY

Clinical intervention involves a deliberate attempt to make desirable changes in a client's behavior or social circumstances; it can take the form of psychotherapy, psychosocial rehabilitation, and prevention.

Psychotherapy is usually conducted in an individual format in which a client in need of help is seen by a therapist with special training in clinical or counseling psychology, psychiatry, psychiatric social work, psychiatric nursing, family counseling, pastoral counseling, or other mental health fields. Most clinicians agree that therapy is facilitated by the development of a supportive, yet objective, relationship which, in turn, is fostered by the therapist's ability to display characteristics that Rogers described as genuineness, empathy, and unconditional positive regard. However, therapists who take differing theoretical approaches differ in their emphasis on and use of the therapeutic relationship. Therapists' using different approaches also tend to use differing treatment methods, but there are some common features, too, including efforts to foster insight, reduce emotional discomfort, encourage catharsis, provide new information, assign extratherapy tasks, and promote clients' faith, hope, and expectations for change.

Psychotherapy can also be conducted with groups, couples, and families, using methods that combine those employed in individual psychotherapy with specialized techniques unique to these special formats. Group therapy seeks to change the way individuals interact in a wide range of interpersonal relationships, while couples therapy addresses these issues within the context of an intimate dyad. Family therapy focuses on understanding and changing the forces within a family that affect the functioning of each of its members.

Psychosocial rehabilitation is a mode of intervention that aims to help people displaying mental disorders to cope with the occupational, economic, family, and environmental effects of those disorders. Intervention programs emphasizing prevention attempt to modify social, economic, and environmental factors that lead to disorders in vulnerable populations or to strengthen qualities that protect individuals from developing disorders.

Community psychology is a field that applies psychological principles to understanding individual and social problems, preventing behavior disorders, and creating beneficial social changes.

Chapter 8

Clinical Intervention: Methods of Psychotherapy

In the previous chapter, we provided an overview of all forms of clinical intervention, from individual treatment to social action through community psychology. In this chapter, we focus more specifically on psychotherapy, the most common form of clinical intervention. Our review will describe the methods of psychotherapy employed by therapists who adopt the psychodynamic, behavioral, and phenomenological approaches to clinical psychology.

PSYCHODYNAMIC THERAPIES

Sigmund Freud was the founder of psychotherapy as we know it today. His one-to-one method of studying and helping people, his systematic search for relationships between a person's developmental history and current problems, his emphasis on conflict, thoughts, and emotions, and his focus on the therapist–patient relationship pervade all other modern treatment methods.

The Beginnings of Classical Psychoanalysis

In 1886, with the help of a senior colleague, Joseph Breuer, Freud began the private practice of medicine in Vienna. Like Breuer, Freud often saw patients with neurological symptoms for which no organic cause could be found. Some, for example, complained of paralysis that affected their entire hand, but not their arm. Others suffered paralysis of the legs during the day, but walked in their sleep. These patients were called *neurotics*, and Freud dealt with the most common type: those displaying *hysterical* (i.e., nonorganic) paralyses, amnesia, anesthesia, blindness, and speech loss. In Freud's day, treatment for hysteria included "wet packs" and baths or electrically generated heat. Freud believed that whatever success these methods had were due to suggestion, so he began experimenting with techniques that maximized the benefits of suggestion, foremost among which was *hypnosis.*

Freud became familiar with hypnosis when he spent six months in Paris studying with Jean Charcot, director of the neurology clinic at the Salpêtrière asylum. Charcot showed that hysterical symptoms could be created and temporarily removed through a hypnotic trance and thus that hysteria and hypnosis were related phenomena. Later, in the French city of Nancy, Freud visited a medical clinic run by Ambrose-August Liebault and Hippolyte Bernheim, who also used hypnotic suggestions to temporarily remove hysterical symptoms. Freud's own use of hypnotic suggestion produced equally temporary results, but around 1890 he began to combine hypnosis with a new technique called the *cathartic method,* which he learned from Breuer.

Breuer had stumbled on this technique while attempting to relieve the hysterical symptoms of a patient known as Anna O. The symptoms—which included headaches, a severe cough, neck and arm paralyses, and other problems—began during her father's illness and intensified following his death. She began to display extremes of

Sigmund Freud (1856–1939). (Courtesy of Historical Pictures Service, Inc., Chicago, Illinois. Reprinted by permission.)

mood which went from agitation and hallucinations during the day to calm, trancelike states in the evenings. Breuer was struck by the fact that these "trances" resembled hypnosis.

> Breuer discovered that if Anna were permitted while in the hypnotic state to recite the contents of all her hallucinations from the day, then she invariably would leave the trance state and enjoy a period of almost normal tranquility and lucidity during the following late night hours.... Anna came to refer to the exercise of reciting her hallucinations as the "talking cure," or ... "chimney sweeping." (Fancher, 1973, p. 48)

This "talking cure" did not eliminate Anna's daytime disorders, however, and to Breuer's dismay, new symptoms began to appear. In attempting to cure one of these, an inability to drink liquids, Breuer made the discovery that would later start Freud on the road to psychoanalysis:

> During one of Anna's hypnotic states ... she began describing to Breuer an Englishwoman whom she knew but did not especially like. The woman had a dog that Anna particularly despised. Anna described how on one occasion she entered the woman's room and observed the dog drinking water from a glass. When the event occurred, Anna was filled with strong feelings of disgust and loathing, but out of politeness she was unable to express them. As she recited this account to Breuer, she for the first time permitted herself the luxury of expressing fully and animatedly her negative feelings about the dog's drinking. When she emerged from the trance she immediately asked for a glass of water, which she ... drank without the slightest difficulty. (Fancher, 1973, p. 49)

Removal of Anna's fear of drinking was apparently brought about by her vivid recollection of a forgotten event while in a trance. It occurred to Breuer that other hysterical symptoms might be caused by forgotten memories and that their recall might cure them. He began hypnotizing Anna and asking her to remember everything she could about her symptoms.

> (H)e discovered that every symptom could be traced to a traumatic or unpleasant situation for which all memory was absent in the waking state. Breuer found that whenever he could induce Anna to recall those unpleasant scenes and, more importantly, to *express the emotions* they had caused her to feel, the symptoms would disappear. (Fancher, 1973, pp. 49–50; italics added)

Freud also found the cathartic method successful, but he encountered serious drawbacks as well. For one thing, not all his patients could be hypnotized. In addition, Freud found that recalling memories and expressing emotions associated with them is most beneficial when patients remember these experiences after their hypnotic sessions, which some did not. To facilitate *conscious* recognition of emotional memories, Freud began looking for a nonhypnotic means of helping patients recall them. He asked his patients to relax with their eyes closed and to report whatever thoughts, feelings, or memories came to mind. Recall was often helped by having the patient lie on a couch. This procedure later became known as *free association,* a mainstay among the psychoanalytic techniques to be described later.[1]

At first, Freud's treatment of neurotic patients focused mainly on helping them remember important, usually unpleasant, memories and emotions that had been protected from recall by various *defense mechanisms* (see Chapter 2). For example, when many of his patients recalled early sexual trauma, usually molestation by a parent or other relative, Freud assumed that such events were the basis for most hysterical symptoms. By the turn of the century, however, he was convinced that this "seduction theory" was incorrect and that there were more important causal factors to be considered. For one thing, he found it hard to believe that the sexual abuse of children was as widespread as was suggested by his patients' reports. Second, Freud began to pay attention to *dreams* (his patients' and his own) and concluded that they represented the fulfillment of fantasies and wishes, many of which are socially unacceptable and thus appear—often in disguised form—only when defenses are relaxed during sleep. He suggested that, like dreams, hysterical symptoms could be based on unconscious wishes and fantasies, not just on memories of real events. Thus, a patient's "memory" of childhood seduction by a parent might actually be a *fantasy* or *wish* about such an encounter. The implications of this new theory altered Freud's approach to therapy as well. His *psychoanalytic* treatment of neurosis shifted from the recovery of memories to the illumination of the unconscious.

Goals of Psychoanalysis

According to Freud, when patients understand the real, often unconscious, reasons why they act in maladaptive ways and see that those reasons are no longer valid, they will not have to continue behaving in those ways. However, it is not enough for the therapist to simply describe the unconscious material that appears to be at the root of clients' problems; with the therapist's guidance, clients must make these discoveries for themselves. The process of self-understanding includes *intellectual* recognition of one's innermost wishes and conflicts, *emotional* involvement in discoveries about oneself, and the *systematic tracing* of how unconscious factors have determined past and present behaviors and affected relations with other people.

Thus, the main goals of psychoanalytic treatment are (1) intellectual and emotional *insight* into the underlying causes of the client's problems, (2) *working through* or fully exploring the implications of those insights, and (3) strengthening the ego's control over the id and the superego (see Chapter 2). Freud saw working through as particularly important because clients need to understand how pervasive their unconscious conflicts and defenses are if they are to be prevented from returning. Thus, it would do little good for a patient to know that she has unconscious feelings of anger toward her mother if she did not also see that she deals with women in the present as if

---

[1]Freud may have hit upon this technique through a lost memory of his own. When still a teenager, he read an essay by Ludwig Borne called "The Art of Becoming an Original Writer in Three Days." Borne suggested that the would-be writer should spend three days writing down everything that comes to mind "without any falsification or hypocrisy" and that amazingly new and surprising thoughts would appear (Fancher, 1973).

they were her mother, and that her problems in relation to these women are based on unconscious hostility and/or attempts to defend against it. Insight provides the outline of a patient's story; working through fills in the details.

Reaching the ambitious goals set by classical psychoanalysis involves the dissection and gradual reconstruction of the patient's personality. This process requires a lot of time (three to five sessions each week for two to fifteen years), a lot of money (fees exceed $100 per hour), and, presumably, a great deal of therapist skill.

Psychoanalytic Treatment Techniques

Classical psychoanalysts assume that the client's most important unconscious feelings and conflicts are protected by psychological defenses. They seek to show their clients how and where to look for important material and to help them understand what emerges. To accomplish these tasks, most analysts depend on a few basic techniques.

Free Association. As noted earlier, free association evolved from Freud's search for a nonhypnotic way to help his patients recover memories. It requires the client to follow a single fundamental rule: to say everything that comes to mind without editing or censorship. It is assumed that, by removing the constraints of logic, social amenities, and other rules, unconscious material will surface more easily.

Still, because of defenses, the unconscious bases for clients' current problems are seldom clearly revealed in the memories, feelings, and wishes arising through free association. It is the therapist's task to try to make sense of the bits and pieces that emerge. *Patterns of association* are often important in doing so:

> CLIENT: My dad called last night. It was nice to hear from him, but I never quite feel comfortable when we talk. Once we get through the usual "hello; how are you" part, there just doesn't seem to be anything to say. (long silence) I almost fell asleep there for a minute. I used to do that a lot in college. I must have slept through half my classes. Once I woke up and saw the professor standing over me, shaking me, and the whole class was laughing.

The fact that thoughts about his father led to memories about a threatening authority figure could have significance, especially if this pattern is repeated in other sessions. It could mean that the client still has unresolved feelings of fear and hatred toward his father, feelings that need to be clarified and dealt with.

What the client says during free association may be defensive in nature. The client whose mind goes blank or who comes up with only trivial details of the day is seen as erecting barriers to self-exploration. According to psychoanalytic theory, these defenses must be recognized by the therapist and made clear to the client if they are to be overcome.

The Use of Dreams. Because unconscious material is believed to be closer to the surface in dreams than during waking consciousness, great importance is attached to them in psychoanalysis. The client's description of a dream—in which, say, she is running through the woods and suddenly falls into a lake—reveals its *manifest content* or obvious features. Manifest content often contains features associated with the dreamer's recent activities that day (called "day residue").

For psychoanalytic purposes, the most interesting aspect of dreams is their *latent content:* the unconscious ideas and impulses that appear in the form of a safe compromise between repression and expression. The process of transforming unacceptable material into acceptable manifest content is called *dream work* (Freud, 1900), so most manifest dream content is viewed as being symbolic of something else—the specifics of which differ from person to person and from dream to dream. In spite of the popular belief that certain dream symbols (e.g., a snake) always mean the same thing (e.g., a penis), Freud believed dreams must be interpreted more flexibly (he is said to have pointed out that "sometimes a cigar is just a cigar").

Dream work can take many forms. For example, an unconscious desire to have extramarital sex might be *displaced* to a position of minor importance in the dream, appearing as an adult bookstore glimpsed from a moving car. Or an apparently innocuous dreamed event—such as one's brother leaving for a vacation—may *substitute* for taboo wishes (e.g., the brother's death). Dream work may also *devalue* significant material. Ruth Munroe (1955) tells of a prudish woman who often dreamed of being unashamedly naked in public. Presumably, the woman defended against unconscious sexual wishes by making them seem unimportant. Unconscious material often appears in *condensed* form, including *alogical sequences* (e.g., in which there is a sudden shift of time or place) or *dramatizations* (as when two people fighting might represent conflicting tendencies within the dreamer).

Waking defense mechanisms also hamper the analyst's attempts to uncover latent content because they alter the client's report of the dream, a process Freud called *secondary revision.* For example, the dreamer might unconsciously reorganize the report to make the dream seem more logical than it really was. To identify those aspects of a dream with the greatest unconscious significance, some analysts ask their clients to describe a dream repeatedly. If later versions differ from the initial telling, the analyst assumes that the changes reflect unconscious efforts to disguise or defend against highly charged material.

Another common procedure is to ask the client to free associate to a dream's manifest content. In the process, unconscious material may be revealed. Consider this dream reported to Dr. Robert Lindner by a female patient whose father and mother (who was confined to a wheelchair by paralysis) had a violently unhappy marriage:

> I was in what appeared to be a ballroom or dance hall, but I knew it was really a hospital. A man came up to me and told me to undress, take all my clothes off. He was going to give me a gynecological examination. I did as I was told but I was very frightened. While I was undressing, I noticed that he was doing something to a woman at the other end of the room. She was sitting or lying in a funny kind of contraption with all kinds of levers and gears and pulleys attached to it. I knew that I was supposed to be next, that I would have to sit in that thing while he examined me. Suddenly he called my name and I found myself

running to him. The chair or table—whatever it was—was now empty, and he told me to get on it. I refused and began to cry. It started to rain—great big drops of rain. He pushed me to the floor and spread my legs for examination. I turned over on my stomach and began to scream. I woke myself up screaming. (Lindner, 1954, pp. 134-135)

Lindner describes how this manifest content is used as raw material for free association:

"Well," she said after a brief, expectant silence, "What does it mean?"

"Laura," I admonished, "you know better than that. Associate and we'll find out."

"The first thing I think of is Ben," she began. "He's an intern at the University, you know. I guess that's the doctor in the dream—or maybe it was you. Anyhow, whoever it was, I wouldn't let him examine me."

"Why not?"

"I've always been afraid of doctors . . . afraid they might hurt me."

"How will they hurt you?"

"I don't know. By jabbing me with a needle, I guess. That's funny, never thought of it before. When I go to the dentist I don't mind getting a needle; but with a doctor it's different . . . I shudder when I think of having my veins punctured. I'm always afraid that's what the doctor will do to me."

"Has it ever been done?"

She nodded. "Once, in college, for a blood test, I passed out cold."

"What about gynecological examinations?"

"I've never had one. I can't bear to think of someone poking around inside me." Again silence; then, "Oh," she said, "I see it now. It's sex. I'm afraid the doctor in the dream *is* Ben. He wants me to have intercourse, but it scares me and I turn away from him." (Lindner, 1954, p. 135)

This "insight" seems to have come too easily and was too obvious. The analyst feels sure there is more to it.

" . . . Other men have made love to you."

"Yes," she said, sobbing now, "but I only let them as a last resort, as a way of holding on to them a little longer . . . I'd do anything to keep them from getting inside me—poking into me . . . like the needle, I guess."

"But why, Laura?"

"I don't know," she cried "I don't know. Tell me."

"I think the dream tells you," I said.

"The dream I just told you?"

"Yes . . . There's a part of it you haven't considered. What comes to your mind when you think of the other woman in your dream, the woman the doctor was examining before you?"

"The contraption she was sitting in," Laura exclaimed, "It was like a—like a wheelchair—my mother's wheel chair—my mother's wheelchair! Is that right?"

"Very likely," I said.

"But why would he be examining *her*? What would that mean?"

"Well, think of what that kind of examination signifies for you."

"Sex," she said. "Intercourse—that's what it means. So that's what it is—that's what it means! Intercourse put my mother in the wheelchair. It paralyzed her. And I'm afraid that's what it will do to me. So I avoid it—because I'm scared it will do the same thing to me. . . . Where did I ever get such a crazy idea?" (Lindner, 1954, pp. 136-137)

Notice how free association to dream content led the patient to an insight that will provoke further exploration of unconscious material not yet revealed. Frequently, a series of dreams is explored in analysis as a way of finding patterns of latent content and of not overemphasizing the importance of a single dream. In other words, dreams provide ideas for further probing more often than they provide final answers.

Analysis of Everyday Behavior. In line with his notion of psychic determinism, Freud believed that unconscious wishes, fantasies, and defenses shape all behavior, including apparently meaningless everyday acts. Accordingly, psychoanalysts are as attentive to clients' reports of activities outside of treatment as they are to what happens during treatment sessions. The analyst tries to maintain an "evenly divided" or "free-floating" attention to trivial as well as momentous events, to purposeful acts and accidental happenings, to body language as well as spoken language. Mistakes in speaking or writing (so-called "Freudian slips"), accidents, memory losses, and humor are seen as especially important sources of unconscious material.

Analysis of Resistance. Any client behavior that interferes with the analytic process is considered a sign of *resistance* against achieving insight. To overcome resistance, psychoanalysts try to help clients recognize its presence—in obstructed free associations, distorted dream reports, missed appointments, lateness for treatment sessions[2], avoidance of certain topics, or failure to pay the therapist's bill (Fine, 1971). Even clients' desire to address troubling symptoms rather than intrapsychic conflicts, or their request for evidence of the value of treatment is likely to be identified by psychoanalysts as an effort to divert attention from the unconscious causes of their problems.

Analysis of the Transference. The client's feelings toward and relationship with the therapist are called the *transference.* Some of these feelings are determined by the therapist's characteristics and behavior, but others are seen as influenced by unconscious conflicts about authority figures from childhood which lie at the root of the client's current problems. To facilitate the transference, many analysts maintain an "analytic incognito," revealing so little about themselves that the client can be free to project onto them the attributes and motives that are unconsciously associated with parents and other important people in their lives. So at various times, the client may see the therapist as a loving caregiver, a vengeful father, a seductive mother, a jealous lover, or the like.

---

[2]It has been jokingly suggested that you cannot win in analysis because you are dependent if you show up early, resistant if you show up late, and compulsive if you are right on time.

When the patient–therapist relationship creates a miniature version of the causes of the client's problems, it is referred to as the *transference neurosis* and becomes the central focus of analytic work. This reproduction of early unconscious conflicts allows the analyst to deal with important problems from the past as they occur in the present. Transference and transference neuroses must be handled with care as analysts try to decode the meaning of their clients' feelings toward them. If an analyst responded "normally" to a client's loving or hostile comments, the client would not learn much about what those comments reflect. Instead, the goal is to focus on and work through the meaning of the client's feelings for the therapist. If this can be done, the transference neurosis will be resolved and, with it, the client's main unconscious conflicts. (Because sensitive handling of the transference is thought so crucial to psychoanalysis, analysts are trained to be keenly alert to their own unconscious feelings toward clients—known as the *countertransference*—so that these feelings do not distort the analytic process.)

Making Analytic Interpretations.   Analysts want clients to gain insight into unconscious conflicts, but they don't want to overwhelm them with potentially frightening material before they are ready to handle it. This is where *analytic interpretation* comes in. Through questions and comments about the client's behavior, free associations, dreams, and the like, the analyst guides the process of self-exploration. Thus, if the client shows resistance to seeing the potential meaning of some event, the therapist not only points this out, but offers an interpretation of what is going on.

The interpretive process is tentative and continuous, a constant encouragement of clients to consider alternative views, to reject obvious explanations, to search for deeper meanings. However, the analyst does not interpret everything of unconscious significance as soon as it is detected. An interpretation is best delivered when the client is nearly aware of something important, but has not yet been able to verbalize it. Interpretations can be blunt or subtle, depending on what the therapist thinks the client can handle. Here is one that falls somewhere in between:

> You know, it's very interesting that whenever you say something that is a little bit nasty to anyone you smile. After you've been a little bit aggressive, you become *very* agreeable and nice, and I notice it here. I wonder if when you were with your father you discovered that the only way to keep him from attacking you was to become more sociable, amiable, in this kind of smiling, passive way. . . . (Barton, 1974, p. 33)

As interpretations help clients understand and work through the transference, the therapeutic relationship changes. Clients not only see how defenses and unconscious conflicts caused problems, they learn to deal differently with the world, beginning with the therapist. They also learn that forces from their past no longer need dictate their behavior in the present. Ideally, this emotional understanding will liberate the patient to deal with life in a more realistic and satisfying manner than before.

Our brief account of classic psychoanalytic techniques has left out many details and oversimplified others. More complete coverage of the approach is contained in numerous standard references (e.g., Freud, 1949; Munroe, 1955; Menninger, 1958; Kernberg, 1976).

Variations on Classical Psychoanalysis

Freud attracted many followers. Some sought to preserve his ideas and techniques in their original form; others advocated changes ranging from minor alterations to whole-sale rejection of fundamental principles. In this section, we describe a few of these treatment variations.

Psychoanalytically Oriented Psychotherapy. Therapists whose psychoanalytic procedures depart only slightly from the guidelines set down by Freud are said to employ *psychoanalytically oriented psychotherapy*. For example, during the 1930s and 1940s, Franz Alexander and his colleagues at the Chicago Psychoanalytic Institute questioned the belief that treatment must be intense, extended, and fundamentally similar in all cases (Alexander & French, 1946). They also sought to apply psychoanalysis to "nontraditional" clients such as the young and the severely disturbed.

In psychoanalytically oriented psychotherapy, not every patient is seen for the standard five sessions per week because daily sessions may foster too much dependence on the analyst or may become so routine that the patient pays too little attention to them. The frequency of sessions varies as circumstances dictate. Early in treatment the patient may be seen every day; later, sessions may take place less often. Alexander even suggested that temporary interruptions in treatment could be beneficial by testing the patient's ability to live without therapy and reducing reliance on the therapist. He noted as well that, while some clients need lengthy psychoanalysis in order to fully explore and work through resistance, insights, and the transference, others—especially those whose problems are either relatively mild or especially severe—are candidates for less extensive treatment aimed at support rather than at the uncovering and reconstructing associated with classical analysis (for a more recent example of this approach, see Davanloo, 1994).

Today, practitioners of psychodynamically oriented therapy (e.g., Strupp, 1989; Strupp & Blinder, 1984) try to create an empathic and supportive atmosphere in which the client feels cared for and understood, a key outcome known as *corrective emotional experiences*. In this context, the patient begins to reenact conflicts from the past with the therapist (the transference). In response to these reenactments, psychodynamically oriented therapists are likely to be more emotionally supportive and less prone to interpretation than are classic psychoanalysts. They also tend to be more active. For example, while Freudian analysts discouraged clients from making major life decisions during treatment (in order to prevent errors born of maladaptive impulses, false insights, or neurotic defenses) the analytically oriented therapist may encourage such decisions. The idea is that the therapeutic relationship provides a stable context in which to form plans for progress that can be tested in real life. Thus, a client who is unhappy about an unsatisfying job might be encouraged to look for a better position.

Psychoanalytically oriented therapists use a number of other unorthodox techniques, including the following:

1. The patient may sit up and face the analyst rather than lie on a couch.
2. Normal conversation may be substituted for free association.
3. Hypnosis may be used to promote self-exploration.

4. The nature of current problems and their solution is emphasized.

5. The patient's family may be consulted (or even offered treatment) as part of a broad-based effort at helping the patient.

Ego Analysis.   While psychoanalytically oriented psychotherapists mainly revised Freud's procedures, another group of therapists known as *ego analysts,* challenged some of his basic principles. They argued, for example, that Freud's preoccupation with sexual and aggressive instincts (the id) as the basis for behavior and behavior disorder is too narrow. Behavior, they said is also determined by the ego, which can function not just to combat id impulses, but also to promote learning and creativity.

These ideas led analysts such as Heinz Hartmann (1958), David Rapaport (1951), Melanie Klein (1960), Erik Erikson (1946), and even Freud's daughter, Anna Freud (1946), to use psychoanalytic techniques to explore patients' adaptive ego functions as well as their id instincts. To them, therapy is more than a means of treating disorders by exploring and working through early childhood experiences; it is a relationship experience that can lead to client self-actualization. As such, ego analysis has much in common with the phenomenological approach to therapy described later. Several excellent references provide more detailed coverage of the theory and practice of ego analysis (Eagle, 1984; Guntrip, 1973; Monroe, 1955; Slipp, 1981).

Alfred Adler's Individual Psychology.   Alfred Adler was an early follower of Freud who was the first to defect from the ranks of orthodox psychoanalysis. As described in Chapter 2, he retained a psychodynamic orientation, but he deemphasized Freud's theory of instincts, infantile sexuality, and the role of the unconscious in determining behavior. Because Adler believed that people's problems (or maladaptive lifestyles, as he called them) were based largely on the misconceptions they held, his treatment methods focused on exploring and altering those misconceptions.

So where a strict Freudian might see a teenage boy's vomiting before school each morning as a defense of some kind, the Adlerian analyst would view the problem as reflecting tension brought about by a misconception such as "I must do better than everyone else." And while the vomiting might be explored in Freudian analysis through free association, a therapist using Adler's individual analysis would discuss the symptom with the client as an illustration of a *style of life* driven by misconceptions which function to protect the client from perceived weaknesses. The youngster would then be helped to form more appropriate attitudes and given encouragement to change his style in a more adaptive direction.

In Adlerian analysis, client and therapist sit face to face in similar chairs. The feelings and reactions expressed toward the therapist (transference) are interpreted not as reflecting unconscious childhood conflicts, but as the client's habitual style of dealing with people *like* the therapist. Similarly, Adlerians view resistance as a sample of how the client usually avoids unpleasant material, and dreams are interpreted—not as symbolic wish fulfillment—but as a "rehearsal" of how the client might deal with problems in the future. And where Freudians offer interpretations designed to promote insight into *past causes* of current problems, Adler interpreted in order to promote insight into the patient's current lifestyle. He often phrased his interpretations as questions, such as, "Could it be that your unhappiness with your work is related to your insistence that everything must go perfectly for you?" This style of interpretation emphasizes the *purpose* of the client's behavior rather than its cause, and it encourages the client to be an active collaborator in the search for this purpose. Once clients see what it is they are doing, it becomes harder to maintain maladaptive ideas and behaviors.

Adlerian therapists are more involved than Freudians are in advising and encouraging their clients to change. For example, once a client realizes that her dependence on her husband is part of her overall style of seeking protection (and thus controlling others), the therapist might point out several alternative ways she might start to change. Adlerians also use modeling, homework assignments, and other techniques to help patients become aware of their lifestyle and to prompt them to change. Many of these methods are similar to tactics employed in the behavioral and phenomenological therapies described later.

Object Relations and Other Psychodynamic Therapies.

One of the most important developments in modern variations on psychoanalysis has been the emergence of *object relations theory,* a movement associated with a group of influential British analysts including Ronald Fairbairn (1952), Donald Winnicott (1965), Melanie Klein (1975), and Margaret Mahler (Mahler, Pine, & Bergman, 1975), as well as Otto Kernberg (1976) and Heinz Kohut (1971, 1977, 1983). Object relations theories, and the therapies based on them, focus on the nature of interpersonal relationships that are built from very early infant–mother interactions and on the nature of the personality characteristics—especially the *self*—that result from these interactions (Blatt & Lerner, 1983; Eagle, 1984).

In Kohut's *self-psychology,* for example, the analyst's task is to provide the type of empathic responding and nurturing that the client is assumed to have missed as an infant. Thus, in contrast to classical psychoanalysts, object relations theorists view the therapeutic relationship not as transference to be analyzed, but as a "second chance" for the client to obtain in a close relationship the gratification that was absent during infancy. This emphasis on ego support, acceptance, and psychological "holding" of damaged selves has made object relations therapies among the most popular versions of psychoanalysis, largely because they allow a friendly, naturally human stance toward the therapeutic relationship which many therapists prefer to traditional Freudian neutrality. It is a stance that is similar to that taken in some of the phenomenological therapies discussed later (Kahn, 1985).

Other variants on psychoanalysis are also related to phenomenological treatments. For example, when Otto Rank, another early follower of Freud, left the fold he developed a therapeutic approach that emphasized the client's innate *will to health* as a vehicle for promoting mature independence. He saw the therapist mainly as a *facilitator* of the patient's inherent potential for growth, not as a relentless explorer of the unconscious. We shall see that Carl Rogers's client-centered therapy was built partly on these concepts.

Similarly, Harry Stack Sullivan, discussed in Chapter 2 as the father of the interpersonal perspective, employed therapy methods that anticipated the cognitive-behavioral approaches described in the next section (Wachtel, 1977). Sullivan believed that the therapist should carefully observe interpersonal relationships and then use these

TABLE 8.1   Variations on Freudian Psychoanalysis

I. Alternate systems of analytic psychotherapy based on theoretical or ideological differences from Freudian classical analysis.

  1. The non-Freudian systems.

    a. The *individual psychology* of Alfred Adler.

    b. The *analytical psychology* of Carl Jung

    c. The *will therapy* of Otto Rank.

  2. Neo-Freudian systems based on the cultural emphasis.

    a. The *holistic* approach of Karen Horney.

    b. The *interpersonal relations* school of Harry Stack Sullivan.

    c. The *cultural* approach of Erich Fromm.

II. Attempts to streamline, abbreviate, and speed up the process of psychoanalytic therapy.

  1. Stekel's *active analytic* psychotherapy.

  2. Ferenczi's experiments with *active* techniques.

  3. The Chicago school of *brief* psychoanalytic therapy.

III. Expansions of Freudian classical analysis in various directions.

  1. The "object-relations approach" of Guntrip, Winnicott, Fairbairn, and the British school.

  2. The "eight stages of man" and Erikson's extension of Freud's theory of character development.

  3. Character analysis of Wilhelm Reich.

  4. Kohut's approach to the treatment of narcissistic character disorders.

IV. Modifications based on the shift in emphasis to ego psychology.

  1. Federn's ego psychology and the psychotherapy of the ego boundaries.

  2. Wolman's interactional psychoanalytic therapy.

SOURCE: Kutash, 1976, pp. 89–90.

observations to clarify for clients how their typical cognitions and behaviors interfere with successful living. Clients would then be able to use this information to stop perpetuating interpersonal conflicts and to develop more adaptive ways of living.

Our review of variations on psychoanalysis has barely scratched the surface of the methods available (see Table 8.1). Far more detailed coverage is available in several excellent texts on psychotherapy (e.g., Corsini & Wedding, 1995).

BEHAVIORAL AND COGNITIVE-BEHAVIORAL THERAPIES

Behavioral and cognitive-behavioral therapies are based on the principles and assumptions of the behavioral approach to clinical psychology (see Chapter 2). This means that:

1. Behavior disorders are seen as developing through the same laws of learning as any other behaviors.

2. Therapy methods should be guided by the results of research on learning. When behavioral treatments first emerged, they relied mainly on the principles of classical

and operant conditioning of overt behavior, but today they have expanded to encompass the latest about what psychologists in cognitive, social, and biological psychology have learned about how people think and feel (Viken & McFall, 1994).

3. Therapy should be aimed at modifying overt, maladaptive behaviors, as well as the cognitions, physical changes, and emotions that accompany overt behavior. The covert aspects of clients' problems should be dealt with as directly as possible.

4. Treatment should address clients' current problems by dealing with the contemporary environmental forces, learned habits, and cognitive factors that maintain them. Treatment can proceed without exploring early childhood experiences, unconscious processes, inner conflicts, or the like.

5. There is a commitment to the experimental evaluation of treatment. Behavioral therapists are particularly likely to employ techniques whose efficacy has been established by the results of controlled research.

This learning-oriented, empirical, here-and-now approach to treatment is not impersonal, however. Like other clinicians, behavioral therapists believe that treatment proceeds best when offered in the context of a supportive and productive therapeutic relationship. Indeed, as noted in Chapter 7, some behavioral therapists believe that the therapeutic relationship serves as the ideal context for modeling, then reinforcing, adaptive client behaviors.

Beginnings of Behavior Therapy

The term *behavior therapy* first appeared in a 1953 paper that described the use of operant conditioning to improve the functioning of chronic schizophrenics (Lindsley, Skinner, & Solomon, 1953). Today, behavior therapy has become one of the most popular approaches to treating all sorts of behavior disorders in adults and children (Wilson, 1995).

Groundwork for the emergence of behavior therapy occurred in the 1920s, when psychologists became interested in studying the role of conditioning and learning in the development of anxiety. For example, Ivan Pavlov observed *experimental neuroses* in his dogs after exposing them to electric shock or requiring them to make difficult sensory discriminations. The dogs' symptoms included agitation, barking, biting the equipment, and forgetting things they had previously learned. In the 1940s, Jules Masserman of Northwestern University studied the conditioning and deconditioning of experimental neuroses in cats.

The discovery of experimental neuroses in animals led to research on similar problems in humans. The most famous of these studies was a classic experiment in 1920 by John B. Watson and his graduate student, Rosalie Rayner. A nine-month-old infant, Albert B., was presented with several stimuli such as a white rat, a dog, a rabbit, a monkey, masks, and a burning newspaper. He showed no fear toward any of these objects, but he did become upset when a loud noise was sounded by striking a steel bar with a hammer. To see whether Albert's fear could be conditioned to a harmless object, Watson and Rayner associated the loud noise with a tame white rat. Albert was shown the rat and, as soon as he began to reach for it, the noise was sounded. After several pairings, the rat alone elicited a strong emotional reaction in the child. This conditioned fear also generalized to some extent to other, previously neutral, furry objects including a rabbit, a fur coat, Watson's own hair, and even a Santa Claus mask. Albert's fear persisted in less extreme form during assessments conducted over a one-month period.

A few years later, Mary Cover Jones, another of Watson's students, investigated several techniques for *reducing* children's fears (Jones, 1924a, b). For example, she used *social imitation* to help a three-year-old named Peter conquer his fear of rabbits. "Each day Peter and three other children were brought to the laboratory for a play period. The other children were selected carefully because of their entirely fearless attitude toward the rabbit. . . ." (Jones, 1924b, p. 310). The fearless examples set by the other children helped Peter become more comfortable with the rabbit, but his treatment was interrupted by a bout of scarlet fever, and his progress was jeopardized by a frightening encounter with a big dog. When treatment resumed, it included *direct conditioning*, a procedure in which Peter was fed his favorite food in a room with a caged rabbit. At each session—some of which were attended by Peter's fearless friends—the bunny was placed a little closer to him. This procedure eliminated Peter's fear of rabbits; Peter summed up the results of the treatment by announcing "I like the rabbit."

The cases of Albert and Peter encouraged the application of conditioning principles to the treatment of fear and many other disorders; the 1920s and 1930s saw learning-based treatments for sexual disorders, substance abuse, and various anxiety-related conditions. However, it was not until the late 1950s and early 1960s that behavior therapy began to achieve its status as a major treatment approach. It was then that treatment research in South Africa, England, and the United States by Joseph Wolpe, Stanley Rachman, Arnold Lazarus, Hans Eysenck, Knight Dunlap, Andrew Salter, and others began to attract widespread attention among clinicians. Their work, which laid the foundation for the behavioral treatment methods described in the following sections, was described in several influential books, including *Psychotherapy by Reciprocal Inhibition* (Wolpe, 1958), *Conditioning Techniques in Clinical Practice and Research* (Franks, 1964); *Case Studies in Behavior Modification* (Ullmann & Krasner, 1965); *Research in Behavior Modification* (Krasner & Ullmann, 1965); and *Behavior Therapy Techniques: A Guide to the Treatment of Neuroses* (Wolpe & Lazarus, 1966). B.F. Skinner's (1953) *Science and Human Behavior* provided a blueprint for the therapeutic use of operant conditioning.

Systematic Desensitization

The anti-anxiety treatment known as *systematic desensitization* (SD) was developed in 1958 by Joseph Wolpe, a South African psychiatrist, as a result of his efforts to help cats overcome laboratory-induced experimental neuroses. The animals had been repeatedly shocked in a special cage, so they resisted being put in that cage and refused to eat while there. Wolpe reasoned that if conditioned anxiety could inhibit eating, perhaps eating might inhibit conditioned anxiety through the principle of *reciprocal inhibition*. According to Wolpe (1958): "If a response antagonistic to anxiety can be made to occur in the presence of anxiety-evoking stimuli so that it is accompanied by a complete or partial suppression of the anxiety responses, the bond between these stimuli and the anxiety responses will be weakened" (p. 71). In fact, when he "counterconditioned" the cats' fear by hand-feeding them in cages that were closer and closer to where their anxiety had been learned, most animals showed greatly diminished emotional reactions.

To try similar methods with humans who suffered phobias and other maladaptive fears, Wolpe needed to create responses other than eating that might be incompatible with anxiety. He chose three: deep muscle relaxation, interpersonal assertion, and sexual arousal. Muscle relaxation became the standard anxiety inhibitor in most cases of systematic desensitization; assertion or sexual arousal is employed mainly when the anxiety to be inhibited relates to interpersonal or sexual problems.

The most common relaxation technique is *progressive relaxation training* (e.g., Bernstein & Borkovec, 1973), a shorter version of a method pioneered by Edmund Jacobson in 1938. It involves tensing and then releasing various groups of muscles while focusing on the sensations of relaxation that follow. (You can get an idea of what the training feels like by clenching your fist for about five seconds and then abruptly releasing the tension.)

The next step in desensitization is for the therapist to create a graduated hierarchy of situations that the client finds increasingly anxiety-provoking. The content and ordering of these items (which are later to be imagined or experienced "live") is guided by the client so that each elicits just a bit more anxiety than the one before it (see Table 8.2). Too large an increase in arousal between items will make progress difficult, while too small an increase may lengthen treatment needlessly.

After relaxation training and hierarchy construction are complete, desensitization itself begins. In *imaginal desensitization*, the client relaxes and then visualizes the easiest item on the hierarchy. If the client can imagine the scene without anxiety for ten seconds, the therapist describes the next one. If not, the client signals the anxiety and stops visualizing the scene. After regaining complete relaxation, the client again pictures the item for a shorter duration, then for gradually longer periods until it no longer creates distress. This sequence is continued until the client can handle all items in the hierarchy. Ideally, reduction of anxiety to imagined scenes transfers to their real-life equivalents, but the client is also urged to seek out real-world counterparts of the visualized scenes in order to reinforce progress and to assess the generality of treatment effects. Completion of a hierarchy typically takes three to five sessions, though it is possible to finish a short hierarchy in a single meeting. In *in vivo* desensitization, clients use their relaxation skills, and the comforting presence of the therapist, to stay calm while actually confronting gradually more threatening versions of what they fear.

Systematic desensitization can be very effective in the treatment of conditioned maladaptive anxiety. Indeed, Gordon Paul (1969b), a pioneer in research on SD, concluded that "for the first time in the history of psychological treatments, a specific therapeutic package reliably produced measurable benefits for clients across a broad range of distressing problems in which anxiety was of fundamental importance" (p. 159).

TABLE 8.2 A Desensitization Hierarchy.

In imaginal desensitization, the client relaxes while visualizing a series of increasingly frightening scenes. In *in vivo* desensitization, the client confronts real hierarchy items unders controlled conditions. Here is an imaginal hierarchy used in the treatment of a seventeen-year-old woman who feared getting lice or other bugs in her hair. The numbers in parentheses indicate the session(s) of desensitization during which each item was presented.

1. Writing the words *bug* and *lice*. (1)

2. While reading in school you notice a small bug on your book. (1)

3. While walking down the sidewalk you notice a comb in the gutter. (1)

4. You are at home watching television when an ad concerning a dandruff-removing shampoo comes on. (2)

5. You are reading a *Reader's Digest* article that goes into detail concerning the catching and curing of a case of lice. (2)

6. You look at your desktop and notice several bobby pins and clips upon it. (3)

7. You are in a department store, and the saleslady is fitting a hat on you. (3)

8. At a store you are asked to try on a wig and you comply. (3)

9. You are watching a movie and they show a scene where people are being deloused. (4, 5, and 6)

10. At school, in hygiene class, the teacher lectures on lice and bugs in people's hair. (4 and 5)

11. A girl puts her scarf on your lap. (5)

12. In a public washroom you touch the seat of a commode. (6)

13. You are in a beauty shop having your hair set. (6)

14. A girl sitting in front of you in school leans her head back on your books. (6 and 7)

15. While sitting at home with your sister, she tells you that she used someone else's comb today. (7 and 8)

16. While sitting in the local snack bar a friend tells you of her experiences when she had a case of lice. (8 and 9)

17. You are combing your hair in the washroom when someone asks to borrow your comb. (9)

18. A stranger asks to use your comb and continues to ask why not when you say no. (9)

19. While standing looking at an ad in a store window, someone comes up beside you and puts their head near yours to see too. (10)

20. A stranger in the washroom at school hands you her comb and asks you to hold it for her. (10)

21. Your sister is fixing your hair when she drops the curlers on the floor, picks them up, and uses them in your hair. (11)

22. A stranger notices a tangle in your hair and tries to help you by combing it out with her comb. (11)

SOURCE: Geer, 1965.

However, SD may be less successful in treating anxiety-related problems, such as panic disorder and obsessive-compulsive disorder, that are more generalized or complex than specific phobias. Indeed, behavioral therapists have found that treatments involving direct exposure of the client to feared stimuli may be the treatment of choice for many of these disorders (Barlow & Wolfe, 1981).

Exposure Techniques

Like *in vivo* desensitization, *exposure treatments* entail direct exposure to frightening stimuli, but the idea here is not to prevent anxiety. Instead, exposure to feared stimuli is arranged so that anxiety occurs and continues until—because no harm comes to the client—it eventually disappears through the process of extinction.

Using *flooding,* for example, clients might be asked to touch and remain in contact with—for hours, if necessary—items they fear are "contaminated." While some therapists favor intense, prolonged exposures to items at the top of the client's anxiety hierarchy, others start with lower items before trying the most frightening ones (Barlow & Waddell, 1985). In either case, exposure times must be long enough for anxiety to dissipate; exposure should not be terminated while the client is still anxious because the resulting anxiety reduction would reinforce avoidance behavior.

Exposure treatments are especially popular in cases of obsessive-compulsive disorder (in which clients experience *obsessions*—persistently fearful ideas or worries—and engage in *compulsions*, which are repeated behavioral rituals designed to reduce or prevent anxiety stemming from their obsessions). In such cases, exposure is usually accompanied by *response prevention*, meaning that clients are not allowed to perform the rituals they normally use to reduce anxiety (Abramowitz, 1996; see Table 8.3). Exposure techniques are also used extensively with *agoraphobia*, a severe disorder involving fear of being away from home or some other safe place, or of being in a public place—such as a theater—from which escape might be difficult. Exposure treatments are also used for the panic attacks that often precede the development of agoraphobia.

Social Skills Training

Some psychological disorders may develop partly because people lack the social skills necessary for participating in satisfying interpersonal relationships and for gaining other reinforcers. If their skill deficits are severe, these people can become demoralized, anxious, angry, or alienated. Accordingly, behavioral therapists often include *social skills training* in the treatment of disorders such as depression (Bellack, Hersen, & Himmelhoch, 1983), anxiety disorders (Ost, Jerremalm, & Johansson, 1981), antisocial and delinquent behavior (Stumphauzer, 1986), schizophrenia (Dilk & Bond, 1996), and social withdrawal and isolation, often with children and adolescents.

Although social skills training encompasses many techniques, *assertiveness training* is one of the most popular, especially with adults whose inability to effectively express their needs and wishes leads to resentment, aggression, or depression. All too often, these people know what they would *like* to say and do in various social situations but, because of thoughts like "I have no right to make a fuss" or "He won't like me if I object," they suffer in silence. Assertion training is designed to (1) teach clients how to express themselves appropriately if they do not already have the skills to do so, and/or (2) eliminate cognitive obstacles to clear self-expression. They are also taught that assertiveness is *the appropriate expression of feeling in ways that do not infringe upon the rights of others* (Alberti & Emmons, 1974; Wolpe & Lazarus, 1966).

TABLE 8.3 Exposure Treatment of Obsessive-Compulsive Disorder

Here is an excerpt from a treatment session in which a client's obsessions about contamination and resulting compulsive cleaning rituals are treated with exposure methods. Notice how the therapist guides and encourages the client to confront a frightening situation (a dead animal by the side of a road) and to stay in contact with it until anxiety begins to subside.

THERAPIST: (*Outside the office.*) There it is, behind the car. Let's go and touch the curb and street next to it. I won't insist that you touch it directly because it's a bit smelly, but I want you to step next to it and touch it with the sole of your shoe.

PATIENT: Yuck! It's really dead. It's gross!

T: Yeah, it is a bit gross, but it's also just a dead cat if you think about it plainly. What harm can it cause?

P: I don't know. Suppose I got germs on my hand?

T: What sort of germs?

P: Dead cat germs.

T: What kind are they?

P: I don't know. Just germs.

T: Like the bathroom germs that we've already handled?

P: Sort of. People don't go around touching dead cats.

T: They also don't go running home to shower or alcoholing the inside of their car. It's time to get over this. Now, come on over and I'll do it first. (*Patient follows.*) OK. Touch the curb and the street, here's a stone you can carry with you and a piece of paper from under its tail. Go ahead, take it.

P: (*Looking quite uncomfortable.*) Ugh!

T: We'll both hold them. Now, touch it to your front and your skirt and your face and hair. Like this. That's good. What's your anxiety level?

P: Ick! Ninety-nine. I'd say 100 but it's just short of panic. If you weren't here, it'd be 100.

T: You know from past experience that this will be much easier in a while. Just stay with it and we'll wait here. You're doing fine.

P: (*A few minutes pass in which she looks*

Thus, telling your boss that you will not agree to an unreasonable request requires assertion, but so does telling your friends that you were moved by their recent expression of sympathy.

Assertion training often takes place in groups and usually includes four components: (1) defining assertion and distinguishing it from aggression and submissiveness, (2) discussing clients' rights and the rights of others in a variety of social situations, (3) identifying and eliminating cognitive obstacles to assertion, and (4) practicing assertive behavior. This last component usually begins with role-playing or rehearsal of various social interactions, with the therapist taking the client's role and demonstrating appropriate assertiveness. Next, the client tries the same behavior. This effort is reinforced and suggestions are made for further improvement. After more refined rehearsals, the client is asked to try the new thoughts and actions outside of therapy. Successes and failures are analyzed at subsequent sessions, where further skill training and practice occur.

Although initially focused on training in the "refusal skills" many clients need to ward off unreasonable requests, assertiveness training is now also aimed at promoting a

---

TABLE 8.3   Exposure Treatment of Obsessive-Compulsive Disorder. (*Continued*)

very upset.) Would you do this if it wasn't for me?

T: Yes, if this were my car and I dropped my keys here, I'd just pick them up and go on.

P: You wouldn't have to wash them?

T: No. Dead animals aren't delightful but they're part of the world we live in. What are the odds that we'll get ill from this?

P: Very small I guess. . . . I feel a little bit better than at first. It's about 90 now.

T: Good! Just stay with it now.

The session continues for another 45 minutes or until anxiety decreases substantially. During this period conversation focuses generally on the feared situation and the patient's reactions to it. The therapist inquires about the patient's anxiety level approximately every 10 minutes.

T: How do you feel now?

P: Well, it is easier, but I sure don't feel great.

T: Can you put a number on it?

P: About 55 or 60 I'd say.

T: You worked hard today. You must be tired. Let's stop now. I want you to take this stick and pebble with you so that you continue to be contaminated. You can keep them in your pocket and touch them frequently during the day. I want you to contaminate your office at work and your apartment with them. Touch them to everything around, including everything in the kitchen, chairs, your bed, and the clothes in your dresser. Oh, also, I'd like you to drive your car past this spot on your way to and from work. Can you do that?

P: I suppose so. The trouble is going home with all this dirt.

T: Why don't you call Ken and plan to get home after he does so he can be around to help you. Remember, you can always call me if you have any trouble.

P: Yeah. That's a good idea. I'll just leave work after he does. OK. See you tomorrow.

SOURCE: Steketee and Foa, 1985.

---

broader range of social skills, including making conversation, engaging in interpersonal problem-solving, and appropriately responding to emotional provocations (e.g., Tisdell & St. Lawrence, 1988).

Modeling

A very important mechanism in human learning is imitation, also known as *modeling* or observational learning (Bandura, 1969). In fact, learning through modeling is usually more efficient than learning through direct reinforcement or punishment. (Imagine if everyone had to be hit by a car before knowing how to cross streets safely!) Observing the consequences of a model's behavior can also *inhibit* or *disinhibit* an observer's imitative behavior (we are unlikely to pet a dog that just bit someone, but we are more likely to cross against a red light after watching someone else do so).

Modeling has been used to treat many clinical problems, including social withdrawal among adults and children, obsessive-compulsive behaviors, unassertiveness, antisocial conduct, physical aggressiveness, and early infantile autism (Rosenthal & Steffek,

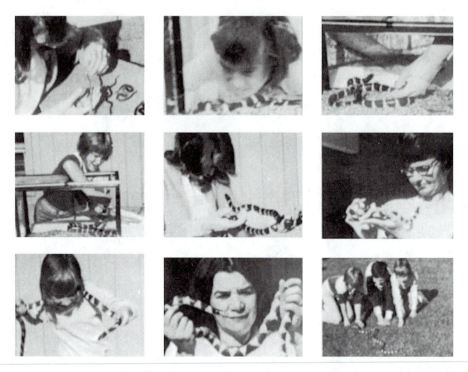

FIGURE 8.1 A modeling film for the treatment of snake phobia. (From A. Bandura, E. B. Blanchard, & B. Ritter, The relative efficacy of desensitization and modeling approaches for inducing behavioral, affective and attitudinal change. *Journal of Personality and Social Psychology*, 1969, *13*, 173–199. Copyright by the American Psychological Association. Reprinted by permission.)

1991). In the tradition of Mary Cover Jones (1924b), it is also commonly used to treat fears. The simplest modeling approach eliminating fearful avoidance involves having a client observe live or videotaped models as they perform behaviors that the client avoids—with the models experiencing no negative consequences (see Figure 8.1). In a common variant on this basic modeling treatment called *participant modeling*, the client first observes live models, then makes guided, gradual contact with the feared object under controlled and protected circumstances.

Modeling treatments appear to be especially effective when the model(s) are similar to the client, have high status, and are rewarded for their actions (Bandura, 1986). One way of making models more similar to clients—while also providing instruction on how to deal successfully with fear—is to present *coping models* who initially display fearfulness, then cope with and overcome it (Meichenbaum, 1971). The effects of modeling treatments have increasingly been linked to their ability to increase *self-efficacy*, the belief that one can successfully perform certain behaviors.

Aversion Therapy

Aversion therapy is a set of techniques in which painful or unpleasant stimuli are used to decrease the probability of unwanted behaviors such as drug abuse, alcoholism, overeating, smoking, and disturbing sexual practices. Following classical conditioning principles, most aversion methods pair stimuli that elicit problematic behavior with a noxious stimulus. So, for example, an alcoholic is exposed to a foul odor as he sits at a simulated bar, smelling a glass of Scotch. Ideally, continued pairings should decrease the attractiveness of the eliciting stimuli until the unwanted behavior is reduced, if not eliminated. When aversion therapy is based on operant conditioning, electric shock or some other aversive stimulus acts as a punisher; it is delivered just after the client performs the problematic behavior (e.g., immediately after taking a drink of alcohol).

In an early example of electrical aversion, alcoholics were shocked on half the occasions they sipped alcohol (Blake, 1965). The shock was terminated only when subjects spat out the alcohol, a procedure known as *aversion relief.* Follow-up interviews indicated a 54% rate of abstinence over six months and 52% abstinence after one year. In another early case, aversion therapy was used with a thirty-three-year-old fetishist who had been attacking women's baby carriages and handbags (Raymond, 1956). After these objects were repeatedly paired with chemically induced nausea, the client reported being repulsed by the objects of his former affections.

Certain types of aversive stimuli tend to work better with behaviors that involve certain sensory systems (Garcia, McGowan, & Green, 1972). For example, it may be easier to establish a conditioned association between nausea and overeating or overdrinking than between, say, overeating and pain. Similarly, it may be easier to associate sexual or aggressive misbehaviors with the pain of shock than with nausea.

The nature of aversive stimuli can be adjusted at will in a form of aversion therapy called *covert sensitization*, in which the client visualizes aversive consequences accompanying unwanted behavior. Joseph Cautela, the originator of covert sensitization, describes the following scene to be visualized by an alcoholic client:

> You are walking into a bar. You decide to have a glass of beer. You are now walking toward the bar. As you are approaching the bar you have a funny feeling in the pit of your stomach. Your stomach feels all queasy and nauseous. Some liquid comes up your throat and it is very sour. You try to swallow it back down, but as you do this, food particles start coming up your throat to your mouth. You are now reaching the bar and you order a beer. As the bartender is pouring the beer, puke comes up into your mouth. You try to keep your mouth closed and swallow it down. You reach for the glass of beer to wash it down. As soon as your hand touches the glass, you can't hold it down any longer. You have to open your mouth and you puke. It goes all over your hand, all over the glass and the beer. You can see it floating around in the beer. . . . You turn away from the beer and immediately you start to feel better and better. When you get out into the clean fresh air you feel wonderful. You go home and clean up. (Cautela, 1966, p. 37)

Covert sensitization offers some advantages over shock or chemically induced aversion (Cautela & Kearney, 1986). For one thing, it can create imagery that approximates more closely than a laboratory could the stimuli encountered in the client's natural environment.

As researchers have continued to study aversion therapy, they have learned how to increase its effectiveness in treating undesirable behaviors. One commentator summarized the effects of this research as follows: "In many quarters and in spite of the continuing controversies, aversion therapy is rapidly achieving the status of re-spectability in the total range of services to be considered by professionals concerned with behavior change objectives" (Sandler & Steele, 1991, p. 241). Still, debate contin-ues over several aspects of aversion methods. First, there is concern about whether the changes produced by aversion therapies are extensive, durable, and generalizable enough to justify the unpleasantness of the treatment. Critics also note that aversion therapy does not teach clients alternative behaviors that can replace their maladaptive ones. Learning such alternatives is particularly important for clients being treated for overeating, smoking, drug abuse, and other pleasure-oriented problems. In the case of fetishes and other paraphilias, for example, clients' problems usually reappear if they do not learn to enjoy sexual outlets that are satisfying to them and acceptable to soci-ety. Third, many therapists find it aversive to use aversion therapies, and a small num-ber of clinicians have called for a ban on them. Their distaste is engendered partly by skepticism about treatment effects, but also by (1) reluctance to intentionally inflict discomfort on clients, (2) worry over possible side effects such as generalized fear or aggressiveness, and (3) overuse of the procedures by therapists who might use them simply because they can bring about quick (but temporary) changes (Masters et al., 1987).

Accordingly, aversive methods tend to be used as a last resort to control danger-ous behavior (such as self-abuse) that has not responded to nonaversive methods, and even then, as part of a broader treatment approach designed to promote more adaptive behavior. Clinicians also use the minimum effective amount of aversive stimulation so as to minimize harm and potential side effects.

Contingency Management

Contingency management is a generic term for any operant technique that modifies a behavior by controlling its consequences. *Shaping, time out, contingency contract-ing, response cost,* and *token economies* are all examples of contingency manage-ment. In practice, contingency management refers to presenting and/or withdrawing reinforcers and aversive stimuli contingent upon the appearance of certain target behaviors. Contingency management has been applied to a broader range of prob-lems than any other behavioral technique. Autism, temper tantrums, learning difficul-ties, hyperactivity, retardation, juvenile delinquency, aggression, hallucinations, delu-sions, depression, phobias, sexual disorders, and physical and psychosomatic complaints are just a few of the targets that have been dealt with through contin-gency management.

Contingency management is so widely applied because it is so flexible. It can be tailored to clients of all ages, to the unique problems of an individual, and to the behav-ior of a group or even a whole community. Because its methods are relatively easy to learn, a client's friends, relatives, teachers, and peers can be trained to employ contin-gency management in real-life settings. Contingency management can also be used by clients to modify their own behavior. This process, known as *self-control,* can be thought of as the ability to regulate personal behaviors by arranging appropriate rein-forcement contingencies. Thus an overweight person who decides to eat only at specified times, only in the kitchen, and only in the presence of family is practicing a form of self-control (Rehm et al., 1981).

Complete accounts of the wide range of contingency management techniques are available in many texts (e.g., Spiegler & Guevremont, 1993). We present five examples here.

Shaping. Also called *successive approximation,* shaping is a procedure for developing new behaviors by initially reinforcing any act that remotely resembles the desired behavior. The criterion for reinforcement is then made gradually more stringent until only those responses matching the final standard are rewarded. Shaping is useful for instigating behaviors that appear to exceed the client's present capacities. It has been used to teach speech to children who are mute, toilet habits to those who are incontinent, and self-help and occupational skills to severely retarded persons.

Time Out. Time out is a special example of extinction that reduces the frequency of unwanted behavior by temporarily removing the person from the setting where that behavior is being reinforced. The most common example is sending a child to a quiet, boring room for a short time following some act of mischief. Time out is based on the principle that ignoring a child's "bad" behavior will decrease it, especially if alternative "good" behavior is also reinforced.

Contingency Contracting. Contracting is a form of contingency management where a formal, often written, agreement between therapist and client spells out the consequences of certain client behaviors. Behavioral contracting has been applied to targets such as marital distress (Wood & Jacobson, 1985), family disruptions (Alexander & Parsons, 1973), drug abuse (Boudin, 1972), obesity (Brownell & Foreyt, 1985), and other problems (Walker et al., 1981). Therapeutic contracts have even been used to prevent clients' dangerous or suicidal behavior; they set up rules that forbid violent behavior or that require the client to take specific precautionary actions (calling the therapist, turning over weapons to the therapist) should he or she consider acting dangerously (Bongar, 1991).

The typical contract includes five components (Stuart, 1971): (1) responsibilities of each of the parties to the contract, (2) rewards for fulfilling the contract, (3) a system for monitoring compliance with the contract, (4) bonuses for unusual accomplishments, and (5) penalties for failures.

Response Cost. Response cost is a punishment contingency that involves the loss of a reward or privilege following some undesirable behavior. Fines for traffic violations are everyday examples of response cost. Response cost methods have been used to decrease the frequency of many clinical problems, including smoking, self-abuse, overeating, academic problems, and a range of inappropriate or aggressive behaviors in adults and children (see Figure 8.2). Two major advantages of these methods are that (1) behaviors decreased through response cost remain suppressed longer than when other types of punishment are employed and (2) response cost does not carry as many unwanted side effects as other, more aversive forms of punishment (Kazdin, 1972).

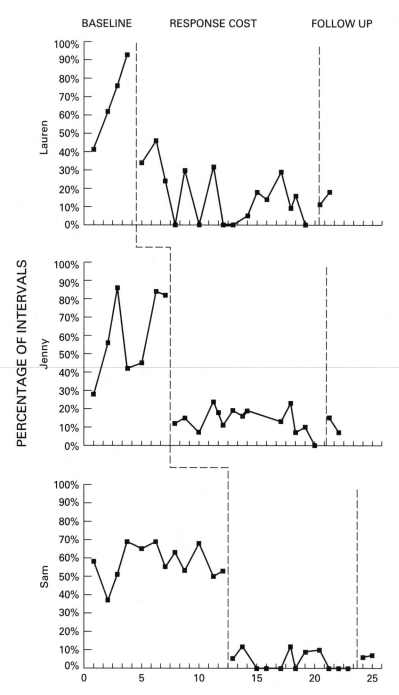

FIGURE 8.2 Effects of response cost methods to reduce noncompliance in children. These graphs show the effects of response cost used by mothers to decrease the rates at which their

Token Economies. A token economy is a system for implementing the principles of contingency management to alter a variety of behaviors, usually the behavior of adults or children in some controlled institutional setting. You might think of it as a monetary system in which clients are paid in a special currency (tokens) for performing designated behaviors.

Token economies usually include four elements, the first of which is for staff (and clients) to decide which *target behaviors* are to be changed. Common targets in hospitalized mental patients are increased social interaction and improved self-care skills. Second, a *token* or other medium of exchange is identified as payment for performing target behaviors. Gold stars and colored stickers are often used with children; for adults, tokens may be poker chips or specially made "coins." Third, *back-up reinforcers* are established; these are the goods or services for which tokens may be exchanged. Snacks, TV or recreational privileges, "vacations" from the hospital, and more luxurious living conditions are common back-ups. Finally, there are *rules of exchange* governing (1) the number of tokens to be given for performing each target behavior and (2) the number of tokens necessary to purchase each back-up reinforcer.

In the first published report on a token economy, hospitalized mental patients showed a significant increase in self-care and completed work assignments (Ayllon & Azrin, 1965). This report stimulated the development of similar token economies in numerous psychiatric hospitals, institutions for retarded people, and elementary school classrooms plagued by disruptive or delinquent behavior (Burchard, 1967; Cohen, 1968; O'Leary & Becker, 1967). Special programs for Head Start participants, alcoholics, drug addicts, and autistic children were also developed according to token economy principles. There have even been token economies designed to promote community-wide conservation and environmental protection efforts (Nietzel et al., 1977).

Biofeedback

The use of behavioral methods to control heart rate, blood pressure, muscle tension and other physiological responses is known as *biofeedback*. The name refers to the fact that the behaviors to be changed are biological in nature and that special equipment is

---

children refused to comply with their requests for appropriate behavior. During baseline sessions, all three children were noncompliant more than 50% of the time. At the beginning of each response-cost training session, the children were given points which were taken away one at a time whenever the child disobeyed. If the child lost 50% of these points, a privilege—such as watching TV or playing a game during the session—was also taken away. As treatment progressed, this 50% criterion was gradually made more stringent—e.g., the child would lose privileges if they lost even 20% of their points. Notice that noncompliance dramatically decreased during treatment, and that it stayed low at a six-week follow-up. [Reproduced from L. M. Little and M. L. Kelley (1989). The efficacy of response cost procedures for reducing children's noncompliance to parental instructions. *Behavior Therapy, 20,* 525–534. Copyright ©1989 by Association for Advancement of Behavior Therapy.]

used to monitor the target response and to give the client feedback about its intensity or frequency in the form of a meter reading, graph, or auditory signal. The monitor and feedback apparatus is attached to the client, who then uses some mental or physical strategy to change the internal target response in a desired direction. In most cases, the reinforcer for improvement is simply knowledge of results provided by the feedback, but praise or monetary rewards have also been used.

Biofeedback has been widely used in the treatment of several clinical disorders, including high blood pressure, migraine headache, Reynaud's disease (a circulatory disorder), stomach problems, bruxism (nocturnal tooth-grinding), irregular heart beat, and other problems that involve disruptions in autonomic or musculoskeletal functioning (e.g., Sedlacek & Taub, 1996). It appears to produce significant improvements in many of these conditions, though it is still not clear how durable these improvements are and whether they are any greater than the benefits of simpler procedures such as relaxation training (Reed, Katkin, & Goldband, 1986).

Cognitive-Behavioral Therapy

All therapeutic interventions involve thought processes, but some procedures are specifically directed toward changing clients' maladaptive cognitions. These techniques, known as *cognitive-behavioral therapy* or simply *cognitive therapy*, attempt to modify maladaptive behavior by influencing a client's cognitions (beliefs, schemas, self-statements, and problem-solving strategies). Cognitive-behavioral therapists see a larger role than traditional behaviorists do for thoughts as causes of overt behavior. Indeed, they assume that emotional problems are largely caused by irrational or maladaptive thinking and that restructuring these cognitions will be therapeutic.

Cognitive therapists also believe that certain cognitions, particularly thoughts about the self, are especially important in the development of disorder (Salovey & Singer, 1991). These thoughts are usually connected to emotions; they affect how we feel about ourselves and our relationships with others. Cognitions influence our outlook on the future and our confidence that we will be able to cope with new demands. They also color how we think about the past and the way we explain events that have happened to us. Cognitive versions of behavioral therapy have surged in popularity in the past ten years (see Dryden & Trower, 1989; Freeman et al., 1989; Goldfried & Davison, 1994; Kendall & Braswell, 1985; Ingram, 1986).

Beck's Cognitive Therapy. One of the most influential types of cognitive therapy is Aaron Beck's approach to the treatment of depression, an approach based on the assumption that depression and other emotions are determined by the way people think about their experiences (Beck et al., 1979; Beck & Weishaar, 1995). His version of cognitive therapy has also been applied to anxiety disorders, personality disorders, and substance use disorders (Beck et al., 1990; Linehan, 1993).

Beck says that depressive symptoms result from logical errors and distortions that clients make about the events in their lives. For example, they draw conclusions about themselves on the basis of insufficient or irrelevant information, as when a woman believes she is worthless because she was not invited to a party. They also exaggerate the importance of trivial events, as when a man decides that his vintage record collection is ruined because one record has a scratch on it. And they minimize the significance of positive events, as when a student believes that a good test score was the result of luck, not intelligence or hard work.

Cognitive therapists work to identify and correct their client's distorted beliefs using five related strategies: (1) recognizing the connections between cognitions, affect, and behavior; (2) monitoring occurrences of cognitive distortions; (3) examining the evidence for and against these distortions; (4) substituting more realistic interpretations for dysfunctional cognitions; and (5) giving "homework assignments" to practice new thinking strategies and more effective problem-coping.

Rational Emotive Behavior Therapy. Another influential cognitive therapy is Albert Ellis's *rational-emotive behavior therapy*, or REBT (Ellis, 1995). Ellis (1973) stated the core principles of REBT as follows:

> When a highly charged emotional Consequence (C) follows a significant Activating Event (A), A may seem to but actually does not cause C. Instead, emotional Consequences are

"Why doesn't she call? I don't understand. She said she'd call at 5:00. It's 5:15 already. Maybe she's been in an accident. Maybe she's lying in a ditch somewhere. I'd better call her and make sure she's ok. No, what if she's not hurt. What if she's with a MAN. I can't call her. She'll think I'm too pushy. They never like pushy men. But it's 5:20 already and she SAID she'd call— I didn't make her say that. She might really be hurt and bleeding somewhere. But what if I call her and she doesn't want to talk to me? God-damned women."

Cognitive-behavior therapy focuses on changing habits of thinking that tend to create problems. (Courtesy of the Western Psychological Association) largely created by B—the individual's Belief System. When, therefore, an undesirable Consequence occurs, such as severe anxiety, this can usually be quickly traced to the person's irrational Beliefs, and when these Beliefs are effectively Disputed (at point D), by challenging them rationally, the disturbed Consequences disappear and eventually cease to reoccur. (p. 167)

To summarize the ABCs of REBT: Psychological problems result not from external stress but from the irrational ideas people hold, which lead them to insist that their wishes must be met in order for them to be happy.

The therapist's task in REBT is to attack these irrational, unrealistic, self-defeating beliefs and to instruct clients in more rational or logical thinking patterns that will not upset them (Ellis, 1962; Ellis & Grieger, 1977; Ellis & Dryden, 1987). The REBT therapist is active, challenging, demonstrative, and often abrasive. Ellis advocates the use of strong, direct communication in order to persuade clients to give up the irrational ideas with which they indoctrinate themselves into misery. Here is a brief excerpt from an initial REBT session between a therapist (T) and a young woman (C) who presented several problems, among them the abuse of alcohol.

C: (after being asked what is wrong) . . . my tendency is to say *everything.* I want to change everything; I'm depressed about everything; et cetera.

T: Give me a couple of things, for example.

C: What I'm depressed about? I, uh, don't know that I have any purpose in life. I don't know what I—what I am. And I don't know in what direction I'm going.

T: Yeah, but that's—so you're saying, "I'm ignorant!" (client nods) Well, what's so awful about being ignorant? It's too bad you're ignorant. It would be nicer if you weren't—if you *had* a purpose and *knew* where you were going. But just let's suppose the worst: For the rest of your life you didn't have a purpose, and you stayed this way. Let's suppose that. Now why would you be so bad?

C: Because everyone *should* have a purpose!

T: Where did you get the *should?*

C: 'Cause it's what I believe in. (silence for a while)

T: I know. But think about it for a minute. You're obviously a bright woman; now, where did that *should* come from?

C: I, I don't know! I'm not thinking clearly at the moment. I'm too nervous! I'm sorry.

T: Well, but you *can* think clearly. Are you now saying, "Oh, it's hopeless! I can't think clearly. What a shit I am for not thinking clearly!" You see: You're blaming yourself for *that.*

C: (visibly upset; can't seem to say anything; then nods)

T: Now you're perfectly *able* to think.

C: Not at the moment!

T: Yes you are! Want to bet?

C: (begins to sob)

T: What are you crying about now?

C: Because I feel so stupid! And I'm afraid!

T: Yeah, but "stupid" means "I'm putting myself down for acting stupidly."

C: All right! I didn't expect to be put on so *fast.* I expected a moment to catch my breath and see who you *were;* and to establish some different kind of rapport.

T: Yeah. And that would be nice and easier; but we would really waste our time.

C: Yes, I guess we would.

T: But you're really upset because you're not giving the right answers—and isn't that *awful!*

C: Yes. And I don't think that anybody likes to be made a fool, a fool of!

T: You *can't* be made a fool of!

C: (chokes a little)

T: You see, that's the *point:* That's impossible. Now why *can't* you be made a fool of?

C: (angry outburst) Why don't you stop asking me?

T: (interrupting) No! You'll never get better unless you *think.* And you're saying, "Can't we do something *magical* to get me better?" And the answer is "No!"

The REBT therapist's frontal assault on the client's irrational beliefs is not restricted to cognitive interventions. Role-playing, sensory-awareness exercises, desensitization, assertion training, and specific homework assignments are also employed in an attempt to provide behavioral complements to cognitive change.

Dialectical Behavior Therapy. Pioneered by Marsha Linehan (Linehan, 1993; Linehan & Kehrer, 1993), *dialectical behavior therapy*, or *DBT*, is a form of cognitive-behavioral therapy often used to help clients who display the impulsive behavior, mood swings, fragile self-image, and stormy interpersonal relationships associated with borderline personality disorder (Nietzel et al., 1998).

Initially, DBT helps these clients develop skill at containing their erratic behaviors, but after these "containment" goals have been reached, the therapist helps the client confront any traumatic experiences—such as physical or sexual abuse in childhood—that might have contributed to their current emotional difficulties. This phase of treatment concentrates on eliminating self-blame for these traumas, reducing post-traumatic stress symptoms, and resolving questions of who *is* to blame for the trauma. By consistently helping borderline clients see that almost all events can be thought about from varying perspectives, the dialectical therapist tries to encourage them to see the world in a more integrated or balanced way.

Relapse Prevention. Alan Marlatt and Judith Gordon's *relapse prevention* treatment is a cognitive-behavioral intervention designed to help clients who are trying to overcome alcoholism or other substance use disorders (Marlatt & Gordon, 1985). Marlatt and Gordon believe that relapse is most likely when clients engage in thoughts (such as "I owe myself a drink.") that lead to relapse. Once a relapse episode occurs, guilt and shame tend to generate a cascade of negative self-evaluations ("I've let my family down."; "I'm a complete failure.") which increases the probability of continued drinking, an outcome known as the *abstinence violation effect* (Marlatt & Gordon, 1985).

Relapse prevention techniques teach the client to monitor risky cognitions and to replace them with different thinking strategies. For example, instead of thinking about how good it would feel to drink, clients are taught to focus on how miserable it felt to be in jail after a drunken driving arrest. They are also taught to view a relapse episode not as an excuse to resume substance use, but as a temporary setback whose recurrence can be prevented by working on better cognitive and behavioral self-control strategies.

PHENOMENOLOGICAL/EXPERIENTIAL THERAPIES

The therapies we have described so far treat human behavior as mainly the product of either intrapsychic conflicts or learning. However, as discussed in Chapter 2, a third force in clinical psychology deemphasizes these factors and focuses instead on *conscious experience* as the basis for human behavior. This *phenomenological* approach views humans as creative, growthful beings who, if all goes well, consciously guide their own behavior toward realization of their fullest potential as unique individuals. When behavior disorders arise, they are usually seen as stemming from disturbances in awareness or restrictions on existence that can be eliminated through various therapeutic experiences (Fischer, 1989; Greenberg, Elliott, & Lietaer, 1994). Treatment approaches aimed at addressing and correcting these problems are known as *phenomenological/experiential (P/E) therapies*.

Common Features in Phenomenological/Experiential Therapies

Several themes unify the goals and techniques associated with phenomenological/experiential treatments.

First, P/E therapists assume that their clients' lives can be understood only when viewed from the point of view of those clients. This theme can be traced to philosophers such as Søren Kierkegaard and Jean-Paul Sartre, who emphasized that the meaning of life is not intrinsic, but is constructed by the perceiver. The idea of individually construed reality was also emphasized by a group of German psychologists—including Koffka, Köhler, and Werthheimer—known as the Gestalt school.

Second, many P/E therapists view human beings not as instinct-driven creatures but as naturally good people who are able to make choices about their lives and determine their own destinies. This optimistic perspective has led some P/E therapies—especially those originating in North America—to be described as *humanistic* therapies. Those P/E therapists committed to European existential philosophies are less likely to argue that all clients naturally strive toward positive goals (Fischer, 1989), but all P/E therapies do aim to promote each client's growth as a unique person. This goal is referred to as *self-actualization*. The assumption is that once clients are allowed to reach their full potential, they will find their own solutions to personal problems.

Third, P/E therapists view the therapeutic relationship as the primary vehicle by which therapy achieves its benefits. It must be a relationship that guarantees honest, emotionally open, interpersonal experiences for both client and therapist. Focusing on the immediate, moment-to-moment experiences in this relationship is what helps clients perceive themselves more positively.

A fourth characteristic of P/E therapies is that clients are regarded as equals. Therapists treat them as responsible individuals who are experts on their own experiences and who must ultimately be the ones to make decisions about their lives.

Finally, many P/E therapists emphasize the importance of experiencing and exploring emotions that are confusing or painful. They use several techniques to promote emotional awareness and experience and, as research documenting the effectiveness of these techniques has accumulated (Greenberg, Elliott, & Lietaer, 1994), many therapists beyond the P/E school have employed them. One example is called the *empty chair technique*. It is designed to increase awareness of unresolved conflicts and emotions by asking the client to imagine that a parent, child, spouse, or other person associated with the conflict or emotion is sitting in an empty chair nearby. The client is then instructed to talk to the imagined person and to express—perhaps for the first time—true feelings about him or her and about events or conflicts in which that person played a part. It is hoped that, in the process, clients will learn to take responsibility for and master these feelings.

The two most prominent examples of phenomenological/experiential therapies are Carl Rogers'(1951) client-centered therapy and Fritz Perls' Gestalt therapy (Perls, 1969).

Client-Centered Therapy

By far, the most influential of the phenomenological/experiential treatments is the *client-centered therapy* of Carl Rogers. First trained in psychodynamic therapy methods in the late 1920s, Rogers eventually became uncomfortable with the idea of therapists as authority figures who searched relentlessly for unconscious material. Rogers felt there had to be a better way to do clinical work, and an alternative began to take shape when he discovered a treatment approach advocated by Otto Rank, whose revision of Freud's ideas was mentioned earlier. To Rank, the client "... is a moving cause, containing constructive forces within, which constitute a will to health. The therapist guides the individual to self-understanding, self-acceptance. It is the therapist *as a human being* who is the remedy, not his technical skill.... The spontaneity and uniqueness of therapy lived in the present carry the patient toward health" (Meador & Rogers, 1973, p. 121; italics added).

As Rogers began to incorporate these ideas about nonauthoritarianism and the value of a good human relationship into his therapy sessions, he came to believe that "it is the *client* who knows what hurts, what directions to go, what problems are crucial, what experiences have been deeply buried" (Rogers, 1961, pp. 11–12). He also began to see therapy as an "if ... then" proposition: *If* the correct circumstances are created by the therapist, the client—driven by an innate potential for growth—will spontaneously improve.

Rogers's approach to treatment reflected his self-actualization theory, which, as described in Chapter 2, assumes that people are thwarted in their growth by judgments imposed on them by others. When these *conditions of worth* force people to distort their real feelings, symptoms of disorder appear. Thus, if a person really wanted to be an artist but had to ignore those feelings because of family pressure to become an accountant, depression might result. Growth would stop as the person's behavior (e.g., professing satisfaction with accounting) became increasingly discrepant, or *incongruent,* with real feelings.

Client-centered therapy is aimed at providing an interpersonal relationship that the client can use to further personal growth, but this growth-enhancing relationship can only appear, said Rogers, if the therapist experiences and expresses three interrelated attitudes: unconditional positive regard, empathy, and congruence.

Unconditional Positive Regard. The therapeutic attitude Rogers called *unconditional positive regard* conveys three messages: that the therapist (1) *cares about* the client, (2) *accepts* the client, and (3) *trusts* the client's ability to change.

The ideal form of unconditional positive regard is *nonpossessive caring,* in which genuine positive feelings are expressed in a way that makes clients feel valued, but still free to be themselves, not obligated to try to please the therapist. The therapist's *willingness to listen* is an important manifestation of unconditional positive regard.

Carl Rogers (1902–1987) by John T. Wood (Courtesy of Carl Rogers).

Patient, warm, and interested in what the client has to say, Rogerian therapists do not interrupt the client or change the subject or give other signs that they would rather be doing something else.

The "unconditional" aspect of unconditional positive regard is manifested in the therapist's willingness to accept clients as they are without judging them. Rogers believed that the experience of being prized as a human being, regardless of one's feelings or behaviors, can be a growth-enhancing experience for clients whose development has been hampered by conditions of worth and other evaluative pressures. Fortunately, expressing unconditional positive regard does not require *approving* of all the things a client says or does, merely *accepting* them as part of a person whom the therapist cares about. This ideal is illustrated in the following interaction:

> CLIENT: That was the semester my brother died and everything seemed to be going down the tubes. I knew how important it was to my parents that I get into medical school, but I also knew that my grades would be lousy that year unless I did something. To make a long story short, I bought a term paper and cheated on almost every exam that semester.
>
> THERAPIST: It was a really rough time for you.

Notice that the therapist focuses on the client's feelings in the situation, not on the ethics of the behavior. In other words, to express unconditional positive regard, the therapist must separate a client's worth *as a person* from the worth of the client's *behavior*.

The "positive" component of unconditional positive regard is reflected in the therapist's *trust* in the client's potential for growth and problem solving. Rogers believed that if clients perceive that their therapist lacks this trust, they will not develop the confidence they need to make changes. So, like other phenomenological/experiential therapists, Rogerians try not to give advice, take responsibility for clients, or make decisions for them. Such restraint is sometimes difficult, especially when therapists feel that they know "what's best" for a client. However, the client must be allowed to make bad decisions or experience problems, even if they could have been averted by following the therapist's advice. That advice might prevent one problem, but would create others: The therapist would become a superior, the client would become more dependent, and, most important, both client and therapist would have less faith in the client's ability to deal independently with problems.

Empathy. To understand a client's behavior and help the client understand it as well, the therapist must try to see the world as the client sees it. In Rogerian terms, this involves striving for *accurate empathy* or *empathic understanding*. To illustrate, let's consider an excerpt from the beginning of a therapy session:

> CLIENT: I don't feel very normal, but I want to feel that way.... I thought I'd have something to talk about—then it all goes around in circles. I was trying to think what I was going to say. I tell you, I just can't make a decision; I don't know what I want. I've tried to reason this thing out logically—tried to figure out

which things are important to me. I thought that there are maybe two things a man might do; he might get married and raise a family. But if he was just a bachelor, just making a living—that isn't very good. I find myself and my thoughts getting back to the days when I was a kid and I cry very easily. The dam would break through. I've been in the Army four and a half years. I had no problems then, no hopes, no wishes. My only thought was to get out when peace would come. My problems, now that I'm out, are as ever. I tell you, they go back to a long time before I was in the Army. . . . I love children. When I was in the Philippines—I tell you, when I was young I swore I'd never forget my unhappy childhood—so when I saw these children in the Philippines, I treated them very nicely. I used to give them ice cream cones and movies. It was just a period—I'd reverted back—and that awakened some emotions in me I thought I had long buried. (A pause. He seems very near tears.) (Rogers, 1951, pp. 32–33)

Many therapists would react to this client using what Rogers called an *external frame of reference*. They would observe the client from the outside and apply their values to what the client says (see the left side of Table 8.4). An empathic therapist, however, would try to adopt an *internal* frame of reference in an effort to understand what it must be like to *be* this client (see the right side of Table 8.4).

TABLE 8.4   Some Therapist Thoughts That Reflect Internal Versus External Frames of Reference

External	Internal
I wonder if I should get him started talking.	You're wanting to struggle toward normality, aren't you?
Is this inability to get under way a type of dependence?	It's really hard for you to get started.
Why this indecisiveness? What could be its cause?	Decision making just seems impossible for you.
What is meant by this focus on marriage and family?	You want marriage, but it doesn't seem to you to be much of a possibility.
The crying, the "dam" sound as though there must be a great deal of regression.	You feel yourself brimming over with childish feelings.
He's a veteran. Could he have been a psychiatric case? I feel sorry for anybody who spent four and one-half years in the service.	To you the Army represented stagnation.
What is this interest in children? Identification? Vague homosexuality?	Being very nice to children somehow has meaning for you; but it was—and is—a disturbing experience for you.

SOURCE: Rogers, 1951, pp. 33–34.

To communicate an empathic attitude to their clients, Rogerian therapists employ the active listening methods described in Chapter 4. Of particular value is *reflection,* which serves the dual purposes of (1) communicating the therapist's desire for emotional understanding and (2) making clients more aware of their own feelings. Reflection is one of the most misunderstood aspects of client-centered therapy because the therapist appears to be stating the obvious or merely repeating what the client has said.[3] But reflection is more than repetition or paraphrasing. As suggested in Chapter 4, it involves distilling and "playing back" the client's feelings. For example, suppose a client says "This has been such a bad day. I've had to keep myself from crying three or four times. I'm not even sure what's wrong!" The therapist's response could be externally oriented (e.g., "Well what exactly happened?"), but a more empathic comment might be: "You really do feel bad. The tears just well up inside. And it sounds like it is scary to not even know why you feel this way."

At first glance, the clinician may seem to be a parrot, but look more closely. The client never *said* she felt bad; the therapist inferred it by taking the client's point of view. Similarly, the client never said her sadness frightened her—it was the clinician's ability to put himself in the client's shoes that led to this speculation. If the therapist's inferences are wrong, the client can correct them, but right or wrong, the clinician has let the client know that he wants to understand her.

Congruence.   Rogers also believed that the more *genuine* the therapist is in relating to clients, the more helpful the therapist will be. The therapist's feelings and actions, he said, should be *congruent,* or consistent, with one another. "This means that I need to be aware of my own feelings . . . [and willing] to express, in my words and my behavior, the various feelings and attitudes which exist in me" (Rogers, 1961, p. 33). According to Rogers, when the therapist is congruent, a *real* human relationship occurs in therapy.

To get an idea of how congruence promotes trust, think of a time when a close friend might have told you something that you did not want to hear, perhaps that you looked silly or were wrong about something. Once you know that a friend will say what he or she really feels even if it does not make you happy, it makes it easier to trust whatever else that friend might say. However, if you know that your friend can be incongruent, telling you what you want to hear instead of what he or she genuinely feels, your faith in that person's reactions ("You really look great.") is likely to be undermined.

Here is one way that congruence can be displayed in a therapist–client interaction:

CLIENT: I just feel so hopeless. Tell me what I'm doing wrong in my life.

THERAPIST: I guess when you are feeling this bad it would be nice if someone could come along and tell you what is going wrong and how you can put everything right again. I wish I could do all that, but I can't. I don't think anyone else can either.

---

[3]In a famous joke, Rogers is supposed to have responded to a livid fellow duck hunter who threatens to shoot Rogers if he doesn't relinquish a disputed kill: "You feel this is your duck."

Notice the therapist's reflection of the client's feeling plus the direct expression of (1) a genuine wish to understand and solve the client's problems, and (2) an admission that she is not capable of such a feat.

The Nature of Change in Client-Centered Therapy.

Rogers argued that as clients experience empathy, unconditional positive regard and congruence in a therapeutic relationship, they become more self-aware and self-accepting, more comfortable and less defensive in interpersonal relationships, less rigid in their thinking, more reliant on self-evaluation than on evaluations by others, and better able to function in a wide variety of roles (Rogers, 1951; see Table 8.5).

An Illustration of Client-Centered Therapy.

The following edited excerpts from Rogers's (1967) case of the "Silent Young Man" should give you a better idea of what actually goes on when the principles underlying client-centered therapy are translated into clinical practice (from Meador & Rogers, 1973, pp. 139–144). "Jim," the client in this case, was twenty-eight years old and had been hospitalized as a "simple schizophrenic." After eleven months of therapy, he had made some progress but was still withdrawn and inarticulate. Where other therapists might have given up, Rogers continued to convey the therapeutic attitudes he believed would ultimately bring about growth.

TABLE 8.5 Stages in the Process of Therapeutic Change

Stage 1: Communication is about externals. There is an unwillingness to communicate self. Feelings and personal meanings are neither recognized as such nor owned. Constructs are extremely rigid. Close relationships are construed as dangerous.

Stage 2: Feelings are *sometimes* described but as unowned past *objects* external to self.

Stage 3: There is much description of feelings and personal meanings which are not now present. These distant feelings are often pictured as unacceptable or bad. . . . There is a beginning recognition that any problems that exist are inside the individual rather than external.

Stage 4: Feelings and personal meanings are freely described as present objects owned by the self. . . . There is a beginning loosening of personal constructs. . . . There is some expression of self-responsibility for problems.

Stage 5: Many feelings are expressed in the moment of their occurrence and are thus experienced in the immediate present. These feelings are owned or accepted.

There is a questioning of the validity of many personal constructs. The person has a definite responsiblity for the problems which exist in him.

Stage 6: Feelings previously denied are now experienced both with immediacy and acceptance.

Stage 7: The individual lives comfortably in the flowing process of his experiencing. New feelings are experienced with richness and immediacy, and this inner experiencing is a clear referent for behavior. Incongruence is minimal and temporary.

Excerpts from "Person-centered therapy," by Betty D. Meador and Carl R. Rogers, in R. J. Corsini, ed., *Current Psychotherapies*, Itasca, IL: F E Peacock Publishers. Copyright 1984 by Peacock Publishers. (Reprinted by permission.)

THERAPIST: Do you look kind of angry this morning, or is that my imagination? (client shakes his head slightly) Not angry, huh? (silence of 1 minute, 26 seconds)

THERAPIST: Feel like letting me in on whatever is going on? (silence of 12 minutes, 52 seconds)

THERAPIST: I kind of feel like saying that "If it would be of any help at all I'd like to come in." On the other hand if it's something you'd rather—if you just feel more like being within yourself, why that's OK too—I guess another thing I'm saying, really, in saying that is, "I do care. I'm not just sitting here like a stick." (silence of 1 minute, 11 seconds)

THERAPIST: And I guess your silence is saying to me either you don't want to or can't come out right now and that's OK. So I won't pester you but I just want you to know, I'm here. (silence of 17 minutes, 41 seconds)

[After two more unanswered comments over the next minute or so, Rogers continues.]

THERAPIST: Maybe this morning you just wish I'd shut up—and maybe I should, but I just keep feeling I'd like to—I don't know, be in touch with you in some way. (silence of 2 minutes, 21 seconds)

[Client yawns.]

THERAPIST: Sounds discouraged or tired. (silence of 41 seconds)

CLIENT: [at last!] No. Just lousy.

THERAPIST: Everything's lousy, huh? You feel lousy? . . .

CLIENT: No.

THERAPIST: No? (silence of 20 seconds)

CLIENT: No. I just ain't no good to nobody, never was, and never will be.

THERAPIST: Feeling that now, hm? That you're just no good to yourself, no good to anybody. Just that you're completely worthless, huh? . . .

CLIENT: Yeah. That's what this guy I went to town with just the other day told me. . . .

THERAPIST: I guess the meaning of that, if I get it right, is that here's somebody that—meant something to you and what does he think of you? Why, he's told you that he thinks you're no good at all. And that really knocks the props out from under you. [Jim weeps quietly] It just brings the tears.

CLIENT: I don't care though.

THERAPIST: You tell yourself you don't care at all, but somehow I guess some part of you cares because some part of you weeps over it. . . .

CLIENT: I guess I always knew it.

THERAPIST: If I'm getting that right, it is that what makes it hurt worst of all is that when he tells you you're no good, well shucks, that's what you've always felt about yourself. Is that—the meaning of what you're saying? [Jim nods in agreement] . . . So that between his saying so and your perhaps feeling it underneath, you just feel about as no-good as anybody could feel.

[The client continues to cry and, after several more minutes of reflecting the sad, hopeless feelings being expressed, Rogers ends the interview. Three days later another session takes place. After some initial comments by the therapist, the client breaks in:]

CLIENT: I'm gonna take off.

THERAPIST: You're going to take off? Really run away from here? . . . I know you don't like the place but it must be something special came up or something?

CLIENT: I just want to run away and die.

THERAPIST: M-hm, m-hm, m-hm. It isn't even that you want to get away from here *to* something. You just want to leave here and go away and die in a corner, hm? . . . Can't help but wonder whether it's still true that some things this friend said to you—are those still part of the thing that makes you feel so awful?

CLIENT: In general, yes.

[The next 30 minutes or so are taken up in further reflection of the client's negative feelings and in silences of up to 13 minutes.]

CLIENT: I might go today. Where, I don't know, but I don't care.

THERAPIST: Just feel your mind is made up and that you're going to leave. (silence of 53 seconds)

CLIENT: That's why I want to go, 'cause I don't care what happens.

THERAPIST: M-hm, m-hm. That's why you want to go, because you really don't care about yourself. You just don't care *what* happens. And I guess I'd just like to say—I care about you. And I care what happens.

After a thirty-second silence, the client bursts into violent sobs. For the next fifteen minutes or so, Rogers reflects the intense emotions that pour forth. According to Rogers, this is an important moment of therapeutic change. "Jim Brown, who sees himself as stubborn, bitter, mistreated, worthless, useless, hopeless, unloved, unlovable, *experiences* my caring. In that moment his defensive shell cracks wide open, and can never again be quite the same" (Meador & Rogers, 1973, p. 145). The client in this case left the hospital after several more months of treatment; eight years later he reported to Rogers that he was happy, employed, and living on his own.

Impressive as case studies can be, Carl Rogers was among the first to recognize the need for scientific research to substantiate the alleged value of any treatment technique, including his own. He pointed out, for example, that although many therapists extol the value of relationship therapy, "since their criteria are largely intangible measures such as the freedom from minor tensions and the greater degree of personal comfort achieved, any measurement of success is difficult indeed." (Rogers, 1939, p. 200). Rogers was the first to record therapy sessions, and he conducted some of the first empirical research on the relationship between treatment outcome and therapist characteristics such as empathy and warmth (Rogers, 1942).

Gestalt Therapy

After Rogers' client-centered approach, the gestalt therapy methods developed by Friedrich S. (Fritz) and Laura Perls is probably the best-known phenomenological/experiential treatment. Like client-centered methods, gestalt therapy aims at enhancing clients' awareness in order to free them to grow in their own consciously guided ways. More specifically, the gestalt therapist seeks to reestablish clients' stalled growth processes by helping them (1) become aware of feelings that they have *disowned* but which are a genuine part of them, and (2) recognize feelings and values that they *think* are a genuine part of themselves, but which in fact are borrowed from other people.

The client is encouraged to assimilate or "re-own" the genuine aspects of self that have been rejected and to reject the "phony" features that do not belong. Ideally, when clients assimilate and integrate all aspects of their personality (both the desirable and the undesirable), they start taking responsibility for themselves as they really are instead of being attached to and defensive of a partially phony, internally conflicted self-image. For example, a person who feels superior to others but who has forced this feeling out of awareness in favor of a more socially acceptable air of humility will become aware of and express both sides of the conflict ("I'm great" versus "I shouldn't brag"). Once both poles of this conflict confront each other, the client may find a resolution ("It's OK to express my feelings of competence, but I need to take the feelings of others into account as well."). As long as one side of the conflict is out of awareness, such resolution is impossible. According to Perls, when conflict resolutions occur with full awareness of both poles, the person begins to grow again.

As the following sections show, the methods of gestalt therapy are much more active and dramatic than those of client-centered treatment.

Focus on the Here and Now.   For one thing, gestalt therapists believe that therapeutic progress is made by keeping clients in contact with their feelings as they occur in the here and now. Perls expressed this belief in a conceptual equation where "Now = experience = awareness = reality" (Perls, 1970). Any attempt by the client to recount the past or anticipate the future obstructs therapy goals. It is an escape from reality. So instead of *reflecting* (as a Rogerian might) the client's nostalgia for the past or thoughts about the future, a gestalt therapist will point out the avoidance and insist that it be terminated.

This method was illustrated in Fritz Perls's filmed interview with "Gloria" (Perls, 1965). At one point Gloria says that what is happening in the interview reminds her of when she was a little girl. Perls immediately asks, "Are you a little girl?" to which Gloria answers, "Well, no, but it's the same feeling." Again Perls asks, "Are you a little girl?" and Gloria says, "The feeling reminds me of it." Perls explodes: "*Are* you a little girl?"

The client finally says, "No." In other words, talking *about* the past or the future gets the client nowhere, but the *immediate* experience of feelings from the past or fears about the future as they occur in the therapy session may be helpful.

Role-Playing. Through *role-playing* or part-taking, clients explore inner conflicts and experience the symptoms, interpersonal games, and psychological defenses they have developed to keep those conflicts—and various other aspects of their genuine selves—out of awareness. By asking clients to "become" their resistance to change, for example, gestalt therapists help them toward an *experiential* awareness of what the resistance is doing *for* and *to* them. So when John, a member of a gestalt therapy group, found it difficult to talk to another group member, Mary, because he says there is a "wall" between them, the therapist asks him to "play" the wall (Polster & Polster, 1973, pp. 53–54):

> JOHN: (as the wall) I am here to protect you against predatory women who will eat you alive if you open yourself up to them.

The therapist asks John to "converse" with his resistance to experience both sides of the conflict that prevents him from relating to others in an intimate way:

> JOHN: (to the wall) Aren't you exaggerating? She looks pretty safe to me. In fact, she looks more scared than anything.
>
> JOHN: (as the wall) Sure she's scared. I'm responsible for that. I'm a very severe wall and I make a lot of people scared. That's how I want it and I have even affected you that way too. You're scared of me even though I'm really on your side.
>
> JOHN: (to the wall) I *am* scared of you and I even feel you inside me, like I have become like you. I feel my chest as though it were iron and I'm really getting mad about that.
>
> JOHN: (as the wall) Mad—at what? I'm your strength and you don't even know it. Feel how strong you are inside.
>
> JOHN: (to the wall) Sure I feel the strength but I also feel rigid when my chest feels like iron. I'd like to beat on you, knock you over, and go over to Mary.

Here, the gestalt therapist urges the client to *do* what he *feels* and resolve the conflict in a growthful way.

> THERAPIST: Beat on your iron.
>
> JOHN: (beats his chest and shouts) Get out of my way—get *out* of my *way!* (silence of a few moments) My chest feels strong—but not like it's made of iron. (after another silence, John begins to cry and talks to Mary) I don't feel any wall between us anymore and I really want to talk to you.

Frustrating the Client. Because it is not always this easy for clients to become aware of hidden feelings, gestalt therapists use many other methods for self-exploration. To help clients give up their maladaptive interpersonal roles and games, for example, Perls deliberately set out to frustrate their efforts to relate to him as they normally would to others. During individual or group therapy, he put his clients on what he called the "hot seat," where all attention was focused on them, and where their symptoms, games, and resistances were pointed out and explored.

Suppose that a client begins a session by saying "I've really been looking forward to having this session. I hope you can help me." Instead of reflecting this feeling or asking *why* the client feels this way, a gestalt therapist would focus on the manipulative aspect of the statement, which seems to contain the message, "I expect you to help me without my having to do much." The therapist might say, "How do you think I could help you?" The client (somewhat taken aback) might respond, "Well, I was hoping you could help me understand why I'm so unhappy." From here, the therapist would continue to frustrate the client's attempt to get the therapist to take responsibility for solving the client's problems and, in the process, would help the client experience his real feelings:

> THERAPIST: Tell me what you mean when you say "unhappy." (Like many behavioral therapists, gestalt therapists tend to focus on specific examples of general problems.)
>
> CLIENT: Oh, I don't know, it's just that I don't ever feel satisfied with myself. I never seem to be able to . . . I don't know—it's very complicated and hard for me to express.
>
> THERAPIST: How old are you?
>
> CLIENT: Thirty-six.
>
> THERAPIST: And as a thirty-six-year-old person, you can't tell me what makes you unhappy?
>
> CLIENT: I wish I could, but I'm too confused about it myself.
>
> THERAPIST: (who infers that the client is "playing stupid" in order to avoid responsibility for problems) Can you play me trying to help you? What would I say and what would I do?
>
> CLIENT: Well, you might say "Don't worry, I'll figure out what your problems are and help you get on the right track."
>
> THERAPIST: OK, tell me how you expect me to do all this *for* you.
>
> CLIENT: OK, I see. I guess I hope you have some magic pill or something.

At this point the therapist might again request a statement of the client's problems and, this time, might get a more genuine answer.

Use of Nonverbal Cues. Gestalt therapists pay special attention to what clients say *and* what they do, because the nonverbal channel often contradicts the client's words. For example:

> CLIENT: I wish I wasn't so nervous with people.
>
> THERAPIST: Who are you nervous with?

CLIENT: With everyone.

THERAPIST: With me, here, now?

CLIENT: Yes, very.

THERAPIST: That's funny, because you don't look nervous to me.

CLIENT: (suddenly clasping his hands) Well I am!

THERAPIST: What are you doing with your hands?

CLIENT: Nothing, I just clasped them together. It's just a gesture.

THERAPIST: Do the gesture again. (client reclasps his hands) And again, clasp them again, harder. (client clasps hands harder) How does that feel?

CLIENT: It feels tight, kind of constricted.

THERAPIST: Can you become that tightness? Can you get in touch with what that tightness might say to you?

CLIENT: OK, ah, I'm tight. I'm holding everything together. I'm keeping the lid on you so that you don't let too much out.

The therapist wondered what the clasped hands meant. Instead of asking *why* the client clasped them, she pointed out *what* the client did. She then asked him to concentrate on the associated feelings by repeating and exaggerating the gesture. Once the client expressed these feelings, the client was asked to elaborate on them. The result was that the client expressed a defensive feeling about being in therapy that he had originally, and inaccurately, described as nervousness.

The Use of Dreams.   In gestalt therapy, a client's dreams are seen as messages from the client to him- or herself. Gestalt therapists help clients become aware of what the message says by asking them to first recount their dream, then to "read" it by playing the part of certain features and characters. In the process, the client may become aware of and assimilate disowned parts of the self.

Other Methods.   There are several other methods that gestalt therapists use to help clients increase awareness and promote "re-owning" of alienated aspects of personality.

One of these is encouraging direct and immediate messages that force clients to take responsibility for their feelings. In group therapy, for example, the client who points to another client and says "She really makes me uncomfortable" would be asked to repeat the message directly to the person involved: "You make me uncomfortable." Similarly, "I" language is substituted for "it" language. "It makes me furious to hear that" contains the message that "it" is responsible for the client's anger. The therapist would ask the client to restate the message as "I am angry at you." Clients are also asked to convert indirect *questions* into direct *statements*. The message behind the question "Do you think I'll ever feel any better than I do now?" may be "I am terrified that I'll always be depressed and maybe kill myself." If so, it is important for the client to be aware of and to express the fear.

Gestalt therapists also turn role-playing into extended "conversations" between various parts of the client, including between the client's superego (what Perls called "topdog") and the part that is suppressed by "shoulds" and "oughts" (the "underdog"). Using the *empty chair* technique described earlier, dialogues also occur between the client and persons from the past with whom the client has unfinished business; the client "talks" to these people while imagining them seated in a nearby chair. This activity is designed to promote here-and-now awareness of strong emotions in a safe environment and, in the process, allows the person to master these feelings rather than be intimidated by them. Here is an example:

> CLIENT: My sister and I used to fight an awful lot when we were kids, but we seemed closer somehow then than we are now.
>
> THERAPIST: Can you put her in that chair and say this to your sister now?
>
> CLIENT: OK. I feel so far away from you now, Rita. I want to have that feeling of being in a family again.

Clients may also be asked to clarify and release feelings toward significant people in their lives via the *unmailed letter* technique. Here, they write—but do not send—a letter in which they express important, but previously unspoken feelings.

Role-played *reversals* also are used to enhance awareness of genuine feelings. So the client who conveys an image of cool self-sufficiency and denies feelings of tenderness toward others might be asked to play a warm, loving person. In the process, this client may get in touch with some feelings that have been suppressed for many years.

An Illustration of Gestalt Therapy. The following edited excerpt from one of Fritz Perls's group sessions gives some idea of the way the gestalt therapy methods are integrated in clinical practice (Perls, 1969). The client, "Jane," had worked with Perls before and thus shows more familiarity with the method than a new client would; otherwise the procedures are representative.

> JANE: I can't say that I'm really aware of what I'm doing. Except physically. I'm aware of what's happening physically to me but—I don't really know what I'm doing.
>
> PERLS: I noticed one thing: When you come up on the hot seat, you stop playing the silly goose.
>
> JANE: Hmm. I get frightened when I'm up here.
>
> PERLS: You get dead.
>
> JANE: . . . I'm wondering whether or not I'm dead. I notice that my legs are cold and my feet are cold. I feel—I feel strange. . . . I notice that my attention is concentrated on that little matchbox on the floor.
>
> PERLS: OK. Have an encounter with the matchbox.
>
> JANE: [as the matchbox] I don't care if you tell the truth or not. It doesn't matter to me. I'm just a matchbox.

PERLS: Try this for size. Tell us, "I'm just a matchbox."

JANE: I'm just a matchbox and I feel silly saying that. I feel kind of dumb, being a matchbox.... A little bit useful, but not very useful. There's a million like me. And you can look at me, and you can like me, and when I'm all used up, you can throw me away. I never liked being a matchbox.... I don't know if that's the truth when I say I don't know what I'm doing. I know there's one part of me that knows what I'm doing.... She's saying (with authority) well, *you* know where you're at. You're playing dumb. You're playing stupid. You're doing this and you're doing that.... She's saying (briskly) now when you get in the chair, you have to be in the here-and-now, you have to do it *right,* you have to be turned on, you have to know everything—

PERLS: "You have to do your job."

JANE: You have to do your job, and you have to do it *right.* And you have to—become totally self-actualized, and you have to get rid of all your hangups.... [Now Jane spontaneously returns to being her frightened self again and talks to her demanding self:] You really make it hard for me.... You're really putting a lot of demands on me.... I don't know everything, and on top of that, I don't know what I'm doing half the time....

PERLS: So be your topdog again.

JANE: Is that—

PERLS: Your topdog. That's the famous topdog. The righteous topdog. This is where the power is.

JANE: Yeah. Well—uh—I'm your topdog. You can't live without me. I'm the one that—I keep you noticed, Jane. If it weren't for me, nobody would notice you. [Jane now responds to "topdog"] Well, I don't want to be noticed, *you* do . . . I don't really want to be noticed, as much as you do.

PERLS: I would like you to attack the righteous side of that topdog.

JANE: Attack—the righteous side?

PERLS: The topdog is always righteous. Topdog *knows* what you've got to do, has all the right to criticize, and so on.

JANE: Yeah.... You're a bitch! Like my mother. You know what's good for me. You make life hard for me....

PERLS: Now please don't change what your hands are doing, but tell us what's going on in your hands.... Let them talk to each other.

JANE: My left hand. I'm shaking, and I'm in a fist, straining forward . . . the fist is very tight, pushing my fingernails into my hand. It doesn't feel good, but I do it all the time. I feel tight.

PERLS: And the right hand?

JANE: I'm holding you back around the wrist.

PERLS: Tell it why you hold it back.

JANE: If I let you go you're gonna hit something. I don't know what you're gonna hit, but I have to—I have to hold back 'cause you can't do that. Can't go around hitting things.

PERLS: Now hit your topdog.

JANE: [gives short, harsh yells]

PERLS: Now talk to your topdog. "Stop nagging—"

JANE: [yells at "topdog"] Leave me alone!

PERLS: Again.

JANE: Leave me alone!

PERLS: Again.

JANE: [screaming and crying] *Leave me alone!*

PERLS: Again.

JANE: [screams and cries): LEAVE ME ALONE! I DON'T HAVE TO DO WHAT YOU SAY! (still crying) I don't have to be that good! . . . I don't have to be in this chair! You make me! You make me come here! . . . I'd like to kill you.

PERLS: Say this again.

JANE: I'd like to kill you.

PERLS: Again.

JANE: I'd like to *kill* you.

PERLS: Can you squash it in your left hand?

JANE: It's as big as me . . . I'm strangling it. [Perls gives Jane a pillow which she strangles while making choking noises and crying]

PERLS: OK. Relax, close your eyes. (long silence) OK, come back to us.

[Later in the session, Perls asks Jane to turn her perfectionist "topdog" into an "underdog" and to talk down to it.]

Jane: [to her perfectionist "topdog"] . . . You don't have to do anything, you don't have to prove anything. (cries) You're only twenty years old! You don't have to be the queen. . . .

JANE: [as her perfectionist "topdog"] OK, I understand that. I know that. I'm just in a *hurry*. . . . You have to keep hurrying and the days slip by and you think you're losing time, or something. I'm *much* too hard on you. I have to leave you alone.

PERLS: . . . Let your topdog say "I'll be a bit more patient with you."

JANE: [as topdog] . . . I'll be a bit more patient with you.

PERLS: Say this again.

JANE: It's very hard for me to be patient. . . . But I'll try to be a bit more patient with you. . . . As I say that, I'm stomping my foot, and shaking my head.

PERLS: OK. Say, "I won't be patient with you." [Perls asks Jane to repeat this and to take responsibility for the feeling by repeating the statement to several group members.]

PERLS: OK, how do you feel now?

JANE: OK.

PERLS: You understand, topdog and underdog are not yet together. But at least the conflict is clear, in the open, maybe a little less violent. (Perls, 1969, pp. 264–272.)[4]

Other Phenomenological/Experiential Therapies

Rogers' and Perls' methods of treatment represent two prominent examples of phenomenological/experiential therapies, but there are others which blend psychodynamic, Rogerian, or gestalt methods with principles from behavioral or existential psychology (Greenberg, Elliott, & Lietaer, 1994; Kahn, 1985; Maslow, 1962, 1968; May, 1969; May, Angel, & Ellenberger, 1958).

For example, the *logotherapy* of Viktor Frankl (1963, 1965, 1967) is based on existential philosophy and is oriented toward helping clients (1) take responsibility for their feelings and actions, and (2) find meaning and purpose in their lives. Frankl believed that people can feel a lack of meaning and purpose without displaying neurotic or psychotic behaviors. He saw his approach as applicable to anyone, whether they were officially suffering mental disorder or not.

METHODS OF PSYCHOTHERAPY AT WORK

Q.: Which approach to clinical treatment or intervention (psychodynamic, behavioral/cognitive-behavioral, phenomenological/experiential), is most important to your work, and why?

DR. SANDY D'ANGELO: Much of my treatment work involves young children with behavioral problems. I typically use a behavioral approach when working with parents to identify target behaviors, analyze contingencies affecting behavior, and help parents restructure their interactions with children. Because of the setting in which I work, I typically do not use a family therapy approach; however, understanding interactions within the family and family structure are extremely important in understanding the child's behavior.

DR. HECTOR MACHABANSKI: My approach to clinical treatment is multifaceted and geared to the specific problems presented by clients. However, I pay special attention to the quality of the therapeutic relationship and I use cognitive-behavioral and interpersonal systems concepts as guides to my interventions.

DR. GEOFFREY THORPE: "Learning theory" is what attracted me to psychology, and I was enthusiastic about applying the findings of research on learning principles to the treatment of mental health problems. Accordingly, I sought out training in behavior therapy. The field has changed a great deal since my graduate school days, but I retain my commitment to learning principles as a solid foundation for therapeutic interventions.

---

[4] For other case examples of gestalt therapy see Perls (1970), Polster & Polster (1973), and Rosenblatt (1975).

CHAPTER SUMMARY

Clinicians offer psychotherapy using methods based on psychodynamic, behavioral, and phenomenological/experiential approaches to clinical psychology.

In Freudian psychoanalysis, clients are helped to explore the unconscious wishes, fantasies, impulses, and conflicts that are presumed to lie at the root of their psychological problems. The goals of psychoanalytic treatment include insight into these underlying causes and then understanding, or working through, the implications of the insight. To get at unconscious material, much of which is based in infancy and childhood, Freud developed a number of treatment techniques, including free association and analysis of the meaning of dreams, of everyday behaviors, of resistance to treatment, and of transference appearing in the therapeutic relationship. Interpretations of the meaning of this material help move clients toward insight and understanding.

Other psychodynamically oriented therapists have developed variations on orthodox Freudian psychoanalysis. Among the most prominent of these methods are Alexander's psychoanalytically oriented psychotherapy, ego analysis, Adler's individual psychology, object relations therapy, and Sullivan's interpersonal therapy. These therapies tend to be briefer than classical psychoanalysis and to focus more on current problems rather than childhood conflicts, more on strengthening ego functions than on analyzing id impulses, more on actively repairing damage from inadequate early caregiver relationships than on gaining insight into them, and more on changing maladaptive interpersonal relationships than on delving into their unconscious origins.

Behavioral and cognitive-behavioral therapies are based on the principles of learning and on research on cognitive psychology. Their treatment methods are aimed at directly modifying overt maladaptive behaviors, as well as the maladaptive thinking patterns that accompany those behaviors. Behavioral methods include various kinds of systematic desensitization, exposure techniques such as flooding, social skills training (including assertiveness training), several types of modeling, aversion therapy, contingency management (including shaping, time out, contingency contracting, response cost, and token economies), and biofeedback. Cognitive-behavioral methods include Beck's cognitive therapy for depression and Ellis's Rational Emotive Behavior Therapy.

Phenomenological/experiential therapies are based on the assumption that people are inherently growthful and that their progress toward unique self-actualization will resume when problems that have impaired it are removed by the experience of a supportive therapeutic relationship. These problems are presumed to arise largely from socialization processes that prompt people to distort or suppress genuine feelings and wishes in order to please others, so therapy is aimed at creating a client–therapist relationship in which clients can become more aware of how they really think and feel. Therapists using Carl Rogers' client-centered therapy create this relationship by using reflection and other active listening methods to convey empathy, unconditional positive regard, and congruence as they work with clients. The same goals of self-awareness and growth are sought in a more active and direct way through Perls' gestalt therapy, whose methods include focusing on the present, having clients role-play suppressed or disowned aspects of the self, frustrating their efforts at resistance, attending to their nonverbal behavior, and having them engage in dialogues with imaginary versions of significant people in their lives.

Chapter 9

Research on Clinical Intervention

In Chapters 7 and 8, we described the wide array of interventions that clinical psychologists employ in their efforts to help troubled clients. How well do these methods work? In this chapter, we first review the research methods that are used to evaluate clinical interventions in general and psychotherapy in particular. Next, we discuss what those methods have revealed about the effects of the various forms of psychotherapy that clinicians offer to individuals, groups, couples, and families. We then consider the results of clinical and community psychologists' efforts to promote psychosocial rehabilitation and to prevent mental disorders. Finally, we summarize the ways in which the results of evaluative research have combined with economic forces to shape today's clinical intervention methods.

The results of research on the effects of psychotherapy and other clinical interventions are of interest to three audiences, each with somewhat differing perspectives on mental health and the criteria used to assess it (Newman & Tejeda, 1996; Strupp & Hadley, 1977).

First, there are *clients*, who have an obvious stake in the success of interventions designed to help them. Clients tend to ask two questions: "Did the intervention help me?" and (if they paid for treatment) "Was it worth the expense?" The second audience is made up of *psychotherapists* and others who implement clinical intervention programs. They want to know whether or not their efforts are worthwhile and whether and how the effects of their efforts can be improved. The third audience evaluating clinical interventions is *society*, by which we mean all "third parties" who are interested in the ability of those interventions to produce desirable changes in clients. Third parties can include the client's spouse or companion, parents, friends, or teachers, as well as police, judges, and the insurance companies or health maintenance organizations responsible for covering mental health care costs. The combined concerns of this third audience are that clinical intervention should not only benefit clients, but—by reducing crime, family stress and violence, human suffering, and health-care related expenses—should also benefit society at large.

METHODS FOR EVALUATING PSYCHOTHERAPY

Because it is the most prominent form of clinical intervention, researchers have tended to focus most of their attention on evaluating the effects of various forms of psychotherapy. For a long time the main question posed by clinical researchers was "Is psychotherapy effective?", but they gradually discovered that this question was too broad. Starting in the 1970s, therapy outcome research began to be influenced by Gordon Paul's (1969a) more specific reformulation: "What treatment, by whom, is most effective for this individual with that specific problem, under which set of circumstances, and how does it come about?" (p. 44).

Alan Kazdin (1982b) translated Paul's "ultimate question" into a list of outcome research goals including (1) determining the efficacy of a specific treatment; (2) comparing the relative effectiveness of different treatments; and (3) assessing the specific components of treatment that are responsible for particular changes. Today, psychotherapy research also seeks to assess the durability of the benefits of particular treatments, identify any negative side-effects associated with a treatment, determine how acceptable a treatment is to various kinds of clients, map the cost-effectiveness of various treatments, and discover whether a treatment's effects are clinically significant and socially meaningful (Howard et al., 1996; Kazdin & Wilson, 1978).

Designing Outcome Experiments on Psychotherapy

To reach all these goals, psychotherapy researchers must design and conduct their treatment outcome evaluations in such a way that the results can be interpreted unambiguously. For example, it is one thing for clients, therapists, relatives, and even test scores to suggest that a client has improved following a program of psychotherapy, but it is quite another to demonstrate scientifically that it was psychotherapy itself that *caused* the improvements. Of all the research designs that can evaluate the presence of a cause–effect relationship between therapy and improvement, the most powerful is the controlled *experiment* (Jacobson & Christensen, 1996).

An experiment is *an attempt to discover the causes of specific events by making systematic changes in certain factors and then observing changes that occur in other factors.* The factors that experimenters manipulate are called *independent variables,* while the factors in which resulting changes are observed are called *dependent variables.* In psychotherapy-outcome research, the independent variable is usually whether (or what type of) therapy is given, and the dependent variable is the amount and kinds of change seen in clients.

Most psychotherapy-outcome experiments employ either *within-subject* or *between-subject* research designs, both of which allow the experimenter to examine the effects of varying treatment conditions (the independent variable) on clients' thinking and behavior (the dependent variables). Generally speaking, within-subject designs alter a treatment variable and observe the effects of that manipulation on the same client(s) at different points in time. In between-subject research, different groups of clients are exposed to differing treatments, whose effects are then compared across the groups.

Within-Subject Research

The within-subject experiment requires that the dependent variables (client behaviors) be measured on several repeated occasions. The first of these observations usually takes place during a pretreatment, or *baseline*, period that provides a measure of the client's problematic behavior against which to compare subsequent changes. Once baseline measures have established a stable picture of the client's typical behavior, the *intervention* phase of the experiment begins. Here, the experimenter manipulates the independent variable by introducing some form of treatment and watches the dependent variable for any changes from its baseline level. Several types of within-subject experiments are used in clinical treatment research (Hayes, 1983; Kazdin, 1982a), but the two most popular versions are the reversal design and the multiple-baseline design.

In the *reversal,* or *ABAB,* design, a no-treatment baseline period (A) is alternated with a treatment period (B). The length of the A and B phases is determined by many factors, but usually each phase continues until the client's behavior becomes relatively stable. What can be learned from repeatedly presenting, then withdrawing, treatment? The logic underlying this design suggests that if behavior changes reliably and substantially *only* during each treatment period, and returns toward the baseline each time treatment is discontinued, the experimenter gains confidence that the treatment is responsible for the changes (see Figure 9.1).

Especially in situations where there are clinical or ethical concerns about interrupting treatment, experimenters may prefer the *multiple-baseline* design, which allows them to evaluate the effect of an intervention without repeatedly discontinuing it. Instead, the researcher observes several dependent measures at once, but applies a treatment to only one of them. If the treatment has a specific effect, the only aspect of the client's behavior that should change is the one that was treated. The treatment is then applied to additional targets, one at a time, and the effect on each is observed. Confidence in the causal effects of the treatment increases if each dependent measure changes when, and only when, treatment is applied to it. However, if behaviors change whether or not they were specifically targeted, the experimenter can assume that improvement may have been caused by some combination of treatment and some more general factors, such as the client's positive expectations about treatment.

To illustrate, suppose an experimenter wants to evaluate the effects of a contingent social-reinforcement program on the behavior of hospitalized mental patients. The dependent variables in this hypothetical experiment are three behaviors needing improvement: personal grooming, attending occupational therapy, and socializing with other patients. Each of these targets is first observed during a pretreatment baseline pe-

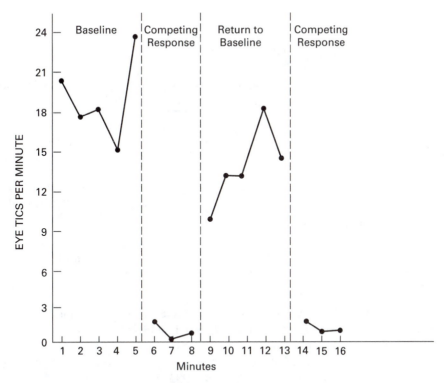

FIGURE 9.1 Evaluating treatment with a reversal design. The client in this study was a nine-year old girl with a severe eye tic. The frequency of tics observed during the first baseline period declined dramatically when the intervention was introduced (it consisted of teaching the girl to blink softly every five seconds as a competing response to the tic). Notice that the tics increased when treatment was withdrawn during the second baseline period, but nearly disappeared when the competing response treatment was resumed during the second treatment period. (From N. H. Azrin & A. L. Peterson, 1989, Reduction of an eye tic by controlled blinking. *Behavior Therapy, 20,* 467–473.)

riod, after which social reinforcement from hospital staff is first provided whenever the patients display improved grooming, then when they attend therapy sessions, and finally when they socialize. If the results of this treatment program are as shown in Figure 9.2, it becomes highly unlikely that factors other than treatment accounted for the outcome.[1]

---

[1]Tests of the statistical significance of treatment effects are not used in single-subject research, partly because such tests require larger numbers of subjects, but also because $N = 1$ researchers are interested mainly in demonstrating that a client's behavior was reliably affected by manipulations of the independent variable. If such results are not obvious in a graph of the client's behavior, statistical significance would be irrelevant. When within-subjects designs employ groups of clients, however, researchers sometimes employ statistical techniques to measure the magnitude and significance of changes appearing over time (Kraemer & Thiemann, 1989; Kratochwill, Mott, & Dodson, 1984).

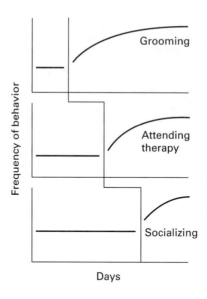

FIGURE 9.2 Hypothetical data from a multiple-baseline design. Notice that each targeted dependent variable improves when, *and only when*, social praise was made contingent on it. Such a pattern of results bolsters confidence that the treatment had a causal effect on behavior. (From A. E. Kazdin & S. A. Kopel, "On resolving ambiguities of the multiple baseline design: Problems and recommendatons," *Behavior Therapy*, 1975, *6*, 601–608. © 1975 by Academic Press, New York. Reprinted by permission.)

Within-subject research can be conducted with a small number of clients, sometimes as few as one at a time. Indeed, "single-subject" or "$N = 1$" research is a popular treatment evaluation strategy because, first, it permits the intensive study of clinical phenomena—such as multiple personality—that are too rare to allow large-group designs (Barlow & Hersen, 1984; Kazdin, 1993, 1994). Second, the $N = 1$ approach encourages the integration of clinical research and clinical practice; it gives individual clinicians a way to empirically evaluate the treatment they deliver to individual clients (Hayes, 1983). Third, the fine-grained study of a particular client over time makes it possible for clinicians to address therapy "process" questions—such as which events in therapy were followed by what changes—as well as the more obvious outcome questions (e.g., *whether* their treatment caused changes in their clients). Indeed, the intensive study of how interactions, events, or sequences within a psychotherapy session are related to important changes in a client has become a major focus of psychotherapy research (e.g., Greenberg, 1986; Greenberg, Elliott, & Lietaer, 1994). A goal of this kind of "process research" is to discover *how* psychotherapy produces change in a client so that therapists can learn how to bring about more therapeutic "good moments" (Mahrer & Nadler, 1986) in which clients show change or improvement.

Between-Subject Research

The simplest example of a between-subjects experiment on therapy outcome is one in which the researcher manipulates an independent variable by giving treatment to one group of clients—the *experimental* group—and compares any observed changes to those seen in members of a *control* group, which received no treatment. Measures of the clients' problematic behavior (the dependent variable) are made for both groups prior to the experiment (the *pretest*), shortly after the treatment period ends (the *posttest*), and perhaps also at longer posttreatment intervals (the *follow-up*).

It is important that clients be *randomly assigned* to experimental or control groups because, given a large enough number of clients, this procedure makes it likely that the treatment and control groups will be approximately equivalent in age, severity of disorder, socioeconomic status, and other important variables that might affect treatment outcome. If clients are not randomly assigned to conditions, any between-group differences in client behavior seen at the end of the experiment might be attributed to differences that existed between groups before the experiment ever began. If, for example, the most disturbed clients were put in the no-treatment group, the cards are stacked in favor of the treatment being evaluated. Thus, treated clients might improve much more than untreated clients, but because they were less disturbed to begin with, the treated clients might have improved even without treatment. When experimental designs are flawed, or *confounded*, in this way, we do not know whether to attribute improvement to treatment or to other uncontrolled factors. Once the pretest equivalence of the experimental and control groups is established, differences between the groups at posttest or follow-up can more confidently be attributed to the treatment that only the experimental group received. The significance of observed differences between treatment and control groups is tested via standard statistical analyses that help the researcher determine how likely it was that these differences might have occurred by chance.

Comparisons between treatment and no-treatment groups is just a first step in therapy-outcome research. After all, even large and statistically significant differences between a treatment and a no-treatment group can tell us little more than giving treatment appears to be more effective than doing nothing. The simple treatment/ no-treatment design cannot shed much light on the more complex questions that psychotherapy-outcome researchers want to address. Was treated clients' improvement due to specific therapeutic techniques, characteristics of the therapist, or the capacity of therapy to generate expectancy for improvement? Is the treatment tested better than various alternative treatments available?

One way of answering questions like these is to design *factorial experiments*, so named because they allow the researcher to examine the impact of various factors that might be responsible for the changes seen in treated clients. In a typical factorial outcome study, one group of clients might receive a complete treatment package, while another gets only that part of treatment thought to be most important to its effectiveness. A third group might be exposed to procedures that are impressive enough to generate expectations for improvement but involve no formal treatment methods (a placebo-control condition). A no-treatment group might also be included to assess the impact of the mere passage of time. By comparing the changes seen in all four groups, the experimenter can begin to determine whether the effects of the complete treatment package is better than no treatment, placebo effects, and a less extensive version of treatment. If a fifth group of clients is given a completely different form of treatment, the experimenter could also compare the first approach with that alternative.

Between-subject research designs have been popular among psychotherapy researchers because they allow manipulation of several independent variables simultaneously rather than sequentially, as required by within-subject designs. Between-subject designs are expensive, however; it usually takes many clients and a large research staff to compose and treat the groups necessary for the statistical analyses used. In addition, between-subject designs are not as suitable for evaluating the effects of a *sequence* of interventions; that type of question is better addressed by within-subject designs.

PRACTICAL PROBLEMS IN PSYCHOTHERAPY RESEARCH

Whether they employ within-subject or between-subject methods, psychotherapy researchers' overriding goal is to design experiments whose results are as high as possible on both internal and external validity so that they can serve as useful guides to clinicians in choosing treatments and charting progress in individual cases (Cook & Campbell, 1979; Goldfried & Wolfe, 1996; Howard et al., 1996; Newman & Tejeda, 1996).

Threats to Internal and External Validity

An experiment is said to have high *internal validity* if its design allows the researcher to confidently assert that observed changes in dependent variable(s) were *caused* by manipulated independent variable(s), not by some unknown, unintended, or uncontrolled confounding factor(s). The experimenter wants to be able to say, for example, that clients' reduced depression was caused by the cognitive therapy they received, not by the confidence they had in the treatment or by a TV show they happened to see.

Experiments are high on *external validity* if their results are applicable, or generalizable, to clients, problems, and situations other than those included in the experiment. External validity does not always follow from internal validity. For example, a study evaluating systematic desensitization for claustrophobia might feature random assignment to groups and include all the control conditions necessary to conclude that desensitization was responsible for clients' improvement. However, suppose this internally valid design employed expert desensitization therapists who treated only European-American female college students with mild cases of claustrophobia. These restrictions on therapist and client variables might reduce the study's external validity because its results may not apply to therapists in general, to clients from varying age or ethnic groups, or to clients who display more disabling phobias.

Most researchers agree that the best way to assess the outcome of psychotherapy is to conduct research on the treatments actually offered by clinicians to clinically disordered clients in real treatment settings. The ideal experimental outcome study, then, would select a large random sample of clients seeking help for depression or some other specific problem, assign them randomly to varying treatments or to specialized control conditions, have practicing therapists give them real or placebo treatments, then have measures of therapeutic change collected by unbiased persons who are unaware of which clients were in which treatment or control groups.

Unfortunately, numerous practical obstacles make these ideal arrangements virtually unachievable. For one thing, both clinical and ethical considerations sometimes prevent randomly assigning real clients to various treatment and control conditions. Few clients seeking treatment would be happy about being placed in a placebo or no-treatment group simply for the sake of promoting good science. Therapists, too, are reluctant to allow clients to be assigned to conditions that have little chance of bringing about beneficial changes. There are other, more basic impediments to research on psychotherapy, as well, including the fact that few clinical settings can offer researchers a sufficient number of clients who meet all the demographic, health, and disorder criteria that are ideal for inclusion in a controlled experiment. Add to these obstacles the practical problems of enlisting experienced therapists to participate in a study, convincing agency administrators to invest resources in the research, preventing subjects from prematurely dropping out of treatment, and collecting meaningful long-term outcome measures from clients, and you can understand why some psychotherapy researchers shy away from attempting to conduct real-life evaluations of treatment outcome.

Dealing With Threats to Validity

There are several approaches to solving these psychotherapy-outcome research problems. The first is for researchers to use all their creativity and tenacity to conduct the best clinical research they can, while recognizing that certain questions about psychotherapy cannot be answered with certainty outside a laboratory. Another approach, as mentioned earlier, is the use of within-subject designs to conduct fine-grained research on the "good moments" that occur in real-world therapy settings. A variant on this approach is the case-study model, in which therapists develop a specific treatment formulation for each client, then assess therapy's effects for that client (Howard et al., 1996; Kazdin, 1993; Persons, 1991).

Clinical Trials.   Investigators can also conduct cooperative outcome studies in which they combine therapy results for similar types of clients being treated by many different therapists at several clinical centers. This type of study, known as a *clinical trial*, allows experimental procedures such as random assignment to be used to investigate psychotherapy as it is practiced in real clinical settings. A prime example of this strategy is the NIMH Collaborative Study on the treatment of depression (Elkin, 1994; Elkin et al., 1989, 1995). Similar multi-site studies are currently evaluating the treatment of other mental disorders.

Laboratory Analogues.   Yet another approach is to bring psychotherapy research questions into the laboratory. Approximating clinical conditions in a controlled experimental setting is called *analogue research*. Its advantages include the ability to (1) control the client, therapist, and environmental variables that tend to fluctuate in unknown ways in clinical settings, (2) recruit (even advertise for) a sufficient number of clients who display a particular problem and who meet other demographic criteria,

(3) train therapists to conduct treatment(s) in specified ways, and (4) keep the number and length of treatment sessions constant for all clients.

The similarity between clinical and analogue settings can be assessed along four dimensions (Bernstein & Paul, 1971). The first of these involves *client characteristics* and *recruitment.* The degree to which an analogue experiment's results can be generalized to a clinical population depends on the extent to which the subjects are similar to clients who seek treatment.

The second dimension is the nature of the *target problem.* Certain target problems selected for analogue study, such as the fear of small animals or insects, may bear so little resemblance to the problems that most clients bring to clinics that they distort our understanding of the potency of therapeutic techniques.

A third dimension of interest relates to *therapist characteristics.* In many analogue studies, the therapists are graduate students in clinical psychology who have far less experience in general, or with the particular treatment being evaluated, than the average practicing clinician. (As we will see later, however, this factor may not necessarily hamper the ability of inexperienced therapists to help their clients).

Finally, clinical and analogue studies can be compared in terms of the *treatment techniques* they employ. As noted, analogue treatments can be standardized for all clients. This often means that therapists are given manuals that specify how a treatment should be conducted during the analogue study (e.g., Moncher & Prinz, 1991). In most clinics, however, therapists use methods that are tailored to the unique needs of each client. If *manualized* treatment techniques are simplified, altered, shortened, or otherwise changed in ways that do not fairly represent their use in clinical practice, the results of these analogue methods may say little about the therapies they were designed to evaluate.

Client Surveys.   A recent and somewhat controversial approach to evaluating psychotherapy has been to conduct surveys of how real clients fared after receiving psychotherapy as it is practiced in their communities. The survey approach obviously places far more emphasis on external rather than internal validity because, unlike within- or between-subject experiments, it exerts no experimental control over anything (Jacobson & Christensen, 1996). A recent example of this approach is a *Consumer Reports Survey*, described later, in which readers of *Consumer Reports* magazine answered a series of questions about the treatment and treatment results they experienced when they sought help for mental health problems (Seligman, 1995).

Necessary Compromises in Therapy Research

Notice the dilemma inherent in *any* approach to designing valid psychotherapy research: In order to exert the experimental control necessary to maximize internal validity, researchers may be forced to study clients, therapists, problems, treatments, and treatment settings that may not allow for high external validity. At the same time, if the researcher tries to maximize external validity by conducting research on real clients with real problems in community treatment settings, the resulting lack of experimental control may be lethal to internal validity. Given this dilemma, we must recognize that the results of well-controlled experiments can be used to draw only limited conclusions about therapies being conducted in clinical practice (Weisz, Weiss, & Donenberg, 1992; Shadish et al., in press). At the same time, we must be wary of evaluative data coming from less well-controlled research in clinical settings. Indeed, any conclusions drawn from the results of any outcome study must be tempered by awareness of the compromises in research design and methods that were made in an effort to strike a reasonable balance between internal and external validity.

In short, answering Paul's ultimate outcome question ("What treatment, by whom, is most effective for this individual, with that specific problem, under which set of circumstances, and how does it come about?") will require many researchers to conduct many different kinds of studies over many years. Let's now consider what they have discovered so far about the outcome of individual psychotherapy.

EFFECTIVENESS OF INDIVIDUAL PSYCHOTHERAPY

Although therapists have studied the outcome of psychotherapy for a long time, the modern era of outcome research began in 1952 when Hans Eysenck, a British psychologist, reviewed several experiments and concluded that the recovery rate is about the same for patients who receive therapy as for those who do not. Eysenck argued that the rate of "spontaneous remission" (improvement without any special treatment) was 72% over two years compared to improvement rates of 44% for psychoanalysis and 64% for eclectic therapy (Eysenck, 1952). In later reviews, Eysenck (1966) evaluated more studies and, while persisting in his pessimism about the effectiveness of traditional therapy, claimed that behavior therapy produced superior outcomes.

Box Score Reviews

Eysenck's conclusions sparked heated debate among clinicians. Many critics attacked his thoroughness, fairness, and his methods of statistical analysis. Others conducted their own reviews of the outcome literature and reached more optimistic conclusions about the effectiveness of psychotherapy. For example, Allen Bergin (1971) asserted that "psychotherapy on the average has modestly positive effects" (p. 228), a belief he later amended to "clearly positive results" (Bergin & Lambert, 1978). Another review found that more than 80% of psychotherapy outcome studies produced positive results (Meltzoff & Kornreich, 1970). Indeed, most reviews have concluded that most forms of psychotherapy produce better outcomes than no treatment and that various types of therapy are equally effective with most clients (e.g., Lambert, Shapiro, & Bergin, 1986; Luborsky, Singer, & Luborsky, 1975; Stiles, Shapiro, & Elliott, 1986). But there were also reviews that supported Eysenck's claim that (1) traditional psychotherapy is no better than no treatment, and (2) for several kinds of problems, behavior therapy *is* especially effective (Kazdin & Wilson, 1978; Rachman & Wilson, 1980).

Among the many reasons for the discrepant, sometimes contradictory results of therapy outcome reviews is the fact that different researchers have used differing standards in (1) selecting the outcome studies they survey, (2) evaluating the quality of these studies, (3) interpreting the magnitude of therapy effects, and (4) combining the results of many studies to reach their conclusions.

The traditional approach to summarizing outcome research has been the *narrative* or *box score* review. In a box score review, the researcher makes categorical judgments about whether each outcome study yielded positive or negative results and then tallies the number of positive and negative outcomes. Reviewers who use this method have been criticized (including by each other) for being subjective and unsystematic in the way they integrate research studies. Another problem with narrative reviews is that the sheer number of outcome studies makes it difficult for reviewers to weigh properly the merits and results of each study. Disagreements over these results made it clear that an alternative to box score analyses was needed, an alternative that would allow researchers to quantify and statistically summarize the effects of each outcome study, separately and in the aggregate.

Meta-Analytic Studies

One such alternative is *meta-analysis,* a quantitative technique that standardizes the outcomes of a large number of studies so they can be compared or combined (Rosenthal, 1983). The first application of meta-analysis to psychotherapy research came in 1977, and it led Mary Smith and Gene Glass to conclude that, on the average, psychotherapy was very effective (Smith and Glass, 1977). Later, they published a much larger meta-analysis which encompassed 475 psychotherapy-outcome studies (Smith, Glass & Miller, 1980). In this monumental meta-analysis, therapy effectiveness was evaluated by computing *effect sizes* for all the treatments used in all the studies. An effect size was defined as the treatment group mean on a dependent measure minus the control group mean on the same measure divided by the standard deviation of the control group. Thus, an effect size indicates the average difference in outcome between treated and untreated groups in each study. There can be as many effect sizes for a treatment as there are measures on which that treatment is evaluated—including clients' self-reports of how they feel, therapists' opinions about how much a client has changed, pre- and posttreatment psychological test scores, and observers' ratings of how well clients are doing—although there are statistical reasons why it is best to derive one average effect size for each treatment (Hedges & Olkin, 1982). Looking at effect sizes measured immediately after therapy ends, or in some cases, months after treatment, indicates how much better off the average treated client was compared with the average person in a no-treatment control group.

On the basis of their meta-analysis, Smith and her colleagues drew the following conclusions:

1. The average effect size for psychotherapy was .85 standard deviations, which they interpreted to mean that "the average person receiving psychotherapy was better off at the end of it than 80% of the persons who do not" (Smith, Glass, & Miller, 1980, p. 29).
2. Only 9% of the effect sizes were negative, indicating that deterioration caused by psychotherapy was not frequent.

3. Specific types of therapy were not associated with significantly different effects. Across all types of problems, psychodynamic, Rogerian, behavioral, and cognitive therapies all tended to yield essentially equivalent effect sizes. The one exception to this pattern was that behavioral therapies were a bit more effective than other approaches in treating certain well-defined problems such as phobias and panic attacks.

4. Effect sizes tended to be larger when (1) more reactive methods were used to measure outcome (e.g., asking clients rather than relatives about progress), (2) experimenters were more committed to the therapy they were evaluating, and (3) measures were taken immediately after therapy (though, even months later, improvement was still evident).

Several other research teams have performed meta-analyses using different statistical methods or differently selected sets of studies (e.g., Andrews & Harvey, 1981; Brown, 1987; Lambert & Bergin, 1994; Landman & Dawes, 1982; Lipsey & Wilson, 1993; Shapiro & Shapiro, 1982). In general, these analyses have confirmed the conclusion that psychotherapy is an effective intervention for a wide variety of psychological disorders. In addition, these second and third-generation meta-analyses have led to the following additional conclusions about the effects of psychotherapy:

1. In general, better-designed research studies yield larger estimates for the effectiveness of psychotherapy (Landman & Dawes, 1982).

2. The effects of psychotherapy tend to be maintained over periods of six to eighteen months (Andrews & Harvey, 1981; Nicholson & Berman, 1983; Robinson, Berman, & Neimeyer, 1990). These data serve to counter fears that gains attributed to psychotherapy might be short lived; there is even some evidence that clients show continuing improvement during follow-up periods (Gallagher-Thompson, Hanley-Peterson, & Thompson, 1990).

3. The problems of a small percentage of clients do become worse after psychotherapy—about 10% of effect sizes in major meta-analytic studies of psychotherapy have been negative (Shapiro & Shapiro, 1982; Smith et al., 1980)—but the causes and course of deterioration or negative change are not well understood.

4. It appears that, for about half of treated clients, the benefits of psychotherapy begin to appear after the first six to eight sessions, and that 75% of those who show improvement typically do so by the twenty-sixth session (Howard et al., 1996). Continued benefits occur as treatment continues, but the rate of progress tends to slow, probably because the client's most difficult problems tend to be addressed in later sessions. The relatively quick response to psychotherapy by most clients has led, as we shall see, to the increased use of "brief therapies" that aim to produce benefits in twenty-five sessions or less (Koss & Shiang, 1994).

5. In line with the findings of the earliest meta-analyses (Smith, Glass, & Miller, 1980), the type of therapy that clients receive makes little difference to overall treatment effectiveness. Indeed, this conclusion has been reached by so many analyses that psychotherapy researchers jokingly call it the "Dodo bird verdict"

(Luborsky et al., 1975), in reference to Lewis Carroll's tale of *Alice in Wonderland*. In the story, Alice and several other characters run a race, but they run in different directions. When they ask the Dodo bird to name the winner, he answers diplomatically: "Everybody has won and all must have prizes." In the race among various psychotherapies, too, all appear to have crossed the outcome finish line together. When differences among treatments *are* found, it tends to be cognitive and behavioral therapies that show slight to moderate advantages over other treatments (e.g., Shapiro & Shapiro, 1982; Svartberg & Stiles, 1991).

6. The amount of professional experience that therapists have—and even whether they are professional or nonprofessional therapists—appears largely unrelated to the success of treatment (Berman & Norton, 1985; Hattie, Sharpley, & Rogers, 1984; Stein & Lambert, 1984). This conclusion, too, is consistent with early meta-analyses (Smith, Glass, & Miller, 1980) which found that nonprofessionals and professionals with less experience did about as well overall as experienced professional therapists. Experienced professionals *sometimes* produce outcomes that are superior to those of novice or nonprofessional therapists (Stein & Lambert, 1995), but the fact that most studies fail to find consistent advantages associated with professional training or experience is remarkable. Of course, in many studies nonprofessional therapists worked under the supervision of experienced professionals, and in others, professional therapists were assigned more difficult cases. Similarly, therapists described as "more experienced" might have been practicing only a year longer than those described as "less experienced" (Nietzel & Fisher, 1981).

Still, therapist training and experience do not appear to affect the success of treatment as much as most clinicians assume (Dawes, 1992; Durlak, 1979; Henry, et al., 1993). This is an important finding because if training is not crucial, it would be difficult to justify the extensive preparation most therapists receive, or the expense associated with professional treatment. Additional well-designed research on this topic is needed, but the burden of proof is clearly on trained professionals to show that they possess special abilities to help people with psychological problems.

Criticisms of Meta-Analysis. Despite its popularity, meta-analysis has been severely criticized on the grounds that it (1) is subject to the same biases and arbitrariness encountered in narrative reviews; that is, certain studies are omitted and others are combined into categories that may not be reliably defined; (2) involves an "apples-and-oranges" approach to evaluation (combining varying treatments for varying problems on varying clients) that obscures important distinctions in treatments and outcomes; (3) pays insufficient attention to the research quality of individual studies of psychotherapy; and (4) is based on several statistical assumptions that, if violated, can invalidate the results obtained (e.g., Eysenck, 1978; Wilson, 1985; Wilson & Rachman, 1983).

Each of these criticisms has been answered by proponents of meta-analysis who argue that (1) meta-analysis makes explicit the rules for selecting and combining studies (in narrative reviews, these rules are often not explicitly defined); (2) if one is interested in evaluating psychotherapy as a general intervention, combining different treatments is not an error (just as it is not an error to combine apples and oranges if one is evaluating fruit); (3) as noted earlier, it is the better-designed studies, not the weaker ones, that are producing the largest therapy effect sizes; and (4) corrections are available for remedying most of the statistical problems that can threaten a meta-analysis.

Client Satisfaction Surveys

The conclusions about psychotherapy reached by most box score analyses and meta-analyses are reflected in the *Consumer Reports* study mentioned earlier. In that survey, about 4,100 of the 7,000 respondents had seen a mental health professional in the past three years. As a group, these clients were well-educated and predominantly middle-class; about half were women, and their average age was forty-six. Although these characteristics are not representative of the U.S. population as a whole, they are a reasonably good approximation of the type of client who normally seeks out professional treatment for psychological problems. The respondents were asked to rate (1) the degree to which formal treatment had helped with the problem that led them to therapy, (2) how satisfied they were with the treatment they received, and (3) how they judged their "overall emotional state" after treatment.

Responses indicated that about 90% of these clients felt better after treatment, that there was no difference in the improvement of clients who had psychotherapy alone versus psychotherapy plus medication, that no particular approach to psychotherapy was rated more highly than others, and that while all types of professionals appeared to help their clients, greater improvements were associated with treatments by psychologists, psychiatrists, and social workers compared to family physicians or marriage counselors.

The Clinical Significance of Treatment Effects

Many psychotherapy outcome studies focus on the question of whether one specific treatment has significantly larger effects than other types of treatment or various control conditions. This is an important question, but it is not the only one. Researchers, and especially clients, also want to know whether psychotherapy produces effects that are *clinically significant*, as well as statistically significant (Sechrest, McKnight, & McKnight, 1996). In other words, did treatment produce changes that are personally and socially meaningful? Do the clients and those around them see improvements that matter in daily life?

Alan Kazdin (1982b) proposed two methods for evaluating the clinical significance of posttreatment change. In the first, called *subjective evaluation,* individuals who regularly interact with or observe clients are asked to rate the extent to which treatment has led to important differences in the clients' behavior and functioning. The second method, called *social,* or *normative comparison,* evaluates clients' posttreatment behavior in relation to that of nondisturbed, "normal" peers. Using this second method, one can quantitatively define clinical significance in terms of the standard deviation units that separate treated clients from the mean of some normative group (Jacobson & Truax, 1991; Kendall, 1984; see Figure 9.3). Quantitative social comparisons have revealed clinically significant results following various forms of psychotherapy for

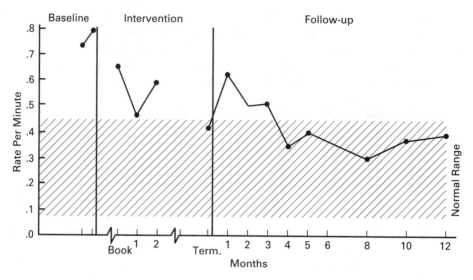

FIGURE 9.3 Assessing clinical significance via normative comparison. (From G. R. Patterson, "Intervention for boys with conduct problems: Multiple settings, treatments, and criteria," *Journal of Consulting and Clinical Psychology,* 1974, *42,* 471–481. Copyright 1974 by the American Psychological Association. Reprinted by permission.)

impulsivity (Kendall & Zupan, 1981), depression (Nietzel et al., 1987), anxiety disorders (Nietzel & Trull, 1988), marital problems (Snyder & Wills, 1989), and schizophrenia (Hansen, St. Lawrence, & Christoff, 1985)

EFFECTIVENESS OF GROUP, COUPLES, AND FAMILY THERAPIES

Less research exists on the outcome of groups, couples, and family therapies, but available results suggest that, in general, these formats for psychotherapy can have benefits that are at least equal to those of individual treatment.

Research on Group Therapy

Empirical evidence confirms that group therapy can be an effective form of treatment, especially when group members clearly understand how the group is run and what will be expected of them (Bednar & Kaul, 1994). Better outcomes are achieved when the group is cohesive, provides accurate feedback to members, and encourages interpersonal learning and supportive interactions. The fact that group treatment is often as beneficial as one-to-one psychotherapy (e.g., Orlinsky, Grawe, & Parks, 1994) will probably lead to increased use of group therapy in the future because of its potential cost savings, both for clients and their health insurance companies.

Effectiveness of Self-Help Groups. The effects of self-help groups (SHGs) are seldom evaluated empirically. Most SHG members are simply convinced that their groups are valuable and thus see formal outcome research on them as unnecessary or even undesirable. Evaluation is further complicated by the fact that the goals of SHGs are often hard to describe precisely. The few outcome evaluations that are available have produced mixed results (Nietzel, Guthrie, & Susman, 1991), but it generally appears that active members value their involvement in the group and experience moderate improvements in some areas of their lives. It would be helpful if SHGs were more receptive to empirical research so that clinicians could learn more about their beneficial effects and how they occur.

Research on Couples Therapy

Compared with no-treatment control groups, almost all forms of marital therapy can produce significant improvements in couples' happiness and adjustment (Alexander, Holtzworth-Monroe, & Jameson, 1994). However, the magnitude or clinical significance of these improvements is frequently disappointing. As many as half of treated relationships remain distressed, and even among couples who show improvement, the changes are often not large enough to allow them to view their relationship as successful or happy. Further, the few available long-term follow-ups on the effects of successful marital therapy indicate that 30% to 40% of couples treated with behavioral marital techniques, at least, relapse into marital discord or divorce (Jacobson, Schmaling, & Holtzworth-Munroe, 1987; Snyder, Wills, & Grady-Fletcher, 1991).

Programs aimed at *enriching* marital relationships or *preventing* marital problems in new marriages generally show positive initial effects relative to no-treatment controls (Giblin, 1986; Halweg & Markman, 1988), but, as with most forms of marital therapy, it has not been shown that these programs can produce lasting changes in long-term relationships (Bradbury & Fincham, 1990).

As with individual therapy, studies comparing the effects of different theoretical approaches to marital therapy have found no significant advantages for any of them in terms of immediate benefits. In one of the most comprehensive of these comparative outcome studies, Doug Snyder and his colleagues assessed the fate of seventy-nine unhappily married couples who had been randomly assigned to behavioral marital therapy, insight-oriented marital therapy, or a wait-list control group (Snyder & Wills, 1989; Snyder, Wills, & Grady-Fletcher, 1991; Wills, Faitler, & Snyder, 1987). All treatments were conducted by well-trained and closely-supervised clinicians. After twenty-five sessions of therapy, both behavioral and insight couples reported significant improvements in marital satisfaction and individual adjustment compared to their pretreatment status and to couples on the waiting list. At a follow-up assessment six months later, these improvements tended to be well-maintained. In short, both therapies proved to be about equally effective (Snyder & Wills, 1989). Four years later, however, about half the remaining couples in both conditions reported substantial marital difficulties since termination of treatment. We say "remaining" because by that time 38% of the couples who had behavioral treatment had divorced; only 3% of the couples in the insight-oriented treatment had done so (Snyder, Wills, & Grady-Fletcher, 1991).

Though these results call into question the long-term benefits of behavioral marital therapy, critics of the study note that the form of behavioral therapy used in Snyder's research excluded many contemporary behavioral techniques, including some procedures that *were* offered in the insight-oriented treatment (Jacobson, 1991). Still, these results suggest to many that achieving long-term gains in a couple's happiness requires understanding and resolving persistent emotional conflicts, not just negotiating solutions to specific problems.

Research on Family Therapy

Families who complete a course of therapy together usually show significant improvements in communication patterns and in the behavior of the family member whose problems prompted therapy in the first place (e.g., Szapocznik et al., 1986). This outcome is typically reported in empirical research on family therapy for several kinds of identified-client and family problems (Hazelrigg, Cooper, & Boudin, 1987; Shadish et al., 1993). Family therapies aimed at improving parental discipline techniques and at decreasing family members' criticism of, and emotional overinvolvement with, mentally ill relatives have proven particularly effective (e.g., Hooley, 1985; Serketich & Dumas, 1996).

Certain types of family therapy appear more successful than others. Behavioral and structural family therapies have received the strongest empirical support. As noted in Chapter 7, each of these approaches emphasizes pragmatic changes in the way families interact and go about solving problems. Psychodynamic or humanistic family therapies that do not stress direct modification of specific symptoms and problems tend to show smaller effects.

EFFECTIVENESS OF PSYCHOSOCIAL REHABILITATION

Recall from Chapter 7 that, unlike individual, group, couples, or family therapy, psychosocial rehabilitation programs are designed to help people with mental disorders cope with—and minimize the impact of—their problems. Do these programs reach their goals?

Several research studies have shown that psychosocial rehabilitation programs can help severely mentally ill patients learn new skills such as administering their own medication, monitoring their symptoms, engaging in appropriate social conversations, and caring for their own health and safety (Benton & Schroeder, 1990; Dilk & Bond, 1996). The evidence is less clear that patients regularly use the skills they have learned to cope with problems in the community (Wallace, 1993). Patients who have received special skill training perform better in their home environments than they did before training, but they tend to not do as well as they had in the training environments.

Comprehensive psychosocial rehabilitation programs have also been shown to reduce relapse rates and other crises such as arrests or imprisonment (Bond et al., 1990; Olfson, 1990). In some cases, these outcomes are achieved even though the overall rate of symptom expression has not declined significantly. In one well-conducted evaluation of Assertive Community Treatment (ACT), severely mentally ill patients were randomly assigned to either ACT or a drop-in center where they could socialize with other patients, obtain food, and engage in recreational activities (Bond et al., 1990). Outcome assessments after one year suggested that there were large differences in how often clients actually participated in their assigned services; 76% of ACT patients were active in treatment, compared to only 7% of drop-in center patients. Further, ACT patients were admitted to the state mental hospital significantly less often during the treatment year than were the drop-in center clients, they had significantly fewer contacts with the legal system, and maintained more stable housing arrangements in the community.

Other research indicates, however, that if rehabilitation programs are not continued for at least two years, clients often deteriorate, rehospitalization rates increase, and overall quality of life declines (Wallace, 1993). These results are not particularly surprising. Given that disorders such as schizophrenia impair almost all aspects of functioning, it is to be expected that, to be effective, treatment should be comprehensive and continuous.

EFFECTIVENESS OF PREVENTIVE INTERVENTIONS

In Chapter 7, we described a number of community psychology programs aimed at preventing mental disorders. Recall that these primary prevention programs are designed to modify social, economic, and environmental risk factors that lead to disorders or to strengthen positive qualities that can protect vulnerable individuals from developing disorders.

Primary prevention programs have focused on almost every conceivable cause of psychological problems (Trickett, Dahiyal, & Selby, 1994). Parents have been taught to cuddle infants, read to toddlers, and closely supervise middle-schoolers. Children have been trained to control their aggressive conduct, become more creative problem-solvers, strengthen their social skills, cope with negative life events, and resist peer pressures for misbehavior. School curricula have been expanded, contracted, specialized, and decentralized. The criminal justice system has experimented with decriminalization, diversion, and neighborhood watches, while the mental health care system has attempted deinstitutionalization, community consultation, and stress management. Teenagers have been educated about the dangers of unprotected sex, single parenthood, substance abuse, and other risky behaviors; and they have been encouraged to turn their energies to prosocial pursuits. Communities have been reorganized, recapitalized, and empowered. Job training, affirmative action, welfare reforms, and new public housing programs have all been justified, in part, by their potential for preventing mental disorders.

The Status of Prevention

Some prevention programs aim at one causal variable, while others address a multitude of influences. Some are small-scale innovations funded on a shoestring; others, like Head Start, are multibillion dollar national efforts. Most important, some of these programs have been flops, while others have produced impressive successes (Burchard & Burchard, 1987; Edelstein & Michelson, 1986; Mrazek & Haggerty, 1994; Price et al., 1988). Evaluative research on prevention programs have taught community psychologists and other mental health professionals several important lessons about what makes these programs work (Coie et al., 1993).

They have learned, first, that certain risk factors—such as poverty, child abuse and family violence, infant–caregiver attachment problems, stressful life events, academic failure, and low self-esteem—can have such widespread effects on human development that they should be the main targets of prevention programs.

Second, because most mental disorders are caused by a host of social, economic, and psychological risk factors (Petraitis, Flay, & Miller, 1995), prevention programs must address these multiple risks if they are to be effective. For example, preventing school failures among low-income children might require study-skill tutoring programs, but these programs will not help children whose parents cannot bring them to the sessions because they lack reliable transportation. An effective prevention program for these families would have to provide transportation as well as tutoring.

Third, researchers have learned that the longer mental-disorder risk factors operate, the more serious their consequences (Rutter, 1997). For example, severe parental conflict early in a child's life may impair the parents' ability to supervise the child and thus make it harder for the child to achieve success in the early school years. As school performance declines, the child may suffer rejection by more successful peers, thus leading the child to affiliate with other children who are doing poorly in school. By early adolescence, these groups of unsuccessful, disaffected youngsters tend to increasingly reject prosocial expectations, which puts them at risk for antisocial behavior and substance abuse. Recognizing this "domino effect," prevention-oriented psychologists now seek to defuse risk factors as early as possible (Zigler, Taussig, & Black, 1992).

They also realize that, partly because of the "domino effect," certain risk factors are particularly dangerous during particular developmental stages. For example, the appearance of criminal activity associated with antisocial behavior disorders is most closely linked to inadequate parental monitoring and discipline in the preschool years, to disengagement, misbehavior, and poor academic performance in the primary school years, and to peer influences in adolescence. To effectively prevent these disorders, psychologists must design their programs to address the right risk factor at the right time in clients' lives (Yoshikawa, 1994).

Fourth, prevention programs must also take into account the cultural norms and traditions of the people they aim to help. African-Americans, Hispanic-Americans, Asian-Americans, and Native Americans now constitute about 18% of the U.S. population; by the year 2050, it is estimated that this figure will be nearly 50%. These demographic changes pose a fundamental challenge to preventionists because programs that work well in one cultural setting may not work well in another. A new rule of thumb has evolved: Preventive interventions should capitalize as much as possible on people's natural strengths, existing resources, and cultural traditions, and not try to change people's coping methods or other behaviors to match the program planners' preconceived ideals.

Obstacles to Progress in Prevention

Progress toward the primary prevention of mental disorders is hampered by several problems. For one thing, many of the people for whom prevention programs are intended do not acknowledge that they are at risk for anything and may view preventive services as unnecessary or intrusive. In other words, those most in need are sometimes the least interested in what prevention scientists have to offer. Community psychologists debate the wisdom of trying to convince these people of their high-risk status because doing so can have unintended consequences that raise serious ethical questions. For example, educating people about their mental health risks might create enough anxiety about the appearance of mental disorder that the warning becomes a self-fulfilling prophecy.

The reluctance of some high-risk people to take part in prevention programs also creates a problem in evaluating these programs. If the people who end up participating in a program are at lower risk for disorder than the population for which the programs were intended, researchers may overestimate what their prevention program can accomplish in the community as a whole (Stein, Bauman, & Ireys, 1991).

Finally, even when a new prevention program demonstrates success with high-risk groups, its results may not be replicable. Demonstration projects—with their full funding and large and enthusiastic staffs—are often hard to duplicate in less well-funded agencies where overworked, underpaid, and unappreciated staffers do not have the time or commitment to follow through on the project (Bauman, Stein, & Ireys, 1991).

CLINICAL INTERVENTIONS TODAY

The clinical interventions offered to troubled or vulnerable people today have been shaped partly by the results of research on psychotherapy, psychosocial rehabilitation, and disorder-prevention programs, and partly by the economic realities of health care in the 1990s. In this final section, we consider some of the outcomes and trends that have appeared in response to these empirical findings and economic forces.

Prevention Programs

Community psychologists and other mental health professionals are using what they have learned to develop preventive interventions that are based on empirically supported theories about which risk factors are associated with which disorders. In 1982, the U.S. National Institute of Mental Health began funding a series of Prevention Intervention Research Centers (PIRCs) to stimulate this kind of research. PIRCs bring together scientists from fields such as psychology, anthropology, sociology, epidemiology, and psychiatry to collaborate on research on the early causes of specific disorders. The centers focus on experiments with at-risk, but not yet disordered, groups such as children living in high-stress environments or adults facing the threat of unemployment (Sandler et al., 1991; Turner, Kessler, & House, 1991).

PIRC research is geared toward first discovering the incidence of disorders, then investigating the causal mechanisms responsible for them. Prevention programs aimed at modifying risk factors for the disorders are then developed and assessed. The programs that prove effective are then transferred to new settings where their impact is again evaluated. This sequence of events has already proven its worth in a number of areas, including, for example, reducing the incidence of aggressive behavior in schoolchildren and reducing depressive disorders in adolescents (Clarke et al., 1995; Kellam et al., 1994).

Prevention-centered research can benefit the entire field of mental health because its longitudinal nature leads to a clearer picture of the way mental disorders emerge and develop. Unfortunately, prevention programs are often very expensive, so unless federal and state legislators are convinced that the effects of these programs justify their cost, the funds to implement them may not be forthcoming. In the long run, preventing disorders in large populations costs less than treating people one at a time, but the long-term perspective is not an easy one for most politicians (and many psychologists) to take (Heller, 1996).

Still, many psychologists continue to pursue prevention programs consistent with the PIRC research model. Their emphasis is no longer on the social and political activism advocated by early community psychologists (Albee, 1996), or even on well-intentioned interventions that *might* have long-term benefits. Instead, the focus will increasingly be on intervention experiments—carried out by teams of researchers from clinical psychology, psychiatry, social work, and other fields—aimed at rigorously evaluating interventions aimed at reducing the biological, developmental, and psychological risk factors that are *known* to lead to specific disorders.

This new focus in the field now known as *prevention science* has been strongly influenced by the research reviews and recommendations contained in the reports of two study groups sponsored by the National Institute of Mental Health and the National Academy of Sciences' Institute of Medicine (Mrazek & Haggerty, 1994; NIMH, 1994). Assuming adequate funding will be allocated for implementing them, these blueprints for prevention science (NIMH, 1995) are sure to chart the course of preventive interventions for many years to come (Reiss & Price, 1996).

Eclecticism in Psychotherapy

In the field of psychotherapy, clinicians must deal with evidence that no single theoretical approach to therapy is better than all others for treating all clinical problems. Accordingly, the majority of therapists pledge allegiance to no single therapy system, preferring to combine methods from several approaches in an effort to meet the perceived needs of each client (Garfield & Kurtz, 1976; Jensen, Bergin, & Greaves, 1990; Norcross, Prochaska, & Gallagher, 1989b).

This hybrid orientation is known as eclecticism or *eclectic psychotherapy.* Eclectics are not anti- or atheoretical clinicians who simply reach into a grab bag and pull out techniques at random. Their choices are principled ones, based on the circumstances of each individual case, not the dictates of a general theoretical system. Increasingly, this approach to psychotherapy is being referred to as *integrationism.* The appearance of the *International Journal of Eclectic Psychotherapy* and the founding of the Society for the Exploration of Psychotherapy Integration provide two indications that integrationism is thriving among today's clinicians.

Because it is not a school of psychotherapy, eclecticism has not had a single famous founder, nor has it attracted a large number of vocal promoters. Frederick Thorne (1967, 1973) is a well-known advocate of an eclectic approach, but even he appears to be a somewhat reluctant spokesman: "Eclecticism carries with it none of the special advantages of uniqueness, newness or proprietorship of special knowledge implicit in the special schools whose adherents often turn such attributes to personal advantage" (Thorne, 1973, p. 449). Other champions of eclecticism include James Prochaska, who has attempted to identify the common therapy processes in any effective psychotherapy (Prochaska & DiClemente, 1984), and Arnold Lazarus (1981), whose *multimodal therapy* illustrates a predominantly behavioral, but still eclectic, approach to treatment.

In formulating multimodal therapy, Lazarus (1981, 1995) advocated "technical eclecticism," meaning that therapists should use whatever techniques are most appropriate for given problems regardless of the theoretical system from which those techniques are derived. Multimodal therapy addresses seven areas of client functioning: behavior, affect (emotion), sensation, imagery, cognition, interpersonal relations, and biology (including health, nutrition, and the impact of medication and other drugs).[2] Lazarus tends to focus multimodal treatment on the behavioral and interpersonal areas, and to use behavioral, cognitive, and rational-emotive methods, but he deals with all seven areas, using techniques drawn from other approaches to therapy as well (Lazarus, 1995; see Table 9.1)

TABLE 9.1   An Example of Multimodal Therapy

Here is a hypothetical client's BASIC ID profile, along with the methods that might be used in multimodal therapy to address each area of problematic functioning (based on Lazarus, 1995).

Area of Functioning	Client's Problem	Treatment Used
Behavior	Withdrawal, avoidance, inactivity	Systematic desensitization; reinforcement of desired behaviors
Affect	Anger, resentment, hostility	Gestalt or other methods of getting in touch with and reliving painful emotional experiences and genuine feelings
Sensation	Headaches, stomach pain, tension	Biofeedback and relaxation training
Imagery	Death images, images of family rejection	Visualization of being healthy and of coping with problems
Cognition	Preoccupation with past failures and perceived worthlessness	Cognitive restructuring; creating and practicing positive self-statements
Interpersonal	Unassertive, passive	Assertiveness training
Drugs/Biological	High blood pressure	Anti-hypertensive medication

---

[2]By substituting "drugs" for "biology," Lazarus summarizes these areas of function with the acronym BASIC ID.

Eclectic Therapy Packages.   Which therapy methods are most popular in eclectic packages? One national survey (Jensen, Bergin, & Greaves, 1990) found that 72% of eclectic therapists reported including psychodynamic principles within their version of treatment, 54% included cognitive approaches, and 45% included behavioral methods. Blends including phenomenological approaches came in fourth. So there are many versions of eclectic therapy, each of which may have a predominant analytical, behavioral, cognitive-behavioral, or phenomenological flavor.

Eclectic therapists' choices about which treatment methods to use are increasingly guided by experimental studies demonstrating that certain well-defined therapies are particularly beneficial in the treatment of specific mental disorders (Chambliss, 1995; Roth & Fonagy, 1996). Some of these *empirically validated treatments* are summarized in Table 9.2.

TABLE 9.2   Empirically Validated Treatments

A special task force of the Clinical Psychology Division of the American Psychological Association reviewed treatment literature to identify those therapies that empirical research had validated as effective interventions for specific disorders. The "well established" treatments had been found effective by a large body of studies. The "probably efficacious" treatments were found to be effective in a smaller number of studies.

Treatment	Source for Evidence of Efficacy
Well-established treatments	
Beck's cognitive therapy for depression	Dobson (1989)
Behavior modification for developmentally disabled individuals	Scotti, Evans, Meyer & Walker (1991)
Behavior modification for enuresis and encopresis	Kupfersmid (1989) Wright & Walker (1978)
Behavior therapy for headache and for irritable bowel syndrome	Blanchard, Schwarz, & Radnitz (1987) Blanchard, Andrasik, Ahles, Teders, & O'Keefe (1980)
Behavior therapy for female orgasmic dysfunction and for male erectile dysfunction	LoPiccolo & Stock (1986) Auerbach & Kilmann (1977)
Behavioral marital therapy	Azrin, Bersalel, et al. (1980) Jacobson & Follette (1985)
Cognitive behavior therapy for chronic pain	Keefe, Dunsmore, & Burnett (1992)
Cognitive behavior therapy for panic disorder with and without agoraphobia	Barlow, Craske, Cerny, & Klosko (1989) Clark et al. (1989)
Cognitive behavior therapy for generalized anxiety disorder	Butler, Fennell, Robson, & Gelder (1991) Borkovec et al. (1987) Chambless & Gillis (1993)

TABLE 9.2   Empirically Validated Treatments (*Continued*)

Treatment	Source for Evidence of Efficacy
Exposure treatment for phobias (agoraphobia, social phobia, simple phobia) and posttraumatic stress disorder	Mattick, Andrews, Hadzi-Pavlovic, & Christensen (1990) Trull, Nietzel, & Main (1988) Foa, Rothbaum, Riggs, & Murdock (1991)
Exposure and response prevention for obsessive-compulsive disorder	Marks & O'Sullivan (1988) Steketee, Foa, & Grayson (1982)
Family education programs for schizophrenia	Hogarty et al. (1986) Falloon et al. (1985)
Group cognitive behavioral therapy for social phobia	Heimberg, Dodge, Hope, Kennedy & Zollo (1990) Mattick & Peters (1988)
Interpersonal therapy for bulimia	Fairburn, Jones, Peveler, Hope, & O'Conner (1993) Wifley et al. (1993)
Klerman and Weissman's interpersonal therapy for depression	DiMascio et al. (1979) Elkin et al. (1989)
Parent training programs for children with oppositional behavior	Wells & Egan (1988) Walter & Gilmore (1973)
Systematic desensitization for simple phobia	Kazdin & Wilcoxin (1976)
Token economy programs	Liberman (1972)
Probably efficacious treatments	
Applied relaxation for panic disorder	Öst (1988) Öst & Westling (1991)
Brief psychodynamic therapies	Piper, Azim, McCallum, & Joyce (1990) Shefler & Dasberg (1989) Thompson, Gallagher, & Breckenridge (1987) Winston et al. (1991) Woody, Luborsky, McLellen, & O'Brien (1990)
Behavior modification for sex offenders	Marshall, Jones, Ward, Johnston, & Barbaree (1991)
Dialectical behavior therapy for borderline personality disorder	Linehan, Armstrong, Suarez, Allmon, & Heard (1991) Johnson & Greenberg (1985)
Emotionally focused couples therapy	Azrin, Nunn, & Frantz (1980)
Habit reversal and control techniques	Azrin, Nunn, & Frantz-Renshaw (1980)
Lewinsohn's psychoeducational treatment for depression	Lewinsohn, Hoberman, & Clarke (1989)

Source: From "Training in and Dissemination of Empirically-Validated Psychological Procedures: Report and Recommendations," by Task Force on Promotion and Dissemination of Psychological Procedures, 1995, *The Clinical Psychologist, 48*, pp. 22–23. Copyright 1995 by Division of Clinical Psychology, American Psychological Association. Reprinted with permission.

The Advent of Managed Care

In the United States today, the kind of treatment clients receive—and the duration of that treatment—is influenced not only by therapists' preferences, but also by the preferences and policies of the insurance companies and health maintenance organizations that pay therapy bills. These "third-party payers" want to cover only treatments that are effective, efficient, and necessary. Accordingly, the type and length of mental health treatment are increasingly controlled by *managed care systems*, which allocate health services to a group of people in a fashion designed to contain the overall cost of these services. (In contrast to fee-for-service plans, most managed health care systems provide health care to their subscribers for a fixed, prepaid price.)

Many managed care companies attempt to contain their costs by doing a *utilization review* of each client. One of their case managers will look at the nature of the client's problems, the therapist's treatment plan, and the therapy progress notes. The case manager—who is *not* likely to be a mental health professional—then determines whether the managed care plan will pay for the treatment and, if so, for how many sessions of which specific types of therapy. A case manager may decide, for example, that a depressed client can receive no more than eight sessions of psychotherapy, even though the therapist says the client's problems require more extensive treatment. (The impact of managed care is discussed in more detail in Chapter 14.)

Time-Limited Therapies

Managed care reviewers' affinity for treatments that are as brief as possible tends to discourage long-term, insight-oriented therapies. However, as described in Chapter 8, the idea of relatively brief treatment and the development of alternatives to psychoanalysis appeared long before the advent of managed care. These trends began in the 1930s with Franz Alexander's psychoanalytically oriented psychotherapy and gained prominence in the 1960s as clinicians found that behavioral, cognitive-behavioral, and phenomenological methods could produce benefits in months rather than years (Garfield & Bergin, 1994). By the 1980s, according to some surveys, the average psychotherapy client was being seen for only eight to ten sessions (Olfson & Pincus, 1994; Taube et al., 1988), but it was not lost on managed care organizations that, when clients paid a fixed health care fee instead of being charged for each session, treatment lasted an average of nearly seventeen sessions (Manning, Wells, & Benjamin, 1986).

Clinicians and managed care personnel who advocate brief treatments point to evidence from meta-analyses and other sources suggesting that most improvements take place early in the therapy process, and they conclude from this evidence that treatment need not be lengthy to be effective (Austed & Berman, 1991; Bloom, 1992; Kopta et al., 1991; Steenbarger, 1994). Other clinicians challenge the validity of this conclusion (e.g., Miller, 1996a) and argue further that even if brief treatments *can* be effective, they may not be right for every client. Choices about the duration of treatment, they say, should reside mainly with clinicians; they are concerned that cost-driven pressure for shorter treatments will discourage comprehensive pretreatment clinical assessments and deprive some clients of the amount of treatment they need to experience long-term benefits. They point to studies showing, for example, that not all symptoms of depression improve at the same rate and that clients who received sixteen therapy sessions show more permanent improvement than those whose treatment lasted only eight sessions (Barkham et al., 1996a, 1996b).

Psychotherapy and Drug Treatments

Managed care organizations' emphasis on brief, efficient treatment has also fostered a trend toward the use of drugs, or drugs plus psychotherapy, as a way of quickly reducing the symptoms of mental disorder, especially in cases of anxiety and depression. Of course, the use of drugs in the treatment of these and many other psychological problems began almost as soon as the drugs appeared in the 1950s, well before managed care came along. But whereas only 27% of psychiatric outpatients were given drugs in 1975, that figure grew to 55% by 1988, and today, psychiatrists prescribe antidepressants, anxiolytics (anti-anxiety), and other psychotropic medication for up to 90% of their patients (Olfson, Pincus, & Sabshin, 1994). These drugs are also routinely prescribed by most general practice physicians for patients complaining of anxiety, depression, eating disorders, sleep disorders, and a wide variety of other problems. In the United States alone, hundreds of millions of drug prescriptions are written every year for the treatment of mental disorders.

Combining drugs and psychotherapy can in fact be quite helpful and, in some cases, may be better than either approach alone (e.g. Hollon, 1993), but most studies have found that, for anxiety disorders and depression, at least, combined treatments do not greatly improve on what either treatment can achieve on its own (Antonuccio, Danton, & DeNelsky, 1995; Conte et al., 1986; Wexler & Cicchetti, 1992). Other studies have found that, for these disorders, psychotherapy—especially cognitive-behavioral and interpersonal therapies—can result in benefits that are greater and more enduring than drug treatments (e.g., Hollon & Beck, 1994; Weissman & Markowitz, 1994). Nevertheless, many clients who might once have received psychotherapy alone are now getting drugs, or drugs and psychotherapy, even though they might have done just as well without them (Barlow, 1996).

The Emergence of Practice Guidelines

How is a therapist to know which form of treatment will be most effective with a given client? This version of Paul's (1969) "ultimate question" about treatment has still not been answered, but day-to-day decisions about treatment planning must be made, and here, too, one can see the growing influence of managed care systems on treatment practices.

Numerous sets of *practice guidelines* are now being published in the United States by health care corporations, by professional organizations such as the American Psychiatric Association (APA, 1995) and the American Association of Applied and Preventive Psychology (Hayes et al., 1995), and by federal government bodies such as the National Institutes of Health and the Agency for Health Care Policy and Research (Depression Guideline Panel, 1993). Guidelines are also appearing in the United Kingdom, Australia, New Zealand, and many other countries (e.g., Barlow, 1996; Roth & Fonagy, 1995; Quality Assurance Project, 1985). These guidelines are designed to steer mental health care providers toward treating specific problems—such as anxiety disorders, depression, schizophrenia, bipolar disorder, eating disorders, and substance-use disorders—with methods that maximize effectiveness while minimizing cost (VandenBos, 1993).

Most practice guidelines encourage the use of therapies that possess efficacy and effectiveness. Treatment *efficacy* is established by evidence from controlled, internally valid research showing that a treatment reliably produces specific effects. A treatment's *effectiveness* is established when research on its beneficial effects are shown to have external validity—that is, when it is shown to have practical usefulness when employed with clients in a variety of settings.

Practice guidelines have proven controversial because (1) they are perceived as restricting clinicians' freedom; (2) the empirical basis, and thus the validity, of some recommendations has been questioned; (3) recommendations from differing sources may be inconsistent; and (4) they tend to "medicalize" the treatment of many disorders that can be effectively treated without drugs. Indeed, the American Psychological Association has recently published a set of suggestions for evaluating recommendations contained in various practice guidelines (APA Board of Professional Affairs Task Force, 1995).

In an attempt to remedy the problems created by the proliferation of numerous uncoordinated practice guidelines, the Association for the Advancement of Behavior Therapy and the American Association for Applied and Preventive Psychology jointly sponsored a National Planning Summit on Scientifically Based Behavioral Health Practice Guidelines (Hayes, 1996). The idea behind this meeting—which took place in November of 1996 and was attended by representatives of managed care organizations, government agencies, and organizations of psychiatrists, psychologists, counselors, nurses, and social workers—was to begin working toward a set of empirically-based treatment guidelines that can be confidently used by all mental health practitioners, regardless of which third-party payer is involved in a client's treatment. Accomplishing this goal is a tall order, to say the least, so it is unlikely that universally agreed-upon practice guidelines will be adopted in the near future.

INTERVENTION RESEARCH AT WORK

Q.: To what extent does research on the effectiveness of various forms of clinical intervention affect your clinical work? Does the availability of a list of empirically validated methods affect your work?

DR. SANDY D'ANGELO: Because of the extensive literature in the child clinical field, I tend to review closely only a limited number of focal topics that frequently occur in my practice; these include treatment of autism, parent training, and attention deficit hyperactivity disorder. However, working in a medical center, I also evaluate many children with rare congenital or acquired syndromes, and with each of these, I must review the literature to determine what types of cognitive deficits are typically found in these children; this information helps me advise parents about their children's prognosis and the educational services the children might need. I generally search for information through on-line services such as Medline; a list of validated methods is helpful, but not essential.

DR. HECTOR MACHABANSKI: Research on various forms of clinical interventions informs my clinical work to the extent that it is useful in dealing with the problems and cultural characteristics of particular clients.

DR. GEOFFREY THORPE: Research on treatment effectiveness has an immense impact on my work. In working with clients to develop a treatment plan, I always recommend that we include methods with demonstrated effectiveness for their problems (when relevant data are available). However, I am opposed to mindlessly linking specific treatments to specific diagnoses; doing so risks ignoring important individual differences among clients. Indeed, such mechanical linking is inconsistent with behavior therapy principles, which stem from experimental psychology and emphasize research with single cases. In any event, we do not yet have all the answers to treating all disorders, so it is important to experiment with new techniques, especially when dealing with relatively unresearched problems (Thorpe & Olson, 1997).

CHAPTER SUMMARY

Evaluative research on clinical interventions has focused mainly on the effects of various forms of psychotherapy. The goals of this research are to answer questions about the efficacy of specific treatments, the relative effectiveness of different treatments, the components of treatment responsible for improvement, the durability of treatment benefits, the negative side-effects associated with treatment, client acceptance of treatment, the cost-effectiveness of various treatments, and their clinical and social significance.

The main method for establishing a causal relationship between therapy and improvement is the controlled experiment, in which the researcher makes systematic changes in certain factors (called independent variables) and then observes changes occurring in other factors (called dependent variables). In psychotherapy-outcome research, the independent variable is usually the type of therapy given, and the dependent variable is the change seen in clients. Within-subject experiments (including reversal, or ABAB, designs) manipulate a treatment variable and observe its effects on the same client(s) at different points in time. Between-subject experiments randomly assign clients to different groups, each of which is exposed to differing treatments whose effects are compared.

Psychotherapy-outcome experiments should be designed to be as high as possible on both internal and external validity. If an experiment is high on internal validity, the researcher can be confident that observed changes in clients were actually caused by treatment, not by uncontrolled confounding factor(s). An experiment is high on external validity if its results are generalizable to clients, problems, and situations other than those included in the experiment. Unfortunately, in order to exert the experimental control necessary to maximize internal validity, researchers are usually forced to use clients, therapists, problems, treatments, and settings that may not be representative enough to allow for high external validity. External validity can be increased by studying real clients with real problems in real treatment settings, but the loss of experimental control in such studies may impair internal validity.

In spite of Hans Eysenck's initial claim that traditional psychotherapy is no more beneficial than receiving no treatment, most subsequent reviews, meta-analyses (studies that quantitatively summarize the results of many outcome experiments), and client surveys suggest that most forms of psychotherapy do produce better outcomes than no treatment, but that various types of therapy are about equally effective. It also appears that the effects of psychotherapy are relatively durable, that the benefits of therapy often begin to appear after six to eight sessions, and that therapists' training and experience has a less-than-expected impact on the success of treatment. The same general conclusions hold for group, couples, and family therapy.

Psychosocial rehabilitation programs can help mental patients function at maximum capacity and avoid rehospitalization, especially if the patients participate in these programs for an extended period. The effects of a wide variety of programs designed to prevent mental disorders are mixed; the best of them tend to intervene early in people's lives in order to alter many of the risk factors known to be associated with specific disorders.

Today's clinical interventions are shaped not only by research on psychotherapy, psychosocial rehabilitation, and prevention programs, but also by the economic realities of health care in the 1990s, especially the trend toward managed care.

Chapter 10

Clinical Child Psychology

Clinical psychology has its roots in the assessment and treatment of childhood disorders. As noted in Chapter 1, for example, Lightner Witmer's goal in establishing the first psychological clinic in the United States was to treat children's academic and behavioral problems. Other early clinical psychologists applied revised versions of Alfred Binet's mental ability tests to identify children with special intellectual needs and gifts. It is surprising, then, that for much of this century, behavior disorders in childhood were largely overlooked in favor of adult disorders (Rubenstein, 1948). Indeed, the study of childhood disorder was, for a long time, simply "... a downward extension and extrapolation from the study of psychopathology in adults." (Garber, 1984, p. 30).

This adult-oriented approach to childhood disorders can be seen in early versions of the *Diagnostic and Statistical Manual* (DSM). With few exceptions (e.g., adjustment reactions), the 1952 DSM-I ignored childhood disorders, while the 1968 DSM-II noted only a few disorders unique to childhood (e.g., hyperkinesis reaction). It was only with the publication of DSM-III in 1980 that childhood disorders received broad coverage in the official diagnostic classification system.

This longstanding adult-oriented perspective on childhood disorders reflects the history of the very concept of childhood itself. Only recently have children been considered and treated as something other than miniature adults. This "adultomorphic" view was reinforced by psychoanalytic and behavioral approaches to therapy, both of which have tended to downplay the unique nature of childhood problems (Gelfand

& Peterson, 1985). Because Freud's theory focused so much on early childhood development, it may seem paradoxical to accuse psychoanalysis of adultomorphism, but Freud did not see children as good candidates for psychoanalytic treatment, and "... many analysts' formulations of patients' problems seem remarkably little affected by their patients' ages" (Gelfand & Peterson, 1985, p. 41). In similar fashion, the radical behavior therapy that was so influential in the 1960s and 1970s ignored the unique nature of childhood disorders. Its guiding principle was "an organism is an organism," be it a rat, a child, or an adult. Because all organisms are subject to the same laws of learning, developmental level became an irrelevant issue in treatment planning (Baer, 1973).

During the last three decades, this adult-oriented approach to children's behavior disorders has given way to a more child-centered approach. This new approach highlights several aspects of childhood that make it inappropriate to try using adult models of psychopathology to understand children's disorders. Clinical child psychologists are also discovering that traditional adult-oriented methods of classification, assessment, and intervention may have limited relevance for childhood disorders. The changing approach to child clients appeared in DSM-III, which was the first version of DSM to make specific recommendations concerning developmental considerations in the diagnostic criteria for childhood disorders. Today, DSM-IV contains more than two dozen Axis I disorders specific to children. In addition, since 1970 several major new journals have appeared—such as the *Journal of Abnormal Child Psychology*, the *Journal of Clinical Child Psychology*, and *Development and Psychopathology*—devoted entirely to research on childhood behavior disorders. APA's Division 12 (Clinical Psychology) now has two sections devoted to children: Section 1 (clinical child) and Section 5 (pediatric). Finally, a new field of study known as *developmental psychopathology* has evolved to study childhood disorders from a developmental perspective. Scientists working in this field focus on how various adaptive and maladaptive patterns of behavior are manifested during various stages of development (Sroufe & Rutter, 1984). Developmental psychopathologists also study how children develop competencies as well as disorders (Masterpasqua, 1989; Strayhorn, 1988), and they try to learn about protective factors that prevent some children at risk for disorders from actually developing them (Mash & Dozois, 1996).

After so many years of neglect, why is so much attention being devoted to understanding and treating childhood psychopathology? There are a number of reasons. First, psychopathology is relatively common in childhood; 8% to 22% of children are diagnosed with a behavioral, emotional, or learning disorder (Mash & Dozois, 1996). Second, many childhood disorders (e.g., conduct disorders, learning disabilities, autism) have lifelong consequences for the affected individual, the family, and society at large. For example, it can cost society over $40,000 a year to keep a child in a residential placement (Zigler et al., 1992). Third, most adult disorders have their roots in childhood disorders that may go undiagnosed and untreated. One recent epidemiological study found that only 26% of adults with a psychiatric disorder had no diagnosable problems in childhood (Newman et al., 1996). Another study found that fewer than 15% of children with a diagnosable psychiatric disorder had received any outpatient mental health services in the preceding year (Goodman et al., in press). Finally, by studying the risk factors, causes, and course of childhood disorders, we may be better able to develop effective early intervention programs that prevent childhood problems from escalating into adult psychopathology.

In this chapter, we discuss several characteristics and concerns that differentiate clinical child psychology from the general field of clinical psychology. We first provide an overview of clinical child psychology, and then focus on the classification, assessment, and treatment of childhood disorders.

CHARACTERISTICS UNIQUE TO CLINICAL CHILD PSYCHOLOGY

In dealing with their young clients, clinical child psychologists must pay special attention to referral issues, developmental considerations, infant temperament factors, the quality of infants' early attachments, the nature of parent–child interactions, and the impact of childhood stressors.

Referral Issues

When adults feel distressed they can seek professional help, but children do not have this option. They must depend on parents, teachers, or other significant people in their lives to determine whether they need the help of a mental health professional. A child may suffer considerable distress, but if the parents are unaware of, or are indifferent to, the problem, the child will not receive needed attention. Conversely, as noted in our discussion of family therapy in Chapter 7, children may be referred to a mental health professional for reasons that have more to do with parental or family problems than with the child's emotional or behavioral characteristics (Christensen, Margolin, & Sullaway, 1992).

Among the parental factors that influence whether children will be referred for psychological help is the parents' level of tolerance for certain behaviors. For example, parents who perceive noncompliance as temporary and manageable are less likely to seek help for their child than are parents who see the same behavior as permanent and unmanageable (Shepherd, Oppenheim, & Mitchell, 1971).

Maternal depression is another factor influencing the referral of children for clinical intervention. Research consistently shows that the more depressed mothers feel, the more likely they are to see their children as behaviorally disordered (Griest, Wells, & Forehand, 1979; Webster-Stratton, 1988). Of course, there are several possible explanations of these correlational findings (Richters, 1992). Maternal depression may indeed lead mothers to view their children as disordered; depressed individuals see many aspects of their world in a negative light. Or, it might be that unmanageable child behavior contributes to the mothers' feelings of helplessness and depression. It may even be that a third factor, such as the father's indifference, could account for both the mother's depression and the child's behavioral problems. Whatever the case, results such as these suggest that mothers' emotional states may influence how they perceive their children's behavior, their own capacity to cope with it, and thus the likelihood of referring children for professional help. (Fathers' emotional states appear less influential; Webster-Stratton, 1988).

Developmental Considerations

The particularly rapid physical, psychological, and social developments that take place in childhood have profound implications for clinical child psychology.[1] For one thing, clinicians must evaluate the appropriateness or inappropriateness of a child's behavior relative to developmental norms in the child's culture. Thus, intense fears or bedwetting might be considered normal in young children, but a symptom of disorder in older children (Campbell, 1989). In fact, most symptoms of childhood disorders tend to be seen as appropriate, or at least typical, behavior at an earlier stage of development. For example, the hallmark symptoms of attention-deficit hyperactivity disorder—including restlessness, overactivity, and distractability—are reported by the parents of about half of nonreferred preschool children (Lapouse & Monk, 1958; Werry & Quay, 1971). With the exception of symptoms associated with autism, mental retardation, and other severe disorders, the appropriateness of children's behavior must be evaluated in light of their developmental stage (Mash & Dozois, 1996).

Theoretical explanations of children's problems must also take developmental factors into account. For example, learned helplessness—the belief that one's actions do not affect events—is a popular model for explaining depression in adults. Adults susceptible to such beliefs tend to attribute their failures to permanent internal characteristics ("I failed the test because I am stupid."), whereas a psychologically healthier response would be to make temporary, external attributions ("The test was unfair." or "I did not study enough this time."). A major premise of this model is that failures produce a sense of helplessness when adults perceive there is nothing they can do to alter outcomes. However, a developmental study of causal attributions found that younger children (kindergarten, first-, third-graders) were less susceptible to helpless attributions following failure than were older children (fifth-graders; Rholes et al., 1980). One reason for the difference may be that younger children do not see ability as a stable attribute, so failures do not imply stable limitations on their likelihood of future successes. Younger children's attributional style may protect them against the onset of perceived helplessness. With increasing age, children may become more realistic—and perhaps more pessimistic—about their capabilities (Ruble & Rholes, 1981).

If clinicians are to avoid making errors in explaining children's disorders, it is important that they familiarize themselves with the developmental literature on the presumed causes of those disorders (Burbach & Peterson, 1986; Furman, 1980).

Infant Temperament

When people who have several children describe their parenting experiences, they are likely to express amazement at how different each child is, from infancy onward.

---

[1]Of course, these developmental processes do not stop when individuals reach adulthood, which is why many developmental psychology courses cover not just childhood, but life-span development. Accordingly, the developmental considerations discussed in this section may also be relevant in varying degrees to the study of psychopathology at any age.

These parental observations are well supported by empirical investigations. Several landmark studies have discovered reliable temperamental differences among infants that appear at birth and have both short-term and long-term implications (Thomas, Chess, & Birch, 1968; Thomas & Chess, 1977; Chess & Thomas, 1986).

Temperament refers to the infant's behavioral style, how the infant reacts to and even produces environmental events. In the New York Longitudinal Study, for example, rating infants on nine dimensions—such as activity level, response to new stimuli, intensity of reactions, disposition, and distractibility—allowed their temperaments to be classified as "easy," "difficult," or "slow-to-warm-up" (Thomas, Chess, & Birch, 1968).

"Easy" children adapt well to new situations, are not easily upset, show regularity in biological functions such as feeding and sleeping, and pose few problems for their parents. Parents whose first child displays this "easy" temperament often wonder why other parents complain so much about child-rearing problems. The reason is that some of them have a "difficult" child, who is easily upset, irregular in biological functioning, shows intense and often negative reactions to environmental changes, and in general drains the parents' energy and patience. Indeed, the parents of a "difficult" first child may wonder at times whether they ever want to have another child. The "slow-to-warm-up" child falls somewhere between the "easy" and "difficult" types.

One of the most important implications of infant temperament for clinical child psychology is that "difficult" infants tend to be at greatly increased risk for developing conduct problems, stormy relationships with peers, and academic difficulties when they enter first grade (Thomas, Chess, & Birch, 1968). Further, temperament at age three has also been found to predict behavioral problems twelve years later (Caspi et al., 1995) and personality traits fifteen years later (Caspi & Silva, 1995). These data suggest that some childhood behavioral problems are partly a function of the child's innate biological characteristics. These findings have created a renewed interest in the *diathesis-stress model* of psychopathology (see Nietzel et al., 1998). As described in Chapter 2, the diathesis-stress model emphasizes the interaction between a biological predisposition and environmental stressors in the appearance of behavioral problems.

Jerome Kagan's (1989) research on overly inhibited children provides an excellent example of how early temperament can act as a diathesis in the development of subsequent clinical difficulties. Kagan found that 10% to 15% of very young children are constitutionally shy and inhibited in unfamiliar situations. Compared to noninhibited children, they tend to be more behaviorally cautious, motorically tense, and physiologically aroused. When asked to fall backwards onto a mattress, for example, overly inhibited children are more likely to fall into a sitting position rather than relax and let gravity take over completely. Similarly, overly inhibited children have higher heart rates and increased cardiac acceleration in response to mild stressors. Being overly inhibited appears to be a stable characteristic that places these children at increased risk for developing various anxiety disorders, much as children with difficult, underinhibited temperaments tend to be at higher risk for conduct disorders (Nietzel et al., 1998). In short, children at opposite ends of the temperament spectrum seem to carry a diathesis for different kinds of disorders. Whether or not they actually display them, of course, depends on the influence of various stressors, parenting practices, and other environmental factors.

Early Attachment

Infant temperament can have an impact on the nature and quality of the *attachment* that develops between babies and their caregivers. According to the object relations theories described in Chapter 8, the nature and quality of this attachment—especially in the first year of life—play a crucial role in shaping the child's personality (Jones, 1996). Attachment theory has led many clinical child psychologists to look for links between the nature of infants' early attachments and the appearance of psychopathology in childhood, adolescence, and adulthood (Cicchetti, Toth, & Lynch, 1995).

According to attachment theory, infants have an innate need to form a strong emotional bond with at least one caregiver, and they arrive with a built-in repertoire of behaviors—such as smiling and cooing—designed to maintain proximity to the caregiver. Separation from the caregiver produces crying and other distress reactions designed to get the caregiver's attention and services (Beck, 1991; Bowlby, 1969). From an evolutionary perspective, these behaviors are adaptive because they increase the likelihood that the caregiver will meet the infant's needs, thereby increasing its chances for survival.

John Bowlby, a British psychiatrist and psychoanalyst, developed an influential version of attachment theory while assessing the mental health needs of very young children who were orphaned and left homeless by World War II (Bowlby, 1969; Zeanah, 1996). Inspired by earlier research on insitutionalized infants, (Spitz, 1946), Bowlby suggested that the depression, weight loss, and other psychological and physical problems shown by some of these infants stemmed from the fact that, while orphanages were meeting their charges' physical needs, there were not enough caregivers available to allow the infants to form a firm attachment to at least one caregiver. This idea is consistent with the results of experiments by Harry Harlow (e.g., Harlow & Zimmerman, 1959) in which monkeys deprived of attachment experiences from infancy displayed a variety of emotional problems.

Mary Ainsworth, an American psychologist, is credited with developing experimental procedures, called the Strange Situation, for measuring the nature and quality of one- to two-year-old children's attachments to their caregivers (Ainsworth & Wittig, 1969). The Strange Situation exposes children to several stressors and observes their reactions to each. First, the mother and child enter a playroom and the clinician observes the child's ability to separate from the mother and explore. Then, a stranger enters the room and starts talking with the mother. Shortly thereafter, the mother leaves the room for approximately three minutes, then returns. In another episode, the baby is left alone in the room for up to three minutes.

The child's responses to separations from the mother and to subsequent reunions with her are the primary targets of measurement. Using the Strange Situation, Ainsworth found that most babies (about 70%) displayed what she called secure attachment, while the rest showed insecure forms of attachment. Subsequent work has identified three types of insecure attachments: avoidant, resistant/ambivalent, and disorganized/disoriented (Beck, 1991). Securely attached babies, even if distressed by their mother's departure, are easily comforted by her return. Insecurely attached infants either avoid the mother when she returns (the avoidant type) or approach her but are not comforted by her (the resistant/ambivalent type). The disorganized/disoriented group display the greatest apparent insecurity, and their responses are often contradictory (e.g., approaching the mother but looking away). According to attachment theory, these different patterns of responding are assumed to be determined by the babies' experiences with their caregivers. Securely attached infants have been found to have warm, loving mothers who are sensitive to their needs, whereas insecurely attached infants tend to have distant, rejecting, or inconsistent mothers (Cicchetti et al., 1995).

Attachment theorists argue that people's view of themselves, as well as the quality of all subsequent relationships, are colored by the kind of attachment they had with their caregiver in infancy. For example, infants whose attachment was impaired by the behavior of distant, insensitive mothers may come to view themselves as unworthy of love, and, in adulthood, they may never find close relationships capable of meeting their emotional needs. Recent work has also suggested that infants who experienced different types of insecure attachments may be at risk for different types of disorders (Cicchetti et al., 1995). Thus, aggressive behavior in children has been found to be associated with the disorganized/disoriented pattern of attachment (Lyons-Ruth, 1996), while depressive disorders tend to be associated with insecure-avoidant attachment (Cicchetti et al., 1995). Recently, researchers have found evidence of early attachment types in the behavior of adolescents and adults (Main, 1996) and have related these patterns to the appearance of a variety of disorders (del Carmen & Huffman, 1996). Preliminary results of new therapeutic interventions designed to improve the quality of infant-caregiver attachment have been encouraging (Cicchetti et al., 1995).

Although caregivers obviously play a crucial role in the attachment process, it is important not to give them all the credit or blame for the kind of attachment that develops with their babies. It is also the case that infants differ in their ability to form attachments with a caregiver, and differences in temperament may make it easier or harder for caregivers to form attachments to them. Indeed, the quality of attachment probably results from the mutual influence of caregiver and infant characteristics (Greenberg, Speltz, & DeKlyen, 1993; Sroufe, 1985).

Parent–Child Interaction Patterns

Research on infant temperament and its role in attachment has changed clinical child psychologists' views of parent–child interactions in general. Specifically, it has caused them to pay closer attention to what the *child* brings to the relationship. While traditional psychodynamic theory stressed parents' influences on their child's development, findings from longitudinal studies on temperament suggest that the child's behavior influences the parents just as much (Thomas & Chess, 1977). These studies showed, for example, that initial assessments of parent–child interactions across the three infant-temperament categories showed few differences. During subsequent assessments, however, the parents of "difficult" infants issued more controlling statements and engaged in more punitive interactions with their children. These results suggest that, to some extent, at least, it is the child's difficult behavior that creates—or triggers—parents' inappropriate reactions.

This temperament-related interpretation of parent–child interactions contrasts with the traditional view that child psychopathology is mainly the result, not the cause, of faulty parenting. For example, the social withdrawal and bizarre behavior associated with childhood autism was once attributed to the cold, indifferent behavior exhibited by these children's so-called "refrigerator" mothers (Bettleheim, 1967; Kanner, 1943). This attribution was derived from observations of mothers with their autistic children, but it appears to have been a case of inferring causation from correlation. It now appears that these mothers' withdrawal and apparent emotional indifference was not the *cause* of their children's autism, but the *result* of having interacted for years with a child who does not communicate and respond normally.[2]

Other researchers have found that the punitive behavior often shown by the parents of hyperactive children has more to do with the children's behavior than the parents' disciplinary style. In one study, for example, when hyperactive children were given medication that improved their behavior, their parents immediately behaved more positively toward them (Barkley & Cunningham, 1979). Similar effects have been seen in the behavior of the teachers and peers of hyperactive children (Cunningham, Siegel, & Offord, 1985; Whalen, Henker, & Dotemoto, 1980).

A final example of the powerful effects of children's behavior on their parents comes from a study which investigated the relationship between adult alcohol consumption and child behavioral problems (Lang et al., 1989). Parental alcohol problems can certainly contribute to behavior disorders in their children, but this study addressed the reciprocal question: Can child behavior disorders contribute to adult alcohol consumption? To find out, sixteen male and sixteen female undergraduate students were asked to interact with either a normal child or a boy trained to act like a hyperactive child. The students were told that the purpose of the study was to examine the effects of adult alcohol consumption on child behavior. After this initial, baseline interaction, the students were allowed to drink as much beer as they wanted before going back for a second interaction. The second interaction never took place, however, because the researchers were interested only in how much beer the students consumed and how distressed they reported feeling during the first interaction. The results indicated that students who interacted with the "hyperactive" child were significantly more distressed than those who spent time with the normal child. Moreover, the males in the "hyperactive" condition consumed significantly more alcohol than did males in the "normal" condition (there were no differences in consumption for female students). So for males, at least, having a distressing interaction with a difficult-to-manage child was associated with significantly greater alcohol consumption. The external validity of this laboratory analogue is threatened by the fact that these students were not parents with an identified alcohol problem (see Chapter 9), but the results are suggestive nevertheless.

---

[2]We are all subject to the kind of fallacious thinking that led to incorrect causal theories about the causes of autism. What did you say to yourself the last time you witnessed a mother yelling at her child? Did you conclude that the child was difficult or that the mother's parenting probably caused the child's misbehavior? A single observation simply does not allow a clear picture of the interacting causes of behavior disorder, especially in children.

In summary, clinical child psychologists now realize that it is overly simplistic to attribute all children's behavioral problems to faulty parenting. It is equally unlikely, however, that all child psychopathology can be understood exclusively in terms of the child's characteristics. The parent–child relationship, like all dyadic interactions, is reciprocal in nature; the child's temperament and behavior affect the parents, and parental tolerance and responses alter the child's behavior. The term *goodness-of-fit* has been used to capture the idea that whether a child develops a behavioral problem is partially a function of the degree to which the child's temperament and the parental response style are concordant (Thomas & Chess, 1977). The greater the mismatch (e.g., rigid parents with a "difficult" infant), the greater the likelihood that the child will be at risk for subsequent problems.

Many of the advances in understanding and treating childhood behavior disorders that have occurred in the last three decades have been made by theorists who take this reciprocal or bidirectional view of parent–child interactions.

The Coercion-Escalation Hypothesis of Aggressive Behavior. Gerald Patterson's (1976, 1982) work on the reciprocal nature of interactions between aggressive children and their parents is an excellent case-in-point. As would be expected from our earlier discussion, his detailed observations in the homes of normal and aggressive children showed that in both kinds of homes, parents' behavior alter the probability of certain child responses, just as the children's behavior alters the likelihood of certain parental responses (Patterson et al., 1969). However, Patterson also saw important differences in the family interactions of normal versus aggressive children. For example, aggressive children were twice as likely as nonaggressive children to persist in their aversive behavior following parental punishment (Patterson, 1976).

Rather than seeing this pattern as reflecting parents' ineffective punishment tactics *or* children's insensitivity to the consequences of their behavior, Patterson looked at how parents and children "teach" each other to adopt and rely on coercive, aversive control tactics that can lead to childhood aggressiveness. Here is a simple example: Suppose that Wanda has just picked up her three-year-old son, Billy, from day-care and they are now at the grocery store, buying food for dinner. As they pass a freezer case, Billy asks for an ice cream bar, but Wanda says "No, you'll spoil your dinner." Billy responds by throwing a temper tantrum, which creates a problem for Wanda because she needs to finish her shopping and, besides, it is embarrassing to have her child acting out-of-control in public. Wanda solves the problem by giving Billy an ice cream bar, but with the admonition that this is the last time he will get one this close to dinner. Billy's tantrum stops immediately, and the shopping proceeds.

What do Billy and his mother learn from this interaction? First, Billy learns that if he throws a temper tantrum when his mom says "No," he can get his way (tantrum-throwing is positively reinforced). At the same time, Wanda is reinforced for giving in to Billy's demands—especially when he throws a tantrum in public—because doing so terminates his aversive and humiliating behavior. The principles of operant conditioning outlined in Chapter 8 suggest that both Billy and his mother will behave in similar ways when confronted with similar situations in the future. Billy will throw tantrums and Wanda, despite her best intentions to the contrary, will give in to them. Indeed, not giving in will probably cause Billy to escalate the intensity of his tantrum—perhaps including physical aggression or damage to property—until Wanda feels she has no choice but to give him what he wants. This family dyad has fallen into what Patterson (1982) called the "reinforcement trap"—each obtains a short-term benefit at the expense of undesirable long-term consequences. As Billy becomes harder to manage, his parents may resort to more aversive methods to control him.

As noted later, Patterson's work on understanding children's aggressive behavior has led to the development of a systematic and widely employed behavioral intervention program for dealing with such problems (Patterson, 1975).

Childhood Stressors

Adopting a diathesis-stress model of psychopathology requires clinical child psychologists to look not only at diatheses (such as temperament, attachment problems, cognitive deficits, and genetic influences), but also at a variety of environmental stressors that are likely to make expression of disorder more likely. Among these stressors are maladaptive parenting (including physical or sexual abuse), parental disability, psychopathology or discord, multiple hospitalizations, loss of a parent through divorce or death, the birth of a sibling, exposure to poverty, and the trauma of war (Freud & Burlingham, 1943; Garmezy, 1983; Lyons, 1971). Here we focus on three common childhood stressors—going to school, parental marital conflict, and abuse.

Going to School.   Because it is mandatory in North America and many other cultures, going to school constitutes the single greatest source of stress for many children. Indeed, the age of six—when most children enter first grade—is the peak referral point for childhood disorders, including learning disabilities, attention-deficit hyperactivity disorder, conduct and oppositional disorders, and peer relationship difficulties. Most of these problems stem from, arise in, or are exacerbated by the school environment.

What is it about school that makes it such a potent stressor? Consider what is required of children entering first grade. They must sit quietly for what seems to them to be long periods of time while focusing their attention on mastering complex new skills (e.g., reading, math) that make heavy demands on the children's cognitive resources. Further, they need a certain amount of social skill in order to be accepted by and succeed with their peers. Finally, children must constantly comply with their teacher's requests. Children who fail at one or more of these tasks are very likely to be labeled as displaying one of the primary behavior disorders of childhood (which tend to involve learning difficulties, noncompliance, peer conflicts or rejection, and attentional problems).

Because most child referrals involve school-related difficulties, clinicians routinely collect assessment data directly from the school setting (usually in the form of teacher ratings or observations) or from school-related measures such as achievement tests. Accordingly, clinical child psychologists must be knowledgeable about what is considered normal and abnormal in school functioning—including how learning disabilities are assessed and diagnosed—as well as about legal issues affecting school referrals and placements. Clinical treatment of children often takes place in the school and may involve training teachers in classroom management procedures (O'Leary & O'Leary, 1972) or helping them develop social-skills training programs for their students. As a result, clinical child psychologists may find themselves seeking compromises between the wishes of the school (e.g., to place a disruptive child in a special class) and the concerns of parents (e.g., to avoid stigmatizing their child with a "special class" label).

Working in school settings helps clinical child psychologists understand how those settings can either increase or decrease the likelihood of behavioral and learning problems (Rutter et al., 1979) and how important school-based programs can be in efforts at primary prevention of behavior disorders (see Chapter 7).

Parental Conflict and Divorce. As of 1990, approximately 45% of children in the United States were not living with both their natural parents. This figure does not begin to represent all the children who are affected by severe parental conflict, because many discordant marriages or other relationships are not dissolved (Emery, 1982). Exposure to parental conflict and divorce creates several sources of stress, all of which can have significant effects on children's physical, psychological, and behavioral functioning. For one thing, the child's standard of living often falls as parents shoulder the financial burden of maintaining two households. Children may also be caught up in the turmoil of a custody battle between their parents, and even if not, may have to shuttle between, and adapt to, differing home environments and parenting practices. Further, parenting skills often deteriorate, partly because each parent may now have to work alone, and partly because they may be experiencing depression, anger, and other psychological problems that impair their effectiveness as sources of discipline, guidance, and support. Finally, should one or both parents remarry, children must deal with a step-parent and, perhaps, step-siblings (Hetherington & Arasteh, 1988). Even then, the children of divorce are not out of the woods, because remarried parents are at increased risk for subsequent separations and divorce (Hetherington, Stanley-Hagan, & Anderson, 1989).

When children are exposed to so many stressors at once, the likelihood of mental health problems increases dramatically (Rutter, 1981). Boys, especially, tend to show marked increases in aggressive and noncompliant behavior, as well as disruptions in school work and peer relations during the two years following their parents' divorce. For girls, the findings are not as dramatic or clear-cut. The post-divorce problems that girls display tend to be less severe and to disappear in a year or so. This gender difference may be attributed to the tendency for boys to act out their problems and for girls to internalize them, thus making them less obvious. However, there is some evidence that divorce-related stress may result in delayed problems for girls, especially regarding heterosexual relations (Hetherington, 1989).

Individual differences in children can influence the effects that divorce has on them. For example, temperamentally "difficult" children show more adverse effects of divorce than do "easy" children (Hetherington, 1989). Age is also a factor. Preschool children often respond to divorce with behavioral regression and separation anxiety, whereas the most striking response of older children is intense anger at one or both parents (Wallerstein, Corbin, & Lewis, 1988).

Exactly how does divorce produce negative consequences in children? Is it the fact that the child now lives mainly with one parent (the mother, typically) and sees the other one much less frequently, if at all? The consensus among clinical child psychologists is that separation *per se* does not produce the adverse behavioral consequences associated with divorce (Emery, 1982). Instead, the active component appears to be the amount and intensity of marital conflict taking place prior to, during, and after the divorce. Divorces that are relatively amicable produce much less psychological and behavioral disturbance in children than those that are stormy.[3] Thus, when parents in distressed relationships ask clinical psychologists whether they should stay together for the benefit of the children, a common response is, "not if there is a high degree of conflict between you."

Clinical child psychologists are paying increasing attention to helping parents and children cope with the stressors associated with the dissolution of marriage or other long-term relationships (Grych & Fincham, 1992). For example, one program designed to help children cope with separation and divorce emphasizes three goals: (1) social support, whereby children are taught to share their feelings with other children facing a similar situation; (2) self-statement modifications, in which the children are trained to identify problem areas which they can and cannot control; and (3) training in appropriate ways of expressing anger (Pedro-Carroll & Cowen, 1985). Intervention programs have also been created for divorcing parents (Bloom, Hodges, & Caldwell, 1982). In these programs, parents are taught how to cope with their own feelings and how to help their children adjust to the disruptions in their lives (Grych & Fincham, 1992).

Child Abuse

The scope and seriousness of child abuse only came to public attention in the United States in the late 1960s and early 1970s, as signaled by the publication of a book called *The Battered Child Syndrome* (Helfer & Kempe, 1968). In 1974, the U.S. Congress passed the Federal Child Abuse Prevention and Treatment Act, and, since then, reports of abuse have increased dramatically. Between 1976 and 1984, for example, the rate of reported abuse rose approximately 10% per year (Wicks-Nelson & Israel, 1991), and it is now estimated that child abuse results in 570,000 serious injuries a year (Sedlak & Broadhurst, 1996). The increase in abuse reports may reflect some increase in the incidence of abusive behavior, but it also reflects major changes in public and professional sensitivity to and awareness of the problem of abuse. Thus, in 1976, only 10% of the U.S. population thought abuse was a serious problem; 90% of the population thought so ten years later (Wicks-Nelson & Israel, 1991). All U.S. states have made it a legal requirement that any teacher, physician, psychologist, or other health professional who suspects abuse must report the case to the appropriate social agencies.

---

[3]Obviously, a major confound in these studies is that conflict-filled divorces are more likely in families in which there had been higher rates of discord and aggression all along. Thus, children in these families may have been predisposed to aggressive and noncompliant behavior (Block et al., 1986).

The battered child syndrome originally centered on severe physical abuse (Helfer & Kempe, 1968). It was diagnosed from evidence of inexplicable or repeated injuries detected in X-rays and physical examinations. However, the definition of child abuse has now broadened to include neglect, psychological abuse, sexual abuse, and exploitation. *Neglect* refers to failure to sufficiently meet children's physical and/or emotional needs. *Psychological abuse* has proven more difficult to define; it consists of verbal and emotional assaults against the child, including rejection, degradation, and terrorizing (Hart & Brassard, 1987). Today, physically battered children make up only a minority of reported abuse cases. Not surprisingly, the primary perpetrators of neglect and physical and sexual abuse are parents, although siblings and other relatives, babysitters and day-care workers may also be responsible.

It is a common misconception among the public and professionals alike that if you were abused as a child, you are doomed to perpetuate the cycle by becoming an abusing parent. However, there is evidence that only about a third of abused children become abusive parents (Kaufman & Zigler, 1987). Though this tragic figure exceeds the rate for nonabused children, it still means that the majority of abused children do not become abusive parents. Another misconception is that the vast majority of abusive parents suffer from mental disorders. In fact, most of these people do not meet diagnostic criteria for any psychiatric disorder. So what *does* cause parents to abuse their children? Three general factors have been identified (Wicks-Nelson & Israel, 1991): (1) social and cultural influences, including poverty, stress, and a tolerance for violence and harsh disciplinary procedures; (2) parents' personal characteristics, including a history of abuse, low frustration tolerance, and aggressiveness; and (3) difficulties in the parent–child interaction, including inappropriate parental expectations or explanations for the child's behavior, ineffective disciplinary practices, and a temperamentally "difficult" child.

Craig Twentyman and his colleagues propose a four-stage cognitive-behavioral sequence to describe abusive incidents: (1) the parent initially sets unrealistic expectations for the child; (2) the child fails to meet these expectations; (3) the parent misattributes the child's inappropriate behavior to intentional characteristics (e.g., deliberate spitefulness); and (4) the parent overreacts to the child's willful disobedience and becomes abusive (Twentyman, Rohrbeck, & Amish, 1984). This pattern is intensified in homes where children are prone to misbehavior and where parents tend to overreact to environmental stressors.

Research suggests that abused children are at increased risk for behavioral and emotional problems, though not for any specific disorder (Browne & Finkelhor, 1986). Abused children are prone to later school failure, aggressiveness, depression, peer problems, and impaired sexual and marital relationships. In addition, these children tend to develop insecure attachments, to view interpersonal relationships as coercive, threatening, and unpredictable, and to interpret the behavior of others in a hostile and suspicious manner (Mash & Dozois, 1996). Finally, as many as 20% of abuse victims show serious psychopathology in adulthood, including depression, substance use, sexual dysfunctions, eating disorders, and personality disorders (Finkelhor & Browne, 1988). Only about a third of victims of childhood sexual abuse show no symptoms of psychopathology (Kendall-Tackett, Williams, & Finkelhor, 1993).

Historically, the primary intervention for abused children was to place them in foster care. The goal, obviously, is to remove children from dangerous environments and provide them with a stable and therapeutic setting. However, foster care has come under criticism for several reasons. First, it is expensive. Second, although it was designed to be short term in nature, it is not uncommon for abused children to spend many years living in a series of foster homes. Foster care placement is also designed to provide a respite for abusing parents during which time they can learn more appropriate parenting skills, but the necessary training often does not occur and when periods of separation are extended, it becomes difficult to reintegrate the child into the family home.

Today, treatment and prevention of child abuse focuses on working with both the victims and their parents (Wolfe, 1987). Intervention with parents usually concentrates on helping them to improve their disciplinary practices so as to reduce out-of-control incidents, on educating them about realistic expectations for their child's behavior, on training them in anger control and stress management, and on providing social support for those who feel isolated. Treatment may also focus on alleviating parents' marital discord, depression, or other problems that heighten the likelihood of child abuse. Interventions with abused children may involve an environmental enrichment program for those who exhibit developmental delays due to neglect or abuse. Alternatively, the intervention may be directed at specific behavioral or emotional problems arising from the abusive environment. For example, social skills training may be offered to socially withdrawn children, while impulse (or anger) control training or supportive therapy may be used with children experiencing emotional problems. Finally, some form of individual or group therapy may be provided for the victims of abuse. The goal of this therapy is to provide a safe environment in which children can express their feelings and gain a better understanding of what happened to them—including the fact that they are not responsible for their parents' abusiveness (Wenar, 1994). The therapy sessions also give children a chance to form a supportive relationship with an adult. There is evidence that having such a relationship with one adult can serve as a buffer against the effects of adverse environmental events, including maladaptive parenting.

Children's Testimony in Abuse Cases.   Probably no area in clinical child psychology is as controversial as that of children's testimony in trials involving charges of physical and sexual abuse. The controversy centers on whether children can give accurate testimony in the courtroom about abuse they have allegedly suffered or observed and whether testifying in court might have a negative impact on their psychological well-being (Saywitz, 1990). Trials can be an unnerving experience for anyone, and they can be especially distressing for children. "When children come in contact with the [legal] system, they typically follow a path of repeated contacts with strangers, in strange situations, governed by a set of unfamiliar rules" (Saywitz, 1990, p. 330). In addition, because children are usually testifying not against strangers, but against a parent, they are subject to conflicting pressures. One or both parents may employ subtle suggestions or even outright coercion to alter the child's testimony, and it is not unusual for child witnesses to be told repeatedly that their testimony may send their parent to prison for a long time. *Sexual abuse accommodation syndrome* (Summit, 1983), a pattern of delayed disclosure, recantation, or other alterations in testimony, may result from these pressures. Testifying in abuse cases can also be traumatic for children because their statements may not be believed. Judges and juries have long been skeptical of child witnesses because of limitations in children's cognitive development that may impair the accuracy of their testimony. They are especially worried about children's memory skills, ability to differentiate truth from fantasy, and susceptibility to suggestion.

Although the debate about whether children are competent to offer testimony in abuse cases is far from resolved (Ceci & Bruck, 1993), both researchers and the courts appear to be moving toward the conclusion that children's testimony, although not perfect, is "good enough" to be relied upon in the courtroom (Wrightsman, Nietzel, & Fortune, 1998). In other words, children's memory capacity may be less than adults, and they may not offer as many details in recalling events as adults do, but research also indicates that children are able to describe accurately the basic events that occurred. Further, when children do make errors in recall, they are likely to be errors of omission rather than errors of commission. That is, they are more likely to leave out information than to add erroneous events or details (Saywitz, 1990). Still, it is important to be cautious in drawing conclusions about the results of laboratory research on children's testimony, because real-life assessments of abuse accusations differ in an important way from these analogue studies (Ceci & Bruck, 1993). Specifically, abuse assessments frequently involve repeated questioning of children, a process that can lead children to believe that their initial answers may have been wrong and prompt them to change their responses to please the questioner. Thus, the fact that one-shot research studies suggest that children are not suggestible does not guarantee that, under repeated questioning, children will not make false accusations.

The growing tendency to accept children as witnesses in child abuse trials has been accompanied by recognition that special procedures may be needed to ensure the accuracy of their testimony and to minimize the stress that giving it may create. Thus, children are sometimes allowed to testify in another room so that they do not have to confront the accused, or they may be allowed to demonstrate alleged acts of abuse using puppets or other play materials (Koocher et al., 1995). The development and evaluation of such procedures provide examples of the roles that clinical child psychologists have played, and will continue to play, in helping the courts balance the rights of the accused and the accuser in child abuse cases.

CLINICAL ASSESSMENT OF CHILDREN

Clinical assessment of childhood and adult disorders share several features. Both are concerned with reliability, validity, and utility, and many of the same assessment procedures—such as interviewing and observations—are used with children and adults. However, as clinical child psychologists take special note of the child referral processes, developmental considerations, mandatory school attendance policies, and

---

TABLE 10.1 Questions Routinely Asked in the Clinical Assessment of Children

1. Why is this child being referred for help at this time?

2. Are there differences between the parents, or between the parents and teachers, in how they perceive this child?

3. Is the child having academic or behavior problems in school?

4. Is the child having problems at home, either with parents or siblings?

5. Are there family factors (e.g., marital discord) that may exacerbate the problem?

6. How does the child get along with his or her peers? Does he or she make social overtures? Are they accepted or are they rejected?

7. Does the child acknowledge that he or she has a problem; what symptoms are admitted?

8. How does the child feel about the referral? What are the child's explanations for the referral problem?

9. Is this a long-standing problem or a stage through which the child is going?

---

social/familial factors just discussed, they find themselves asking assessment questions about child clients that they would usually not ask about adults (see Table 10.1).

Recognition of these special issues also influences how clinicians collect assessment data on childhood disorders. For one thing, because parents and teachers refer children for mental health services, paramount attention is given to information supplied by these adults during interviews and on behavior rating scales. The value of interviews and tests to elicit children's self-reports about their problems tends to be limited by the children's often-unreliable memories and concrete cognitive styles. Second, because the majority of child referrals pertain to school-based problems, the clinical assessment of children routinely includes an evaluation of school performance, including intelligence and achievement testing. Third, children's emotional and behavioral states depend heavily on the nature of their family life. Accordingly, assessment of children often includes exploration of the child's behavior within the family (e.g., observations of mother–child interactions), as well as assessment of parental functioning (e.g., maternal depression, marital discord). A standard assessment battery for children includes behavior rating scales, clinical interviews, intelligence and achievement testing, structured observations, and family and peer interaction measures.

Behavior Rating Scales

Behavior rating scales are inexpensive and easy to administer. The forms can be completed and returned in advance of a clinic appointment so the information can be evaluated before the formal assessment begins, or parents can complete the forms while they are in the clinic's waiting room. Some scales, such as the Child Behavior Checklist (CBCL) (Achenbach & Edelbrock, 1981), can be computer-scored.

Standard rating scales cover most childhood behavioral problems, so they give clinicians a broad overview of the child, including conduct and anxiety problems as well as social relations and school functioning. In addition, normative data are available on rating scales such as the CBCL, thus allowing the child's behavior to be evaluated in comparison to a large group of children of similar age and gender. Finally, because they are easy to administer, rating scales can be used on repeated occasions, such as when monitoring the effectiveness of an ongoing treatment program. They also allow for the collection of standardized follow-up data, even after families have moved away.

The most frequently used behavior rating scales show high test–retest reliability and good validity (Achenbach, 1988). For example, scores on the Conners (1973) Ten-item Teacher Rating Scale can differentiate attention-deficit hyperactivity disorder (ADHD) children from children with other behavior problems, and can distinguish ADHD children on medication from those on placebo. These scale ratings can even detect behavioral changes associated with differing dosages of medication (Ross & Ross, 1982). However, rating scale data are subject to the information-processing biases discussed earlier, as well as to errors stemming from rater characteristics (Cairns & Green, 1979). Parents' mood, tolerance or intolerance of their child's behavior, and their desire to make their child look "good" or "bad" can all influence ratings (Webster-Stratton, 1988). The value of behavior ratings are also limited by the fact that they convey global impressions of children's behavior, but little information about important situational determinants of that behavior (Cairns & Green, 1979). Information about global traits may be helpful in diagnosing a child's problems, but it does not say what environmental factors trigger or reinforce problematic behavior. As we shall see later, knowing about those factors is crucial to establishing an effective treatment program.

Clinical Interviews

As in adult cases, clinical interviews are central to the assessment of childhood disorders. The clinician will usually interview the parents, as well as the referred child. When interviewing the parents, the clinician has the following goals in mind (Achenbach, 1988):

1. Establish rapport. Developing a close working relationship with the parents will make it easier for them to reveal personal information about themselves, the referred child, and the family. This relationship will also be valuable if the clinician ends up helping the parents with their own psychological and parenting problems.

2. Obtain specific details about the child's problem. What is it? When and where and how often does it occur? How do the parents and siblings respond? Interviews allow the clinician to follow up on rating scale responses by obtaining specific examples of problematic behaviors and situations.

3. Chart the course of the problem. When did it start? What triggered it? Is it continuous or sporadic?

4. Gather a developmental history of the child, including information on major developmental milestones, transition periods (e.g., starting school), and factors that may have disrupted normal development (e.g., hospitalizations, parental divorce).

5. Explore family factors that may exacerbate the child's problem. These factors might include marital discord, sibling rivalry, and parental mental disorder. When both parents are interviewed, the clinician will evaluate the degree to which they agree about the nature and origins of their child's problems, and will estimate the parents' abilities to participate in programs for dealing with those problems.

As described in Chapter 4, the validity of any interview can be threatened by various kinds of bias or error, and this is certainly true when parents describe their child's problems. Their memories are fallible, they have limited normative data on which to base judgments about the appropriateness of their child's behavior, they may have emotional problems that distort their responses, and they may be motivated to present their child in either a positive or negative light (especially during interviews relating to child custody battles or school placement decisions). Still, information from parental interviews is often helpful in piecing together the diagnostic puzzle.

Interviews with referred children, too, can offer valuable information about them and the environments in which their problems occur (La Greca, 1990; Mash & Terdal, 1988). The goals of child interviews include the following:

1. Establish rapport. Children often do not know why they are being interviewed and may misunderstand what their parents told them about the clinical evaluation. Some parents tell the child nothing about the clinic visit, or present only vague information (e.g., "We're going to take you to the doctor's office."). It is important to correct any misconceptions the child may have.

2. Evaluate the child's understanding of the problem that led to referral. Does the child feel there is a problem and, if so, what does he or she think is the cause?

3. Evaluate the child's explanations of problematic behavior. This goal is important in assessing the child's habitual way of thinking about the world. For example, does the child see others as hostile and threatening (see Figure 10.1)? Does the child believe that he or she is powerless to forestall failure at school (Diener & Dweck, 1978)?

4. Obtain a description of the fear, sadness, anxiety, anger, or low self-esteem associated with problems such as childhood depression and anxiety disorders (Ialongo et al., 1994).

5. Observe the child during the interview. By doing so, clinicians can confirm or revise impressions gained from interviewing the child's parents. These observations can also provide information about the child's cognitive maturity, activity level, and degree of compliance (Edelbrock et al., 1985). Informal observational assessments have limited validity, however. For example, one study found that 80% of hyperactive children displayed no signs of overactivity in the physician's office (Sleator & Ullmann, 1981).

Valuable as child interviews can be, clinicians do not usually rely on them very much in determining the severity of behavioral problems, in making a diagnosis, or in choosing a treatment approach because—especially when children are under the age

Imagine the following scenario: You are a third grader eating lunch in a school cafeteria. You look away and the next thing you know, milk is spilt all over your tray. You look at the boy next to you and he is laughing. How would you explain the milk getting onto your tray?

According to Dodge (1986), there are important differences between how aggressive and nonaggressive children explain this ambiguous event. Nonaggressive children would assume it was done by accident, while aggressive children would claim it was done on purpose. This tendency of the aggressive children to assume hostile intent in ambiguous situations (a *hostile attributional bias*) perpetuates their aggressive behavior and exacerbates their social difficulties. By assuming hostile intent, aggressive children feel more justified in retaliating. However, peers see this retaliation as unjustified, given the event was accidental. This retaliation therefore reinforces the peers' belief that these children are inappropriately aggressive and should be avoided. Thus, a vicious cycle is created in which the aggressive children think their peers are out to get them. They respond to this perceived threat by retaliating, which increases the likelihood that they will continue to have social difficulties.

FIGURE 10.1 Hostile attributional biases in aggressive children.

of ten—these interviews tend to have low reliability (Edelbrock et al., 1985). The reliability of child interviews increases with age of the child; adolescents are as reliable as, and sometimes more reliable than, their parents in reporting their behavioral problems. A new set of interview methods known as narrative elaboration has recently been shown to improve the accuracy of young children's self-reports (Saywitz & Snyder, 1996), but it will take further research to determine if these methods—which include visual recall cues as well as training in, practice with, and reminders to use memory retrieval skills—can aid memory without influencing its content.

Intelligence and Achievement Tests

If you only had one session to evaluate a child, your time might best be spent administering tests of IQ and academic achievement (e.g., reading, math, spelling) because:

1. Compared to any other test or interview procedure, IQ and achievement tests have the best normative data available, allowing for precise statements about the child's functioning relative to other children of the same age.
2. Excellent reliability and validity data exist for both types of tests. IQ scores are the single best predictor of children's current and future academic and occupational functioning.
3. The majority of child referrals involve academic and/or behavioral difficulties in the classroom, so it is necessary to determine what contribution learning problems, low intelligence, or inappropriate parent or teacher expectations may make to these problems.
4. These tests assess specific strengths and weaknesses in the child's academic and cognitive functioning (e.g., memory or visual-spatial deficits) and this information

can be used to make recommendations concerning treatment, special school placement or remediation.

5. Testing gives the clinician a standardized situation in which to observe the child's activity level, ability to follow instructions, speed of response, distractibility and attention span, friendliness, flexibility in thinking, anxiety, and response to feedback about success and failure (Sattler, 1988).

Against these advantages, the clinician must balance the following limitations on intelligence and achievement testing (Sattler, 1988):

1. The test environment is somewhat artificial and may yield an inaccurate picture of the child's performance in the classroom. Test anxiety may impair the performance of some children, while for others—such as ADHD children—the structured nature of testing may raise performance above what normally appears in the classroom.

2. IQ and achievement tests may be biased against minority children or children for whom English is a second language.

3. Too much credence can be given to a single IQ score, so that lowered expectations about a child's ability become self-fulfilling prophesies that lead to declining performance (Rosenthal & Rubin, 1978). Factors other than intelligence influence success in the classroom.

Projective Tests

Projective testing with children represents the domain in which the discrepancy is greatest between what research findings support and what clinicians actually do. Many clinicians' assessment batteries still include the Rorschach inkblot test, as well as projective tests specifically designed for children—including story-telling procedures such as the Children's Apperception Test (Bellak, 1954) and the Mutual Story-Telling Technique (Gardner, 1971), and drawing techniques such as the Draw-a-Person (Koppitz, 1968) and House-Tree-Person techniques (Buck, 1948; see Figure 10.2)—in spite of research showing that projectives fail to offer much useful assessment information about children (Martin, 1988).

Test–retest and interrater reliabilities for these tests are often unacceptably low (Gelfand, Jenson, & Drew, 1982; Gittelman, 1980), and there is little evidence that the tests measure what they purport to measure (Gittelman, 1980). Finally, there is no evidence for the *incremental validity* of projective tests. In other words, even if they did allow valid inferences about children (e.g., that signs of aggression on the CAT predicted aggressive behavior), it is usually the case that this same information is already available through interviews, observations, or other means. One investigator put it this way: projective tests with children "sometimes . . . tell us poorly something we already know" (Gittelman, 1980, p. 434).

Given their dismal track record, why do projective tests remain popular in the assessment of children? The answer is partly that drawing pictures or telling stories offer excellent ways for children to express themselves. As Jean Piaget (1962) pointed out,

FIGURE 10.2 An example of a drawing made by a child taking the House-Tree-Person Test. Adapted from Cummings (1986).

the nonverbal aspects of play allow children to create and understand their world. Many clinical child psychologists would agree that "[drawings] must be looked upon as a universal language of childhood whereby children of all races and cultures express their ideas of the world about them" (Goodenough, 1931, p. 505). The courts also recognize the importance of children's nonverbal expressions; judges routinely allow child witnesses to use anatomically correct dolls to help describe incidents of sexual abuse (Haugaard & Reppucci, 1988). Similarly, clinicians who work with children know that, often, the best way to break the ice and build rapport is to ask the child to draw a picture or tell a story. Unfortunately, there is no good evidence that clinical interpretations of these pictures or stories offer especially accurate insights into children's personalities, or especially accurate predictions about children's behavior outside the testing situation.

Behavioral Observations

More so than for adult disorders, behavioral observations are an integral part of the assessment of childhood disorders. Because children's problems usually occur in the home or school, observations in these settings give clinicians the opportunity to validate, or get new perspectives on, reports made by parents and teachers through rating scales and interviews. Thus, observations allow a more naturalistic assessment of the child's behavior, providing real-world information that interviews and tests cannot offer. Observational assessments are also vital to the behavioral techniques that have become the treatment of choice for many childhood disorders. These techniques require systematic observation of behaviors that are the targets of treatment, as well as of the environmental stimuli that elicit and reinforce those behaviors. Unlike rating scales, which offer global impressions, observations allow fine-grained analyses of these important stimulus–behavior–consequence relationships (Cairns & Green, 1979).

As noted in Chapter 6, Gerald Patterson and his colleagues were pioneers in the development of home observation systems. They first recorded the rate of noxious child behaviors (e.g., noncompliance, teasing, whining), then compared rates of inappropriate (and appropriate) behaviors across deviant and nonreferred children to quantify the characteristics of disturbed family interactions. They also tried to isolate those parent or sibling behaviors that elicited noxious responses from referred children. One important finding was that "sibling teases" can be a powerful stimulus for deviant responses. Observational data allowed Patterson and his colleagues to develop a theoretical model, discussed earlier, of how children's aggressive behavior begins and is maintained. Later, we describe an intervention program they developed for altering disturbed family interactions.

School observation systems focus primarily on classroom behavior (Abikoff et al., 1977), although playground behavior may also be monitored (Pelham & Bender, 1982). Classroom observations often concentrate on behaviors associated with ADHD.

Despite the benefits offered by observational assessment in the home or school, many clinicians hesitate to use these methods. For one thing, observation is expensive and time-consuming. Obtaining reliable and representative observational data requires a professional or paraprofessional observer to travel to the child's home or school and remain there for extended periods. If interrater reliability data are to be obtained, a second observer is needed. Home observations usually require that observers visit during the evening, when the entire family is present (and when hourly pay rates may be higher). Many clinicians also worry that placing observers in the child's home can change the environment enough to alter the family's interactions and thus undermine the validity of observational data. For example, Patterson's (1982) system requires that all family members be in sight, and that they not watch television or talk on the telephone. In such circumstances, if everyone tries to be on their best behavior, the clinician may not learn much about typical family life, or the child's problems.

To overcome some of these problems, clinicians often arrange for observations to be made in a clinic (Mash & Barkley, 1986). Clinic observations can be recorded on videotape by hidden cameras, making it unnecessary for trained observers to be present when the family comes in; tapes of several families can be evaluated later, at an observational analysis session. Further, clinic observations can be made under standardized conditions in which each child or family can be exposed to identical situations. For example, some clinics feature a simulated classroom that can be used to assess child behaviors related to ADHD (Milich et al., 1982). Similarly, Rex Forehand and his colleagues have employed a clinic observation system for assessing children's rates of noncompliance with parental commands (Forehand & McMahon, 1981).

Family and Peer Interaction Measures

Children live in different social worlds at home, at school, and at play, and clinicians often attempt to assess the impact of these multiple social environments.

Assessment of Children's Peer Relations. In the last three decades, interest among clinical child psychologists in the assessment of children's peer relations has increased (Landau & Milich, 1990). This is not surprising; just thinking back to childhood can help us recall how our emotional development was affected by how well, or how poorly, we got along with our peers (Hartup, 1983). Martha Putallaz and John Gottman (1983, p. 13) provide a poignant example of this point (spelling errors in the original):

> I can hide. i am a little boy. i don't have friends but i have som friends but win i wait at the busstop som people haet me and some like me . . . one day i was moveing so people would not tesz me in ne mor but again they tesz me.

Clinicians are also interested in children's peer relations because many social skills (e.g., sharing, taking turns, cooperating) are learned best through peer interactions, and because disturbed peer relations are one of the strongest predictors of later behavioral and psychological problems (Cowen et al., 1973).

Although mothers, teachers, or children themselves can provide some information about peer relations, a child's peer group offers the most reliable and valid data. In an assessment procedure known as *peer sociometics*, children evaluate their classmates or playmates by answering two simple questions: "Whom do you like?" and "Whom don't you like?". The answers to these questions allow any child in a group to be assigned two scores: a *popularity* index, which is the total number of classmates indicating they like the child; and a *rejection* index, which is the total number who dislike the child. Isolated children (low popularity, low rejection) differ in important ways from rejected (low popularity, high rejection) and popular (high popularity, low rejection) children. Isolated children make few social overtures, whereas both rejected and popular children initiate many social interactions. The overtures of popular children are successful, while those of the rejected children are rebuffed.

Although peer sociometric data tend to be reliable and valid, collecting these data can be difficult, and there are concerns that—especially at school—the use of sociometry risks stigmatizing rejected children (Hayvren & Hymel, 1984). Accordingly some clinicians prefer to assess a child's social interactions via teacher ratings (Greenwood et al., 1979) or by asking the child for self-reports on social anxiety, loneliness, and social goals (Asher & Wheeler, 1985; La Greca et al., 1988; Renshaw & Asher, 1983).

Assessment of Family Interactions. Clinical assessment of social interactions in children's families has a long history (Jacob & Tennenbaum, 1988). Early work in this area focused on parental behavior because faulty parental communication was presumed to produce child psychopathology (Mishler & Waxler, 1968). As this view was replaced by one in which parent–child interactions are seen as reciprocal (Bell & Harper, 1977), the primary assessment procedure involved observations of parent–child interactions (Patterson, 1982). More recently, there has been renewed interest in broader familial communication patterns (Alexander & Parsons, 1982; Foster & Robin, 1988). For example, communications by parents and siblings that are critical, hostile, or emotionally overinvolved may exacerbate a child's psychopathology even if they do not play a causal role (e.g., Rosenfarb et al., 1995). The next decade should see a further refinement of these assessment procedures. In addition, virtually all clinical child psychologists recognize that parental factors, such as marital discord, maternal depression, or paternal substance abuse, can influence a child's functioning and shape the focus of intervention strategies. Thus, measures of these characteristics are becoming a standard part of the assessment of referred children.

CLASSIFICATION OF CHILDHOOD DISORDERS

Assessment of childhood problems often results in the diagnosis of a childhood mental disorder. Classification of childhood disorders has followed a different path than adult disorders, even though they both have the same objectives (see Chapter 1). There has been a greater emphasis on *empirically derived* classification systems for children, while adult disorders have mainly been classified into *clinically derived* diagnostic categories. Empirically derived systems rely on statistical analyses of large amounts of data to determine the symptoms that make up a diagnostic category. In contrast, clinically derived systems rely on the judgments of experts, who use their clinical and research experience to determine the diagnostic criteria.

There are at least two reasons for the emphasis on the empirical approach among childhood researchers. First, as already noted, early versions of the clinically derived DSM systems virtually ignored the unique aspects of childhood disorders. DSM-I (APA, 1952) had only two categories specifically associated with childhood disorders, and one of these, Adjustment Reaction, was so nonspecific as to be virtually useless. DSM-II (APA, 1968) was little better. Beginning with DSM-III and DSM-III-R (APA 1980; 1987) childhood disorders were given serious attention, but even DSM-IV (APA, 1994) retains several of the shortcomings typical of its predecessors.

The empirical approach to classifying childhood disorders arises also from the referral process described earlier. Because children do not refer themselves for help, standard assessment procedures rely on information from parents, teachers, and other significant people in the child's life. The most common procedure for gathering this information is to have knowledgeable adults complete behavior rating scales on the referred child. Child psychiatry clinics routinely collect such data on large numbers of children. The advent of high-speed computers made it possible to quickly analyze these data to determine which symptoms tend to cluster together in children.

Here, we consider both empirical and clinical approaches to the classification of childhood disorders, as well as the similarities and differences in the disorder category systems derived from each.

Empirically Derived Systems

In contrast to the clinical approach, the empirical approach to classification makes no initial assumptions about which symptoms are interrelated, or what diagnostic categories may exist, although *a priori* decisions are involved in determining which behavioral symptoms to enter into the statistical analyses. In other words, the data are allowed to speak for themselves about the extent to which symptoms appear in the same child. The primary statistical technique for determining the interrelationship among behavioral symptoms is *factor analysis*. This procedure involves examining the correlations among all symptoms and determining which behaviors tend to occur together. Those symptoms which show the highest correlations among themselves form factors or dimensions. This is a *dimensional* approach to psychopathology which assumes that all children can display all of the behaviors being studied, but to varying degrees. Children who score high on particular disorder factors are considered to suffer to a greater degree from the problems associated with those factors. This approach contrasts with clinically derived *categorical* systems which assume that children either do or do not have a given disorder.

The empirical approach to the diagnosis of childhood psychopathology is embodied in the work of Thomas Achenbach (1978; Achenbach & Edelbrock, 1979, 1981) who developed rating scales for assessing more than 100 of the most common problems of childhood. He asked thousands of parents and teachers to complete these rating scales in relation to both referred and nonreferred boys and girls ranging in age from four to sixteen. Although the results differed somewhat depending on the child's age and gender, several factors emerged which reflect a variety of childhood behavioral problems. Figure 10.3 offers examples of the factors that typically arise from such analyses, along with the behavioral characteristics associated with each.

Two factors in particular seem to encompass the majority of childhood behavior disorders (Achenbach & Edelbrock, 1978; Quay, 1986). One of these factors describes *externalizing* or *undercontrolled* problems; the other, *internalizing* or *overcontrolled* problems. The externalizing factor refers to acting-out behavior—such as hyperactivity, aggression, and delinquency—that is aversive to others in the child's environment. The internalizing factor refers to problems in which the child experiences depression, anxiety, somatic problems, and other significant discomfort that may not be evident, let alone disturbing, to others. These two broad factors offer a reliable and valid way of differentiating childhood behavioral problems. Generally, children who display externalizing problems tend to be male, to have a poorer academic record, and to show a poorer prognosis than those with internalizing disorders. Given the aversive nature of the externalizing disorders, as well as their more negative prognosis, it is not surprising that, until recently, more attention has been devoted to these problems than to the internalizing disorders.

The computer-driven empirical approach avoids the biases in judgment that may be associated with the clinical approach. As noted in Chapter 3, clinicians sometimes misperceive associations between symptoms; they sometimes even perceive correlations that do not exist. For example, clinician's biases have often led to a perceived association between bedwetting and firesetting even though there is, in fact, no

Conduct Disorder
  Fighting, hitting
  Disobedient, defiant
  Temper tantrums
  Destructiveness
  Impertinent, imprudent
  Uncooperative, resistant

Attention Problems
  Poor concentration, short attention span
  Daydreaming
  Clumsy, poor coordination
  Preoccupied, stares into space
  Fails to finish, lacks perseverance
  Impulsive

Motor Overactivity
  Restless, overactive
  Excitable, impulsive
  Squirmy, jittery
  Overtalkative
  Hums and makes other odd noises

Social Ineptness
  Poor peer relations
  Likes to be alone
  Is teased, picked on
  Prefers younger children
  Shy, timid, lacks self-confidence
  Stays with adults, ignored by peers

Somatic Complaints
  Headaches
  Vomiting, nausea

Stomach aches
Muscle aches and pains
Elimination problems

Socialized Aggression
  Has "bad" companions
  Truant from home
  Truant from school
  Steals in company with others
  Loyal to deliquent friends
  Belongs to a gang

Anxious-Depressed Withdrawal
  Anxious, fearful, tense
  Shy, timid, bashful
  Withdrawn, seclusive
  Depressed, sad, disturbed
  Hypersensitive, easily hurt
  Feels inferior, worthless

Schizoid Unresponsive
  Won't talk
  Withdrawn
  Sad
  Stares blankly
  Confused

Psychotic Disorder
  Visual hallucinations
  Auditory hallucinations
  Bizarre, odd, peculiar
  Strange ideas and behavior
  Incoherent speech
  Repetitive speech

This table lists nine factors typically obtained from factor analyses of behavior rating scales. The behavioral items that frequently load on each factor are listed under the factor name.

SOURCE: Quay (1986).

FIGURE 10.3 Factors typically derived from factor analysis of rating scales, and characteristics frequently associated with each.

association (Achenbach, 1985). The problem is compounded when clinicians are asked to make judgments about associations among numerous symptoms and disorders.

A second strength of empirical classification systems is their quantitative approach to decision making. Large-scale normative investigations have resulted in objective, operational rules for defining inclusion and exclusion criteria for specific syndromes. In one study, for example, rating scale data from 1,300 parents of nonreferred children (aged four to sixteen) allowed researchers to calculate means and standard deviations for disorder factor scores (Achenbach & Edelbrock, 1981). This normative information was then used to compare referred children's scores on specific factors to peers of the same age and sex (see Figure 10.4).

A final strength of the empirical approach is that it allows evaluation of childhood disorders from the perspectives of both parents and teachers. Factor analyses of these separate ratings can show, for example, that certain behavioral problems are more significant in some situations than others, meaning that teachers may be less aware of delinquency problems than mothers, but the converse may be true for problems in peer relationships.

A major problem with the empirical approach to classifying childhood disorders relates to the data used in the factor analyses. Most of the conclusions about the dimensions underlying childhood disorders have been based on symptom ratings by parents and teachers. These ratings may be biased by personal factors, such as parental depression, that have little to do with the child's behavior. The factors derived from rating scale items also depend on how parents and teachers interpret those items. For example, DSM-IV includes "often doesn't seem to listen" as an example of inattention. However, mothers tend to interpret "doesn't seem to listen" to mean active noncompliance and thus tend to associate it with oppositional or conduct disorders (Milich, Widiger, & Landau, 1987).

Another problem with the empirical approach is that it is not good at identifying rare disorders. For example, empirical analyses of behavior checklist data almost never generate factors describing autism (see Nietzel et al., 1998), yet this disorder does exist.

Clinically Derived Systems

As described in Chapter 3, clinically derived disorder-classification systems such as the DSM are developed by panels of experts who identify appropriate diagnostic categories, as well as the specific symptoms most typical of each. These experts rely on their clinical experience with a variety of disorders, as well as their reading of the research literature, to arrive at an agreed-upon classification system. However, even when experts observe similar patients and read the same empirical reports, they may not always agree on the diagnostic criteria for a given disorder. In short, reaching a consensus on these decisions often involves compromise, just as legislators must amend proposed legislation to produce a bill that will receive support sufficient for passage.

Clinicians and researchers interested in childhood disorders have had differing responses to the way these disorders have been classified in the various editions of the DSM. Many felt satisfied that, beginning with DSM-III, childhood problems were finally recognized as unique and worthy of clinical attention. Others questioned whether the revisions were a step forward or backward in terms of classifying childhood disorders (Rutter & Shaffer, 1980). Let's consider the improvements and shortcomings of DSM-III, DSM-III-R, and DSM-IV classifications of childhood disorders.

One improvement has been greater breadth of coverage; DSM-IV contains more than four times as many childhood categories as DSM-II (Bemporad & Schwab, 1986). These categories reflect five domains of functioning: intellectual problems (e.g., mental retardation), behavioral problems (e.g., conduct disorders), emotional problems (e.g.,

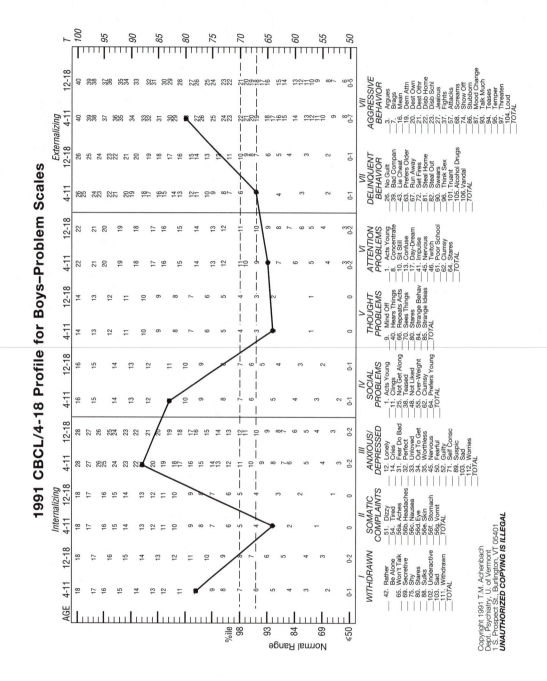

1991 CBCL/4-18 Profile for Boys–Problem Scales

anxiety disorders), physical problems (e.g., enuresis), and developmental problems (e.g., autism). However, some clinicians have criticized this increased breadth of coverage. They argue that disorders such as mental retardation and learning disabilities, which are included in recent versions of the DSM, are educational problems rather than psychiatric disorders and therefore should not be included in a psychiatric classification system (Rutter & Shaffer, 1980). Some psychologists fear that broadening coverage of childhood disorders represents an attempt by psychiatrists to assume control of problems outside their expertise (Garmezy, 1978).

As noted in Chapter 3, operational criteria for defining mental disorders began appearing in DSM-III, an improvement that benefitted the diagnosis of childhood as well as adult problems. For example, whereas DSM-II contained only one sentence listing the possible symptoms of hyperactivity, DSM-IV includes explicit diagnostic criteria about the number and types of specific symptoms that must appear before this diagnosis can be made, along with information about onset and duration of the disorder, as well as exclusionary criteria (see Table 10.2).

Still, even DSM-IV falls short of using fully operational criteria. It does not specify how to measure criterion behaviors, and terms such as *often* and *easily* are used without guidance about the severity of the problems they represent. A major goal of the newest DSM was to introduce a developmental framework to the classification of the childhood disorders. Unfortunately, the only consistent developmental data offered are age of onset and course of disorders. The diagnostic criteria are not adjusted to reflect developmental differences for any disorder. For example, DSM-IV offers the clinician no guidelines for diagnosing the presence of attention problems in children of differing ages. In addition, for several disorders (e.g., depression, generalized anxiety), no specific childhood criteria are offered. Instead, the clinician is instructed to use the adult criteria. Finally, the recent DSM versions offer too little coverage of disorders seen in infancy and early childhood (Mash & Dozois, 1996).

The developers of DSM-IV have relied far more than their predecessors on empirical investigations to identify the symptoms of specific disorders (Widiger et al., 1991), and this is especially the case for childhood disorders (Mash & Dozois, 1996). Still, to the clinical child psychologist, perhaps the most frustrating aspect of the DSM approach to diagnosis is that the criteria for given disorders change, often substantially, with each edition of the manual. For example, in DSM-III, a diagnosis of ADHD required that a child display inattention, impulsivity, *and* hyperactivity. In DSM-III-R, the symptoms from these three subcategories were collapsed into one list, and a child could receive the ADHD diagnosis merely by displaying a certain *number* of them, regardless of which subcategories they represented. DSM-IV contains only two

---

FIGURE 10.4 An example of a profile from the 1991 Child Behavior Checklist (CBCL). Here is the profile of a six-year-old boy's scores on the mother's rating version of the Child Behavior Checklist (CBCL). The CBCL contains scales for two age groups: four to eleven and twelve to eighteen. Scores falling above the dotted line occur in less than 2% of nonreferred children in the age range and are considered especially problematic. This type of profile resembles, and offers many of the same diagnostic features as, those generated by the MMPI (see Chapter 5). In this case, the profile is typical of a young child displaying aggression, peer difficulties, and depression. (Adapted from Achenbach, 1991).

TABLE 10.2 Diagnostic Criteria Used in DSM-IV for Attention-Deficit Hyperactivity Disorder

These criteria are typical of those used in clinically derived systems for classifying childhood mental disorders.

A. Either 1 or 2:

1. six (or more) of the following symptoms of *inattention* have persisted for at least six months to a degree that is maladaptive and inconsistent with developmental level:

    Inattention

    a. often fails to give close attention to details or makes careless mistakes in schoolwork, work, or other activities
    b. often has difficulty sustaining attention in tasks or play activities
    c. often does not seem to listen when spoken to directly
    d. often does not follow through on instructions and fails to finish schoolwork, chores, or duties in the workplace (not due to oppositional behavior or failure to understand instructions)
    e. often has difficulty organizing tasks and activities
    f. often avoids, dislikes, or is reluctant to engage in tasks that require sustained mental effort (such as schoolwork or homework)
    g. often loses things necessary for tasks or activities (e.g., toys, school assignments, pencils, books, or tools)
    h. is often easily distracted by extraneous stimuli
    i. is often forgetful in daily activities

2. six (or more) of the following symptoms of *hyperactivity-impulsivity* have persisted for at least six months to a degree that is maladaptive and inconsistent with developmental level:

Hyperactivity

a. often fidgets with hands or feet or squirms in seat
b. often leaves seat in classroom or in other situations in which remaining seated is expected
c. often runs about or climbs excessively in situations in which it is inappropriate (in adolescents or adults, may be limited to subjective feelings of restlessness)
d. often has difficulty playing or engaging in leisure activities quietly
e. is often "on the go" or often acts as if "driven by a motor"
f. often talks excessively

Impulsivity

g. often blurts out answers before questions have been completed
h. often has difficulty awaiting turn
i. often interrupts or intrudes on others (e.g., butts into conversations or games)

B. Some hyperactive-impulsive or inattentive symptoms that caused impairment were present before age seven years.

C. Some impairment from the symptoms is present in two or more settings (e.g., at school [or work] and at home).

D. There must be clear evidence of clinically significant impairment in social, academic, or occupational functioning.

E. The symptoms do not occur exclusively during the course of a Pervasive Developmental Disorder, Schizophrenia, or other Psychotic Disorder and are not better accounted for by another mental disorder (e.g., Mood Disorder, Anxiety Disorder, Dissociative Disorder, or a Personality Disorder).

symptom subcategories (inattention and impulsivity/hyperactivity), and a child can receive one of three ADHD diagnoses—Inattentive Type, Hyperactive/Impulsive Type, or Combined Type—depending on whether they meet the criteria for one or both of the subcategories listed in Table 10.2.

SPECIFIC CHILDHOOD DISORDERS

In this section, we offer descriptions of four types of childhood disorders that clinical child psychologists often encounter in their assessment and treatment activities: ADHD (an externalizing disorder), childhood depression, (an internalizing disorder), learning disabilities (a developmental disorder), and childhood autism (a pervasive developmental disorder).

Attention-Deficit Hyperactivity Disorder

Attention-deficit hyperactivity disorder (ADHD) is considered the most common childhood behavior disorder, affecting approximately 5% of school-age children. While this figure represents, on the average, only one child per classroom, it is enough to seriously disrupt the learning environment, as any teacher will confirm. ADHD primarily affects boys (the boy-to-girl ratio ranges from 5:1 to 10:1) and, though it appears prior to first grade, the problems it creates are intensified by the demands of the school environment.

As already noted, the core features of ADHD are inattention, impulsivity, and overactivity. The attention problems consist primarily of children having difficulty sustaining their focus; they fail to finish school assignments, and they do not stay on task in the classroom (Abikoff, Gittelman-Klein, & Klein, 1977). Impulsivity refers to the fact that these children act before they think. Although it is agreed that ADHD children are impulsive, operationally defining this construct is difficult (Milich & Kramer, 1984). Behaviors typical of this problem include difficulty waiting to take turns, interrupting, and being impatient. ADHD children exhibit overactivity in both gross motor movements (e.g., running around the room, standing on chairs), and fine motor movements, such as fidgeting and squirming, restlessness, and playing with objects.

In addition to these core features, ADHD children display a myriad of other behavioral and learning problems, including aggressive and delinquent behavior, oppositional and noncompliant reactions to adult requests, and problems in social interactions. The reputation that these children develop is so negative that merely telling a normal child that he or she is about to meet an ADHD boy will adversely affect the subsequent interaction, even if the boy does not actually display ADHD (Harris et al., 1990).

As ADHD children grow, the primary features of the disorder lessen and, in adulthood, some show few effects of their childhood disorder. Others are at significant risk for residual academic, social, and emotional problems. For example, they may work at jobs that are below what their socioeconomic background would predict, and report having fewer friends and being less happy than their age mates (Weiss & Hechtman, 1986). Still others experience more serious legal or psychiatric complications. Anywhere from one-third to one-half of adults who had displayed ADHD will be arrested at least once for a serious offense, compared to 10% of a non-ADHD control group (Satterfield, Hoppe, & Schell, 1982). Having a stable family background, a high IQ, and low levels of aggression in childhood seem to protect ADHD children against this last outcome.

Childhood Depression

Only recently have internalizing disorders such as childhood depression received the kind of attention that has long been focused on ADHD and other externalizing disorders. This relative neglect stems first from the fact that, as noted earlier, internalizing disorders create little discomfort for the parents and teachers responsible for referring children for help. Second, early follow-up studies suggested that children displaying internalizing disorders were not at risk for subsequent psychiatric problems. Third, some clinicians insisted that clinical depression simply did not, or could not, occur among children. Orthodox psychoanalysts believed, for example, that children did not have sufficient superego development to internalize the anger necessary for clinical depression (Cantwell, 1983). Others argued that depressive symptoms in childhood merely reflected temporary developmental phenomena (Lefkowitz & Burton, 1978).

Increased attention to internalizing disorders has made it clear that childhood depression is similar to adult depression in terms of its emotional, cognitive, behavioral, and physical manifestations, but that the specific symptom picture may differ depending on the child's developmental stage (Kaslow & Rehm, 1985). Indeed, there is considerable debate over the fact that DSM-IV lists the same criteria for diagnosing depression in both children and adults. Research on assessment of childhood depression has focused on the reliability and validity of children's self-reports (Saylor et al., 1984), as well as on the validation of behavioral observation measures (Kazdin et al., 1985). Researchers are also looking at whether causal theories of adult depression, such as learned helplessness, apply to childhood depression (Kaslow, Rehm, & Siegel, 1984; Seligman et al., 1984).

Learning Disabilities

Learning disabilities refer to the problems some children have in mastering one or more basic academic tasks (such as reading or math), despite having average or above intelligence and sufficient motivation and environmental stimulation. Learning disabilities appear in all cultures, although the rates may differ from one to another. It is estimated that learning disabilities affect from 5% to 10% of school-age children, with many more boys than girls being identified. These developmental disorders have been around for as long as children have been going to school, but it was not until the 1970s that they were officially recognized. Prior to that time, children with learning disabilities were considered either unmotivated or oppositional and were often repeatedly held back in school until they either dropped out or were expelled.

Clinicians agree that there are several types of learning disabilities, although there is less agreement on how to describe them. One approach is to categorize children by the subject matter in which they have a problem (e.g., reading disability, math disability). Another is to refer to the mental processing problems involved (e.g., language disorder, visual-spatial disorder). Children with language disorders tend to show a verbal IQ lower than their performance IQ, a good sight vocabulary, but problematic phonetic skills. Thus, they can easily read familiar words, but have great difficulty with new ones. In contrast, children with visual-spatial problems tend to have a performance IQ lower than their verbal IQ and to display good phonetic skills but have a problematic sight vocabulary.

Federal Public Law 94-142 (1977) guarantees that all handicapped children, including those with learning disabilities, receive a free public education designed to meet their unique needs. Because the law's definition of learning disabilities is vague, the U.S. states have developed operational definitions that usually incorporate three basic features. First, there must be a significant discrepancy between a child's potential and actual performance (e.g., obtaining a reading achievement score that is at least two standard deviations below the level predicted by the child's IQ). Second, the child's deficit must be due to "basic psychological processes." These deficits must be inferred from the child's performance on tests, but unfortunately, no tests exist that can offer reliable and valid assessments of such processing deficits (Wong, 1986). Accordingly, attention has shifted to a third definitional feature, namely exclusionary criteria. This involves inferring a deficit in basic psychological processes when subpar academic performance cannot be explained by emotional disturbance, educational disadvantage, or other alternative causes. Because it is impossible to rule out many of these alternative causes, many states, fearing litigation, define learning disabilities exclusively in terms of a significant, and quantifiable, discrepancy between a child's aptitude and achievement.

Childhood Autism

The pervasive developmental disorder known as autism is one of the most unusual and baffling disorders seen in childhood. It is unusual because of the symptom picture it presents, and baffling because no adequate theory has been proposed to account for these symptoms. Autistic children have severe problems in social functioning and language, and display a variety of bizarre behaviors.

Their social difficulties consist of complete indifference to others. They do not seek out others and, even as infants, they avoid making eye contact, resist physical contact, and they show little or no emotion. They do not play with other children and do not imitate the behavior of others.

Approximately half of these children do not develop normal, useful language and those who do speak in an unusual manner, occasionally using language for noncommunicative purposes. For example, they may engage in *echolalia*, in which they repeat whatever they hear. Unlike hearing-impaired children, they will not sign or point to get their message across. They also have great difficulty talking about situations or events that are not present, and are very poor at understanding the perspective of other individuals. Finally, their speech sounds different from that of other children, often being flat and lacking inflection, so that it has been described as sounding similar to computer generated language.

Autistic children's bizarre behaviors often involve abnormally under- or overreactivity to environmental events. Thus, the child may be oblivious to the comings and goings of other individuals but may be hypersensitive to the rustling of paper. In addition, they often are overly sensitive to any changes in their environment and may scream in protest if one of their favorite objects is touched or moved. They also engage in unusual, repetitive behaviors that appear to serve a self-stimulatory purpose. Thus, they may repeatedly flap their hands or engage in self-injurious behavior, such as hitting or biting themselves. In addition, these children may gaze at spinning objects (e.g., fans) for long periods of time, or constantly twirl an ashtry or a piece of string.

Autism is presumed to be present at birth, although it may not become evident until around the age of 2. Fortunately, it is a relatively rare disorder, only occurring in approximately 4 children per every 10,000. The majority of children with autism are mentally retarded, with only approximately 20% with an IQ score above 70. Obviously, these children are difficult to test, and, for some, their IQ scores may be underrepresentations of their actual abilities. However, for most of these children, their IQ scores and adaptive functioning levels (e.g., self-care skills) are consistent with a diagnosis of mental retardation.

A CLINICAL CASE

So far, our discussion of the assessment and classification of childhood disorders has remained mainly at an abstract, conceptual level. However, the assessments and disorders we have described involve not abstract entities, but real children whose problems do not always fit neatly into diagnostic categories, and for whom clinical assessment data are not always clear or unambiguous. To highlight these realities, and to illustrate how various sources of assessment data are combined in making decisions about diagnostic classification and treatment, we offer the case of "Billy," a boy who was seen by one of the authors. As is common in clinical case presentations, our description will be organized in terms of referral questions, history of the problem, behavioral observations, assessment results, diagnostic conclusions, and treatment recommendations.

Referral Questions

When first seen, Billy was eleven years and eight months old and in the fifth grade at school. He was referred by the school social worker because he was displaying a number of behavioral problems, both at home and in class. He was sometimes quite aggressive, he did not do what others asked of him, he was manipulative, and he was cruel to animals. Billy was described as having a high activity level, being difficult to discipline, often displaying temper tantrums when he did not get his way. The teacher in his special, "behavior problem" classroom described him as impulsive, difficult to motivate, likely to fail to complete assignments, and having poor attentional skills. He was also said to constantly move his head and make unusual noises. Billy had little self-confidence, had difficulty making friends, and had even talked about killing himself.

In a complex clinical case like Billy's a number of diagnoses must be considered, including both externalizing (i.e., ADHD, conduct disorder, oppositional defiant disorder) *and* internalizing (i.e., depression) disorders. In addition, the clinical child psychologist must consider whether a learning disorder may be involved in the clinical picture and, whether the constant head movements and unusual noises might be an early indication of Tourette's syndrome, a neurological disorder. To evaluate all these possibilities, clinical assessment must address a number of questions: (1) what is the nature and extent of Billy's aggressive behavior?; (2) how serious is his suicidal ideation?; (3) what is the nature of his home life and what skills do his parents have for handling him?; and (4) how are his attentional problems, his poor motivation and his academic difficulties related—what is causing what?

History of the Problem

Billy's parents said that he had no real problems until he entered school at age five, but teachers have had great difficulty disciplining him ever since. School records include repeated references to problems of inattention and impulsivity, while the parents noted that his "motor was running all of the time." For a time, he had been treated with Ritalin (a hyperactivity drug described later), but this only made him worse. In the fifth grade, when he was placed in the behavior problem class, his suicidal talk began. Billy's medical history and exam were considered unremarkable, except that he was somewhat slow in developing. He did not walk until the age of sixteen months. At three standard deviations above the mean weight for his age, he was markedly obese. He also needed glasses to do school work, but he often refused to wear them.

Behavioral Observations

Billy frequently whined, complained, and displayed other strikingly immature behavior during the testing phase of clinical assessment. He was noncompliant and oppositional, constantly testing the patience of the examiner. However, as testing progressed and limits were firmly enforced, his oppositional behavior diminished. Billy showed a generally short attention span and was easily distracted. He also often responded to test materials too quickly and without sufficient regard for his responses. The examiner also noted intermittent shoulder shrugs, which may be consistent with the head movements reported by the school.

Assessment Results

An interview with the parents, who have been married for fifteen years, revealed that they were in constant conflict with Billy at home, and that—consistent with Patterson's coercion-escalation hypothesis—these encounters frequently escalate into verbal fights. They said that Billy displayed a number of conduct disorder symptoms, including bullying neighbor children, setting fires, frequently lying, and stealing money from home. His mother reported that she was held back in school because of math difficulties and that her father was an alcoholic. The father reported no significant problems, although he quit school after the tenth grade. Finally, the parents said that, while they are "getting to the end of their rope" in dealing with Billy, his only sibling, a sister, displays no significant problems.

The results of Billy's intellectual and achievement tests presented an inconsistent and somewhat confusing picture. His Full Scale IQ was 81, which puts him in the borderline-low range of normal functioning. However, there was considerable inconsistency in his scores on various subtests, with scores ranging from 4 to 11 (10 is average). This variability suggests that his intellectual capabilities are probably somewhat greater than the score of 81 he received, but that poor motivation and/or learning problems may be impairing his performance. Achievement testing presented a somewhat different picture. Billy tested at his age-appropriate grade level, and above what his IQ results would predict, for both reading and spelling. However, he was two years below grade level in arithmetic. Thus, while he clearly did not have a learning disability in reading and spelling, he may have had one in arithmetic. It is hard to be sure about this, however. His arithmetic score of 71 is not significantly below his IQ score, but the IQ itself may be spuriously low because of his motivational problems. As noted earlier, such considerations often complicate the diagnosis of learning disabilities.

Observations made at school revealed that Billy did indeed have difficulty settling down to tasks and that he constantly fiddled with objects. He also complained a great deal and could be quite "mouthy." He was observed to be "off task" 41% of the time during seatwork and 61% of the time during classroom instruction time. However, in a small group setting he was only off task 4% of the time.

Conclusions and Recommendations

On the basis of all the assessment information available, the clinician concluded that Billy clearly demonstrated a significant conduct disorder, as well as attention-deficit hyperactivity disorder. The possibility of a learning disability in math was considered but not diagnosed, pending further testing. Additional neurological testing was also required before any conclusion could be drawn about whether Billy was showing signs of Tourette's disorder. He was not judged to be clinically depressed, although it was obvious that he did have self-esteem problems resulting from academic and behavioral difficulties.

Because of the severe nature of Billy's conduct disorder, his large size (which made him difficult to manage), and the fact that his parents acknowledged that they were no longer confident about being able to handle him, the clinician recommended that Billy be placed in a residential treatment center.

Follow-up Evaluation

The clinician evaluated Billy again two years after the initial assessment program. Unfortunately, his problems had continued. He was still at the residential treatment center, and he was not doing well there. In addition, his movement disorder symptoms had worsened, and he was being given medication for Tourette's. Billy was also exhibiting signs of anxiety, insecurity, and low self-esteem, so that concern about depression was raised again and became a focus of further attention.

TREATMENT OF CHILDHOOD DISORDERS

The treatment of childhood disorders differs in important ways from clinical interventions for adults. As is the case with assessment, child therapy poses a special challenge for clinicians because children do not self-evaluate or self-report effectively, and because they do not refer themselves for help, their contact with a therapist requires parental motivation and cooperation. The significance of these and related issues will be apparent in the following brief review of the major forms of therapy for childhood disorders.

Psychodynamic Therapy

Children are usually not appropriate candidates for traditional psychoanalytic therapies (Johnson, Rasbury, & Siegel, 1986), partly because they are seldom motivated to participate in such an intensive therapy experience. Further, they are unlikely to understand the need for introspection and the active role they must play in orthodox psychoanalysis. Their immature language and incomplete cognitive development, too, may hamper verbal reasoning and abstract problem solving, thus limiting their ability to profit from a therapist's interpretations.[4] In addition, psychoanalysis assumes the presence of established psychological defenses and a relatively stable personality structure. Depending on their age and developmental status, children may not exhibit such consistencies. Finally, many childhood problems appear to result from environmental forces (e.g., school, parents) rather than intrapsychic conflicts.

Given that research evidence and clinical practice suggest that standard psychoanalytic therapies are not well suited to children (Achenbach, 1982; Johnson et al., 1986), psychodynamically-oriented therapists tend to adopt variations on usual analytical procedures—such as using play rather than free association as the main communication medium between client and therapist. They may also pursue less ambitious treatment goals, such as helping a child successfully pass through a crucial stage of development rather than focusing on prior fixations (Gelfand & Peterson, 1985).

Various forms of psychodynamically-oriented *play therapy* focus on helping children become aware of and resolve inner conflicts without relying heavily on the verbal skills required in adult treatment. Play therapy allows children to express their inner concerns not by talking about them directly, but through the way they play with, and the voices they give to, puppets, dolls, and modeling clay. All the while, the therapist creates an accepting and empathic atmosphere in which children can feel secure to explore their feelings (Axline, 1976). Traditional psychoanalysts tend to interpret the child's verbal and nonverbal behavior during play as revealing unconscious motivation and conflicts, while object-relations therapists (see Chapter 8) are more likely to see it as indicative of the quality of a child's attachment to caregivers. Therapists who adopt a client-centered therapy approach are also likely to use play as a method for helping children explore their feelings and their problems.

Behavioral Therapy

Various forms of behavioral therapy, especially operant procedures, have been the most frequently employed interventions for childhood problems during the last three decades. Approximately 50% of child therapists identify with this approach (Mash, 1989), which is

---

[4]In the case of Little Hans, which was important to the development of Freud's psychoanalytic theory and methods, Freud talked only to the father, never to Hans.

characterized by several notable features reminiscent of adult versions of behavioral treatment. These include (1) an emphasis on the principles of learning as the basis of behavior disorder and treatment; (2) a focus on observable situational determinants of behavior (e.g., rewards and punishments, not inferred intrapsychic problems); (3) treating problems by altering observable stimuli that control behavior today, not by exploring hypothesized underlying problems from the past; and (4) using empirically validated treatments and collecting objective, observable outcome data on treatment results.

Behavioral interventions often involve teaching parents or teachers to administer behavior management procedures (Dangel & Polster, 1984; O'Leary & O'Leary, 1972). The rationale for this aspect of behavioral treatment is that parents and teachers are often in a better position than therapists to control the environmental antecedents and consequences that maintain problem behaviors in children at home and at school (see Figure 10.5).

There are several reasons why behavioral interventions have become the treatment of choice for many childhood disorders. First, the community mental health movement of the 1960s emphasized preventive interventions, including training nonprofessionals as change agents. Behaviorally oriented parent and teacher training programs fit well with these goals. Second, there was dissatisfaction with traditional psychodynamic treatment methods, especially for children with externalizing disorders or severe psychopathology (e.g., autism). Operant conditioning procedures, in particular, gave parents and teachers concrete solutions for previously intractable child behavioral problems. Third, in the late-1970s the federal government began to stress accountability in the treatment of handicapped children in school. Public Law 94-142 requires Individual Education Plans (IEPs) for all special education children. For every identified handicapped child, schools must develop an IEP that contains a list of treatment goals for the child, a plan for reaching those goals, and a report on the outcome. Behavioral interventions, with their clearly defined targets, specific treatment strategies, and systematic data collection components, lend themselves well to such an accounting.

There is evidence that behavioral therapies are effective for a wide range of childhood disorders, especially for externalizing disorders involving aggression (Patterson, 1976), stealing (Reid & Patterson, 1976), and hyperactivity (Pelham & Murphy, 1986). Behavioral procedures have also proven effective for a number of internalizing problems, including bedwetting (Doleys, 1983), fears (Morris & Kratochwill, 1983), and school avoidance (Last & Francis, 1988). Finally, operant approaches have shown they effectively maximize the skills and potential of children with severe mental disorders, including mental retardation and autism (Lovaas, 1987). Behavioral interventions are also cost effective; most can be completed in less than twenty sessions. In addition, by training parents and teachers as change agents in the natural environment, clinicians increase the likelihood that positive changes will be maintained after therapy is terminated, and that positive effects may generalize to other, nonreferred children (siblings, classmates). Finally, the theory behind the behavioral approach is easy to understand, the treatments can be implemented in a relatively straightforward manner (Weisz et al., 1987), and the results can be quantified in a way that allows parents and teachers to chart improvements as they occur.

Because many childhood behavioral disorders reflect problems in the home, behavioral parent training procedures focus on systematically teaching parents how to manage their children better (Polster & Dangel, 1984). A variety of approaches have been proposed, although those developed by Patterson (1975) and Forehand and McMahon (1981) are the most widely implemented. Whatever the specific orientation, all behavioral parent training procedures include the following five steps.

1. *Pinpoint the target behavior.* Parents must define the problem behavior explicitly so that it can be measured. Often, parents present vague or global complaints about their child's behavior ("He won't mind," "He's got a bad attitude") that make it difficult for the clinician to design the intervention. Parents are encouraged to identify inappropriate behaviors to be decreased as well as appropriate behaviors to be increased.

2. *Chart the target behavior.* Parents are then asked to keep records of the target behaviors. There are two purposes to this data collection. First, these data offer a baseline against which subsequent interventions can be assessed. Second, merely by observing their child's behavior more systematically, parents begin to note the stimuli and consequences that elicit or reinforce the undesirable behavior

("Whenever his sister teases him he hits her and she starts crying").

3. *Develop an intervention.* Behavioral parent training employs an operant perspective, which assumes that behaviors are elicited by the stimuli that precede them and maintained by the consequences that follow. Separating where two children sit at the dinner table is an example of altering antecedents to decrease the rate of fighting during dinner. Giving the children extra TV time for each 5 minutes of dinner that passes without fighting is an example of altering the consequences to modify the same behavior.

4. *Assess the intervention.* Throughout the intervention, the parents keep records of the target behaviors. These data indicate whether the intervention is effective or whether changes need to be made. For example, if a shaping procedure is employed, the data indicate when the parents should increase the behavior criterion required to earn reinforcement.

5. *Fade out the program.* The ultimate goal of all behavioral interventions is that naturally occurring antecedents and consequences will elicit and maintain the desired behaviors. Therefore, if an intervention is successful, the therapist will help the parents fade out the program so that the treatment gains can be maintained after the treatment has ended.

FIGURE 10.5 Behavioral parent training.

Despite its popularity and proven effectiveness, the behavioral approach does have some limitations. For one thing, it does not help all children. For example, Patterson (1982) found that he was unsuccessful with at least one-third of the aggressive children he treated. These children tended to live in families in which there was serious parental psychopathology (e.g., maternal depression) or powerful environmental stressors (e.g., poverty, divorce). Indeed, behaviorally oriented therapists have recognized that simple parent training may not be sufficient for *insular* families (those with few social resources), and that a multimodal approach, addressing parental as well as child problems, may be necessary (Griest et al., 1982). A second limitation of the behavioral approach is that although producing generalized treatment effects is a desirable goal, achieving that goal is often difficult. Often, initial successes are not maintained, or behavioral changes seen in one setting (e.g., school) do not carry over to other settings (e.g., home). Finally, there are some childhood problems—depression and certain anxiety disorders, for example—that may not lend themselves to operant conditioning or other traditional behavioral interventions. Behavioral clinicians are now turning to cognitive-behavioral interventions to help them deal with such disorders.

Cognitive-Behavioral Interventions

Adult versions of the cognitive-behavioral treatment approach have focused on anxiety disorders and depression, where they have a long history of significant success (see Chapter 9). The use of cognitive-behavioral methods with children, however, has appeared only relatively recently. At first, these methods were used almost exclusively in cases of externalizing disorders (especially impulsivity, hyperactivity, and conduct disorders; Abikoff & Gittelman, 1985; Kazdin et al., 1987; Lochman, 1992; Meichenbaum & Goodman, 1971), but today they are as likely to be applied to children's anxiety and depressive disorders as to ADHD and conduct disorders (Kendall & Panichelli-Mindel, 1995).

The cognitive-behavioral approach to externalizing disorders involves training children to improve their problem-solving and to engage in careful planning before making verbal responses in social situations (Johnson et al., 1986). In other words, children with behavior disorders are taught to bring their inappropriate behavior under cognitive (rational) control. Several techniques are employed in these interventions, including:

1. Problem-solving training (Kazdin et al., 1987). Here, the child is taught to assess the problem (e.g., Billy teased me); generate possible responses (ignore him, hit him, discuss the problem with him); and evaluate consequences of the alternative responses (if I hit him, I may get in trouble).

2. Impulse-control training. This approach involves training hyperactive or impulsive children to slow down and evaluate response alternatives before responding—to "stop, look, and listen" (Douglas, 1972).

3. Perspective-taking. Children are trained to evaluate the effects of their misbehavior (e.g., stealing, lying) on others, and to be sensitive to the thoughts and feelings of others. This approach is frequently employed with delinquent and aggressive children (Chandler, 1973; Kazdin et al., 1987).

Initially, cognitive-behavioral approaches were heralded as a clinical breakthrough for treating the externalizing disorders. Training children to think carefully before they act was assumed to produce the kind of generalizable treatment effects that had been missing from more traditional operant interventions. Further, whereas operant approaches require a parent, teacher, or other adult to elicit and reinforce the desired behavior, cognitive interventions are designed to help children carry out a change strategy within themselves, whether or not an adult is present. Unfortunately, this does not always happen. A review of cognitive-behavioral interventions with ADHD children led to the conclusion that, "The expectation that the development of internalized self-regulation skills would facilitate generalization and maintenance has not been realized" (Abikoff, 1985, p. 508). Although other reviews are less pessimistic (Dush, Hirt, &

Shroeder, 1989), the general conclusion has been that these interventions are not very effective with seriously disturbed children (Baer & Nietzel, 1991).

One promising line of work has been reported by Alan Kazdin and his colleagues, who employed cognitive-behavioral therapy to treat severely conduct-disordered children (Kazdin et al., 1987, 1989). In two studies, intensive problem-solving training (compared to social-relationship therapy) significantly improved the children's behavior, as indicated by parent and teacher ratings. Even more noteworthy, these improvements were maintained at a one-year follow-up.

The cognitive-behavioral approach to internalizing disorders tends to focus on the following skills:

1. Recognizing anxiety-arousing feelings and the thoughts that may trigger these feelings. Once the feelings and thoughts are identified, problem-solving procedures are employed to counter them (Kendell, 1994).

2. Identifying biased, dysfunctional, and misguided cognitions and learning to make more appropriate and adaptive cognitions (Mash & Dozois, 1996). Dysfunctional cognitions may include helpless attributions, self-blame for uncontrollable events, and overly harsh self-judgments (Kaslow, Rehm, & Siegel, 1984).

Cognitive-behavioral interventions for internalizing disorders are still quite new, and not enough studies are available to draw firm conclusions about their effectiveness (Kendell & Panichelli-Mindel, 1995).

Biological Interventions

Although they are very popular in the treatment of adult mental disorders, drugs tend not to be widely employed in the treatment of childhood disorders. For example, when antidepressants are prescribed for children, it is often in relation to problems other than depression (bedwetting, school avoidance, hyperactivity). Drug treatments are used less frequently with children than with adults mainly because still-developing children may be especially vulnerable to the adverse side-effects associated with various drugs.

Stimulant Medication Treatment of ADHD Children. The main exception to physicians' tendency not to medicate children for behavior disorders is seen in the use of methylphenidate (Ritalin) and other stimulant medications in the treatment of attention-deficit hyperactivity disorder. As many as 2 million school-age children in the United States are currently taking these medications for behavioral or learning problems, and hundreds of careful studies have shown that stimulant medication dramatically improves the behavior of ADHD children (DuPaul & Rapport, 1993; Whalen et al., 1985). The children remain seated longer, finish more academic work, give correct answers more often, and show improved social interactions with peers, parents, and teachers. ADHD boys even pay attention better while playing baseball when on medication than on placebo (Pelham et al., 1990).

Nevertheless, controversy continues to surround the use of stimulants for children. It seems that, at least once a year, Ritalin makes the cover of a major news magazine (e.g., *Newsweek*, March 18, 1996), and a number of lawsuits have claimed that stimulant medication is responsible for a variety of negative outcomes, including suicides and homicides. Most professionals dismiss these claims as overly sensational, but there still are many questions about stimulant medication that have not been resolved.

For example, even though medication may produce behavioral improvements, it may also give children the message that these improvements are attributable not to their own efforts, but to the medication. Critics worry that children who get such a message may exert less effort at self-control when they are not being medicated, thus creating a form of dependency on the drug. This may not always be the case, however. One study examined the impact of medication on ADHD boys' self-evaluations, self-esteem, and mood, as well as on the explanations they offered for improved performance (Pelham et al., 1992). On medication days, as compared to placebo days, these boys were significantly more likely to report positive behavioral changes, including increased compliance and fewer rule violations. They also reported feeling happier and liking themselves better on medication days. However, when asked to account for their good performance on medication days, the boys were likely to say that they tried hard, rather than that the pill helped them. These results indicate that ADHD children recognize the effects of medication, but are also willing to take personal credit for improved behavior.

Dietary Modifications. Besides medication, one of the major biological interventions for children's behavioral problems involves dietary modifications. This approach is based on the assumption that refined sugar (Charlton-Seifert, Stratton, & Williams, 1980) and other foods or food additives (Feingold, 1975) are responsible for causing or exacerbating childhood behavioral problems, especially hyperactivity. Indeed, many parents and teachers are convinced that eating a candy bar, for example, will inevitably make problem children overactive and out of control. Efforts to reduce or eliminate such children's intake of these substances continue in spite of the fact that carefully controlled studies suggest that the foods in question have little or no impact on the children's behavior (Harley et al., 1978; Milich, Wolraich, & Lindgren, 1986).

An Integrative Approach to Treating Childhood Disorders

Even this brief review shows that a variety of approaches have been employed in the treatment of childhood disorders. Although these interventions are often beneficial in the short-run (Casey & Berman, 1985), long-term improvement in most serious childhood problems—especially attention-deficit hyperactivity disorder, conduct disorder, and delinquency—is not nearly as likely (Pelham & Murphy, 1986; Zigler, Taussig, & Black, 1992).

Why have psychological interventions so consistently failed to demonstrate long-term gains? First, interventions for serious childhood disorders tend to be reactive rather than proactive. Regardless of whether the problem is delinquency, school failure, or child abuse, there has been a tendency for clinicians to wait until the problem is well established before taking action. As described in Chapter 7, a more effective approach would be to identify at-risk children and then try to intervene before their problem has become entrenched and resistant to treatment.

The second problem with current approaches to childhood treatment is that they are often not comprehensive enough. Serious childhood disorders such as delinquency are caused by a multitude of economic, social, and psychological factors, and for interventions to be effective, they must address as many of these factors as possible (Zigler et al., 1992). Too many treatments today address only one or two causal factors. In delinquency, for example, a large number of causal factors have been identified, including temperament, inhibitory control problems, faulty or abusive parenting, school failure, poverty, parental discord, and peer difficulties (Zigler et al., 1992). A comprehensive treatment package for this disorder should include interventions that focus on many, if not all, of these factors. It might consist of medication to decrease the child's inhibitory problems, academic tutoring to lessen the risk of school failure, training in problem solving to improve peer interactions, anger-control training to decrease inappropriate responses to frustration, marital therapy for parents to decrease discord in the home, parent training to improve disciplinary procedures, and early childhood education to decrease the adverse effects of poverty.

A third factor limiting the long-term effectiveness of psychological treatments for serious childhood disorders is their relatively brief duration. For example, the typical parent-training program lasts from eight to twenty weeks. However, as Alan Kazdin (1985) persuasively argues, chronic disorders need continual treatment. Using an analogy from medicine, he notes that a physician treating diabetes would not discontinue insulin treatment after the diabetes comes under control. Similarly, psychological interventions with children should not end when the problem shows initial improvement.

In short, serious childhood disorders require early, comprehensive, and long-term interventions. Unfortunately, the expense of such interventions makes it difficult to find funding for early prevention strategies, even though the initial expenditures would save money in the long run. For example, insurance companies generally do not pay for treating children who are *at risk* for problems, and while governments will spend $40,000 a year to incarcerate a juvenile offender (Zigler et al., 1992), they tend to refuse to spend a fraction of that amount on programs to prevent delinquent behavior. This short-sighted perspective may be changing, however. The U.S. government has awarded a major grant for a pilot project designed to evaluate the long-term effectiveness of comprehensive treatments for at-risk conduct-disordered children (Conduct Problems Prevention Research Group, 1992). These treatments include many of the procedures described above (the intervention even pays for telephones to be installed in children's homes to help decrease their mothers' social isolation). If this pilot project proves effective in decreasing the risk of delinquency among these children, the government may decide to provide broader support for such programs.

THE FUTURE OF CLINICAL CHILD PSYCHOLOGY

Predicting the future is a hazardous business. However, the history of clinical child psychology clearly shows that its advancements have lagged several decades behind developments in adult clinical psychology. Therefore, the future of clinical child psychology is likely to shadow recent developments in the adult area. Specifically, we predict that child neuropsychology, pediatric psychology, and cognitive-behavioral interventions—especially for internalizing disorders—will see dramatic growth in the near future (see also Kazdin, 1989).

In child neuropsychology, recent advancements in the assessment of adult functioning are now being applied in the evaluation of children (Hynd, Snow, & Becker, 1986). In addition, high-technology advances are allowing major breakthroughs in the understanding of the role of brain functioning in the development of many childhood disorders, such as learning disabilities (see Shaywitz et al., 1995). In pediatric psychology, programs are being developed to help children cope with diabetes and other chronic illnesses (Delameter, 1986). Further, now that it is recognized that children infected with the AIDS virus suffer profound social and psychological problems, clinicians will be working on interventions designed to help children cope with the prolonged hospitalization, social stigma, and physical disabilities associated with this disease (Task Force on Pediatric AIDS, 1989). In the area of cognitive-behavioral therapy, more attention will be directed toward the identification and subsequent treatment of children with internalizing disorders, especially anxiety and depression (Kendell & Panichelli-Mindel, 1995).

Societal changes also will shape the future of clinical child psychology (Kazdin, 1989). For example, the dramatic rise in rates of divorce and remarriage will increase the need to help children cope with these significant stressors (Hetherington & Arasteh, 1988). Further, with teenage pregnancy at epidemic levels, the children of teenage mothers are at great risk for behavioral and learning problems (Furstenberg, Brooks-Gunn & Chase-Lansdale, 1989). Similarly, the increased number of mothers who are working outside the home is producing a generation of "latchkey" children for whom effective child-care strategies need to be developed (Peterson, 1989). Finally, promising leads are now being explored for the prevention of drug and alcohol use among children (Christiansen et al., 1989).

CLINICAL CHILD PSYCHOLOGY AT WORK

Q.: To what extent do the principles, methods, and research results associated with clinical child psychology affect your work?

DR. SANDY D'ANGELO: Mainly in relation to assessment. Research in assessment can be very helpful to the clinician, especially when working with special populations such as children under three, in which there has been an explosion of new measures. It is also important to remain up-to-date with research on existing tests, such as validation with specific populations, test revisions, etc.

DR. HECTOR MACHABANSKI: The principles, methods, and research results in clinical child psychology affect my work with our population of children at the Medical Center and in all aspects of my school consultations. Specifically, recent research findings on attention-deficit hyperactivity disorder have assisted my approach to assessing children and providing early intervention services to them.

DR. GEOFFREY THORPE: They do not have any direct effect, because I do not work with children. But our doctoral program has an active developmental/clinical psychology track, and in recruiting colleagues as professors and clinical supervisors in that area, it is important to select clinician/researchers with expertise in the area of clinical child psychology.

CHAPTER SUMMARY

Clinical psychologists' longstanding focus on assessing and treating adults has changed over the last three decades to the point that clinical child psychologists have become a prominent subgroup in the field. Clinical psychologists have developed methods of classification, assessment, and intervention that are specialized for use with young clients.

In dealing with these clients, clinical child psychologists pay special attention to referral issues, developmental considerations, infant temperament factors, the quality of infants' early attachments, the nature of parent–child interactions, and the impact of childhood stressors.

Taking all these special considerations into account leads clinical child psychologists to ask assessment questions about child clients that they would usually not ask about adults, and to use assessment methods (e.g., behavior rating scales, third-party interviews, intelligence and achievement tests, and family and peer interaction measures) that are less frequently used with adult clients.

Unlike the clinically derived disorder classification systems used with adults (which rely on the judgments of experts to determine diagnostic criteria), classification of childhood disorders has tended to emphasize empirically derived systems which rely on statistical analyses of large amounts of data to determine the symptoms of given diagnostic categories. Empirically derived systems have identified two main kinds of childhood disorders: externalizing problems such as hyperactivity, aggression, and delinquency and internalizing problems such as depression, anxiety, and somatic problems. Other significant childhood problems include developmental disorders such as learning disabilities, and pervasive developmental disorders such as childhood autism.

Treatment of child clients poses special challenges because they may not give accurate self-reports and because their presence in therapy requires parental motivation and cooperation. Specialized forms of psychodynamic, behavioral, and cognitive-behavioral treatment have been developed for use with children, and while some (such as operant and cognitive-behavioral approaches) have proven successful with a wide range of problems, the benefits may be of rather short duration and may not generalize beyond the settings in which treatment took place. While, in general, drugs tend to be used only rarely in treating childhood disorders, methylphenidate (Ritalin) and other stimulant medications are widely prescribed and widely effective in dealing with attention-deficit hyperactivity disorder. Rather than dealing with childhood disorders after they appear, clinical child psychologists would prefer early, comprehensive, and long-term interventions designed to prevent these disorders before they emerge.

Chapter 11

Health Psychology

Some of the questions first addressed by ancient philosophers were What is mind?, What is body?, and Are mind and body related, and if so, how? Clinical psychologists, too, have addressed this *mind–body problem*. For example, the notion of "psychosomatic disorders" (physical diseases that have psychological causes) has a long history, reflecting clinicians' observations that emotional problems sometimes lead to physical illnesses. Indeed, research on the ways in which psychological factors can affect physical health has made it clear that mind and body interact reciprocally: mental processes and behavior can affect bodily functions and the condition of the body can affect the way we think and act.

In this chapter and the next, we discuss two specialized areas of clinical psychology—health psychology and neuropsychology—that illustrate how important it is for psychologists to study relationships between psychological and biological factors. We have selected these areas because they have been some of clinical psychology's best "growth stocks" in the past twenty-five years. New research discoveries and expanding professional roles for clinicians have increasingly attracted psychologists to these areas.

WHAT IS HEALTH PSYCHOLOGY?

Health psychology is a specialty that emerged in the 1970s and is devoted to studying "psychological influences on how people stay healthy, why they become ill, and how they respond when they do get ill" (Taylor, 1995, p. 3). This subfield has enjoyed such rapid growth over the last twenty-five years that it now has its own division in the APA (Division 38) and its own journal, *Health Psychology*. Health psychology research is also often published in the *Journal of Behavioral Medicine* and *Psychological Medicine*. Related professional organizations include the Society of Behavioral Medicine and the American Psychosomatic Society. Many clinical psychology training programs now include a "track" that specializes in the training of health psychologists, and some programs have developed health psychology as their major focus. Health psychology is closely related to the larger field of *behavioral medicine*, which involves the integration of knowledge from the social/behavioral sciences (e.g., psychology, sociology, and anthropology), the biological sciences, and medicine into an interdisciplinary science focused on understanding and treating all types of medical disorders in the broadest possible ways. Health psychology and behavioral medicine follow a *biopsychosocial* model which holds that physical illness is the result of biological, psychological, and social disruptions. They study how psychological conditions and behavioral processes are linked to illness and health.

Sir William Osler, a physician, is generally considered the father of modern behavioral medicine because he insisted that psychological and emotional factors must be considered in order to understand and treat various diseases. In 1910, Osler gave a lecture in which he suggested that many symptoms of heart disease "are brought on by anger, worry, or sudden shock." These ideas are remarkably similar to contemporary proposals about how key psychological factors may be linked to heart disease.

Osler's views were made more relevant by significant changes in the nature of illness in Western cultures during the twentieth century. As recently as a hundred years ago, most Americans died of acute infectious diseases such as pneumonia, typhoid fever, and tuberculosis. However, advances in education, sanitation, and vaccination have all but eliminated these diseases, leaving *chronic* illnesses—heart disease and cancer, for example—as the major threats to life (Blumenthal, 1994). Further, the major risk factors for developing chronic illnesses are *behaviors* such as smoking, unhealthy eating, and alcohol abuse.

These changes in the major threats to health, along with changing ideas about illness, spurred research on how psychological, behavioral, and medical conditions are related. It became clear, for example, that psychological factors contribute to the onset or severity of heart disease, ulcers, asthma, stomach disorders, cancer, arthritis, headaches, and hypertension. Indeed, until recently, these illnesses were called *psychosomatic* or *psychophysiological*, disorders in recognition of the mixture of psychological and biological determinants operating in them. But categorizing just a few illnesses as psychosomatic implies that psychological factors are not relevant in other conditions. Today's health psychologists consider psychological factors to be potential influences on almost all diseases.

The more we learn about any human disorder, the more difficult it becomes to draw a line that clearly divides those that are "physical" from those that are "mental." For example, schizophrenia and major depression, two of our most serious mental disorders, almost always entail a mixture of physical and psychological causes and symptoms. Further, depression often adversely affects the course of diseases such as diabetes; and many cases of diabetes ultimately lead to clinical depression.

Several books provide more detailed discussions of the history of health psychology and behavioral medicine (e.g., Ogden, 1996; Taylor, 1995). In this chapter, we discuss four areas of research and practice that occupy many health psychologists (Blumenthal, Matthews, & Weiss, 1994):

1. Understanding how environmental stressors, psychological processes, social forces, and physiological factors interact to influence illness and health,
2. Identifying risk factors for sickness as well as protective factors for health,
3. Developing and evaluating techniques for promoting healthy behaviors and preventing unhealthy ones, and
4. Developing and evaluating psychological interventions that contribute to the effective treatment of illness.

STRESS, HEALTH, AND ILLNESS

Stress is the negative emotional and physiological process that occurs as people try to adjust to or deal with environmental circumstances that disrupt, or threaten to disrupt, their daily functioning (Taylor, 1995). The environmental circumstances (such as job demands, exams, personal tragedies, or even annoying daily hassles) that cause people to make adjustments are called *stressors*. The physical, psychological, and behavioral responses (such as increased heart rate, anger, and impulsiveness) that people display in the face of stressors are called *stress reactions*.

Barbara Dohrenwend (1978) suggested a four-stage model of how stressors and stress reactions contribute to physical illness and/or psychological disorder. In the first stage, stressful life events occur, followed in the second stage by a set of physical and psychological stress reactions. In the third stage, these stress reactions are mediated by environmental and psychological factors that either amplify or reduce their intensity. Factors likely to reduce stress reactions include things like adequate financial resources, free time to deal with stressors, a full repertoire of effective coping skills, the help and support of friends and family, a strong sense of control over stressors, a tendency to be optimistic, and a view of stressors as challenges. Stress-amplifying factors include things like poverty, lack of social support, inadequate coping skills, pessimism, a sense of helplessness, and seeing stressors as terrifying threats. In stage four, the interaction of particular stressors, particular people, and particular circumstances results in physical and/or psychological problems that may be mild and temporary (some anxiety, a headache, or a few sleepless nights) or severe and persistent (e.g., an anxiety or mood disorder, or physical illness). Exactly how stressors and stress reactions might contribute to physical illness is not clearly understood, but part of the story is told by their impact on the nervous system and the immune system.

Stress and the Nervous System

Physiological reactions to stress include a pattern of responses in the central and autonomic nervous system that Hans Selye (1956) called the *general adaptation syndrome* or GAS. The GAS begins with an *alarm reaction* which is often called the fight-or-flight response because it helps us combat or escape stressors. The alarm reaction releases into the bloodstream a number of "stress hormones," including adrenal corticosteroids, catecholamines (e.g., adrenaline), and endogenous opiates (the body's natural painkillers), all of which cause increases in heart rate, blood pressure, and respiration, pupillary dilation, muscle tension, release of glucose reserves, and concentration of attention on the stressor.

If the stressor persists, or if new ones occur in quick succession, alarm is followed by the *stage of resistance*, during which less dramatic, but more continuous biochemical efforts to cope with stress can have harmful consequences. For example, prolonged release of stress hormones can create chronic high blood pressure, damage muscle tissue, and inhibit the body's ability to heal.

If stressors continue long enough, the *stage of exhaustion* appears as various organ systems begin to malfunction or break down. Here, people experience physical symptoms ranging from fatigue, weight loss, and indigestion to colds, heart disease, and other more serious problems.

Stress and Immune System

Another important effect of prolonged stress is suppression of the immune system, the body's defense against disease-causing agents (Herbert & Cohen, 1993; Maier, Watkins, & Fleshner, 1994). For example, chronic stressors (e.g., taking care of a seriously ill relative) have been shown to lower immune system functioning, and even brief stressors like final-exam periods have been associated with a decline in the activity of immune system cells that fight viruses and tumors (Kiecolt-Glaser & Glaser, 1992). In one particularly interesting study of the relationship between stress and illness, researchers injected volunteer subjects with cold viruses or a placebo and then measured the amount of stress experienced by the volunteers over a given time period (Cohen, Tyrell, & Smith, 1991). The results showed that the appearance of colds and infections was correlated with the amount of stress the subjects encountered. Many researchers now suspect that *immunosuppression* is the basis for the association between stressors and increased risk for some forms of cancer and other illnesses (e.g., Cohen, 1996).

Measuring Stressors

To study the relationship between stress and illness, it is necessary to measure stress accurately, and health psychologists have tried to do so in several ways. One example is a questionnaire called the Schedule of Recent Experiences (SRE) (Amundson, Hart, & Holmes, 1986), which contains a list of forty-two events involving health, family, personal, occupational, and financial matters (see Table 11.1). Respondents check the events that have happened to them during the past six, twelve, twenty-four, and thirty-six months, and then give each event a weight based on the amount of adjustment needed to deal with it (1 = very little adjustment; 100 = maximal adjustment). These weights are summed to give a Life Change Unit Score.

Criticism of the SRE led other researchers to develop stress assessment instruments that differ in how they weight the occurrence of an event, the time periods surveyed, and the content of the events themselves (Zimmerman, 1983). For example, the

---

TABLE 11.1   The Schedule of Recent Experiences

In the Schedule of Recent Experiences (Amundson, Hart, & Holmes, 1986) subjects indicate which of 42 stressful events have happened to them in the past 6-, 12-, 24-, and 36-month periods. After subjects check the events that have occurred, the amount of adjustment each event required is assigned a value on a 100-point scale. The stressful events are organized into five categories. Examples from each category are listed below.

A. Health
  A major change in eating habits
  A major change in sleeping habits
B. Work
  Changed to a new line of work
  Experienced being fired from work
  Changed work hours or conditions
C. Home and family
  A change in family "get togethers"
  Death of a close friend
  A divorce

  Gaining a new family member
D. Personal and Social
  Sexual difficulties
  A minor violation of the law
  A vacation
  A major change in church activities
E. Financial
  Major business readjustment
  Foreclosure on a mortgage or loan
  Taking out a mortgage or loan for a major purchase, such as a home, business, property, etc.

Life Experiences Survey (Sarason, Johnson, & Siegel, 1978) allows respondents to rate the positive or negative impact of each listed event, and to add stressful events that are *not* listed. These more individualized ratings are designed to make the LES and similar instruments more sensitive to the stressors experienced by people of diverse ethnic and cultural backgrounds.

Health psychologists have theorized that the effects of many minor daily stressors can be as cumulatively significant as one major one, so they have also developed "chronic strain" inventories, such as the Hassles Scale (Kanner et al., 1981). On this scale, respondents indicate how severely they have been hassled in the past month by events such as "misplacing or losing things," "unexpected company," "auto maintenance," "too many meetings," and "filling out forms." Another approach to measuring stress involves examining the effects of specific life crises such as crime victimization (e.g., Burnam et al., 1988) on later adjustment. Further discussion of these and other methods of measuring stress can be found in a number of sources (e.g., Kessler, Price, & Wortman, 1985; Zimmerman, 1983).

The results of research with even the best stress assessment scales shows that while there is undoubtedly a relationship between stress and illness, the strength of that relationship is relatively weak. In other words, even though people who are exposed to significant stressors are more likely overall to become ill than those exposed to fewer stressors, most people who experience stressors do not become ill. This realization has led health psychologists to search for variables that might explain how people are protected from the assumed health-harming effects of stress. Among several *vulnerability* or *resistance* factors (Kessler et al., 1985), two variables—coping strategies and social support—have sparked the most interest.

Coping Strategies

Coping refers to people's cognitive, emotional, and behavioral efforts at modifying, tolerating, or eliminating stressors that threaten them (Folkman & Lazarus, 1980). People vary in how they cope with stress. Some try to eliminate or otherwise deal with stressors directly; others attempt to change the way they think about stressors to make them less upsetting; still others concentrate on managing the emotional reactions that stressors cause (Lazarus, 1993).

Research groups at the University of California (Berkeley) and at the State University of New York at Stony Brook have developed instruments to measure how people cope with stress. At Berkeley, Richard Lazarus and Susan Folkman developed a Ways of Coping checklist consisting of sixty-eight items that describe how 100 middle-aged adults said they coped with stressful events in their lives (Folkman & Lazarus, 1980). These items fall into two broad categories: *problem-focused* and *emotion-focused* coping (see Table 11.2). The 100 respondents reported on a total of 1,332 stressful episodes, and in 98% of them, said they used both coping methods. Their choice was not random, however. The typical respondent emphasized problem-focused methods for coping with some stressors and emotion-focused methods for others. Problem-focused coping was favored for stressors related to work, while emotion-focused coping was used more often when the stressors involved health. Men tended to use problem-focused coping more often than women in certain situations, but men and women did not differ in their use of emotion-focused coping.

TABLE 11.2   Ways of Coping

Problem-focused and emotion-focused coping are two major ways in which people deal with stressors.

Coping Skills	Example
Problem-focused coping	
Confronting	"I stood my ground and fought for what I wanted."
Seeking social support	"I talked to someone to find out more about the situation."
Planful problem solving	"I made a plan of action and I followed it."
Emotion-focused coping	
Self-controlling	"I tried to keep my feelings to myself."
Distancing	"I didn't let it get to me; I tried not to think about it too much."
Positive reappraisal	"I changed my mind about myself."
Accepting responsibility	"I realized I brought the problem on myself."
Escape/avoidance (wishful thinking)	"I wished that the situation would go away or somehow be over with.

SOURCE: Adapted from Folkman, S., Lazarus, R. S., Gruen, R. J., & DeLongis, A. (1986). Appraisal, coping, health status, and psychological symptoms. *Journal of Personality and Social Psychology*, 50, 571–579.

At Stony Brook, Arthur Stone and John Neale developed an alternative instrument that asked respondents open-ended questions about how they handled particular stress-related problems on a given day. It also provided a one-sentence description of each of eight coping styles used to handle a problem on a given day: distraction, situation redefinition, direct action, catharsis, acceptance, seeking social support, relaxation, and religion. Respondents were also asked to describe in their own words the particular thoughts or actions they had used for each category of coping (Stone & Neale, 1984).

Despite differences in their methodologies, both research teams reached similar conclusions about coping. Men tended to use direct action a little more—and distraction, catharsis and seeking social support a little less—than women. The way a given problem was cognitively appraised or defined was significantly related to the ways in which people tried to cope with it. Finally, most people appeared to be flexible copers; although they may have one favorite coping style, they combine it with other strategies as their view of a problem requires.

Effective coping can lessen some effects of stress, but its success depends on several factors, including the type of stress to be reduced. For example, coping through denial (e.g., viewing a failed exam as being unimportant) appears to be an effective response to short-term stress but an ineffective strategy for handling the chronic stress of a marital problem (Mullen & Suls, 1982).

Are particular types of stressors better managed by particular coping strategies? Possibly. For example, people who face painful illnesses such as arthritis appear to do better with problem-focused coping, such as actively seeking information about the stressors so they can anticipate and try to control them (Revenson & Felton, 1989). On the other hand, when faced with a truly uncontrollable condition, emotion-focused coping, including ventilation of feelings but also occasional distraction from the trauma, might be an effective strategy (Meyerowitz, Heinrich, & Schag, 1983).

Social Support

Social support has been defined in many ways (Schradle & Dougher, 1985), but its essential element appears to be the experience of being cared for, loved, esteemed, and part of a network of communication and mutual obligation (Baumeister & Leary, 1995). Social support, then, involves more than the presence of others. It provides relationships in which emotional support, feedback, guidance, assistance, and values are exchanged.

Several studies have shown that the relationship between stress and illness is weaker among individuals who perceive high levels of social support in their lives (e.g., Broman, 1993; Wickrama, Conger & Lorenz, 1995). There are several possible reasons why this might be so (Cohen & Wills, 1985; Uchino, Cacioppo, & Kiecolt-Glaser, 1996). The most popular explanation is that social support acts as a *buffer* against stress. The buffer model claims that social support enables people who face intense stressors to neutralize their harmful effects. By serving as an additional resource in a person's attempts at managing stressful problems, social support bolsters their efforts at constructive coping (Thoits, 1986), and may lessen the chances of self-defeating strategies such as excessive drinking. In short, people's *perception* of social support can strengthen their belief that others care for and value them; it may also enhance their self-esteem and increase feelings of confidence about handling stress in the future (Heller, Swindle, & Dusenbury, 1986). Another view, sometimes termed the *direct-effect model*, holds that social support is helpful regardless of whether stressful events are experienced because there is a general benefit to being embedded in supportive relationships that manifests itself in better health (Baumeister & Leary, 1995). A third explanation for the apparent benefits of social support is that high levels of support, good health, and low levels of stress all reflect the influence of some underlying characteristic such as *social competence*, which has positive effects on many areas of functioning.

Of course, some combination of all three models may be operating. What does seem clear is that *lack* of social support, particularly lack of emotional support, puts people at higher risk for both physical and psychological disorders (Cohen & Wills, 1985; Kessler et al., 1985) and even death (House, Robbins, & Metzner, 1982).

Despite its general advantages, social support is not always associated with protection against illness. Social ties can create conflicts if others' helping efforts leave the recipient feeling guilty, overly indebted, or dependent. If a recipient is not able to reciprocate helping efforts, she or he may feel disadvantaged in future interactions with the donor. In other instances, potential helpers may behave in misguided ways (giving too much advice or becoming upset when their advice is not followed) that lead the recipient to feel invaded, incompetent, or rejected (Broman, 1993; Malarkey et al., 1994; Wortman & Lehman, 1985).

RISK FACTORS FOR ILLNESS

Anything that increases a person's chances of developing an illness is called a risk factor for that illness. Some risk factors stem from biological and environmental conditions such as genetic defects or exposure to toxic chemicals (Stokols, 1992). Others come in the form of health–risky patterns of behavior. For example, smoking, overeating, lack of exercise, and consumption of a high-fat, low-fiber diet have all been identified as risk factors for two of North America's leading killers: cardiovascular disease and cancer (VandenBos, DeLeon, & Belar, 1991). Conversely, certain behaviors or lifestyles tend to promote health. For example, people who eat breakfast regularly, rarely snack between meals, exercise regularly, do not smoke, get seven to eight hours of sleep per night, and do not use alcohol excessively live an average of eleven years longer than people who practice none of these behaviors (Breslow, 1979).

There are a number of ways in which psychological risk factors, too, can influence illness and health. To take but one example, aggressive people are likely to seek out competitive situations which, because they often entail conflict, frequently produce physiological arousal. This arousal may ultimately increase the risk of illness. At the same time, aggressive people may be less likely to receive stress-reducing social support from others. Because they are often competitive and in a hurry, aggressive people may be less likely to take time to get medical check-ups that might detect diseases in their early stages. So a personality trait such as aggressiveness may make three contributions to an illness—especially in people who are genetically predisposed toward it—by increasing physiological arousal, by suppressing social support, and by interfering with healthy behavior.

Behavioral and psychological risk factors appear to combine with other risks to create a strong overall relationship between socioeconomic status (SES) and health. (SES, which reflects a person's social standing relative to others in a society, is measured in terms of income, education, and occupation.) The lower one's SES, the greater one's chances of suffering chronic illness and unexpectedly early death (e.g., Adler et al., 1994). This relationship makes sense when viewed in light of the fact that low SES is linked to poorer nutrition, greater exposure to environmental hazards, and less adequate medical care. These factors may explain the health disadvantages suffered by poor people compared to rich people, but why is it also true that rates of chronic illness differ between middle- and upper SES levels, where nutritional, environmental, and health care differences are not as great?

The answer may lie in differences across SES levels in terms of psychological functioning, environmental stressors, and health-risky behaviors, all of which can have an impact on people's vulnerability to illness. For example, negative emotions are significantly linked to greater risks for serious illnesses (e.g., Appels & Otten, 1992; Markowitz et al., 1991). Social class is inversely related to certain strong negative emotions, such as depression, hostility, and chronic antagonism (e.g., Scherwitz, et al., 1992). Therefore, the consistent association between SES and health may be mediated through their common relationship to differential levels of chronic negative emotion. People at each successively lower SES level also face more negative life events than those above them (McLeod & Kessler, 1990), thereby increasing the number and intensity of stressors with which they must cope. People at lower SES levels are also likely to have fewer financial and other material resources at hand to cope with these stressors, thereby further increasing their impact. Finally, the prevalence of health-risky behaviors tends to be inversely related to SES. Smoking, for example, is more common among less educated people, and people who work in lower status occupations are less likely to engage in physical exercise. Each of these habits have direct negative effects on health, but they can also act in concert with each other, and with other variables, to magnify health problems. Thus, lack of exercise is associated with obesity, which itself is more common among low SES groups (Ernst & Harlan, 1991). Obesity, in turn, significantly increases risks for serious illnesses such as hypertension, diabetes, and coronary heart disease (e.g., Foster & Kendall, 1994). Similarly, people who drink alcohol excessively or abuse illegal drugs are also much more likely to smoke (Sobell, Toneatto, & Sobell, 1994), thereby constituting a double dose of behavioral risk.

The negative physical consequences of unhealthy behaviors may also lead to increased levels of stress, depression, discouragement, and consequent impairment in coping skills (Valliant, 1994). For people in lower socioeconomic classes, then, years of engaging in harmful behaviors may slowly but surely lead to a cluster of bad outcomes that include physical illness.

The multifaceted influence of behavioral, psychological, and social risk factors is seen in several serious illnesses, including heart disease, cancer, and AIDS.

Risk Factors for Cardiovascular Disease

About half of the deaths each year in North America result from cardiovascular diseases, which include coronary heart disease (CHD), high blood pressure, and stroke. There are several risk factors for these diseases, including genetic predisposition, cigarette smoking, and high levels of low-density lipoprotein cholesterol (the so-called "bad" cholesterol). Ethnicity is also a factor; CHD is about half as common among Chinese- or Japanese-Americans as among European- or African-Americans, while high blood pressure is about twice as common among African-Americans as European-Americans. Important as they are, genetic, sociocultural, and behavioral risk factors cannot fully account for the majority of cases of CHD or hypertension. Accordingly, scientists have studied the role of stressors and psychological characteristics in these diseases.

The Role of Stressors.   Some of the first strong evidence about the role of stress in cardiovascular disease came from research on monkeys' responses to various types of stress (Manuck, Kaplan, & Clarkson, 1983; Manuck et al., 1988). Researchers wanted to know whether increases in cardiovascular and endocrine reactivity caused by stressors can, if repeated many times over several years, produce the kinds of changes in the heart or peripheral arteries seen in cardiovascular diseases. The answer appears to be yes; animals showing the greatest increase in heart rate in response to stressors also had significantly more plaque—a build-up of cholesterol and other fatty substances—in their coronary arteries than did animals whose reaction was less extreme.

As noted earlier, people, too, react to threatening stimuli and other stressors with increases in heart rate—as well as with pronounced changes in blood pressure, and secretion of epinephrine, norepinephrine, and other stress hormones (Anderson, 1989; Krantz & Manuck, 1984). In the short run, these changes have little significance for cardiovascular functioning, which returns to normal soon after a stressor ends. However, if repeated stressors continually stimulate cardiac activity, the small arteries at the body's periphery may undergo permanent constrictions that result in increased blood pressure (Obrist, 1981).

Demographic variables such as ethnicity, gender, and age are related to a tendency to overreact physiologically to stressors (Adler & Matthews, 1994). This relationship may explain why certain people are at greater risk for heart disease than others. Males, African-Americans of both genders, and older people all suffer higher-than-average rates of heart disease *and* have larger-than-average blood pressure responses to certain stressors. Why these differences occur is not yet clear, although physical factors—such as diet—and cultural factors such as living in stressful environments are almost certainly important contributors. In one study, persons living in crowded urban environments showed more cardiovascular reactivity to laboratory stressors than did residents of lower stress areas (Fleming et al., 1987). Thus, the heightened risk of cardiovascular disease among African-Americans may be related to the fact that many of them are, because of lower socioeconomic status, exposed to higher-stress environments. Because they face more social adversity and obstacles than other groups, African-Americans may also be more likely to feel anger and express hostility. The increased risk of CHD for men in general may stem from their tendency to behave aggressively or competitively in social situations, while the risk for older people may lie in a gradual erosion of social support that increases the impact of stressors.

Psychological Factors in CHD. As noted earlier, the impact of stressors can be mediated by psychological factors, including whether we think about stressors as threats or challenges, and whether we believe we can control them. People who feel helpless in the face of what they see as threats are likely to experience more intense physiological reactivity and emotional upset. On the other hand, those who view stressors as challenges, and feel confident about coping with them, may experience less reactivity and distress (Lazarus & Folkman, 1984).

The psychological risk factors for CHD that have attracted the most attention in the past twenty years are associated with the *Type-A* behavior pattern that a pair of cardiologists noticed was typical of many patients with heart disease (Friedman & Rosenman, 1974). Type-A people are described as displaying (1) explosive, accelerated speech; (2) a heightened pace of living; (3) impatience with slowness; (4) attempts to perform more than one activity at a time; (5) preoccupation with self; (6) dissatisfaction with life; (7) evaluation of accomplishments in terms of numbers; (8) competitiveness; and (9) free-floating hostility (Matthews, 1982). In contrast to Type-A persons, *Type-B* persons are more relaxed and feel less time pressure. They appear less competitive, controlling, and hostile.

There are three main procedures for measuring Type-A behavior. The *Structured Interview* (Rosenman, 1978) consists of about twenty-five questions that tap how a person responds to frustrating situations (some of the questions are asked in a slow, halting manner designed to provoke Type-A behavior). The *Jenkins Activity Survey* (Jenkins, Zyzanski, & Rosenman, 1971) contains approximately fifty questions that assess competitiveness, impatience, and job involvement (sample item: Do you ever have trouble finding time to get your hair cut or styled?) The *Framingham Type A Scale* (Haynes et al., 1978) is a ten-item self-report measure that concentrates on competitiveness, time urgency, and sense of job pressure. These three measures tend not to agree well with one another in classifying the Type-A pattern (Matthews & Haynes, 1986), which makes it more difficult to summarize the results of research on the relationship between Type A and CHD. Although the Jenkins Activity Survey is used frequently because of its convenience, the Structured Interview appears to be the superior measure because its results are more strongly related to illness measures (Matthews, 1988).

Early research suggested that the entire constellation of Type-A behavior and thinking is an important risk factor for the development of CHD. For example, in the Western Collaborative Group Study (WCGS), 3,500 men between the ages of thirty-nine and fifty-nine were classified as Type A or Type B. Of 257 men who suffered heart attacks during the eight-and-a-half-year study, 178 (69%) of them were Type A's. In other words, Type A's were more than twice as likely to have had heart attacks as Type B's (Rosenman et al., 1975). The impact of Type A on CHD risk remained even after the researchers statistically controlled for several other risk factors, including family history of heart disease, high cholesterol, high blood pressure, and cigarette smoking. Another major epidemiological research project called the Framingham Heart Study found essentially the same results in relation to about 1,600 healthy men and women (Haynes, Feinleib, & Kannel, 1980).

However, we now know that the relationship between Type-A behavior and CHD is much more complex than was originally believed. For one thing, being a Type-A person does *not* mean that you are highly likely to suffer a heart attack or other form of CHD. Notice that even though Type A's in the WCGS and Framingham studies were twice as likely to develop CHD as Type B's, the vast majority of Type A's never developed CHD. Second, careful re-analysis of the Framingham study (Eaker et al., 1989), more recent follow-up on the WCGS sample (Ragland & Brand, 1988) and data from prospective studies conducted with Asian-American men (Cohen & Reed, 1985) suggest that not all aspects of Type-A behavior are risk factors for CHD (Matthews, 1988; Miller et al., 1991). Recent research suggests that the most health-risky aspect of the Type-A pattern is hostility, a feature that not all Type A's display (Williams & Barefoot, 1988). Some researchers suggest that the role of hostility in CHD may be especially strong when it is combined with cynicism and chronic suspiciousness or distrust (Dembroski et al., 1985).

Most research on Type-A behavior was first focused on men, but the pattern appears to be very similar in women. (Source: Shirley Zeiberg/Simon & Schuster/PH College.)

Others argue that the data are not yet clear enough to single out hostility as the major CHD risk factor (Thoresen & Powell, 1992). Indeed, it may be that chronic negative emotions, whether part of the Type-A pattern or not, carry the greatest risks for CHD, and physical illness in general. One review of research on psychological predictors of CHD found that people chronically experiencing one or more negative emotions such as depression, aggressive competitiveness, and anger were more likely to develop CHD than the hurried, impatient workaholics typically labeled as Type A (Booth-Kewley & Friedman, 1987). Another study showed that anxiety scores significantly predicted the twenty-year incidence of hypertension in middle-aged men in the Framingham Heart Study even when variables such as age, obesity, smoking, and alcohol use were statistically controlled for (Markowitz et al., 1991). Still other studies have found that men who reported fatigue, dejection, defeat, and increased irritability—a condition termed *vital exhaustion* or what is commonly called "burnout"—were at higher risk for later chest pain and heart attacks (Appels & Otten, 1992; Appels & Schouten, 1991).

Combining the results of research on psychological risk factors and CHD, it appears that when encountering a stressor, Type A's experience faster heart rates and higher blood pressure than Type B's (Harbin, 1989; Lyness, 1993), and that these differences in reactivity are strongest in response to stressors that generate interpersonal conflict, mobilize competitiveness, or involve criticism. Of course, these are just the kinds of situations most likely to lead to anger and hostility. Likewise, chronically hostile people experience high levels of cardiovascular reactivity, most notably in response to interpersonal stressors (Suls & Wang, 1993). Perhaps Type-A behavior or chronic negative emotions are linked to CHD because people with these characteristics consistently overreact physiologically to situations that threaten them or make them angry. In addition, their competitiveness and hostility create ever more opportunities for conflict, to which they then overreact. In the long-run, this physiological overarousal could put a strain on arteries and increase the chances for other cardiovascular defects. The link between these psychological characteristics and CHD might also be forged in another way. Frequent angry outbursts or other negative emotions may be accompanied by rapid swings in the levels of stress hormones, the corticosteroids and catecholamines. A constant barrage of hormonal changes could, in turn, bring about various chemical changes that weaken arteries. In addition, many of these people are "too busy" to go to a doctor, eat a balanced diet, get enough sleep, or engage in regular exercise; they may also consume excessive caffeine and smoke tobacco. The interaction of these unhealthy behaviors with emotionally driven wear and tear may prove to be the most complete explanation of the psychological risks for CHD.

Risk Factors for Cancer

About 1 million people are diagnosed with cancer each year in the United States alone, and one out of three Americans will develop some form of cancer at some time in their lives. Indeed, cancer is the second leading cause of death in the United States.

It is widely known that the risk of developing various forms of cancer is increased by behavior patterns such as smoking tobacco and eating a high-fat diet (Bodmer & McKie, 1994), and it has also been suggested that there may be psychological risk factors as well. Since the early 1960s, a few researchers have claimed that cancer is associated with the so-called *Type-C*, or cancer-prone personality (Kissen & Eysenck, 1962). People displaying this personality are said to be overly conforming and emotionally blunted, appearing calm and collected, but engaged in vigorous efforts to deny and repress inner turmoil. Type-C people are also said to feel hopeless and powerless in the face of life's stressors. However, empirical evidence for a link between Type-C personality and cancer is weak. For example, longitudinal studies that have tried to use personality assessments to predict the appearance of cancer have yielded conflicting results. Thus, it appears that behavioral risk factors are more significant than psychological ones in elevating cancer risk.

Risk Factors for AIDS

It has been estimated that as many as 1 million people in the United States are infected with HIV, the virus that causes acquired immune deficiency syndrome (AIDS), and that, worldwide, over 20 million people are infected. By the year 2000, the total number may exceed 30 million (Shariff, 1995). In the United States, homosexual males and intravenous drug users are at highest risk, but the incidence of HIV infection is growing especially fast among low-income African-Americans and Hispanic-American adolescents. HIV is also spreading among young women at such a rate that, today, HIV/AIDS is the fourth leading killer of women in the United States.

Health psychologists have helped focus attention on the fact that most cases of AIDS can be prevented by avoiding several risky behavior patterns: (1) sexual activity without the use of condoms or other protective devices, (2) sexual contact with multiple partners and/or partners with an unknown sexual history, (3) heavy use of alcohol or other drugs prior to sexual activity (because drugs impair judgment about the necessity of using condoms), and (4) for intravenous drug users, sharing injection needles.

ILLNESS PREVENTION AND TREATMENT PROGRAMS

Health psychologists have collaborated with physicians, health educators, and other professionals to develop programs for preventing and treating a variety of illnesses. The prevention programs are designed to reduce behavioral and psychological risk factors in specified populations, typically by helping people make healthy changes in diet, exercise, and smoking and drinking habits (Matarazzo & Carmody, 1983). The scope of illness-prevention programs ranges from one-to-one consultations on a particular person's lifestyle, to workplace programs aimed at groups of at-risk employees, to large-scale interventions that use mass media campaigns to influence the health–risky behaviors of whole communities. Health psychology treatment programs usually focus on helping medical patients, individually or in small groups, minimize or cope with the symptoms of their illnesses. The success of these methods and the promise of new advances account in part for the rapid increase in the number of health psychologists employed in hospitals and other health-care settings.

In this section, we highlight health psychology interventions related to cardiovascular diseases, gastrointestinal problems, pain, cancer, and AIDS. More extensive discussions of these activities can be found in health psychology textbooks (e.g., Taylor, 1995).

Cardiovascular Diseases

As noted earlier, many people who do not currently have CHD or hypertension are at risk for these diseases because of the way they tend to behave and think. These people can benefit from preventive interventions designed to reduce their risk.

For example, several treatment programs have been developed to reduce Type-A behavior (Nunes, Frank, & Kornfeld, 1987; Thoreson & Powell, 1992). Among the many techniques available, relaxation training, self-monitoring, and training in coping skills appear to have the largest effects on Type-A behavior. Interventions aimed at changing Type-A behavior can also have beneficial effects on some of the biological factors presumed to be at the root of CHD; reduced cholesterol, lowered systolic blood pressure, and slowed heart rate have all been associated with reductions in Type-A behavior. (Type-A readers who are anxious about their status and obsessing about whether they can change their behavior—by tonight, if possible—should read the recommendations for reducing Type-A behavior contained in Table 11.3—slowly, please.)

TABLE 11.3   Changing Type-A Behavior

Is it the case that "once a Type A always a Type A" or can a Type-A person slow down, loosen up, learn to relax, and become more like a B? Friedman and Rosenman (1974) believe that Type-A behavior can be changed if people practice changing their ways of thinking and behaving. Here are a few examples of the changes that they recommend.

Philosophical Guidelines

1. Make an honest self-appraisal of your strengths and weaknesses so that you will be less dependent on the opinions of others and less driven to please them.
2. Develop broader interests in activities outside your career preoccupations—e.g., art, literature, making new friends.
3. Accept the fact that life consists of many unfinished processes, jobs, and events. Only some of these tasks will ever be finished no matter how compulsively you work at them.

Reengineering Your Day

1. Arrange your work environment so as to promote peace—e.g., schedule more time for appointments than you think they will require, keep a clean desk, don't be a slave to the telephone.
2. Talk less.
3. Reserve periods of time each week when you can be alone.

Drills

1. Go to a restaurant with a companion where you know you will have to wait in line to be served.
2. Whenever you go faster in your car to beat a red light at the intersection, punish yourself by circling the block and coming back to the same intersection.
3. Read books that demand patience and your full attention. For example, the prose of Proust and Faulkner moves at a pace that forces Type-A persons to stop their tendency to skim.

Many studies have evaluated the effects of programs for changing Type-A behavior. For example, in the Recurrent Coronary Prevention Project, over 800 patients who had already suffered a heart attack received periodic counseling over a three-year period (Friedman et al., 1986). For some, the counseling focused on the importance of changing diet, exercise, and smoking habits, and adherence to prescribed medications. Others received this counseling along with advice on how to reduce Type-A behavior. At the end of the three-year program, only 7.2% of the patients who regularly attended the counseling-plus-Type A modification sessions had suffered another heart attack. The heart attack rate was 13.2% for those who had received counseling alone. It is not yet clear, however, if similar programs with healthy Type-A people would have similar effects.

In another approach to preventing CHD, health psychologists have developed programs aimed at eliminating smoking and other harmful habits and at promoting regular exercise, good diet, and other healthy habits (e.g., Jeffery, 1988). Some of these programs focus on a specific risk factor, such as obesity; others address several risk factors at once. The settings for implementing these programs also vary. Workplace interventions have become popular because corporations believe they reduce the cost of health care and because occupational health promotion programs permit the control and investigation of several motivational and environmental variables (Glasgow & Terborg, 1988). Mass media, correspondence, and agricultural extension programs have also been attempted.

A prime example of a community-wide project aimed at preventing multiple risk factors associated with cardiovascular disease was the Stanford Heart Disease Prevention Program (SHDPP) (Meyer et al., 1980). Approximately 500 persons in three Northern California towns were identified as being at high risk for heart disease. In Community #1 (Watsonville), fifty-six subjects were assigned to a mass media campaign (TV and radio spots) that acquainted the audience with probable causes of heart disease and the changes in smoking, diet, and exercise that could reduce the risk. One hundred and thirteen additional people in Watsonville were exposed to the same media campaign, but also got "intensive instruction" involving face-to-face behaviorally oriented counseling about how to make risk-lowering changes. In Community #2 (Gilroy), 139 people received the media campaign alone, while in Community #3 (Tracy) 136 people served as a no-treatment control group which received neither media nor intensive instructional intervention. The health status of all participants was assessed at three annual follow-up surveys.

All treated groups showed decreases in cardiovascular disease risk factors and increased knowledge about those factors. The largest and longest-lasting overall risk reductions appeared in the people of Watsonville who got the mass media campaign and intensive instruction. The investigators concluded that "intensive media plus face-to-face instruction had greater impact on cardiovascular disease risk and related knowledge and behavior than did the media-only treatment or control" (Meyer et al., 1980). The SHDPP has been subjected to several criticisms, however. A major difficulty was the high *attrition* or drop-out rate (around 25%), especially in the Watsonville intensive instruction group (e.g., when dropouts are considered in this group, its smoking cessation rate, for example drops from 50% to 32%).

Other prominent examples of multiple-component prevention programs are the Multiple Risk Factor Intervention Trial (MRFIT, 1982) which attempted to lower blood pressure, smoking, and blood cholesterol in thousands of high-risk individuals; the North Karelia, Finland project (designed in the context of the international Know Your Body Program; Williams, Arnold, & Wynder, 1977); and the Minnesota Heart Health Program, a five-year educational intervention targeting multiple heart disease risk factors (Blackburn et al., 1984). A special feature of the latter two programs is that their interventions were aimed at children and adolescents. Schools were the primary setting for these interventions, which concentrated on improving knowledge about health, changing peer norms about habits like cigarette smoking, and educating families about risk factors (Perry et al., 1988).

Gastrointestinal Problems

Among the gastrointestinal disorders addressed by health psychologists are fecal incontinence, irritable bowel syndrome, inflammatory bowel disease, and repetitive vomiting among infants and retarded adults. Psychotherapy, stress management, and hypnosis have all proven to be effective in relieving symptoms of irritable bowel syndrome. Biofeedback and conditioning techniques (see Chapter 8) which teach patients to monitor and control internal sensations and reflexes are highly successful treatments for fecal incontinence and repetitive vomiting (Whitehead, 1992). Gastrointestinal problems are often symptoms of such chronic illnesses as cancer and diabetes; therefore, successful treatment methods are also useful in managing these disorders.

Pain

Pain may be the single most common physical symptom experienced by medical patients (Turk & Rudy, 1990), so pain management is an important objective in psychological interventions with many disorders. Health psychologists have concentrated their pain research and treatment on three areas: chronic pain conditions, headache, and rheumatoid arthritis. For headache and chronic pain, biofeedback and relaxation training methods have a long record of success, and cognitive-behavioral techniques have also proved effective (e.g., Azar, 1996; Blanchard, 1992). Arthritis pain has generally been treated effectively via stress management and cognitive-behavioral therapy techniques (Young, 1992). These treatments also have some positive effects on the overall physical impairment associated with arthritis.

Cancer

Health psychologists have developed a number of interventions designed to address several aspects of cancer (Andersen, 1992). Their goal is to promote a higher quality of life for cancer patients by helping them (1) understand and confront the disease more actively, (2) cope more effectively with stressors associated with cancer, and (3) develop emotionally supportive relationships in which they can disclose their fears about the disease (Andersen, 1992). Behavioral techniques, such as relaxation training, hypnosis, stress management, and cognitive restructuring have proven especially useful.

For example, many drugs used to treat cancer cause severe nausea and vomiting. After several treatments, some patients become nauseated even before they receive the drugs, an effect known as *anticipatory nausea*. This reaction, in turn, makes some of these patients reluctant to continue treatment. (Anticipatory nausea is probably a conditioned response elicited by cues associated with the sights and smells of the hospital environment where the unconditioned stimulus—chemotherapy—is delivered.) Standard antiemetic drugs have not proven very successful in reducing or preventing anticipatory nausea and vomiting, so attention has turned to the use of behaviorally oriented psychological treatments such as relaxation training with guided imagery, systematic desensitization, and biofeedback (Redd et al., 1987).

In one study, patients receiving chemotherapy were randomly assigned to receive either psychological treatment or no treatment (Burish et al., 1987). Before their first session of chemotherapy, patients in the treatment group were trained to use muscle relaxation and calming imagery to cope with the stress of the cancer-treatment procedures. No-treatment patients were told about the advantages of staying relaxed during chemotherapy and were urged to do so, but they were given no training in relaxation or coping skills. Patients receiving the relaxation training reported significantly less nausea, vomiting, and anxiety than did no-treatment control patients. These improvements were still apparent as long as three days after chemotherapy sessions.

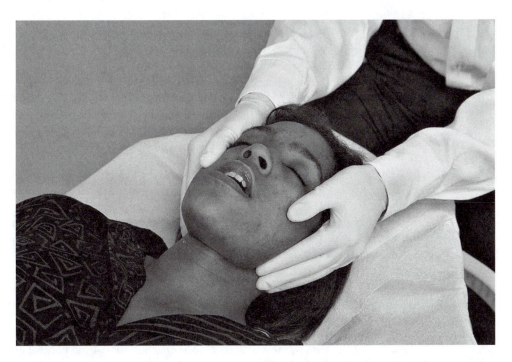

The benefits of relaxation training and pleasant imagery probably stem from the fact that they help distract patients from focusing on aversive stimuli and engender patients' confidence that they can exert control over these stimuli.(Source: Michal Heron / Simon & Schuster/PH College.)

A number of other psychological interventions, including educational programs and various kinds of individual and group therapy, have been shown to improve the mental and physical well-being of cancer patients (Fawzy et al., 1995). One of the most influential studies of such interventions was conducted with eighty-six women suffering metastatic breast cancer (Spiegel, Bloom, & Yalom, 1981; Spiegel & Bloom, 1983). The women were randomly assigned either to no psychological treatment or to weekly group therapy that emphasized mutual support, self-disclosure, and discussion of death and dying; half of those in the treatment group were randomly assigned to also receive training in self-hypnosis for pain reduction. Because many of these women were in the advanced stages of cancer, not all of them completed the twelve-month treatment. However, among those who did, patients receiving group therapy reported significantly less emotional distress and fatigue, a higher energy level, and fewer maladaptive efforts at coping with cancer than the no-treatment controls. The self-hypnosis component also appeared to have its own benefits. The women who received group therapy without hypnosis reported increased pain during the year, while those in the self-hypnosis subgroup reported no change in pain. On average, the group therapy patients lived almost twice as long after treatment began than control subjects did (36.6 months versus 18.9 months). At ten-year follow-up, the three surviving patients from the original sample had all been in the group therapy condition.

In another study, eighty patients who had recently undergone surgical treatment for malignant melanoma, a serious form of skin cancer, were randomly assigned either to no treatment or to a six-week group program of educational information about skin cancer, training in stress management (including relaxation and enhancement of personal coping strategies), and social support (Fawzy et al., 1990). Six months later, patients in the group program showed significantly more effective coping skills, less emotional distress, and greater anti-pathogen activity in the immune system than did those in the no-treatment group. Five to six years after surgery, the death rate among the thirty-four group treatment patients tested at six-month follow-up was only 8.8%, while the rate for thirty-four no-treatment patients was 29.4% (four treated and three non-treated patients suffered recurrences of their cancer; Fawzy et al., 1993). The researchers suggested that the success of their treatment lies in helping patients reduce feelings of anxiety and inadequacy, increase their sense of personal control over the illness, and improve active participation in their treatment.

It has been suggested that behaviorally oriented psychotherapy might help prevent cancer in Type-C personalities, or prolong the lives of patients who already have cancer (Grossarth-Maticek & Eysenck, 1991). For example, Hans Eysenck and his colleagues used *creative novation therapy*, also called *autonomy training* to help Type-C people become more autonomous and assertive, more skilled at coping with stress, and better able to express emotion. In one study, 100 healthy Type-C adults were randomly assigned to a program of autonomy training or no treatment. About thirteen years later, 32% of control participants were reported to have died of cancer, but there were no cancer deaths among the treated group. Another 30% of the control group had died of other causes, while the overall death rate for the treated group was only 10% (Eysenck & Grossarth-Maticek, 1991).

Unfortunately, descriptions of this study are not detailed enough to be sure that the autonomy training was responsible for the differences observed, and the effects have not been replicated by other researchers. Additional well-controlled research will be necessary, therefore, before we can conclude that any form of psychotherapy can help prevent cancer.

AIDS

The main focus for health psychologists working on the problem of AIDS is to reduce the unprotected sexual contact and needle sharing that are known risk factors for HIV infection (e.g., Bowen & Trotter, 1995).

In one program, for example, gay men participated in twelve group sessions of role-playing, behavioral rehearsal, and problem-solving techniques designed to promote condom use and other safe sex practices—including more assertively resisting partners' efforts to coerce them into high-risk behaviors (Kelly et al., 1989). Compared to a control group of gay men who did not receive training, program participants significantly increased their use of condoms, their resistance to sexual coercion, and their knowledge of AIDS risks.

In a study of an HIV/AIDS program aimed at African-American teenagers at risk for HIV infection, participants were randomly assigned to either a single class on the basic facts about HIV transmission and prevention, or to an eight-session program combining the same basic information with behavioral skill training, role-playing, and group support for sexual abstinence, safe sex practices, and resisting pressure to engage in unsafe sex (St. Lawrence et al., 1995). Teenagers in the behavioral skills group decreased their rate of unprotected intercourse significantly more than those in the single-class group, and this difference was still evident a year later. Further, among those who had been sexually abstinent when the study began, 88.5% of the teens in the behavioral training program remained so during the follow-up, while only 69% of the one-session information group were still abstinent. Success has also been reported following similar programs aimed at adult African-American women in inner cities (e.g., Kalichman, Rompa, & Coley, 1996).

With the help of health psychologists, many large U.S. cities have established AIDS education programs, clean needle exchanges, condom distributions, and publicity campaigns encouraging safe sex (Kelly & Murphy, 1992). There are also AIDS prevention programs in many other countries, including those of sub-Saharan Africa, Asia, and parts of the Caribbean where women's AIDS risks are increasing dramatically. In addition to lack of basic knowledge about how AIDS is transmitted, women in these countries often face additional obstacles to lowering their AIDS risk. These obstacles include lack of economic or social power to exert control over their sexual activity and their concern that asking partners to use condoms will lead to accusations of sexual infidelity. Accordingly, a major goal of AIDS prevention programs in these countries is to empower women to (1) learn about HIV transmission, (2) take greater control of their sexual lives, (3) obtain protective devices such as female condoms or vaginal microbicides, and (4) become less economically dependent on men and therefore less subject to coerced or commercialized sex.

Other psychological interventions attempt to help patients cope with HIV/AIDS itself. For example, in a study conducted at the University of Miami, forty-seven gay men who were unaware of their HIV status agreed to be tested for HIV (Anntoni et al., 1991; LaPerriere et al., 1990). Five weeks before being notified of their HIV status, the men were randomly assigned to either a ten-week cognitive-behavioral stress management (CBSM) program, a ten-week group aerobic exercise program, or a no-treatment control group. The main goals of treatment were to buffer the anxiety and depression associated with being notified of HIV infection and to lessen the immunological impairments that often occur with the stress of being notified that one has HIV. Men receiving CBSM training received assertiveness role-playing, training in muscle relaxation, cognitive restructuring to help reduce feelings of stress and helplessness, and basic information about HIV risks and transmission. Men in the CBSM group whose tests showed they had HIV displayed less depression and less significant impairments in immune system functioning than did HIV-positive subjects in the no-treatment group. In fact, measures of two kinds of cells that are specifically attacked by HIV and a general measure of immunity actually showed increases for CBSM participants; these measures either decreased or showed no change in the controls. (Two other measures of immune system functioning revealed no significant effects). The more often the CBSM men practiced relaxation training at home, the lower their post-notification depression scores and the higher their HIV-specific measures of immune competence. Relaxation training appears to be an especially important part of this treatment package, but the reasons for its specific effectiveness need further study. Research on how permanent and how large a change in immune functioning such treatments can bring and whether such changes can alter the course of AIDS are continuing (e.g., Lutgendorf et al., 1997).

Some Comments on Risk Reduction Programs

Psychological interventions aimed at disease prevention or symptom reduction often result in immediate improvements that, unfortunately, may not be maintained long enough to promote a healthier life (Blanchard, 1994). For example, smoking cessation programs are usually followed by significant rates of abstinence, but more than 50% of smokers resume their habit within a year (Jason et al., 1995; Shiffman et al., 1996). A similar picture exists for the treatment of obesity. Although behavior modification appears to be the most effective psychological intervention for obesity, maintenance of weight loss and learning new eating habits are major difficulties for most people. For example, most psychologically oriented weight-reduction interventions can achieve reductions of about one pound per week, but it is much more difficult to maintain these reductions beyond one or two years (Brownell & Wadden, 1992). Finally, the success of programs to reduce the risk of HIV infection is difficult to gauge. Marked reductions in unsafe sexual practices have been reported by gay men in urban areas (e.g., Kelly et al., 1989), but among other inner-city men and women, gay men in smaller communities, and lower SES and minority adolescents, HIV prevention efforts have not been nearly as successful (Kelly & Murphy, 1992). Improving the long-term effects of risk reduction programs remains a major challenge in health psychology.

IMPROVING COMPLIANCE WITH MEDICAL TREATMENT REGIMENS

The effectiveness of treatment of an illness depends first on its being the correct treatment, and second on the patient's cooperation with the treatment. The extent to which patients adhere to medical advice and treatment regimens is called *compliance* or *adherence* (Rodin & Salovey, 1989). Noncompliance in taking prescribed medication may occur in up to half of all patients, at least part of the time (Haynes, 1982), and this figure may be as high as 80% among adolescents (Rickert & Jay, 1995). They may not take prescribed medications at all, may take it less frequently or more frequently than instructed, or they may ignore rules about the need to take medicine with food or not to consume alcohol while on medication. Noncompliance tends to be even more common in relation to treatments that are complicated or involve substantial lifestyle changes. Indeed, noncompliance has been called "the best documented but least understood health-related behavior" (Becker & Maiman, 1975). Health psychologists have been involved in efforts to understand the causes of noncompliance and in developing interventions to improve compliance.

Causes of Noncompliance

The chief cause of noncompliance appears to be miscommunication between physicians and patients. Patients frequently do not understand what physicians tell them about their illnesses or their treatments. As a result, they are confused about what they should do or they forget what they have been told. One study showed that, five minutes after seeing their physician, general-practice patients had forgotten 50% of what the doctor had told them (Ley et al., 1973). The emotional aspects of patient–physician communication also are correlated with compliance. A common pattern of troubled communication involves patient antagonism toward the physician, accompanied by physician withdrawal from the patient. Compliance may also be reduced by the sheer complexity, inconvenience, or discomfort associated with some kinds of treatment. Finally, noncompliance with treatment may appear because patients do not have a good system for reminding themselves about what to do, and when to do it.

A social-psychological theory called the Health Belief Model (HBM) (Rosenstock, 1966) has been applied to understanding the reasons for patient noncompliance (Becker & Maiman, 1975). According to the HBM, patients' compliance with treatment depends on factors such as (1) how susceptible to a given illness they perceive themselves to be and how severe the consequences of the illness are thought to be; (2) how effective and feasible versus how costly and difficult the prescribed treatment is perceived to be; (3) the influence of internal cues (physical symptoms) plus external cues (e.g., advice from friends) in triggering health behaviors; and (4) demographic and personality variables that modify the influences of the previous three factors.

Interventions to Improve Compliance

Attempts to improve compliance with treatment can be classified into three general approaches: (1) educating patients about the importance of compliance so that they will take a more active role in maintaining their own health, (2) modifying treatment plans to make compliance easier, and (3) using behavioral and cognitive-behavioral techniques to increase patients' ability to comply (Masur, 1981).

Education.   One direct and effective intervention for improving compliance with short-term treatments is to give patients clear, explicit, written instructions that supplement oral instructions about how treatment is to proceed. Educating *physicians* about the causes and management of noncompliance may also be beneficial. In one study (Inui, Yourtee, & Williamson, 1976), physicians who had been educated about the HBM and ways to improve compliance had more compliant patients at a six-month reassessment.

Modification of Treatment Plans.   A second strategy for increasing compliance is to reorganize treatment to make it easier for patients to comply with it. Examples include timing daily doses of medication to coincide with daily habits (e.g., taking pills right after brushing teeth), giving the treatment in one or two injections rather than in several doses per day, packaging medicine in dosage strips or with pill calendars, and scheduling more frequent follow-up visits to supervise compliance. These procedures have shown promise (e.g., Boczkowski, Zeichner, & DeSanto, 1985), but many of them entail additional manufacturing costs and extra time from service providers, two characteristics that tend to limit their usefulness.

Behavior Modification.   Health psychologists have used a number of behavioral techniques, including the use of postcard reminders, telephone calls, wristwatch alarms and other *environmental cues* to prompt patients to take pills or perform other aspects of treatment plans (Rickert & Jay, 1995). They have also set up written *contingency contracts* between patient and physician that specify what behaviors the patient must perform in order to earn rewards (e.g., more conveniently timed office appointments). Such contracts encourage a more collaborative relationship between patient and physician and have been successful in improving compliance (Swain & Steckel, 1981). *Token economies* (see Chapter 8) have also been employed to encourage compliance. In one study, three children with kidney failure were given points for maintaining recommended weight, potassium, and nitrogen levels (Magrab & Papadopoulou, 1977). The points could be exchanged for rewards in the hospital. In comparison to baseline levels, these children were able to achieve substantial weight gains, and two of them showed improvements in the other indices.

Behavior modification procedures have also been used to reduce noncompliance motivated by the discomfort associated with essential medical procedures or treatments. The best-known illustration of these methods was described earlier in relation to behavioral treatments for the control of anticipatory nausea in cancer patients undergoing chemotherapy. Other examples include teaching children to use breathing exercises and distraction techniques to help them overcome fear of routine vaccination shots (Blount et al., 1992), employing hypnosis to reduce pain in burn patients who are undergoing debridement procedures (Patterson et al., 1992), and using relaxation, systematic desensitization, and participant modeling to help fearful patients get the dental work they need, but have been avoiding (e.g., Kleinknecht & Bernstein, 1978).

HEALTH PSYCHOLOGY AT WORK

Q.: To what extent do the principles, methods, and research results associated with health psychology affect your work?

DR. SANDY D'ANGELO: Research and methods in health psychology are important to me because I work with many children who have congenital syndromes, chronic illness, or learning problems and developmental delay associated with medical factors. In fact, the majority of children in my clinical practice have some type of medical disorder or risk factor, so I frequently review recent publications on the psychosocial aspects of children's disorders.

DR. HECTOR MACHABANSKI: Health psychology is especially relevant to my hospital work. I work with children who have some of type of chronic illness, and my collaboration with pediatricians, neurologists, and geneticists makes it important for me to stay abreast of the latest developments in health psychology.

DR. GEOFFREY THORPE: Health psychology is not directly relevant to my work. I tend to refer students whose clients have health-related problems to a colleague of mine who specializes in this area.

CHAPTER SUMMARY

Health psychology is a specialty devoted to studying psychological influences on health, illness, and coping with health problems. It is closely related to the larger field of behavioral medicine, which involves the integration of knowledge from many disciplines in understanding and treating medical disorders. Both fields adopt a biopsychosocial model, seeing physical illness as the result of biological, psychological, and social disruptions. Health psychologists seek to (1) understand how these factors interact to influence illness and health, (2) identify risk factors for sickness and protective factors for health, (3) promote healthy behaviors and prevent unhealthy ones, and (4) create interventions that contribute to medical treatment of illness.

Stress is the negative emotional and physiological process that occurs as people try to deal with environmental circumstances, called stressors, that disrupt or threaten daily functioning. Stress reactions can be physical, psychological, and behavioral. Physical stress reactions include the general adaptation syndrome, which begins with an alarm reaction and, if stressors persist, continues into the stages of resistance and exhaustion. Prolonged stress can result in immunosuppression, impairment of the body's disease-fighting immune system. Stressors can be measured by the Life Experiences Survey and other paper and pencil tests.

People's stress-coping efforts can be problem-focused (aimed at modifying or eliminating stressors), emotion-focused (aimed at blunting the emotional impact of stressors), or both. The impact of stressors tends to be lessened in people with better social support systems. Lack of social support increases risk for physical disorders.

Anything that increases the chances of developing an illness is called a risk factor for that illness. Behaviors associated with risk for cardiovascular disease (CHD) and cancer include smoking, overeating, lack of exercise, and consumption of a high-fat diet. Stressors, Type-A personality, and especially the negative emotions associated with both, also appear to be a risk factor for CHD. Risk factors for AIDS include unprotected sexual activity and, for intravenous drug users, sharing injection needles.

Illness prevention programs in health psychology seek to reduce risk factors for cardiovascular disease, gastrointestinal problems, pain, cancer, AIDS, and other diseases by working with individuals, groups, and whole communities to alter health-risky behaviors. These programs usually result in short-term improvements that may not be maintained in the long run.

Health psychologists' efforts to improve patients' compliance with prescribed medical treatments include education about the importance of compliance, modifying treatment plans to make compliance easier, and using behavioral techniques to increase patients' ability to comply.

Chapter 12

Clinical Neuropsychology

Neuropsychology is the field of study that endeavors to define the relationship between brain processes and human behavior and psychological functioning. Neuropsychologists are interested in a wide range of functions, including cognitive abilities (language, mathematical, and visual-spatial skills); motor abilities (gross and fine motor skills); emotional characteristics, such as the ability to express and understand feelings; personality traits (e.g., extraversion and hypnotic susceptibility); and mental disorders (e.g., depression and schizophrenia).

Historically, the main source of data in neuropsychology has been the study of behavior after brain damage. By observing the effects of specific kinds of brain damage on behavior, neuropsychologists were able to make inferences about the organization of the brain. More recently, the development of behavioral methods that allow neuropsychologists to study the organization of the brain in non-brain-damaged people has made it possible to confirm and expand our understanding of brain–behavior relationships. The power of the neuropsychological approach is revealed by the insights it has provided about brain damage and about psychological disorders such as learning disabilities, depression, schizophrenia, and psychopathy.

Knowledge that has been garnered from neuropsychological research is often applied by *clinical neuropsychologists*, who work with children and adults who have had trauma or injury to the brain, or who are experiencing problems in some area of functioning that may be related to a brain impairment. Often, the clinical neuropsychologist is called upon to assess how damage to the brain expresses itself in behavioral, cognitive, and emotional deficits. (A *deficit* is a deficiency in a patient's performance relative to the level shown by a normative, or average, group of people, or relative to the level shown by a patient on an earlier occasion.) Clinical neuropsychologists typically seek to answer one or more of the following questions (Jones & Butters, 1983):

1. Does the client show deficits that suggest organic brain damage?
2. If there is impairment, how severe is it and what is its prognosis or likely course?
3. Can the impairment be localized to a certain area of the brain?
4. What is the probable cause of the impairment?
5. What are the consequences of the impairment for the client's personal, occupational, and interpersonal functioning?
6. What recommendations are there for rehabilitation of the impairment?

To answer these questions, clinical neuropsychologists must integrate data and knowledge from several sources. First, they must be proficient in the general assessment skills that we described in Chapters 3 through 6. Indeed, neuropsychological assessment should not be isolated from an assessment of the entire person, including social and family background, intellectual functioning, personality dynamics, and emotional reactions to possible brain dysfunction. Second, the clinical neuropsychologist must be well versed in the neurosciences, including neuroanatomy (the study of the structures of the nervous system and the functions of these structures), neuropharmacology (the study of drugs that affect the functioning of the nervous system), and neurophysiology (the study of the physiology of the nervous system, including the chemistry of nerve tissue and the relationship between the nervous system and endocrine functions). Third, clinical neuropsychologists must be knowledgeable about a wide range of human abilities—including cognition, language, and perception—and developmental psychology (including behavioral genetics and life-span psychology). Fourth, the clinical neuropsychologist must have an in-depth understanding of clinical psychology in order to distinguish brain impairments from other causes of psychopathology and to design effective rehabilitative programs for individual clients. Finally, clinical neuropsychologists must be thoroughly trained in the specialized methods of neuropsychological assessment.

The increasing demand for clinical neuropsychologists has stimulated many clinical psychologists to list neuropsychology as one of their specialties. All too often, however, these individuals do little more than take one or two courses in neuropsychological assessment as part of their graduate training in clinical psychology and then begin to "do neuropsychologicals." Even more troubling are those who acquire all of their experience in neuropsychology through clinical workshops or other brief training. These patterns are problematic because the education of a competent clinical neuropsychologist is a lengthy process requiring courses in several disciplines, a large body of basic knowledge, research sophistication, supervised experience, and clinical acumen. Although various models are available for such preparation, all of them require extensive coordinated training for which there simply are no shortcuts (APA Division of Clinical Neuropsychology, 1989; Meier, 1981). Clinical neuropsychologists who work with children need even further specialized training, since many disorders have particular manifestations in children, and the problems that arise are unique (for example, family dynamics can play an important role in managing children with seizure disorders). Pediatric clinical neuropsychologists also need to be experienced in evaluating the educational programs and resources available to the client.

HISTORICAL DEVELOPMENT OF NEUROPSYCHOLOGY

Neuropsychology has only recently been defined as a field of study; the term appears to have been used first in the late-1940s. Behind it, however, lies a long history of thinking and speculation about the mind and its relation to the brain. As far back as 500 B.C., scholars debated about whether the mind was localized in the brain (the "brain hypothesis") or the heart (the "cardiac hypothesis") (Kolb & Whishaw, 1990). In the fourth century B.C., Aristotle decided that the mind must reside in the heart, because it was warm and active; the brain, which was cool and inert, was a "radiator" that cooled the blood. In the second century A.D., after studying the effects of brain damage on the behavior of wounded gladiators, the famous Roman physician, Galen, localized the mind in the brain. Later, debate focused on exactly where in the brain the mind was localized. Galen believed that the mind resided in the fluid of the ventricles. In the sixteenth century, Anreas Vesalius put this theory to rest by dissecting brains and discovering that the ventricles are the same size in animals and people. Since people were considered far more rational than animals, he reasoned that the mind must therefore reside in the tissue of their far larger brains.

Of greatest importance to neuropsychology were several lines of research in the 1800s that focused on possible relationships between specific behaviors and specific areas of the brain. As noted in Chapter 1, the study of *localization of function* was popularized by anatomists Franz Gall and his associate, Johann Spurzheim, through the "science" of phrenology, which claimed that individual differences in personality and intelligence could be assessed by measuring the bumps and indentations of the skull's surface. These features supposedly corresponded to the part of the brain responsible for the characteristic in question. Though very popular with the public, phrenology was disdained by most scientists.

Pierre Flourens's discoveries about localization of function earned greater scientific respect. Flourens surgically destroyed parts of animals' brains and then observed the behavioral consequences of the loss. He concluded that although there was some localization of cortical function, the hemispheres of the cortex functioned more like an interrelated unit. This view was later supported by the work of Karl Lashley, who emphasized the capacity of one area of the cortex to take over for the functions of a destroyed area, a capacity he described as *equipotentiality.*

Although the folly of phrenology discredited early ideas about localization of brain functions, careful work in behavioral neurology eventually provided convincing support for it. For example, in 1825, Jean Baptiste Bouillaud presented a paper in which he argued that the capacity for speech was localized in the frontal lobes. A few years later, Marc Dax reportedly presented a similar paper, but apparently, no one paid much attention until 1861, when Bouillaud's son-in-law, Ernest Auburtin, described yet another case demonstrating speech deficits associated with damage to the frontal lobes. Shortly thereafter, Paul Broca, a French physician who was present at the meeting of the Anthropological Society of Paris where Auburtin gave his paper, had the opportunity to confirm, by autopsy, that a patient with a profound speech deficit but otherwise normal intelligence had damage to the left frontal lobe. By 1863, Broca had examined eight such patients and had argued the case in such a way that localization of function was indisputable.

Another early clinical insight into localization of function was made by two Italian ophthalmologists: Antonio Quaglino, a professor at the University of Pavia, and Giambattista Borelli, a practicing ophthalmologist in Turin. In 1867, they published a paper describing the case of a man who lost the ability to recognize familiar faces after a cerebral hemorrhage that mainly damaged the right hemisphere of the brain. The loss of the capacity for facial recognition is known today as *prosopagnosia;* its precise cause is still a matter of great interest to researchers (Young & De Haan, 1992).

Development of Neuropsychological Assessment Techniques

By the turn of the twentieth century, Alfred Binet had begun assessing brain-damaged children in Paris. Although these tests are usually considered the beginning of modern intelligence testing (see Chapter 5), they also foreshadowed neuropsychological assessment. Many of the disorders commonly assessed today with neuropsychological techniques had been identified by Binet's time. As of the 1920s, *aphasia* (disordered language abilities), *apraxias* (impaired abilities to carry out purposeful movements), *amnesias* (disorders of memory), and seizure disorders had all been classified, studied, and, in some cases, treated. In Russia, a Psychoneurological Institute was formed in 1907 to study the behavioral consequences of brain damage, and throughout the first decade of the 1900s, several investigators in the United States had begun to use psychological tests to study the effects of brain damage on behavior.

A crucial development in the history of neuropsychology was the work of Ward Halstead, who, in 1935, established a neuropsychology laboratory at the University of Chicago. By observing brain-damaged persons in natural settings, Halstead was able to identify several characteristics in their disordered behavior which he then tried to assess more thoroughly through existing psychological tests or new ones he developed himself. Next, Halstead compared the test results from a large number of brain-damaged patients to those of a group of normal control subjects and selected a battery of ten neuropsychological assessments based on their ability to discriminate the brain-damaged patients from the controls (Reitan & Davison, 1974). Halstead's first graduate student, Ralph M. Reitan, started his own neuropsychology laboratory in 1951 at the Indiana University Medical Center. Reitan revised Halstead's test battery by dropping two tests and adding several new ones, including the Wechsler intelligence scale and the MMPI. The resulting *Halstead-Reitan Battery* is still the world's most widely used package of neuropsychological tests.

Basic research in neuropsychology and advances in assessment methods grew dramatically following World War II. Five groups of scientists made especially noteworthy contributions to the field in this period (Jones & Butters, 1983):

1. The Montreal Neurological Institute-McGill University Group, especially Brenda Milner and Doreen Kimura, who studied the effects of many types of specific, or focal, brain lesions on behavior. The Montreal investigators developed several neuropsychological assessment techniques, and their research (e.g., Branch, Milner, & Rasmussen, 1964; Kimura, 1967) led to widespread acceptance of the view that each hemisphere of the brain has special importance for certain types of behavior.

2. Hans-Lukas Teuber who, along with several colleagues at the New York University College of Medicine and the Massachusetts Institute of Technology, studied the behavioral effects of combat injuries to the brains (particularly the frontal lobes) of World War II veterans.

3. The Boston Veterans Administration and Boston University School of Medicine group, including Edith Kaplan, Nelson Butters, and Harold Goodglass, who carefully classified various forms of aphasia and amnesia and who emphasized the need to study the process that contributes to objective performance deficits. Noting that patients may do poorly on the same neuropsychological tests for different reasons, the Boston group advocated assessments that measure not only the extent of deficits but also the qualitative problems that lead to the deficits. This approach has come to be known as the process approach.

4. Arthur L. Benton, at the University of Iowa, who, in 1945, developed the Benton Visual Retention Test, a test of visual memory still in use today. Benton also made numerous discoveries about the different behavioral effects of lesions in the right versus the left hemisphere and developed a number of other neuropsychological tests with admirable psychometric properties (e.g., Benton et al., 1983).

5. Alexander Luria, a Russian scientist whose unique approach to neuropsychology became enormously influential in the West following the translation of his book, *Higher Functioning in Man,* in 1966 and the systematic description of his assessment methods by the Danish psychologist Anna-Lise Christensen in 1975. Luria's theory of functional systems in the brain is founded on important principles of brain functioning which we will examine in more detail later.

Research with Split-Brain Patients

Another important part of the history of neuropsychology is the work of Roger Sperry and his colleagues at the California Institute of Technology (Sperry, 1961, 1982). These investigators studied the behavioral effects of cutting the corpus callosum, the band of fibers that connects the brain's two hemispheres and allows them to communicate with each other. This surgical procedure is occasionally used—when drug treatment is ineffective—to prevent the spread of epileptic seizures from one side of the brain to the other. When the corpus callosum is severed, there is no direct pathway between the hemispheres, rendering incommunicado vast sections of brain tissue devoted to complex information processing. Yet, previous research failed to note any significant differences between normal people and so-called split-brain patients. It was not until Sperry (who won the Nobel Prize in 1981 for his work) used more sophisticated experimental procedures to test split-brain patients that it became possible to identify a disconnection syndrome (e.g., Sperry, 1968).

Normative Studies

Research with split-brain patients stimulated an enormous number of studies investigating the brain organization of non-brain-damaged people. These studies often used a *tachistoscope*, which is a stimulus presentation device that takes advantage of the fact that when the eyes are focused on a central point, stimuli in the left visual field are perceived first by the right hemisphere, whereas stimuli in the right visual field are perceived first by the left hemisphere. To get the information *directly* to both hemispheres, a person would have to move the eyes so as to place the information that was formerly in one visual field in the other. To forestall this possibility, the tachistoscope is designed to present visual stimuli for less than about 200 milliseconds, which is how long it takes for the eyes to move. Researchers can thus be fairly certain that the only way each hemisphere can obtain information from the opposite hemisphere's visual field is to receive a "second-hand copy" via the fibers of the corpus callosum.

Using tachistoscopic methods, experimenters were able to direct visual stimuli to one hemisphere or the other and measure a person's accuracy of performance or reaction time in response. Similarly, dichotic listening techniques, which direct auditory input simultaneously to both ears, rely on the tendency to ignore or suppress information in the ear opposite the hemisphere that is less adept at the task. By measuring the relative accuracy of responses for the two visual fields (for tachistoscopic presentation) or for the two ears (dichotic presentation), researchers have documented and confirmed unique hemispheric superiorities for a wide variety of cognitive and perceptual tasks (Kimura, 1961, 1966, 1967; Pirozzolo & Rayner, 1977).

The Emergence of Clinical Neuropsychology

Our understanding of brain–behavior relationships has been enriched and expanded remarkably in the last few decades by research and scholarship that have provided converging evidence for many insights. At the same time, these insights have been increasingly applied in the interests of individual clients through clinical neuropsychology, which emerged as a distinctive professional specialty in the 1970s. Two events marked the development of clinical neuropsychology: The first was the founding of the *Journal of Clinical Neuropsychology* by Louis Costa and Byron Rourke; the second was the formation of the Division of Clinical Neuropsychology (Division 40) within the American Psychological Association. Division 40 now has more than 3,900 members and is specifically concerned with neuropsychology as a field of professional practice.

Clinical neuropsychologists are likely to see a wide variety of clients. Many adult clients are referred by the staff of rehabilitation, psychiatric, or geriatric facilities. Child and adolescent clients may be referred by teachers, school psychologists or social workers, or family physicians. Perhaps most often, however, clients are referred to clinical neuropsychologists by physicians or other medical staff because of brain damage caused by a head injury or a stroke.

The following example of a head injury case is typical, and provides a focal point for our discussion of basic principles of neuropsychology and neuropsychological assessment. Mary Ellen was an athletic young woman and a skilled sailor. Sailing with some friends on Lake Michigan one day, her boat was hit by a sudden, violent squall. As she desperately tried to change to a smaller sail, a severe wind shift and an accompanying wave caused the boom, a heavy aluminum spar, to swing violently from one side of the boat to the other, striking Mary Ellen on the right side of her head and knocking her unconscious. She remained in a coma for about a week. Some time later, a clinical neuropsychologist was asked to help evaluate the effects of Mary Ellen's head injury on her cognitive, attentional, and emotional functions. The regions of her brain that had been injured were the parietal, temporal, and frontal lobes. In the following sections, we describe some of the effects of damage to these parts of the brain, as well as some of the things that clinical neuropsychologists do to evaluate their functioning.

BASIC PRINCIPLES OF NEUROPSYCHOLOGY

Thorough coverage of brain functioning is beyond the scope of this chapter, but certain principles of brain–behavior relationships are so fundamental to neuropsychology that it is essential to review them before describing neuropsychological assessment procedures. One of the most important of these relationships involves localization of function.

Localization of Function

As noted earlier, localization of function refers to the fact that the brain is organized in a compartmentalized fashion, with different parts responsible for different skills or senses. Historically, disagreement has existed regarding the extent to which the brain should be viewed as a set of independent information processors versus an integrated unit. Theorists who emphasized the interrelatedness of brain areas stressed the global, holistic quality of brain functioning. Alexander Luria, for example, proposed a theory of brain organization that emphasized its integration rather than its specificity. Luria's theory was that the brain is organized into three functional systems: (1) a brain stem system for regulating a person's overall tone or waking state; (2) a system located in the posterior (back) portion of the cortex for obtaining, processing, and storing information received from the outside world; and (3) a system for planning, regulating, and verifying mental operations that is located mainly in the anterior (front) portion of the cortex.

Today, when neuropsychologists map the brain according to specific functions, they do so in a way that reflects both localization and global perspectives (Walsh, 1987). For example, the concept of *modularity* implies that different regions of the brain function as specialized units that process particular types of information or perform specific kinds of tasks. Different modules interact with each other to produce a seamless sequence of behaviors. Modules are organized in a fashion that reflects both the structure and function of the brain. Thus, the brain can be conceptualized as having several levels of organization, ranging from the global to the local. For example, the various areas identified in Figure 12.1 are associated with functions that can be distinguished by whether they primarily process incoming information (sensory) or program outgoing behavior (motor). They can also be distinguished by modality (for example, whether they primarily process visual or auditory information). In general, brain regions behind the central sulcus are more involved in the reception of sensory information involving touch, pressure, temperature, and body position, whereas brain regions in front of the central sulcus are more involved in programming motor output.

The lobes of the cerebral cortex are also associated with particular functions. For example, the *occipital lobes* are involved in processing visual information. Signals from the eyes' retinas are carried by the optic nerves to the thalamus and then to several regions in the occipital lobes. Because of the way the nervous system is organized, visual information is represented *topographically* in the brain; in other words, neighboring parts of the brain respond to neighboring areas of the visual field. (A similar arrangement for other types of specific sensory and motor information has given rise to the rather comical maps of the *homunculus*, or "little man," which show the relative

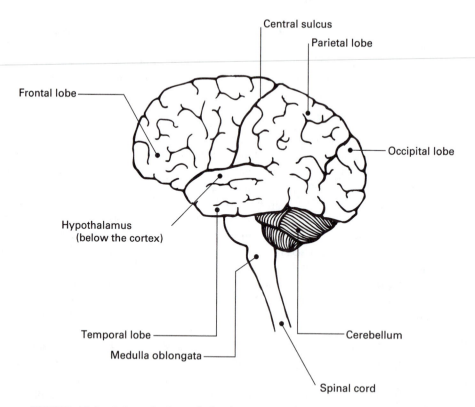

FIGURE 12.1 A lateral view of the human cerebral cortex and other brain structures.

size of cortical areas representing sensory information from or motor output to various regions on the opposite side of the body; see Figure 12.2).

After visual information is processed in the occipital lobes, it is relayed to association areas in the *parietal lobes*. They are called "association" areas because they combine and integrate sensory information from a variety of sources. Because the parietal lobes are the meeting ground for visual, auditory, and sensory input, they are uniquely involved in creating a unified perception of an object. For example, when we pick up a rose, the pathways that convey its smell are separate from those that convey its visual image, and these are separate from the ones that convey the painful prick of its thorns. Yet we experience the rose as a single, unified object. Patients with damage to the parietal lobes often have difficulty recognizing objects, even highly familiar ones, in this unified way (see Figure 12.3).

The parietal lobes are also involved in creating a spatial map of our environment and the objects in it, an organization that doesn't depend on the orientation or position of our bodies. Because of this specialty, the parietal lobes play a unique role in attention and awareness of spatial location. Patients with damage to the parietal lobe on only one side of the brain often display an intriguing deficit called *hemi-neglect,* in which they

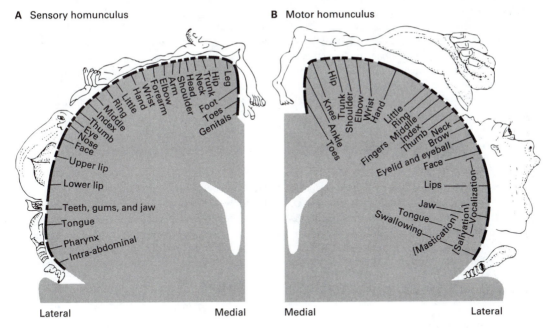

A Sensory homunculus

B Motor homunculus

FIGURE 12.2 Sensory and motor areas of the human brain. These maps show where on the human cortex sensory information is received (left) and where motor functions are controlled (right). Note that areas of the body that are more sensitive to sensory information (such as the tip of the tongue or the fingers) are represented by more cortical area than areas that are less sensitive (such as the back of the head or the upper leg). Source: Kandel, Schwartz, and Jessell (1991). Reprinted with the permission of Macmillan Publishing Company from *The Cerebral Cortex of Man* by Wilder Penfield and Theodore Rasmussen. Copyright 1950 Macmillan Publishing Company; copyright renewed © 1978 Theodore Rasmussen.

The effects of brain damage can take an almost infinite number of forms. A common pattern following severe damage includes deficits in large realms of behaviors, such as language, motor coordination, or memory. In other cases, there are milder deficits involving narrower functions, and, sometimes, these deficits are of great interest because they permit neuroscientists to map specific brain–behavior relationships more precisely than ever.

In some instances these narrow deficits are so unusual that they defy common sense, as in the case of Doctor P., "the man who mistook his wife for a hat" (Sacks, 1985). Dr. P. was a distinguished musician, a man of superior intelligence, refinement, and wit. In fact, his reputation as a person with an offbeat sense of humor may have hidden for a time the neurological significance of a strange set of symptoms that Dr. P.'s students and family began to observe—symptoms that included difficulty recognizing familiar people when he looked at them, but not when he heard them speak, and mistakenly seeing faces in fire hydrants, parking meters, furniture knobs, and other inanimate objects. Dr. P.'s ophthalmologist, who suspected brain damage after examining Dr. P.'s eyes, referred him to Dr. Oliver Sacks, a neurologist. Dr. Sacks found Dr. P. to be a charming, healthy man, but one who showed a "teasing strangeness" in the way he looked at, but seemed to not really see, the neurologist's face. Other oddities included Dr. P.'s mistaking his foot for his shoe, and, upon leaving Sacks's office, attempting to lift his wife's head off and put it on his head like a hat!

Intrigued, Dr. Sacks visited the patient's home. There, he observed that Dr. P.'s musical abilities were intact, as was his perception of abstract shapes, but his reactions to faces on television or in family photographs were very bizarre. Dr. P. seemed incapable of visually perceiving real, three-dimensional objects; instead, he saw only abstractions. His visual world was empty except for lifeless features which he could describe in almost geometric detail. An interesting confirmation of Dr. P.'s visual problems came in a series of paintings he had done over the years and had displayed throughout his house. Sacks (1985, p. 16) described them as follows: "All his earlier work was naturalistic and realistic, with vivid mood and atmosphere.... Then, years later, they became less vivid, less concrete, less realistic and naturalistic; but far more abstract, even geometrical and cubist. Finally, in the last paintings, the canvasses became intense—mere chaotic lines and blotches of paint."

Dr. P.'s disorder, of which he seemed to be almost happily unaware, was diagnosed as *visual agnosia*; he was unable to derive a meaningful perception of objects by looking at them. Although he never ascertained the cause of the defect, Dr. Sacks speculated that it was a tumor or degenerative process in the part of the cortex responsible for object perception. Despite his difficulties, Dr. P. lived for several more years and played and taught music until the final days of his life.

Although Dr. P.'s case is remarkable, deficits in the ability to recognize familiar faces have often been reported in the literature. Indeed, while researching the problem, Dr. Sacks encountered reports of a farmer who suddenly could no longer distinguish the faces of his once-familiar cows and a museum worker who thought his own reflection was a three-dimensional picture of an ape.

FIGURE 12.3 A case of brain damage: The man who mistook his wife for a hat.

ignore the side of the body and the side of space opposite the damaged hemisphere. Thus, Mary Ellen, who had damage to the right parietal region, did not eat the food on the left side of her plate, forgot to comb her hair on the left side of her head, and neglected to button the shirt-sleeve on her left arm. She also tended to ignore words on the left side of the page, and failed to notice when a doctor or family member approached from the left. Hemi-neglect can be so extreme that patients sometimes believe that parts of their bodies belong to other people. In one case (Sacks, 1990), a patient woke up in the middle of the night and tried to throw his leg out of bed, thinking that a stranger had gotten into bed with him. This syndrome is most common after damage to regions of the right parietal lobe (probably because of the unique specialization of the right hemisphere for processing spatial information), but it can occur after damage to the left parietal lobe as well.

Clinical neuropsychologists typically assess the presence of parietal lobe deficits by using tests such as the Benton Test of Facial Recognition, tests of object recognition in which the patient is shown an object and asked to name it or point to it, and tests of visual-spatial skills. Because the abilities to tell right from left and to comprehend abstract concepts are often disrupted by left parietal damage, these skills are carefully tested in cases where such damage is suspected. Hemi-neglect is often assessed by asking the patient to draw a clock or a flower. Mary Ellen's problems were revealed when she put all the numbers on the clock, and all the petals on the flower, on the right side of the paper (opposite the intact left hemisphere). Mary Ellen also performed poorly on a letter cancellation task (which required her to cross out all the letters or symbols on a page), and on a line bisection task, in which she was asked to mark the middle of a straight line. She missed most of the letters on the left side of the page and bisected the line well to the right of midline.

Once information is integrated in the parietal lobes, the *temporal lobes* come into play by categorizing, classifying, and storing the information in long-term memory. Accordingly, the most dramatic effect of temporal lobe damage is the disruption of memory. For example, researchers at McGill University discovered that patients who underwent brain surgery that removed a structure called the *hippocampus* from both temporal lobes, had complete amnesia for all new information (Scoville & Milner, 1957). These patients cannot remember how to find their way around in unfamiliar places, nor can they remember the name of someone they met minutes earlier. Every event, no matter how often repeated, is perceived as if it is happening for the first time. Recent research has demonstrated that their memory loss is most evident on a conscious level. Thus, while these patients may not be *aware* of having seen a particular object in the past, they sometimes show *unconscious* recognition, as evidenced by changes in heart rate or skin conduction in response to familiar stimuli (Gazzaniga, Fendrich, & Wessinger, 1994; Jacoby & Kelley, 1987).

The temporal lobes are also important in attaching appropriate emotional or motivational significance to particular stimuli. People with temporal lobe epilepsy, for example, often display a collection of emotional traits which some researchers have termed the "temporal lobe personality" (Bear & Fedio, 1977). One of these traits is a tendency to see mundane events as imbued with personal emotional significance, a tendency that can lead to paranoid thinking. Patients with temporal lobe epilepsy have also been described as "hypergraphic," which refers to their tendency to do a lot of writing, or to be "sticky" (a tendency to have difficulty disengaging from a conversation).

Clinical neuropsychologists typically assess problems associated with temporal lobe pathology by using a variety of memory tests, such as Benton's Visual Retention Test, the Wechsler Memory Scale-Revised, or the California Verbal Learning Test. They also compare patients' memory for verbal material, which would indicate left temporal lobe disorder, with their memory for visual-spatial material, which would indicate right temporal lobe disorder. Mary Ellen, who sustained damage to her right hemisphere, did poorly on tests of memory for visual-spatial material, but performed normally on tests of memory for verbal material.

The brain's *frontal lobes* are seen as primarily involved in the planning, organization, and direction of complex sequences of behavior (Kolb & Whishaw, 1990). As befits a position of such responsibility, the frontal lobes receive input from most other parts of the brain. This input is necessary because making appropriate decisions about responses and actions requires taking into account as much current information as possible from the environment (including the position and current state of the body). This new information must also be compared to previous information, and its motivational and affective significance must be assessed.

It is no wonder, then, that frontal lobe damage can produce highly disruptive, and often intriguing, effects. In one case, for example, a patient's frontal lobe damage did not impair his performance on any of a battery of neuropsychological tests; yet he was unable to hold down a job, plan or conduct chores around the house, or even decide what to do next (Eslinger & Damasio, 1985). Despite wholly intact perceptual abilities and intellectual skills, he was unable to integrate all the information available to him and apply it to daily activities in a constructive manner. In other cases, frontal lobe damage can result in changes in personality, failure to correctly judge the timing of events, and inability to use feedback from the environment to guide and modify behavior. Mary Ellen, our head-injured client, found herself having difficulty planning activities that she had previously carried out almost instinctively. For example, making dinner became an ordeal. She had trouble timing her activities so that all the food was done at the same time.

Typically, clinical neuropsychologists test for frontal lobe function by examining sequences of motor behavior, the ability to generate behavioral strategies, and the tendency to *perseverate* (an inability to inhibit behavior even when it is inappropriate). Two tests commonly used to assess frontal lobe damage are the Wisconsin Card Sorting Test and the Categories Test from the Halstead-Reitan Battery. In both tests, the examiner cues patients as to how to proceed by informing them on each trial whether they were right or wrong. This feedback is designed to signal them to change their strategy for matching or categorizing information. Patients with frontal lobe lesions will often perseverate in the same strategy, whether it is successful or not.

Lateralization of Function

As already noted, each hemisphere of the cerebral cortex is associated with different kinds of functions. At one time it was assumed that the left is the dominant hemisphere overall, while the right is the nondominant, or minor, hemisphere. We now know, however, that each hemisphere is dominant for certain types of functions or processes.

Specialization of the Left Hemisphere.   In most right-handers, the left hemisphere is specialized to handle spoken language and other aspects of linguistic processing, such as the ability to understand and produce speech. Thus, in right-handers, the right hemisphere has no direct access to speech mechanisms. Brain organization in left-handed people is more variable.

Evidence that the left hemisphere is specialized for speech comes from a variety of sources. In addition to studies documenting language deficits in patients with left hemisphere damage (Rasmussen & Milner, 1975), a number of neurosurgical procedures have provided comprehensive evidence for the left hemisphere's special language abilities. For example, before beginning brain surgery, neurosurgeons typically locate, and then try to avoid, regions of the brain that are crucial for language. They do this by electrically stimulating particular areas, and, if this renders the patient unable to speak when instructed to, they conclude that the area is important for language. Such explorations have shown that stimulation of the left, but usually not the right, hemisphere leads to disruptions in speech production and language processing. Furthermore, the disruptions are consistent with the general area of function subserved by particular regions of the brain reviewed earlier. Thus, stimulation of the left *temporal* lobe disrupts verbal memory functions, whereas stimulation of the left *frontal* lobe disrupts speech production (since it involves complex motor sequences).

Another technique often used to investigate language lateralization involves injecting sodium amytal into the internal carotid artery (Wada & Rasmussen, 1960). This procedure temporarily puts one hemisphere "to sleep," during which time the neuropsychologist or neurologist can test the patient. When the left hemisphere is "sleeping" in this way, nearly all right-handers lose their ability to speak (e.g., Milner, 1974).

Research with split-brain patients has also provided powerful evidence for left hemisphere dominance in language functions. For example, split-brain patients might be asked to sit in front of a screen that makes it impossible to see objects that are placed in their hands. To identify the object, these patients must depend entirely on tactile information carried by the sensory nerves from the hand to the brain. Like most nerve pathways, these sensory nerves cross over the midline before they reach information processing areas in the cortex. As a result, information from the left hand is initially sent to the right side of the brain, and information from the right hand is sent to the left side of the brain. In a normal brain, the corpus callosum transfers this information to the opposite hemisphere in a split second, but because the corpus callosum is severed in split-brain patients, the only way their opposite hemisphere can obtain information about a touched object is if they look at it. What happens when the screen blocks the split-brain patients' view? Roger Sperry and his associates (e.g., Sperry, 1974) found that these patients have no difficulty naming objects being held in the right hand (which is connected to their left hemisphere), but when asked to name objects they were holding in the left hand (which is connected to the right hemisphere), the patients were reduced to silence. When they were asked to use their left hand to pick out a picture of the object, however, they could do so correctly every time. The obvious conclusion is that the right hemisphere is mute—it does not contain speech mechanisms like those housed within the left hemisphere.

Specialization of the Right Hemisphere.   Although the right hemisphere appears to lack speech functions, it is not stupid. As Sperry and his colleagues showed, given a nonverbal means of communication, the right hemisphere is able to perform on

a level equal to that of the left. Indeed, one of the greatest contributions of research with split-brain patients has been to demonstrate the right hemisphere's high-level information-processing capability. We now know that the right hemisphere is crucial for analyzing a vast array of spatial and nonverbal information, including the highly complex signals involved in social communication. The right hemisphere is superior to the left in its understanding of the relationships between objects in space and time. It seems to specialize in perceiving the *gestalt,* or whole picture presented by the world. Thus, when we look at a wooded landscape the left hemisphere would be more likely to focus on individual trees, but miss the perception of a forest. The right hemisphere will be likely to see the forest, but to ignore the trees. These tendencies are revealed in the drawings produced by brain-damaged patients. Patients with right hemisphere damage, like our client Mary Ellen, are reasonably good at drawing the *parts* of an object, but they are likely to place the parts incorrectly relative to each other. Patients with left hemisphere damage are reasonably good at drawing an object's overall shape, but they tend to leave out the details.

As just noted, the right hemisphere is much better than the left at understanding the signals that are involved in interpersonal communication (Perecman, 1983). Only part of the important information in a conversation is carried by the actual content of the utterances; a great deal of information is conveyed by *how* words are said rather than by *what* is said (Bates, 1976). The right hemisphere is especially good at perceiving and decoding gestures, tone of voice, facial expressions, body language, and other nonverbal information, and then integrating them into a coherent message.

Even the domain of language, long thought to be under the sole purview of the left hemisphere, depends, in part, on the right hemisphere. Recent research has shown that the right hemisphere plays an important role in understanding metaphors and other linguistic devices. For example, right-brain-damaged patients interpret statements like "I cried my eyes out" as if they were literally true. Nor do they appreciate humor, often losing the ability to "get a joke" (Gardner et al., 1983).

The difficulties right-brain-damaged patients have in judging situations appropriately, in relating to others, and in accurately perceiving social cues is compounded by another problem—they are often unaware of their deficits. The inability to comprehend the magnitude and severity of one's difficulties is called *anosognosia.* This problem poses a serious obstacle to rehabilitation programs because few remedial strategies will be effective for patients who do not perceive that they even have a problem.

NEUROPSYCHOLOGICAL ASSESSMENT TECHNIQUES

Neuropsychologists employ a number of techniques to assess patients' cognitive, emotional, or behavioral deficits, and to link these deficits to what is known about brain functioning. They usually follow one of two approaches to assessing deficits in patients suspected of having suffered brain damage. One approach—called the *fixed battery*— is to administer a predetermined, standardized set of tests to all patients. In the second, *individualized* approach, a flexible battery is administered. A few tests may be routinely given to all patients, but the remaining tests are selected with the special characteristics of a particular patient in mind. The individualized approach tailors the choice of tests to specific diagnostic questions as well as to what is discovered about a patient from the initial set of tests.

Both approaches have advantages and disadvantages. Batteries are comprehensive, their standardization is useful for research, and they can be given by paraprofessionals, since there is no need for expert judgments about what tests to use. (It is worth noting that a federal court recently accepted evidence from a Halstead-Reitan Neuropsychological Battery, but barred evidence from two flexible batteries; Reed, 1996). But fixed batteries can be inefficient because they assess functions that are not impaired in many patients; also, because of their fixed nature, batteries may become obsolete; it is difficult to revise them to incorporate new and potentially better tests. Individualized approaches allow in-depth assessment of particular problems, permit the use of new tests as they are developed, and focus more thoroughly on specific deficits. However, the individualized approach requires testers who have more training and sophistication, and because of the different combinations of tests it employs, it is more difficult to use in research comparing the performance of different patients.

Nowadays, few clinical neuropsychologists are wedded to a single fixed battery, although many will administer one and then give a selected set of additional measures. It appears likely that controversy will continue over what is the ideal approach. At present, at least, it appears that a fixed battery may be the better choice in cases involving court proceedings. Whichever approach neuropsychologists use, it is particularly important that they interpret test results with each patient's cultural background in mind. As noted in Chapter 5 in relation to intelligence testing, cultural factors can influence neuropsychological test performance in ways that the uncritical assessor might interpret as indicative of brain damage when, in fact, no such damage exists.

It would be ideal if the neuropsychologist could compare a patient's current level of functioning to that same person's performance prior to any suspected brain damage. Because standardized assessments of a patient's behavioral and cognitive abilities have usually not been performed prior to brain damage, the clinical neuropsychologist must usually rely on the alternative strategy of estimating *premorbid* abilities from whatever clues can be assembled. One way to estimate premorbid functioning is to look at patients' current best performance and assume that it provides a general reflection of their overall level of premorbid function. Another way to make such estimates is to consider the correlations that are known to exist between cognitive abilities and demographic variables such as age, ethnicity, sex, and socioeconomic status. These correlations provide a general basis for presuming what a particular person's premorbid functioning probably was (e.g., Barona & Chastain, 1986). Thus, a near-average score on a mental ability test might not be unexpected for a patient with a high school education working at a blue-collar job, but that same score would be surprising in a college professor.

Batteries

As noted earlier, the Halstead-Reitan Neuropsychological Test Battery is the most widely used battery. It is suitable for persons aged fifteen and older, but there are two other versions that can be used for children aged nine to fourteen, and five to eight, respectively.

The Halstead-Reitan Battery.   When used with adults, the Halstead-Reitan neuropsychological battery usually combines the MMPI and the Wechsler Adult Intelligence Scale-Revised (WAIS-R) (see Chapter 5) with the following ten Halstead-Reitan tests (Boll, 1981):

1. *The Categories Test* requires a patient to form correct categorizations of the visual stimuli presented in 208 slides. Initially the task is simple but becomes more difficult as it goes along. This test measures mental efficiency, the ability to derive a rule from experience, and the ability to form abstract concepts. A more convenient booklet form of this test has been developed, and there is also a booklet short form containing a subset of the stimulus items.

2. *The Tactual Performance Test* presents a board with spaces into which ten blocks of various shapes can be fitted, somewhat like a big jigsaw puzzle. The patient is asked to fit the blocks into the spaces as quickly as possible, while blindfolded. The patient performs this task three times; first with the preferred hand, next with the nonpreferred hand, and finally with both hands. Following the final trial, the blindfold is removed, the board is removed from view, and the patient is asked to draw the board and its blocks in their proper places from memory. This test measures abilities such as motor speed, tactile and kinesthetic perception, and incidental memory.

3. *The Seashore Rhythm Test* presents thirty pairs of rhythmic beats. The patient's task is to say whether the rhythms are the same or different. The test measures nonverbal auditory perception, attention, and concentration.

4. *The Speech-Sounds Perception Test* requires that the patient match spoken nonsense words to words on written lists. Language processing, verbal auditory perception, attention, and concentration are measured by this task.

5. *The Finger Tapping Test* is a simple test of motor speed in which the patient taps a small lever with the index finger as fast as possible for ten seconds. Several trials with each hand are used, allowing comparison of lateralized motor speed.

6. *The Trail Making Test* is a kind of "connect-the-dots" task involving a set of circles that are numbered or lettered. The circles must be connected in a consecutive sequence, thus requiring speed, visual scanning, and the ability to use, and switch between, different sets.

7. *The Strength of Grip Test* gives a right- versus left-side comparison of physical strength. The patient simply squeezes a dynamometer twice with each hand.

8. *The Sensory-Perceptual Exam* assesses whether the patient can perceive tactile, auditory, and visual stimulation when presented on one side of the body at a time (unilaterally) and on both sides simultaneously (bilaterally). Each of the three senses is assessed separately and with standard variations in the location of the stimulation used.

9. *Tactile Perception Tests* employ various methods to assess the patient's ability to identify objects when they are placed in the right and left hand, to perceive touch

in different fingers of both hands, and to decipher numbers when they are traced on the fingertips while the patient's eyes are closed.

10. The *Aphasia Screening Test* measures several aspects of language usage and recognition, as well as abilities to reproduce geometric forms and pantomime simple actions. Twelve of the thirty-two tasks from this test are presented in Table 12.1. Although widely used, the test has recently been criticized (Lezak, 1995; Snow, 1987b), and it has been suggested that neuropsychologists should use a shorter version of it. Indeed, the test appears to discriminate only poorly between left- and right-brain-damaged patients; significant differences between the two groups appear on only one item, copying the drawing of a key.

Reitan recommended four procedures for evaluating performance on the Halstead-Reitan Battery. These procedures are generally followed by practitioners today, although there are variations in the extent each of them is emphasized. First, *level of performance* is assessed by comparing the patient's performance to that of normative groups; an impairment index is calculated based on the number of tests for which the patient's performance falls into a clinically deficient range. Second, *patterns of performance* are analyzed. Pattern analysis examines variations in performance on different components of a test; the most common example is the comparison of scores on verbal versus performance scores on the WAIS-R IQ test. Third, emphasis is placed on *comparing right-side to left-side performance* and drawing inferences about hemispheric functioning when large differences appear. Fourth, the neuropsychologist looks for *pathognomonic signs*, which are specific deficits that are so strongly indicative of organic problems that their presence almost always indicates a disorder.

The Luria-Nebraska Neuropsychological Battery. Charles Golden and his colleagues at the University of Nebraska (Golden, 1981; Golden, Purisch, & Hammeke, 1985) compiled a neuropsychological test battery based on Luria's methods, but which presents explicit rules for presenting the test items and quantitatively scoring the results. The latest version of this battery, known as the Luria-Nebraska Neuropsychological Battery, consists of 279 items and can be completed in about two and a half hours, or roughly half the time it takes to administer the Halstead-Reitan. The items in the Luria-Nebraska Battery are those that, in validation studies, best discriminated control subjects (psychiatric patients and normal individuals) from neurological patients. The items are organized into twelve content scales, which test motor functions, rhythm and pitch, tactile and kinesthetic functions, visual functions, receptive language, expressive language, reading, arithmetic, writing, memory, intermediate memory, and intelligence. In addition, there is a pathognomonic scale composed of items that are rarely missed by normal subjects but rarely passed by brain-damaged ones. There is also a left-hemisphere scale and a right-hemisphere scale that measure motor and sensory functions of the right and left sides of the body, respectively. Scales for localization and lateralization have also been described, but have not been as thoroughly validated as the initial scales (e.g., McKay & Golden, 1979).

TABLE 12.1   Sample Items From the Aphasia Screening Test

Patient's Task	Examiner's Instructions to the Patient
Copy Square	First, draw this on your paper (examiner points to picture of a square). I want you to do it without lifting your pencil from the paper. Make it about this same size (points to square).
Name Square	What is that shape called?
Spell Square	Would you spell that word for me?
Copy Cross	Draw this on your paper (examiner points to picture of a cross). Go around the outside like this until you get back to where you started (examiner draws a finger line around the edge of the stimulus figure). Make it about this same size (points to cross).
Name Cross	What is that shape called?
Spell Cross	Would you spell that word for me?
Name Baby	What is this? (examiner points to picture of baby)
Repeat/Explain "He shouted the warning"	I am going to say something that I want you to say after me. So listen carefully: He shouted the warning. Now you say it. Would you explain what that means? (Sometimes it is necessary to amplify by asking the kind of situation to which the sentence would refer. The patient's understanding is adequately demonstrated when he brings the concept of impending danger into his explanation.)
Write "He shouted the warning"	Now I want you to write that sentence on the paper. (Sometimes it is necessary to repeat the sentence so that the patient understands clearly what he is to write.)
Name Key	What is this? (examiner points to picture of key)
Demonstrate Use of Key	If you had one of these in your hand, show me how you would use it (points to key).
Draw Key	Now I want you to draw a picture that looks just like this. Try to make your key look enough like this one so that I would know it was the same key from your drawing (points to key).

SOURCE: Filskow and Boll, 1981. (© Copyright 1981. Used by permission of John Wiley & Sons.)

A patient's performance on each test item is scored 0 (normal performance), 1 (borderline performance), or 2 (defective performance). The summed items from each scale are then converted to *T*-scores, allowing creation of a profile much like those derived from the MMPI (see Chapter 5). In addition to profile analysis, the Luria-Nebraska can be interpreted qualitatively by analyzing patterns of item failures or the presence of pathognomonic signs. *T*-scores can also be adjusted for age and education, making the score cutoffs used to assess impairment specific to such characteristics.

Although strong claims have been made for the Luria-Nebraska's ability to discriminate brain-damaged from schizophrenic patients, this battery has been severely criticized for flawed test construction, improper data analysis, inadequate standardization, and a distortion of Luria's original methods, which simply may not be translatable into items on a battery (see Adams, 1980a, b; Golden, 1980; and Spiers, 1980, for the flavor of this sometimes bitter controversy).

Individualized Approaches

One of the most thorough and best-described individualized approaches is that of Murial D. Lezak, a psychologist at the Oregon Health Sciences University and the Portland, Oregon, Veterans Administration Hospital. Lezak's strategy, as described in her book, *Neuropsychological Assessment* (1995), is to give all patients several standard tests that assess major functions in the auditory and visual receptive modalities as well as in the spoken, written, graphic, and constructional response modalities. Following this initial battery, which usually takes two to three hours, Lezak proceeds with "hypothesis testing," during which she shifts the focus of the assessment from one set of functions to another as the data indicate what may be the most impaired abilities.

> The addition of specialized tests depends on continuing formulation and reformulation of hypotheses as new data answer some questions and raise others. Hypotheses involving differentiation of learning from retrieval, for instance, will dictate the use of techniques for assessing learning when retrieval is impaired. . . . every other function can be examined across modalities and in systematically varied formats. In each case, the examiner can best determine what particular combinations of modality, content, and format are needed to test the pertinent hypothesis. (Lezak, 1995, p. 125)

The other well-known individualized approach to neuropsychological assessment was developed by the Boston group, including Edith Kaplan, Harold Goodglass, and Nelson Butters. Their assessment begins with a core set of eleven tests that measure areas such as intelligence, memory, attention, construction, and sensory-perceptual abilities. The additional tests that are administered depend on the nature of the referral plus the results of initial testing. Attention to the strategies and processes involved in patients' failures and successes in test performance partially determines the selection of additional tests. Even more importantly, the emphasis on process and strategy contributes to a more than usually detailed analysis of patients' deficits, with the recognition that superficially similar deficits can reflect quite distinct underlying processes (Jones & Butters, 1983; Kaplan, 1990).

It is difficult to assess the validity of individualized approaches because they are tailored to each patient's needs and hence are not given in exactly the same form to sufficient numbers of patients to permit large-scale comparisons. Furthermore, individualized approaches depend much more than batteries do on the skill of the examiner using them. It thus becomes difficult to separate the validity of the tests from the clinical acumen of the examiner. Despite these limitations, individualized approaches offer a promising strategy when they are based on theoretical models that specify the impairments that one is likely to encounter with various types of brain damage (Satz & Fletcher, 1981). In other words, individualized approaches usually reflect a theoretical justification for the use of particular tests while the typical neuropsychological battery does not; its construction depends only on the ability of its items to empirically differentiate brain-damaged patients from others. This difference is another example of the distinction between empirical versus rational approaches to test construction that we outlined in Chapter 5.

Neurodiagnostic Procedures

The neuropsychological assessments we have described have often been compared to and validated against methods used by neurologists. Their *neurodiagnostic procedures* are designed to directly observe damage to central nervous system tissue or to monitor some biophysical function of the brain that suggests impairment. In other words, while the neuropsychologist examines how patterns of behavior are related to possible brain lesions, the neurologist either observes lesions themselves or looks for chemical or physical evidence that a lesion is present.

Despite growing sophistication in recent years, neurological methods are not infallible. First, some neurological procedures are valid indicators of certain disorders but not of others. For example, the EEG is an excellent test for patients with seizure disorders, but it is not sensitive to Alzheimer's disease or brain infections. Second, some tests may show abnormalities in patients who have no brain damage. The EEG is susceptible to this "false positive" mistake, particularly in children. A third difficulty with some of the neurodiagnostic techniques listed below is that they are risky for the patient. This is especially true of exploratory surgery, arteriograms, and repeated X-rays.

Neurological Clinical Examination. As Oliver Sacks did with Dr. P., physicians conducting neurological clinical examinations screen patients' sensory abilities, eye movements, cognitive and perceptual abilities, language, motor and postural irregularities, and symptom history. The examination is a preliminary investigation of brain disturbance.

Lumbar Puncture. Spinal fluid is extracted from the spinal cord by inserting a needle. Examination of the fluid's chemistry as well as its pressure upon extraction can help diagnose brain infections, hemorrhages, and some tumors. It is often not performed when any of several conditions are present (e.g., brain abscess), and it has some complications, the most common of which is headaches.

Electroencephalogram (EEG). The EEG monitors the electrical activity of the cerebral cortex. It is especially useful in the diagnosis of seizure disorders and some vascular diseases affecting large blood vessels in the brain. It is safe, but it yields a relatively high rate of false positives.

Other Electrical Tests. Electromyogram (EMG), evoked potentials, and nerve conduction velocities all measure electrical activity of some sort—in muscles (EMG), in the brain when elicited by an external stimulus (evoked potentials), or in peripheral nerves (nerve conduction velocities). These tests are useful in the diagnosis of muscle disease, nerve disease caused by conditions such as diabetes, and certain sensory deficits.

X-rays.   There are many variations of X-ray pictures of brain structure. The technology of X-rays was revolutionized in the 1970s by the introduction of *computerized tomography* (CT scans), which provides computer-enhanced three-dimensional pictures of successive "slices" of the living brain. CT scans are very valuable in the diagnosis of tumors, traumatic damage, degenerative diseases like Alzheimer's, and cerebrovascular disease.

Positron Emission Tomography (PET).   PET scans show changes not just in the structure of the brain, but also in its metabolic function. It does this by tracking the rate at which a radioactive chemical injected into the brain is consumed by brain cells. Since diseased tissue uses the chemical at a different rate than normal tissue, PET scans can reveal specific areas of abnormal brain physiology. In addition to making neurological diagnoses, PET scans may help differentiate schizophrenics from bipolar patients.

Single Photon Emission Computed Tomography (SPECT).   The SPECT procedure is similar to the PET scan, but because it uses a radioactive chemical that lasts longer than those used in PET, it permits imaging of cortical and subcortical brain sections from several different angles. It, too, may prove useful in the diagnosis of disorders like schizophrenia.

Arteriography.   To make arteriograms, a dye is injected into the patient's arteries and a series of X-rays is taken to reveal the condition of those arteries as the dye passes through them. This test is used primarily to diagnose cerebrovascular disease, especially strokes and hemorrhages. Arteriograms can be very uncomfortable.

Magnetic Resonance Imaging (MRI) and Functional MRI (fMRI).   MRI works by tracking the activity of atoms in the body as they are "excited" by magnets in a chamber or coil placed around the patient's head. MRI allows imaging of brain structure whereas functional MRI (fMRI) is similar to PET and SPECT in that it measures the activity of the brain. MRI is advantageous in that it does not require exposure to X-rays or radioactive substances.

Biopsies and Exploratory Surgery.   These procedures involve direct examination of suspect brain tissue. Although they are risky, they can give a definite diagnosis of some neurological conditions.

NEUROPSYCHOLOGICAL APPROACHES TO PSYCHOPATHOLOGY

Recently, research in neuropsychology has begun to shed light on a number of psychological disorders, including depression and schizophrenia. Neuropsychologists are also beginning to expand our understanding of several childhood problems, especially learning disabilities.

Depression

Neuropsychologists have been interested in depression ever since the 1970s, when it was systematically documented that different kinds of brain damage produce different kinds of emotional reactions (Gainotti, 1972). For example, right-brain-damaged patients often show a rather cheerful, inappropriate, unconcerned reaction to their impairment and hospitalization. This "euphoric" or "indifference" reaction is often accompanied by anosognosia, or unawareness of deficit. In contrast, left-brain-damaged patients often show a "catastrophic" reaction, which is characterized by tearfulness, despair, and other symptoms of depression (Gainotti, 1972). More recent studies have confirmed that one-third to two-thirds of patients become depressed after experiencing damage to the left side of the brain (Starkstein & Robinson, 1988). These studies have also shown that the probability of depression rises with increasing proximity of the lesion to the front part of the brain. The closer the lesion is to the frontal pole of the left hemisphere, the more severe the depression.

It appears that these emotional responses are not simply a reaction to the experience of being impaired. In one study comparing stroke patients to orthopedic patients suffering similar degrees of disability, four times as many stroke patients were depressed (Folstein, Maiberger, & McHugh, 1977). Furthermore, the degree of depression doesn't correlate with the severity of the disability (e.g., aphasia), suggesting that if there is a relationship, it is not a simple, linear one. These findings have been corroborated by research measuring EEG activity in the left versus the right hemisphere. The left hemisphere in clinically depressed people is typically less active than the right; similarly, when nondepressed people are just feeling sad, the left hemisphere is less active than the right hemisphere. These differences in EEG activity are most evident over the frontal regions of the brain, confirming their importance for these emotional effects.

Tachistoscopic studies have also shown that, when visual stimuli are projected to both hemispheres, the left hemisphere typically rates pictures as more positive than the right hemisphere—even though each hemisphere has seen the exact same pictures (Heller, 1990). These results suggest that in the normal brain, frontal regions of the left hemisphere play some role in maintaining a positive perspective on things. It may well be that negative mood states result when a lesion or other condition causes these left-side areas to be underactive relative to those in the right hemisphere.

Researchers have speculated that these effects may be mediated by the neurotransmitter dopamine, more of which has been found in the left hemispheres of both animals and people. Dopamine seems to play a special role in allowing people to find things rewarding or enjoyable; for example, the euphoric effects of amphetamine have been shown to be mediated by an increase in dopamine in the brain. It is possible, therefore, that interfering with the transmission of dopamine may affect the activity level of the left hemisphere, which, in turn, may produce depression.

Other studies have found depression associated with reduced functioning of the *right* hemisphere, but there, regions further toward the rear appear to be most involved (Heller, 1990). People who are depressed show some of the same cognitive deficits displayed by patients with damage to parietal-temporal regions of the brain. They have difficulty with visual-spatial information processing and show a number of attentional problems that are similar to right-brain-damaged patients. These effects may be caused by the interrelationship of the frontal and posterior regions of the brain. Since frontal regions often inhibit activation in posterior regions, relatively greater activation in the right frontal region compared to the left may be producing too much inhibition of the right posterior regions.

It is possible that some of the characteristic cognitive and psychomotor symptoms of depression are due to these underlying neuropsychological patterns. For example, the frontal regions of the left hemisphere are involved in programming fine motor activities, and depressed patients display slowed responses and reduced activity.

These neuropsychological findings have implications not only for our understanding of depression, but also for its diagnosis and treatment in brain-damaged people and normals. For example, it is important to consider the possibility that in addition to having problems with impaired language comprehension or expression, a brain-damaged patient may also be depressed. This is why neuropsychologists typically ask family members whether a patient is sleeping and eating normally, or recovering as expected. If not, an underlying depression may be present, and may require treatment with antidepressant medication. It is also possible that depressed people without brain damage can display neuropsychological deficits that suggest brain impairment. With proper treatment of the depression, these deficits are typically reduced.

Schizophrenia

Neuropsychologists have been deeply involved in studying brain functioning in schizophrenics. Early studies, most of which used tachistoscopic methods, suggested the possibility that schizophrenia is characterized by an overactivation of the brain's left hemisphere (Gur, 1978). Current studies continue to implicate the left hemisphere, but the picture is now more complicated.

Studies comparing regional cerebral blood flow and glucose metabolism in schizophrenics versus normal controls suggest that the left prefrontal region of schizophrenics is abnormal because it is not activated during performance on tests like the Wisconsin Card Sort Test. In contrast, subcortical regions of the same hemisphere show a hyperactivation compared to controls (Rubin et al., 1991).

These results are compatible with several observations regarding the symptoms of schizophrenia. First, many schizophrenics display what are termed *negative* symptoms, which include flat affect, lack of initiative, lack of energy, absence of social engagement, and loss of spontaneity. These same symptoms are encountered in certain patients with prefrontal lesions. Second, the disruption in linear reasoning, logical thought, and language typically seen in schizophrenia is consistent with some kind of damage to the specialized regions of the left hemisphere. We must be cautious in drawing conclusions, however, because the prefrontal region is intricately connected to many other parts of the brain, and damage or dysfunction elsewhere could cause the prefrontal region to malfunction. Furthermore, most of the studies we have mentioned are based on small samples, because schizophrenia is relatively rare in the general population, the patients are difficult to test, and the technology is expensive and complicated. Nonetheless, many researchers believe that the results of neuropsychological studies point to the possibility that schizophrenia is related to damage or dysfunction of the prefrontal regions of the left hemisphere (Andreasen et al., 1986; Buschbaum et al., 1992; Rubin et al., 1991).

Learning Disabilities

Given their interest in intellectual abilities and mental performance, it is not surprising that neuropsychologists are interested in learning disabilities. Several neuropsychological studies have found, for example, that *dyslexia* (disruptions in the ability to read) is usually related to dysfunction of the left hemisphere. Tachistoscopic studies and other behavioral measures have found that children with reading problems tend to show a reduction in the advantage normally seen in the left hemisphere relative to the right (Obrzut, 1988). Indeed, these children tend to rely more on right than left hemisphere processes in learning to read. Dyslexia is correlated with other deficits in language skills; for example, children with reading difficulties often are slow to acquire spoken language.

Autopsy studies of people who were known to have had dyslexia reveal that the structure of their left hemispheres is different from that of most people, and researchers have also found evidence for misplaced brain cells, called *ectopias,* in the left hemisphere. These misplaced cells are likely to "get lost" during the development of the brain, when cells normally migrate to their proper places in the cortex. Such misplacements could cause developmental delays and deficits in the functioning of the left hemisphere. Pediatric clinical neuropsychologists can often help document left hemisphere deficits in children with reading difficulties. They also help design remedial programs for such children and consult with teachers and parents on how best to get academic information across.

A different type of learning disability involves deficits in visual-spatial and visual-motor skills, as well as in other abilities that depend on the right hemisphere. This syndrome of *nonverbal learning disability* was first described about twenty years ago (Myklebust, 1975), but neuropsychological research is only now helping to delineate this disorder and communicate its significance to teachers and mental health professionals. Children with nonverbal learning disabilities may have long escaped the notice of professionals because they are often talkative and show high levels of verbal intelligence. Consequently, they sound as though they should be more skillful in the nonverbal realm than they actually are. Children with nonverbal learning disabilities often have difficulty keeping up with other children on nonverbal tasks. They are slow to learn skills like tying shoes, dressing, eating, and organizing their time and their environment. Because their deficits are less obvious, they are likely to be labeled as having an emotional or behavioral problem, not a learning disability. Unfortunately, when these children have been viewed as bad, uncooperative, or "a problem" long enough, they may end up behaving accordingly. Early diagnosis and treatment of children with nonverbal learning disabilities should help prevent some of these subsequent psychological and behavioral problems.

Nonverbal learning disabilities may result from right-hemisphere deficits early in childhood which can dramatically interfere with normal development (Rourke, 1989). These deficits inhibit a child from exploring the environment, learning the consequences of actions, and gaining essential experience in coordinated visual-motor skills. Wendy Heller and her colleagues (e.g., Heller, Hopkins, & Cox, 1991) have studied infants with brain hemorrhages caused by immature development of the vascular system. They found that right-brain-damaged babies were less facially expressive and showed less reciprocity in interactions with their mothers than left-brain-damaged babies or non-brain-damaged controls. Since mother–infant interaction predicts the quality of attachment at slightly older ages, and since quality of attachment predicts social adjustment in childhood, these results suggest that right-brain problems can not only create early motoric and cognitive handicaps, but can also lead to the early abnormalities in social relationships that place the children at risk for emotional difficulties later in life. Their difficulties in social development are probably related to their inability to meet the intense demands for nonverbal information processing in social situations. Overwhelmed by the task of integrating information about other children's facial information, tone of voice, physical activity, and verbal content, they fail to follow even simple exchanges. Over time, their lack of experience and interaction with other children can cause them to feel isolated, lonely, and depressed. It has even been suggested that nonverbal learning disability may be a risk factor for the development of schizophrenia.

In assessing nonverbal learning disabilities, pediatric clinical neuropsychologists look first for a discrepancy between Verbal and Performance IQ on the Wechsler Intelligence Scale for Children. Often, Verbal IQ will be average or well above average, with Performance IQ significantly lower. If the pattern persists on other tests comparing verbal and visual-spatial/visual-motor skills, a nonverbal learning disability is likely to be diagnosed. Often, although not always, the pattern of poor performance on right hemisphere tasks is accompanied by signs on the Halstead-Reitan Battery suggesting impaired right-hemisphere performance.

As in the case of verbal learning disabilities, pediatric clinical neuropsychologists work to devise remedial programs for children with nonverbal learning disabilities. They encourage parents and teachers to take advantage of the child's verbal skills in ways that can help compensate for a lack of understanding in nonverbal domains. They also recommend that these children get individual attention from a learning disabilities specialist or tutor; otherwise, like children with verbal learning disabilities, their academic achievement is likely to fall behind as the demands of school increase. The children's impaired social skills can often be addressed by group therapy, social skills workshops, individual therapy, or facilitation of structured peer interactions such as scouting or participation in after-school programs.

TRAINING IN CLINICAL NEUROPSYCHOLOGY

Part of the task of APA's Division of Clinical Neuropsychology has been to define the training and educational experiences necessary to become a competent clinical neuropsychologist, and to institute a procedure by which to obtain the credentials to demonstrate such competence. As a result, an American Board of Clinical Neuropsychology has been established as a component of the American Board of Professional Psychology (see Chapter 14). Individuals who have undergone the proper training and have had sufficient experience in the practice of clinical neuropsychology (currently five years of postdoctoral practice) can apply to take the examination for *diplomate* status in clinical neuropsychology. The following statement defining a clinical neuropsychologist was adopted by the Executive Committee of Division 40 at the APA meeting on August 12, 1988:

> A Clinical Neuropsychologist is a professional psychologist who applies principles of assessment and intervention based upon the scientific study of human behavior as it relates to normal and abnormal functioning of the central nervous system. The Clinical Neuropsychologist is a doctoral-level psychology provider of diagnostic and intervention services who has demonstrated competence in the application of such principles for human welfare following:
>
> A. Successful completion of systematic didactic and experiential training in neuropsychology and neuroscience at a regionally accredited university;
>
> B. Two or more years of appropriate supervised training applying neuropsychological services in a clinical setting;
>
> C. Licensing and certification to provide psychological services to the public by the laws of the state or province in which he or she practices;
>
> D. Review by one's peers as a test of these competencies.

Attainment of the ABCN/ABPP Diploma in Clinical Neuropsychology is the clearest evidence of competence as a clinical neuropsychologist because it assures that all of these criteria have been met.

This statement, along with a series of important documents relating to clinical neuropsychology, appears in a volume entitled *The TCN Guide to Professional Practice in Clinical Neuropsychology* (Adams & Rourke, 1992). This volume contains the Division 40 guidelines for doctoral training programs in neuropsychology and a listing of such programs at the doctoral, postdoctoral, and internship levels. Undergraduates interested in pursuing the field of clinical neuropsychology can refer to a section describing the experiences that are useful to seek at the college level.

FUTURE DIRECTIONS IN NEUROPSYCHOLOGY

One of the most obvious trends in neuropsychological research and practice is the increasing reliance on measures of brain functioning such as PET, fMRI, and other indices of regional cerebral activation and organization. Continued development and refinement of these techniques are likely, and they will become more accessible to researchers and clinicians. In combination with other measures of neuropsychological, cognitive, attentional, and emotional functioning, brain activity measures will provide a new database for the field.

Joseph Matarazzo (1992) predicted that these measures will eventually be used to assess individual differences in brain structure and mental ability, "thus heralding the first clear break from test items and tests in the Binet tradition in a century" (p. 1012). Matarazzo also argued that the future will bring refinement in the specificity of tests of ability as psychologists learn more about cognitive organization. At the same time, the links between specific kinds of abilities and the parts of the brain involved in those abilities will become clearer. Consequently, it will become easier to design tasks to measure even more precisely the functioning of particular brain regions, and to link these to individual differences in ability levels.

Increasing the sensitivity of the measures we have available, along with an improved ability to link these measures to specific brain regions, bodes well for our understanding of brain–behavior relationships in a variety of conditions. For example, as the elderly population increases, the incidence of Alzheimer's and other dementing illnesses will increase. Mapping the relationship between memory functions and the activity of specific brain regions promises to advance both basic knowledge about the problem as well as efforts to improve clinical assessment and intervention. Similarly, our understanding of the neural architecture in schizophrenia and other mental disorders will be advanced by future research which couples performance on neuropsychological tests with the measurement of brain activity.

NEUROPSYCHOLOGY AT WORK

Q.: To what extent do the principles, methods, and research results associated with neuropsychology affect your work?

DR. SANDY D'ANGELO: Pediatric neuropsychologists have studied the cognitive consequences of many medical disorders and medical treatments. For example, we now know much about typical cognitive profiles of children with Williams syndrome, fetal alcohol syndrome, untreated phenylketonuria, and children exposed to anticonvulsant medication in the womb. We also are learning more about the negative effects of some medical treatments—such as radiation used in bone marrow transplantation—on children's cognitive development. Because I work in a Department of Pediatrics, neuropsychological research applied to medical disorders is very useful to me as I consult with professional colleagues, schools, and parents about children's learning and behavioral problems, prognoses, and need for supportive interventions.

DR. HECTOR MACHABANSKI: Neuropsychology has some impact on my work, as I am always attempting to refine assessment techniques in working with chronically ill and organically involved children.

DR. GEOFFREY THORPE: It does not directly affect my work. However, our doctoral students may choose to take specialized clinical practica in neuropsychology in community settings, and one of the supervisors with neuropsychological expertise teaches an elective graduate course on this topic.

CHAPTER SUMMARY

The field of neuropsychology seeks to define the relationship between brain processes and human behavior and psychological functioning—including cognitive and motor abilities, emotional characteristics, personality traits, and mental disorders. Clinical neuropsychologists apply the results of neuropsychological research in their work with children and adults who have had trauma or injury to the brain, or who are experiencing other problems related to a brain impairment.

Speculation about the mind's relation to the brain goes back to ancient times, but neuropsychology was not defined as a scientific field until the late 1940s, and clinical neuropsychology did not emerge as a distinctive professional specialty until the 1970s.

One of most important organizational principles underlying brain–behavior relationships is localization of function, which refers to the fact that different parts of the brain are responsible for different skills or senses. For example, the occipital lobes of the cerebral cortex are involved in processing visual information; association areas in the parietal lobes combine and integrate sensory information from a variety of sources; the temporal lobes are involved in categorizing, classifying, and storing information in long-term memory; and the frontal lobes are primarily involved in the planning, organization, and direction of complex sequences of behavior. Lateralization of function is another vital feature of the brain's organization that has important implications for behavior. In most right-handers, the left hemisphere is specialized to handle speech and other linguistic processing, including the ability to understand and produce spoken language. The right hemisphere is crucial for analyzing spatial and other nonverbal information, including complex signals involved in social communication.

Clinical neuropsychologists use a variety of tools and one of two main approaches to assess patients' cognitive, emotional, or behavioral deficits, and to relate these deficits to specific impairments in brain functioning. In the "fixed battery" approach, a standardized set of tests is given to all patients, while in the individualized approach, a flexible battery of tests is selected depending on the characteristics of each patient. The most widely used fixed battery is the Halstead-Reitan Neuropsychological Test Battery. It consists of ten specific tests, and is combined with the MMPI and an IQ test. The Luria-Nebraska Neuropsychological Battery can be given in less time and the scores on its 279 items can be organized into an MMPI-like profile. Two prominent individualized approaches have been developed by Murial D. Lezak, and by Edith Kaplan, Harold Goodglass, and Nelson Butters. The results of neuropsychological assessments are often compared to and validated against neurological assessments, including EEG, various brain imaging techniques, arteriograms, and even exploratory surgery.

Today neuropsychology research is helping clinicians better understand a variety of psychological disorders, including depression, schizophrenia, and verbal and nonverbal learning disabilities.

APA's Division of Clinical Neuropsychology has defined the training and educational experiences necessary to become a clinical neuropsychologist and established criteria for demonstrating competence in this specialty.

Chapter 13

Forensic Psychology

As noted in Chapter 1, clinicians are likely to be increasingly involved in a variety of the specialty areas that will help to define clinical psychology in the twenty-first century. This trend has already helped to shape the contents of this book. The first edition, published in 1980, did not include chapters on clinical child psychology, health psychology, or neuropsychology; these were added, however, in subsequent editions. In the fourth edition, published in 1994, we predicted that forensic psychology—a specialty that applies psychological principles and knowledge to legal issues and proceedings—would be a "growth stock" for clinical psychologists, but we did not include a separate chapter on the topic.

Our prediction was accurate. It is now clear that the demand for psychologists to contribute in various ways to the legal system has grown to the point that forensic psychology has become a major professional activity and a focal point of scholarship among clinical psychologists. There are numerous indicators of this growth surge. For example, the American Psychology-Law Society (Division 41 of the American Psychological Association) now lists almost 2,000 members and publishes its own journal, *Law and Human Behavior*. In 1995, APA itself inaugurated publication of *Psychology, Public Policy, and Law*, another journal devoted to psychology and the law.

THE SCOPE OF FORENSIC PSYCHOLOGY

Clinical psychologists play a variety of roles in the legal system, including in the areas of (1) law enforcement psychology, (2) the psychology of litigation,

(3) correctional psychology, and (4) forensic psychology, the area we will focus on in this chapter.

Law enforcement psychology involves conducting research on the activities of law enforcement agencies and providing direct clinical services in support of these agencies. A clinician working in this area might test candidates for police work to screen out those who are not psychologically fit, offer crisis intervention to police officers involved in violent encounters, consult with detectives about what kind of individual might have committed a certain type of crime, or help question witnesses in ways that enhance their recollection of crimes (e.g., Saywitz & Snyder, 1996).

The *psychology of litigation* is concerned with the effects of various legal procedures, usually those used in civil or criminal trials. Clinicians working in this area may offer advice to attorneys about jury selection, study the factors that influence jury deliberations and verdicts, and analyze the effects of specific portions of trials, such as opening statements, cross-examination of witnesses, or closing arguments.

Correctional psychology is concerned primarily with the delivery of psychological services to individuals serving jail sentences after having been convicted of a crime. Most clinicians working as correctional psychologists are employed in prisons, penitentiaries, or special juvenile facilities, but they may also operate out of a probation office or be part of a special community-based correctional program.

Forensic psychology (and forensic psychiatry) involves the application of mental health knowledge and expertise to questions about individuals who are involved in some type of legal proceeding. These questions can cover an enormous range of issues, including, for example, (1) is an individual sufficiently mentally ill and potentially dangerous to justify involuntary hospitalization?; (2) is a person charged with a crime mentally competent to stand trial?; (3) as a result of an injury or trauma, has a person suffered psychological harm, and if so, how serious is it?; and (4) did a person possess adequate mental capacity and understanding at the time he or she drafted a will? Clinical psychologists answer these and many other forensic questions that arise in particular cases by applying the results of empirical research and the skills and techniques of their profession, and then offer their opinions during testimony at civil and criminal trials or other legal proceedings.

In this chapter, we illustrate the practice of forensic psychology by describing five areas in which clinicians often offer expert testimony. These include:

1. Competence to stand trial and criminal responsibility;
2. Psychological damages in civil trials;
3. Civil competencies;
4. Psychological autopsies and criminal profiling; and
5. Child custody and parental fitness.

Our discussion will include a description of the basic psycho-legal questions experts must address in each area, coverage of the techniques clinicians typically use to evaluate these questions, and a summary of the empirical evidence and legal status associated with psychologists' activities in these areas. Remember, though, that our review of these five areas merely scratches the surface of what is going on at the interface of psychology and law. New research issues are constantly being addressed, and professional psychological services are continually expanding in the legal arena. You can review these advancements in journals such as *Law and Human Behavior, Forensic Reports,* or *Psychology, Public Policy, and Law,* as well as in textbooks on law and psychology (e.g., Bartol & Bartol, 1994; Monahan & Walker, 1993; Sales & Shuman, 1996; Wrightsman, Nietzel, & Fortune, 1998).

CRIMINAL COMPETENCE AND RESPONSIBILITY

No area of law illustrates the controversies surrounding expert testimony as dramatically as the question of whether a defendant was insane while committing an illegal act. Proving insanity can result in a defendant's being acquitted or, if convicted, protected from the punishment that would otherwise ensue.

Why do courts allow defendants' mental condition to be considered at trial? The basic reason is that most societies believe it is immoral to punish people who, as a result of a mental disorder, either do not know that their actions are wrong or cannot control their conduct. Societies see punishment as fully deserved only by those who can understand the nature and wrongness of their criminal behavior.

Criminal Competence

In the United States, it is not even permissible to continue criminal proceedings against a defendant who is unable to understand the nature and purpose of those proceedings. Thus, before a court ever considers whether a defendant was sane or insane during an alleged criminal act, it must first decide about the defendant's *competence to stand trial.* Defendants are considered incompetent if, as a result of a mental disorder, they cannot (1) understand the nature of their trial, (2) participate meaningfully in their own defense, or (3) consult with their attorney. Competence refers to the defendant's mental condition at the time of the trial, whereas insanity, described next, refers to the defendant's mental condition at the time of an alleged offense.

Because competence refers to an understanding of legal proceedings, the criteria for competence depend to some extent on the proceeding to be understood. Table 13.1 describes several kinds of competencies, other than competence to stand trial, that mental health experts are asked to evaluate in criminal defendants. Different questions are involved in each of these evaluations because each requires different capabilities of defendants. (Questions about the competencies listed in Table 13.1 also arise in civil law; we discuss these later.)

The law requires defendants to be competent for several reasons (Melton et al., 1987). First, legal proceedings are more likely to arrive at accurate results with the participation of competent defendants. Second, punishment of convicted defendants is morally acceptable only if they understand why they are being punished. Finally, the perceived fairness of our adversary system of justice requires participation by defendants who have the capacity to defend themselves against charges brought by the state.

TABLE 13.1   Legal Competencies

Because questions about competence can be raised at any point in the criminal process, a variety of competencies may be at issue in deciding whether a defendant can participate in different functions. Competence for any legal function involves (1) determining what abilities are necessary, (2) assessing the context in which these abilities must be demonstrated, (3) evaluating the implications of deficiencies in the required abilities, and (4) deciding whether the deficiencies warrant concluding that the defendant is incompetent (Grisso, 1986).

Mental health professionals are sometimes asked to evaluate any of the following competencies:

Competence to confess. Competence to confess requires that defendants, once in police custody, make a confession only after having waived their *Miranda* rights—knowingly, intelligently, and voluntarily. A mental health professional's assessment of these abilities is difficult because, in most cases, the waiver and confession occur months before the professional's evaluation. This situation requires many assumptions about the defendant's psychological condition at the time of arrest. As a result,

professional evaluations of competence to confess are given less weight than evidence about the police methods used to obtain the confession.

Competence to waive the right to an attorney. Can defendants decide they do not want a lawyer to represent them at trial? The Supreme Court has held that defendants have a Constitutional right to waive counsel and represent themselves at trial, providing that this decision is made competently (*Faretta v. California*, 1975). The standard for this competence is that the defendant waives the right to counsel with understanding and while voluntarily exercising informed free will.

Competence to waive the right to counsel was at issue in the trial of Colin Ferguson, a man charged with murdering six passengers and wounding nineteen more when, on a December evening in 1993, he went on a killing rampage aboard a Long Island Railroad train. Ferguson insisted on serving as his own attorney, after rejecting the "black rage" defense suggested by his two lawyers, Ron Kuby and the late William Kunstler. At first, Ferguson proved rational and effective enough to have several of his objections to the prosecutor's case sustained. But

---

Here is one example of a case in which the question of competence to stand trial was raised (Wrightsman, Nietzel, and Fortune, 1994, pp. 250–251):

Jamie Sullivan was a twenty-four-year-old clerk charged with arson, burglary, and murder in connection with a fire he set at a small grocery store in Kentucky. Evidence in the case showed that, after closing time, Sullivan returned to the store where he worked and forced the night manager, Ricky Ford to open the safe and hand over $800. Sullivan then locked Ford in a small office, doused the store with gasoline, and set it on fire. Ford was killed in the blaze. Police arrested Sullivan within hours at his grandmother's apartment on the basis of a lead from a motorist who saw Sullivan running from the scene.

If convicted on all charges, Jamie Sullivan could have faced the death penalty, but he was mentally retarded. He had dropped out of school in the eighth grade, and a psychologist's evaluation at that time reported his IQ to be 68. He could read and write only his name and a few simple phrases. He had a history of drug abuse and had spent several months in a juvenile correctional camp at the age of fifteen after vandalizing five homes in his neighborhood. When he tried to enlist in the Army, he was turned down because of his

TABLE 13.1 Legal Competencies (*Continued*)

then, giving new meaning to the old saying that defendants who act as their own lawyers have a fool for a client, Ferguson opened his case by claiming that "There were ninety-three counts to that indictment, ninety-three counts only because it matches the year 1993. If it had been 1925, it would have been a twenty-five-count indictment." This was a prelude to Ferguson's attempt at cross-examining a series of eyewitnesses, who, in response to his preposterous suggestion that someone else had been the murderer, answered time after time to the effect that "No, I saw the murderer clearly. It was you."

Competence to refuse the insanity defense. In cases where there is a likelihood that the defendant was insane at the time of an alleged offense, can the defendant refuse to enter a plea of insanity? Courts are divided on this question. Some have suggested that society's stake in punishing only mentally responsible persons requires the imposition of an insanity plea even on unwilling defendants (*Whalen v. United States*, 1965). Others (*Frendak v. United States*, 1979) have approached this question within the general framework of competency—if defendants understand the alterna-

tive pleas available and the consequences of those pleas, they should be permitted to reject an insanity plea.

Competence to be sentenced and punished. For legal and humanitarian reasons, convicted defendants should not be sentenced to punishment unless they are competent to understand the punishment being imposed and the reasons it is being imposed. For clinicians, evaluating competence for punishment is often a more straightforward matter than evaluating competence to stand trial, because in the latter case, issues arise about whether the accused can interact effectively with counsel and appreciate alternative courses of action.

The most controversial aspect of establishing competence for punishment appears in death penalty cases. In *Ford v. Wainwright* (1986), the U.S. Supreme Court decided that the Eighth Amendment ban against cruel and unusual punishments prohibits the execution of defendants while they are incompetent. Therefore, mental health professionals are sometimes called upon to evaluate inmates who have been sentenced to death in order to determine whether they are competent to be executed.

limited intelligence and drug habit. Jamie's attorney believed that Sullivan's mental problems might render him incompetent to stand trial and therefore asked a psychologist to conduct an evaluation. The psychologist asked Jamie a series of questions about his upcoming trial, to which he gave the following answers:

QUESTION: What are you charged with?

ANSWER: Burning down that store and stealing from Ricky.

Q: Anything else?

A: They say I killed Ricky too.

Q: What could happen to you if a jury found you guilty?

A: Electric chair, but God will watch over me.

Q: What does the judge do at a trial?

A: He tells everybody what to do.

Q: If somebody told a lie about you in court, what would you do?

A: Get mad at him.

Q: Anything else?

A: Tell my lawyer the truth.

Q: What does your lawyer do if you have a trial?

A: Show the jury I'm innocent.

Q: How could he do that best?

A: Ask questions and have me tell them I wouldn't hurt Ricky. I liked Ricky.

Q: What does the prosecutor do in your trial?

A: Try to get me found guilty.

Q: Who decides if you are guilty or not?

A: That jury.

After interviewing and testing Sullivan, the psychologist found that his current IQ was 65, which fell in the mentally retarded range, that he did not suffer any hallucinations or delusions, but that he expressed strong religious beliefs that "God watches over his children and won't let nothing happen to them." At a hearing to determine whether Jamie was competent to stand trial, the psychologist testified that the defendant was mentally retarded and consequently his understanding of the proceedings was not as accurate or thorough as it might otherwise be. However, the psychologist also testified that Sullivan did understand the charges against him as well as the general purpose and nature of his trial. The judge ruled that Jamie Sullivan was competent to stand trial. A jury convicted him on all the charges and sentenced him to life in prison.

It is estimated that, like Jamie Sullivan, 30,000 or more defendants are evaluated annually to determine their competence to stand trial or plead guilty, both of which are governed by the same standard (Nicholson & Kugler, 1991). The question of criminal competence can be raised at any point in the criminal process—by the prosecutor, the defense attorney, or the presiding judge. This question is usually raised by defense attorneys who believe that a client may be suffering from a mental disorder. Defense attorneys have questions about the competence of clients in up to 15% of all felony cases and about half that often in misdemeanor cases (Poythress et al., 1994). However, in many of these cases, the attorney does not seek a formal evaluation.

If a question of competence is raised, the judge is obligated to order an evaluation. Typically, when the judge orders a competency assessment, the defendant is taken to a special hospital for observation and examination. In fact, most mentally disordered offenders who have been committed to hospitals are there either because they are waiting for a competency evaluation or because they have been found incompetent and are receiving treatment to restore their competence. In most states, psychiatrists, psychologists, and social workers are authorized to perform competency evaluations, and they often use special structured interviews to do so (see Table 13.2).

Over 70% of defendants referred for such evaluations are ultimately found competent to stand trial (Nicholson & Kugler, 1991), and judges seldom disagree with the consensus of the clinicians who examined a given defendant.

What sort of person is usually judged to be incompetent? One study showed that of more than 500 defendants who were found incompetent, many were "marginal" men—undereducated, deficient in job skills, and with long histories of contact with

TABLE 13.2 The Competency Assessment Instrument

The Competency Assessment Instrument (Laboratory for Community Psychiatry, 1974) is a special instrument that is widely used by psychologists to assess defendants' competence. This structured interview, which takes about one hour, taps thirteen functions relevant to competence to stand trial.

1. Appraisal of available legal defenses: This item calls for an assessment of the accused's awareness of possible legal defenses, and how consistent these are with the particular circumstances of the case.

2. Unmanageable behavior: This items calls for an assessment of the appropriateness of the defendant's current motor and verbal behavior, and the degree to which this behavior would disrupt a trial. Any inappropriate or disruptive behavior must arise from a substantial degree of mental illness or mental retardation.

3. Quality of relating to attorney: This item calls for an assessment of the interpersonal capacity of the accused to relate to the average attorney, including the ability to trust and to communicate relevantly.

4. Planning of legal strategy, including guilty pleas to lesser charges where pertinent: This item calls for an assessment of the degree to which the accused can understand, participate, and cooperate with counsel in planning a strategy for the defense which is consistent with the reality of case circumstances.

5. Appraisal of role of defense counsel, prosecuting attorney, judge, jury, defendant, and witnesses: This set of items calls for a minimal understanding of the adversary process by the accused. The accused should be able to identify the prosecuting attorney and prosecution witnesses as foes, the defense counsel as a friend, the judge as neutral, and the jury as the determiners of guilt or innocence.

6. Understanding of court procedure: This item calls for an assessment of the degree to which the defendant understands the basic sequence of events in a trial and their importance (e.g., the different purposes of direct and cross examination).

7. Appreciation of charges: This item calls for an assessment of the accused's concrete understanding of the criminal charges, and to a lesser extent the seriousness of the charges.

8. Appreciation of the range and nature of possible penalties: This items calls for an assessment of the accused's concrete understanding and appreciation of the punishing conditions and restrictions that could be imposed and of their possible duration.

9. Appraisal of likely outcome: This item calls for an assessment of how realistically the accused perceives the likely outcome, and the degree to which impaired understanding contributes to a less than adequate or inadequate participation in efforts at defense. Evaluating the accused on this item requires the clinician to be familiar with the facts and circumstances of the alleged offense.

10. Capacity to disclose to an attorney pertinent facts surrounding the alleged offense, including information about the defendant's mental state, movements and their timing, and actions at the time of the alleged offense: This item calls for an assessment of the accused's capacity to give a basically consistent, rational, and relevant account of the motivational and external facts surrounding the case.

11. Capacity to realistically challenge prosecution witnesses: This item calls for an assessment of the accused's capacity to recognize distortions in prosecution testimony. Relevant factors include attentiveness and

(*continued*)

TABLE 13.2   The Competency Assessment Instrument (*Continued*)

memory. In addition there is an element of initiative. If false testimony is given, the degree of activism with which the defendant will apprise counsel of inaccuracies is important.

12. Capacity to give relevant testimony: This item calls for an assessment of the accused's ability to testify with coherence, relevance, and independence of judgment.

13. Self-defeating vs. self-serving motivation, in a legal sense: This item calls for an assessment of the accused's motivation to ade-

quately defend against the prosecution's charges and to appropriately utilize available legal safeguards to this end. It is recognized that accused persons may appropriately be motivated to seek expiation and appropriate punishment in their trials. Of concern here is the pathological seeking of punishment and the deliberate failure by the accused to use appropriate legal protection. Passivity or indifference do not justify low scores on this item; actively self-destructive manipulation of the legal process arising from mental pathology does.

both the legal and mental health systems (Steadman, 1979). Substance abuse problems were common, and minorities were overrepresented relative to their presence in the general population. Other studies have found relatively high percentages of psychosis and lower intelligence among incompetent defendants (Nicholson, Briggs, & Robertson, 1988; Roesch & Golding, 1980; Ustad et al., 1996). One other consistent finding is that incompetent defendants are charged with more serious crimes than defendants in general. Overall then, the typical incompetent defendant is likely to have a history of psychosis for which treatment has been received, to currently exhibit symptoms of serious mental disorder, and to be single, unemployed, and poorly educated (Nicholson & Kugler, 1991).

If a competency evaluation finds a defendant competent, the legal process resumes and the defendant again faces the possibility of trial. If the defendant is found incompetent, the picture becomes more complicated. For crimes that are not serious, the charges might be dropped, sometimes in exchange for requiring the defendant to receive treatment. If the charges are serious, the defendant usually will be returned to an institution for treatment designed to restore competence, which, if successful, will result in the defendant ultimately standing trial. In most states, this mandatory treatment can last up to six months, after which, if the person is still judged incompetent, a different form of hospitalization will be arranged, or the person might be released. Outpatient treatment of incompetent defendants is used less often, even though it can often be justified.

How successful are efforts to restore defendants' competence? One study evaluated an experimental group treatment with a sample of incompetent defendants sent to one of three Philadelphia facilities (Siegal & Elwork, 1990). In addition to receiving the usual psychiatric care, defendants assigned to these special treatment groups watched videotapes and received special instructions on courtroom procedures. They also discussed various ways of resolving the problems a defendant might face during a trial. A matched control group received treatment for their general psychiatric needs, but no specific training aimed at improving competence. Following treatment, defendants in the competence-restoration group showed significant increases compared to controls in their knowledge of competence-relevant information. In addition, hospital staff judged 43% of the experimental subjects to be competent to stand trial after treatment compared to 15% of the control subjects.

The Insanity Defense

Criminal defendants are presumed to be mentally responsible for the crimes with which they are charged. Therefore, if defendants plead *not guilty by reason of insanity* (NGRI), they must present evidence that they lacked the state of mind necessary to be held responsible for a crime. Because *insanity* is a legal term, not a psychological concept, it is defined by legal standards that have evolved over time, and vary from state to state and country to country.

These standards began to be formalized in 1843, when an Englishman named Daniel McNaughton tried to assassinate the British prime minister, Robert Peel. McNaughton suffered paranoid delusions that Peel was conspiring against him, so he waited outside the prime minister's house at Number 10 Downing Street, where he shot and killed Peel's secretary, whom he mistook for the prime minister. McNaughton was charged with murder, but pleaded not guilty by reason of insanity, claiming that he did not know the difference between right and wrong. Nine medical experts testified that McNaughton was insane and, after hearing instructions from the judge, the jury did not even leave the courtroom before deciding that McNaughton was not guilty by reason of insanity. This verdict infuriated the British public, and Queen Victoria was particularly upset because she herself had been the target of several assassination attempts. She demanded that Britain toughen its definition of insanity.

After extended debate in the House of Lords and among the nation's highest judges, a definition of insanity known as the *McNaughton rule* was enacted: ". . . to establish a defense on the grounds of insanity it must be clearly proved that, at the time of committing the act, the accused was laboring under such a defect of reason, from disease of the mind, as not to know the nature and quality of the act he was doing or, if he did know it, that he did not know what he was doing (was) wrong" (quoted in Post, 1963, p.113).

McNaughton remains the standard for insanity in about twenty U.S. states. It "excuses" criminal conduct by defendants whose mental illness either (1) causes them to not know what they are doing (e.g., believing they are shooting a space alien rather than a person) or (2) leaves them incapable of knowing that what they are doing is wrong (e.g., having the delusion that the victim is about to abduct them). However, the McNaughton rule has been criticized over the years because it focuses only on cognition—knowing right from wrong—and ignores how mental illness might affect motivation or emotions.

An alternative to *McNaughton* was proposed in a 1954 U.S. case involving Monte Durham. Durham had been in and out of prisons and mental hospitals most of his life. He was a car thief, a burglar, and a bad check artist. At one of his trials for residential burglary, Durham's plea of not guilty by reason of insanity was rejected by the judge, who believed the defendant still knew right from wrong. Durham's lawyers appealed

Daniel McNaughton, the man whose successful *not guilty by reason of insanity* plea in a nineteenth-century British murder case led to the legal definition of insanity that prevailed in most states for many years. His case also set the stage for controversy and continuing changes in the way courts deal with mentally ill people charged with crimes. (Source: The Bethlem Royal Hospital.)

this decision, claiming that the McNaughton rule was obsolete. Judge David Bazelon of the United States Court of Appeals in Washington, D.C. reviewed *McNaughton* and ruled that Durham should have a new trial in which the standard for judging insanity would be "that an accused is not criminally responsible if his unlawful act was the product of a mental disease or mental defect." This became known as the *Durham rule*, or the *product test*.

Initially, the Durham rule was popular with mental health professionals, but it soon ran into trouble with attorneys and judges who believed that it gave too much weight to the testimony of clinicians about any kind of mental illness that could cause criminal behavior. As a result, the Durham rule was never accepted by more than a few states; in 1972, the Bazelon court replaced it with the Brawner rule, also known as the *ALI rule*.

The ALI rule was developed by the American Law Institute (ALI) in a case in which the defendant, Archie Brawner, Jr., had been convicted of murdering Billy Ford. This rule holds that a defendant is not responsible for criminal conduct if, "at the time of such conduct as a result of mental disease or defect [the defendant] (lacks) substantial capacity either to appreciate the criminality (wrongfulness) of his conduct or to conform his conduct to the requirements of the law." The ALI Rule, or something close to it, is used by about half the states in the United States, and one part of it is used in all federal courts as the test of insanity. The ALI rule differs from McNaughton in three main ways:

1. By using the term "appreciate" instead of "know," the ALI Rule acknowledges that emotional factors as well as cognitive ones influence criminal conduct.
2. The ALI Rule does not require that offenders have a total lack of appreciation for the wrongfulness of their behavior—only that they lack "substantial capacity."
3. The ALI Rule defines insanity in both cognitive and volitional terms. Defendants can be considered insane even if they appreciated that certain conduct was wrong, as long as a mental illness rendered them unable to control their conduct.

After John Hinckley was found not guilty by reason of insanity for shooting President Ronald Reagan, press secretary James Brady, and three other people in 1982, an ABC News poll showed that 67% of Americans believed that justice had not been served in the case. Highly publicized cases like Hinckley's (and McNaughton's) are often followed by widespread public dissatisfaction with the insanity defense. Among the greatest concerns are that large numbers of defendants use the insanity defense to avoid punishment, that defendants found NGRI are quickly released from the hospital after their trials, and that insane criminals are more dangerous than other criminals. The public also worries that the insanity defense favors the rich and that juries rely too much on the testimony of expert witnesses. How realistic are these concerns?

Prevalence and Success of the Insanity Defense. The insanity defense is used much less frequently than most people assume, and with far less success than defendants would wish. One study in Wyoming found that the public assumed that the insanity defense was raised in half of all criminal cases and was successful about 20% of the time. In fact, the insanity defense was used by only 102 of 22,102 felony defendants studied (less than .005%), and was successful only once (Pasewark & Pantle, 1981). Across the United States, experts estimate that fewer than 1% of all criminal cases result in a finding of NGRI (Silver, Cirincione, & Steadman, 1994). Generally, the more often the insanity defense is used, the lower its rate of success (Appelbaum, 1994). Simply put, juries are reluctant to find violent offenders NGRI.

The Likelihood of Early Release. Defendants found NGRI seldom go "scot free." One New York study found that NGRI defendants were hospitalized for an average of three-and-a-half years and that defendants who had committed more serious offenses tended to be confined longer (Steadman & Braff, 1983). In many states, the norm is to keep NGRI defendants in a mental institution until a judge is convinced that it is safe to release them. One survey of more than a million indictments across seven states showed that (1) defendants found guilty were *more likely* to be released from confinement than those acquitted on the basis of insanity, and (2) compared to convicted defendants, insanity acquittees spent less time in confinement in four states and more time in confinement in three states (Silver, 1995).

Does hospital confinement and treatment produce benefits for defendants found NGRI? Some studies show that individuals who complete their hospital treatment do better than those who run away from the institution (Nicholson et al., 1991), but another found no difference in the post-hospitalization behavior of NGRI defendants who were officially discharged and those who escaped (Pasewark et al., 1982). Robert Nicholson and his colleagues (1991) collected data on all NGRI defendants in Oklahoma who had been treated in the state forensic hospital over a five-year period. Within two-and-a-half years of their release, half of these patients had been rearrested or rehospitalized, a rate that is about the same as for criminals in general. These data confirm the results of earlier studies (Cohen et al., 1988; Melton et al., 1987).

In an effort to err on the side of caution, judges often use criteria for releasing NGRI defendants that are stricter than those set for other kinds of involuntary commitments. In the 1992 case of *Foucha v. Louisiana*,[1] the U.S. Supreme Court eliminated this discrepancy, ruling that it is unconstitutional to keep a defendant in an institution who no longer meets the standard for involuntary civil commitment—that is, who is no longer mentally ill *and* dangerous. This ruling seems fair, but cases like that of E.E. Kemper III raise certain doubts about it. Kemper was released from a California hospital for the insane after spending five years there for murdering his grandparents. He petitioned a court to seal his psychiatric records, which it did after psychiatrists pronounced him sane. Neither the court nor the examining psychiatrists knew that, since his release, Kemper had killed his mother and seven other women. The last murder occurred three days before the court hearing that sealed his records (Gleick, 1978).

Dangerousness of Insane Defendants. Cases like Kemper's are rare, but they add fuel to the argument that the insanity defense puts the public at risk of violence by NGRI defendants. The dangerousness of NGRI defendants is difficult to deter-

---

[1]112 S.Ct. 1780 (1992).

mine, partly because it is hard to know how dangerous *anyone* might be (Lidz, Mulvey, & Gardner, 1993; Mossman, 1994). Assessing the dangerousness of NGRI defendants is further complicated by the fact that most of them are immediately removed from their communities and confined in a hospital where they receive drugs and other treatment. Although people with serious mental disorders (including NGRI defendants) are a bit more likely to be violent than people without such disorders, this relationship is typically found *only for people who are currently experiencing psychotic symptoms* (Link, Cullen, & Andrews, 1993; Monahan, 1992). If drugs or other treatments reduce these symptoms, the potential for violence is reduced as well.

The Economics of the Insanity Defense. The parents of John Hinckley, Jr. spent about $1,000,000 on psychiatric evaluations and expert testimony to support their son's insanity plea. His case contributed to the perception that the insanity defense is so costly that the average defendant cannot afford it. There are almost no data to support this view; in fact several studies have found no socioeconomic or ethnic bias in the use or success of the insanity plea (Boehnert, 1989; Howard & Clark, 1985; Nicholson et al., 1991; Pasewark & Pantle, 1981; Steadman et al., 1983).

Equal access to the insanity plea is assured by the 1985 U.S. Supreme Court decision in *Ake v. Oklahoma*,[2] which held that poor defendants who plead insanity are entitled to the assistance of mental health professionals at state expense. Of course, a person who can afford more than one expert, or the most expensive expert, might mount a more impressive insanity defense than a less affluent defendant, but this economic reality applies to any kind of defense. Defendants who can afford to hire a squadron of attorneys, detectives, DNA experts, or ballistic specialists have advantages over poor defendants, but hardly anyone suggests that this fact justifies eliminating defenses based on mistaken identity or ballistic tests.

The Role of Expert Witnesses. There is great public concern that testifying about insanity allows mental health experts to give opinions for which they lack proper competence or certainty. Three issues are pertinent to this problem. First, can experts reliably and validly diagnose mental illness and, therefore, identify this component of legal insanity? Second, can experts accurately assess a defendant's criminal responsibility for acts committed in the past, sometimes in the distant past? Third, even if the answer to the first two questions is "yes," are clinicians any more capable than nonprofessionals of making these judgments?

As noted in Chapter 3 in relation to assessment in general, many psychologists and psychiatrists doubt that their fields have any special expertise in determining a defendant's sanity at the time of an alleged offense (Dawes, Faust, & Meehl, 1989; Ziskin & Faust, 1988). They are also concerned that experts have too much influence on the outcomes of insanity trials. These critics contend that decisions about criminal responsibility are legal questions best left in the hands of juries or judges. Finally, they worry that the public loses confidence in the behavioral sciences when juries see, and the media report, a parade of mental health experts who contradict one another about a defendant's sanity. We discuss some of these issues in more detail later.

---

[2]105 S.Ct. 977 (1985).

Revisions and Reforms in the Insanity Defense

Several changes have been made in insanity defense rules and procedures over the past fifteen years. Three of these changes have received the most attention.

The Guilty But Mentally Ill Verdict. For many decades, juries deliberating cases involving the insanity defense could only reach verdicts of guilty, not guilty, or not guilty by reason of insanity. Since 1976, however, about a quarter of the states in the United States have passed laws giving juries a fourth possible verdict: *guilty but mentally ill* (GBMI). A defendant found GBMI is usually sentenced to the same period of confinement as any other defendant convicted of the same crime. Ideally, however, the GBMI prisoner's confinement begins in a treatment facility, and transfer to a prison occurs only after treatment is complete. The real intent of GBMI laws is to offer a compromise verdict that will decrease the number of defendants found NGRI. It is unclear how successful these laws have been in this respect; there have been decreases in NGRI verdicts in some states, but not others (Callahan et al., 1992; Roberts & Golding, 1991).

Several other problems have been identified with the GBMI verdict and have caused authorities to take a second look at this reform. First, it complicates an already confusing situation for juries who must evaluate insanity pleas. GBMI laws require jurors to distinguish between mental illness that results in insanity and mental illness that does not. Second, the claim that the GBMI verdict would result in more treatment for mentally ill prisoners has proven to be unfounded. Overcrowding at most facilities prevents adequate treatment from ever taking place. In one Michigan study, 75% of GBMI offenders went directly to prison without any treatment (Sales & Hafemeister, 1984). Finally, the GBMI verdict—and any opportunity for treatment it might bring—is available only to the small proportion of defendants who raise an insanity defense. A severely disturbed defendant who does not claim insanity cannot be found GBMI.

The Insanity Defense Reform Act. In 1984, in the wake of the John Hinckley trial, Congress passed the *Insanity Defense Reform Act* (IDRA). Its purpose was to limit the number of defendants in federal courts who could successfully use insanity as a defense. The IDRA did not abolish the insanity defense, but it did change its use in the federal courts in three important ways:

First, the IDRA places the burden on the *defendant* to prove insanity, rather than on the prosecution to prove sanity, which had previously been the case.

Second, it eliminates the volitional prong of the ALI rule. Lack of behavioral control because of mental illness is no longer a basis for insanity in federal cases. Insanity is restricted to the cognitive part of the ALI rule, namely that as a result of mental illness the defendant could not appreciate the nature or wrongfulness of his acts. This change essentially makes the federal test of insanity the same as the old McNaughton rule. This reform was introduced because of claims that (1) the ability to control one's acts cannot be assessed reliably and (2) the issue of volition provides a loophole through which many criminal offenders were walking to freedom. However, there is substantial empirical research that contradicts both of these claims.

John Hinckley was found not guilty by reason of insanity in the shooting of President Ronald Reagan. Shortly afterward, the U.S. Congress passed the Insanity Defense Reform Act (IDRA), which was designed to close what were perceived as legal loopholes in federal laws governing the insanity plea. (Source: AP/Wide World Photos.)

Third, the IDRA prohibits experts from giving *ultimate opinion* testimony about insanity. As a result, experts may describe a defendant's mental condition and the effects it might have on behavior, but they may not state any *conclusions* about a defendant's insanity. The reformers hoped that this change would prohibit experts from having too much control over verdicts, but empirical studies suggest that the prohibition might not have much effect on juries. In one study, for example, research participants read one of several versions of a trial in which a defendant pleaded NGRI in the killing of his boss (Fulero & Finkel, 1991). One group of participants read a transcript in which mental health experts for both sides offered only *diagnostic* testimony, that is, that the defendant was mentally ill at the time of the offense. A second group read a version in which the experts testified about their diagnosis and also gave a *penultimate opinion* about how the disorder might have affected the defendant's understanding of the wrongfulness of his act. A third group read a transcript in which the experts discussed diagnosis, gave penultimate opinions, and then offered an *ultimate opinion* as to whether the defendant was sane or insane at the time he killed his boss. In this study, participants' verdicts were not affected by the type of testimony they read. These results could mean that a ban on ultimate opinion testimony does not accomplish much (Rogers & Ewing, 1989), but it could also mean that the ban can shorten expert testimony without sacrificing essential information.

In theory, varying rules for insanity should influence jurors to come to different verdicts, but psychologists have questioned whether the typical juror comprehends these legal definitions and then applies them as intended by the courts. In one study, jurors scored only 51% correct on a series of questions testing their comprehension of the McNaughton rule (Elwork, Sales, & Suggs, 1981). Other research found similar results: Regardless of which insanity rule was used, college students showed low rates of accurate recall and comprehension of the crucial components in various insanity definitions (Arens, Granfield, & Susman, 1965; Ogloff, 1991).

Most mock jury studies of the IDRA have found that verdicts are little affected by whether jurors hear ALI instructions, IDRA instructions, or no instructions at all about the definition of insanity (Finkel, 1989). Jurors appear to depend on their own views about what constitutes insanity and interpret the evidence according to those views, regardless of the formal instructions judges give them (Roberts & Golding, 1991).

Abolition of the Insanity Defense.   A few U.S. states, such as Idaho and Montana, have abolished the insanity defense. Has this drastic step solved the problem of holding mentally ill people responsible for criminal acts? Not really. Issues associated with insanity remain because, to be convicted of a crime in *any* state, one must have *intended* the illegal act. Defendants can be found guilty of theft, for example, only if it can be proved that they intended to steal. Accordingly, even states where there is no insanity defense must allow evidence to be introduced about a defendant's *mens rea*— or guilty mind—during alleged crimes. If, because of a mental disorder, defendants lack the *mens rea* for a crime, they should be found not guilty. To help juries decide about *mens rea*, experts continue to offer testimony about the effects of mental illness on defendants, even if those defendants are not allowed to use an insanity defense.

In short, a defendant's mental state can never be entirely eliminated from jurors' consideration, simply because it makes no sense to talk about "guilt" without knowing something about a person's state of mind at the time of an alleged crime. In one form or another, then, the issue of insanity is likely to remain a part of court decisions about criminal responsibility.

PSYCHOLOGICAL DAMAGES IN CIVIL TRIALS

When one person is injured by the actions of a second party, the injured individual can sue that second party to recover money damages as a compensation for the injury. Such legal actions are covered by an area of civil law known as torts. A *tort* is a wrongful act that causes harm to an individual. Tort law provides a mechanism for *individuals* to seek redress for the harm they have suffered from the wrongful acts of another party. It thus differs from criminal law which—acting on behalf of *society as a whole*—prosecutes defendants for wrongful behavior and seeks to punish them in an attempt to maintain society's overall sense of justice.

The O.J. Simpson case provides an illustration of how both criminal punishment and civil remedies can be sought for the same act. Simpson was prosecuted by the State of California under *criminal* law for the murder of his former wife, Nicole Brown Simpson, and her friend, Ronald Goldman. He was found not guilty of murder, but the Brown and Goldman families sued him for money damages under *civil* law, alleging that he caused their relatives' wrongful deaths. The civil trial resulted in a $33.5 million judgment against Simpson.

Definition of a Tort

Many kinds of behavior can constitute a tort. Slander and libel are torts, so are cases of medical malpractice, the manufacture of defective products resulting in a personal injury, and intentional or negligent behavior producing harm to another person.

Four elements are involved in proving that a tort has occurred. First, there must be a situation in which one person owes a duty to another. For example, a physician has a duty to treat patients according to accepted professional standards, and private citizens have a duty to not physically or psychologically harm others.

Second, a tort typically requires proving that one party intentionally or negligently violated a duty owed to other parties. *Negligence* is behavior that is often measured by asking whether a "reasonable person" would, under similar circumstances, have acted as the defendant did. *Intentional* behavior refers to conduct in which a person meant the outcome of a given act to occur. (In some tort cases, a defendant can be held *strictly liable* even if the defendant did not act negligently or intentionally. This standard is often used in product liability cases; if a company manufactures a product that harms an innocent user, it will be held liable for the harm regardless of whether it acted negligently or intended the harm to occur.)

Third, the violation of a duty had to be the proximate cause of the harm suffered by the plaintiff. A *proximate cause* is one that constitutes an obvious or substantial reason why a given harm occurred. A proximate cause is sometimes said to be one that leads to "foreseeable" outcomes—results that would be expected given certain events or actions.

Fourth, the harm has to involve a legally protected right or interest for which the person can be compensated for damages suffered; if it does, then it can be the subject of a civil lawsuit.

A person can suffer various kinds of damage from a tort, including destruction of personal property, physical injuries, and/or emotional distress (sometimes called "pain and suffering"). Civil law has always compensated victims who are physically hurt or who sustain property losses, but, in the past, had been reluctant to compensate emotional distress, largely out of concern that emotional damages are too easy to fake and too hard to measure. When recovery for emotional damages was allowed, the courts often required that emotional or psychological harm had to be accompanied by a physical injury, or that a plaintiff who was not physically injured had at least to be in a "zone of danger." For example, a plaintiff can recover emotional damages without being physically injured by an escaped wild animal, *if* she was standing close to her children when *they* were attacked (Weissman, 1985). In recent years, civil courts have not only taken the view that psychological symptoms and mental distress can be compensated even in the absence of physical damage to the plaintiff, but the "zone of danger" appears to be expanding. Two types of mental injuries are now commonly claimed in civil lawsuits: those arising from "extreme and outrageous" conduct that is intended to cause distress and those arising from "negligent" behavior. In both kinds of cases, clinical psychologists are often called upon to give expert testimony on the nature and extent of the psychological damages suffered by the plaintiff.

In negligence cases, the plaintiff is allowed to sue for psychological damages suffered when witnessing an injury to a loved one, whether or not the plaintiff was in danger. Thus a parent can seek compensation for psychological damages after seeing his child crushed to death by a defective roller coaster. To receive compensation for psychological damages in the case of intentional torts, a plaintiff has to prove that a defendant intentionally or recklessly acted in an extreme and outrageous fashion (sometimes defined as "beyond all bounds of decency") in order to cause the plaintiff emotional distress. The plaintiff must also prove that the distress is severe; in other words, the psychological effects of the defendant's actions must be more than merely annoying or temporarily upsetting (Merrick, 1985).

What kinds of behavior might qualify as intentional or reckless? There are all-too-many examples. One court found that a bill collector acted outrageously when, to locate a debtor, he posed as a hospital employee, lied to the debtor's mother about her grandchildren having been injured, and asked where the debtor could be found and informed about the "accident" (*Ford Motor Credit Co. v. Sheehan*).[3]

In recent years, an increasing number of intentional tort cases have dealt with sexual harassment in the workplace. A plaintiff who claims to have been sexually harassed at work can sue the workers allegedly responsible for the harassment, and the company itself, if the plaintiff can show that the company knew (or should have known) about the harassment and did not take adequate measures to stop it. Plaintiffs in these cases can seek both *compensatory damages* for emotional harm as well as *punitive damages* that punish the company for its failure to respond properly to the misconduct. The law recognizes two kinds of sexual harassment. The first, called *quid pro quo* harassment, consists of cases in which a supervisor promises job benefits to an employee in return for sexual favors or denies job opportunities to an employee who refuses the supervisor's sexual overtures. The second kind of harassment involves the creation of a *hostile work environment* for an employee based on that employee's gender.

Intentional torts can also stem from harassment based on factors other than gender. In a case in which one of the authors was involved, a car salesman sued his employer for permitting, and participating in, a pattern of harassment based on the salesman's physical disability. The plaintiff, whom we shall call "Lyle," suffered injuries as a teenager that forced him to walk slowly and with a severe limp. It seems that, when business was slow, the other salesmen at the dealership where Lyle worked would amuse themselves by "goosing" one another. They took special pleasure in "goosing"

---

[3]373 So. 2d. 956 (Fla. App. 1979).

Lyle, however, because he could not get away from them and also because he would shriek "Oops!" each time it happened (inevitably, his co-workers gave him the nickname "Oops"). At his trial, Lyle testified that he was "goosed" several times an hour, and estimated that it happened as many as 1,500 times during his employment, including while he was talking to potential customers. On one occasion when he was "goosed" while standing next to a vehicle in the showroom, Lyle's knee struck the vehicle, resulting in an injury that kept him off work for two weeks. Even this did not deter his tormentors; they teased Lyle about drawing "gooseman's compensation." After repeated complaints to his sales manager brought no relief, Lyle quit his job and sued his employer for outrageous conduct causing physical and psychological damages.

At his trial, Lyle testified about the anger and humiliation he suffered from the harassment, about his suicidal thoughts, and about the revenge fantasies that plagued him. Following his testimony, and that of a clinical psychologist confirming that Lyle suffered from a mixed anxiety and mood disorder brought on by workplace harassment, the jury returned a verdict for the plaintiff and awarded Lyle $795,000 for physical and psychological injuries.

Assessing Psychological Damage in Tort Cases.

When clinical psychologists conduct assessments with civil plaintiffs, they typically perform an evaluation that, like most clinical assessments, includes a social history, a clinical interview, psychological testing, and perhaps interviews with others and a review of available records (see Chapter 3). Based on these data, the clinician will reach a decision about what, if any, psychological problems, the person might be suffering. This aspect of the forensic evaluation is not much different from what a clinician might do with any client, whether or not the client is involved in a lawsuit.

The far more difficult additional question the clinician must answer is whether the psychological problems were caused by the tort, were aggravated by the tort, or existed prior to the tort. While there is no established procedure for answering this question, most clinicians try to locate all clinical records and other sources of data that might help establish the point in time at which any diagnosed disorder began to appear. When plaintiffs allege that they were targeted for harassment or some other intentional tort because the defendants knew they had a psychological problem that made them especially vulnerable, the clinician must take this prior condition into account in reaching conclusions about the effects of the tort.

Workers' Compensation Cases

When a worker is injured on the job, the law provides for the worker to be compensated, but it does so via a streamlined system that avoids the necessity of proving a tort. This system, known as *workers' compensation law*, is in place in all fifty states and in the federal government. In workers' compensation systems, employers contribute to a fund that insures their workers who are injured at work, and they also waive their right to blame the worker or some other individual for the injury. For their part, workers give up their right to pursue a tort against their employers, and agree that, if they are compensated for their injury, the award they receive will be determined by the type and duration of the injury and the amount of their salary at the time of the injury. Workers can seek compensation for (1) physical and psychological injuries sustained at work, (2) the cost of the treatment they receive for their injuries, (3) lost wages, and (4) the loss of future earning capacity.

Because psychological injuries or mental disorders arising from employment can be compensated, clinical psychologists are often asked to evaluate injured workers and render an opinion about the existence, cause, and implications of any mental disorders that might appear in a given case. Claims for mental disability usually arise in one of three ways.

First, a physical injury or job-related threatening event can cause a mental disorder and psychological disability. A common pattern in these *physical–mental* cases is for a worker to sustain a serious physical injury—a broken back or severe burns, for example—that results in chronic pain. As the pain continues, the worker experiences an overlay of psychological problems, usually depression and anxiety (see Chapter 11). These problems worsen until they become full-fledged mental disorders, resulting in further impairments in overall functioning.

The second work-related pathway to mental disability is for an individual to suffer a traumatic incident at work or to undergo a long period of continuous stress that leads to psychological difficulties. The night clerk at a convenience store who is the victim of an armed robbery and subsequently develops post-traumatic stress disorder exemplifies such *mental–mental* cases, as does the clerical worker who, after years of overwork and job pressure, experiences an anxiety disorder.

In a third kind of case, known as *mental–physical*, work-related stress is blamed for the onset of a physical disorder such as high blood pressure. Many states have placed special restrictions on these types of claims, and psychologists are seldom asked to evaluate them.

In recent years, the number of psychological claims arising in workers' compensation litigation has increased dramatically; much of the increase has been attributed to a surge in mental–mental cases (Barth, 1990). In the 1980s, stress-related mental disorders became the fastest growing occupational disease category in the United States (Hersh & Alexander, 1990). It is not clear what accounts for this surge in psychological claims, but three explanations have been proposed. It might be due, first, to the growing proportion of women in the work force; women are more often diagnosed with anxiety and depressive disorders than men (Sparr, 1995). A second possibility is that shifts in the job market from manufacturing and industrial jobs to service-oriented jobs have produced corresponding increases in interpersonal and other psychological stressors and decreases in physical injuries. Third, claims of psychological impairments might be motivated primarily by financial incentives, producing a range of cases in which genuine impairments are mixed in with exaggerated, or even false, claims of disability.

CIVIL COMPETENCIES

The concept of mental competence extends to many decisions that individuals must make throughout their lives. In our earlier discussion of competence to stand trial, we focused on the tasks required of defendants during the course of a criminal trial. However, the question of mental competence is raised in several noncriminal situations as well; we refer to these other situations as involving *civil competencies*.

Questions of civil competency focus on whether an individual has the capacity to understand information relevant to making a particular decision and then making an informed choice about what to do. For example, civil competency questions are commonly asked about whether a person is capable of managing personal financial affairs, making decisions about accepting or refusing medical or psychiatric treatment, or executing a will which directs how property should be distributed to heirs or other beneficiaries.

The legal standards used to define competence have evolved over many years, but scholars who have studied this issue agree that four abilities are essential to competent decision-making (Appelbaum & Grisso, 1995). A competent individual is expected to be able to (1) understand basic information relevant to making a decision, (2) apply that information to a specific situation in order to anticipate the consequences of various choices that might be made, (3) use logical, rational thinking to evaluate the pros and cons of various strategies and decisions, and (4) communicate a personal decision or choice about the matter under consideration.

The specific abilities associated with each of these general criteria vary, depending on the decision the person must make. Deciding whether to have risky surgery demands different kinds of information and thinking processes than does deciding whether to leave one's estate to one's children versus a charitable organization.

Clinical psychologists interested in psycho-legal issues have focused considerable research attention on the competence of individuals with severe mental disorders to make decisions and give informed consent about their own psychiatric treatment. Can persons with serious mental disorders make competent treatment decisions? Do their decision-making abilities differ from persons who do not suffer mental disorders? These are some of the questions being explored in the MacArthur Treatment Competence Study, whose ongoing aim is to develop structured interview measures that can be used to assess the four basic abilities—understanding information, applying information, thinking rationally, and expressing a choice—that are necessary to establish legal competence (Grisso et al., 1995).

In one phase of this study, standardized interviews were conducted with patients suffering from either schizophrenia, major depression, or heart disease and also with healthy persons who were matched on various demographic variables with the three patient groups (Grisso & Appelbaum, 1995). Only a minority of the persons *in any group* showed significant impairments in competent decision-making about the various treatment options they were asked to consider. However, compared to the heart patients or the healthy people, patients with schizophrenia or major depression tended to have a poorer understanding of treatment information and to use less adequate reasoning in considering the consequences of treatment. These impairments were more severe and consistent for the patients with schizophrenia than for those with depression, and the more serious the symptoms of mental disorder (especially those involving disturbed thinking), the poorer the understanding.

These results have obvious implications for social policies relating to persons with mental disorders. First, contrary to what many people might assume, the majority of patients suffering from severe disorders such as schizophrenia and major depression appear to be capable of competent decision-making about their treatment. However, a significant number of patients—particularly those with severe forms of schizophrenia—do show some impairments in their decision-making abilities.

The question of treatment-related competence usually arises when a patient refuses a treatment that seems medically and psychologically justified. Under these circumstances, some medical staff try to make the patient's decision-making task easier by presenting information about treatment options in simpler ways. These revised presentations can help patients better appreciate how a recommended treatment would be in their best interests, but time constraints may not allow for this slower process. When an impasse develops between the patient's expressed wishes and the recommendations of treating professionals, it would be ideal to have a brief interview instrument available for assessing whether the patient lacks the cognitive abilities necessary to reach a competent decision. The initial results of the MacArthur Treatment Competence Study are being used to develop such an instrument (Grisso & Appelbaum, 1995).

Questions relating to civil competencies illustrate that mental health laws and policies are not just theoretical concepts or abstract principles; these laws and policies can have significant positive or negative effects on the treatment that individual patients receive, and how well that treatment works. Accordingly, many mental health professionals and attorneys point out that legal rulings in this area have implications not only for case law or for broad social issues—such as balancing individual rights against those of society—but for individual patients' lives. This perspective, known as *therapeutic jurisprudence* (Wexler & Winnick, 1991), views the law as having the potential for being therapeutic for patients and suggests that all mental health laws should be evaluated to determine their therapeutic impact. In other words, therapeutic jurisprudence would frame decisions about the issues discussed in this section partly in terms of the impact various solutions would have for individual patients.

PSYCHOLOGICAL AUTOPSIES AND CRIMINAL PROFILING

As already mentioned, most forensic assessments, like most other clinical assessments, include interviewing, observing, and testing clients in order to arrive at an understanding of them. In a few unusual circumstances, however, clinicians may be called upon to give opinions about a deceased person's state of mind prior to death. In such cases, obviously, the clinician must conduct the evaluation without that person's participation. These postmortem psychological evaluations are known as *psychological autopsies* or *equivocal death analyses* (Ogloff & Otto, 1993).

Psychological Autopsies

The first psychological autopsies are believed to have been done in the 1950s, when a group of social scientists in Los Angeles began assisting the County Coroner's Office in determining whether suicide, murder, or accident was the most likely cause of death in certain equivocal cases. Since then, psychological autopsies have become commonplace, especially when it is important to determine whether someone died by accident or suicide (this question is often raised by insurance companies that could deny death benefits if their policy holder committed suicide). They are also used (1) in workers' compensation cases when an employee's family claims that stressful working conditions or work-related trauma contributed to their relative's suicide or accidental death, (2) to decide whether a deceased individual had the mental capacity necessary to competently execute or modify a will, and (3) to support the argument made by criminal defendants that the person they allegedly killed died by suicide, not homicide.

There is no standard format for conducting psychological autopsies, but most clinicians rely heavily on documents and other life records that a person leaves behind, as well as on interviews with those who knew the decedent (Ebert, 1987). Some clinicians concentrate on evidence from the time just before the person's death. What was the person's mood? How was the person doing at work? Were there any pronounced changes in the person's behavior? Others, especially those who take a psychodynamic approach to clinical psychology, look for evidence about family dynamics and personality traits appearing early in the person's life. As a child, how did the person interact with parents or other caregivers? What was the individual's approach to school? To competition with peers?

How valid are psychological autopsies—that is, do they accurately portray a person's state of mind at the time of death? There are certainly reasons to doubt their validity. For one thing, most of the assessment information comes "second hand," because the person about whom inferences are to be made is not available for interviewing or testing. Further, as noted in Chapter 4, information obtained through third-party interviews may be distorted by memory lapses or by efforts to describe a person in an especially good, or bad, light. Unfortunately, no empirical research is available concerning the validity of psychological autopsies, mainly because the decedent's "true" state of mind prior to death is unknown, and thus cannot be compared to conclusions later drawn by clinicians. This problem may be partially solved if, in future studies, researchers were to see how well-reputed experts do when given psychological autopsy information about cases in which the cause of death appears ambiguous, but is actually known. Studying the accuracy of these experts' conclusions, and the reasons behind them, may go a long way toward establishing the validity of psychological autopsies.

In the absence of such research, judges have had mixed reactions to psychological autopsy evidence. In cases involving workers' compensation claims and questions of whether insurance benefits should be paid, the courts have usually admitted psychological autopsy testimony; they have been much more reluctant to do so in criminal cases and in cases involving the question of whether a person had the mental capacity to draft a will (Ogloff & Otto, 1993). Indeed, many judges are generally more skeptical about allowing expert testimony in criminal cases than in civil ones, perhaps because the risks of prejudicial testimony are greater when one's liberties can be taken away. The courts' hesitancy in permitting psychological autopsy testimony in cases involving the validity of wills may stem from concern that, in such cases, the deceased's state of mind is the critical legal question to be decided by the jury. Allowing expert testimony on this matter might be viewed as invading the province of the jury, something that judges want to avoid.

Criminal Profiling

In some ways, psychological autopsies resemble a technique known as criminal profiling. In both cases, clinicians draw inferences about an individual's motives and state of mind on the basis of life records or other data a person has left behind. In psychological autopsies, however, the identity of the person being assessed is known, and the question is what they did, and why. In *criminal profiling*, the person's behavior is known, and the question is "who did it."

Clinicians' involvement in criminal profiling is based on the assumption that criminals commit their crimes in distinctive ways, leaving clues to their psychological makeup—much as DNA or fingerprints point to their physical identity or ballistics tests reveal the kind of firearm they used. Indeed, evidence is accumulating that certain psychological characteristics are linked to certain patterns of criminal behavior and that these links can be detected by a psychological analysis of crime scenes. Accordingly, police are now using criminal profiling to focus their search for suspects in certain kinds of crimes to people who possess the behavioral and psychological characteristics that tend to be associated with such crimes. Profiles have also been developed to help investigators identify persons who are likely to be hijackers, drug couriers, and illegal aliens (Monahan & Walker, 1990).

One of the first examples of successful criminal profiling came in 1957, with the arrest of George Matesky, the so-called "Mad Bomber" of New York City. After trying for over a decade to identify the person responsible for more than thirty bombings in the New York area, the police consulted Dr. James Brussel, a local psychiatrist. Brussel examined pictures of the bomb scenes and analyzed letters sent to police by the bomber. Based on these data, Brussel advised the police to look for a heavyset, middle-aged, Eastern European, Catholic man who was single and lived with a sibling or an aunt. Brussel also concluded that the man loved his mother and valued neatness. He even predicted that, when the man was found, he would be wearing a buttoned double-breasted suit. When the police finally arrested Matesky, this profile turned out to be uncannily accurate, right down to the suit (Brussel, 1968).

Not all early profiles were so useful, however. For example, a committee of experts charged with profiling the "Boston Strangler" concluded that there was not one, but two killers, each of whom lived alone and was a schoolteacher. The experts also suggested that one of the men would be homosexual. Albert De Salvo, the man who ultimately confessed to these killings was a married, heterosexual construction worker who lived with his wife and two sons (Porter, 1983).

Today, the major source of research and development on criminal profiling is the FBI's Behavioral Science Unit, which has been working on criminal profiles since the 1970s. Now part of the National Center for the Analysis of Violent Crime, this unit employs special FBI agents trained in the behavioral sciences, as well as mental health consultants. The unit has amassed large amounts of data on the backgrounds, family characteristics, current behaviors, and psychological traits of various types of criminal offenders (Douglas & Olshaker, 1995). A key element of the unit's research is the interviewing of various types of known offenders in order to discover how each type selects and approaches their victims, how they react to their crimes, what demographic or family characteristics they share, and what personality features predominate among them. For example, as part of its study of mass and serial killers, the FBI has conducted detailed interviews with many notorious killers, including Charles Manson, Richard Speck, and David Berkowitz (Ressler & Shachtman, 1992).

How valid are psychological profiles of criminals? Are expert profilers more accurate than other groups in their descriptions of suspects? Compared to other investigators, do expert profilers use special processes to evaluate information? In one study that provides some initial data on these questions, four groups of people evaluated two criminal cases—a homicide and a sex offense—that had already been solved but were unknown to the people examining them (Pinizzotto & Finkel, 1990). The first group consisted of four expert criminal profilers with a total of forty-two years of experience and six police detectives who had recently been trained as profilers. In the second group were six police detectives with fifty-seven years of experience in criminal investigations but no training or experience in profiling. The third group was composed of six clinical psychologists who had no experience in either profiling or criminal investigation. The final group consisted of six students in undergraduate psychology classes.

For each case, all participants were given the array of materials that profilers typically use, including crime scene photographs and descriptions, autopsy and toxicology reports (in the murder case), and descriptions of the victims. After studying these materials, each participant was asked to write down all the details of each crime they could recall and to indicate how important these details would be in creating a profile of the criminal. All participants were then asked to (1) prepare a profile of the most likely suspect in each case, (2) answer fifteen questions about the gender, age, employment status, and other characteristics of these suspects, and (3) after reading written descriptions of a "lineup" of five suspects, rank them from "most likely" to "least likely" to have committed each of the crimes.

Compared to the other three groups, the expert profilers wrote longer profiles that contained more specific predictions about suspects, included more accurate predictions, and were rated as more helpful by other police detectives. Although they did not differ substantially in the way they thought about the evidence, expert profilers were more accurate than the other groups in answering specific questions about the sex-offense suspect; the groups did not differ in their accuracy about the homicide suspect. These results suggest that, in certain kinds of cases, at least, profilers can produce more useful and valid criminal profiles, even when compared to experienced crime investigators.

Unfortunately, criminal profiling in the real world is fraught with many difficulties and does not always bear fruit. For example, after a bomb exploded at the 1996 Atlanta Olympics, police almost immediately—and incorrectly, as it turned out—focused their suspicions on a Centennial Olympic Park security guard named Richard Jewell. Jewell was singled out because he fit an FBI profile for this kind of bombing; he is a white, single, middle-age male who craves the limelight, sometimes as a police "wannabe." In this case, the profile was wrong, and at this writing the identity of the bomber or bombers remains unknown.

CHILD CUSTODY AND PARENTAL FITNESS

One of the fastest growing areas for clinical psychologists in forensic psychology is the assessment of families in crisis.

Parental Fitness

Sometimes clinicians are asked to conduct evaluations of *parental fitness*. In these cases, the evaluator must determine if a parent's custody rights over their children should be terminated—and the children removed from their home—because the individual is unfit to be a parent. The legal definition of parental unfitness varies from state to state (Azar & Benjet, 1994), but in general, the law makes it rather difficult to take children away from their biological parents. To prove parental unfitness in Kentucky, for example, it must be shown that the parent (1) inflicted, or allowed someone else to inflict, physical injury, emotional harm, or sexual abuse on the child, (2) is morally delinquent, (3) abandoned the child, (4) is mentally ill, or (5) fails to provide essential care for the child for some reason other than poverty (*Davis v. Collinsworth*,[4] 1989). In most other states, too, it must be shown that one or more of these conditions is substantially threatening a child's welfare, and the evidence proving this threat must usually be "clear and convincing" (Azar & Benjet, 1994).

Child Custody Disputes

More commonly, clinical psychologists' involvement in the legal aspects of family crises comes when parents are separating or divorcing. Here, the clinician is usually asked to conduct a *child custody* evaluation and to offer recommendations to help a court settle disputes over which parent can best meet their children's needs and which, therefore, should retain custody of them. The growth in these assessment activities is attributable, first, to the fact that, with half of all marriages in the United States now ending in divorce, child custody issues arise in millions of families. More than a third of United States children will spend some time living in a stepfamily and over half will spend time in a single-parent household (Bray, 1991). Second, fathers have been challenging the long-held assumption that the best interests of young children are usually served by awarding custody to their mothers. As we approach the twenty-first century, many courts want to know about the parenting abilities of *each* parent before making custody decisions.

Most states permit two kinds of custodial arrangements. The most common arrangement is *sole custody*, in which one parent is awarded legal custody of the child and the other parent is granted rights of visitation and other types of contact with the

---

[4]Ky. 771 S.W. 2d 329 (1989).

child. In *joint-custody* arrangements, both parents retain parental rights concerning decisions about the child's general welfare, education, health care, and other matters. Joint custody does not mean that the child spends an equal amount of time with each parent. Usually, one parent is given physical custody of the child, and the child spends more time living with that parent. Thus, compared to sole custody, joint custody distributes the frequency of child contact more evenly between the two parents, leads to more interaction between the divorced parents (and generates more demands for cooperation concerning their children), and results in more variation in caregiving arrangements, including more frequent separations and reunions between children and parents (Clingempeel & Repuccci, 1982).

Clinicians conduct custody evaluations under any of three sets of circumstances. In some cases, a judge appoints a clinician to conduct a custody evaluation that will be available to all the parties. In others, each party retains a different expert to conduct independent evaluations, and in still others, the two sides agree to share the cost of hiring one expert to conduct a single evaluation (Weissman, 1991). Most informed observers prefer either the first or third option because they minimize the hostilities and adversarial pressures that usually arise when separate experts are hired by each side (Keilin & Bloom, 1986).

Although the methods used in custody evaluations vary a great deal depending on the specific issues in each case, the American Psychological Association and the Association of Family and Conciliation Courts have published guidelines for conducting custody evaluations. Most evaluations include the following components:

1. Clinical, social-history, and mental status interviews of the parents and the children;
2. Standardized testing of the parents and the children;
3. Observation of interactions between each parent and the children, especially when the children are minors;
4. Interviews or other assessments with individuals who have had opportunities to observe family members (e.g., the children's grandparents, adult children of the parents, neighbors, the family physician, school teachers); and
5. Documents that might be relevant to the case, including medical records of children and parents, school report cards, and arrest records.

A national survey of mental health professionals who conduct child custody evaluations found that these experts devoted an average of nineteen hours to each custody evaluation (Keilin & Bloom, 1986). (By the mid-1990s, this figure had increased to more than twenty-six hours, largely because of more time devoted to reviewing records and writing more elaborate reports; Ackerman & Ackerman, 1997). A substantial amount of this time is spent interviewing and observing the parties in various combinations. More than two-thirds of the respondents indicated that they conducted individual interviews with each parent and each child, observed each parent interacting (separately) with each child, and conducted formal psychological testing of the parents and the children. The MMPI was the test most often used with parents; intelligence tests and projective personality tests were the most common instruments used with the children (see Chapter 5).

These experts also reported how often they recommended different kinds of custodial arrangements. The most common recommendation was limited joint custody, in which parents share the decision making, but one parent maintains primary physical custody. Single-parent custody without visitation was the least recommended alternative.

Do children adapt and function better when raised in joint custody or sole custody arrangements? One might expect it could go either way, because while joint custody allows the child to maintain close ties to both parents, sole custody simplifies custodial arrangements and minimizes children's confusion over where their home is. Indeed, most studies report either no major differences between children in the two types of custody or only somewhat better adjustment by joint-custody children (Crosbie-Burnett, 1991; Shiller, 1986; Wolchik, Braver, & Sandler, 1985). For example, in a study of seventy-eight step-families with adolescent children, Margaret Crosbie-Burnett (1991) found that joint custody was associated with greater family cohesion, improved adjustment by these adolescents, and better relationships with their step-parents. However, the gender of the child moderated the impact of the custodial arrangement on adjustment. Girls tended to feel more upset in sole-custody families; boys expressed more anxiety in joint-custody families.

Consistent with the results of earlier research (Emery, 1982; Hetherington & Arasteh, 1988), Crosbie-Burnett (1991) found that continuing hostility and conflicts between the parents—regardless of the type of custody in force—was associated with poorer adjustment on the part of the children. It appears that the quality of the relationship between divorced parents is more important to the adjustment of their children than whether the children are raised in sole-custody or joint-custody arrangements.

Many mental health professionals believe evaluations regarding child custody and parental fitness are among the most ethically challenging and clinically difficult of all forensic cases. For one thing, the emotional stakes are extremely high, and both parents are often willing to spare no expense or tactic in the battle over who will win custody. Associated with this conflict is the fact that the children are usually forced to live, for months if not years, in an emotional limbo where they do not know with whom they will eventually live, where they will be going to school, or how often they will see each parent. Second, to conduct a thorough family assessment, the clinician must evaluate the children, both parents, and, when possible, other people who have observed the family's interaction. Often, not all parties agree to such evaluations or do so only under coercion, a fact that often creates a lengthy and unfriendly assessment process. Third, to render an expert opinion, the clinician must possess a great deal of knowledge—not only about the particular children and parents being evaluated—but also about infant–parent attachment, child development, family systems, the effects of divorce on children, adult and childhood mental disorders, and several different kinds of testing. Complicating the situation, too, are changes in traditional definitions of a "family." Increasing tolerance of variability in lifestyles has forced clinicians to confront questions about whether parents' sexual orientation or ethnicity should have any bearing on custody decisions. Finally, child custody evaluations are usually highly adversarial processes, in which one side will challenge the procedures or opinions of any expert with whom it disagrees. Clinicians who conduct custody evaluations must therefore brace themselves for all sorts of attacks on their clinical methods, scholarly competence, personal character, and professional ethics.

Custody Mediation

Because divorce is such a potent stressor for children and because protracted custody battles tend to leave a trail of emotionally battered family members in their wake, clinicians are devoting increasing attention to helping parents and children cope with these transitions or to finding alternatives to custody battles (Grych & Fincham, 1992; Kelly, 1991).

Custody mediation services are now being used more often in lieu of adversarial court procedures. The supposed benefits of custody mediation are that resolutions are reached more quickly and with better compliance among the participants than with adversarial procedures. It is not clear, however, that mediation always leads to better adjustment in divorcing parents or in their children. To assess the impact of mediated versus adversarial child custody procedures, Robert Emery and his colleagues at the University of Virginia randomly assigned divorcing couples to settle their custody disputes either through mediation or litigation. They found that while mediation greatly reduced the number of hearings and total amount of time required to reach a resolution, parents who mediated did not differ in terms of psychological adjustment from those who litigated. There was a consistent gender difference in satisfaction with the two methods, however. Fathers who went through mediation were much more likely to report feeling satisfied with the process than did fathers who litigated; mothers who went through mediation, on the other hand, were less likely to express satisfaction with its effects, and some measures showed better adjustment for mothers who litigated their dispute (Emery, Matthews, & Wyer, 1991; Emery, Matthews, & Kitzmann, 1994).

MENTAL HEALTH EXPERTS IN THE LEGAL SYSTEM

Testifying as an expert witness is one of the most visible of clinical psychologists' forensic activities. Clinical psychologists (and psychiatrists) have testified in some of the most notorious trials in recent U.S. history, including those of the Menendez brothers, O.J. Simpson, Jeffrey Dahmer, Susan Smith, and John Hinckley.

Such testimony is controversial, however. Judges, lawyers, and psychologists have all expressed a great deal of concern about the reliability, validity, propriety, and usefulness of expert testimony by mental health professionals. For example, in his 1994 book, *The Abuse Excuse*, attorney Alan Dershowitz denounced much of this type of testimony as providing obviously guilty defendants with a way to avoid being held responsible for their crimes. Another commentator summed up such skepticism when he referred to trial testimony by mental health experts as the time to "send in the clowns." Former federal appellate judge David T. Bazelon (1974) once complained that "Psychiatry . . . is the ultimate wizardry . . . in no case is it more difficult to elicit productive and reliable testimony than in cases that call on the knowledge and practice of psychiatry." This view was echoed by Warren Burger (Burger, 1975), a former Chief Justice of the Supreme Court who chided experts for the "uncertainties of psychiatric diagnosis."

At the trial of Susan Smith, who was eventually convicted of murder for rolling her car into a South Carolina lake with her two young sons strapped inside, expert witnesses gave conflicting testimony about whether her crime was the result of mental illness. (Source: Dave Martin / AP/Wide World Photos.)

Sharply worded critiques of psychologists' expert testimony can be found in several other sources (Bonnie & Slobogin, 1980; Ennis & Litwack, 1974; Morse, 1978), and one well-known guidebook is devoted entirely to the subject of how to cross-examine the "highly dubious" expert testimony of psychologists (Ziskin & Faust, 1988). So popular is this resource that experts who have been cross-examined according to its principles are often said to have been "Ziskinized."

Steven Smith (1989) lists eight specific concerns about testimony by mental health experts:

1. The scientific foundations for much of the testimony offered in court is often less than adequate, leading to unreliable information and potentially incorrect verdicts.

2. Much of the testimony is of limited relevance, thus wasting the court's time and burdening an already crowded docket.

3. Experts are too often permitted to testify about "ultimate issues" (e.g., Is the defendant insane? Was the plaintiff emotionally damaged?) that are more appropriate for juries to decide.

4. Expert testimony is frequently used to introduce information that would otherwise be prohibited because it is hearsay. (Experts are permitted to share this information with juries if it is the kind of information they routinely rely on in reaching their opinions.)

5. The adversary system compromises experts' objectivity. Experts readily testify to opinions that favor the side that hired them, becoming little more than "hired guns" whose testimony can be bought.

6. Because expert testimony is expensive, reliance on experts gives an advantage to the side with the most money.

7. Testing the reliability and validity of expert opinions through cross-examination is inadequate because attorneys are usually not well-equipped to conduct such cross-examinations and juries often fail to understand the significance of the information uncovered in the process.

8. The spectacle of experts disagreeing with one another in trial after trial ultimately reduces the public's esteem for mental health professionals.

Despite public skepticism, psychological and psychiatric expert testimony has grown rapidly. It is estimated that psychologists and psychiatrists testify in approximately 8% of all trials held in federal civil courts, and mental health witnesses participate in as many as a million cases each year (O'Connor, Sales, & Shuman, 1996). Three factors appear especially responsible for the widespread use of forensic experts from psychology.

Expert testimony is frequent, first, because there are many topics for psychologists to testify about (see Table 13.3). As scientists learn more about human behavior, attorneys are likely to find their research results helpful in court cases. The press usually focuses on testimony concerning criminal competence and responsibility, but testimony about these topics is actually relatively rare compared to those involving experimental, developmental, industrial/organizational, and social psychology.

TABLE 13.3 **Topics for Expert Psychological Testimony**

Expert witnesses from psychology testify about topics in criminal trials, civil litigation, and domestic disputes. In fact, expert testimony is given on these topics much more often than on claims of insanity. Here are sixteen of the more common subjects of expert psychological testimony.

Topic of Testimony	Main Question Addressed in Testimony
Insanity	What is the relationship between the defendant's mental condition at the time of the alleged offense and the defendant's responsibility for the crime?
Criminal competency	Does the defendant have an adequate understanding of the legal proceedings in which he or she is involved?
Sentencing	What are the prospects for the defendant's rehabilitiation? What deterrent effects do certain sentences have?
Eyewitness identification	What factors affect the accuracy of eyewitness indentification?
Trial procedure	What effects are associated with variations in pretrial and/or trial procedures?
Civil commitment	Does a mentally ill person present a danger, or threat of danger, that requires treatment no less restrictive than hospitalization?
Psychological damages in civil cases	What psychological consequences has an individual suffered as a result of wrongful conduct? To what extent are the psychological problems attributable to a preexisting condition?
Psychological autopsies	In equivocal cases, do a deceased person's personality and circumstances of death indicate a likely mode of death?
Negligence and product liability	How do environmental factors and human perceptual abilities affect an individual's use of a product?
Trademark litigation	Is a certain product name or trademark confusingly similar to that of a competitor?
Class-action lawsuits	What psychological evidence is there that effective treatment is being denied or that testing procedures are discriminatory?
Guardianship and conservatorship	Does an individual possess the necessary mental ability to make decisions concerning living conditions, financial matters, health, etc.?
Child custody	What psychological factors will affect the best interests of the child whose custody is in dispute?
Adoption and termination of parental rights	What psychological factors affect the best interests of a child whose parents' disabilities may render them unfit to raise and care for the child?
Professional malpractice	Did a defendant's professional conduct fail to meet the standard of care owed to the plaintiff?
Social issues in litigation	What are the effects of pornography, violence, spouse abuse, etc., on the behavior of a defendant who claims that his or her misconduct was caused by one of these influences?

Based on Nietzel & Dillehay (1986)

Second, expert testimony flourishes because the law encourages it. Since the mid-1970s, U.S. courts have relaxed their standards for admitting the testimony of experts. In general, a qualified expert can testify on a topic if "scientific, technical, or other specialized knowledge will assist the trier of fact to understand the evidence or to determine a fact in issue" (Federal Rule of Evidence 702). In 1993, the U.S. Supreme Court ruled in *Daubert v. Merrell Dow*[5] that judges can decide when expert testimony is based on scientific evidence that is sufficiently relevant and reliable to be admitted. This opinion encourages consideration of innovative opinions, and many critics, including experts themselves, fear that it will lead judges—especially those who cannot distinguish valid from invalid research—to occasionally expose jurors to testimony based on "junk science" rather than standard empirical methods and sound scientific principles.

Finally, expert testimony thrives because it can be very lucrative. At hourly rates ranging from $100 to $400, forensic experts can earn thousands of dollars per case. If one party in a trial hires an expert, the other side usually feels compelled to do so as well. Consequently, the use of psychological experts feeds on itself and has become a significant source of income for many professionals.

In response to concerns about the value and impact of mental health experts' testimony, several reforms and remedies have been proposed. Most of these suggestions are aimed at reducing the undue influence or excessive partisanship thought to plague expert testimony. For example, several commentators have recommended that experts not be allowed to testify about the "ultimate issue" in forensic cases. As noted earlier, this recommendation was included in federal reforms concerning the insanity defense. However, there is little evidence that limiting expert testimony in this way has had much impact on the use or success of the insanity defense, and it is no more certain that it would have any greater impact in other kinds of cases.

Another suggestion has been to reduce the overly adversarial nature of expert testimony by limiting the number of experts each side may introduce to testify about a given topic, by requiring that the experts be chosen from an approved panel of individuals reputed to be objective and highly competent, or by allowing testimony only from experts who have been appointed by a judge—not those hired by opposing attorneys. These changes would appear to reduce the "hired gun" problem, but it is not clear that consensus could be easily reached on which experts belong on an "approved" list or that being appointed by a judge guarantees an expert's objectivity.

Several scholars have suggested that courts not permit clinical opinion testimony unless it can be shown that it passes the scientific reliability standard established by the *Daubert* decision (Faust & Ziskin, 1988; Imwinkelreid, 1994). Such a requirement might lead to a dramatic decline in testimony by forensic psychologists and psychiatrists, but unless attorneys and lawyers are more thoroughly educated about scientific methodology, it is not clear that they can make informed distinctions between "good" and "bad" science (Gless, 1995).

---

[5]113 S.Ct. 2786 (1993).

A more modest reform is to simply ban any reference to witnesses as providing *expert* testimony, a term that seems to suggest that jurors should pay extra attention to it. Instead, whenever the jury is present, judges would always refer to *opinion* testimony or *opinion* witnesses (Richey, 1994).

FORENSIC PSYCHOLOGY AT WORK

Q.: To what extent do the principles, methods, and research results associated with forensic psychology affect your work?

Dr. Sandy D'Angelo: Very little.

Dr. Hector Machabanski: Forensic psychology does have some impact on my consulting work with attorneys. With each client and referral question, I attempt to become familiar with the relevant legal issues. For example, in consulting with an attorney who is defending a family under threat of deportation, I must become familiar with immigration issues and laws as part of the process of preparing to conduct a psychological assessment with the family.

Dr. Geoffrey Thorpe: I conduct forensic evaluations as part of my clinical work, and our doctoral program has a formal link with a state agency that coordinates such evaluations. Through this link, some students are hired as research assistants to apply state-of-the-literature findings in developing protocols for conducting child abuse and neglect evaluations and evaluating convicted sex offenders. With one of my graduate students, I am currently conducting a research project on factors affecting the credibility of psychologists as expert witnesses.

CHAPTER SUMMARY

Clinical psychologists are becoming increasingly involved in forensic psychology, a specialty that applies mental health knowledge and expertise to questions about individuals involved in legal proceedings. The nature of forensic assessment depends on the questions being asked, but, like most clinical assessments, it often includes a social history, a clinical interview, psychological testing, a review of life records, and perhaps interviews with a variety of third parties.

Evaluating competence to stand trial requires assessment of whether defendants can understand the nature of their trial, participate in their defense, or consult with their attorney. Most defendants referred for such evaluations are ultimately found competent.

At their trials, defendants who plead not guilty by reason of insanity (NGRI) must present evidence that they lacked the state of mind necessary to be held responsible for a crime. Psychologists and other mental health experts evaluate these defendants to determine if they meet the legal definition of insanity. This definition has changed over time, and can vary from one state or country to another. Some use the McNaughton rule—which requires proof that mental illness left the defendant unable to understand the nature of criminal act, or to know that the act was wrong. A somewhat larger number employ a rule developed by the American Law Institute, which says a defendant is not responsible for criminal conduct if, at the time of the act, mental illness left the defendant without the capacity either to appreciate the criminality of the act or to control it. Both rules have been criticized, and a variety of reforms—including abolition of the insanity defense, further changes in the definition of insanity, and the advent of the guilty but mentally ill verdict—have been tried to deal with the criminally insane.

In tort lawsuits, where plaintiffs seek compensatory and punitive damages for wrongful acts they claim caused them psychological harm, psychologists often testify about the nature, extent, and impact of that harm.

Psychologists also conduct assessments designed to determine questions about civil competency, such as whether a person is mentally capable of making decisions about financial affairs, medical or psychiatric treatment, or disposition of assets in a will.

Sometimes clinicians are called upon to conduct "psychological autopsies," in which they give opinions about a deceased person's state of mind prior to death. These evaluations, based on life records and third-party interviews, help resolve such questions as whether someone died by accident or suicide, whether workplace stress contributed to death, or whether the deceased was mentally competent when writing a will. Some clinicians even do criminal profiling to help police focus on suspects whose characteristics tend to be associated with particular kinds of crimes. The validity of these enterprises is not firmly established.

A growing area of forensic activity for clinical psychologists is assessing families in crisis. They offer opinions about the fitness of parents to retain custody over their children, and whether joint custody, sole custody, or some other arrangement would be best for the children when parents divorce. Many clinicians are also involved in efforts to mediate, rather than litigate, custody battles.

Expert testimony by psychologists is common, partly because many judges and lawyers encourage it, but critics doubt the reliability, validity, propriety, and usefulness of such testimony. A variety of reforms in the rules governing mental health experts' testimony have been proposed, but they may or may not solve the problems associated with this aspect of forensic psychology.

Chapter 14

Professional Issues
in Clinical Psychology

If Lightner Witmer returned from the dead to review the field he founded, he would not recognize many modern clinicians as his colleagues. A few might match his original psychoeducational, child-oriented model. But many others would bewilder Witmer, because they practice something very different from the clinical psychology of the early twentieth century.

After reading the previous thirteen chapters, you should be able to sympathize with Witmer's confusion. Clinical psychology is an expanding profession that is becoming more and more difficult to summarize in a single volume. As we saw in Chapter 1, clinicians now fill a long list of professional roles. However, no list does full justice to the complexity of clinical psychology, because it does not indicate either the multiple functions required by each job or the new specialties yet to emerge in the years to come. Noting an almost geometric growth in the number of clinicians, a proliferation of alternative roles, and increasing specialization, commentators struggle for an apt description of clinical psychology's current status. A favorite summary is that clinical psychology is in a transitional state.

This claim understates the changes in clinical psychology on at least two counts. First, it suggests that transition is a novel era in an otherwise tranquil history. This, of course, is not correct. Clinical psychology has been in constant transition. Witmer would not have had to wait until the 1990s to be surprised by changes in clinical psychology; he would have seen them by the 1920s.

The words "transitional state" also underestimate the pace of change in clinical psychology. The rate of transition has been accelerating like an object falling through space. Each decade since World War II has seen more extensive changes in the field than any preceding period.

Consider just three examples. First, in 1947 there were 787 members in American Psychological Association's Division 12, the Division of Clinical Psychology. In 1964, there were 2,883 members (Shakow, 1968), and in 1996 the membership of Division 12 stood at more than 6,500, over eight times its original size. (The largest APA division—the Division of Psychologists in Independent Practice—has more than 8,000 members, mainly clinical psychologists.) Second, in the first fifty years of clinical psychology, there was only one conference on professional training. Since that time there have been five national training conferences. In addition, several other conferences addressing specific issues in the training of clinical psychologists have been held; we discuss some of these conferences later in this chapter. Finally, early proposals for training in clinical psychology discouraged clinicians from entering private practice; only a handful of psychologists did so. In the 1990s, independent practice is the leading type of employment for clinical psychologists, with more than one-third of clinicians employed full-time or part-time in some type of independent practice.

These changes—along with the community mental health movement, health-care reform, the appearance of behavioral medicine and other new psychological specialties, and society's demand for mental health services—suggest that it is more accurate to portray clinical psychology not so much in transition, as in an entirely new era.

The first era of clinical psychology extended from its birth in 1896 to World War II. During that era, clinical psychology appeared as a subfield of scientific psychology and as a contributing member of the mental health team under the supervision of psychiatry. The approximately fifty years since the end of World War II have constituted clinical psychology's second era. During this period, the field's identity became established and expanded vigorously. This modern era has seen the field largely transformed from an academic discipline into a service profession. It has seen clinical psychology liberate itself from the opposition of some members of nonclinical psychology and from the domination of psychiatry. It has been an era in which clinicians struggled for autonomy, got it, and became determined to retain it.

The professionalization and current status of clinical psychology are our primary topics in this final chapter. It is a story that has many subplots because the professionalization of clinical psychology involves several overlapping developments that have reshaped clinical psychology's identity. We focus on five issues crucial to clinical psychology's struggle for professional recognition:

1. *Professional training.* What training does one need to become a clinical psychologist, and what are the options for obtaining it?
2. *Professional regulation.* What are the mechanisms for insuring that a clinical psychologist possesses minimum skills and meets minimum requirements to function professionally?
3. *Professional ethics.* What principles guide clinicians in determining the ethical standards for their profession? How is unethical behavior handled?

4. *Professional independence*. What is the relationship between clinical psychology and other mental health professions?

5. *Perils of professionalization*. Has the professionalization of clinical psychology been an asset or a detriment? Has the public benefited? Has the quality of clinical psychology improved?

PROFESSIONAL TRAINING

The first four decades of the twentieth century saw little progress in the creation of advanced training for clinical psychologists. For clinicians of that period, experience was not only the best teacher, it was practically the only one. Psychologists were involved increasingly in clinical work during this time, but their training for these activities was unsystematic.

The APA took a few tentative, and mostly ineffective, steps toward formalizing clinical training during the 1930s and early 1940s. In 1931, an APA Committee on Standards of Training for Clinical Psychologists was formed, and in 1935 this committee published several recommendations for clinical training. In 1936, the psychology department at Columbia University proposed a training curriculum for clinical psychologists that involved two years of graduate work and a one-year internship (Shakow, 1948). In 1943, a Committee on Training in Clinical Psychology released a report entitled "Proposed Program of Professional Training in Clinical Psychology"; two years later a report on graduate internship training in psychology was published. However, little was accomplished with respect to training clinical psychologists until the late-1940s, when the social needs brought about by World War II and the financial support provided by the Veterans Administration and the U.S. Public Health Service combined to offer clinical psychology a unique opportunity to establish its identity, expand its functions, and elevate its status.

The psychologist most influential in the development of clinical training programs was David Shakow, for many years the chief psychologist at Worcester State Hospital in Massachusetts and later an important figure at the National Institute of Mental Health. As early as 1942, Shakow saw the need for a four-year doctoral-level training program in clinical psychology that included an internship during the third year (Shakow, 1942). Shakow attracted the attention of Carl Rogers, who was then president of the APA. Rogers asked Shakow to chair a Committee on Training in Clinical Psychology, with the task of formulating a recommended clinical training program. The committee prepared a report entitled "Recommended Graduate Training in Clinical Psychology," which APA accepted in September 1947 and published that same year in APA's official journal, the *American Psychologist*. The Shakow report set the pattern for clinical training and remains, with surprisingly few exceptions, a standard against which modern clinical programs can be evaluated.

Three important recommendations of the Shakow report on clinical training were:

1. A clinical psychologist should be trained first and foremost as a psychologist.

2. Clinical training should be as rigorous as that for nonclinical areas of psychology.

3. Preparation of the clinical psychologist should be broad and directed toward assessment, research, and therapy.

The Shakow report also advocated several other principles for graduate clinical programs:

4. The core of clinical training programs should involve six areas: general psychology, psychodynamics of behavior, diagnostic methods, research methods, related disciplines, and therapy.
5. The program should offer basic courses in principles as opposed to a large number of courses on special techniques.
6. Training should integrate theory with practice. This emphasis on integrated training was a hallmark of Shakow's plan; mechanisms for integrating theory with practice are suggested in every one of his many articles on training.
7. Throughout the entire program, beginning in the first year, students should have contact with clinical material.
8. Opportunities should also be provided for contact with "normal" persons who never establish clinical contacts.
9. The training atmosphere should encourage maturity and the continued growth of desirable personality characteristics.
10. The program should promote a sense of responsibility for clients.
11. Representatives of related disciplines should teach clinical trainees, and joint study with students in these related disciplines should be arranged.
12. The program must emphasize the research implications of clinical phenomena.
13. Trainees "must acquire the ability to see beyond the responsibilities they owe the individual patient, to those they owe society" (Shakow, 1978, p. 151).

The Shakow report suggested a year-by-year curriculum to achieve these goals. This schedule was not offered as a blueprint for training but as an illustration of an adequate clinical program. In this model, first-year clinical students would become acquainted with the foundations of general psychology. They would also be trained in observational techniques. The second year would be devoted primarily to the experimental, diagnostic, and therapeutic content of clinical psychology. In addition to didactic material, students would acquire direct, practical experience through practicum courses and clinical placements. The third year would be the internship, a year of intensive and extensive experience with clinical phenomena at a hospital, clinic, or medical center. Shakow regarded the internship as an essential component that fostered students' sense of professional identity and immersed them in practical clinical experience. Several objectives were to be met during the fourth year. The dissertation would be completed; the student would take a seminar on professional problems and ethics as well as seminars involving related disciplines; and the student would undergo a period of self-evaluation. Self-evaluation usually meant being in individual psychotherapy, which would help the student uncover biases, attitudes, and personality problems that might interfere with later clinical work.

Many of today's clinical training programs are much like Shakow's prototype (see Table 14.1). However, it usually takes about six-and-a-half, rather than four, years to complete the entire training sequence (Gaddy et al., 1995), and the internship is now usually taken in the fourth or fifth year. The major reasons for the extra years are that most programs require a master's thesis (usually in the second year), some universities still retain requirements such as a foreign language, and many clinical programs have added required courses on professional ethics as well as such specialty areas as human diversity, substance abuse, sexual problems, and organic disorders.

The greatest impact of the Shakow report was that it prescribed that special mix of scientific and professional preparation that has typified most clinical training programs ever since. This recipe for training—described as the scientist–professional model—was officially endorsed at clinical psychology's first major training conference held in Boulder, Colorado in 1949 (Raimy, 1950).

The Boulder Conference

The Boulder Conference on Training in Clinical Psychology was convened with the financial support of the Veterans Administration and the U.S. Public Health Service, which requested APA to (1) name those universities that offered satisfactory training programs and (2) develop acceptable programs in universities that did not have them.

The Boulder conferees accepted the recommendations of Shakow's committee for a scientist–professional model of training. Clinical psychologists were expected to be proficient in research and professional practice and to have earned a Ph.D. in psychology from a university-based graduate program. A supervised, year-long internship would also be required. Shakow's plan thus became known as the *Boulder model*.

The Boulder conferees further agreed that some mechanism was necessary for monitoring, evaluating, and officially accrediting clinical training programs and internship facilities. As a result, APA formed an Education and Training Board whose Committee on Accreditation was charged with these tasks. Currently, clinical training sites are visited by an APA accreditation team about every five years; the longest permissible interval between site visits is seven years. The team consists of three psychologists (selected by the visited program from a list of available choices) who evaluate how well the program is meeting its own training goals and APA's training standards. The most recent version of APA's criteria for accreditation was published in 1996 (Office of Program Consultation and Accreditation, APA, 1996). These new standards, developed by APA over several years, apply to areas of "professional psychology," which include clinical, counseling, and school psychology (Sheridan, Matarazzo, & Nelson, 1995). Programs that emerge in new areas of professional psychology would also be subject to these accreditation guidelines.

The results of accreditation site visits are published each year in the *American Psychologist*. In 1996 there were more than 300 accredited doctoral programs (most of

TABLE 14.1   Sample Schedule for Ph.D. Program in Clinical Psychology

Although there are many variations in the curricula of APA-accredited clinical training programs, the schedule shown here approximates what students encounter in most of them.

Fall Semester	Spring Semester
First year	
Psychological Statistics I	Psychological Statistics II
Introduction to Interviewing	Clinical Assessment II
Clinical Assessment I	Selected Proseminar (Social Psychology, Developmental Psychology, Psychology of Learning, Physiological Psychology)
Practicum in Assessment	
History and Systems of Psychology	Theories and Research in Personality
Second Year	
Psychopathology	Psychotherapy Practicum
Selected Proseminar (choose one from list above)	Clinical Seminar (Group Therapy, Behavior Modification, Child and Family Therapy, Health Psychology, Community Psychology)
Systems of Psychotherapy	
MA research	MA research
Third Year	
Psychotherapy Practicum	Advanced nonclinical seminar
Clinical Seminar (choose one from list above)	Clinical or nonclinical research seminar
Clinical Research Seminar (Research in Personality, Psychopathology Research, Research in Psychotherapy	Psychotherapy Practicum
Advanced nonclinical Seminar	

A written qualifying examination is to be taken during the third year of graduate work, but no later than the beginning of the fourth year. Only those students who have completed their MA thesis are permitted to register for the qualifying examination.

Fourth Year	
Internship	
Fifth Year	
Clinical or nonclinical research seminar	Same as Fall Semester
Advanced nonclinical seminar	
Research on dissertation	

them in clinical psychology) and more than 400 accredited internships.[1] In addition, many doctoral training programs function without APA approval, either because the program has not requested a site visit or because approval has not been granted after an accreditation visit.

The Conferences at Stanford, Miami, and Chicago

Although the Boulder model remains dominant, some clinicians have expressed discontent with it ever since its birth in 1949. This discontent has grown in recent years, and major alternatives to the Boulder model now exist. We will describe these later; for now, let's examine the post-Boulder training conferences that set the stage for these alternatives.

The Stanford Conference.   Named for its location at Stanford University, the 1955 Stanford conference (Strother, 1956), offered no new direction for clinical training, but did anticipate some of the effects that the community mental health movement would later have on clinical psychology, and it stressed the need to prepare clinicians for the new professional roles community mental health would offer.

The Miami Conference.   The Miami Beach training conference was held in 1958 (Roe et al., 1959). By then, clinical psychology had undergone enough changes to warrant reevaluation of the scientist–professional model. The conferees again concluded that the Ph.D. program should be retained as the primary training vehicle, although departments were encouraged to develop programs that best suited their own resources and needs. The need for psychology to train its graduates in the techniques of empirical research was also emphasized.

The Chicago Conference.   The 1965 Chicago Conference on the Professional Preparation of Clinical Psychologists was the first conference to seriously consider alternative models of clinical training. A theme of this conference was that, while the scientist–professional model should be continued, the value of a purely *professional* model of training should also be appreciated.

Interest in a professional model that stressed training in the delivery of clinical services stemmed from two sources. First, the need for psychological service providers was burgeoning, due in large part to the community mental health movement. Second, only a small minority of psychologists, probably about 10%, publish research in psychology. Critics of the Boulder model argued that too much time was being spent training students for activities that, as professionals, they were unlikely to actually perform.

---

[1]To acquaint prospective clinical students with the array of training possibilities, APA publishes annual editions of a book called *Graduate Study in Psychology and Associated Fields*, which lists all graduate programs in psychology, along with a brief description of requirements and training features. In addition, almost all clinical programs offer information—through brochures and/or homepages on the internet—about their orientation, faculty interests, admission and course requirements, and financial support opportunities (see Appendix).

At the same time, research-oriented departments of psychology were accepting increasing numbers of practice-oriented graduate students. The fit was often a bad one, which left both students and faculty dissatisfied.

Participants at the Chicago conference debated the wisdom of replacing the scientist–professional with a professional program (Zimet & Throne, 1965):

> The distinctive feature of this pattern of doctoral training would be the effort to prepare a broadly trained psychological clinician prepared to intervene in a wide variety of settings for the purpose of fostering change and forestalling psychological problems. His training would include psychological science but would stress those areas in which clinical methods find their support. It would also include relevant material from related disciplines such as medicine and sociology. He would be introduced to a variety of diagnostic, remedial, and preventive procedures. His training would include analysis of the manner in which clinical methods are developed with the intent to make him a sophisticated evaluator of new methods developed in the future. Because he would not carry out a doctoral dissertation or learn foreign languages, he would have more time available for professional training and experience. Should he wish to develop the competence of a specialist in specified diagnostic, remedial, or preventive procedures he will need additional training—either on the job or in formal postdoctoral training programs.
>
> We would expect a clinical psychologist trained in this manner to devote full time to professional practice oriented toward treatment, prevention, or both. He would use diagnostic instruments, carry out psychotherapy, engage in milieu therapy, use behavior therapy, consult in community mental health projects, work with groups, organizations, and communities—as the occasion demanded. He would, as far as his limited scientific training would permit, keep abreast of new methods as they developed and critically appraise them prior to adoption. He would contribute to the development of methods of practice by exchanging his professional experience with that of his colleagues. (pp. 21-22)

In the end, the conferees refused to endorse a purely professional model, preferring instead a flexible scientist–professional plan that would not short-change training in clinical activities. Training programs were urged to add faculty who were practicing clinicians and also to broaden their criteria for acceptable research activities.

Diversity in training was encouraged by calling for pilot programs that would experiment with innovative ways of implementing the professional model. Special interest focused on the first Psy.D. (Doctor of Psychology) program, then under development at the University of Illinois at Urbana-Champaign. The appropriate levels (doctoral and subdoctoral) and locations (department of psychology, medical center, independent professional school) of clinical training were also debated at Chicago.

The Chicago conference was important because, while professional training models and subdoctoral programs were not officially endorsed, they had gained considerable support among clinical psychology's leadership. Many of the ideas considered for the first time at Chicago were adopted by the participants at psychology's next training conference.

The Vail Conference

The National Conference on Levels and Patterns of Professional Training in Psychology was held in 1973 in Vail, Colorado. Supported by a grant from the National Institute of Mental Health (NIMH), the Vail conference brought together representatives from a wide range of psychological specialties and training orientations, and included graduate students and psychologists from various ethnic minority groups. In only five days the conference passed 150 resolutions, which introduced sweeping changes in the training of psychologists. These recommendations addressed professional training models, levels of training, and desirable characteristics of training programs (Korman, 1976).

Professional Training Models. The conference officially recognized professional training as an acceptable model for programs that defined their mission as the preparation of students for the delivery of clinical services. These "unambiguously professional" programs were to be given status equal to their more traditional scientist–professional counterparts. Professional programs could be housed in a number of settings, including academic psychology departments, medical schools, or specially established professional schools. When emphasis was on the delivery and evaluation of professional services, the Psy.D. would be the appropriate degree. When emphasis was on the development of new knowledge in psychology, the Ph.D. would be preferred.

Levels of Training. The conferees believed that priority should be given to programs that provided multiple levels of training or demonstrated coordination with degree programs at varying levels. They advocated the idea of a *career lattice*, a structure that would allow upward professional mobility through continued, integrated training.

One of the most controversial of the Vail recommendations was that persons trained at the master's level should be considered professional psychologists. This sentiment reversed the opinion of previous conferences, which envisioned psychology as strictly a doctoral-level profession. The Vail participants, however, felt that many services performed by doctoral psychologists could be performed just as well by personnel trained at the master's or submaster's level. The conference called for professional master's programs and full membership in APA for people trained at the master's level. Soon, universities in several states developed MA training programs in clinical psychology. Today, master's-level clinicians continue to outnumber Ph.D.s in some states. Over 200 programs offer an "MA-only" curriculum in psychology (Quereshi & Kuchan, 1988), and master's-level psychologists graduate at the rate of 6,000 per year (Humphreys, 1996).

The MA proposal was short-lived because the tide later turned against the MA as a recognized degree for the professional psychologist. In 1977 the APA voted that the title of *psychologist* should be reserved for those who have completed a doctoral training program, a policy that remains in effect today, although it is coming under intense attack as the number of MA psychology graduates continues to grow.

The status of the MA clinician was also jeopardized by Vail advocates who, while willing to endorse MA-trained persons as professionals, were unwilling to recommend that they be eligible for licensing as psychologists (a process described later). Another obstacle for the master's-level clinician has been a political one. Quite simply, the status of psychology as a profession vis-a-vis psychiatry is threatened by lumping MA holders along with Ph.D. psychologists. Most observers agree that the professional autonomy of psychology is best preserved by defining it exclusively as a doctoral-level enterprise. Financial considerations have also militated against granting full standing to MA recipients. Psychologists' eligibility for reimbursement as health-care providers is strengthened by portraying clinical psychology as a doctoral-level profession (we return to this topic later).

Desirable Characteristics of Professional Training. The Vail conference considered many issues related to the social obligations of psychology, affirmative action, racism and sexism, and the need for continuing professional development. Although those issues are beyond the scope of this chapter, the attention paid to them at Vail proves that this conference, more than any of its predecessors, seriously challenged both the history and the future of professional psychology.

The Salt Lake City Conference. The sixth national conference on graduate education in psychology was held in July, 1987 at the University of Utah in Salt Lake City. The conference was convened for several reasons, chief among which was the need to evaluate several changes that had taken place in the training of professional psychologists since the Vail conference. There was also a desire to reduce growing tensions between scientists and practitioners over numerous training and organizational issues. Some of the most important of the conference's sixty-seven resolutions are listed below (see also Bickman, 1987, and a special issue of the *American Psychologist*, December 1987):

1. Students in graduate programs seeking accreditation must be trained in a core of psychological knowledge that should include research design and methods; statistics; ethics; assessment; history and systems of psychology; biological, social, and cognitive-affective bases of behavior; and individual differences.

2. By 1995, in order to be accredited by the APA, doctoral training programs must be academic units within a regionally accredited institution of higher education or must be formally affiliated with a regionally accredited university. This resolution was aimed at gaining tighter control of over "free-standing" professional schools of psychology not associated with a university. We discuss those schools in more detail later.

3. Education in psychology occurs along a continuum that includes precollege, undergraduate, graduate, and postdoctoral levels. Training at the lower levels should be broad, with greater depth and specialization introduced at the advanced levels.

What does training in clinical psychology look like after six national training conferences, several smaller conferences, countless hours of discussion, debate, and argument among clinicians, educators, and students, and, most recently, a lengthy process of revising APA's accreditation guidelines? There is no easy answer to that question, but we can provide a general summary.

First, the scientist–professional model has proven to be a tough competitor that is still "the champ" in terms of the number of programs professing it as their training philosophy (O'Sullivan & Quevillon, 1992). The original Boulder model now comes in an increasing number of different packages, however. Most programs have increased the time devoted to professional training in psychotherapy, usually at the expense of courses in psychodiagnostics or general psychology. Some follow a particular theoretical approach—cognitive-behavioral or psychoanalytic, for example—which offers students a relatively narrow perspective on clinical psychology. Other programs emphasize a specialty such as health psychology, clinical-child psychology, or community psychology.

Second, many programs that favor the scientist–professional model are still struggling to find the best way to train clinical psychologists so that their practical skills are well integrated with a solid foundation of scientific knowledge. This struggle stems from at least two sources: (1) the increasing tendency for accreditation standards to create additional course requirements that may not promote integration of science and practice and (2) the difficulty that clinical faculty members have in providing a scientist-professional role model for students.

In 1990, concern over these issues led to the calling of a National Conference on Scientist-Practitioner Education and Training for the Professional Practice of Psychology. Taking place in Gainesville, Florida, this conference reaffirmed the Boulder model as the best foundation for training clinicians and stressed the need for such training to involve more than just equal attention to practice and science (Belar & Perry, 1992). The basic principle for scientist–practitioner training, said the conferees, is that students must be trained to "embody a research orientation in their practice and a practice relevance in their research" (p.72). This principle should be realized in all aspects of the curriculum, including coursework, research training, and practicum experiences, they said, and must be modeled as much as possible by clinical faculty.

The ideals put forth at the Gainesville conference were reflected in the establishment, in 1994, of the Academy of Psychological Clinical Science. This academy, affiliated with the American Psychological Society and made up of graduate training programs committed to clinical science, was created in response to concerns that recent developments in health care reform and licensure and accreditation requirements are threatening to erode the role of science and empirical research in the education of clinical psychologists. Representatives of programs in the academy were particularly concerned that professional training—divorced from its research base—is beginning to dominate accreditation decisions. The goals of the academy, which included twenty-six member programs by 1996, are to strengthen the role of science-based education by:

1. Encouraging the training of students for careers in clinical research;
2. Improving the integration of clinical science research with other scientific areas;
3. Developing new opportunities for training, funding, and careers in clinical science;

4. Providing for the dissemination of clinical science knowledge to policy-makers, consumers, and other professionals; and

5. Fostering the application of clinical science to human problems in responsible, empirically justifiable ways (APS, 1996).

For example, one special issue endorsed by many Academy programs is a commitment to training students in interventions that are empirically validated (see Chapter 9).

As mentioned earlier, other training programs with different philosophies about how to train clinicians have also been created in the past few decades. These programs envision clinicians mainly as health-care or human-service professionals and therefore tend to deemphasize the integration of science and practice. Two training models of this type—the Psy.D. program and the professional school of psychology—are discussed next.

The Doctor of Psychology (Psy.D.) Degree

One of the earliest and most influential professional training programs was the Doctor of Psychology (Psy.D.) program begun by the Department of Psychology at the University of Illinois (Urbana-Champaign) in 1968, and discontinued there in 1980. Unlike Boulder model programs, Psy.D. programs provide training that concentrates on professional skills and clinical services. The emphasis is on the skills necessary for the delivery of a range of assessment, intervention, and consultation services. A master's thesis is not required, nor is a research-oriented dissertation, although most Psy.D. programs do require a written, doctoral-level report of professional quality.

The number of APA-accredited Psy.D. programs continues to grow; by 1992, fifteen were fully accredited and by 1996, the figure had doubled to thirty. Nonetheless, many clinicians have leveled a number of criticisms at Psy.D. training. One observer summarized these early objections: (1) the Psy.D. program is likely to acquire second-class status in the eyes of faculty, students, and the public; (2) the fact that support for the alternate doctorate comes from the unlikely quarter of academic psychology is suspected as being a device for shunting aside the bothersome problem of professional training in clinical psychology; (3) the profession of clinical psychology is in a state of flux, with new roles and practices emerging, making this a particularly inappropriate time to create a new profession with activities that are only dimly foreseeable at present and whose present clinical skills may soon be obsolete; (4) two parallel programs, producing two different degrees, will tend to separate clinical practice from the rest of psychology even further, thus cutting the profession off from its scientific roots; (5) expert practitioners, necessary in a professional degree program, are likely to find it as difficult to be appointed and later promoted at the university as is the case now of competent clinical professors who do not publish research findings; and (6) future graduates of such programs are likely to be stigmatized because of their different degree and different training (Goldenberg, 1973, p. 85).

Were these concerns justified? One study at the University of Illinois found that Psy.D. and Ph.D. students there performed equivalently on qualifying exams and course grades, and showed similar attrition rates (Peterson & Baron, 1975). However, students in Ph.D. programs tend to take about one-and-a-half years longer than Psy.D.

students to finish their clinical programs and are also much more likely to be involved in research activities than Psy.D. students (Gaddy et al., 1995). Other research showed that clinical internship supervisors did not differentiate the quality of work by Ph.D. versus Psy.D. interns (Shemberg & Leventhal, 1981; Snepp & Peterson, 1988). Although very limited in scope, these data belie the gloomy predictions that were made about Psy.D. programs, and proponents continue to call for expanded Psy.D. training opportunities (Shapiro & Wiggins, 1994). However, serious questions about the quality of training in some Psy.D. programs continue to be raised (Strickland, 1985), even among advocates for the degree itself (Peterson, 1985). Of greatest concern is the fact that too many Psy.D. programs employ part-time faculty to train large numbers of students in settings that do not encourage comprehensive education.

Professional Schools of Psychology

As noted earlier, professional schools of psychology are free-standing clinical training units, some with no ties to university departments of psychology. This independent arrangement is thought to free clinical psychology training from the academic constraints of the university, to allow rewards for professional as well as scholarly achievements, and to provide students with faculty role models who are actively practicing clinicians.

Though some professional schools of psychology (at Rutgers or Yeshiva, for example) are housed within a university, most of the more than fifty professional schools in the United States—such as the Minnesota or Chicago Schools of Professional Psychology—are free-standing organizations. The first of these free-standing schools was the California School of Professional Psychology, founded in 1969 under the auspices of the California Psychological Association. With campuses at Los Angeles, Berkeley, San Diego, and Fresno, it is generally regarded as the leading free-standing professional school in the United States. Some free-standing schools award the Ph.D., while others grant the Psy.D. (Peterson, 1985); the Fresno, Los Angeles, and San Diego campuses of the California School offer both.

Professional schools are estimated to enroll over 40% of all students in doctoral training programs in psychology (Kohout, Wicherski, & Pion, 1991), mainly because the average entering class of a professional school is about five times larger than the typical first-year class in a university psychology department (the average Psy.D. program tends to enroll two to three times the number of students as the average Ph.D. program). Further, compared to university-based Ph.D. programs, professional schools and Psy.D. programs accept a higher percentage of those who apply for admission and are less likely to offer them financial aid (Norcross, Hanych, & Terranova, 1996; Peterson, 1985).

The appearance and growth of the professional schools was stimulated by several influences. First, well-intentioned, competent psychologists have had honest disagreements among themselves about the best way to educate clinical students (Bourg et al., 1989). Second, the curricula of professional schools reflect the desire—expressed by most clinical graduate students—to be trained as providers of psychological services rather than as academicians and researchers. Third, professional schools provide a training atmosphere that many students find more comfortable than what they expect to find in academic programs. The professional schools' emphasis on clinical practice and the availability of faculty who are practitioner role models create a culture in tune with the applied interests of most of today's clinical students. Fourth, economic factors and changing employment opportunities encouraged more psychologists to start independent and group practices, work in health-care facilities, and take other clinical service positions for which professional school training appears especially relevant. Finally, professional schools provided the further-training venue sought by large numbers of people who hold master's degrees in psychology but who have not been admitted to traditional Ph.D. training programs in clinical psychology. In short, professional schools challenged the nature of clinical training. They forced clinicians to consider seriously the type of knowledge upon which their services should be based and the standards against which they should evaluate their practices.

Despite the appeal of programs that focus on producing practitioners, we believe that the single most important goal in training clinical psychologists is to teach them to choose and evaluate whatever services they offer in light of research that employs the empirical methods of science. We think that training programs should emphasize the teaching of those clinical services that have been empirically confirmed as effective; they should not offer training in services or roles that, while perhaps being professionally appealing or financially lucrative, lack research support. We also believe that if clinical training moves too far from its foundation in psychological science and concentrates only on teaching therapy techniques, assessment methods, and other professional skills, the clinical psychologist of the twenty-first century will become a narrowly specialized practitioner for whom research is of only passing interest. As a result, clinical psychology will become a poorer science, and ultimately, a weaker profession. If you are interested in further discussions of the pros and cons of professional and Boulder model training, there are several excellent sources available (e.g., Belar & Perry, 1991; Bickman & Ellis, 1990, Fox, 1994; Matarazzo, 1987; Peterson, 1985, 1995; Shapiro & Wiggins, 1994; Stricker, 1992; Stricker & Trierweiler, 1995).

PROFESSIONAL REGULATION

One major responsibility of any health-care or human-service profession is to establish standards of competence that members of the profession must meet before they are authorized to practice. The primary purpose of such *professional regulation* is to protect the public from unauthorized or incompetent practice of psychology by impostors, untrained persons, or psychologists who are unable to function at a minimum level of competence. Although some critics doubt the value of regulation in meeting this goal (e.g., Gross, 1978; Hogan, 1983), psychology has developed an active system of professional regulation.

Certification and Licensure

The most important type of regulation lies in state laws that establish requirements for the practice of psychology and/or restrict the use of the term *psychologist* to persons with certain qualifications. This legislative regulation comes in two kinds of statutes: certification and licensure. The legal basis of these laws rests in the right of the state to pass legislation that protects its citizens. Caveat emptor ("let the buyer beware") is an inadequate protection when buyers are not sufficiently informed about the services to know what to beware of.

Certification laws restrict use of the title *psychologist* or *certified psychologist* to people who have met requirements specified in the law. Certification protects only the *title* of psychologist; it does not regulate the practice of psychology. *Licensure* is a more restrictive type of statute. Licensure laws define the practice of psychology by specifying the services that a psychologist is authorized to offer to the public. The requirements for licensure are usually more comprehensive than for certification. To distinguish between certification and licensure, remember the following rule of thumb: a certification law does not prevent a nonpsychologist from doing the same things as a certified psychologist; it only prevents the person from being called a psychologist. A licensure law not only prevents a nonpsychologist from using the title *psychologist*, it also prohibits the person from offering services that the average citizen believes are among the professional functions of a psychologist.

Licensing laws are administered by state boards of psychology, which are charged by legislatures to regulate the practice of psychology in the states. State boards of psychology have two major functions: (1) determining the standards for admission to the profession and administering procedures for the selection and examination of candidates, and (2) regulating professional practice and conducting disciplinary proceedings involving alleged violators of professional standards.

Thus, in the United States and Canada, having a Ph.D. in clinical psychology does not automatically allow a person to "hang out a shingle" and start to practice psychology. The steps involved in becoming licensed differ somewhat from place to place, but there is enough uniformity in the procedures of most U.S. states to offer a rough sketch of how the aspiring clinical psychologist would approach this task (see Table 14.2).

In 1945, Connecticut enacted the first psychology licensing law; Virginia, Kentucky, and Ohio followed suit within five years (Carlson, 1978). Today, all fifty states, the District of Columbia, and all Canadian provinces have certification or licensure laws. Many states combine their certification and licensure laws into one statute.

As more states passed licensing statutes, there evolved an obvious need for an organization to coordinate the activities of the state boards of psychology and to bring about uniformity in standards and procedures. To answer these needs, the American Association of State Psychology Boards (AASPB) was formed in 1961. In 1991, this organization was renamed the Association of State and Provincial Psychology Boards (ASPPB). ASPPB has also developed a Code of Conduct for psychologists that consists of rules of professional behavior intended to protect the public from unscrupulous, incompetent, and unethical psychologists. The ASPPB has also developed a standardized, objective test for use by state boards in examining candidates for licensure. First released in 1964 and revised frequently since then, this Examination for Professional Practice in Psychology is sometimes called the *multistate* or *national* exam because all jurisdictions can use it as a part of their examination procedure. Finally, the ASPPB helped develop a system of *reciprocity*, meaning that someone licensed in one state can usually transfer licensure to another jurisdiction.

In most states, psychologists are required to keep their license or certificate up to date by paying a periodic renewal fee. By the early 1990s, twenty-seven U.S. states also

---

TABLE 14.2 So You Want to Be a Licensed Psychologist?

Imagine you have just completed a doctoral program in clinical psychology and are now interested in becoming a licensed clinical psychologist. What steps would you have to take? The following hurdles will be encountered in most states. First, you must ask that the state board of psychology review your credentials to determine your eligibility for examination. Their decision is based on several criteria:

1. *Administrative Requirements.* You must have reached a certain age, be a U.S. citizen, and have been a resident in the state for some minimum period. Not too much can be done about these requirements; you either meet them or you do not. One bit of advice: Don't commit any felonies, engage in treason, or libel your governor. These activities are judged to be indicative of poor moral character and may leave you plenty of time to fantasize about licensure while in prison.

2. *Education.* Most states require a doctoral degree in psychology from an accredited university (accreditation in this case refers not to APA approval but to accreditation of the university by a recognized accrediting agency). Official graduate and undergraduate transcripts are required.

3. *Experience.* This usually amounts to one, or more commonly two, years of supervised professional experience in a setting approved by the board. Some of the experience must be postdoctoral; letters of reference will be required from your supervisor(s). If, after scrutinizing your credentials, the board finds you are eligible for examination, you will be invited to take an exam. Here is what to expect:

   Examination Fee. There is a charge for the examination; it is usually between $200 and $300.

   The Examination. Many states use a national exam that contains about 200 objective items covering general psychology methodology, applications of psychology, and professional conduct and ethics. Because many candidates want to practice a specialty like clinical, school, or industrial psychology, boards also prepare essay examinations in these areas. You may also be required to take an oral examination given by the board in which any material relevant to psychology may be covered.

   Reexamination. If you fail any part of the exam, you will be given another chance to take that portion. Most boards feel that twice is enough, however; so if you fail the second time, it might be wise to reconsider the advantages of the family business.

---

required *continuing professional education* (CPE) as a condition for maintaining licensure (VandeCreek, Knapp, & Brace, 1990). Continuing professional education is usually provided in special postdoctoral institutes, seminars, or workshops conducted by experts on particular topics. The purpose of this continuing education activity is to keep the practicing psychologist abreast of current progress in important professional areas. In states requiring CPE, psychologists must document their participation in a certain number of units of CPE instruction. Although psychology has not yet developed its CPE plan to the level of professions such as law or medicine, most psychologists agree that the future will see a strengthening of CPE requirements in their field.

Over the years, licensure of psychologists has been criticized on several grounds. A major objection is that licensure does not assure competence of practitioners because the examination procedures do not adequately assess professional abilities. Some critics further contend that licensure may be detrimental to the public interest because it functions to curtail competition and increase the cost of psychologists' services. Legal challenges to licensure of psychologists involving alleged due process violations and antitrust considerations have been attempted by disgruntled parties, but these attacks have had limited success.

In the 1970s, as part of a general sentiment favoring governmental deregulation of various activities, psychology licensure statutes were eliminated in some states (they have since been reenacted) through so-called "sunset" laws that require unnecessary regulations to be terminated, or have "the sun set" on them, after a certain period. Today, licensure laws are applauded by a majority of clinicians and are upheld by courts if there is a plausible reason to believe they protect the public.

In 1975, the first edition of the *National Register of Health Service Providers in Psychology* was published. The register is a listing of psychologists who possess the training and experience adequate to qualify them as health service providers. The register is used primarily to (1) identify psychologists who specialize in delivering health services and (2) help various organizations identify those psychologists whose mental health services are eligible for reimbursement. Thousands of psychologists are listed in the register, and hundreds of organizations, including many of the largest insurance companies, subscribe to it.

ABPP Certification

Another type of professional regulation is certification by the American Board of Professional Psychology (ABPP). ABPP was founded in 1947 as a national organization that certifies the professional competence of psychologists. Its certification is signified by the award of a diploma in one of several specialty areas including clinical, counseling, industrial/organizational, school, family, forensic, health, and neuropsychology. In 1992, the ABPP reorganized itself so that each of these specialty areas has its own board (all organized under the ABPP umbrella) that develops and administers its own exams and awards its diplomas.

Though it carries no special legal authority, an ABPP diploma is considered more prestigious than licensure. While licensure signifies a *minimal* level of competence, diplomate status is an endorsement of professional expertise, an indication that the person so designated possesses a masterful knowledge of some specialty field. Accordingly, requirements for the ABPP diploma are more rigorous than for licensure. Three years of experience is a prerequisite to even take the ABPP examination, which is conducted by a group of diplomates who observe the candidate dealing directly with clinical situations (e.g., giving a test or interacting with a therapy client).

Other Forms of Legal Regulation

An interesting by-product of psychology's increasing professionalization is greater legal scrutiny of the profession. Historically, courts have been disinclined to pass judgment on what constitutes acceptable psychological treatment, but this reluctance has recently given way to a willingness to evaluate the legality of mental health care. Courts are no longer willing to permit what they see as violations of clients' rights, despite the hazards inherent when nonexperts try to evaluate treatment methods. A comprehensive review of the legal status of psychological treatments would be beyond our purposes here, but we will highlight four legal principles that have been used to challenge some forms of intervention. The first two, known as *right to treatment* and *informed consent*, are usually concerned with institutionalized persons such as mental patients or prison inmates. The third, known as *privileged communication* is particularly relevant to outpatient psychotherapy clients. The fourth form of legal control over professional interventions is through *malpractice litigation*.

Right to Treatment.   The concept of a right to treatment for patients committed to psychiatric hospitals found legal support in the landmark *Rouse v. Cameron*[2] decision. In this case, the patient, Charlie Rouse, had been confined in a hospital for four years after being found not guilty by reason of insanity on a weapons charge. Rouse was not receiving any treatment, and his period of confinement was longer than the one-year maximum prison sentence he would have received if convicted. He petitioned the court to release him from the institution, and the appellate court agreed, further ruling that hospitals must make at least a reasonable effort to treat committed patients.

The court considered the standards for treatment in the case of *Youngberg v. Romeo*[3], which involved a profoundly retarded, thirty-three-year-old man named Nicholas Romeo who had been committed to the Pennhurst State Hospital in Pennsylvania after his father died and his mother could no longer care for him. Nicholas frequently engaged in self-mutilation and was injured several times during his first few years in the hospital, both by his own actions and by other patients. As a protective step, he was restrained in bed for long periods. Upset with how her son was being "treated" at Pennhurst, Nicholas' mother filed suit, alleging that Pennsylvania had violated his 14th Amendment due process rights by not providing him a safe environment and by failing to train him adequately. The case ultimately reached the U.S. Supreme Court which held that the Constitution guarantees involuntarily committed patients the following rights: (1) adequate food, shelter, and clothing, (2) adequate medical care, (3) a safe environment, (4) freedom from restraint, unless restraint is necessary to protect the patient or others, and (5) such training as may be required to ensure the above rights. The Court also concluded that the form of training provided should remain largely a matter of professional judgment.

Although *Youngberg* laid a constitutional "floor" below which no state can fall in treating committed patients, individual states are free to set higher standards of care for the mentally ill, and several states have done so. Some federal courts have also ordered additional treatment rights for patients, but the Supreme Court has not yet ruled that these are required. For example, in the celebrated 1971 case of *Wyatt v. Stickney*[4], a federal court in Alabama ruled that involuntarily committed patients have the right to

---

[2]2373 F. 2d 451 (D.C. Cir. 1966).
[3]457 U.S. 307 (1982).
[4]344 F. Supp. 373 (1972).

individualized treatment which they can help plan, to clothing of their choice, and to a certain number of mental health professionals per patient in order to assure that treatment will be provided. Other state and federal courts have ruled that mental patients have the right to receive visitors, to enjoy a zone of personal privacy (except in emergencies), to receive reasonable payment for work they do in the hospital and, within limits discussed later, to refuse treatment.

Wyatt also directed that a patient is entitled to the "least restrictive conditions necessary to achieve the purposes of commitment." The "least restrictive conditions" doctrine (*Lessard v. Schmidt*[5]) holds that a state cannot stifle a person's civil liberties any more than is necessary for accomplishing legitimate treatment goals. Whenever less drastic means of effective treatment are available, they should be implemented before trying more drastic means. Like many well-intentioned reforms, the "least restrictive conditions" requirement can sometimes pose problems for mental health professionals. For example, many young chronic mental patients have a history of frequent substance abuse and acting out, which makes it difficult to treat them in noninstitutional settings.

In 1975, the U.S. Supreme Court considered the case of *O'Connor v. Donaldson*[6]. Kenneth Donaldson was a forty-nine-year-old man who had been diagnosed with paranoid schizophrenia and confined to the Florida State Hospital at Chattahoochee for fifteen years. His father had him committed because he was supposedly delusional and dangerous, but the evidence for his dangerousness at the time of commitment was questionable. Indeed, hospital staff notes and testimony later revealed that Donaldson was never dangerous to himself or anyone else. Donaldson repeatedly asked to be released from the hospital on the grounds that he was not receiving treatment, that he was not a threat, and that he could live effectively outside the hospital. After his requests were denied, Donaldson filed a lawsuit against Dr. J.B. O'Connor, the superintendent of the hospital for most of the time Donaldson was confined. A jury agreed with Donaldson that he had been improperly confined and awarded him $38,500 in damages. The wisdom of this decision was supported by the fact that, immediately upon his release, Donaldson obtained a job in hotel administration.

The state of Florida appealed the jury's verdict to the U.S. Supreme Court. *O'Connor* was a landmark case because it was the first time the Supreme Court heard arguments about the constitutional rights of a civilly committed mental patient, and it required the Court to evaluate a state's justifications for involuntarily committing the mentally ill to a hospital. Writing for the Court, Justice Potter Stewart ruled that a "state cannot constitutionally confine . . . a nondangerous individual who is capable of surviving safely in freedom by himself or with the help of willing and responsible family and friends." The effect of this decision, and others since then (*Foucha v. Louisiana*[7]), is to limit the state's powers such that it can not force the hospitalization of persons who, even though mentally ill, are not dangerous and can live outside the hospital on their own or with the support of others.

---

[5]349 F. Supp. 1078 (E.D. Wis. 1972).
[6]422 U.S. 563 (1975).
[7]112 S.Ct. 1780 (1992).

Kenneth Donaldson successfully sued to be released from a Florida mental hospital. In affirming the jury's decision, the U.S. Supreme Court decreed that mental illness and the need for treatment alone were not enough to justify involuntary commitment. (Source: AP/Wide World Photos.)

The Right to Refuse Treatment and Informed Consent.   The claim that institutionalized persons have a right to treatment is complicated by the suggestion that they also may have a right to refuse at least some treatments. Fundamental questions are raised when a mental patient does not want to take medication that a physician has prescribed. Should society "help" such patients by ordering treatment against their will? Does the need for treatment outweigh an individual's right to privacy and autonomy? Does it make sense to commit patients to a hospital and then allow them to refuse treatments that could help them regain their freedom?

People's control over their treatment usually takes the form of giving or withholding *informed consent.* Full informed consent involves several elements, including full specification of the nature of treatment; a description of its purpose, risks, and likely outcomes; notification that consent may be terminated at any time without prejudice to the individual; and, as discussed in Chapter 13, demonstration of a mental capacity to consent. Written informed consent is usually required for treatments of an experimental, intrusive, or aversive nature. The rules of informed consent assume that patients are competent to make decisions about their treatment. However, for many decades, informed consent procedures were not applied to mental patients because it was presumed that they were incompetent to make such important decisions.

However, concerns about the side effects of psychoactive drugs, about patients' rights to privacy, and about patients' control over what goes into their bodies led federal district courts in Massachusetts (*Rogers v. Okin*[8]) and New Jersey (*Rennie v. Klein*[9]) to hold that mentally ill patients do have the right to refuse medications, even if those medications are likely to be beneficial. However, the courts held that this right to refuse was not absolute. A patient's desire not to be medicated can be overridden in three general situations: (1) if the patient is behaving dangerously toward self or others, (2) if the patient is so ill as to be unable to make a competent decision about treatment, and (3) if there is an emergency that, in a physician's judgment, makes forced medication necessary. In the 1990 case of *Washington v. Harper*[10], for example, the U.S. Supreme Court held that a mentally ill prisoner cannot be medicated against his will *unless* it is determined by the application of professional standards that the medication was necessary for safety reasons.

The U.S. Supreme Court has also refused to hold that mentally ill patients have a Constitutional right to refuse treatment. Instead, it has used a doctrine of deferring to the professional judgment of physicians who are treating the patient. Thus, in the *Youngberg v. Romeo* case mentioned earlier, the Court held that honoring the rights of patients cannot be used to restrict unnecessarily the professional judgment of treating physicians. Some states still allow patients a right to refuse treatment, but there are so many ways to override a patient's refusal, that the right to refuse is actually more of a right to *object* to treatment and to have the treating physician review the medical necessity of the treatment (Brooks, 1986). In reality, few patients refuse medication over a long period of time (Appelbaum, 1994), and those who persistently do so typically have their refusal ultimately overridden (Appelbaum & Hoge, 1986; Godard et al., 1986).

Privileged Communication. Numerous states have laws establishing a psychotherapist–client privilege. *Privilege* is a legal right granted in order to protect clients from having therapists publicly disclose confidences without the clients' permission. Privilege is similar but not identical to confidentiality. The main difference is that *confidentiality* is an ethical obligation imposed on members of a profession, not a legal requirement. Therapist–client privilege statutes are on the books mainly because of the widespread belief that successful psychotherapy depends in part on assuring clients that the information they reveal to a therapist in confidence will remain private.

Prior to 1996, federal judges had been free to decide on a case-by-case basis whether to protect communications between therapists and clients or to force therapists to reveal their contents. In that year, however, a U.S. Supreme Court decision in the case of *Jaffee v. Redmond*[11] assured protection of confidential communications

---

[8]478 F. Supp. 1342, 1369 (Mass. 1979).
[9]462 F. Supp. 1131 (D.N.J. 1978).
[10]494 U.S. 210 (1990).
[11]133 L. 2d 758 (1996).

between a therapist and client in federal cases. The case involved the death of Ricky Allen, a young man who was killed by Mary Lu Redmond, a police officer in Illinois. Redmond had been called to an apartment to break up a fight. When she arrived and saw Allen about to stab another man, she shot Allen. His family claimed that Allen was unarmed and sued officer Redmond and her police department for violating his civil rights. When the family discovered that Redmond had undergone therapy with a social worker after the shooting, they petitioned to have the therapy notes made available. Both Redmond and her social worker refused to turn over the notes. After trial jurors were told by the judge that they could assume these notes contained material unfavorable to officer Redmond, they returned a verdict for the plaintiff in the amount of $545,000. In its review of the case, the U.S. Supreme Court held that therapists could not be forced to testify about confidential communications. Writing for the Court, Justice John Paul Stevens stated, "effective psychotherapy ... depends upon an atmosphere of confidence and trust in which the patient is willing to make a frank and complete disclosure of facts, emotions, memories, and fears."

As desirable as it may be, a client's right to privileged or confidential communications—like the right to refuse treatment—is not absolute. A therapist may be forced to breach confidentiality in the following situations:

1. If a therapist believes that a client needs to be involuntarily committed to a hospital;
2. If a client raises the issue of his or her mental condition in a trial and the therapist testifies on the client's behalf;
3. If a client has undergone a court-ordered evaluation of his or her psychological condition;
4. If the therapist learns that a client is abusing other people;
5. If a client tells a therapist of an intent to harm another person.

This last exception to maintaining confidentiality poses a particularly difficult situation for clinicians. On the one hand, therapists cannot be expected to treat a client's impulses toward violence without discussing them. On the other hand, if therapists know they might be compelled to disclose such information despite their clients' wish to keep it confidential, they have a reason to avoid the topic of violence in therapy, even if it is important. One specific dilemma brings this issue into particularly sharp focus: Should a therapist who has heard a client threaten to harm another person be required to break confidentiality in order to protect the intended victim? This was the question raised in the now-famous case of *Tarasoff vs. Regents of the University of California.*[12] The answer, in several states at least, is yes.

In the Tarasoff case, a couple sued the University of California, psychotherapists employed by the university, and the campus police to recover damages for the murder

---

[12]529 P. 2d 553 (Col. 1974) Vac. reheard in bank and affirmed 131 Cal. Rptr. 14, 551 P. 2d 334 (1976).

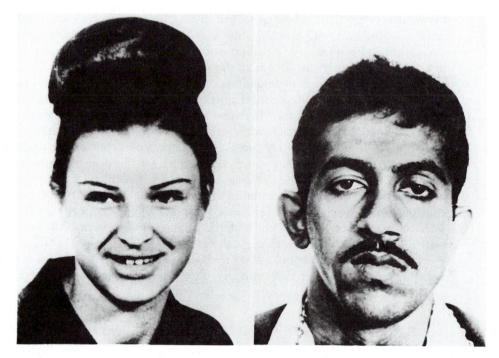

Prosenjit Poddar told his therapist that he intended to murder Tatiana Tarasoff, but Ms. Tarasoff was never warned. The question of whether, and when, therapists should act to protect those who might become victims of their clients' actions is one of the thorniest legal issues in clinical psychology. (Source: AP/Wide World Photos.)

of their daughter (a UC student) by a client of one of the psychotherapists. A lower court sustained the defendants' answers to the suit, but the Supreme Court of California reversed that decision and found for the plaintiffs.

Here are the facts of the case. The client, Prosenjit Poddar, told his psychotherapist, Dr. Lawrence Moore, that he intended to kill a young woman, Tatiana Tarasoff. The therapist informed his superior, Dr. Harvey Powelson, of this threat. The campus police were called and were also asked, in writing, to confine the client. They did so briefly, but then released him after concluding that he was rational and believing his promise that he would stay away from the Tarasoff's home. He didn't do so. After terminating his relationship with his therapist, Poddar killed Tatiana. He was later convicted of murder. No one had warned the woman or her parents of the threat. In fact, Powelson had asked the police to return Moore's letter and further ordered that all copies of the letter and Moore's therapy notes be destroyed.

In reaching its decision, the court weighed the importance of confidential therapy relationships against society's interest in protecting itself from dangerous persons. The balance was struck in favor of society's protection. The therapist's situation was like that of a physician who would be held liable for failing to warn persons about a contagious disease: "The protective privilege ends where the public peril begins."

The *Tarasoff* decision that therapists have a duty to protect specific victims from clients that the therapist believes or should believe to be dangerous has been implemented in some other U.S. states, but it is not legally binding in all states—a fact that even many psychologists misunderstand. About a third of the states have now passed laws that specify the conditions under which a therapist is liable for failing to take precautions to protect third parties from the dangerous acts of the therapist's clients. Some other states have *extended* "Tarasoff liability" to persons other than those specifically threatened. For example, in *Peterson v. State*[13], the Supreme Court of Washington held that therapists are responsible "to protect anyone who might foreseeably be endangered" by their clients.[14] One thing is clear: Therapists are responsible for knowing what their state requires regarding protection of third parties.

More than twenty years have passed since the *Tarasoff* case was decided. What impact has it had? It appears that the decision has made therapists more aware of the potential complications involving client dangerousness and how they should respond to it. At the same time, considerable evidence suggests that *Tarasoff* has not had the adverse impact that many clinicians predicted. For one thing, therapists have not stopped seeing potentially dangerous clients (Givelber, Bowers, & Blitch, 1984). When therapists have had to break confidentiality because of a client's dangerousness, it has not inevitably led to negative effects on the client, particularly when the therapist has first discussed with the client the need to take precautionary steps. Finally, even before *Tarasoff*, many therapists had been breaking confidentiality to warn potential victims in emergency situations, so the decision did not necessarily require clinicians to change their existing practices.

Regulation Through Malpractice Lawsuits. Civil lawsuits brought by clients who allege they have been harmed by the malpractice of professionals constitute another form of regulating clinical psychologists. If a jury agrees with the client's claim, it may order the clinician to pay the client monetary damages to compensate for the harm. To prove a claim of professional malpractice, four elements must be established:

1. A *special professional relationship* had to exist between the client/plaintiff and the therapist. Establishing this element usually requires proving that the plaintiff was receiving formal services from the clinician in exchange for a fee.

2. It must be shown that the clinician was *negligent* in treating the client. Negligence does not simply mean that a bad outcome occurred; nor does it require that the therapist intended any harm to occur. Negligence involves a violation

---

[13]100 Wn. 2d 421, 671 P. 2d 320 (1983).

[14]A related issue concerns therapists' possible obligation to protect third parties from the behavior of their clients who have AIDS (Totten, Lamb, & Reeder, 1990).

of the *standard of care*, defined as the treatment that a reasonable practitioner facing circumstances similar to those of the plaintiff's case would be expected to give.

3. Even if the professional was negligent, it must be shown that the client suffered *harm*.

4. The therapist's negligence must then be shown to be the *cause* of the harm suffered by the client.

Until about thirty years ago, malpractice claims against clinical psychologists were almost nonexistent. Plaintiffs were reluctant to sue a therapist if it meant they might have to talk about their psychological problems in court. Further, there were few agreed-upon standards of care for treating mental disorders so it was difficult to show that a therapist had violated accepted practice. The tide began to turn, however, during the turbulent 1960s, and malpractice charges against clinical psychologists (and psychiatrists) are now much more common—although they are still not nearly as frequent as those against medical specialists in obstetrics, gynecology, and surgery.

Malpractice actions against clinicians often arise over claims that they (1) failed to prevent a client from committing suicide, (2) failed to carry out *Tarasoff* duty-to-protect obligations, (3) failed to make a proper referral of a client when the therapist terminated treatment, or (4) misrepresented their professional qualifications (Smith, 1996). Still, the most common basis for malpractice claims against psychotherapists involves charges that they engaged in sexual intimacies with a current or recently terminated client. Since the ethical codes of all mental health professions strictly forbid such behavior, and since there is empirical evidence that sexual contact between therapist and client is usually harmful to the client (Feldman-Summers & Jones, 1984; Pope & Tabachnick, 1994), plaintiffs who prove such contact can win large malpractice awards. According to several surveys, about 5% to 8% of mental health professionals have engaged in intercourse or other sexual intimacies with a client (Haspel et al., 1997). The rate of sexual contact with clients is about four to five times greater for male therapists compared to female therapists, and therapists who have engaged in sex with clients once are likely to do so again (Pope & Vasquez, 1991).

There are several reasons why sexual contact between therapist and client is unethical. First, most clients who have engaged in sex with their therapists report it was harmful. Second, acting on sexual attraction to clients means that therapists are putting their own needs before those of their clients, another ethical taboo. Third, a therapist who engages in sexual contact with a client is not likely to objectively make judgments about the care of that client. Fourth, therapy clients are often in the midst of psychological crises that impair their ability to make fully informed, independent judgments about their behavior. Finally, sexual relationships between therapist and client are exploitive because the therapist's power and control in the relationship is always much greater than the client's.

A few large malpractice verdicts have also been returned in cases in which therapists are accused of influencing clients to falsely recall allegedly repressed memories of physical or sexual abuse in childhood. Such "de-repression" techniques have been advocated by popular books on incest and by therapists who believe that unless severe childhood traumas are recalled and defused, they will continue to cause mental problems. In addition to being asked to dredge up repressed memories of trauma, suspected victims are often encouraged by their therapists to join special support groups—such as Survivors of Incest Anonymous—that urge their members to aggressively search for buried memories of abuse.

Many researchers are skeptical about the accuracy of memories of trauma that resurface years after the alleged incidents—and only after aggressive memory-recovery therapy (Loftus, 1993; Wakefield & Underwager, 1992). These skeptics point out that most people who suffer severe trauma do not lose their memory of it; in fact, many of them suffer intrusive recollections of it for years afterward. Skepticism is also fueled by the fact that some alleged victims claim to recall traumas that happened when they were less than one year old, a feat contradicted by almost all research on memory and amnesia.

In one highly publicized trial, Gary Ramona—once a highly-paid executive in the California wine industry—sued family counselor Marche Isabella and psychiatrist Richard Rose for planting false memories of trauma in his daughter, Holly, when she was their nineteen-year-old patient. Ramona claimed that the therapists told Holly that her bulimia and depression were caused by having been repeatedly raped by him when she was a child. They also told her that the memory of this molestation was so traumatic that she had repressed it for years. According to Ramona, Dr. Rose then gave Holly sodium amytal (a so-called truth serum) to confirm her "recovered memory." Finally, Isabella was said to have told Holly's mother that up to 80% of all bulimics had been sexually abused (a statement for which there is no scientific support).

At the trial, the therapists claimed that Holly suffered flashbacks of what seemed to be real sexual abuse. She also became increasingly depressed and bulimic after reporting these frightening images. Holly's mother, Stephanie, who divorced her husband after Holly's allegations came to light, testified that she suspected her husband had abused Holly and listed several pieces of supposedly corroborating evidence. Gary Ramona emotionally denied ever sexually abusing his daughter.

The mental health experts who testified on Romana's behalf criticized the therapists for engaging in dangerous techniques. Elizabeth Loftus (1993), a leading critic of aggressive memory therapy, testified that therapists often either suggest the idea of trauma to their clients, or are too uncritical in accepting the validity of trauma reports that occur spontaneously. Another defense witness, Martin Orne, a renowned authority on hypnosis, condemned the use of sodium amytal interviews as "inherently untrustworthy and unreliable" and concluded that Holly's memory had been so distorted by her therapists that she no longer knew what the truth was.

The jury decided that Holly's therapists had planted false memories in her and, in May of 1994, awarded damages to Gary Ramona in the amount of $500,000. Since then, according to the False Memory Syndrome Foundation, a group devoted to un-covering abuses associated with memory recovery therapy, the number of "false memory" cases against therapists has grown. The increase in "false memory" litiga-tion adds to the already-difficult challenges therapists face when trying to help adult clients who have suffered a traumatic childhood. It is obvious that recovered memory therapy has led to some very bad outcomes and very real damage to clients and their families. It is also obvious that the trauma of child abuse does occur and that it can leave deep, painful, and long-lasting emotional scars. Accordingly, therapists must be sympathetic listeners and helpful counselors when clients remember only too well real horrors from childhood; these clients need support in talking about and coping with what they remember. At the same time, therapists must be cautious and avoid suggesting that clients' problems come from traumas that might never have happened.

PROFESSIONAL ETHICS

A code of professional ethics is a set of principles that encourages or forbids certain professional conduct. Ethics are normative statements that justify certain goals and be-haviors. All professions have ethical principles about the proper way for professionals to behave toward the public and toward each other. As psychology moved into its pro-fessional era, it needed to articulate its own ethical principles.

Ethical Standards of The American Psychological Association

Psychology's first code of ethics was published in 1953 (APA, 1953). A unique feature of this code was the way it was developed. True to their empirical foundations, psy-chologists submitted to an APA committee a large number of "critical incidents" in-volving some ethical dilemma that had occurred in a professional context. By analyz-ing this real-life material, the committee distilled a comprehensive ethical code, which was summarized in a set of general principles six years later (APA, 1959). After this version was used for three years, it was amended and formally adopted (APA, 1963). The ethical principles underwent several revisions through the 1960s, 1970s, and 1980s. The current version of the ethical principles, entitled *Ethical Principles of Psy-chologists and Code of Conduct*, became official on December 1, 1992 after six years of debate and revision. This document consists of a Preamble, six General Principles, and a large number of specific Ethical Standards. The Preamble and General Principles presented in Table 14.3 are not enforceable rules; they are statements of the aspira-tions of psychologists to attain their highest ideals, and they provide guidance to psychologists who are evaluating what would be ethically desirable behavior in cer-tain situations.

It is the Ethical Standards that establish enforceable rules of conduct for psycholo-gists. They apply to members of APA and may be used by other organizations, such as state boards of psychology and courts, to judge and sanction the behavior of a

TABLE 14.3   Preamble and General Principles in the APA Ethical Principles of Psychologists and Code of Conduct

Preamble

Psychologists work to develop a valid and reliable body of scienctific knowledge based on research. They may apply that knowledge to human behavior in a variety of contexts. In doing so, they perform many roles, such as researcher, educator, diagnostician, therapist, supervisor, consultant, administrator, social interventionist, and expert witness. Their goal is to broaden knowledge of behavior and, where appropriate, to apply it pragmatically to improve the condition of both the individual and society. Psychologists respect the central importance of freedom of inquiry and expression in research, teaching, and publication. They also strive to help the public in developing informed judgments and choices concerning human behavior. This Ethics Code provides a common set of values upon which psychologists build their professional and scientific work.

This Code is intended to provide both the general principles and the decision rules to cover most situations encountered by psychologists. It has as its primary goal the welfare and protection of the individuals and groups with whom psychologists work. It is the individual responsbility of each psychologist to aspire to the highest possible standards of conduct. Psychologists respect and protect human and civil rights, and do not knowingly participate in or condone discriminatory practices.

The development of a dynamic set of ethical standards for a psychologist's work-related conduct requires a personal commitment to a lifelong effort to act ethically; to encourage ethical behavior by students, supervisees, employees, and colleagues, as appropriate; and to consult with others, as needed, concerning ethical problems. Each psychologist supplements, but does not violate, the Ethics Code's values and rules on the basis of guidance drawn from personal values, culture, and experience.

General Principles

Principle A: Competence

Psychologists strive to maintain high standards of competence in their work. They recognize the boundaries of their particular competencies and the limitations of their expertise. They provide only those services and use only those techniques for which they are qualified by education, training, or experience. Psychologists are cognizant of the fact that the competencies required in serving, teaching, and/or studying groups of people vary with the distinctive characteristics of those groups. In those areas in which recognized professional standards do not yet exist, psychologists exercise careful judgment and take appropriate precautions to protect the welfare of those with whom they work. They maintain knowledge of relevant scienctific and professional information related to the services they render, and they recognize the need for ongoing education. Psychologists make appropriate use of scientific, professional, technical, and administrative resources.

Principle B: Integrity

Psychologists seek to promote integrity in the science, teaching, and practice of psychology. In these activities psychologists are honest, fair, and respectful of others. In describing or reporting their qualifications, services, products, fees, research, or teaching, they do not make statements that are false, misleading, or deceptive. Psychologistis strive to be aware of their own belief systems, values, needs, and limitations and the effect of these on their work. To the extent feasible, they attempt to clarify for relevant parties the roles they are performing and to function appropriately in

(continued)

TABLE 14.3   Preamble and General Principles in the APA Ethical Principles of Psychologists and Code of Conduct (*Continued*)

accordance with those roles. Psychologists avoid improper and potentially harmful dual relationships.

Principle C: Professional and Scientific Responsibility

Psychologists uphold professional standards of conduct, clarify their professional roles and obligations, accept appropriate responsibility for their behavior, and adapt their methods to the needs of different populations. Psychologists consult with, refer to, or cooperate with other professionals and institutions to the extent needed to serve the best interests of their patients, clients, or other recipients of their services. Psychologists' moral standards and conduct are personal matters to the same degree as is true for any other person, except as psychologists' conduct may compromise their professional responsibilities or reduce the public's trust in psychology and psychologists. Psychologists are concerned about the ethical compliance of their colleagues' scientific and professional conduct. When appropriate, they consult with colleagues in order to prevent or avoid unethical conduct.

Principle D: Respect for People's Rights and Dignity

Psychologists accord appropriate respect to the fundamental rights, dignity, and worth of all people. They respect the rights of individuals to privacy, confidentiality, self-determination, and autonomy, mindful that legal and other obligations may lead to inconsistency and conflict with the exercise of these rights. Psychologists are aware of cultural, individual, and role differences, including those due to age, gender, race, ethnicity, national origin, religion, sexual orientation, disability, language, and socioeconomic status. Psychologists try to

eliminate the effect on their work of biases based on those factors, and they do not knowingly participate in or condone unfair discriminatory practices.

Principle E: Concern for Others' Welfare

Psychologists seek to contribute to the welfare of those with whom they interact professionally. In their professional actions, psychologists weigh the welfare and rights of their patients or clients, students, supervisees, human research participants, and other affected persons, and the welfare of animal subjects of research. When conflicts occur among psychologists' obligations or concerns, they attempt to resolve these conflicts and to perform their roles in a responsible fashion that avoids or minimizes harm. Psychologists are sensitive to real and ascribed differences in power between themselves and others, and they do not exploit or mislead other people during or after professional relationships.

Principle F: Social Responsiblity

Psychologists are aware of their professional and scientific responsibilities to the community and the society in which they work and live. They apply and make public their knowledge of psychology in order to contribute to human welfare. Psychologists are concerned about and work to mitigate the causes of human suffering. When undertaking research, they strive to advance human welfare and the science of psychology. Psychologists try to avoid misuse of their work. Psychologists comply with the law and encourage the development of law and social policy that serve the interests of their patients and clients and the public. They are encouraged to contribute a portion of their professional time for little or no personal advantage.

psychologist, whether an APA member or not. These standards are organized under the following headings:

General Standards. Rules prohibiting discrimination, sexual and other types of harassment, and misuse of work products are included here, as are rules about maintaining competence, recognizing the limits of one's competence, proper recordkeeping, fees, and financial relationships.

Evaluation, Assessment, or Intervention. Rules pertaining to the use and interpretation of tests are listed here.

Advertising and Other Public Statements. Standards that control the way psychologists publicize their services and their professional credentials are presented under this category.

Therapy. Rules about the structuring, conduct, and termination of therapy are identified here. Specific standards prohibit psychologists from having sexual intimacies with current clients and from accepting persons as clients if they have had previous sexual intimacies with them. Furthermore, psychologists should not have sexual intimacies with former therapy clients for at least two years after the termination of therapy, and even then only if the psychologist can demonstrate that no exploitation of the client has occurred.

Privacy and Confidentiality. These rules cover psychologists' obligations to protect their clients' rights to confidentiality and privacy.

Teaching, Training, Supervision, Research and Publication. This section contains several ethical standards that control psychologists' conduct as they teach and supervise students and perform psychological research.

Forensic Activities. When performing forensic evaluations or other services, psychologists must comply with special rules about such services.

Resolving Ethical Issues. This last section contains standards about how psychologists are to resolve ethical questions or complaints.

APA's Casebook on Ethical Standards

In 1967, the APA published its first *Casebook on Ethical Standards of Psychologists*, which contained a restatement of the 1963 ethical principles as well as descriptions of actual cases drawn from discussions of the APA's Committee on Scientific and Professional Ethics and Conduct between 1959 and 1962. The *Casebook*, now in a revised edition (APA, 1987a) is intended as a guide to applying APA's ethical principles and standards in situations that psychologists face in their everyday professional activities. It is the source most psychologists study in order to educate themselves about the profession's ethical standards. Periodically, summaries of actual ethical cases and their resolutions are published in the *American Psychologist*, and several books on psychology ethics are now available (Bersoff, 1995; Canter et al., 1994; Keith-Spiegel & Koocher, 1985; Pope & Bouhoutsos, 1986).

A Case Example of an Ethical Dilemma.   As illustrated in the following case from the original *Casebook* APA, 1967, Case 6A, pp. 29–30), most clinicians believe in and are guided by APA's Ethical Principles. It deals with the difficult issue of a clinician protecting the welfare of a client while remaining sensitive to the social interests inherent in criminal conduct. Here are the facts:

A fully trained clinical psychologist in private practice was referred a patient for treatment because of a "near nervous breakdown." The background of the patient revealed many stressful and traumatic circumstances. After a few visits the patient admitted to having committed murder, something that weighed heavily on his conscience. The psychologist wrote to the [APA Ethics] committee for advice, pointing out that no ethical principle fitted the case exactly, the closest being one dealing with [*Tarasoff-*type] situations in which knowledge and intent are revealed but in which an act has not yet been committed. The psychologist wrote further as follows:

> I find myself in a very uncomfortable position of not knowing whether accepting him in a treatment basis would be in effect condoning his act. It is possible to understand the internal pressures and the dynamics which led him to behave as he did. Nor am I sure when he says that he thinks he ought to make public what he has done and bear punishment for it that it is my responsibility to encourage this action. Theoretically I know that I should help him to clarify his own thinking to the point where he can take the course of action which he deems most suitable. However, as he himself states, not only is he involved, but the public knowledge of his act would have to be borne by his wife and daughters. From a psychotherapeutic point of view there is no doubt that this man is in intense psychic pain and regardless of what course he decides to follow I suppose that I could justify seeing him in a professional role in an attempt to make him more comfortable. Yet I do not find it possible to completely encapsulate his act. There is no indication that he is suspected of the act or that he would ever do it again. I am afraid that my own ethical values and social conscience are being intruded, and in a sense I suppose I am asking whether, in this case, they should not be. I do hope that I have outlined the situation clearly enough that your committee can help me to ascertain my ethical responsibilities as a psychologist.

The Committee felt the client should be accepted in therapy without condoning his act, but that the decision in such a case rested with the psychologist involved. In reaching such a decision, it is necessary to take into account responsibilities to both the profession and the community, in addition to recognizing the legal considerations as well. Since the laws in the different states vary with respect to privileged communication, the Committee also recommended that the psychologist confronted with such a question consult an attorney about his legal obligations under the particular circumstances.

Dealing With Ethical Violations

As exemplified by the case just described, most psychologists take great pains to deal with complex and ethically ambiguous situations in accordance with the highest standards of professional conduct. On those rare occasions when, as fallible human beings, psychologists behave in a questionable manner, they are subject to censure by local, state, and national organizations whose task it is to deal with violations of ethical practice.

Once a complaint of unethical behavior is brought against an APA member and the appropriate committee has decided that the conduct in question was in fact unethical, the question of punishment must be decided. The most severe APA sanction is to dismiss the offender from the association and to inform the membership of this action. This penalty is embarrassing for most transgressors, humiliating for a few, but seldom devastating for any. Unethical conduct can also cause psychologists to be threatened with the loss of their professional license by the board of psychology in the state where they practice.

The largest number of ethical violations involve (1) sexual intimacy between a therapist and a client, (2) violations of state or federal laws (e.g., fraudulent billing practices), and (3) breaches of confidentiality. In addition to clear-cut violations, a large number of questionable behaviors often occur that raise possible ethical problems. One survey of 1,319 members of APA asked them to describe any ethical dilemmas they or a colleague had recently encountered (Pope & Vetter, 1992). A total of 679 psychologists returned the questionnaire and indicated the following three areas to be the most ethically troubling for them:

1. *Confidentiality.* Eighteen percent of the troubling incidents involved problems of confidentiality. Reporting suspected child abuse and warning victims about the potential violence of a client were common examples. Here is a typical response:

   > One girl underwent an abortion without the knowledge of her foster parents. . . . I fully evaluated her view of the adults' inability to be supportive and agreed but worried about our relationship being damaged if I was discovered to know about the pregnancy and her action (Pope & Vetter, 1992, p. 599).

2. *Dual or conflictual relationships with clients.* Seventeen percent of the incidents involved difficulties in maintaining the proper boundaries around professional relationships. Here is an example:

   > I was conducting therapy with a child and soon became aware that there was a mutual attraction between myself and the child's mother. The strategies I had used and my rapport with the child had been positive. Nonetheless, I felt it necessary to refer to avoid a dual relationship (at the cost of the gain that had been made) (Pope & Vetter, 1992, p. 400).

3. *Trouble collecting payments for services and conflicts with insurance carriers.* Fourteen percent of the incidents focused on difficulties collecting fees or providing adequate treatment under insurance policy limitations. The following example illustrates this type of problem:

   > A 7 year old boy was severely sexually abused and severely depressed. I evaluated the case and recommended 6 months treatment. My recommendation was evaluated by a managed health care agency and approved for 10 sessions by a nonprofessional in spite of the fact that there is no known treatment program that can be performed in 10 sessions on a 7 year old that has demonstrated efficacy (Pope & Vetter, 1992, p. 401).

Other Ethical Standards

Because of increasing public concern, new governmental research regulations, and outrage about the alleged mistreatment of animals in some laboratories, APA has found it necessary to supplement its ethical standards with a detailed set of guidelines covering psychologists' research with animals, called the *Guidelines for Ethical Conduct in the Care and Use of Animals* (APA, 1992).

Clinical psychologists are also responsible for knowing about other standards that govern their research and delivery of psychological services. The major sources for these various standards are *Ethical Principles in the Conduct of Research with Human Participants* (APA, 1982), *General Guidelines for Providers of Psychological Services* (APA, 1987b), *Specialty Guidelines for the Delivery of Services by Clinical Psychologists* (APA, 1981), *Standards for Educational and Psychological Testing* (APA, 1985), *Guidelines for Providers of Psychological Services to Ethnic, Linguistic, and Culturally Diverse Populations* (APA, 1993), and the *Publication Manual of the American Psychological Association* (APA, 1994).

PROFESSIONAL INDEPENDENCE

Clinical psychologists must consult and collaborate with other professionals in many aspects of clinical practice. They often work closely with educators, attorneys, ministers, social workers, nurses, physicians, and other psychologists. For the most part, psychology's interprofessional relationships are healthy, profitable, and characterized by good will. The most obvious sign of this harmony is the frequency of referrals made across groups. A teacher with a child whose classroom misbehavior is related to a serious emotional problem is likely to suggest that the family consult a psychologist. Similarly, when psychologists encounter clients who are in legal trouble, they urge such clients to hire an attorney.

Psychologists *have* had considerable friction with physicians, particularly psychiatrists. In fact, clinical psychology's most persistent interprofessional problem has been its wary, often stormy, relationships with the medical profession. Saul Garfield (1965) observed that as early as 1917, psychiatrists were critical of psychologists, particularly "those who have termed themselves 'clinical psychologists'" and work in "so-called 'psychological clinics'" and provide "so-called expert testimony." It is no wonder, then, that clinical psychology and psychiatry have waged several battles. The first involved the independent practice of psychotherapy by psychologists. Later, the two fields argued over whether psychologists should have privileges to practice independently in hospitals (*CAPP v. Rank*[15]). More recently, the squabble has concentrated on psychologists' eligibility for reimbursement under an increasing array of public, private, and prepaid mental health plans. Although these controversies are related, we will look at

---

[15]CAPP v. Rank, 51 Cal. 3d, 793 P.Sd (1990).

two of them—the independent practice of psychotherapy and reimbursement issues—in separate sections that clarify the development of each.

Independent Practice of Psychotherapy

As long as psychologists confined themselves to research, consultation, and testing, physicians did not interfere. Psychologists, by the same token, found no problem with the fact that physicians were the authority on physical disorders or organic treatments such as medication, electroconvulsive therapy, and surgery. Disagreement, when it came, centered on psychotherapy, which both professions (along with several others) offered to the public.

When psychologists began to engage in the independent practice of psychotherapy, psychiatrists objected and insisted that a psychotherapist must be either a physician or under the supervision of a physician. The psychiatrists' rationale is that physicians are the experts on the functioning of the *whole person* and that with many types of abnormal behaviors it is essential that the therapist differentiate mental and physical aspects of the disorder and treat both aspects thoroughly. For their part, psychologists contend that the vast majority of mental disorders involve psychological and social processes rather than physical ones, and that they are better trained about these processes than physicians are. In addition, when physical causes and/or medical treatments are indicated, psychologists are aware of their ethical obligations to refer such clients to physicians. Finally, psychologists point out that many of the most influential therapists over the years have been nonphysicians (e.g., Anna Freud, Carl Rogers, Erich Fromm, Erik Erickson).

Ironically, psychologists themselves were once opposed to practicing psychotherapy independently (Humphreys, 1996). In 1949, the APA discouraged the practice of psychotherapy by psychologists who were not working in collaboration with psychiatrists (Goldenberg, 1973). Psychologists reconsidered their position on the independent practice of psychotherapy (APA, 1958), but psychiatrists did not. In fact, the American Medical Association (AMA, 1954) adopted an official policy that psychotherapy was a medical procedure to be performed only by medically trained personnel. The strategy of the AMA in this battle was to oppose certification and licensure of psychologists. This strategy was unsuccessful, a fact for which most clinical psychologists are grateful. By the end of the 1950s, psychology had ended psychiatry's dominance over psychotherapy, and psychologists now provide more office-based mental health care than do psychiatrists (McGuire, 1989).

Relations between psychologists and psychiatrists improved throughout the 1970s and early 1980s. Psychiatrists came to accept psychologists as professionals and were less inclined to treat them with the condescension of earlier days. In turn, psychologists shed some of their defensive armor and were less prone to feel that they constantly must guard against psychiatrists. Both fields were strengthened by the growing number of well-qualified persons who entered the two professions.

In the 1990s, relationships between psychologists and psychiatrists have again become strained. This time the tensions are primarily economic, although they also involve questions about whether psychologists should continue to be excluded from offering professional services—primarily the prescription of psychoactive medications—historically reserved for physicians. These issues are made more urgent by changes occurring in the way health care is funded in the United States.

The Economics of Mental Health Care

Having won the battles over licensure and recognition of psychology as an independent profession in the 1970s and 1980s, clinicians turned to struggles involving the economic aspects of mental health care. The initial focus of these struggles was whether psychologists should be eligible for reimbursement for their services by insurance companies. Physicians opposed psychologists' inclusion, claiming that it would be too costly to third-party payers and consumers. Physicians also argued that if psychologists were to be included, their services should be reimbursed *only* when they were treating clients referred and supervised by physicians. As a result, many major health insurance companies (such as Blue Cross/Blue Shield), run by and for physicians, excluded psychologists from third-party payments except when billing under a physician's supervision.

Of course, psychologists found this arrangement intolerable for a profession that aspired to full autonomy. As a result, in the late-1960s and early-1970s psychologists began lobbying state legislatures to pass *freedom-of-choice* laws, which mandate that services rendered by qualified mental health professionals licensed to practice in a given state shall be reimbursed by insurance plans covering such services regardless of whether the provider is a physician. Physicians fought hard against such legislation, using the term *medical psychotherapy* to refer to the only services they believed should be reimbursable. This term was condemned by psychology as a political maneuver intended to guarantee that physicians would be the only professionals identified as appropriate providers of psychotherapy.

Psychologists argued that there is nothing "medical" about psychotherapy. They also presented data to counter claims that including them as providers or even including coverage of mental disorders treated by any provider would be too costly for third-party payers. For example, one study showed that a *single session of psychotherapy* reduced subsequent use of medical resources by 60% among the recipients, and that there was about a 75% reduction in medical utilizations by patients receiving two to eight sessions of psychotherapy (Cummings, 1977; see also Olbrisch, 1977). Psychologists contended that, far from being economically disadvantageous, reimbursing for psychotherapy can be cost effective because it saves money that would otherwise be spent for more expensive medical services. This reduction, known as *medical offset* has been replicated in larger studies (e.g., Holder & Blose, 1987) and has become a rallying point for clinical psychologists who claim that psychotherapy is a highly effective and efficient addition to the health care system (Fraser, 1996; Groth-Marnat & Edkins, 1996).

Over the years psychologists have succeeded in having freedom-of-choice laws enacted in most U.S. states. By 1983, forty states covering 90% of the U.S. population had passed legislation that provided free choice of licensed psychologists as reimbursable providers of mental health services (Lambert, 1985). Additional legislation at the federal level promoted recognition of psychologists as independent clinicians. The

Rehabilitation Act of 1973 (PL 93-112) provided parity for psychologists with physicians in both assessment and treatment services. Services provided by clinical psychologists are reimbursable under both the Federal Employee Health Benefits Act (PL 93-363) and the Federal Work Injuries Compensation Program (PL 94-212). Licensed psychologists are also recognized as *independent providers* by CHAMPUS (The Civilian Health and Medical Program of the Uniformed Services), a federal program covering several million beneficiaries in all fifty states and the District of Columbia.

For three decades, psychologists have fought for legislative changes that would make it possible for them to be directly reimbursed for their services under Medicaid (a shared federal/state program for the medically needy) and Medicare (a federal program for elderly and disabled clients). Physicians have strenuously lobbied against such amendments, repeating the refrain that including psychologists would be too costly and that psychologists are not qualified to diagnose and treat many mental disorders without the supervision of a physician.

However, the tide has turned at last. With respect to Medicare, the federal program that provides health care funds for more than 30 million aged and 3 million disabled recipients, an amendment allowing psychologists to be included and reimbursed as direct Medicare providers was signed into law in 1989 by President George Bush. Psychologists have been less successful in obtaining coverage for their services under Medicaid (DeLeon et al., 1992). This program, established by Congress in the 1960s to help the states supply health care to the poor and needy, grew dramatically in the last decade; federal expenditures for Medicaid increased from $14 billion to $41 billion. The individual states are free to determine their own criteria for recipient eligibility and to control which services will be covered at what cost. As a result, states that have been concerned about excessive use of mental health services have limited the kinds of treatment they will reimburse. As of 1989, only half the states reimbursed psychologists for their services under Medicaid (DeLeon et al., 1992). During the 1990s, the states began experimenting with new ways of delivering mental health services to Medicaid recipients. One popular approach is known as the *carve out*, in which a state creates a separate organization that is responsible for "carving out," delivering, and integrating all the mental health services to which Medicaid recipients are entitled. These carve out systems are usually designed according to managed care principles (discussed below) and typically make extensive use of clinical psychologists.

Even though a state or the federal government passes a freedom-of-choice law, some insurance companies will ignore it unless forced to comply. For example, it took nearly four years of litigation to force Blue Cross/Blue Shield of Virginia to comply with that state's freedom-of-choice law (Resnick, 1985). A related area of litigation lies in suits challenging the practice of denying hospital staff privileges to nonphysicians. California, North Carolina, Washington, D.C., Georgia, and several other states have passed laws allowing hospital privileges for psychologists, but physician-based attacks on California's law required psychologists to go to court to protect the original law.

The Effects of Changing Health Care Systems.   As noted in Chapter 1, the delivery, financing, and organization of health care—including mental health care—has changed at an unprecedented rate in the 1990s. Several forces have given rise to these changes. First, the costs of health care have skyrocketed and now account for almost 15% of the U.S. gross national product (Frank, 1993). These increases have led to several proposals for national health reform, but the most recent attempts, by the 102nd Congress (1993–1994), to make sweeping reforms in public financing of health care led to few substantial changes. As a result, health care reform has been taken up by the states and by private businesses who see the reform movement as an opportunity for expanded profits. Insurance companies have invented new reimbursement plans and various self-insurance packages to curtail the costs and extent of health-care coverage. Many new forms of health insurance put a cap on how much reimbursement is allowed for such services.

With these changes have come numerous challenges to the practice of clinical psychology. In particular, psychologists are being forced to recognize that (1) the nature, quality, and availability of health care is determined by health care economics, and (2) changes in health care financing can nullify all the victories psychologists won in freedom-of-choice legislation battles. If clinical psychology is to remain an active player in the health care market, clinicians have to be prepared to adjust to the financing changes already in place, and those likely to come in the near future (Humphreys, 1996).

There is continuing debate over how to reform the organization and financing of the U.S. health care system so as to provide basic health care for all citizens while controlling health care costs. The outcome of this debate will have a tremendous impact on mental health services. The two questions of greatest interest to clinical psychologists are what mental health services will be covered in the basic package of guaranteed care and whether psychologists delivering these services will be reimbursed as independent professionals. Whatever system ultimately appears, containing costs and easing people's access to care will be primary goals. Accordingly, clinical psychologists will need to become increasingly able to integrate their *mental* health services into general health care approaches (DeSantis & Walker, 1991; Johnstone et al., 1995) involving systems similar to those we describe next.

Managed Care Systems. The latest trend in health care reform is known as managed care. A *managed care* system develops methods of allocating health services to a group of people in order to provide the most appropriate care while still containing the overall cost of these services. Managed care can be organized in several different ways, including, for example, as employee assistance programs (EAPs), health maintenance organizations (HMOs), preferred provider organizations (PPOs), integrated delivery systems (IDSs), and independent practice associations (IPAs). In general, these organizations provide specific packages of health care services to subscribers for a fixed, pre-paid price. This arrangement contrasts with more traditional systems in which providers could be reimbursed on a fee-for-service basis for whatever kinds of health care they chose to offer. As noted in Chapter 1, these new plans derive more profits if they can keep subscribers healthy, and thus minimize their utilization of services (Tulkin & Frank, 1985).

Mental health care, too, is increasingly being offered in the context of one of these *managed behavioral health care* plans; more than a third of U.S. citizens receive their mental health coverage in this way (Rosenberg, 1996), and it is estimated that by the year 2000, this figure will rise to 65% (Johnstone et al., 1995).

The various formats seen in managed care organizations have evolved in three stages (Miller, 1995). Initially, managed care relied on organizing health care providers into networks such as HMOs or PPOs that offered reduced fees to consumers who agreed to get their health services only from providers who are members of the network. In the second stage, *utilization review* was added. This is a system in which case managers working for the network review each patient's case, determine how much treatment is necessary, and then authorize payment for only that amount of treatment. In other words, the case manager, rather than the mental health professional, determines the clinical needs and appropriate level of care for clients, usually with an eye toward minimizing costs and maximizing profits for the organization. The third stage in the development of managed care systems has seen the increasing use of plans designed to shift financial risks to the care providers, thereby creating an incentive for them to limit the care they give in order to increase profits.

An increasingly popular way of shifting financial risks in this way is through *capitation* systems. Here is how a simple capitation system might work: The Acme Insurance Company agrees to pay a mental health corporation $3.00 per month for every subscriber to its Positive Mental Health Plan. This arrangement limits the insurance company's financial risk by putting a "cap" on its costs. If the Positive Mental Health Plan enrolls 60,000 members, Acme pays it $180,000 every month from the premiums Acme collects from its customers. Obviously, the fewer treatment sessions Positive Plan clients receive from therapists working for the Plan, the more profit it will make. The more clients that must be treated, or the longer their treatments last, the smaller the profit to Positive.

As part of its utilization review system, a case manager working for Positive will review each client's problem, the therapist's treatment plan, and the therapy progress notes. The case manager, who more than likely is *not* a mental health professional, will then determine whether Positive will pay for the treatment and, if so, for how many sessions, and which specific types of therapy will be reimbursed. Generally, managed care reviewers discourage comprehensive clinical assessments and insight-oriented, longer term therapies in favor of medications and short-term therapies. Thus, a case manager may decide, for example, that a depressed client can receive no more than eight sessions of psychotherapy, even if the therapist believes that the client's problems require more extensive treatment.

As you might imagine, the advent of managed care has caused great concern among mental health professionals. Some of their most serious criticisms are that managed care systems (1) are more interested in cutting costs and raising profits than in assuring excellent heath care, (2) result in many clients receiving too little treatment, (3) threaten the confidentiality of therapy by requiring that too much information about clients be included in the utilization review, (4) allow untrained personnel to conduct the utilization reviews, (5) collect inadequate data on the outcomes of their treatments, and (6) exclude from the system clients who have pre-existing disorders.

So while most clinicians welcome incentives that encourage their use of the most effective and efficient treatments available (Patricelli & Lee, 1996), they oppose incentives that put profits before quality of treatment and that are determined by case managers who know very little about the nature and treatment of mental disorders. Indeed, the major concern about managed care is that it usually focuses on management of costs, not quality health care. If cost containment is promoted over treatment quality, if inappropriate limits are set on the duration of psychotherapy, and if case managers intrude too often into the confidentiality of therapy, managed mental-health care systems will ultimately fail to bring about the cost-effective treatment they promise.

How is the shift toward managed care affecting the practice of clinical psychology? For one thing, increasing numbers of clinicians are abandoning their private or group practices and joining the staffs of HMOs or PPOs. They are also creating their own health care organizations and aggressively marketing their services to businesses and industries. A larger question concerns the effects of managed care on the quality of clinical services. Will quality suffer under profit-driven managed care plans, or will mental health services become more cost effective and responsive to consumer needs? As heated debate over this question continues (Barlow, 1996; Cantor, 1996; Cool, 1996; Miller, 1996)[16], the APA has responded to the managed care environment by developing an aggressive marketing strategy aimed at:

1. Educating consumers and employers about several perceived dangers and shortcomings of most managed care systems, including emphases on cost containment rather than improved service, evaluations of services by nonprofessional reviewers, inappropriate limits on the amount of allowable treatment, and violations of client confidentiality rights.

2. Educating consumers and employers about the value of psychology in any comprehensive health care system. This effort involves extensive advertising and other public relations activities focusing on psychology's effectiveness in treating the problems of children, the elderly, the seriously mentally ill, and substance abusers.

3. Helping psychologists diversify their services so they can expand their practice. These specialty training programs are aimed at areas such as health psychology, sports psychology, drug and alcohol abuse, and severe mental disorders.

This campaign has been welcomed by many practitioners as politically necessary if clinical psychology is to ensure its professional identity and economic survival. However, aggressive marketing runs the risk of making claims for psychology that go beyond available scientific data (Sechrest, 1992). The skeptical attitude that underlies the scientist's insistence on empirical proof is difficult to maintain in the face of pressures to promise effective interventions for every type of social problem and mental disorder. In the long run, the profession of clinical psychology will prosper most if it makes only those claims that are clearly tied to a scientific base (Garfield, 1992; Sechrest, 1992).

---

[16]For a more complete discussion of the range of opinions that clinical psychologists hold about managed mental health care, see a special section on managed care in the February, 1991 and August, 1996 issues of the journal *Professional Psychology: Research and Practice*. See also the March 1993 issue of the *American Psychologist*.

The Costs of Protecting Professional Independence

It is almost inevitable that the legal struggles and political combat over issues of professional independence will have negative effects on psychology in general, and clinical psychology in particular. For one thing, litigation is very expensive for the APA, the state psychological associations, or the other organizations of psychologists that bear most of the costs[17]. Further, money spent on litigation cannot be spent for other activities (e.g., sponsorship of research or prevention programs) that might be of greater interest to academic or nonclinical psychologists, who are justifiably concerned that clinicians will bankrupt psychological associations by expending their resources in court cases. Clinicians need to take seriously the questions that nonclinical psychologists raise about the best use of organized psychology's limited resources.

Another risk of litigation is that, as previously described in relation to psychology's high-profile marketing strategy, psychologists may be tempted to exaggerate their accomplishments and claims for success, particularly in psychotherapy. The profession will not be well served by promising more than it can deliver, especially when consumers must bear whatever additional costs expanding health care coverage might bring. Finally, there are disadvantages in maintaining an adversarial stance toward psychiatry. As one observer put it, "today's adversaries are tomorrow's allies" (Resnick, 1985, p. 983). Psychology and psychiatry have mutual interests in several areas and these interests will be jeopardized by continued interprofessional sparring. For example, some forms of managed care might omit mental health services, an exclusion that both psychology and psychiatry should oppose. Members of both professions may find that the most serious threats to their status as mental health care providers come not from each other, but from outside forces and that countering these threats requires a cooperative and unified response.

PERILS OF PROFESSIONALISM

Have the first fifty years of clinical psychology's professional era made it a better profession, or have they simply made it more of a guild that employs meaningless membership criteria? Has clinical psychology become a better profession by endorsing standards of training, competence, and service, or is it merely a more closed profession? We consider such questions in these final pages.

The ultimate justification for the professionalization of any discipline is that the public will benefit from the standards that govern the profession. Of course these restrictions also benefit members of the profession because they control the profession's population and thus reduce competition. There is little objection to this latter function when it is a by-product of protecting the public from unqualified

---

[17]Currently, for example, a group of New Jersey practitioners and the New Jersey Psychological Association are suing a behavioral health care company to regain clinician control over treatment decisions (Sleek, 1997).

practitioners. The problem arises when the priorities of a profession are reversed, so that the promotion of its members' interests takes precedence over its obligations to the public.

As early as 1951, Fillmore Sanford, then executive secretary of the APA, warned about the perils of professionalization. In an effort to call psychology's attention to its obligations as a profession, Sanford proposed sixteen principles that should be considered "the criteria of a good profession" (Sanford, 1951, p. 667; see Table 14.4). He hoped that these criteria would guide the development of psychology as a socially useful and responsive profession.

Sanford's statement remains timely. Although it was written as an idealistic vision of what psychology should strive for, it can be used today as a yardstick for measuring what psychology has become. The first two criteria deal with the need for psychologists to adjust to social needs and changes. At several points we have emphasized that

Table 14.4   Fillmore Sanford's Criteria for a Good Profession

1. A good profession is motivated by a sense of social responsibility.

2. A good profession is sufficiently perceptive of its place in society to guide its practices and policies so they conform to the best and changing interests of that society.

3. A good profession is continually on guard lest it represent itself as able to render services that are beyond its demonstrable competence.

4. A good profession continually seeks to find its unique pattern of competence and concentrates its efforts on the rendering of the unique service based on its pattern of competencies.

5. A good profession devotes relatively little of its energy to "guild" functions, to the building of its own in-group strength, and relatively much of its energy to the serving of its social function.

6. A good profession engages in rational and non-invidious relations with other professions having related competencies and common purposes.

7. A good profession devotes a proportion of its energies to the discovery of new knowledge.

8. A good profession develops channels of communication between the discoverers of knowledge and the appliers of knowledge.

9. A good profession does not relegate its discoverers of knowledge to positions of second-rate status.

10. A good profession is free of nonfunctional entrance requirements.

11. A good profession provides preparatory training which is validly related to the ultimate function of the members of the profession.

12. A good profession is one in which the material benefits accruing to its members are proportional to social contributions.

13. A good profession is one whose members are socially and financially accessible to the public.

14. A good profession has a code of ethics designed primarily to protect the client and only secondarily to protect the members of the profession.

15. A good profession facilitates the continuing education and training of all its members.

16. A good profession is continually concerned with the validity of its techniques and procedures.

clinical psychology has responded to the social, political, and economic events surrounding it. The growth of the profession itself was a reaction to social upheaval and virtually unprecedented human needs. In a similar fashion, the evolution of such disparate psychological activities as assessment, psychotherapy, community psychology, and behavior modification was rooted in the fact that psychology has always been well tuned to the current *zeitgeist*.

Several criteria (3, 4, 13, and 14) are concerned with professional ethics. Psychologists are justifiably proud of their code of ethics because it remains the only set of professional standards developed through explicitly empirical procedures. This pride has not fostered complacency, however, and the code continues to be revised and supplemented with other statements about ethics in specific areas.

Three criteria (10, 11, and 15) relate to professional training. Clinical psychology is committed to training programs that are appropriate for the roles clinicians are asked to fill. The Boulder model of training is still valued, but in the context of experimentation with other systems of training intended to prepare psychologists who will deliver clinical services.

The sixth of Sanford's criteria concerns interprofessional relationships. This issue, especially the relationship between clinical psychologists and psychiatrists, continues to be the focus of much attention. An adequate response to our sometimes troubled relations with psychiatry requires a balancing act. Clinicians must search for new opportunities to collaborate and cooperate with all professions, but at the same time, psychology must also be a free profession, unwilling to enter into a Faustian pact where the goodwill of the medical profession is purchased with acquiescence to its domination of psychology.

The largest number of Sanford's criteria discuss the priorities of the profession, the essential contributions it should make to the public. Like many psychologists before and after him, Sanford affirmed research and advancement of new knowledge as psychology's primary activity. The creation of basic knowledge is the one function that separates the professional from the technician, who applies methods based on existing knowledge. This conclusion seems especially important for a relatively new profession like clinical psychology, where "the fewer its techniques of demonstrable utility, the more of its resources it should devote to research" (Sanford, 1951, p. 669).

THE FUTURE OF CLINICAL PSYCHOLOGY

When authors reach the end of their books, they often assume the role of prophets who cast an eye toward the future and predict the development of their fields. We, too, cannot resist this temptation. Our outlook for the future of clinical psychology emphasizes the following expectations:

1. The number of clinicians will continue to increase, although at a slower pace than in the past. Clinical psychology has had a growth spurt over the past few decades. Whether one considers the number of training programs established, the number of students graduated, or the number of psychologists licensed to

practice, the field has expanded enormously. Some analysts suggest that the number of clinical psychologists (one for every 100,000 persons) already exceeds national needs and predict economic hard times for clinicians about to start their careers (Robiner, 1991). Others disagree, arguing that such dire predictions neglect the need for researchers and prevention-oriented psychologists as opposed to practitioners offering traditional clinical services (Pion, 1991; Schneider, 1991). Still others respond that the knowledge base about professional supply and consumer demand is currently inadequate for answering questions about how many clinical psychologists are needed (VandenBos, DeLeon, & Belar, 1991).

Although we believe the rate of increase in the production of clinical psychologists will slow over the next decade, the number of clinicians available is not as important an issue as two others—for what roles will clinicians be trained and how good will their training be?

Several areas will continue as "growth stocks" for clinicians. As described in Chapters 11 and 12, health psychology, behavioral medicine, and clinical neuropsychology should remain important specialty areas because of the contributions psychologists can make to treatment and the promotion of physical health (Johnstone et al., 1995). Although these activities pose exciting opportunities for psychologists, we must be realistic in our claims of success so as not to promise more than our knowledge allows us to deliver. Another burgeoning specialty area, described in Chapter 13, is forensic psychology. Psychologists will continue to be consulted on a range of topics relevant to the legal system (Sales & Shuman, 1996; Wrightsman, Nietzel, & Fortune, 1998). Demand for psychologists' expertise in litigation and general mental health law is growing dramatically. Although this demand is gratifying and potentially lucrative, psychologists must be careful not to testify on matters that exceed their competence and not to exaggerate the scientific support for the conclusions they report.

A third specialty area in which clinical psychologists' services will be in increasing demand is clinical child psychology. Assessment and treatment of childhood disorders have advanced remarkably in the past decade, as has basic research on child development and the etiology of child psychopathology. As we discussed in Chapter 10, this greater attention to children has generated much knowledge about their unique qualities and problems and has led to an emphasis on early interventions designed to prevent emotional and academic problems (Zigler, Taussig, & Black, 1992). Recently, these efforts increasingly include programs for the prevention of drug and alcohol abuse among children and adolescents.

2. Clinical psychology will take on a more notable consumer orientation. This trend is apparent in the growing emphasis on professional accountability to clients and in the expectation that psychologists must develop their own standards as health service providers. As a result of these developments, clinicians will need to better evaluate both the effectiveness of their interventions and the financial costs of producing certain outcomes (Banta & Saxe, 1983; Newman & Tejeda, 1996). Increasingly, psychologists will be expected to prove that their services lead to

substantial improvements in clients' health and functioning. The psychologist as researcher will always have a place in the future.

3. The growing emphasis on service evaluation will be accompanied by abandonment of a "brand name" approach to psychotherapy and a shift toward offering treatments that have been empirically validated as effective. As research indicates the effectiveness of behavior-change techniques, regardless of their theoretical origins, clinicians may find little advantage in identifying themselves as behaviorists, gestaltists, or analysts.

4. Controversy will continue over the question of how clinical psychologists should be trained. Currently, there is enthusiasm for preparing clinicians to work with specialty problems and/or groups such as the chronically mentally ill, children and youth, rural populations, substance abusers, and older patients. NIMH has directed training grant funds toward these "underserved groups," and they will probably remain a focus of training for some clinical programs in the future.

   As for more general training trends, we anticipate a widening gap between Boulder model programs that stress training in research methods and psychology's scientific traditions and more professionally oriented programs that concentrate on developing practitioner skills. This gap may ultimately be accompanied by the development of alternative or competing systems of accreditation—one for clinical scientist programs and one for professional practitioner programs. Programs of all types should expect to face rising expectations that their students are trained in interventions that enjoy the highest levels of empirically validated effectiveness (Crits-Christoph, et al. 1995).

   Other training proposals include lengthening clinical internships from one year to two years (Belar et al., 1989), and developing a formal system of postdoctoral education that would emphasize training in specialty skills (Graham & Fox, 1991).

5. Psychologists will continue to push for the freedom of their profession. Not only will organized psychology intensify its political efforts for inclusion in all types of health-care plans, but individual psychologists will strive to keep abreast of the most modern clinical techniques so that they can continue to offer top-quality services.

   The most controversial of these efforts will be the one aimed at enabling psychologists to prescribe psychoactive medication for their clients. The idea that, like psychiatrists, psychologists should have *prescription privileges* emerged in the mid-1980s and was based on two main arguments: (1) it is in clients' interests that psychologists be able to offer a full range of treatment alternatives; and (2) it worked out well when optometrists, podiatrists, physician assistants, dentists, nurses, and other nonphysician groups acquired prescription privileges (Cullen & Newman, 1997).

   For some time now, a few psychologists employed by the federal government have been authorized to prescribe drugs—under the supervision of a physician—aboard Navy ships and in the Indian Health Service. The Department of Defense has also explored the possibility that psychologists might be prepared to prescribe psychotropic medications more widely. In 1991, it established a Psychopharmacology Demonstration Project (PDP) at the Uniformed Services Hospital of the Health Sciences and Walter Reed Army Medical Center to train and supervise a small number of clinical psychologists in the prescribing of psychotropic medications (DeLeon, Fox, & Graham, 1991). Initially structured as a three-year program, the curriculum eventually consisted of one year of didactic work and one year of clinical practicum (Sammons & Brown, 1997). As of June, 1996, seven psychologists had graduated from the program, but it was met by fierce opposition from organized psychiatry and physicians in general (Bell, Digman, & McKenna, 1995). Controversy over the PDP led Congress to order the General Accounting Office to perform a cost-benefit analysis of the program. The recently released results of that study raised questions about the value of and need for the PDP, leaving its future in doubt. As of 1997, no new students were being enrolled in the program.

Psychology itself remains divided over the question of prescription privileges for its practitioners. Advocates see it as a necessary and socially responsible step (DeLeon et al., 1991), and, in 1996, the American Psychological Association's Council of Representatives officially endorsed the pursuit of prescriptive authority for psychologists. The Council also recommended a draft of model legislation to be introduced in states seeking authorization of psychologist prescribers and a model postdoctoral curriculum (covering neurosciences, pharmacology, physiology, physical and laboratory assessments, and clinical pharmacotherapeutics) to be used in training prescribers (Cullen & Newman, 1997).

Opponents of prescription privileges for psychologists (DeNelsky, 1996; Hayes & Heiby, 1996; May & Belsky, 1992) question the value of its long-term impact, either for clinical psychology or for the clients it serves. They are concerned that prescription authority would detract from the nonmedical identity and services that psychology has traditionally offered to the public. Psychologist educators also remain skeptical about prescription privileges, largely because they fear it would unduly lengthen training time, displace other important subject matter in the traditional clinical psychology curriculum, and be too expensive (Evans & Murphy, 1997).

The pros and cons of prescription privileges for psychologists are listed in Table 14.5. Although the debate is far from resolved, it does appear that the pro-prescription contingent is gaining support. Surveys indicate that psychologists' attitudes toward prescription privileges have become more favorable recently, and that the more they learn about the prescription privilege, the more they tend to endorse it (Pimental et al., 1997). A growing number of state psychological associations are working to secure prescription privilege legislation, and, while none of the laws proposed so far in Hawaii, Missouri and California have been passed, psychologists in several other states are also preparing bills for their legislatures to consider and are developing curricula to train psychologists in prescribing medication (Cullen & Newman, 1997).

TABLE 14.5   Should Psychologists Be Trained to Prescribe Psychoactive Medication?

Clinical psychologists have not reached a consensus on the question of whether they should have prescription privileges. Although many psychologists remain ambivalent (Jarrett & Fairbank, 1987), surveys suggest a shift toward a more favorable opinion (Frederick/Schneiders, 1990). Here are the major arguments for and against prescription privileges for psychologists.

Arguments For	Arguments Against
1. Helps provide a fuller range of mental health services to underserved groups (e.g., elderly, chronically mentally ill, rural populations).	1. Produces an increase in malpractice insurance rates.
2. Compensates for the shortage of physicians in many areas.	2. Increases the length and expense involved in training clinical psychologists.
3. Allows psychologists to use a technique that is necessary for effective treatment of some clinical problems.	3. Increases the medicalization of problems that are primarily economic, social, and/or psychological in nature.
4. Is a logical extension of psychologists' increasing interest in the reciprocal influence of psychological and physiological factors.	4. Erodes psychologists' traditional expertise in the area of assessment and research.
5. Ensures the economic survivability and professional autonomy of psychology.	5. Pulls psychology away from its distinctive emphasis as the science of human behavior.

Of course, none of these forecasts tells us what clinical psychology should strive for and what it should avoid. For this wisdom we continue to rely on the ideas of a clinical psychologist who gave the question a career's worth of serious attention:

> Clinical psychology, after a long period spent as part of an academic discipline, is in the early stages of becoming a profession. It is going through the natural disturbances and difficulties which attend a growth process of this kind. However, if it selects its students carefully, for personality as well as intellect; if it trains thoroughly, in spirit as well as letter; if it trains broadly, recognizing that "specialists" . . . are not clinical psychologists; if it remains flexible about its training and encourages experimentation; if it does not become overwhelmed by immediate needs at the cost of important, remoter goals; if it maintains its contact with its scientific background, remaining aware of the importance of theory as well as practice; if it remains modest in the face of the complexity of its problems, rather than becoming pretentious—in other words, if it finds good people and gives them good training—these disturbances and difficulties need not be of serious concern. Its future, both for itself as a profession and for society in the contribution it can make, is then assured. Fortunately, there are many reasons for believing that these are the prevailing aspirations in clinical psychology. (Shakow, 1948, p. 246)

These comments were written by David Shakow in 1948. We believe that the aspirations Shakow expressed can be realized by clinical psychology only if, in the future, it firmly establishes itself, in Stanley Schneider's (1991) eloquent phrase, as "a profession based on science that is informed by practice." We hope this book plays a role in moving some of you to join in the creation of that future.

PROFESSIONAL ISSUES AT WORK

Q.: How is your daily work affected by issues such as professional ethics, clinical training models, professional regulation (licensing), right-to-treatment laws, informed consent rules, privileged communication, independent practice status for psychologists, prescription privileges, managed care and other financial aspects of clinical psychology, and trends toward specialization?

DR. SANDY D'ANGELO: Perhaps the ethical principles that come to the fore most frequently when working in a medical center are informed consent and confidentiality. Informed consent is a requisite for both treatment and research; when working with children, psychologists must decide in what way to provide children with information and to document the child's consent to participate in research or treatment. When working with children, issues of confidentiality can often be thorny: With whom can information be shared? Who should have access to information? Who is a part of the treatment team? To what extent can one converse with other professionals also treating the child? Clinical work with children and adolescents also raises questions about the extent and type of information to be shared with parents.

DR. HECTOR MACHABANSKI: Professional issues affect my daily work mainly in terms of professional ethics and regulation. All of the professional issues you mentioned become relevant at various times, depending on the clients being dealt with and the problems they present.

DR. GEOFFREY THORPE: A colleague and I co-teach a required graduate seminar on Ethics and Professional Problems. We do our best to keep up to date with all relevant professional issues because we are responsible for ensuring that our doctoral graduates will be license-eligible in every state. Thus, teaching this course is invaluable to our own professional development. Ethical issues arise every day in my clinical practice. It is incumbent upon all practitioners to maintain ethical competence, a challenging task in a climate of rapid change. Journals such as *Professional Psychology: Research and Practice*, and *Law and Human Behavior* are extremely helpful resources, as is *The Psychologist's Legal Handbook* and related publications. As a member of my state's psychology licensing board, I assist my fellow board members in oral examinations during which we ask applicants about their knowledge of ethics and other aspects of professional practice. In short, it would be hard to overstate the importance of sound ethical training and a commitment to ethical standards in the preparation of a clinical psychologist.

CHAPTER SUMMARY

Five professional issues are of prime importance as clinical psychology continues to develop its scientific and professional identity in the twenty-first century. These issues involve training, regulation, ethics, independence, and the perils associated with the professionalization of clinical psychology.

Beginning in the late-1940s, clinical training programs have typically followed some version of the Boulder model, a scientist–practitioner curriculum which emphasizes psychology's scientific foundation more than the development of clinical service skills. Several training conferences since that time have reaffirmed the Boulder model, but training models that emphasize professional skills are also available now. These include Doctor of Psychology (Psy.D.) programs and practice-oriented Ph.D. programs offered in psychology departments, medical schools, and, especially, in free-standing schools of professional psychology.

Professional regulation of clinical psychologists comes in several forms, including (1) laws that establish criteria for who may use the title of "psychologist" (certification laws) and perform psychological services (licensing laws), (2) laws and court rulings that give institutionalized clients the right to receive treatment and the right to give informed consent for it, (3) laws establishing client–therapist discussions as privileged communication, and (4) lawsuits alleging clinical malpractice.

Psychology's code of ethics is unique because it was developed on the basis of psychologists' experiences with real ethical dilemmas. The current version, called "Ethical Principles of Psychologists and Code of Conduct," includes a Preamble, six General Principles, and a large number of Ethical Standards covering a wide range of specific topics, from advertising services and testing to rules about confidentiality and sexual contact with clients.

Clinical psychology's struggle to gain, and retain, its status as a profession that is authorized to offer independent services has been long, difficult, and continuing. It first involved the right of clinicians to offer psychotherapy. Later, the issue was whether clinical psychologists could practice independently in hospitals, and whether psychologists should be eligible for reimbursement under various public, private, and pre-paid mental health insurance plans. While these rights are now reasonably well established in most states, some of them may be made irrelevant by the continuing growth of managed care systems whose provisions are making it increasingly difficult for clinical psychologists to function outside of HMOs, group medical practices, or other health-related organizations.

Today, clinical psychology confronts the formidable challenge of shaping its training programs and service functions to meet client needs in the era of managed care while still maintaining the highest standards of professionalism, which includes letting itself be guided by the empirical research tradition that launched the field a hundred years ago.

Appendix

Getting into Graduate School in Clinical Psychology

John P. Fiore, M.Ed.
Associate Head for Undergraduate Affairs
Department of Psychology
University of Illinois at Urbana-Champaign

Students ask a number of questions when they are thinking of applying to graduate school in clinical psychology. The purpose of this Appendix is to answer some of those questions. The first step in applying to graduate school is to ask yourself: (1) Do I want to go to graduate school at this time? (2) Are my credentials strong enough for admission to graduate school? (3) In what type of program am I interested? (4) Given my credentials, to what type of program can I realistically aspire? Let's consider some things you should take into account as you answer these questions, and others related to them.

Do I Want to Go to Graduate School at This Time?

A Ph.D. program in clinical psychology requires that you make major emotional, financial, and time commitments. At least five years are needed to complete such a program, during which time you will be living on subsistence wages, at best. In addition, you will be asked to work harder than you have in previous academic endeavors. For example, typical requirements may involve a full course load of academic work, a twenty-hour-per-week placement at a clinical agency, as well as independent research toward completion of your thesis or dissertation.

It is not only the time and effort that make graduate school so demanding. The academic expectations and requirements are aimed at a higher level than those with which most students are familiar. Compared to undergraduate school, much more independent thinking is expected of graduate students. Finally, the method of instruction shifts dramatically compared to that encountered in undergraduate courses. Most graduate classes are taught in a seminar format, which involves discussion and student-directed presentations rather than faculty lectures. Journal articles, rather than textbooks, are the primary reading material.

How can you determine whether you are ready for graduate school? The answer may depend on how you feel about the prospect of graduate study. It is appropriate to be apprehensive; indeed, a certain amount of anxiety can serve as an effective motivator for increased effort. However, if you are ambivalent about entering graduate school, consider taking some time off before pursuing further education. Most graduate programs are so demanding and stressful that ambivalence on your part is likely to interfere with your ability to successfully complete one.

Will a Delayed Application Hurt My Chances for Admission?

Contrary to what you might have heard, your application to graduate school in clinical psychology will probably not be jeopardized if you decide to take some time off after completing your undergraduate studies. Graduate admissions committees are seeking the best candidates for their programs, and what you do during your "time off"—along with accompanying changes in your attitude, commitment, maturity, and motivation—may actually enhance your application, thus making admission more, not less, likely. In fact, some clinical programs prefer applicants who have had work experience after completing the undergraduate degree. A period of time off may also help you to realize if graduate study in clinical psychology is not for you. Whatever the case—whether you need to be away from school for a while before making a final decision about applying, or you need to work for a year or more in order to accumulate sufficient funds to pay for your education, rest assured that your delayed application will be taken seriously.

If I Choose Not to Apply to Graduate School, What Human Service Jobs Are Available at the Bachelor's Degree Level?

Bachelor's-level jobs and career opportunities exist in a variety of fields for graduates who are interested in clinical psychology and related human service professions. Some of these jobs require formal training in, and are open mainly to graduates of undergraduate programs in community mental health work. Others seek graduates of undergraduate programs in related fields, including elementary education, special education, and the teaching of psychology in secondary schools. Still other job opportunities exist for graduates with an orientation toward, and experience in, various human services. Such jobs are likely to be found in schools, community centers, social service agencies, half-way houses, crisis intervention programs, youth services, and general outreach programs. Here are just a few of the jobs open to students who have an undergraduate degree in psychology and related fields.

Community Relations Officer	Police Officer
Affirmative Action Officer	Public Safety Officer
Recreation Worker	Behavior Modification Specialist
Health Educator	Behavioral Observer
Rehabilitation Counselor	Social Service Worker
Psychiatric Assistant	House-parent
Volunteer Service Director	Youth and Family Counselor
Probation and Parole Officer	Case Aide Worker
High School Psychology Teacher	Teacher Aide
Residential Youth Specialist	Vocational Program Coordinator
Community Worker	Interviewer
Sustaining Case Worker	Clinical Intake Worker
Foster Home Recruiter	Residence Advisor
Aging/Rehabilitation Specialist	Student Affairs Officer
Camp Director	Financial Aid Counselor
Group Worker	Admissions Counselor
Child-Care Worker	Employment Counselor
Residence Hall Director	Development Officer
Drug Abuse Counselor	Alcohol Abuse Counselor
Program Specialist for Developmentally Disabled	Counselor in Mental Health Settings

Career advancement possibilities in human service and mental health fields for those without graduate or professional degrees vary. It is possible for bachelor's-level employees to advance in a mental health field; many become mental health administrators, for example. One cannot officially become a psychologist through promotion, of course, but if your purpose in entering a bachelor's-level mental-health-related job is to gain experience that will help you to decide whether or not to pursue a graduate degree in clinical psychology, these promotion issues are unlikely to be important to you.

In What Types of Programs Am I Interested?

Many students seem to think that if they want to do clinical work, they must enter a graduate program in clinical psychology. In fact, there are many different types of programs that offer training leading to careers in the mental health professions. Programs in counseling psychology, school psychology, and social work all offer extensive training and experience in clinical work. Graduates of these programs enter many of the same positions as do clinical psychologists. As noted in Chapters 1 and 14, recent trends in our health care system have led to increased enrollment in health maintenance organizations (HMOs), many of which are hiring increasing numbers of master's-level professionals trained in clinical psychology, social work, psychiatric nursing, counseling, and related fields. Indeed, there are those who believe that master's-level professionals from these fields will enjoy increased opportunities for direct service roles, while Ph.D. clinical psychologists will tend to take on more administrative, supervisory, and consulting roles. Thus, before investing all of your efforts in applying to doctoral programs in clinical psychology, you should explore the clinical job opportunities available to professionals trained at the master's level, and to doctoral and sub-doctoral professionals trained in related fields.

Are My Credentials Strong Enough for Graduate School in Clinical Psychology?

In order to evaluate your credentials objectively, and to be aware of your strengths and weaknesses, it is important to understand the criteria employed by graduate admissions committees in clinical psychology. A recent survey of directors of clinical training programs suggests that the four main criteria applied in the selection of new graduate students are, in order of importance, (1) Graduate Record Exam (GRE) scores; (2) grade point average (GPA); (3) letters of recommendation; and (4) research experience, publications, and presentations. Each graduate program may weigh these criteria differently, of course, but all of them tend to be used, to some extent, at least. Notice that clinical experience was not included on the list. Indeed, such experience may help students decide whether clinical psychology is the field for them, but—other than as a source of relevant letters of recommendation—it appears not to be deemed especially important in the graduate selection process.

GRE Scores.   Students do not like to hear this, but performance on the GRE is an important predictor of success in graduate school, and thus one of the most important selection criteria used by graduate admissions committees. One study found, for example, that GRE scores were more useful than college GPA in predicting performance in a graduate program in clinical psychology (Dollinger, 1989). GRE scores represent the only data for which comparisons can be made across all applicants. All students take the exact same test, so performance is not influenced by differences in collegiate standards, as are letters of recommendation and college grades. A score of 1,200 for a student in Alaska means the same as a 1200 in Florida. Thus, the GRE is widely viewed as providing a summary of a student's potential for successful performance in graduate school. Keep in mind, however, that scores on the GRE and other standardized quantitative tests tend not to be given as much weight when evaluating applications from members of ethnic minority groups, people from nonpsychology backgrounds, and other "nontraditional" students whose potential might not be captured by such tests.

Letters of Recommendation.   When reading letters of recommendation, admissions committee members tend to look for comments relating to the applicant's overall potential for graduate school, willingness to work hard, level of interpersonal skills, and likelihood of success in clinical work. Letter writers are not likely to learn these things about you through classroom contacts alone, so it is crucial that you develop means of interacting with faculty outside the classroom. The best way to do this is to get involved as a paid or unpaid member of one or more faculty member's research groups.

Research Experience. There are many reasons why you should gain research experience prior to applying to graduate school in clinical psychology. First, in universities, the Ph.D. in clinical psychology is both a research degree and a clinical degree. Therefore, admissions committees want to ensure that applicants understand what is involved in research, and that they enjoy participating in such activities. Second, as just noted, working with faculty on their research is an excellent way to obtain letters of recommendation that define more precisely your potential for graduate school. Third, working on research projects will help you decide which areas you would (and would not) like to pursue in graduate school. This information, in turn, will help you apply to those psychology departments whose faculty are working in the areas of your greatest interest. Finally, research experience may serve as the basis for discussion with faculty during any campus visits that you might make.

Given My Credentials, to What Type of Program Can I Realistically Aspire?

One of the most difficult things you need to do when applying to graduate school is to be realistic about evaluating your credentials. Unfortunately, the credentials of many applicants are not strong enough to gain entry to Ph.D. programs in clinical psychology. Unless you have pursued other options as well, you may be setting yourself up for disappointment. Fortunately, several such options are available. For example, master's (MA) programs in clinical psychology usually have lower criteria for admission than Ph.D. programs. You might want to consider these programs either to earn a terminal master's degree or as the first step toward a Ph.D. program. Counseling, school, or other psychology programs that offer clinical training also tend to be somewhat less competitive than Ph.D. programs in clinical psychology. As noted earlier, students in these programs often receive as much applied training and experience as students in clinical psychology programs, and master's-level job openings may be on the rise. Finally, nonclinical Ph.D. programs in psychology (e.g., developmental, social) tend to attract fewer applicants than do clinical programs. If you are committed to the field of psychology, and want to remain in a research environment, you may find a nonclinical Ph.D. program in psychology more rewarding than a mental-health-related doctoral program in another field.

In short, Ph.D. programs in clinical psychology are not for everyone; they are highly competitive, they place great demands on their students, and they emphasize research training as much as clinical experience. Having offered some guidelines to help you assess your credentials and aspirations, and to determine whether you should apply to programs in clinical psychology, we now consider some more general issues that you will need to address before beginning the application process.

GENERAL ISSUES

I Have Decided to Apply to Graduate School in Clinical Psychology. What Should I Do First?

In choosing graduate programs, you will want to make sure they provide the training and professional environment that will meet your needs. Therefore, you should clarify your personal goals, objectives, and plans. Are you most interested in research, balanced training in clinical practice and research, or primarily in clinical practice? Are you interested in doctoral-level or master's-level programs? Do you have an interest in a specific client population? Do you have preferences related to types and/or locations of future employment? These are but a few of the questions you should be asking yourself before the application process begins. You will not have definitive answers for all possible questions, but you will have some, and these will probably indicate what is most important to you in choosing a graduate program.

Should I Apply to a Master's Degree Program and Complete It Before I Apply to a Doctoral Program?

As noted earlier, there are various routes you can take to earn the doctorate in clinical psychology. A number of graduate programs provide master's degree training only. Many graduates from these programs terminate their formal education at the master's-degree level; others apply to doctoral programs.

Some graduate schools have separate training programs at the master's and doctoral levels and accept students for each. The master's program in these schools sometimes serves as a "feeder" to the doctoral program. However, each program is separate, so the student who does not enter the doctoral program will have completed training similar to that offered at "master's only" schools.

Other programs are designed to prepare doctoral-level clinicians only. They may award the master's degree after a minimum number of credits and a master's thesis have been completed, but it is important to recognize that these departments accept applications for the doctoral degree only.

How Does Earning a Master's Degree Affect My Chances for Admission to a Doctoral Program Later On?

Generally, the possession of a master's degree has little impact on a student's application. Graduate schools are interested in the best candidates they can find. If your credentials are excellent, your chances for being admitted to a doctoral program are good. Some students who feel they need to improve their credentials may find master's-degree work helpful in achieving that goal, but doctoral admission committees consider all academic work when making their decision. A mediocre undergraduate academic record is not disregarded because it has been supplemented with a master's degree and good graduate school grades, but these graduate credentials can improve a student's chances for being seriously considered.

If I Chose to Terminate my Training After Earning a Master's Degree, Will my Opportunities for Doing Clinical Work be Limited?

Though there are many good clinical psychologists whose highest academic degree is the master's, the doctorate is still the standard of the profession. The following resolution was recently adopted by the American Psychological Association (APA) Council of Representatives.

> The title "Professional Psychologist" has been used so widely and by persons with such a wide variety of training and experience that it does not provide the information the public deserves.
>
> As a consequence, the APA takes the position and makes it a part of its policy that the use of the titles "Professional Psychologist," "School Psychologist," and "Industrial Psychologist" is reserved for those who have completed a doctoral training program in psychology in a university, college, or professional school of psychology that is APA or regionally accredited. In order to meet this standard, a transition period will be acknowledged for the use of the title "School Psychologist," so that ways may be sought to increase opportunities for doctoral training and to improve the level of the educational codes pertaining to the title.
>
> The APA further takes the position and makes it a part of its policy that only those who have completed a doctoral training program in professional psychology in a university, college, or professional school of psychology that is APA or regionally accredited are qualified to independently provide unsupervised direct delivery of professional services including prevention, assessment, and therapeutic services. The exclusions mentioned above pertaining to school psychologists do not apply to the independent, unsupervised, direct delivery of professional services discussed in this paragraph.
>
> Licensed or certified master's-level psychologists, having met earlier standards of the profession (i.e., were accorded grandmother/grandfather recognition) are to be regarded as comparably qualified through education, experience, examination, and the test of time, as are present and future doctoral psychologists, and shall be entitled under APA guidelines to include as part of their title the word "psychologist." (APA, 1996, p. vii)

You also need to consider that all U.S. states employ some form of licensing or certification for psychologists (see Chapter 14). Though requirements vary from state to state, an earned doctorate is a prerequisite in most of them. So while the growth of managed care systems has stimulated the job market at the master's-degree level for those seeking a career in direct service, be certain that such jobs match your career expectations before deciding to prepare for clinical work by earning a master's degree.

Are All Doctoral Programs in Clinical Psychology Research-Oriented?

All university-based Ph.D. programs in clinical psychology provide training in research as well as in clinical functions, but there are differences in emphasis from one institution to another. It is worth your effort to learn of each program's emphasis when you are gathering other information about the program. Programs that are strictly research-oriented make this fact clear in their descriptive information and may even refrain from using "clinical psychology" as a program title (experimental psychopathology is a common substitute).

Some graduate programs offer a doctor of psychology (Psy.D.) degree in addition to, or instead of, a traditional Ph.D. As noted in Chapter 14, this degree puts the emphasis on clinical training while reducing the emphasis on research. These programs still require their students to acquire knowledge of research tools, but do not require students to do basic research. In other words, students still develop their knowledge of statistics and research methods but are not required to do an empirically based thesis or dissertation.

How Do I Identify "Good" Graduate Programs?

It is difficult to label graduate programs as "good" or "bad." The real question to be answered is whether a particular university, department, and program fit your needs. Part of the answer will lie in the "research" versus "clinical" emphasis of each program and you can gather information about that by corresponding with current graduate students and faculty located there. You should also consider the size of the department and the program, the student/faculty ratio, opportunities for a variety of practicum experiences, the size and location of the campus and the community, the type and extent of department resources, and the theoretical orientation(s) or approaches which may exist in or dominate the program.

Finally, be cautious about generalizing about the quality of a clinical program on the basis of the reputation of the department in which it resides. There are some psychology departments which are considered to be the "best" by many psychologists, but if your interest is in clinical psychology, do not assume that the clinical program is also one of the best. It very well may be, but be sure to identify what is the best for you and to judge each program against your own personal criteria.

What Does American Psychological Association (APA) Accreditation of a Clinical Psychology Graduate Program Mean?

APA accreditation means the program has met a minimum standard of quality (see Chapter 14). The APA publication *Graduate Study in Psychology* explains that APA accreditation should be interpreted to mean:

1. The program is recognized and publicly labeled as a doctoral program in clinical, counseling, or school psychology (or combination thereof). It is located in and supported by an institution of higher education, which itself is accredited by one of six regional accrediting bodies also recognized by COPA.

2. The program voluntarily applied for accreditation and, in so doing, engaged in extensive self-study of its program objectives, educational and training practices, its resource support base, and its faculty, students, and graduates. The program also participated in a peer review of its operations by a site-visit team of distinguished professional colleagues.

3. The program was thoroughly evaluated by the APA Committee on Accreditation (comprised of professional and public members) and judged to be in sufficient

compliance with the APA Criteria for Accreditation to warrant accreditation status. Those criteria against which a program is evaluated include institutional support; sensitivity to cultural and individual differences; training models and curricula; faculty; students; facilities; and practicum and internship training.

Accreditation, in summary, applies to educational institutions and programs, not to individuals. It does not guarantee jobs or licensure for individuals, though being a graduate of an accredited program may facilitate such achievement. It does speak to the manner and quality by which an educational institution or program conducts its business. It speaks to a sense of public trust, as well as professional quality. (APA 1996, p. ix).

A list of APA-accredited programs in clinical psychology is published each year in the December issue of the APA's main journal, the *American Psychologist*, but be aware that there may be excellent departments that have not applied for accreditation or that have not had a doctoral program in clinical psychology long enough to be eligible for approval.

APPLICATION PROCEDURES

It is now time to review the steps you will need to take in order to file admission applications for graduate programs in clinical psychology.

How Do I Get Initial Information About Graduate Schools?

There are several sources of information and you should use *all* of them. Some of the best of these are the psychology faculty you know, especially those who are clinical psychologists. In preparing for courses, doing research, and keeping current for clinical practice, these faculty carefully review new ideas and research, attend professional meetings, and participate in continuing education workshops. This exposure to the field helps faculty members learn about various departments, programs, schools, training and research staff, the nature and theoretical orientations of different programs, recent changes in the direction of certain departments, and other pertinent information. Though it is not reasonable to expect the faculty to know about all or even most doctoral programs, they will be able to provide you with good information about many of them.

Professional journals and related publications are information sources which many applicants overlook. An excellent way to find programs that meet your needs is to use these sources to identify faculty who are studying topics and using approaches which interest you. A thorough search of the literature—using journals such as *Psychological Abstracts*, CD-ROM services such as *Psychlit*, and various on-line search services—will very likely highlight faculty with whom you might like to study, and indicate where they are located. For specific address information, consult the American Psychological Association and the American Psychological Society membership directories (most psychology departments have recent editions), or visit these organizations' Worldwide Web Homepages.

Some colleges or psychology departments have a special advising staff for their students. These advisors or counselors may or may not be faculty, but if part of their job is to help with graduate school applications, you can benefit from their experience with former students. Even if your school does not have this source of information available, all departmental offices receive pamphlets, notices, and general information brochures from many graduate psychology programs in the United States and Canada. Make full use of this information to help answer some of your questions and inform yourself about new programs.

There are also numerous books that list graduate schools and programs. We have already mentioned the best of these for psychology: the American Psychological Association's *Graduate Study in Psychology*. This book, which is revised semi-annually, contains over 500 pages of information, including application addresses, types of programs and degrees offered by each institution, number of faculty, financial aid information, tuition costs, degree and admission requirements, average grades and entrance test scores for students admitted the previous year, comments about the program, and other valuable information. If your departmental or school library does not have a copy, or if you want your own copy, you may purchase one from the American Psychological Association, 750 First Street, N.E., Washington, D.C. 20002. In 1997, the cost of *Graduate Study in Psychology* was $24.95 (including postage and handling); there is a discount if you are an APA student affiliate.

Other good sources of information about graduate schools are your library and campus career/placement office. They usually have university catalogs other material that help identify graduate programs. Once you have identified clinical psychology programs that interest you, look at the graduate catalogs from their universities to get some idea of their general administrative structure and academic requirements. If departmental course descriptions are listed, you may be able to identify a particular clinical program's emphasis.

Finally, the Internet and the World Wide Web offer an enormous amount of information about many universities, psychology departments, and clinical programs. With a few clicks of a mouse, you can quickly gather information about graduate programs, faculty rosters and research programs, departmental facilities, and the e-mail addresses, FAX numbers, and telephone numbers you might need in order to request additional information. In many cases, you can even download the application forms you will need, a feature of some homepages that eliminates the need to wait for material to arrive by mail.

How Many Potential Programs in Clinical Psychology Should Be on My Initial Application List?

Your *initial* list should include as many programs as possible. The APA's *Graduate Study in Psychology* lists almost every clinical psychology program in the United States and Canada. As you use the various sources of information mentioned above and decide about location preferences, degree preferences, and the like, you will begin to systematically eliminate programs from your initial list. Once you have eliminated as many programs as possible by using the information you have compiled, you should contact each remaining program to request more detailed descriptions. This will allow you to continue to reduce the list on the basis of new information.

When Should I Contact Graduate Programs for Information?

You should request information in August or September, approximately a year before your desired admission date (e.g., September 1998 for Fall 1999 admission). Requesting material earlier than this sometimes gets you old information or merely places you on a waiting list until material is available. If you make a request too late, the material may not arrive in time for you to make effective use of it. Remember, you may have questions which arise from your reading of the material and you may wish to correspond with some departments before a final decision is made about whether or not to apply to them. This all takes some time—give yourself plenty!

What Application Information Should I Ask for and What Format Should I Use?

At minimum, you should ask for information about the clinical psychology program, and request appropriate department and graduate school application forms, a graduate school program and course catalog, financial aid information, financial aid application forms, and a list of faculty and their research interests.

Your request for information need not be elaborate. A post card, form letter, or e-mail message addressed to the department's graduate admission committee can be used, but be sure it includes a request for all the information you will need.

When Should I Apply?

Department application deadlines vary, but most fall between January 15 and February 15. A few come as early as December while others (mostly for master's degree programs) run as late as August. Some departments that have later deadlines often select students as applications arrive for processing. If you apply to schools that use this "rolling admissions" plan, it is to your advantage to submit your application early in the process.

Submitting *very* early applications (September or October) is usually of no particular value since departments are not "tooled-up" for the admission process until later in the fall. Also, required testing (to be discussed later) may not be available to you this early in the school year.

How Many Programs Should I Apply To?

It is difficult to identify a specific number of applications which is appropriate for all students. We are reminded of two cases: One student applied to six schools and was admitted to all of them, while another applied to twenty-seven and was admitted to one. Since competition for admission to Ph.D. programs is keen, the general rule is to apply to as many programs as you can reasonably afford. The larger the number of applications, the better your chances of being accepted.

Once you have decided on a final list of schools, ask yourself what you will do if you are not accepted by any of them. Perhaps at this point you may want to add one or two "safety valve" programs to fall back on. However, do not apply to programs which are really not acceptable to you. Such applications waste admission committee time, your time (and money), and may prevent a serious applicant from being admitted.

How Much Does It Cost to Apply?

Total GRE and other testing costs usually run somewhere around $160.00. Departmental application fees usually vary from nothing to $75.00. Transcript costs (usually $2.00 to $5.00 each), additional test report fees, postage, and phone calls can add up very quickly. Someone applying to ten graduate programs can expect an average cost of $75.00 per application.

QUALIFICATIONS AND CREDENTIALS

What Kinds of Courses and Experiences Will Help My Application?

Your undergraduate department will have designed a graduate preparatory major to meet your course needs. This will probably include a core program of introductory psychology, statistics, and experimental psychology (including a laboratory). These are the minimum requirements for most graduate programs, regardless of specialization area. In addition to looking for these core courses and some breadth in psychology, Ph.D. programs often look for applicants who have had course work in mathematics, laboratory work in sciences outside psychology, and computer science courses. Remember, graduate programs are looking for the best students they can find, so a strong academic preparation is essential.

In addition to standard course work, independent research such as an honors or bachelor's thesis and/or experience as a faculty research assistant is very helpful, in general, and essential for Ph.D. programs. As noted earlier, such research activity not only provides you with desirable experience, but also allows faculty supervisors to observe your potential for scholarly endeavors and to include their evaluations and impressions in letters of recommendation.

As also noted earlier, having clinical experience may not be a very important criterion for admission—psychology departments do not expect you to be a trained clinician when you arrive—but it is helpful to provide some evidence of experience in "helping relationships." Clinically relevant volunteer work, for example, will assist you in establishing that your career decision is based partly on firsthand knowledge of the field. Remember, impressions of what it is like to work in a field and actual working experiences are often very different. It is important that you know what you are getting into when you choose clinical psychology as a career.

Participation in extra-curricular activities, including psychology clubs and honor societies is not usually considered in the admission process except as it might indicate your involvement in psychology, your interpersonal skills, your willingness to work hard, and the like. Thus, simply being a member of Psi Chi or Psi Beta, for example, will not strengthen your application much. However, it could help a lot if your participation as a member showed your creative leadership in developing effective and impressive programs and led to strong letters of support from faculty advisors and campus or community leaders. These activities, and glowing letters about them, will not substitute for the grades, GRE scores, and research experience required for admission, but they may make a difference when admissions committees are trying to decide between candidates who are equally strong on quantitative criteria.

What Grade Average Is Necessary in Order to Be Accepted?

Grade average requirements vary across programs, degrees, and institutions. Some admissions committees will be concerned with a four-year average, while others will consider only the grades from your last two years of course work. For clinical psychology doctoral programs, a 3.5 grade average (on a 4-point system) is generally considered a *minimum*. At highly competitive schools, a 3.7 grade average may be more common among accepted students, but other criteria are also taken into consideration. It is not unusual for a clinical program to reject a student with a 4.0 grade average in favor of one with a 3.5 grade average *if* the lower average is compensated for by other credentials (test scores, research experience, course selection, and the like) which are more in line with the program's goals, requirements, and theoretical orientation.

Admission to master's degree programs is less competitive than for doctoral programs. Many master's programs have a minimum grade average requirement of B- (approximately 2.75 on a 4-point system), though the typical student admitted to such programs is likely to have a solid B (3.25) grade average.

What Testing Is Involved in Applying to Graduate School?

Most graduate schools use standardized tests to assist them in evaluating applicants. As already noted, the most common example is the Graduate Record Examination (GRE). The Miller Analogies Test (MAT) is required by some graduate programs, but not by nearly as many as require the GRE. The MAT is given on an individual basis. It is scheduled for fifty minutes and consists of 100 very difficult verbal analogy items. As with the GRE, MAT testing is often available on college and university campuses. There are MAT preparation books available and you should use one if for no other reason than to gain experience in this form of testing. However, be sure that the schools to which you are applying require the MAT before spending time and money on taking this exam.

Further information about the MAT and testing locations can be obtained by writing to:

The Psychological Corporation
304 East 45th Street
New York, New York 10017

In its *1996–97 General Test Descriptive Booklet*, the more widely required GRE General Test is described as follows:

The GRE General Test measures certain developed verbal, quantitative, and analytical abilities that are important for academic achievement. In doing so, the test necessarily reflects the opportunities and efforts that have contributed to the development of those abilities.

The General Test is only one of several means of evaluating likely success in graduate school. It is not intended to measure inherent intellectual capacity or intelligence. Neither is it intended to measure creativity, motivation, perseverance, or social worth. The test does, however, make it possible to compare students with different backgrounds. A GRE score of 500, for example, has the same meaning whether earned by a student at a small private liberal arts college or by a student at a large public university.

Because several different editions of the paper-based test or pools of questions for the computer-adaptive test are in active use at any one time, not all students receive the same test edition. However, all editions and question pools measure the same skills and meet the same specifications for content and difficulty. The scores from different editions are made comparable to one another by a statistical procedure known as equating. This process makes it possible to assure that all reported scores of a given value denote the same level of developed ability regardless of which edition of the test is taken.

Since students have wide-ranging backgrounds, interests, and skills, the *verbal sections* of the General Test use questions from diverse areas of experience. The areas tested range from the activities of daily life to broad categories of academic interest such as the sciences, social studies, and the humanities. The content areas included in the *quantitative sections* of the test are arithmetic, algebra, geometry, and data analysis. These are content areas usually studied in high school. Questions in the *analytical sections* measure reasoning skills developed in virtually all fields of study. No formal training in logic or methods of analysis is needed to do well in these sections. (ETS, 1996, p. 3)

The GRE Subject Test In Psychology is described in the *1997–98 Information and Registration Bulletin* as follows:

The test has about 218 questions drawn from courses most commonly offered at the undergraduate level, in three categories:

1. Experimental or natural science oriented (about 43% of the questions), including learning, language, memory, thinking, perception, ethology, comparative, sensation, and physiological psychology.
2. Social or social science oriented (about 43% of the questions), including clinical and abnormal, developmental, personality, and social psychology.
3. General (about 14% of the questions), including the history of psychology, applied psychology, measurement, research designs, and statistics. (ETS, 1997, p. 31)

Paper-based GRE testing is given on specific dates throughout the world. On these dates, the general test is given in the morning and the subject test is given in the afternoon. The general test takes about three and one-half hours and the subject test takes slightly less than three hours.

A computer-based version of the GRE General Test is also available. In October of 1996, more than 250 test centers around the world gave the GRE General Test, by appointment, using PC-type computers. One advantage of taking the test on a computer is that you can learn the results immediately after you have finished; written score reports are then mailed to you and the schools you designate within fifteen days. Remember, however, that the computerized option is available only for the GRE General Test.

GRE Information Bulletins include all application material for scheduled test dates and for computer-based testing. They are available at most colleges and universities, or you may obtain a copy by writing to:

Graduate Record Examinations
Educational Testing Service
P. O. Box 6000
Princeton, New Jersey 08541-6000

The basic fees in 1997–98 for GREs given in the U.S., U.S. Territories, and Puerto Rico were $96.00 for the paper-based general test, $96.00 for the subject test, and $96.00 for computer-based testing (general test only). All other locations required a fee of $120.00 for each test.

Should I Take Both the GRE General Test and the GRE Subject Test?

Since the general test is almost always required, there is little choice but to take it. As for the subject test, your decision will be determined, in part, by your choice of the schools to which you will be applying. If you know which these will be, the application information from these graduate programs will indicate whether or not the subject test is required. If you have not decided on a specific list of schools, you had better take both the general test and the subject test, just to be on the safe side. If you wish, the Educational Testing Service will send only general test results or only subject test results to particular schools.

When Should I Take the Graduate Record Exam?

Before answering this question, it is important to discuss the availability of the two forms used to give the GRE General Test. The Educational Testing Service has been reducing the number of dates on which they give the paper-based version the Graduate Record Examination. In 1997–98 the general test was scheduled for early November and mid-April, while the subject tests were scheduled for those two dates, plus an additional date in December. Educational Testing Service is clearly encouraging students to select the computer-based version of the GRE general test, however, and it should not come as a surprise if the paper-based testing is eliminated in the near future.

One feature of the computer-based GRE testing that worries some students is the fact that it is not possible during the test to reconsider, and change, answers to completed questions. Indeed, once a computer-generated question is answered, the computer program selects the next question based on the answer given for the previous question. Thus, it is also not possible to make a first pass through the test to answer "easy" questions and then go back and spend more time on those that take more thought. This restriction has tended to raise the pretest anxiety level of some students because it forces them to change the way they have learned to take multiple-choice examinations. Others report that they like the computer-based general test because it (1) takes significantly less time than the paper-based approach (2) provides immediate results which are sent to graduate schools in ten to fifteen days and (3) can be taken by appointment throughout the year at a date that is convenient for the student. Research by ETS shows that the results of the paper-based and computer-based forms are comparable.

As noted earlier, the GRE subject test is not currently available in a computer-based format, so you must sign up to take it on one of the three standard testing dates. The Educational Testing Service reports that it takes approximately six weeks to score paper-based tests and have the results in the mail, so the latest you can take the subject test (and the paper-based general test, if that is your preference) is on a scheduled date that is at least six weeks before your earliest application deadline. If February 1 is the deadline date for any school to which you are applying, only the November and December test dates will meet that deadline.

Traditionally, most students applying to doctoral programs and electing all-paper-based testing take the entire GRE exam on the November date in the fall of their senior year. This strategy usually puts the test results in the mail to the student and to all designated schools by mid-December. When selecting GRE testing dates, keep in mind that you are very likely to be taking both the general test and the subject test. Three hours of testing in the morning and three more hours in the afternoon can be tiring, so many students choose to take the general test on one date and the subject test on another. Of course, if you have elected to take the computer-based option for the general test, then you need only sign up for the November or December subject test.

Another consideration in selecting test dates is whether or not you wish to use the results to shape decisions about where to apply. If you choose test dates that are sufficiently early, you will be able to look over your scores, consult with advisors, and review resource material such as APA's *Graduate Study in Psychology* book, which lists average GRE scores for students admitted to specific programs. Applying to certain graduate programs before you know what your GRE scores are can be a waste of time and money. Having scores at the 90th percentile makes it reasonable to apply to the most competitive schools; scores at the 40th percentile require a more conservative strategy.

One test-scheduling strategy that has worked well for some students who prefer not to use computer-based testing is to take the paper-based general test in April, near the end of their junior year. They then spend the summer reviewing for the subject test in psychology which they take early in their senior year. This plan allows time for retaking both tests, if necessary, and for using test results in deciding where to apply.

Can I Study for the GRE?

The 1997-1998 GRE *Information and Registration Booklet* describes the types of questions found on the general test, along with some strategies you can use in taking the computer-based and paper-based versions. A free full-length sample GRE general test, which includes instructions for evaluating your performance, is available from the GRE program at the Educational Testing Service. ETS also sells practice material, including GRE general tests and GRE subject tests actually administered in previous years. All of this material can help you become familiar with the types and forms of questions you are likely to encounter on the GRE and it can also give you practice at pacing yourself during the actual examination.

You should review for the quantitative portion of the General Test, especially if you have been away from mathematics for a while. Brushing up on basic algebra and geometry will help you during this part of the exam by reducing the time you will need to recall how to solve particular problems. Students report that the quantitative portion of the GRE is not difficult, but that it is fast paced. Know your basic math "cold," so you can work quickly and accurately.

You can also prepare for the GRE general test via test preparation courses (presented live or on videotape) and annually-revised test preparation books. Because courses and tapes can be quite expensive, most students tend to use the test preparation books. These books usually provide a mathematics and vocabulary review, tips on test taking, and a set of sample test items. Some of the more frequently used "how to prepare" books are published by Barron's Educational Series, Arco Publishing Company, and Monarch Press. They are readily available at most bookstores.

Deciding on test preparation courses versus self-preparation is an individual decision. Some students do not have the time or inclination to design a disciplined preparation study schedule and, for them, the expense of test preparation courses is worth it because they provide needed structure. Whether you decide on a formal course or a do-it-yourself approach, it is important to prepare for the GRE general test in some way!

As for the subject test in psychology, remember that it covers all areas of the discipline. Names, theories, and definitions are likely to be covered on the test, as are basic concepts. No one is expected to know about every area, so if you have not been exposed to certain aspects of psychology, you will no doubt have trouble with some questions. You can prepare for the subject test in psychology by thoroughly reviewing a comprehensive introductory psychology textbook. In addition, books that present the history of psychology, and/or systems and theories in psychology, provide information that is particularly useful in preparing for the psychology subject test.

Can I Take the GRE Tests More Than Once?

You may take the GRE tests as often as you want—but doing so may not be helpful, because the Educational Testing Service's research shows that, in general, GRE scores increase only slightly when the test is retaken. If you plan to retake the computer-based general test, note that you have to wait at least sixty days after the first testing before trying it again. You can take paper-based versions each time they are scheduled, if you wish. We suggest, however, that you plan on taking each part of the GRE only once. A second testing should be done only if special circumstances affected you in a way that you are *sure* led to an artificially low score.

Given the minimal chances of significantly raising your score on a second testing, and the possibility that you might get a lower score, the retake strategy *could* have the effect of reducing the average GRE score a graduate school might use for admission purposes. It may be a better idea to "practice" the GRE—and identify areas of weakness—by buying and taking the previously used GRE tests sold by the Educational Testing Service.

Will I Need Letters of Recommendation for Graduate School Application? If So, How Many and From Whom?

Three letters of recommendation are usually required by the overwhelming majority of graduate programs in clinical psychology. At least two letters should be academic references—that is, from psychology faculty familiar with your academic ability. If faculty from other disciplines can provide a better picture of your academic achievement and potential for graduate study, feel free to ask them for letters. The quality of the recommendation could be more important than whether or not the writer is a psychologist.

A letter from someone who supervised a clinically-related experience or (relevant) job you had can also be helpful, because it helps establish your interest, motivation, and success at working within the mental health field. Letters from "important people" such as senators, governors, and other political figures do not help your application. Generally, these say nothing more than "I've been asked to write ... " and "please give this student full consideration." Such letters are likely to leave the impression that you feel incapable of "making it" on your own. Unless the writer is in a position to judge the candidate's potential as a graduate student or a clinician, such "prestige" letters should not be submitted.

What Should I Know About Asking for Letters of Recommendation?

First, ask permission before you use someone's name as a reference. Many faculty will want to talk with you about your academic and career plans and objectives before agreeing to write a letter. Some will ask you to provide additional written information about yourself and may want to discuss this information with you. Be prepared to do this!

It is appropriate for you to provide faculty with information about yourself because faculty meet many students and can easily forget what each individual did in class, when they took courses, and other details. Also, it is not unusual for faculty to know little about a student other than what they have observed in the classroom. Information about your activities, accomplishments, and job experiences can supplement classroom contacts in a way that enhances the tone and thrust of a recommendation letter.

Here is a list of items you should provide to faculty who are writing letters of recommendation for you:

1. Your full name.
2. Major, minor, curriculum, and specialization.
3. A computation of the grade average in your major, in all college work, and in courses taken since the end of your sophomore year.
4. A transcript of your college courses and grades.
5. A list of the psychology laboratory courses you have had.
6. A description of other research experiences, including comments about the full extent of your participation (include a copy of any major research papers you wrote or contributed to).

7. A list of honor societies, clubs, and organizations to which you belong, along with comments on your participation (be sure to mention positions of responsibility you held).

8. A brief discussion of jobs you have held and volunteer work you have done. Some students carry heavy work loads while being enrolled as full-time students in order to pay for their education; this information should be included, too.

9. An outline of your personal and professional plans and goals.

10. Any other information that might be helpful to the person in writing your letter of recommendation.

Be sure to ask for letters and provide all appropriate recommendation information and other materials *early*. Remember, faculty often write letters for many students; give them plenty of time to prepare yours. To reduce the possibility of error and to speed the process:

1. Include a stamped, addressed envelope for each program for which a recommendation is to be sent.

2. When forms are included, be sure to *type* your name and other information which is not part of the formal recommendation in the appropriate spaces. *Do not hand blank forms to the recommender.*

3. Include a list of all the schools—and their application deadlines—to which a recommendation letter is to be sent. Indicate which schools have provided forms to be completed and which have not provided such forms. This information can then be used by the letter writer as a checklist as the letters and forms are completed.

Will I be Able to See My Recommendation Letters?

Letters of reference are not confidential unless you waive your right to see them. We encourage you to consider doing so because many admissions committee members feel that letter writers are more likely to provide candid evaluations when they know that the student will not see them. If you are concerned about what the letter might include, ask potential letter-writers if they can write in *support* of your application, not just if they will write a letter of reference.

Are Personal Interviews Required?

Interviews may be part of the admissions procedure, but if so, they are likely to come only after the admissions committee has considerably narrowed the number of applicants. Interviews are usually held on the school's campus, but, when a visit requires long-distance travel, a representative of the school may interview applicants at or near the student's place of residence. Telephone interviews are the exception rather than the rule, but a student who has already been interviewed in person should be prepared for a follow-up telephone call. When final decisions are being made, the committee may want to ask some candidates a few more questions.

You might want to try a bit of strategy used by one successful applicant. Near his telephone at home, he kept information about each of the programs to which he had applied (e.g., faculty names, particular emphases and strengths) along with notes about his career interests and goals. He felt that if he received a call from a school to which he had applied, having this information handy would reduce his anxiety about the conversation and help him organize his responses so that his emphasis would be appropriate for each institution. This plan also assured that he would include *all* the points he wanted to make during a call, and thus avoid regret over failing to mention something important. He did receive a call and his strategy worked.

Though interviews are not always part of the applicant review process, once you have received a letter of acceptance it is appropriate to visit the school and talk with department representatives and graduate students about their program. It is *not* appropriate to show up unannounced and expect department representatives to be available. Make an appointment well ahead of time by calling the director of clinical training and asking to meet with clinical psychology faculty and graduate students. Be prepared to outline briefly the nature of your questions and have a number of alternative dates in mind before you call.

Often, students want to schedule interview appointments before they apply to a school or before they are admitted. Some departments, especially those offering only a master's degree, welcome early interviews. However, other departments have so many applicants that it is impossible for them to accommodate such requests. Usually, the information you gather through the methods mentioned earlier—including collecting printed material from various programs—will be sufficient to help you decide whether or not to apply to each of them. If the written material you received is not sufficiently informative to give you a clear picture of a particular program, contact the department for additional details. (Before doing so, be sure to carefully read what you have in hand so that you do not ask about things a department has already covered in its printed material.) Once you are admitted, however, campus visits and interviews can help you to compare programs and make your "accept" or "reject" decisions.

Are My College Transcripts Required?

Most programs will ask for a transcript of courses and grades from each institution at which you have studied after high school. Notations of transfer credit summarized on the transcript from the last school you attended is not usually accepted—separate transcripts are required from each school. Call all the schools you have attended, find out how much they charge to send transcripts, and then send a letter to the director of student records at each school, enclosing a list of institutions to which a copy of your transcript is to be sent. Include a check to cover the cost.

FINANCIAL AID

What Kind of Financial Aid is Available for Graduate Study?

Financial aid comes in three forms: loans, grants, and work programs. The major source of financial aid for graduate students is the university in which they are enrolled, though aid may also be available through guaranteed loan programs (many of which are government sponsored) and national awards which are competitive and have specific criteria for application. These awards are given directly to students for use at the school of their choice.

An example of this latter type of aid is the Danforth graduate fellowship. It provides support for four years and is awarded to seniors who intend to obtain the highest degree in their fields and who have serious interest in college teaching. Students applying to clinical psychology programs with the intention of teaching at a college or university are eligible.

The availability of awards and loans changes regularly, so you should check with the financial aid officer at your college or at the institutions to which you are applying for current information. Because your financial support is most likely to come through the program to which you are admitted, the aid information you will receive with your application material is very important—read it carefully!

Loan programs exist on most campuses as a way of assisting students to invest in their own futures. These loans usually carry a low interest rate, and repayment begins only after the student leaves graduate school.

Fellowships and *scholarships* are given on many campuses as outright grants to support and encourage very bright students with excellent potential. These are few in number and competition for them is fierce.

Assistantships come in two forms: research assistantships and teaching assistantships. As their names imply, both entail working at *jobs* which require the graduate student to assist faculty in research projects or in teaching responsibilities (e.g., as a discussion leader, laboratory instructor, or paper grader). Assistantships usually require ten to twenty hours of work each week.

Some graduate programs receive grants from the federal government to provide *traineeships* in clinical psychology. As a result, there may be training grant funds available for a limited number of students at some institutions. Like fellowships, these are usually outright gifts, but they require that you carry a full academic load. They, too, are few in number and there is keen competition for them.

Not all types of aid are offered at all schools. Again, carefully read the financial aid information you receive to be sure you understand what is potentially available at each school you are considering.

Are There Assistantships Available From Departments Other Than the One to Which I Have Applied?

Assistantships of various types may be available on a campus. If you are accepted to a clinical psychology program that offers little or no financial aid, it is well worth your time to check on the availability of assistantships in departments outside psychology. For example, administrators of campus residence halls may hire graduate students to serve as hall counselors. Further, departments offering large undergraduate courses may not have enough graduate students in their programs to fill the teaching assistantships available and thus may "import" assistants from related areas. Identify your skills and experiences and seek out jobs that fit them.

Do All Financial Aid Packages Involve About the Same Amount of Money?

Financial aid will vary from campus to campus and among departments on the same campus. For example, one school may give more money than others, but also require graduate students to pay their own tuition. Others will give a smaller sum of money, but pay tuition and fees. Some residence hall assistantships provide room and board only, while others provide room, board, tuition, and fees. If financial aid is an important factor in your selection of a graduate program, be sure you know both the amount you will receive and the costs you will incur before you make a final decision to accept or reject an offer of admission.

Are Separate References Required When Applying for Financial Aid?

Sometimes, separate application deadlines and reference letters are involved in the process of seeking financial aid. Usually, any required letters of recommendation are simply copies of those used by departments in the admission process. Still, read your application material carefully to determine exactly what is required in order to apply for financial aid, and remember that *deadlines for financial aid applications are sometimes earlier than deadlines for applying to clinical psychology graduate programs.*

OTHER IMPORTANT QUESTIONS

Are There Any Last-Minute Things I Need to Do When Applying?

Once you have sent in your applications, check with each department to which you have applied to assure that your application has been received *and is complete*. Each year, some applications are not considered because students were unaware that their applications were incomplete. Some departments notify students when letters of reference or GRE scores are missing, but many do not. To eliminate this potential problem, be sure to enclose with each application a stamped, self-addressed envelope for the department to use to verify that your application is complete. Also include something similar to the brief note and checklist shown in Figure A.1.

When I Am Admitted to a Program, How Long Will I Have to Make a Decision About Whether to Accept?

Most admissions offers are made with a specific deadline for accepting or rejecting them. For doctoral programs, this is usually April 15 and is tied to financial aid offers. This date was adopted by the Council of Graduate Departments of Psychology to protect students from being pressured to make decisions before having full information about their alternatives. The Council's statement reads as follows:

Graduate Admissions Committee
Department of Psychology
University of Illinois
Champaign, Illinois 61820

To Whom It May Concern:

    I have applied to your graduate program in clinical psychology. Since I am very interested in being accepted to your program, I would like to verify that my application file is complete. I have enclosed a checklist and a self-addressed, stamped envelope to assist you in providing me with that information. Thank you for your cooperation.

                           Sincerely,

                           Mary Smith

Date: _____   (PLEASE CHECK APPROPRIATE LINES)

                                     Received

Application for Admission   _____
Application for Financial Aid   _____
GRE General Test Scores   _____
GRE Subject Test Scores   _____
Miller Analogies Test Score   _____
Recommendation letters from: _____
    Professor Abigail Jones   _____
    Professor Herbert Long   _____
    Mr. Ben Wright   _____
Transcripts from:
    City Junior College   _____
    University of Colorado   _____

Are there other required materials which have not been received?

_____
_____
_____

    (PLEASE RETURN IN ENCLOSED STAMPED AND ADDRESSED ENVELOPE.)

FIGURE A.1   An example of a brief note and checklist to send to the admissions committee when applying to a graduate program in clinical psychology.

Acceptance of an offer of financial aid (such as graduate scholarship, fellowship, traineeship, or assistantship) for the next academic year by an actual or prospective graduate student completes an agreement which both student and graduate school expect to honor. In those instances in which the student accepts the offer before April 15 and subsequently desires to withdraw, the student may submit in writing a resignation of the appointment at any time through April 15. However, an acceptance given or left in force after April 15 commits the student not to accept another offer without first obtaining a written release from the institution to which a commitment has been made. Similarly, an offer by an institution after April 15 is conditional on presentation by the student of the written release from any previously accepted offer. It is further agreed by the institutions and organizations subscribing to the above Resolution that a copy of the Resolution should accompany every scholarship, fellowship, traineeship, and assistantship offer. (APA, 1996, p. viii)

However, this resolution was subsequently modified by the Council of Graduate Departments of Psychology to read:

An acceptance given or left in force after April 15 commits the student not to solicit or accept another offer. Offers made after April 15 must include the proviso that the offer is void if acceptance of a previous offer from a department accepting this resolution is in force on that date. These rules are binding on all persons acting on the behalf of the offering institution. (APA, 1996, p. viii)

Most recently, the following motion was passed:

That the currently prevailing procedures dealing with the offering and acceptance of financial aid are intended to cover graduate admissions as well as offers of financial aid. To protect candidates against the need to make premature decisions, graduate programs should allow applicants until April 15 to make final decisions. (APA, 1996, p. viii)

Still, if you have decided not to accept an offer, courtesy dictates that you inform the department of your decision as soon as possible. This will be appreciated by the department and may provide space for another student. If you do not receive an acceptance letter in April, you may receive one later because space does become available as accepted students decline offers.

Will I Be Successful in Gaining Admission?

Obviously, we can't answer this question with certainty, but we hope the information and suggestions presented here are helpful to you. A careful examination of your own credentials and the advice of those who have experience with students applying to graduate school in clinical psychology will help you apply to appropriate programs, and to maximize your chances of admission. We wish you success!

References

Abdel, K. A. M. (1994). Normative results on the Arabic Fear Survey Schedule III. *Journal of Behavior Therapy and Experimental Psychiatry, 25,* 61-67.

Abikoff, H. (1985). Efficacy of cognitive training interventions in hyperactive children: A critical review. *Clinical Psychology Review, 5,* 479-512.

Abikoff, H., & Gittelman, R. (1985). Hyperactive children maintained on stimulants: Is cognitive training a useful adjunct? *Archives of General Psychiatry, 42,* 953-961.

Abikoff, H., Gittelman-Klein, R., & Klein, D. (1977). Validation of a classroom observation code for hyperactive children. *Journal of Consulting and Clinical Psychology, 45,* 772-783.

Ables, B. S., & Brandsma, J. M. (1977). *Therapy for couples.* San Francisco: Jossey-Bass.

Abood, L. G. (1960). A chemical approach to the problem of mental illness. In D. D. Jackson (Ed.), *The etiology of schizophrenia* (pp. 91-119). New York: Basic Books.

Abramowitz, J. S. (1996). Variants of exposure and response prevention in the treatment of obsessive-compulsive disorder: A meta-analysis. *Behavior Therapy, 27,* 583-600.

Abramson, L. Y., Seligman, M. E. P., & Teasdale, J. D. (1978). Learned helplessness in humans: Critique and reformulation. *Journal of Abnormal Psychology, 87,* 49-74.

Achenbach, T. M. (1978). The Child Behavior Profile: I. Boys aged 6-11. *Journal of Consulting and Clinical Psychology, 46,* 478-488.

Achenbach, T. M. (1982). *Developmental psychopathology* (2nd ed.). New York: John Wiley.

Achenbach, T. M. (1985). *Assessment and taxonomy of child and adolescent psychopathology.* Newbury Park, CA: Sage.

Achenbach, T. M. (1988). Integrating assessment and taxonomy. In M. Rutter, A. H. Tuma, & I. S. Lann (Eds.), *Assessment and diagnosis in child psychopathology* (pp. 300-343). New York: Guilford Press.

Achenbach, T. M., & Edelbrock, C. S. (1978). The classification of child psychopathology: A review and analysis of empirical efforts. *Psychological Bulletin, 85,* 1275-1301.

Achenbach, T. M., & Edelbrock, C. S. (1979). The child behavior profile: II. Boys aged 12-16 and girls aged 6-11. *Journal of Consulting and Clinical Psychology, 47,* 223-233.

Achenbach, T. M., & Edelbrock, C. S. (1981). Behavioral problems and competencies reported by parents of normal and disturbed children aged four to sixteen. *Monographs of the Society for Research in Child Development, 46,* Serial No. 188.

Achenbach, T. M., & Edelbrock, C. S. (1991). *Manual for the Childhood Behavior Checklist and Revised Child Behavior Profile.* Burlington: University of Vermont Press.

Ackerman, M. J., & Ackerman, M. C. (1997). Custody evaluation practices: A survey of experienced professionals (revisited). *Professional Psychology: Research and Practice, 28,* 137-145.

Ackerman, N. W. (1958). *The psychodynamics of family life.* New York: Basic Books.

Adams, H. E., Doster, J. A., & Calhoun, K. S. (1977). A psychologically based system of response classification. In A. R. Ciminero, K. S. Calhoun, and H. E. Adams (Eds.), *Handbook of behavioral assessment* (pp. 47-78). New York: John Wiley.

Adams, K. M. (1980a). An end of innocence for behavioral neurology? Adams replies. *Journal of Consulting and Clinical Psychology, 48,* 522-524.

Adams, K. M. (1980b). In search of Luria's battery: A false start. *Journal of Consulting and Clinical Psychology, 48,* 511-516.

Adams, K. M., & Rourke, B. P. (1992). *The TCH guide to professional practice in clinical neuropsychology.* The Netherlands: Swets & Zeitlinger.

Adler, A. (1933). *Social interest: A challenge to mankind.* Vienna, Leipzig: Rolf Passer.

Adler, N. E., Boyce, T., Chesney, M. A., Cohen, S., Folkman, S., Kahn, R. L., & Syme, S. L. (1994). Socioeconomic status and health: The challenge of the gradient. *American Psychologist, 49,* 15-24.

Adler, N. E., & Matthews, K. (1994). Health psychology: Why do some people get sick and some stay well. *Annual Review of Psychology, 45,* 229-259.

Ainsworth, M. D. S., & Wittig, B. A. (1969). Attachment and the exploratory behavior of one-year-olds in a strange situation. In B. M. Foss (Ed.), *Determinants of infant behavior,* (Vol. 4, pp. 113-136). London: Methuen.

Albee, G. W. (1959). *Mental health manpower trends.* New York: Basic Books.

Albee, G. W. (1996). Revolutions and counterrevolutions in prevention. *American Psychologist, 51,* 1130-1133.

Alberti, R. E., & Emmons, M. L. (1974). *Your perfect right: A guide to assertive behavior.* San Luis Obispo, CA: Impact.

Alexander, F. M., & French, T. M. (1946). *Psychoanalytic therapy.* New York: Ronald Press.

Alexander, J. F., & Parsons, B. V. (1982). *Functional family therapy.* Monterey, CA: Brooks/Cole.

Alexander, J. F., Holtzworth-Munroe, A., & Jameson, P. B. (1994). The process and outcome of marital and family therapy: Research review and evaluation. In A. E. Bergin & S. L. Garfield (Eds.), *Handbook of psychotherapy and behavior change* (pp. 595-630). New York: John Wiley and Sons.

Alexander, J. F., & Parsons, B. V. (1973). Short-term behavioral intervention with delinquent families: Impact on family process and recidivism. *Journal of Abnormal Psychology, 81,* 219-225.

Allen, G. J. (1971). The effectiveness of study counseling and desensitization in alleviating test anxiety in college students. *Journal of Abnormal Psychology, 77,* 282–289.

Allen, K. W. (1996). Chronic nailbiting: A controlled comparison of competing response and mild aversion treatments. *Behaviour Research and Therapy, 34,* 269–272.

Alliger, G. M., Lillienfeld, S. O., & Mitchell, K. E. (1996). The susceptibility of overt and covert integrity tests to coaching and faking. *Psychological Science, 7,* 32–39.

Allport, G. W., Vernon, C. E., & Lindzey, G. (1970). *Study of values* (rev. manual). Boston: Houghton-Mifflin.

American Medical Association. (1954). Report of committee on mental health. *Journal of the American Medical Association, 156,* 72.

American Psychiatric Association. (1952). *Diagnostic and statistical manual of mental disorders.* Washington, DC: Author.

American Psychiatric Association. (1968). *Diagnostic and statistical manual of mental disorders* (2nd ed.). Washington, DC: Author.

American Psychiatric Association. (1980). *Diagnostic and statistical manual of mental disorders* (3rd ed.). Washington, DC: Author.

American Psychiatric Association. (1987). *Diagnostic and statistical manual of mental disorders* (3rd ed.-Revised). Washington, DC: Author.

American Psychiatric Association (1994). *Diagnostic and statistical manual of mental disorders (DSM-IV).* (4th ed.). Washington, D.C.: American Psychiatric Association.

American Psychiatric Association (1995). Practice guideline for the treatment of patients with substance abuse disorders: Alcohol, cocaine, opiods. *American Journal of Psychiatry, 152,* (Suppl. 11), 5–59.

American Psychological Association. (1947). Recommended graduate training programs in clinical psychology. *American Psychologist, 2,* 539–558.

American Psychological Association. (1953). *Ethical standards of psychologists.* Washington, DC: Author.

American Psychological Association. (1958). Committee on Relations with Psychiatry, Annual Report, *American Psychologist, 13,* 761–763.

American Psychological Association. (1959). Ethical standards of psychologists. *American Psychologist, 14,* 279–282.

American Psychological Association. (1963). Ethical standards of psychologists. *American Psychologist, 18,* 56–60.

American Psychological Association. (1967). *Casebook on ethical standards of psychologists.* Washington, DC: Author.

American Psychological Association. (1981). *Specialty guidelines for the delivery of services by clinical psychologists.* Washington, DC: Author.

American Psychological Association. (1982). *Ethical principles in the conduct of research with human subjects.* Washington, DC: Author.

American Psychological Association. (1985). *Standards for educational and psychological tests.* Washington, DC: Author.

American Psychological Association. (1986). *Guidelines for computer-based tests and interpretations.* Washington, DC: Author.

American Psychological Association. (1987). General guidelines for providers of psychological services. *American Psychologist, 42,* 712–723.

American Psychological Association (1987a). *Casebook on ethical standards of Psychologists.* (Rev. ed.) Washington, DC: Author.

American Psychological Association (1987b). *General Guidelines for Providers of Psychological Services.* Washington, DC: Author.

American Psychological Association. (1992a). Ethical principles of psychologists and code of conduct. *American Psychologist, 47,* 1597-1611.

American Psychological Association (1992b). *Guidelines for ethical conduct in the care and use of animals.* Washington, DC: Author.

American Psychological Association (1993). Guidelines for providers of psychological services to ethnic, linguistic, and culturally diverse populations. *American Psychologist, 48,* 45-48.

American Psychological Association. (1994). *Publication manual of the American Psychological Association* (4th ed.). Washington, DC: Author.

American Psychological Association. (1995a). *Report of the task force on the changing gender composition of psychology.* Washington, D.C.: APA.

American Psychological Association. (1995b). *1993 directory survey, with new member updates for 1994 and 1995.* Washington, D.C.: APA Research Office.

American Psychological Society (1996). A new alliance of doctoral training programs form. *APS Observer 9,* pp. 22, 37, 39, 44.

American Psychological Association Board of Professional Affairs Task Force (1995). *Template for developing guidelines: Interventions for mental disorders and psychosocial aspects of physical disorders.* Washington, D.C.: American Psychological Association.

American Psychological Association Division of Neuropsychology. (1989). Definition of a neuropsychologist. *The Clinical Neuropsychologist, 3,* 22.

Amundson, M. E., Hart, C. A., & Holmes, T. H. (1986). *Manual for the schedule of recent experience.* Seattle: University of Washington Press.

Anastasi, A. (1988). *Psychological testing* (6th ed.). New York: Macmillan.

Anastasi, A. (1992). What counselors should know about the use and interpretation of psychological tests. *Journal of Counseling and Development, 70,* 610-615.

Anastasi, A., & Urbina, S. (1997). *Psychological testing.* (7th ed.) Upper Saddle River, N.J.: Prentice Hall.

Anchin, J. C., & Kiesler, D. J. (Eds.). (1982). *Handbook of interpersonal psychotherapy.* New York: Pergamon Press.

Andersen, B. L. (1992). Psychological interventions for cancer patients to enhance the quality of life. *Journal of Consulting & Clinical Psychology, 60,* 552-568.

Anderson, N. B. (1989). Racial differences in stress-reduced cardiovascular reactivity and hypertension: Current status and substantive issues. *Psychological Bulletin, 105,* 89-105.

Andreasen, N. C., Arndt, S., Swayze II, V., Cizadlo, T., Flaum, M., O'Leary, D., Ehrhandt, J. C., & Yuh, W. T. C. (1994). Thalamic abnormalities in schizophrenia visualized through magnetic resonance image averaging. *Science, 266,* 294-298.

Andreasen, N., Nasrullah, H., Dunn, V., Olson, S., Grove, W., Erhardt, J, Coffman, J., & Crosett, J. (1986). Structural abnormalities in the frontal system in schizophrenia *Archives of General Psychiatry, 43,* 136-144.

Andrews, G., & Harvey, R. (1981). Does psychotherapy benefit neurotic patients? A re-analysis of the Smith, Glass, and Miller data. *Archives of General Psychiatry, 38,* 1203-1208.

Andrews, J. D. W. (1989). Integrating visions of reality: Interpersonal diagnosis and the existential vision. *American Psychologist, 44,* 803–817.

Anson, D. A., Golding, S. L., & Gully, K. J. (1993). Child sexual abuse allegations: Reliability of criteria-based content analysis. *Law and Human Behavior, 17,* 331–341.

Antoni, M. H., Baggett, L., Ironoson, G., Laperriere, A., August, S., Klimas, N., Schneiderman, N., & Fletcher, M. A. (1991). Cognitive-behavioral stress management intervention buffers distress responses amd immunologic changes following notification of HIV-1 seropositivity. *Journal of Consulting and Clinical Psychology, 59,* 906–915.

Antonuccio, D. O., Danton, W. G., & DeNelsky, G. Y. (1995). Psychotherapy vs. medication for depression: Challenging the conventional wisdom with data. *Professional Psychology: Research and Practice, 26,* 574–585.

Appelbaum, P. (1994). *Almost a revolution: Mental health law and the limits of change.* New York: Oxford University Press.

Appelbaum, P. S. (1994). *Almost a revolution: Mental health law and the limits of change.* New York: Oxford University Press.

Appelbaum, P. S., & Grisso, T. (1995). The MacArthur Treatment Competence Study. I: Mental illness and competence to consent to treatment. *Law and Human Behavior, 19,* 105–126.

Appelbaum, P. S., & Hoge, S. K. (1986). The right to refuse treatment: What the research reveals. *Behavioral Services and the Law, 4,* 279–292.

Appels, A., & Otten, F. (1992). Exhaustion as precursor of cardiac death. *British Journal of Clinical Psychology, 31,* 351–356.

Appels, A., & Schouten, E. (1991). Burnout as a risk factor for coronary heart disease. *Behavioral Medicine, 17,* 53–59.

Archer, R. P., Maruish, M., Imhof, E. A., & Piotrowski, C. (1991). Psychological test usage with adolescent clients: 1990 survey findings. *Professional Psychology: Research and Practice, 22,* 247–252.

Arens, R., Granfield, D. D., & Susman, J. (1965). Jurors, jury charges, and insanity. *Catholic Univeristy Law Review, 14,* 1–29.

Arkes, H. A. (1981). Impediments to accurate clinical judgment and possible ways to minimize their impact. *Journal of Consulting and Clinical Psychology, 49,* 323–330.

Asher, S. R., & Wheeler, V. A. (1985). Children's loneliness: A comparison of rejected and neglected peer status. *Journal of Consulting and Clinical Psychology, 53,* 500–505.

Atkinson, D. R., Brown, M. T., Parham, T. A., Matthews, L. G., Landrum-Brown, J., & Kim, A. U. (1996). African American client skin tone and clinical judgments of African American and European American psychologists. *Professional Psychology: Research and Practice, 27,* 500–505.

Atkinson, J. W. (1981). Studying personality in the context of an advanced motivational psychology. *American Psychologist, 36,* 117–128.

Auld, F., Jr., & Murray, E. J. (1955). Content-analysis studies of psychotherapy. *Psychological Bulletin, 52,* 377–395.

Austed, C. S., & Berman, W. H. (1991). Managed health care and the evolution of psychotherapy. In C. S. Austed & W. H. Berman (Eds.), *Psychotherapy in managed health care: The optimal use of time and resources.* (pp. 3–18). Washington, D.C.: American Psychological Association.

Axin, W. G. (1991). The influence of interviewer sex on responses to sensitive questions in Nepal. *Social Science Research, 20,* 303–318.

Axline, V. M. (1976). Play therapy procedures and results. In C. Schaefer (Ed.), *The therapeutic use of child's play.* New York: Jason Aronson.

Ayllon, T., & Azrin, N. H. (1965). The measurement and reinforcement of behavior of psychotics. *Journal of the Experimental Analysis of Behavior, 8,* 357-383.

Azar, B. (1996). Behavioral interventions are proven to reduce pain. *APA Monitor,* December, p. 22.

Azar, S. T., & Benjet, C. L. (1994). A cognitive perspective on ethnicity, race, and termination of parental rights. *Law and Human Behavior, 18,* 249-267.

Azrin, N. H., & Peterson, A. L. (1989). Reduction of an eye tic by controlled blinking. *Behavior Therapy, 20,* 467-473.

Babiker, G. (1993). Projective testing in the evaluation of the effects of sexual abuse in childhood: A review. *British Journal of Projective Psychology, 38,* 45-53.

Backer, T. E., & Richardson, D. (1989). Building bridges: Psychologists and families of the mentally ill. *American Psychologist, 44,* 546-550.

Baekeland, F., & Lundwall, L. (1975). Dropping out of treatment: A critical review. *Psychological Bulletin, 82,* 738-783.

Baer, D. M. (1973). The control of development process: Why not? In J. R. Nesselroade & H. W. Reese (Eds.), *Life-span developmental psychology.* New York: Academic Press.

Baer, R., & Nietzel, M. T. (1991). Cognitive and behavioral treatment of impulsivity in children: A meta-analytic review of the outcome literature. *Journal of Clinical Child Psychology, 20,* 400-412.

Bandura, A. (1969). *Principles of behavior modification.* New York: Holt, Rinehart & Winston.

Bandura, A. (1977). Self-efficacy: Toward a unifying theory of behavioral change. *Psychological Review, 84,* 191-215.

Bandura, A. (1978). The self system in reciprocal determinism. *American Psychologist, 33,* 344-358.

Bandura, A. (1982). Self-efficacy mechanism in human agency. *American Psychologist, 33,* 122-147.

Bandura, A. (1986). *Social foundations of thought and action: A social cognitive therapy.* Englewood Cliffs, NJ: Prentice Hall.

Bandura, A., Ross, D., & Ross, S. A. (1963). Imitation of film-mediated aggressive models. *Journal of Abnormal and Social Psychology, 66,* 3-11.

Banta, H. D., & Saxe, L. (1983). Reimbursement for psychotherapy: Linking efficacy research and public policymaking. *American Psychologist, 38,* 918-923.

Barker, R. G., Dembo, T., & Lewin, K. (1941). Frustration and regression: An experiment with young children. *University of Iowa Student Child Welfare, 18,* No. 1.

Barker, R. G., & Wright, H. F. (1951). *One boy's day.* New York: Harper.

Barker, R. G., & Wright, H. F. (1955). *Midwest and its children: The psychological ecology of an American town.* New York: Row, Peterson.

Barkham, M., Rees, A., Shapiro, D. A., Stiles, W. B., Agnew, R. M., Halstead, J., Culverwell, A., & Harrington, V. M. G. (1996b). Outcomes of time-limited psychotherapy in applied settings: Replicating the second Sheffield psychotherapy project. *Journal of Clinical and Consulting Psychology, 64,* 1079-1085.

Barkham, M., Rees, A., Stiles, W. B., Shapiro, D. A., Hardy, G. E., & Reynolds, S. (1996a). Dose-effect relations in time-limited psychotherapy for depression. *Journal of Clinical and Consulting Psychology, 64*, 927–935.

Barkley, R. A., & Cunningham, C. E. (1979). The effects of Ritalin on the mother-child interaction of hyperactive children. *Archives of General Psychiatry, 36*, 201–208.

Barlow, D. H. (1996). Health care policy, psychotherapy research, and the future of psychotherapy. *American Psychologist, 51*, 1050–1058.

Barlow, D. H., & Hersen, M. (1984). *Single-case experimental designs: Strategies for studying behavior* (2nd ed.). New York: Pergamon Press.

Barlow, D. H., & Waddell, M. T. (1985). Agoraphobia. In D. H. Barlow (Ed.), *Clinical handbook of psychological disorders* (pp. 1–68). New York: Guilford Press.

Barlow, D. H., & Wolfe, B. (1981). Behavioral approaches to anxiety disorders: A report on the NIMH-SUNY, Albany, research conference. *Journal of Consulting and Clinical Psychology, 49*, 448–454.

Barona, A., & Chastain, R. L. (1986). An improved estimate of premorbid IQ for blacks and whites on the WAIS-R. *International Journal of Clinical Neuropsychology, 8*, 169–173.

Barr, C., Mednick, S., & Munk-Jorgensen, P. (1990). Exposure to influenza epidemics during gestations and adult schizophrenia: A 40-year study. *Archives of General Psychiatry, 47*, 869–874.

Barrett, G. V., & Depinet, R. L. (1991). A reconsideration of testing for competence rather than for intelligence. *American Psychologist, 46*, 1012–1024.

Barrick, M. R. & Mount, M. K. (1996). Effects of impression management and self-deception on the predictive validity of personality constructs. *Journal of Applied Psychology, 81*, 261–272.

Barth, P. S. (1990). Workers' compensation for medical stress cases. *Behavioral Sciences and the Law, 8*, 349–360.

Barthell, C. N., & Holmes, D. S. (1968). High school yearbooks: A nonreactive measure of social isolation in graduates who later became schizophrenic. *Journal of Abnormal Psychology, 73*, 313–316.

Bartlett, C. J., & Green, C. G. (1966). Clinical prediction: Does one sometimes know too much? *Journal of Counseling Psychology, 13*, 267–270.

Bartol, C. R., & Bartol, A. M. (1994). *Psychology and law: Research and application.* Pacific Grove, CA: Brooks/Cole.

Barton, A. (1974). *Three worlds of therapy: An existential-phenomenological study of the therapies of Freud, Jung, and Rogers.* Palo Alto, CA: National Press Books.

Basic Behavioral Science Task Force of the National Advisory Mental Health Council (1996). Basic behavioral science rsearch for mental health. *American Psychologist, 51*, 722–731.

Bates, E. (1976). *Language and context: The acquisition of pragmatics.* New York: Academic Press.

Bateson, C., Jackson, D. D., Haley, J., & Weakland, J. H. (1956). Toward a theory of schizophrenia. *Behavioral Science, 1*, 251–264.

Baucom, D. H., Epstein, N., Sayers, S., & Sher, T. G. (1989). The role of cognitions in marital relationships: Definitional, methodological, and conceptual issues. *Journal of Consulting and Clinical Psychology, 57*, 31–38.

Baum, C. G., Forehand, R., & Zeigob, L. E. (1979). A review of observer reactivity in adult-child interactions. *Journal of Behavioral Assessment, 1*, 167–178.

Bauman, L. J., Stein, R. E. K., & Ireys, H. T. (1991). Reinventing fidelity: The transfer of social technology among settings. *American Journal of Community Psychology, 19,* 619-640.

Baumeister, R. F., & Leary, M. R. (1995). The need to belong: Desire for interpersonal attachments as a fundamental human motivation. *Psychological Bulletin, 117,* 497-529.

Bayley, N. (1965). Comparisons of mental and motor test scores for ages 1-15 months by sex, birth order, race, geographic location, and education of parents. *Child Development, 36,* 379-411.

Bayne, R. (1995). *The Meyers-Briggs type indicator: A critical review and practical guide.* New York: Chapman & Hall.

Bazelon, D. (1974). Psychiatrists and the adversary process. *Scientific American, 230,* 18-23.

Bear, D. M. & Fedio, P. (1977). Quantitative analysis of interictal behavior in temporal lobe epilepsy. *Archives of Neurology, 34,* 454-467.

Beck, A. T. (1976). *Cognitive therapy and the emotional disorders.* New York: International Universities Press.

Beck, A. T. (1987). Cognitive models of depression. *Journal of Cognitive Psychotherapy, 1,* 5-37.

Beck, A. T., Freeman, & Associates (1990). *Cognitive therapy of personality disorders.* New York: Guilford Press.

Beck, A. T., Rush, A. J., Shaw, B. F., & Emery, G. (1979). *Cognitive therapy of depression.* New York: Guilford Press.

Beck, A. T., Ward, C. H., Mendelson, M., Mock, J., & Erbaugh, J. (1961). An inventory for measuring depression. *Archives of General Psychiatry, 4,* 561-571.

Beck, A. T. & Weishaar, M. E. (1995). Cognitive therapy. In R. J. Corsini & D. Wedding, D. (Eds.). *Current psychotherapies* (5th ed.). Itasca, Illinois: Peacock Publishers, Inc. (pp. 229-261).

Beck, L. E. (1991). *Child development.* (2nd Ed.). Boston: Allyn and Bacon.

Beck, S. J. (1952). *Rorschach's test: Vol. 3. Advances in interpretation.* New York: Grune & Stratton.

Becker, M. H., & Maiman, L. A. (1975). Sociobehavioral determinants of compliance with health and medical care recommendations. *Medical Care, 13,* 10-24.

Bednar, R. L., & Kaul, T. (1994). Experiential group research. In A. E. Bergin & S. L. Garfield (Eds.), *Handbook of psychotherapy and behavior change* (pp. 631-663). New York: Wiley & Sons.

Belar, C. D. (1995). Collaboration in capitated care: Challenges for psychology. *Professional Psychology: Research and Practice, 26,* 139-146.

Belar, C. D., Bieliauskas, L. A., Larsen, K. G., Mensh, I. N., Poey, K., & Roelke, H. J. (1989). The National Conference on internship training in psychology. *American Psychologist, 44,* 60-65.

Belar, C. D., & Perry, N. W. (1992). National conference on scientist-practitioner education and training for the professional practice of psychology. *American Psychologist, 47,* 71-75.

Belar, C. D., & Perry, N. W. (Eds.). (1991). *Proceedings: National conference on scientist-practitioner education and training for the professional practice of psychology.* Sarasota, FL: Professional Resource Press.

Bell, P. F., Digman, R. H., & McKenna, J. P. (1995). Should psychologists obtain prescribing privileges? A survey of family physicians. *Professional Psychology: Research and Practice, 26,* 371-376.

Bell, R. Q., & Harper, L. V. (1977). *Child effects on adults.* Lincoln and London: University of Nebraska Press.

Bellack, A. S., & Hersen, M. (Eds.). (1988). *Behavioral assessment: A practical handbook* (3rd ed.). New York: Pergamon Press.

Bellack, A. S., Hersen, M., & Himmelhoch, J. M. (1983). A comparison of social skills training, pharmacotherapy and psychotherapy for depression. *Behaviour Research and Therapy, 21,* 101–107.

Bellack, A. S., Hersen, M., & Kazdin, A. E. (Eds.). (1990). *International handbook of behavior modification and therapy* (2nd ed.). New York: Plenum Press.

Bellak, L. (1954). *The Thematic Apperception Test and the Children's Apperception Test in clinical use.* New York: Grune & Stratton.

Bellak, L. (1986). *The Thematic Apperception Test, the Children's Apperception Test, and the Senior Apperception Technique in Clinical Use* (4th ed.). New York: Grune & Stratton.

Bellak, L. (1992). *The TAT, CAT, and SAT in clinical use* (5th ed.). Odessa, FL: Psychological Assessment Resources.

Bemporad, J. R., & Schwab, M. E. (1986). The DSM-III and clinical child psychiatry. In T. Millon & G. L. Klerman (Eds.), *Contemporary directions in psychopathology: Toward the DSM-IV* (pp. 135–150). New York: Guilford Press.

Bender, L. A. (1938). A visual motor Gestalt test and its clinical use. *American Orthopsychiatric Association Research Monograph, No. 3.*

Benjamin, L. S. (1980). *INTREX users' manual.* Madison, WI: INTREX Interpersonal Institute.

Benjamin, L. S. (1993). *Interpersonal diagnosis and treatment of personality disorders.* New York: Guilford Press.

Bennett, C. C. (1965). Community psychology: Impressions of the Boston conference on the education of psychologists for community mental health. *American Psychologist, 20,* 832–835.

Ben-Porath, Y. S., & Butcher, J. N. (1991). The historical development of personality assessment. In C. E. Walker (Ed.), *Clinical psychology: Historical and research foundations* (pp. 121–158). New York: Plenum Press.

Ben-Porath, Y. S., & Waller, N. G. (1992). "Normal" personality inventories in clinical assessment: General requirements and potential for using the NEO Personality Inventory. *Psychological Assessment, 4,* 14–19.

Benton, A. L. (1974). *Revised visual retention test: Clinical and experimental applications* (4th ed.). New York: Psychological Corporation.

Benton, A. L., Hamsher, K., Varney, N. R., & Spreen, O. (1983). *Contributions to neuropsychological assessment: A clinical manual.* New York: Oxford University Press.

Benton, M. K., & Schroeder, H. E. (1990). Social skills training with schizophrenia: A meta-analytic evaluation. *Journal of Consulting and Clinical Psychology, 58,* 741–747.

Berg, I. A. (1955). Response bias and personality: The deviation hypothesis. *Journal of Psychology, 40,* 61–71.

Bergin, A. E. (1971). The evaluation of therapeutic outcomes. In A. E. Bergin & S. L. Garfield (Eds.), *Handbook of psychotherapy and behavior change: An empirical analysis* (pp. 217–270). New York: John Wiley.

Bergin, A. E., & Lambert, M. J. (1978). The evaluation of therapeutic outcomes. In S. L. Garfield & A. E. Bergin (Eds.), *Handbook of psychotherapy and behavior change: An empirical analysis* (2nd ed., pp. 139–190). New York: John Wiley.

Berman, J. S., & Norton, N. C. (1985). Does professional training make a therapist more effective? *Psychological Bulletin, 98,* 401–406.

Bernstein, D. A. (1973). Behavioral fear assessment: Anxiety or artifact? In H. Adams & P. Unikel (Eds.), *Issues and trends in behavior therapy* (pp. 225–267). Springfield, IL: Charles C. Thomas.

Bernstein, D.A., & Borkovec, T. D. (1973). *Progressive relaxation training.* Champaign, IL: Research Press.

Bernstein, D. A., & Carlson, C. R. (1993). Progressive relaxation: Abbreviated methods. In P. M. Lehrer & R. Woolfolk (Eds.), *Principles and practices of stress management* (2nd ed., pp. 53–87). New York: Guilford Press.

Bernstein, D. A., Clarke-Stewart, A., Roy, E. J., & Wickens, C. D. (1997). *Psychology.* (4th ed.) Boston: Houghton Mifflin Company.

Bernstein, D. A., & Nietzel, M. T. (1977). Demand characteristics in behavior modification: A natural history of a "nuisance." In M. Hersen, R. M. Eisler, & P. M. Miller (Eds.), *Progress in behavior modification* (Vol. 4, pp. 119–162). New York: Academic Press.

Bernstein, D. A., & Paul, G. L. (1971). Some comments on therapy analogue research with small animal "phobias." *Journal of Behavior Therapy and Experimental Psychiatry, 2,* 225–237.

Berry, D., Baer, R., & Harris, M. (1991). Detection of malingering on the MMPI: A meta-analysis. *Clinical Psychology Review, 11,* 585–598.

Bersoff, D. (Ed.). (1995). *Ethical conflicts in psychology.* Washington, DC: American Psychological Association.

Bettleheim, B. (1967). *The empty fortress.* New York: Free Press.

Bickman, L. (1987). Graduate education in psychology. *American Psychologist, 42,* 1041–1047.

Bickman, L., & Dokecki, P. R. (1989). Public and private responsibility for mental health services. *American Psychologist, 44,* 1133–1137.

Bickman, L., & Ellis, H. (Eds.). (1990). *Preparing psychologists for the 21st century.* Hillsdale, NJ: Erlbaum.

Bieri, J., Atkins, A. L., Briar, S., Leaman, R. L., Miller, H., & Tripoldi, T. (1966). *Clinical and social judgment: The discrimination of behavioral information.* New York: John Wiley.

Bijou, S. W., Peterson, R. F., & Ault, M. H. (1968). A method to integrate descriptive and experimental field studies at the level of data and empirical concepts. *Journal of Applied Behavior Analysis, 1,* 175–191.

Blackburn, H., Luepker, R. V., Kline, F. G., Bracht, N., Carlaw, R., Jacobs, D., Mittelmark, M., Stauffer, L., & Taylor, H. L. (1984). The Minnesota Heart Health Program: A research and demonstration project in cardiovascular disease prevention. In J. D. Matarazzo et al. (Eds.), *Behavioral health: A handbook of health enhancement and disease prevention* (pp. 1171–1178). New York: John Wiley.

Blake, B. G. (1965). The application of behaviour therapy to the treatment of alcoholism. *Behaviour Research and Therapy, 3,* 75–85.

Blanchard, E. B. (1992). Psychological treatment of benign headache disorders. *Journal of Consulting and Clinical Psychology, 60,* 537–551.

Blanchard, E. B. (1994). Behavioral medicine and health psychology. In A. E. Bergin & S. L. Garfield (Eds.), *Handbook of psychotherapy and behavior change* (pp. 701–733). New York: Wiley & Sons, Inc.

Blatt, S. J., & Lerner, H. (1983). Psychodynamic perspectives on personality theory. In M. Hersen, A. E. Kazdin, & A. S. Bellack (Eds.), *The clinical psychology handbook* (pp. 87–106). New York: Pergamon Press.

Blau, T. H. (1988). *Psychotherapy tradecraft: The technique and style of doing therapy.* New York: Brunner/Mazel.

Block, J. H., Block, J., & Gjerde, P. F. (1986). The personality of children prior to divorce: A prospective study. *Child Development, 57,* 827–840.

Bloom, B. L. (1992). *Planned short-term psychotherapy: A clinical handbook.* Boston: Allyn & Bacon.

Bloom, B. L., Hodges, W. F., & Caldwell, R. A. (1982). A preventive program for the newly separated: Initial evaluation. *American Journal of Community Psychology, 10,* 251–264.

Blouke, P. S. (1997). Musings of a bureaucratic psychologist. *Professional Psychology: Research and Practice, 28,* 326–328.

Blount, R. L., Bachanas, P. J., Powers, S. W., Cotter, M. C., Franklin, A., Chaplin, W., Mayfield, J., Henderson, M., & Blount, S. D. (1992). Training children to cope and parents to coach them during routine immunizations: Effects on child, parent, and staff behavior. *Behavior Therapy, 23,* 689–705.

Blumenthal, S. J. (1994). Introductory remarks. In S. J. Blumenthal, K. Matthews, & S. M. Weiss (Eds.), *New research frontiers in behavioral medicine* (pp. 9–15). Washington, DC: National Institute of Mental Health.

Blumenthal, S. J., Matthews, K., & Weiss, S. W. (Eds.). (1994). *New research frontiers in behavioral medicine.* Washington, DC: National Institute of Mental Health.

Boczkowski, J. A., Zeichner, A., & DeSanto, N. (1985). Neuroleptic compliance among chronic schizophrenic outpatients: An intervention outcome report. *Journal of Consulting and Clinical Psychology, 53,* 666–671.

Bodmer, W., & McKie, R. (1994). *The book of man: The human genome project and the quest to discover our genetic heritage.* New York: Scribner.

Boehnert, C. (1989). Characteristics of successful and unsuccessful insanity pleas. *Law and Human Behavior, 13,* 31–40.

Bogels, S. M. (1994). A structured-training approach to teaching diagnostic interviewing. *Teaching of Psychology, 21,* 144–150.

Boice, R., & Myers, P. E. (1987). Which setting is healthier and happier, academe or private practice? *Professional Psychology: Research and Practice, 18,* 526–529.

Boll, T. J. (1981). The Halstead-Reitan Neuropsychology Battery. In S. B. Filskov & T. J. Boll (Eds.), *Handbook of clinical neuropsychology* (pp. 577–607). New York: John Wiley.

Bond, G. R., Witheridge, T. F., Dincin, J., Wasmer, D., Webb, J., & Graff-Kaser, R. (1990). Assertive community treatment for frequent users of psychiatric hospitals in a large city: A controlled study. *American Journal of Community Psychology, 18,* 865–891.

Bongar, B. (1988). Clinicians, microcomputers, and confidentiality. *Professional Psychology: Research and Practice, 19,* 286–289.

Bongar, B. (1991). *The suicidal patient: Clinical and legal standards of care.* Washington, DC: American Psychological Association.

Bonnie, R., & Slobogin, C. (1980). The role of mental health professionals in the criminal process: The case for informed speculation. *Virginia Law Review, 66,* 427–522.

Boone, D. E. (1993). WAIS-R scatter with psychiatric patients: II. Intersubtest scatter. *Psychological Reports, 73*, 851–860.

Booth-Keweley, S., & Friedman, H. S. (1987). Psychological predictors of heart disease: A quantitative review. *Psychological Bulletin, 101*, 343–362.

Boothby, H., Mann, A. H., & Barker, A. (1995). Factors determining interrater agreement with rating global change in dementia: The CIBIC-plus. *International Journal of Geriatric Psychiatry, 10*, 1037–1045.

Bootzin, R. (1996). Random samplings. *APS Observer*, January.

Boring, E. G. (1950). *A history of experimental psychology* (2nd ed.). New York: Appleton-Century-Crofts.

Borkovec, T. D., & O'Brien, G. T. (1976). Methodological and target behavior issues in analogue therapy outcome research. In M. Hersen, R. M. Eisler, & P. M. Miller (Eds.), *Progress in behavior modification* (pp. 133–172). New York: Academic Press.

Borum, R. (1996). Improving the clinical practice of violence risk assessment. *American Psychologist, 51*, 945–956.

Borum, R. & Grisso, T. (1995). Psychological test use in criminal forensic evaluations. *Professional Psychology: Research and Practice, 26*, 465–473.

Bouchard, T. J. (1984). Twins reared together and apart: What they tell us about human diversity. In S. W. Fox (Ed.), *Individuality and Determinism*. New York: Plenum.

Boudin, H. (1972). Contingency contracting as a therapeutic tool in the deceleration of amphetamine use. *Behavior Therapy, 3,* 604–608.

Bourg, E. F., Bent, R. J., McHolland, J., & Stricker, G. (1989). Standards and evaluation in the education and training of professional psychologists: The National Council of Schools and Professional Psychology Mission Bay Conference. *American Psychologist, 44,* 66–72.

Bourne, L. E., & Ekstrand, B. R. (1976). *Psychology: Its principles and meanings* (2nd ed.). New York: Holt, Rinehart & Winston.

Bowen, A. M. & Trotter, R. T. II (1995). HIV risk in intravenous drug users and crack cocaine smokers: Predicting stage of change for condom use. *Journal of Consulting and Clinical Psychology, 63*, 238–248.

Bowlby, J. (1969). *Attachment and loss, Vol 1: Attachment*. New York: Basic Books.

Bowlby, J. (1988). Developmental psychiatry comes to age. *American Journal of Psychiatry, 145*, 1–10.

Boyle, G. J. (1995). Meyers-Briggs type indicator (MBTI): Some psychometric limitations. *Australian Psychologist, 30*, 71–74.

Bradbury, T. N., & Fincham, F. D. (1990). Attributions in marriage: Review and critique. *Psychological Bulletin, 107*, 3–33.

Braginsky, B. M., Braginsky, D. D., & Ring, K. (1969). *Methods of madness: The mental hospital as a last resort.* New York: Holt, Rinehart & Winston.

Braginsky, B. M., Grosse, M., & Ring, K. (1966). Controlling outcomes through impression management: An experimental study of the manipulative tactics of mental patients. *Journal of Consulting Psychology, 30,* 295–300.

Branch, C., Milner, B., & Rasmussen, T. (1964). Intracarotid sodium Amytal for the lateralization of cerebral speech dominance. *Journal of Neurosurgery, 21,* 399–405.

Brand, J. L. (1995). Does contemporary cognitive psychology favor or oppose psychoanalytic theory? *American Psychologist, 9,* 799–800.

Brauer, B. A. (1993). Adequacy of a translation of the MMPI into American Sign Langauge for use with deaf individuals: Linguistic equivalency issues. *Rehabilitation Psychology, 38,* 247-260.

Bray, J. H. (1991). Psychological factors affecting custodial and visitation arrangements. *Behavioral Sciences and the Law, 9,* 419-437.

Bray, J. H., & Rogers, J. C. (1995). Linking psychologists and family physicians for collaborative practice. *Professional Psychology: Research and Practice, 26,* 132-138.

Breier, A., Buchanan, R. W., Elkashef, A., Munson, R. C., Kirkpatrick, B., & Gellad, F. (1993). Brian morphology and schizophrenia: A magnetic resonance imaging study of limbic, prefrontal cortex, and caudate structures. *Archives of General Psychiatry, 49,* 921-926.

Brems, C., Thevenin, D. M., & Routh, D. K. (1991). The history of clinical psychology. In C. E. Walker (Ed.), *Clinical psychology: Historical and research foundations* (pp. 3-36). New York: Plenum Press.

Breslow, L. (1979). A positive strategy for the nation's health. *Journal of the American Medical Association, 242,* 2093-2094.

Broman, C. L. (1993). Social relationships and health-related behavior. *Journal of Behavioral Medicine, 16,* 335-350.

Brooks, A. (1986). Law and antipsychotic medications. *Behavioral Sciences and the Law, 4,* 247-264.

Brotemarkle, B. A. (1947). Fifty years of clinical psychology: Clinical psychology 1896-1946. *Journal of Consulting Psychology, 11,* 1-4.

Brown, J. (1987). A review of meta-analyses conducted on psychotherapy outcome research. *Clinical Psychology Review, 7,* 1-24.

Brown, L. S. (1990). Taking account of gender in the clinical assessment interview. *Professional Psychology: Research and Practice, 21,* 12-17.

Brown, R., & Herrnstein, R. J. (1975). *Psychology.* Boston: Little, Brown.

Brown, W. H., Odom, S. L., & Holcombe, A. (1996). Observational assessment of young children's social behavior with peers. *Early Childhood Research Quarterly, 11,* 19-40.

Browne, A., & Finkelhor, D. (1986). Impact of child sexual abuse: A review of the research. *Psychological Bulletin, 99,* 66-77.

Brownell, K. D. (1981). Assessment of eating disorders. In D. H. Barlow (Ed.), *Behavioral assessment of adult disorders* (pp. 329-404). New York: Guilford Press.

Brownell, K. D., & Foreyt, J. P. (1985). Obesity. In D. H. Barlow (Ed.), *Clinical handbook of psychological disorders* (pp. 299-343). New York: Guilford Press.

Brownell, K. D., & Wadden, T. A. (1992). Etiology and treatment of obesity: Understanding a serious, prevalent, and refractory disorder. *Journal of Consulting and Clinical Psychology, 60,* 505-517.

Brunswick, E. (1947). *Systematic and representative design of psychological experiments with results in physical and social perception.* Berkeley: University of California Press.

Brussel, J. A. (1968). *Casebook of a crime psychiatrist.* New York: Bernard Geis Associates.

Buck, J. N. (1948). The H-T-P technique: A qualitative and quantitative scoring manual. *Journal of Clinical Psychology, 4,* 319-396.

Burbach, D. J., & Peterson, L. (1986). Children's concepts of physical illness: A review and critique of the cognitive-developmental literature. *Health Psychology, 5,* 307-325.

Burchard, J. D. (1967). Systematic socialization: A programmed environment for the habitation of antisocial retardates. *Psychological Record, 17,* 461-476.

Burchard, J. D., & Burchard, S. N. (Eds.). (1987). *Prevention of delinquent behavior.* Newbury Park, CA: Sage.

Burger, W. E. (1975). Dissenting opinion in *O'Connor v. Donaldson. U.S. Law Week, 42,* 4929-4936.

Burisch, M. (1984). Approaches to personality inventory construction: A comparison of merits. *American Psychologist, 39,* 214-227.

Burish, T. G., Carey, M. P., Krozely, M. G., & Greco, F. A. (1987). Conditioned side effects induced by cancer chemotherapy: Prevention through behavioral treatment. *Journal of Consulting and Clinical Psychology, 55,* 42-48.

Burnam, M. A., Stein, J. A., Golding, J. M., Siegel, J. M., Sorenson, S. B., Forsythe, A. B., & Telles, C. A. (1988). Sexual assault and mental disorders in a community population. *Journal of Consulting and Clinical Psychology, 56,* 843-850.

Buros, O. K. (Ed.). (1938). *The 1940 mental measurements yearbook.* Highland Park, NJ: Gryphon Press.

Buschbaum, M., Haier, R., Potkin, S., Nuechterlein, K., Bracha, H., Katz, M., Lohr, J,m Wu, J., Lottenberg, S., Jerabek, P., Trenary, M., Tafalla, R., Reynolds, C., & Bunney, W. (1992). Frontostriatal disorder of cerebral metabolism in never-medicated schizophrenics. *Archives of General Psychiatry, 49,* 935-942.

Butcher, J. N. (Ed.). (1987). *Computerized psychological assessment: A practitioner's guide.* New York: Basic Books.

Butcher, J. N., Dahlstrom, W. G., Graham, J. R., Tellegen, A., & Kaemmer, B. (1989). *Manual for administration and scoring of the MMPI-2.* Minneapolis: University of Minnesota Press.

Butcher, J. N., & Keller, L. S. (1984). Objective personality assessment. In G. Goldstein & M. Hersen (Eds.), *Handbook of psychological assessment* (pp. 307-331). New York: Pergamon Press.

Butcher, J. N., & Williams, C. L. (1992). *Essentials of MMPI-2 and MMPI-A interpretation.* Minneapolis: University of Minnesota Press.

Butcher, J. N., Williams, C. L., Graham, J. R., Archer, R., Tellegen, A., Ben-Porath, Y. S., & Kaemmer, B. (1992). *MMPI-A: Manual for administration, scoring, and interpretation.* Minneapolis, MN: University of Minnesota Press.

Cairns, R. B., & Green, J. A. (1979). How to assess personality and social patterns: Observations or ratings? In B. Cairns (Ed.), *The analysis of social interactions: Methods, issues, and illustrations* (pp. 209-226). Hillsdale, NJ: Lawrence Erlbaum Associates.

Callaghan, G. M. (1996). The clinical utility of client dream reports from a radical behavioral perspective. *The Behavior Therapist, 19,* 49-52.

Callahan, V. A., McGreevey, M. A., Cirincione, C., & Steadman, H. J. (1992). Measuring the effects of the guilty but mentally ill (GBMI) verdict: Georgia's 1982 GBMI reform. *Law and Human Behavior, 16,* 447-462.

Campbell, D. T., & Fiske, D. W. (1959). Convergent and discriminant validation by the multitrait-multimethod matrix. *Psychological Bulletin, 56,* 81-105.

Campbell, S. B. (1989). Developmental perspectives in child psychopathology. In M. Hersen & T. Ollendick (Eds.), *Handbook of child psychopathology* (2nd ed., pp. 5-28). New York: Plenum Press.

Canter, M. B, Bennett, B. E., Jones, S. E., & Nagy, T. F. (1994). *Ethics for psychologists: A commentary on the APA ethics code.* Washington, DC: American Psychological Association.

Cantor, D. W. (1996). Lowering the standard of care. *APA Monitor*, November, p. 2.

Cantwell, D. P. (1983). Depression in childhood: Clinical picture and diagnosis criteria. In D. P. Cantwell & G. A. Carlson (Eds.), *Affective disorders in childhood and adolescence* (pp. 3-18). New York: Spectrum.

Caplan, G. (1964). *Principles of preventive psychiatry.* New York: Basic Books.

Carlson, H. S. (1978). The AASPB Story: The beginnings and first 16 years of the American Association of State Psychology Boards, 1961-1977. *American Psychologist, 33,* 486-495.

Carroll, J. B. (1993). *Human cognitive abilities: A survey of factor-analytic studies.* Cambridge, England: University of Cambridge Press.

Carson, R. C. (1969). *Interaction concepts of personality.* Chicago: Aldine.

Carson, R. C. (1991). Dilemmas in the pathway of the DSM-IV. *Journal of Abnormal Psychology, 100,* 302-307.

Casey, R. J., & Berman, J. S. (1985). The outcome of psychotherapy with children. *Psychological Bulletin, 98,* 388-400.

Caspi, A., Henry, B., McGee, R. O., Moffitt, T. E., & Silva, P. A. (1995). Temperamental origins of child and adolescent behavior problems: From age 3 to age 15. *Child Development, 66,* 55-68.

Caspi, A., & Silva, P. A. (1995). Temperamental qualities at age 3 predict personality traits in young adulthood: Longitudinal evidence from a birth cohort. *Child Development, 66,* 486-498.

Cattell, R. B., Eber, H. W., & Tatusoka, M. M. (1970). *Handbook for the Sixteen Personality Factor Questionnaire.* Champaign, IL: Institute for Personality and Ability Testing.

Cattell, R. B., Eber, H. W., & Tatusoka, M. (1992). *Handbook for the sixteen personality factor questionnaire (16PF).* Champaign, Ill: Institute for Personality and Ability Testing.

Cautela, J. R. (1966). Treatment of compulsive behavior by covert sensitization. *Psychological Record, 86,* 33-41.

Cautela, J. R., & Kastenbaum, R. A. (1967). A reinforcement survey schedule for use in therapy, training, and research. *Psychological Reports, 20,* 1115-1130.

Cautela, J., & Kearney, A. J. (1986). *The covert conditioning handbook.* New York: Springer.

Ceci, S. J., & Bruck, M. (1993). Suggestibility of the child witness: A historical review and synthesis. *Psychological Bulletin, 113,* 403-439.

Chambliss, D. L. (1995). Training in and dissemination of empirically-validated psychological treatments: Report and recommendations. *The Clinical Psychologist, 48,* 3-23.

Chambliss, D. L., Babich, K., Crits-Christoph, P., Frank, E., Gilson, M., Montgomery, R., Rich, R., Steinberg, J., & Weinberger, J. (1995). Training in and dissemination of empirically-validated psychological treatments: Report and Recommendations. *The Clinical Psychologist, 48,* 3-23.

Chan, D. W., & Lee, H. B. (1995). Patterns of psychological test use in Hong Kong in 1993. *Professional Psychology: Research and Practice, 26,* 292-297.

Chandler, M. (1973). Egocentrism and antisocial behavior: The assessment and training of social perspective-taking skills. *Developmental Psychology, 9,* 326-332.

Chapman, L. J., & Chapman, J. P. (1967). The genesis of popular but erroneous psychodiagnostic observations. *Journal of Abnormal Psychology, 72,* 193-204.

Charlton-Seifert, J., Stratton, B. D., & Williams, M. G. (1980). Sweet and slow: Diet can affect learning. *Academic Therapy, 16,* 211-217.

Chesler, P. (1972). *Women and madness.* New York: Doubleday.

Chess, S., & Thomas, A. (1986). *Temperament in clinical practice.* New York: Guilford Press.

Christensen, A., Margolin, G., & Sullaway, M. (1992). Interparental agreement on child behavior problems. *Psychological Assessment, 4,* 419-425.

Christiansen, B. C., Smith, G. T., Roehling, P. V., & Goldman, M. S. (1989). Using alcohol expectancies to predict adolescent drinking behavior after one year. *Journal of Consulting and Clinical Psychology, 57,* 93-99.

Cicchetti, D., Toth, S. L., & Lynch, M. (1995). Bowlby's dream comes full circle: The application of attachment theory to risk and psychopathology. In T. H. Ollendick & R. J. Prinz (Eds.), *Advances in clinical child psychology* (pp. 1-75). New York: Plenum.

Ciminero, A. R., Calhoun, K. S., & Adams, H. E. (1986). *Handbook of behavioral assessment* (2nd ed.). New York: John Wiley.

Clark, B. J., & Abeles, N. (1994). Ethical issues and dilemmas in the mental health organization. *Administration and Policy in Mental Health, 22,* 7-17.

Clarke, G. N., Hawkins, W., Murphy, M., Sheeber, L. B., Lewinsohn, P. M., & Seeley, J. R. (1995). Targeted prevention of unipolar depressive disorder in an at-risk sample of high school adolescents: A randomized trial of a group cognitive intervention. *Journal of the American Academy of Child and Adolescent Psychiatry, 34,* 312-321.

Clarke-Kudless, D. (1996). Bringing psychology to the table—issues facing the American Psychological Association as psychology approaches the millenium: A conversation with Dorothy W. Cantor. *Professional Psychology: Research and Practice 27,* 252-258.

Clay, R. A. (1996). Psychology continues to be a popular degree. *APA Monitor,* September.

Clingempeel, W. G., & Reppucci, N. D. (1982). Joint custody after divorce: Major issues and goals for research. *Psychological Bulletin, 91,* 102-127.

Clum, G. A. & Curtin, L. (1993). Validity and reactivity of a system of self-monitoring suicide ideation. *Journal of Psychopathology and Behavioral Assessment, 15,* 375-385.

Cohen, B. B. & Vinson, D. C. (1995). Retrospective self-report of alcohol consumption: Test-retest reliability by telephone. *Alcoholism: Clinical and Experimental Research, 19,* 1156-1161.

Cohen, H. L. (1968). Educational therapy: The design of learning environments. *Research in Psychotherapy, 3,* 21-58.

Cohen, J. & Servan-Schreiber, D. (1992). Context, cortex, and dopamine: A Connectionist approach to behavior and biology in schizophrenia. *Psychological Review, 99,* 45-77.

Cohen, J. B., & Reed, D. (1985). Type A behavior and coronary heart disease among Japanese men in Hawaii. *Journal of Behavioral Medicine, 8,* 343-352.

Cohen, M. I., Spodak, M. K., Silver, S. B., & Williams, K. (1988). Predicting outcome of insanity acquittees released to the community. *Behavioral Sciences and the Law, 6,* 515-530.

Cohen, R. J., Swerdlik, M. E., & Smith, D. K. (1992). *Psychological testing and measurement.* Mountain View, CA: Mayfield.

Cohen, S. (1996). Psychological stress, immunity, and upper respiratory infections. *Current Directions in Psychological Science, 5,* 86-90.

Cohen, S., Mermelstein, R., Kamarck, T., & Hoberman, H. (1985). Measuring the functional components of social support. In I. G. Sarason & B. R. Sarason (Eds.), *Social support: Theory, research, and application* (pp. 73-94). The Hague: Nijhoff.

Cohen, S., Tyrrell, D. A., & Smith, A. P. (1991). Psychological stress in humans and susceptibility to the common cold. *New England Journal of Medicine, 325,* 606-612.

Cohen, S., & Wills, T. A. (1985). Stress, social support, and the buffering hypothesis. *Psychological Bulletin, 98,* 310-357.

Coie, J. D., Watt, N. F., West, S. G., Hawkins, J. D., Asarnow, J. R., Markman, H. J., Ramey, S. L., Shure, M. B., & Long, B. (1993). The science of prevention: A conceptual framework and some directions for a national research program. *American Psychologist, 48,* 1013-1022.

Collins, R. L., Parks, G. A., & Marlatt, G. A. (1985). Social determinants of alcohol consumption: The effects of social interactions and model status on the self-administration of alcohol. *Journal of Consulting and Clinical Psychology, 53,* 189-200.

Colmen, J. G., Kaplan, S. J., & Boulger, J. R. (1964, August). *Selection and selecting research in the Peace Corps.* (Peace Corps Research Note No. 7).

Comer, J. P. (1987). New Haven's school-community connection. *Educational Leadership, 44,* 13-16.

Conduct Problems Prevention Research Group. (1992). A developmental and clinical model for the prevention of conduct disorder: The FAST Track Program. *Development and Psychopathology, 4,* 509-527.

Cone, J. D. (1988). Psychometric considerations and the multiple models of behavioral assessment. In A. S. Bellack & M. Hersen (Eds.), *Behavioral assessment: A practical handbook* (3rd ed., pp. 42-66). New York: Pergamon Press.

Cone, J. D., & Foster, S. L. (1982). Direct observation in clinical psychology. In P. C. Kendall & J. N. Butcher (Eds.), *Handbook of research methods in clinical psychology* (pp. 311-354). New York: John Wiley.

Conners, C. K. (1973). Rating scales for use in drug studies with children. *Psychopharmacology Bulletin* (Special issue, Pharmacotherapy of Children), 24-84.

Conte, H. R., Plutchik, R., Wild, K., & Karasau, T. B. (1986). Combined psychotherapy and pharmacotherapy for depression: A systematic analysis of evidence. *Archives of General Psychiatry, 43,* 471-479.

Conway, J. B. (1988). Differences among clinical psychologists: Scientists, practitioners, and scientist-practitioners. *Professional Psychology: Research and Practice, 19,* 642-655.

Cook, T. D., & Campbell, D. T. (1979). *Quasi-experimentation: Design and analysis issues for field settings.* Chicago: Rand-McNally.

Cool, L. C. (1996). Shrink and tell: Is your confidentiality being compromised? *American Health,* December, pp. 16-18.

Coontz, P. D., Lidz, C. W., & Mulvey, E. P. (1994). Gender and the assessment of dangerousness in the psychiatric emergency room. *International Journal of Law and Psychiatry, 17,* 369-376.

Cooper, N. A., & Clum, G. A. (1989). Imaginal flooding as a supplementary treatment for PTSD in combat veterans: A controlled study. *Behavior Therapy, 20,* 381-392.

Cormier, W. H., & Cormier, L. S. (1991). *Interviewing strategies for helpers: Fundamental skills and cognitive behavioral interventions* (3rd ed.). Pacific Grove, California: Brooks/Cole.

Cornblatt, B., & Erlenmeyer-Kimling, L. E. (1985). Global attentional deviance in children at risk for schizophrenia: Specificity and predictive validity. *Journal of Abnormal Psychology, 94,* 470-486.

Corsini, R. J., & Wedding, D. (1995). *Current psychotherapies* (5th ed.). Itasca, Illinois: Peacock Publishers, Inc.

Costa, P., & McCrae, R. (1985). *NEO-Personality Inventory manual*. Odessa, Florida: Psychological Assessment Resources.

Costa, P. T., & McCrae, R. R. (1992a). *Manual for the Revised NEO Personality Inventory (NEO-PIR) and the NEO Five-Factor Inventory (BEO-FFI)*. Odessa, FL: Psychological Assessment Resources.

Costa, P. T., & McCrae, R. R. (1992b). Normal personality inventories in clinical assessment: General requirements and potential for using the NEO Personality Inventory. *Psychological Assessment, 4,* 5-13.

Couch, R. D. (1995). Four steps for conducting a pregroup screening interview. *Journal for Specialists in Group Work, 20,* 18-25.

Covner, B. J. (1942). Studies in phonographic recordings. I. The use of phonographic recordings in counseling practice and research. *Journal of Consulting Psychology, 6,* 105-113.

Cowen, E., Pederson, A., Babigian, H., Izzo, L., & Trost, M. (1973). Long-term follow-up of early detected vulnerable children. *Journal of Consulting and Clinical Psychology, 41,* 438-446.

Coyne, J. C. (1976). Toward an interactional description of depression. *Psychiatry, 39,* 28-39.

Craig, R. J. (1993). *Psychological assessment with the Millon clinical multiaxial inventory (II): An interpretive guide*. Odessa, Florida: Psychological Assessment Resources.

Crews, F. (1996). The verdict on Freud. *Psychological Science, 7,* 63-68.

Crits-Cristoph, P., Frank, E., Chambless, D. L., & Karp, J. F. (1995). Training in empirically validated treatments: What are clinical psychology students learning? *Professional Psychology: Research and Practice, 26,* 514-522.

Cronbach, L. J. (1946). Response sets and test validity. *Educational and Psychological Measurement, 6,* 475-494.

Cronbach, L. J. (1960). *Essentials of psychological testing* (2nd ed.). New York: Harper & Row.

Cronbach, L. J. (1970). *Essentials of psychological testing* (3rd ed.). New York: Harper & Row.

Cronbach, L. J., Gleser, G. C., Nanda, H., & Rajaratnam, N. (1972). *The dependability of behavioral measurements*. New York: John Wiley.

Cronbach, L. J., & Meehl, P. E. (1955). Construct validity in psychology tests. *Psychological Bulletin, 52,* 281-302.

Crosbie-Burnett, M. (1991). Impact of joint versus sole custody and quality of co-parental relationship on adjustment of adolescents in remarried families. *Behavioral Sciences and the Law, 9,* 439-449.

Crumbaugh, J. C. (1968). Cross-validation of the Purpose in Life test based on Frankl's concepts. *Journal of Individual Psychology, 24,* 74-81.

Cuesta, M. J., & Peralta, V. (1995). Psychopathological dimensions in schizophrenia. *Schizophrenia Bulletin, 21,* 473-482.

Cullen, E. A., & Newman, R. (1997). In pursuit of prescription privileges. *Professional Psychology: Research and Practice, 28,* 101-106.

Cummings, N. A. (1977). The anatomy of psychotherapy under national health insurance. *American Psychologist, 32,* 711-718.

Cummings, N. A. (1995). Unconscious fiscal convenience. *Psychotherapy in Private Practice, 14,* 23-28.

Cunningham, C. E., Siegel, L. S., & Offord, D. R. (1985). A developmental dose-response analysis of the effects of methylphenidate on the peer interactions of Attention Deficit Disordered boys. *Journal of Child Psychology and Psychiatry, 26,* 955-971.

Dahlstrom, W. G. (1992). The growth in acceptance of the MMPI. *Professional Psychology: Research and Practice, 23*, 345-348.

Dahlstrom, W. G., Lachar, D., & Dahlstrom, L. E. (1986). *MMPI patterns of American minorities.* Minneapolis: University of Minnesota Press.

Dahlstrom, W. G., Welsh, G. S., & Dahlstrom, L. E. (1972). *An MMPI handbook: Vol. 1. Clinical interpretation* (rev. ed.). Minneapolis: University of Minnesota Press.

Dahlstrom, W. G., Welsh, G. S., & Dahlstrom, L. E. (1975). *An MMPI handbook: Vol. 2. Research applications.* Minneapolis: University of Minnesota Press.

Dana, R. H., & Leech, S. (1974). Existential assessment. *Journal of Personality Assessment, 38,* 428-435.

Dangel, R. F., & Polster, R. A. (Eds.). (1984). *Parent training.* New York: Guilford Press.

Davanloo, H. L. (1994). *Basic principles and techniques in short-term dynamic psychotherapy.* Northdale, NJ: Jason Aronson, Inc.

Davidson, W. S., Redner, R., Blakely, C., Mitchell, C. M., & Emshoff, J. G. (1987). Diversion of juvenile offenders: An experimental comparison. *Journal of Consulting and Clinical Psychology, 55,* 68-75.

Davis, K. L., Kahn, R. S., Ko, G., & Davidson, M. (1991). Dopamine in schizophrenia: A review and reconceptualization. *American Journal of Psychiatry, 148*, 1474-1486.

Dawe, H. C. (1934). An analysis of two-hundred quarrels of pre-school children. *Child Development, 5,* 139-157.

Dawes, R. M. (1986). Representative thinking in clinical judgment. *Clinical Psychology Review, 6,* 425-442.

Dawes, R. M. (1992). *Psychology and psychotherapy: The myth of professional expertise.* New York: Free Press.

Dawes, R. M. (1994). *House of cards.* New York: The Free Press.

Dawes, R. M., Faust, D., & Meehl, P. E. (1989). Clinical versus actuarial judgment. *Science, 243,* 1668-1674.

del Carmen, R., & Huffman, L. (1996). Epilogue: Bridging the gap between research on attachment and psychopathology. *Journal of Consulting and Clinical Psychology*, *64*, 291-294.

Delameter, A. M. (1986). Psychological aspects of diabetes mellitus in children. In B. B. Lahey & A. E. Kazdin (Eds.), *Advances in clinical child psychology* (Vol. 9, pp. 333-375). New York: Plenum Press.

DeLeon, P. H., Fox, R. E., & Graham, S. R. (1991). Prescription privileges: Psychology's next frontier. *American Psychologist, 46,* 384-393.

DeLeon, P. H., Wedding, D., Wakefield, M. K., & VandenBos, G. R. (1992). Medicaid policy: Psychology's overlooked agenda. *Professional Psychology: Research and Practice, 23,* 96-107.

Dembroski, T. M., MacDougall, J. M., Williams, R. B., Haney, T. L., & Blumenthal, J. A. (1985). Components of Type A, hostility, and anger-in: Relationship to angiographic findings. *Psychosomatic Medicine, 47*, 219-233.

DeNelsky, G. Y. (1996). The case against prescription privileges for psychologists. *American Psychologist, 51*, 207-212.

Dennis, W. (1948). *Readings in the history of psychology.* New York: Appleton-Century-Crofts.

Depression Guideline Panel (1993). *Depression in primary care: Vol. 2. Treatment of major depression* (Clinical practice guideline, No. 5; AHCPR Publication No. 93-0551). Rockville, MD: U.S. Department of Health and Human Services, Public Health Service, Agency for Health Care Policy and Research.

Derksen, J. J., Hummelen, J. W., & Bouwens, P. J. (1994). Interrater reliability of the structural interview. *Journal of Personality Disorders, 8,* 131-139.

DeSantis, B. W., & Walker, C. E. (1991). Contemporary clinical psychology. In C. E. Walker (Ed.), *Clinical psychology: Historical and research foundations* (pp. 513-535). New York: Plenum Press.

Diener, C. I., & Dweck, C. S. (1978). An analysis of learned helplessness: Continuous changes in performance, strategy, and achievement cognitions following failure. *Journal of Personality and Social Psychology, 36,* 451-462.

DiLalla, D. L., & Gottesman, I. I. (1995). Normal personality characteristics in identical twins discordant for schizophrenia. *Journal of Abnormal Psychology, 104,* 490-499.

Dilk, M. N., & Bond, G. R. (1996). Meta-analytic evaluation of skills training research for individuals with severe mental illness. *Journal of Consulting and Clinical Psychology, 64,* 1137-1146.

DiNardo, P. A., & Barlow, D. H. (1988). *Anxiety disorders interview schedule-revised (ADIS-R).* Albany: Center for Stress and Anxiety Disorders.

DiNardo, P. A., Moras, K., Barlow, D. H., Rapee, R. M., et al. (1993). Reliability of DSM-III-R anxiety disorder categories: Using the Anxiety Disorders Interview Schedule-Revised (ADIS-R). *Archives of General Psychiatry, 50,* 251-256.

Dipboye, R. L., Stramler, C. S., & Fontenelle, G. A. (1984). The effects of the application on recall of information from the interview. *Academy of Management Journal, 27,* 561-575.

Dodge, K. A., McClaskey, C. L., & Feldman, E. (1985). Situational approach to the assessment of social competence in children. *Journal of Consulting and Clinical Psychology, 53,* 344-353.

Dohrenwend, B. S. (1978). Social stress and community psychology. *American Journal of Community Psychology, 6,* 1-14.

Doleys, D. M. (1983). Enuresis and encopresis. In T. Ollendick & M. Hersen (Eds.), *Handbook of child psychopathology* (pp. 210-226). New York: Plenum Press.

Dollinger, S. J. (1989). Predictive validity of the Graduate Record Examination in a clinical psychology program. *Professional Psychology: Research and Practice, 20,* 56-58.

Douglas, J., & Olshaker, M. (1995). *Mind hunter: Inside the FBI's elite serial crime unit.* New York: Scribner's.

Douglas, V. I. (1972). Stop, look and listen: The problem of sustained attention and impulse control in hyperactive and normal children. *Canadian Journal of Behavioral Science, 4,* 259-282.

Dryden, W., & Trower, P. (1989). *Cognitive psychotherapy.* New York: Springer.

DuBois, P. H. (1970). *A history of psychological testing.* Boston: Allyn & Bacon.

Dulany, D. E. (1968). Awareness, rules, and propositional control: A confrontation with S-R behavior theory. In T. R. Dixon & D. L. Horton (Eds.), *Verbal behavior and general behavior theory* (pp. 340-387). Englewood Cliffs, NJ: Prentice-Hall.

Dunlap, G., Koegel, R. L., & O'Neill, R. (1985). Pervasive developmental disorders. In P. H. Bornstein & A. E. Kazdin (Eds.), *Handbook of clinical behavior therapy with children* (pp. 499-540). Homewood, IL: Dorsey Press.

DuPaul, G. J., & Rapport, M. D. (1993). Does methylphenidate normalize the classroom performance of children with attention deficit disorder? *Journal of the American Academy of Child and Adolescent Psychiatry, 32*(1), 190-198.

Durlak, J. (1979). Comparative effectiveness of paraprofessional and professional helpers. *Psychological Bulletin, 86,* 80–92.

Dush, D. M., Hirt, M. L., & Schroeder, H. (1983). Self-statement modification with adults: A meta-analysis. *Psychological Bulletin, 94,* 408–422.

Dush, D. M., Hirt, M. L., & Schroeder, H. E. (1989). Self-statement modification in the treatment of child behavior disorders. A meta-analysis. *Psychological Bulletin, 106,* 97–106.

Eagle, M. (1984). *Recent developments in psychoanalysis: A critical evaluation.* New York: McGraw-Hill.

Eaker, E. D., Abbott, R. D., Kannel, W. B. (1989). Frequency of uncomplicated angina pectoris in Type A compared with Type B persons (the Framingham study). *American Journal of Cardiology, 63,* 1042–1045.

Ebert, B. W. (1987). Guide to conducting a psychological autopsy. *Professional Psychology: Research and Practice, 18,* 52–56.

Edelbrock, C., Costello, A. J., Duncan, M. K., Kalas, R., & Conover, N. C. (1985). Age differences in the reliability of the psychiatric interview of the child. *Child Development, 56,* 265–275.

Edelstein, B. A., & Eisler, R. M. (1976). Effects of modeling and modeling with instructions and feedback on the behavioral components of social skills. *Behavior Therapy, 7,* 382–389.

Edelstein, B. A., & Michelson, L. (Eds.) (1986). *Handbook of prevention.* New York & London: Plenum Press.

Edwards, A. L. (1957). *The social desirability variable in personality assessment and research.* New York: Dryden.

Ehmann, T. S., Higgs, E., Smith, G. N., Au, T., Altman, S., Llyod, D., & Honer, W. G. (1995). Routinue assessment of patient progress: A multiformat, change-sensitive nurses instrument for assessing psychotic inpatients. *Comprehensive Psychiatry, 36,* 289–295.

Einhorn, H. J., & Hogarth, R. M. (1978). Confidence in judgment: Persistence of the illusion of validity. *Psychological Review, 85,* 395–416.

Elkin, I. (1994). The NIMH treatment of depression collaborative research program: Where we began and where we are. In A. E. Bergin & S. L. Garfield (Eds.), *Handbook of psychotherapy and behavior change* (4th ed.), pp. 114–139.

Elkin, I., Gibbons, R. D., Shea, M. T., & Sotsky, S. M. (1995). Initial severity and different treatment outcomes in the National Institute of Mental Health Treatment of Depression Collaborative Research Program, *Journal of Clinical and Consulting Psychology, 63,* 841–847.

Elkin, I., Shea, M. T., Watkins, J. T., Imber, S. D., Sotsky, S. M., Collins, J. F., Glass, D. R., Pilkonis, P. A., Leber, W. R., Docherty, J. P., Fiester, S. J., & Parloff, M. B. (1989). National Institute of Mental Health Treatment of Depression Collaborative Research Program. General effectiveness of treatments. *Archives of General Psychiatry, 46,* 971–982.

Ellis, A. (1962). *Reason and emotion in psychotherapy.* New York: Lyle Stuart.

Ellis, A. (1973). Rational-emotive therapy. In R. Corsini (Ed.), *Current psychotherapies* (pp. 167–206). Itasca, IL: F. E. Peacock.

Ellis, A. (1993). Changing rational-emotive therapy (RET) to rational-emotive behavior therapy (REBT). *The Behavior Therapist, 16,* 257–258.

Ellis, A. (1995). Rational emotive behavior therapy. In R. J. Corsini & D. Wedding, D. (eds.). *Current psychotherapies* (5th ed.). Itasca, Illinois: Peacock Publishers, Inc. (pp. 162–196).

Ellis, A., & Dryden, W. (1987). *The practice of rational-emotive therapy.* New York: Springer.

Ellis, A., & Grieger, R. (Eds.). (1977). *Handbook of rational-emotive therapy.* New York: Springer.

Elwork, A., Sales, B. D., & Suggs, D. (1981). The trial: A research review. In B. D. Sales (Ed.), *The trial process* (pp. 1-68). New York: Plenum.

Emery, R. E. (1982). Interparental conflict and the children of discord and divorce. *Psychological Bulletin, 92,* 310-330.

Emery, R. E., Matthews, S. G., & Kitzmann, K. M. (1994). Child custody mediation and litigation: Parents' satisfaction and functioning one year after settlement. *Journal of Consulting and Clinical Psychology, 62,* 124-129.

Emery, R. E., Matthews, S. G., & Wyer, M. M. (1991). Child custody medication and litigation: Further evidence on the differing views of mothers and fathers. *Journal of Consulting and Clinical Psychology, 59,* 410-418.

Emmelkamp, P. M. G., & Felten, M. (1985). The process of exposure *in vivo:* Cognitive and physiological changes during treatment of acrophobia. *Behaviour Research and Therapy, 23,* 219-224.

Endicott, J., & Spitzer, R. L. (1978). A diagnostic interview: The schedule for affective disorders and schizophrenia. *Archives of General Psychiatry, 35,* 837-844.

Englemann, S. (1974). The effectiveness of direct verbal instruction on IQ performance and achievement in reading and arithmetic. In R. Ulrich, T. Stachnik, & J. Mabry (Eds.), *Control of human behavior* (Vol. 3, pp. 69-84). Glenview, IL: Scott, Foresman.

Ennis, B. J., & Litwack, T. R. (1974). Psychiatry and the presumption of expertise: Flipping coins in the courtroom. *California Law Review, 62,* 693-752.

Epstein, S. (1994). Integration of of the cognitive and the psychodynamic unconscious. *American Psychologist, 49,* 709-724.

Erikson, E. H. (1946). Ego development and historical change. *The psychoanalytic study of the child* (Vol. 2, pp. 359-396). New York: International Universities Press.

Erikson, E. H. (1959). Identity and the life cycle. *Psychological Issues,* Monograph 1. New York: International Universities Press.

Erikson, E. H. (1963). *Childhood and society* (rev. ed.). New York: W. W. Norton.

Ernst, N. D., & Harlan, W. R. (1991). Obesity and cardiovascular disease in minority populations: Executive summary. Conference highlights, conclusions, and recommendations. *American Journal of Clinical Nutrition, 53,* 1507S-1511S.

Eron, L. D. (1950). A normative study of the thematic apperception test. *Psychological Monographs, 64* (9).

Eslinger, P. J., & Damasio, A. R. (1985). Severe disturbance of higher cognition after bilateral frontal lobe ablation: Patient EVR. *Neurology, 35,* 1731-1741.

Esterson, A. (1993). *Seductive mirage: An exploration of the work of Sigmund Freud.* Chicago: Open Court.

Evans, G. D., & Murphy, M. J. (1997). The practicality of predoctoral prescription training for psychologists: A survey of directors of clinical training. *Professional Psychology: Research and Practice, 28,* 113-117.

Exner, J. E. (1969). *The Rorschach systems.* New York: Grune & Stratton.

Exner, J. E. (1976). Projective techniques. In I. B. Weiner (Ed.), *Clinical methods in psychology* (pp. 61-121). New York: John Wiley.

Exner, J. E. (1978). *The Rorschach: A comprehensive system, Vol. 2: Current research and advanced interpretation.* New York: John Wiley.

Exner, J. E. (1986). *The Roschach: A comprehensive system, Vol. 1: Basic foundations* (2nd ed.). New York: John Wiley.

Exner, J. E. (1993). *The Rorschach: A comprehensive system: Vol. 1. Basic foundations* (3rd ed.). New York: Wiley.

Exner, J. E. (1996). A comment on "the comprehensive system for the Rorschach: a critical examination." *Psychological Science, 7,* 11-13.

Eysenck, H. J. (1952). The effects of psychotherapy: An evaluation. *Journal of Consulting Psychology, 16,* 319-324.

Eysenck, H. J. (1966). *The effects of psychotherapy.* New York: International Science Press.

Eysenck, H. J. (1978). An exercise in mega-silliness. *American Psychologist, 33,* 517.

Eysenck, H. J. (1982). Neobehavioristic (S-R) theory. In G. T. Wilson & C. M. Franks (Eds.), *Contemporary behavior therapy: Conceptual and empirical foundations* (pp. 205-276). New York: Guilford Press.

Eysenck, H. J., & Eysenck, S. B. G. (1975). *Manual for Eysenck Personality Questionnaire.* San Diego, CA: Educational and Individual Testing Service.

Eysenck, H. J., & Grossarth-Maticek, R. (1991). Creative novation behaviour therapy as a prophylactic treatment for cancer and coronary heart disease (Part II): Effects of treatment. *Behaviour Research and Therapy, 29,* 17-31.

Fagan, T. K. (1996). Witmer's contribution to school psychological services. *American Psychologist, 51,* 241-243.

Fairbairn, W. R. D. (1952). *Psychoanalytic studies of the personality.* London: Tavistock Publications/Routledge & Kegan Paul.

Fairweather, G. W. (1980). *New directions for mental health services: The Fairweather lodge: A twenty-five year retrospective.* San Francisco: Jossey-Bass.

Fairweather, G. W., Sanders, D. H., & Tornatzky, L. G. (1974). *Creating change in mental health organizations.* New York: Pergamon Press.

Fallon, T., & Schwab-Stone, M. (1994). Determinants of reliability in psychiatric surveys of children aged 6-12. *Journal of Child Psychology and Psychiatry and Allied Disciplines, 35,* 1391-1408.

Fancher, R. E. (1973). *Psychoanalytic psychology: The development of Freud's thought.* New York: W. W. Norton.

Farrington, D. P. (1991). Childhood aggression and adult violence: Early precursors and later-life outcomes. In D. J. Pepler & K. H. Rubin (Eds.), *The development of childhood aggression* (pp. 5-29). Hillsdale, NJ: Erlbaum.

Faust, D., & Ziskin, J. (1988). The expert witness in psychology and psychiatry. *Science, 242,* 31-35.

Fawzy, F. I., Cousins, N., Fawzy, N. W., Kemeny, M. E., Elashoff, R., & Morton, D. (1990). A structured psychiatric intervention for cancer patients: I. Changes over time in methods of coping and affective disturbance. *Archives of General Psychiatry, 47,* 720-725.

Fawzy, F. I., Fawzy, N. W., Arndt, L. A., & Pasnau, R. O. (1995). Critical review of psychosocial interventions in cancer care. *Archives of General Psychiatry, 52,* 100-113.

Fawzy, F. I., Fawzy, N. W., Hyun, C. S., Guthrie, D., Fahey, J. L., & Morton, D. (1993). Malignant melanoma: Effect of an early structured psychiatric intervention, coping and affective state on recurrence and survival 6 years later. *Archives of General Psychiatry, 50,* 681-689.

Feingold, A. (1989). Assessment of journals in social science psychology. *American Psychologist, 44,* 961-964.

Feingold, B. F. (1975). *Why your child is hyperactive.* New York: Random House.

Feldman-Summers, S., & Jones, G. (1984). Psychological impacts of sexual contact between therapists and other health care professionals and their clients. *Journal of Consulting and Clinical Psychology, 52,* 1054-1061.

Felner, R. D., Farber, S. S., & Primavera, J. (1983). Transitions and stressful life events: A model for primary prevention. In R. D. Felner, L. A. Jason, J. N. Moritsugu, & S. S. Farber (Eds.), *Preventive psychology: Theory, research, and prevention* (pp. 191-215). New York: Pergamon Press.

Ferro, T., Klein, D. N., Norden, K. A., Donaldson, S. K., et al. (1995). Development and reliability of the Family History Interview for Personality Disorders. *Journal of Personality Disorders, 9,* 169-177.

Fine R. (1971). *The healing of the mind: The technique of psychoanalytic psychotherapy.* New York: David McKay.

Fine, S., & Glasser, P. H. (1996). *The first helping interview: Engaging the client and building trust.* Thousand Oaks, California: Sage.

Finkel, N. J. (1989). The Insanity Defense Reform Act of 1984: Much ado about nothing. *Behavioral Sciences and the Law, 7,* 403-419.

Finkelhor, D., & Browne, A. (1988). Assessing the long-term impact of child sexual abuse: A review and conceptualization. In L. Walker (Ed.), *Handbook on sexual abuse in children* (pp. 55-71). New York: Springer.

First, M. B., Spitzer, R. L., Gibbon, M., Williams, J. B. W., et al. (1995). The Structured Clinical Interview for DSM-III-R personality disorders (SCID-II): II. Multi-site test-retest reliability study. *Journal of Personality Disorders, 9,* 92-104.

Fisher, C. T. (1985). *Individualizing psychological assessment.* Monterey, CA: Brooks/Cole.

Fisher, C. T. (1989). A life-centered approach to psychodiagnostics: Attending to lifeworld, ambiguity, and possibility. *Person-Centered Review, 4,* 163-170.

Fisher, C. T., & Fisher, W. F. (1983). Phenomenological-existential psychotherapy. In M. Hersen, A. E. Kazdin, & A. S. Bellack (Eds.), *The clinical psychology handbook* (pp. 489-505). New York: Pergamon Press.

Fleisig, W. E. (1993). The development of the Illustrated Fear Survey Schedule (IFSS) and an examination of its reliability and validity with children with mild mental retardation. *Dissertation Abstracts International, 54,* 1719.

Fleming, I., Baum, A., Davidson, L. M., Rectanus, E., & McArdle, S. (1987). Chronic stress as a factor in psychologic reactivity to challenge. *Health Psychology, 6,* 221-238.

Flynn, J. R. (1984). The mean IQ of Americans: Massive gains 1932 to 1978. *Psychological Bulletin, 95,* 29-51.

Foa, E. B., Riggs, D., Dancu, C., & Rothbaum, R. (1993). Reliability and validity of a brief instrument for assessing post-traumatic stress disorder. *Journal of Traumatic Stress, 6,* 459-473.

Folkman, S., & Lazarus, R. S. (1980). An analysis of coping in a middle-aged community sample. *Journal of Health and Social Behavior, 21,* 219-239.

Folkman, S. & Lazarus, R. S. (1988). *Manual for the ways of coping questionnaire*. Palo Alto, CA: Consulting Psychologists Press.

Folkman, S., Lazarus, R. S., Gruen, R. J., & DeLongis, A. (1986a). Appraisal, coping, health status, and psychological symptoms. *Journal of Personality and Social Psychology, 50*, 571-579.

Follette, W. C. (1996). Introduction to the special section on the development of theoretically coherent alternatives to the DSM system. *Journal of Consulting and Clinical Psychology, 64*, 1117-1119.

Follette, W. C., & Houts, A. C. (1996). Models of scientific progress and the role of theory in taxonomy development: A case study of the DSM. *Journal of Consulting and Clinical Psychology, 64*, 1120-1132.

Follette, W. C., Naugle, A. E., & Callaghan, G. M. (1996). A radical behavioral understanding of the therapeutic relationship in effecting change. *Behavior Therapy, 27*, 623-642.

Folstein, M. F., Maiberger, P., & McHugh, P. R. (1977). Mood disorders as a specific complication of stroke. *Journal of Neurology, Neurosurgery & Psychiatry, 40*, 1018-1020.

Ford, M. & Widiger, T. (1989). Sex bias in the diagnosis of histrionic and antisocial personality disorders. *Journal of Consulting and Clinical Psychology, 57*, 301-305.

Forehand, R., Lautenschlager, G. J., Faust, J., & Graziano, W. G. (1986). Parent perceptions and parent-child interactions in clinic-referred children: A preliminary investigation of the effects of maternal depressive moods. *Behaviour Research and Therapy, 24*, 73-76.

Forehand, R., & McMahon, R. J. (1981). *Helping the noncompliant child: A clinician's guide to parent training*. New York: Guilford Press.

Foster, G. D., & Kendall, P. C. (1994). The realistic treatment of obesity: Changing the scales of success. *Clinical Psychology Review, 14*, 701-736.

Foster, S. L., Bell-Dolan, D. J., & Burge, D. A. (1988). Behavioral observation. In A. S. Bellack & M. Hersen (Eds.), *Behavioral assessment: A practical handbook* (3rd ed., pp. 119-160). New York: Pergamon Press.

Foster, S. L., & Robin A. L. (1988). Family conflict and communication in adolescence. In E. J. Mash & L. G. Terdal (Eds.), *Behavioral assessment of childhood disorders* (2nd ed., pp. 717-775). New York: Guilford Press.

Fowler, R. D. (1985). Landmarks in computer-assisted psychological assessment. *Journal of Consulting and Clinical Psychology, 53*, 748-759.

Fowles, D. C. (1992). Schizophrenia: Diathesis-stress revisited. *Annual Review of Psychology, 43*, 303-336.

Fox, R. (1994). Training professional psychologists for the twenty-first century. *American Psychologist, 49*, 855-867.

Fox, R. E. (1995). The rape of psychotherapy. *Professional Psychology: Research and Practice, 26*, 147-155.

Foy, D. W., Nunn, L. B., & Rychtarik, R. G. (1984). Broad-spectrum behavioral treatment for chronic alcoholics: Effects of training controlled drinking skills. *Journal of Consulting and Clinical Psychology, 52*, 218-230.

Frances, A. J., First, M. B., Widiger, T. A., Miele, G. M., Tilly, S. M., Davis, W. W., & Pincus, H. A. (1991). An A to Z guide to DSM-IV conundrums. *Journal of Consulting and Clinical Psychology, 100*, 407-412.

Frances, A. J., Pincus, H. A., & Widiger, T. A. (1996). DSM-IV and international communication in psychiatric diagnosis. In Y. Honda, M. Kastrup, & J. E. Mezzich (eds.) *Psychiatric diagnosis: A world perspective*. New York: Springer.

Frances, A. J., Widiger, T. A., & Pincus, H. A. (1989). The development of DSM-IV: Work in progress. *Archives of General Psychiatry, 46,* 373-375.

Frank, J. D. (1957). Some determinants, manifestations, and effects of cohesiveness in therapy groups. *International Journal of Group Psychotherapy, 7,* 53-63.

Frank, J. D. (1973). *Persuasion and healing* (rev. ed.). Baltimore, MD: Johns Hopkins University Press.

Frank, L. K. (1939). Projective methods for the study of personality. *Journal of Psychology, 8,* 343-389.

Frank, R. G. (1993). Health-care reform: An introduction. *American Psychologist, 48,* 258-260.

Frankl, V. (1963). *Man's search for meaning.* New York: Washington Square Press.

Frankl, V. (1965). *The doctor and the soul.* New York: Knopf.

Frankl, V. (1967). *Psychotherapy and existentialism: Selected papers on logotherapy.* New York: Washington Square Press.

Franks, C. M. (1964). *Conditioning techniques in clinical practice and research.* New York: Springer.

Fraser, J. S. (1996). All that glitters is not always gold: Medical offset effects and managed behavioral health care. *Professional Psychology: Research and Practice, 27,* 335-344.

Frederick/Schneiders, Inc. (1990). *Survey of American Psychological Association members.* Washington, DC: Author.

Freeman, A., Simon, K. M., Beutler, L. E., & Arkowitz, H. (1989). *Comprehensive handbook of cognitive therapy.* New York: Plenum Press.

Freud, A. (1946). *The ego and mechanisms of defense.* New York: International Universities Press.

Freud, A., & Burlingham, D. T. (1943). *War and children.* London: Medical War Books.

Freud, S. (1900). *The interpretation of dreams.* (Avon Edition, 1965). New York: Avon Books.

Freud, S. (1901). *The psychopathology of everyday life.* New York: Macmillan.

Freud, S. (1904). *On psychotherapy.* Lecture delivered before the College of Physicians in Vienna. Reprinted in S. Freud, *Therapy and technique.* New York: Collier Books, 1963.

Freud, S. (1905). Jokes and their relation to the unconscious. In the *Standard edition of the complete psychological works of Sigmund Freud* (Vol. 8). London: Hogarth Press, 1953-1964.

Freud, S. (1912). Recommendations for physicians on the psychoanalytic method of treatment. *Zentralblatt,* DS. II. Reprinted in S. Freud, *Therapy and technique.* New York: Collier Books, 1963.

Freud, S. (1949). *An outline of psychoanalysis.* (J. Strachey, trans.). New York: W. W. Norton.

Freud, S. (1953-1964). *The standard edition of the complete psychological works of Sigmund Freud* (24 vols.). London: Hogarth Press.

Freund, K., & Watson, R. J. (1991). Assessment of the sensitivity and specificity of a phallometric test: An update of phallometric diagnosis of pediophilia." *Psychological Assessment, 2,* 254-260.

Friedman, M. et al. (1986). Alteration of Type A behavior and its effect on cardiac recurrences in post-myocardial infarction patients: Summary results of the Recurrent Coronary Prevention Project. *American Heart Journal, 112*, 653–665.

Friedman, M., & Rosenman, R. H. (1974). *Type A behavior and your heart.* New York: Knopf.

Fulero, S. M., & Finkel, N. J. (1991). Barring ultimate issue testimony: An "insane" rule? *Law and Human Behavior, 15*, 495–508.

Furman, W. (1980). Promoting appropriate social behavior: A developmental perspective. In B. Lahey & A. Kazdin (Eds.), *Advances in clinical child psychology* (Vol. 3, pp. 1–41). New York: Plenum Press.

Furstenberg, F. F., Brooks-Gunn, J., & Chase-Lansdale, L. (1989). Teenaged pregnancy and child-bearing. *American Psychologist, 44,* 313–320.

Gaddy, C. D., Charlot-Swilley, D., Nelson, P. D., & Reich, J. (1995). Selected outcomes of accredited programs. *Professional Psychology: Research and Practice, 26*, 507–513.

Gaffney, L. R., & McFall, R. M. (1981). A comparison of social skills in delinquent and nondelinquent girls using a behavioral role-playing inventory. *Journal of Consulting and Clinical Psychology, 49*, 959–967.

Gainotti, G. (1972). Emotional behavior and hemispheric side of lesion. *Cortex, 8,* 41–55.

Galanter, M. (1988). Zealous self-help groups as adjuncts to psychiatric treatment: A study of Recovery, Inc. *American Journal of Psychiatry, 145*, 1248–1253.

Gallagher-Thompson, D., Hanley-Peterson, P., & Thompson, L. W. (1990). Maintenance of gains versus relapse following brief psychotherapy for depression. *Journal of Consulting & Clinical Psychology, 58*, 371–374.

Galton, F. (1883). *Inquiries into the human faculty and its development.* London: Macmillan.

Garb, H. N. (1984). The incremental validity of information used in personality assessment. *Clinical Psychology Review, 4,* 641–656.

Garb, H. N. (1989). Clinical judgment, clinical training, and professional experience. *Psychological Bulletin, 105,* 387–396.

Garb, H. N. (1992). The trained psychologist as expert witness. *Clinical Psychology Review, 12,* 451–468.

Garb, H. N. (1995). Sex bias and the diagnosis of borderline personality disorder. *Professional Psychology: Research and Practice, 26*, 526.

Garb, H. N. (1996). The representativeness and past-behavior heuristics in clinical judgment. *Professional Psychology: Theory and Practice, 27*, 272–277.

Garb, H. N., & Schramke, C. J. (1996). Judgment research and neuro psychological assessment: A narrative review and meta-analysis. *Psychological Bulletin, 120,* 140–153.

Garber, J. (1984). Classification of childhood psychopathology: A developmental perspective. *Child Development, 55,* 30–48.

Garcia, J., McGowan, B., & Green, K. (1972). Biological constraints on conditioning. In A. H. Block & W. F. Prokasky (Eds.), *Classical conditioning* (pp. 3–27). New York: Appleton-Century-Crofts.

Gardiner, R. A. (1971). *Therapeutic communication with children: The mutual story-telling technique.* New York: Jason Aronson.

Gardner, H., Brownell, H. H., Wapner, W., & Michelow, D. (1983). Missing the point: The role of the right hemisphere in the processing of complex linguistic materials. In E. Perecman (Ed.), *Cognitive processing in the right hemisphere* (pp. 169–191). New York: Academic Press.

Gardner, W., Lidz, C. W., Mulvey, E. P., & Shaw, E. C. (1996). Clinical versus actuarial predictions of violence in patients with mental illnesses. *Journal of Consulting and Clinical Psychology, 64*, 602–609.

Garfield, S. L. (1965). Historical introduction. In B. B. Wolman (Ed.), *Handbook of clinical psychology* (pp. 125–140). New York: McGraw-Hill.

Garfield, S. L. (1974). *Clinical psychology: The study of personality and behavior.* Chicago: Aldine.

Garfield, S. L. (1992). Comments on "Retrospect: Psychology as a profession." *Journal of Consulting and Clinical Psychology, 60*, 9–15.

Garfield, S. L., & Bergin, A. E. (1994). Introduction and historical overview. In A. E. Bergin, & S. L. Garfield (Eds.), *Handbook of psychotherapy and behavior change* (pp. 3–22). New York: Wiley & Sons.

Garfield, S. L., & Kurtz, R. (1976). Clinical psychologists in the 1970s. *American Psychologist, 31,* 1–9.

Garmezy, N. (1978). Never mind the psychologists: Is it good for the children? *Clinical Psychologist, 31,* 1–6.

Garmezy, N. (1983). Stressors of childhood. In N. Garmezy and M. Rutter (Eds.), *Stress, coping, & development in children* (pp. 43–84). New York: McGraw-Hill.

Gazzaniga, M. S., Fendrich, R., and Wessinger, C. M. (1994). Blinsight reconsidered. *Current Directions in Psychological Science, 3,* 93–95.

Geer, J. H. (1965). The development of a scale to measure fear. *Behaviour Research and Therapy. 3,* 45–53.

Gelfand, D. M., Jenson, W. R., & Drew, C. J. (1982). *Understanding child behavior disorders* (2nd ed.). New York: Holt, Rinehart & Winston.

Gelfand, D. M., & Peterson, L. (1985). *Child development and psychopathology.* Beverly Hills, CA: Sage.

Gelles, R. J., & Straus, M. A. (1988). *Intimate violence.* New York: Simon & Schuster.

Gergen, K. J. (1985). The social constructionist movement in modern psychology. *American Psychologist, 40,* 266–275.

Getka, E. J., & Glass, C. R. (1992). Behavioral and cognitive-behavioral approaches to the reduction of dental anxiety. *Behavior Therapy, 23,* 433–448.

Giblin, P. (1986). Research and assessment in marriage and family enrichment: A meta-analysis study. *Journal of Psychotherapy and the Family, 2,* 79–96.

Gittelman, R. (1980). The role of tests for differential diagnosis in child psychiatry. *Journal of the American Academy of Child Psychiatry, 19,* 413–438.

Givelber, D. J., Bowers, W. J., & Blitch, C. L. (1984). Tarasoff, myth and reality: An empirical study of private law reaction. *Wisconsin Law Review, 1984,* 443–497.

Glaser, R., & Bond, L. (1981). Introduction to the special issue: Testing: Concepts, policy, practice, and research. *American Psychologist, 36,* 997–1000.

Glasgow, R. E., & Terborg, J. R. (1988). Occupational health promotion programs to reduce cardiovascular risk. *Journal of Consulting and Clinical Psychology, 56,* 365–373.

Gleick, J. (1978, August 21). Getting away with murder. *New Times,* pp. 21–27.

Gless, A. G. (1995). Some post-*Daubert* trial tribulations of a simple country justice: Behavioral science evidence in trial courts. *Behavioral Sciences and the Law, 13,* 261–292.

Godard, S. L., Bloom, J. D., Williams, M. H., & Faulkner, L. R. (1986). The right to refuse treatment in Oregon: A two-year statewide experience. *Behavioral Sciences and the Law, 4,* 293–304.

Goffman, E. (1961). *Asylums.* Garden City, NY: Doubleday.

Goins, M. K., Strauss, G. D., & Martin, R. (1995). A change measure for psychodynamic psychotherapy outcome research. *Journal of Psychotherapy Practice and Research, 4,* 319–328.

Goldberg, L. R. (1959). The effectiveness of clinicians' judgments: The diagnosis of organic brain damage from the Bender-Gestalt test. *Journal of Consulting Psychology, 23,* 25–33.

Goldberg, L. R. (1968). Simple models or simple processes? Some research on clinical judgments. *American Psychologist, 23,* 483–496.

Golden, C. J. (1980). In reply to Adams' "In search of Luria's battery: A false start." *Journal of Consulting and Clinical Psychology, 48,* 517–521.

Golden, C. J. (1981). A standardized version of Luria's neuropsychological tests: A quantitative and qualitative approach to neuropsychological evaluation. In S. B. Filskov & T. J. Boll (Eds.), *Handbook of clinical neuropsychology* (pp. 608–642). New York: John Wiley.

Golden, C. J., Purisch, A. D., & Hammeke, T. A. (1985). *Luria-Nebraska Neuropsychological Battery: Forms I and II Manual.* Los Angeles: Western Psychological Services.

Goldenberg, H. (1973). *Contemporary clinical psychology.* Monterey, CA: Brooks/Cole.

Goldfried, M. R. (1980). Toward the delineation of therapeutic change principles. *American Psychologist, 35,* 991–999.

Goldfried, M. R. (1995). Toward a common language for case formulation. *Journal of Psychotherapy Integration, 5,* 221–244.

Goldfried, M. R., & Davison, G. C. (1976). *Clinical behavior therapy.* New York: Holt, Rinehart & Winston.

Goldfried, M. R., & Davison, G. C. (1994). *Clinical behavior therapy* (2nd ed.). New York: Wiley-Interscience.

Goldfried, M. R., & D'Zurilla, T. J. (1969). A behavior-analytic model for assessing competence. In C. D. Spielberger (Ed.), *Current topics in clinical and community psychology* (Vol. 1, pp. 151–196). New York: Academic Press.

Goldfried, M. R., & Sprafkin, J. N. (1974). *Behavioral personality assessment.* Morristown, NJ: General Learning Press.

Goldfried, M. R., Stricker, G., & Weiner, I. B. (1971). *Rorschach handbook of clinical and research applications.* Englewood Cliffs, NJ: Prentice-Hall.

Goldfried, M. R., & Wolfe, B. E. (1996). Psychotherapy practice and research: Repairing a strained alliance. *American Psychologist, 51,* 1007–1016.

Golding, S. L., Roesch, R., & Schreiber, J. (1984). Assessment and conceptualization of competency to stand trial: Preliminary data on the Interdisciplinary Fitness Interview. *Law and Human Behavior, 8,* 321–334.

Golding, S. L., & Rorer, L. G. (1972). Illusory correlation and subjective judgment. *Journal of Abnormal Psychology, 80,* 249–260.

Goldsmith, J. B., & McFall, R. M. (1975). Development and evaluation of an interpersonal skill-training program for psychiatric inpatients. *Journal of Abnormal Psychology, 84,* 51–58.

Goldstein, A. J. (1973). Behavior therapy. In R. Corsini (Ed.), *Current psychotherapies* (pp. 207–249). Itaska, IL: F. E. Peacock.

Goldstein, G., & Hersen, M. (Eds.). (1990). *Handbook of psychological assessment.* New York: Pergamon Press.

Goodenough, F. L. (1931). Children's drawings. In C. Murchison (Ed.), *A handbook of child psychology* (pp. 480–514). Worcester, MA: University Press.

Goodenough, F. L. (1949). *Mental testing.* New York: Rinehart.

Goodman, S. H., Lahey, B. B., Fielding, B., Dulcan, M., Narrow, W., & Regier, D. (in press). Representativeness of clinical samples of youth with mental disorders: A preliminary population-based study. *Journal of Abnormal Psychology.*

Gottesman, I. I. (1991). *Schizophrenia genesis.* New York: W. H. Freeman.

Gottesman, I. I., & Shields, J. (1982). *Schizophrenia: The epigenetic puzzle.* Cambridge: Cambridge University Press.

Gottfredson, G. D., & Holland, J. L. (1989). *Dictionary of Holland occupational codes.* Odessa, Florida: Psychological Assessment Resources.

Gottfredson, L. S. (1994). The science and politics of race-norming. *American Psychologist, 49,* 955–963.

Gottlieb, B. H., & Peters, L. (1991). A national demographic portrait of mutual aid group participants in Canada. *American Journal of Community Psychology, 19,* 651–666.

Gottman, J. M. (1979). *Marital interaction: Experimental investigations.* New York: Academic Press.

Gottman, J. M., & Krokoff, L. J. (1989). Marital interaction and satisfaction: A longitudinal view. *Journal of Consulting and Clinical Psychology, 57,* 47–52.

Gottman, J. M., & Levenson, R. W. (1992). Marital processes predictive of later dissolution: Behavior, physiology, and health. *Journal of Personality and Social Psychology, 63,* 221–233.

Gottman, J. M., & Markman, H. J. (1978). Experimental designs in psychotherapy research. In S. Garfield & A. Bergin (Eds.), *Handbook of psychotherapy and behavior change* (2nd ed., pp. 12–62). New York: John Wiley.

Gottman, J. M., Markman, H. J., & Notarius, C. (1977). The topography of marital conflict: A sequential analysis of verbal and nonverbal behavior. *Journal of Marriage and the Family, 39,* 461–477.

Gottman, J. M., & Roy, A. K. (1990). *Sequential analysis: A guide for behavioral researchers.* New York: Cambridge University Press.

Gough, H. (1987). *California Psychological Inventory: Administrator's guide.* Palo Alto, CA: Consulting Psychologists Press.

Graham, F. K., & Kendall, B. S. (1960). Memory-for-designs test: Revised general manual. *Perceptual and Motor Skills, 11,* 147–188.

Graham, J. R. (1990). *MMPI-2: Assessing personality and psychopathology.* New York: Oxford University Press.

Graham, S. R., & Fox, R. E. (1991). Postdoctoral education for professional practice. *American Psychologist, 46,* 1033–1035.

Grant, B. F., Harford, T. C., Dawson, D. D., Chou, P. S., et al. (1995). The Alcohol Use Disorder and Associated Disabilities Interview Schedule (AUDADIS): Reliability of alcohol and drug modules in a general population sample. *Drug and Alcohol Dependence, 39,* 37–44.

Grantham, R. J. (1973). Effects of counselor sex, race, and language style on black students in initial interviews. *Journal of Counseling Psychology, 20,* 553–559.

Greenberg, L. (1986). Change process research. *Journal of Consulting and Clinical Psychology, 54*, 4-9.

Greenberg, L. S., Elliot, R. K., & Lietaer, G. (1994). Research on experiential psychotherapies. In A. E. Bergin & S. L. Garfield (Eds.) *Handbook of psychotherapy and behavior change* (pp. 509-512). New York: John Wiley.

Greenberg, L. S., & Johnson, S. M. (1988). *Emotionally focused couples therapy*. New York: Guilford.

Greenberg, L. S., & Safran, J. D. (1989). Emotion in psychotherapy. *American Psychologist, 44*, 19-29.

Greenberg, M. T., Speltz, M. L., & DeKlyen, M. (1993). the role of attachment in the early development of disruptive behavior problems. *Development and psychopathology, 5*, 191-214.

Greenblatt, M. (1959). Discussion of papers by Saslow, Matarazzo, & Lacey. In E. A. Rubinstein & M. B. Parloff (Eds.), *Research in psychotherapy* (Vol. 1, pp. 209-220). Washington, DC: American Psychological Association.

Greenspoon, J. (1962). Verbal conditioning and clinical psychology. In A. J. Bachrach (Ed.), *Experimental foundations of clinical psychology* (pp. 510-553). New York: Basic Books.

Greenwood, C. R., Carta, J. J., Kamps, D., Terry, B., & Delquadri, J. (1994). Development and validation of standard classroom observation systems for school practitioners: Ecobehavioral assessment systems software. *Exceptional Children, 61*, 197-210.

Greenwood, C. R., Walker, H. M., Todd, N. M., & Hops, H. (1979). Selecting a cost-effective screening measure for the assessment of preschool social withdrawal. *Journal of Applied Behavior Analysis, 12*, 639-652.

Griest, D. L., Forehand, R., Rogers, T., Breiner, J., Furey, W., & Williams, C. A. (1982). Effect of parent enhancement therapy on the treatment outcome and generalization of a parent training program. *Behaviour Research and Therapy, 20*, 429-436.

Griest, D. L., Wells, K. C., & Forehand, R. (1979). An examination of predictors of maternal perceptions of maladjustment in clinic-referred children. *Journal of Abnormal Psychology, 88*, 277-281.

Grisso, T. (1986). *Evaluating competencies: Forensic assessments and instruments*. New York: Plenum.

Grisso, T., & Appelbaum, P. S. (1995). The MacArthur Treatment Competence Study. III: Abilities of patients to consent to psychiatric and medical treatments. *Law and Human Behavior, 19*, 149-174.

Grisso, T., Appelbaum, P. S., Mulvey, E. P., & Fletcher, K. (1995). The MacArthur Treatment Competence Study. II: Measures of abilities related to competence to consent to treatment. *Law and Human Behavior, 19*, 127-148.

Gross, M. L. (1962). *The brain watchers*. New York: Random House.

Gross, S. J. (1978). The myth of professional licensing. *American Psychologist, 33*, 1009-1016.

Grossarth, M. R., Eysenck, H. J., & Boyle, G. J. (1995). Method of test administration as a factor in test validity: The use of a personality questionnaire in the prediction of cancer and coronary heart disease. *Behaviour Research and Therapy, 33*, 705-710.

Grossarth-Maticek, R., & Eysenck, H. J. (1991). Creative novation behaviour therapy as a prophylactic treatment for cancer and coronary heart disease. Part 1: Description of treatment. *Behaviour Research and Therapy, 29*, 1-16.

Groth-Marnat, G. & Edkins, G. (1996). Professional psychologists in general health care settings: A review of the financial efficacy of direct treatment interventions. *Professional Psychology: Research and Practice, 27,* 161-174.

Grove, H. (1987). The reliability of psychiatric diagnosis. In C. G. Last & M. Hersen (Eds.), *Issues in diagnostic research* (pp. 99-117). New York: Plenum Press.

Grych, J. H., & Fincham, F. D. (1992). Interventions for children of divorce: Toward greater integration of research and action. *Psychological Bulletin, 111,* 434-454.

Guerney, B. G. (Ed.). (1969). *Psychotherapeutic agents: New roles of nonprofessionals, parents, and teachers.* New York: Holt, Rinehart & Winston.

Gullone, E., & King, N. J. (1992). Psychometric evaluation of a revised fear survey schedule for children and adolescents. *Journal of Child Psychology and Psychiatry and Allied Disciplines, 33,* 987-998.

Guntrip, H. (1973). *Psychoanalytic theory, therapy, and the self.* New York: Basic Books.

Gur, R. E. (1978). Left hemisphere dysfunction and left hemisphere overactivation in schizophrenia. *Journal of Abnormal Psychology, 87,* 225-238.

Gurman, A. S., Kniskern, D. P., & Pinsof, W. M. (1986). Research on marital and family therapies. In S. L. Garfield & A. E. Bergin (Eds.), *Handbook of psychotherapy and behavior change* (3rd ed., pp. 565-624). New York: John Wiley.

Hahlweg, K., Revenstorf, D., & Schindler, L. (1984). Effects of behavioral marital therapy on couples' communication and problem-solving skills. *Journal of Consulting and Clinical Psychology, 52,* 553-566.

Hall, G. C. N. (1990). Prediction of sexual aggression. *Clinical Psychology Review, 10,* 229-245.

Halleck, S. L. (1969). Community psychiatry: Some troubling questions. In L. M. Roberts, S. L. Halleck, & M. B. Loeb (Eds.), *Community psychiatry* (pp. 58-71). Garden City, NY: Doubleday, Anchor Books.

Halweg, K., & Markman, H. J. (1988). Effectiveness of behavioral marital therapy: Empirical status of behavioral techniques in preventing and alleviating marital distress. *Journal of consulting and clinical Psychology, 56(3),* 440-447.

Hammond, K. R., & Allen, J. M. (1953). *Writing clinical reports.* Englewood Cliffs, NJ: Prentice-Hall.

Handler, L. (1974). Psychotherapy, assessment, and clinical research: Parallels and similarities. In A. I. Rabin (Ed.), *Clinical psychology: Issues of the seventies* (pp. 49-62). East Lansing: Michigan State University Press.

Hansen, J. C. (1984). Interest inventories. In G. Goldstein & M. Hersen (Eds.), *Handbook of psychological assessment* (pp. 157-177). New York: Pergamon Press.

Hansen, J. C., & Campbell, D. P. (1985). *Manual for the SVIB-SCII* (4th ed.). Palo Alto, CA: Consulting Psychologist Press.

Hansen, D. J., St. Lawrence, J. S., & Christoff, K. A. (1985). Effects of interpersonal problem-solving training with chronic aftercare patients on problem-solving component skills and effectiveness of solutions. *Journal of Consulting and Clinical Psychology, 53,* 167-174.

Harbeck, C., Peterson, L., & Starr, L. (1992). Previously abused child victims' response to a sexual abuse prevention program: A matter of measures. *Behavior Therapy, 23,* 375-388.

Harbin, T. J. (1989). The relationship between the Type A behavior pattern and physiological responsivity: A quantitative review. *Psychophysiology, 26,* 110-119.

Harley, J. P., Ray, R. S., Tomasi, L., Eichman, P. L., Matthews, C. G., Chun, R., Cleeland, C. S., & Traisman, E. (1978). Hyperkinesis and food additives: Testing the Feingold hypothesis. *Pediatrics, 61,* 818-828.

Harlow, H. F., & Zimmerman, R. (1959). Affectional responses in the infant monkey. *Science, 130,* 421-432.

Harris, F. C., & Lahey, B. B. (1982). Recording system bias in direct observational methodology: A review. *Clinical Psychology Review, 2,* 539-556.

Harris, M. J., Milich, R., Johnston, E. M., & Hoover, D. W. (1990). Effects of expectancies on children's social interactions. *Journal of Experimental Social Psychology, 26,* 1-12.

Harris, V. W., & Sherman, J. A. (1973). Effects of peer tutoring and consequences on the math performance of elementary classroom students. *Journal of Applied Behavior Analysis, 6,* 587-598.

Harrison, R. (1965). Thematic apperceptive methods. In B. B. Wolman (Ed.), *Handbook of clinical psychology* (pp. 562-620). New York: McGraw-Hill.

Harrower, M. R. (1965). Clinical psychologists at work. In B. B. Wolman (Ed.), *Handbook of clinical psychology* (pp. 1443-1458). New York: McGraw-Hill.

Hart, S. N., & Brassard, M. R. (1987). A major threat to children's mental health: Psychological maltreatment. *American Psychologist, 42,* 160-165.

Hartmann, H. (1939). Psychoanalysis and the concept of health. *International Journal of Psychoanalysis, 20,* 308-321.

Hartmann, H. (1958). *Ego psychology and the problem of adaptation.* New York: International Universities Press.

Hartshorne, H., & May, M. A. (1928). *Studies in deceit.* New York: Macmillan.

Hartup, W. W. (1983). Peer relations. In E. M. Hetherington (Ed.), *Handbook of child psychology* (Vol. 4): *Socialization, personality, and social development* (pp. 103-198). New York: John Wiley.

Hasemann, D., Nietzel, M. T., & Golding, J. (1996). Clinicians' beliefs about reprocessed memory: Effects of tough and tender-mindedness. Paper presented at the annual meeting of the American Psychological Society. San Francisco.

Haspel, K. C., Jorgenson, L. M., Wincze, J. P., & Parsons, J. P. (1997). Legislative intervention regarding therapist sexual misconduct: An overview. *Professional Psychology: Research and Practice, 28,* 63-72.

Hathaway, S. R. (1958). A study of human behavior: The clinical psychologist: *American Psychologist, 13,* 255-265.

Hathaway, S. R., & McKinley, J. C. (1967). *The Minnesota Multiphasic Personality Inventory Manual.* New York: Psychological Corporation.

Hattie, J. A., Sharpley, C. F., & Rogers, H. J. (1984). Comparative effectiveness of professional and paraprofessional helpers. *Psychological Bulletin, 95,* 534-541.

Hauggard, J. J., & Reppucci, N. D. (1988). *The sexual abuse of children.* San Francisco: Jossey-Bass.

Hayes, S. C. (1983). The role of the individual case in the production and consumption of clinical knowledge. In M. Hersen, A. E. Kazdin, & A. S. Bellack (Eds.), *The clinical psychology handbook* (pp. 181-195). New York: Pergamon Press.

Hayes, S. C. (1996). AABT and AAAPP sponsor national planning conference on practice guidelines. *The Behavior Therapist, 19,* 170.

Hayes, S. C., Follette, V. M., Dawes, R. M., & Grady, K. E. (Eds.). (1995). *Scientific standards of psychological practice: Issues and recommendations.* Reno, NV: Context Press.

Hayes, S. C., & Heiby, E. (1996). Psychology's drug problem: Do we need a fix or should we just say no? *American Psychologist, 51,* 198-206.

Haynes, R. B. (1982). Improving patient compliance: An empirical view. In R. B. Stuart (Ed.), *Adherence, compliance, and generalization in behavioral medicine* (pp. 56-78). New York: Brunner/Mazel.

Haynes, S. G., Feinleib, M., & Kannel, W. B. (1980). The relationahip of psychosocial factors to coronary heart disease in the Framingham study: III. Eight-year incidence of coronary heart disease. *American Journal of Epidemiology, 111,* 37-58.

Haynes, S. G., Levine, S., Scotch, N., Feinleib, M., & Kannel, W. B. (1978). The relationship of psychosocial factors to coronary heart disease in the Framingham study: I. Methods and risk factors. *American Journal of Epidemiology, 107,* 362-383.

Haynes, S. N. (1984). Behavioral assessment of adults. In G. Goldstein & M. Hersen (Eds.), *Handbook of psychological assessment* (pp. 369-401). New York: Pergamon Press.

Haynes, S. N. (1990). Behavioral assessment of adults. In G. Goldstein & M. Hersen (Eds.), *Handbook of psychological assessment* (2nd ed., pp. 423-463). New York: Pergamon Press.

Haynes, S. N. (1993). Treatment implications of psychological assessment. *Psychological Assessment, 5,* 251-253.

Haynes, S. N., & Horn, W. F. (1982). Reactivity in behavioral assessment: A review. *Behavioral Assessment, 4,* 369-385.

Haynes, S. N., & Uchigakiuchi, P. (1993). Incorporating personality trait measures into behavioral assessment: Nuts in a fruitcake or raisins in a mai tai? *Behavior Modification, 17,* 72-92.

Hayvren, M., & Hymel, S. (1984). Ethical issues in sociometric testing: Impact of sociometric measures on interaction behavior. *Developmental Psychology, 20,* 844-849.

Haywood, T. W., Grossman, L. S., & Cavanaugh, J. L. (1990). Subjective versus objective measurements of deviant sexual arousal in clinical evaluations of alleged child molesters. *Psychological Assessment, 2,* 269-275.

Hazelrigg, M. D., Cooper, H. M., & Boudin, C. M. (1987). Evaluating the effectiveness of family therapies: An integrative review and analysis. *Psychological Bulletin, 101,* 428-442.

Heal, L. W., & Sigelman, C. K. (1995). Response biases in interviews of individuals with limited mental ability. *Journal of Intellectual Disability Research, 39,* 331-340.

Hedges, L. V., & Olkin, L. (1982). Analyses, reanalyses, and meta-analysis. *Contemporary Education Review, 1,* 157-165.

Heidegger, M. (1968). *Being and time* (J. Macquarrie & E. Robinson, Trans.). New York: Harper & Row. (Original work published 1927)

Helfer, R. E., & Kempe, C. H. (Eds.). (1968). *The battered child.* Chicago: University of Chicago Press.

Heller, K. (1996). Coming of age of prevention science. *American Psychologist, 51,* 1123-1127.

Heller, K., Swindle, R. W., Jr., & Dusenbury, L. (1986). Component social support processes: Comments and integration. *Journal of Consulting and Clinical Psychology, 54,* 466-470.

Heller, W. (1990). The neuropsychology of emotion: Developmental patterns and implications for psychopathology. In N. L. Stein, B. L. Leventhal, & T. Trabasso (Eds.), *Psychological and biological approaches to emotion* (pp. 167-211). Hillsdale, NJ: Lawrence Erlbaum Associates.

Heller, W., Hopkins, J., & Cox, S. (1991). Effects of lateralized brain damage on infant socioemotional development. *Journal of Clinical and Experimental Neuropsychology, 13,* 64.

Helmes, E., & Reddon, J. R. (1993). A perspective on developments in assessing psychopathology: A critical review of the MMPI and MMPI-2. *Psychological Bulletin, 113,* 453–471.

Henry, W. E. (1956). *The analysis of fantasy: The thematic apperception technique in the story of personality.* New York: John Wiley.

Henry, W. P., Strupp, H. H., Butler, S. F., Schacht, T. E., & Binder, J. L. (1993). Effects of training in time-limited dynamic psychotherapy: Changes in therapist behavior. *Journal of Consulting & Clinical Psychology, 61,* 434–440.

Herbert, T. B., & Cohen, S. (1993). Stress and immunity in humans: A meta-analytic review. *Psychosomatic Medicine, 55,* 364–379.

Herink, R. (Ed.). (1980). *The psychotherapy handbook: The A to Z guide to more than 250 different therapies in use today.* New York: New American Library.

Herrnstein, R. J., & Murray, C. (1994). *The bell curve: Intelligence and class structure in American Life.* New York: Free Press.

Hersch, P. D., & Alexander, R. W. (1990). MMPI profile patterns of emotional disability claimants. *Journal of Clinical Psychology, 46,* 795–799.

Herz, M. I., & Melville, C. (1980). Relapse in schizophrenia. *American Journal of Psychiatry, 137,* 801–805.

Hetherington, E. M. (1989). Coping with family transition: Winners, losers, and survivors. *Child Development, 60,* 1–14.

Hetherington, E. M., & Arasteh, J. D. (Eds.). (1988). *Impact of divorce, single parenting, and stepparenting on children.* Hillsdale, NJ: Lawrence Erlbaum Associates.

Hetherington, E. M., Stanley-Hagan, M., & Anderson, E. R. (1989). Marital transitions: A child's perspective. *American Psychologist, 44,* 303–312.

Hinshaw, S. P., Simmel, C., & Heller, T. L. (1995). Multimethod assessment of covert antisocial behavior in children: Laboratory observations, adult ratings, and child self-report. *Psychological Assessment, 7,* 209–219.

Hodgson, R. J., & Rachman, S. (1977). Obsessional-compulsive complaints. *Behaviour Research and Therapy, 15,* 389–395.

Hoelscher, T. J., Lichstein, K. L., & Rosenthal, T. L. (1986). Home relaxation practice in hypertension treatment: Objective assessment and compliance induction. *Journal of Consulting and Clinical Psychology, 54,* 217–221.

Hoffman, P. J. (1960). The paramorphic representation of clinical judgment. *Psychological Bulletin, 57,* 116–131.

Hogan, D. B. (1983). The effectiveness of licensing: History, evidence, and recommendations. *Law and Human Behavior, 7,* 117–138.

Holder, H. D., & Blose, J. D. (1987). Changes in health care costs and utilization associated with mental health treatment. *Hospital and Community Psychiatry, 38,* 1070–1075.

Holland, J. L. (1994). *The self-directed search.* Odessa, Florida: Psychological Assessment Resources.

Holland, J. L. (1996). Exploring careers with a typology. *American Psychologist, 51,* 397–406.

Holland, J. L., & Gottfredson, G. D. (1994). *Career attitudes and strategies inventory: An inventory for understanding adult careers.* Odessa, Florida: Psychological Assessment Resources.

Hollon, S. D., & Beck, A. T. (1994). Cognitive and cognitive-behavioral therapies. In A. E. Bergin & S. L. Garfield (Eds.), *Handbook of psychotherapy and behavior change* (pp. 428–466). New York: Wiley & Sons.

Hollon, S. D. (1993). Review of psychosocial treatments for mood disorders. In D. D. Dunner (Ed.), *Current psychiatric therapy* (pp. 240–246). Philadelphia, PA: W. B. Saunders Co.

Holmes, M. R., Hansen, D. J., & St. Lawrence, J. S. (1984). Conversational skills training with aftercare patients in the community: Social validation and generalization. *Behavior Therapy, 15,* 84–100.

Holt, R. R. (1958). Formal aspects of the TAT: A neglected resource. *Journal of Projective Techniques, 22,* 163–172.

Holt, R. R. (1978). *Methods in clinical psychology: Projective assessment* (Vol. 1). New York: Plenum Press.

Holt, R. R., & Luborsky, L. (1958). *Personality patterns of psychiatrists: A study of methods for selecting residents* (Vol. 1). New York: Basic Books.

Holtzman, W. H., Thorpe, J. W., Swartz, J. D., & Herron, E. W. (1961). *Inkblot perception and personality: Holtzman Inkblot Technique.* Austin: University of Texas Press.

Holtzworth-Monroe, A. (1992). Social skill deficits in maritally violent men: Interpreting the data using a social information processing model. *Clinical Psychology Review, 12,* 605–618.

Hooley, J. M. (1985). Expressed emotion: A review of the critical literature. *Clinical Psychology Review, 5,* 119–139.

Horowitz, L. M., Rosenberg, S. E., Baer, B. A., Ureno, G., & Villasenor, V. S. (1988). The Inventory of Interpersonal Problems: Psychometric properties and clinical applications. *Journal of Consulting and Clinical Psychology, 56,* 885–892.

Horowitz, L. M., & Vitkus, J. (1986). The interpersonal basis of psychiatric symptoms. *Clinical Psychology Review, 6,* 443–469.

House, J. S., Robbins, C., & Metzner, H. L. (1982). The association of social relationships and activities with mortality: Prospective evidence from the Tecumseh Community Health Study. *American Journal of Epidemiology, 116,* 123–140.

Howard, A., Pion, G. M., Gottfredson, G. D., Flattau, P. E., Oskamp, S., Pfafflin, S. M., Bray, D. W. (1986). The changing face of American psychology: A report from the Committee on Employment and Human Resources. *American Psychologist, 41,* 1311–1327.

Howard, K. I., Lueger, R. J., Maling, M. S., & Martinovich, Z. (1993). A phase model of psychotherapy outcome: Causal mediation of change. *Journal of Consulting and Clinical Psychology, 61,* 678–685.

Howard, K. I., Moras, K., Brill, P. L., Martinovich, Z., & Lutz, W. (1996). Evaluation of psychotherapy: efficacy, effectiveness, and patient progress. *American Psychologist, 51,* 1059–1064.

Howard, R. C., & Clark, C. R. (1985). When courts and experts disagree: Discordance between insanity recommendations and adjudications. *Law and Human Behavior, 9,* 385–395.

Hughes, C. F., Uhlmann, C., & Pennebaker, J. W. (1994). The body's response to processing emotional trauma: Linking verbal text to autonomic activity. *Journal of Personality, 62,* 565–585.

Hull, C. L. (1943). *Principles of behavior.* New York: Appleton.

Humphrey, L. L., Apple, R. F., & Kirschenbaum, D. S. (1986). Differentiating bulimic-anorexic from normal families using interpersonal and behavioral observational systems. *Journal of Consulting and Clinical Psychology, 54,* 190–195.

Humphreys, K. (1996). Clinical psychologists as psychotherapists: History, future, and alternatives. *American Psychologist, 51,* 190–197.

Humphreys, L. G. (1988). Trends in levels of academic achievement of blacks and other minorities. *Intelligence, 12,* 231–260.

Hunt, W. A., & Jones, N. F. (1962). The experimental investigation of clinical judgment. In A. J. Bachrach (Ed.), *Experimental foundations of clinical psychology* (pp. 26–51). New York: Basic Books.

Hunter, R. H. (1995). Benefits of competency-based treatment programs. *American Psychologist, 50,* 509–513.

Husserl, E. (1969). *Ideas: General introduction to pure phenomenology.* New York: Humanities Press. (Original work published 1913)

Hutt, C., & Hutt, S. J. (1968). Stereotypy, arousal and autism. *Human Development, 11,* 277–286.

Hynd, G. W., Snow, J., & Becker, M. G. (1986). Neuropsychological assessment in clinical child psychology. In B. B. Lahey & A. E. Kazdin (Eds.), *Advances in clinical child psychology* (Vol. 9, pp. 35–86). New York: Plenum Press.

Ialongo, N., Edelsohn, G., Wertheimer-Larsson, L., Crockett, L., & Kellam, S. (1994). The significance of self-reported anxious symptoms in the first grade. *Journal of Abnormal Child Psychology, 22,* 441–455.

Ilsley, J. E., Moffoot, A. P. R., & O'Carroll, R. E. (1995). An analysis of memory dysfunction in major depression. *Journal of Affective Disorders, 35,* 1–9.

Imwinkelried, E. J. (1994). The next step after *Daubert:* Devel oping a similarly epistemological approach to ensuring the reliability of nonscientific expert testimony. *Cardozo Law Review, 15,* 2271–2294.

Ingram, R. E. (Ed.). (1986). *Information processing approaches to clinical psychology.* Orlando, FL: Academic Press.

Institute of Personality Assessment and Research. (1970). *Annual report: 1969–1970.* Berkeley: University of California.

Inui, T., Yourtee, E., & Williamson, J. (1976). Improved outcomes in hypertension after physician tutorials. *Annuals of Internal Medicine, 84,* 646–651.

Isenhart, C. E., & Silversmith, D. J. (1996). MMPI-2 response styles: Generalization to alcoholism assessment. *Psychology of Addictive Behaviors, 10,* 115–123.

Jackson, D. N. (1984). *Personality Research Form manual.* Port Huron, MI: Research Psychologists Press.

Jackson, D. N., & Messick, S. (1958). Content and style in personality assessment. *Psychological Bulletin, 55,* 243–252.

Jackson, D. N., & Messick, S. (1961). Acquiescence and desirability as response determinants on the MMPI. *Educational and Psychological Measurement, 21,* 771–790.

Jacob, T., & Tennenbaum, D. L. (1988). Family assessment methods. In M. Rutter, A. H. Tuma, & I. S. Lann (Eds.), *Assessment and diagnosis in child psychopathology* (pp. 196–231). New York: Guilford Press.

Jacobs, M. K., & Goodman, G. (1989). Psychology and self-help groups: Predictions on a partnership. *American Psychologist, 44,* 536–545.

Jacobson, N. S. (1991). Behavioral versus insight-oriented marital therapy: Labels can be misleading. *Journal of Consulting and Clinical Psychology, 59(1),* 142–145.

Jacobson, N. S., & Christensen, A. (1996). Studying the effectiveness of psychotherapy: How well can clinical trials do the job? *American Psychologist, 51,* 1031-1039.

Jacobson, N. S., Holtzworth-Monroe, A., & Schmaling, K. B. (1989). Marital therapy and spouse involvement in the treatment of depression, agoraphobia, and alcoholism. *Journal of Consulting and Clinical Psychology, 57,* 5-10.

Jacobson, N. S., Schmaling, K. B., & Holtzworth-Munroe, A. (1987). Component analysis of behavioral marital therapy: 2-year follow-up and prediction of relapse. *Journal of Marital and Family Therapy, 13(2),* 187-195.

Jacobson, N. S., & Truax, P. (1991). Clinical significance: A statistical approach to defining meaningful change in psychotherapy research. *Journal of Consulting and Clinical Psychology, 59,* 12-19.

Jacoby, L. L., & Kelley, C. M. (1987). Unconscious influences of memory for a prior event. *Personality and Social Psychology Bulletin, 13,* 314-336.

James, J. W., & Haley, W. E. (1995). Age and health bias in practicing clinical psychologists. *Psychology & Aging, 10,* 610-616.

Jarrett, R. B., & Fairbank, J. A. (1987). Psychologists' views: APA's advocacy of and resource expenditure on social and professional issues. *Professional Psychology, 18,* 643-646.

Jason, L. A., McMahon, S. D., Salina, D., Hedeker, D., Stockton, M., Dunson, K., & Kimball, P. (1995). Asssessing a smoking cessation intervention involving groups, incentives, and self-help manuals. *Behavior Therapy, 26,* 393-408.

Jeffery, R. W. (1988). Dietary risk factors and their modification in cardiovascular disease. *Journal of Consulting and Clinical Psychology, 56,* 350-357.

Jenkins, C. D., Zyzanski, S. J., & Rosenman, R. H. (1971). Progress toward validation of a computer-scored test for the Type A coronary-prone behavior pattern. *Psychosomatic Medicine, 33,* 193-202.

Jensen, J. P., Bergin, A. E., & Greaves, D. W. (1990). The meaning of eclecticism: New survey and analysis of components. *Professional Psychology: Research and Practice, 21,* 124-130.

Johansson, C. B. (1982). *Manual for Career Assessment Inventory* (2nd ed.). Minneapolis: National Computer Systems.

Johnsen, B. H., & Hugdahl, K. (1990). Fear questionnaires for simple phobias: Psychometric evaluations for a Norwegian sample. *Scandinavian Journal of Psychology, 31,* 42-48.

Johnson, J. H., Rasbury, W. G., & Siegel, L. J. (1986). *Approaches to child treatment: Introduction to theory, research, and practice.* New York: Pergamon Press.

Johnson, M. L. (1953). Seeing's believing. *New Biology, 15,* 60-80.

Johnson, S. L., & Jacob, T. (1997). Marital interactions of depressed men and women. *Journal of Consulting and Clinical Psychology, 65,* 15-23.

Johnson, S. M., & Bolstad, O. D. (1973). Methodological issues in naturalistic observation: Some problems and solutions for field research. In L. A. Hamerlynck, L. C. Handy, & E. J. Mash (Eds.), *Behavior change: Methodology, concepts and practice* (pp. 7-67). Champaign, IL: Research Press.

Johnson, S. M., & Lobitz, G. K. (1974). Parental manipulation of child behavior in home observations. *Journal of Applied Behavior Analysis, 7,* 23-32.

Johnstone, B., et al. (1995). Psychology in health care: Future directions. *Professional Psychology: Research and Practice, 26,* 341-365.

Jones, B. P., & Butters, N. (1983). Neuropsychological assessment. In M. Hersen, A. E. Kazdin, & A. S. Bellack (Eds.), *The clinical psychology handbook* (pp. 377-396). New York: Pergamon Press.

Jones, E. (1953, 1955, 1957). *The life and work of Sigmund Freud* (Vols. 1-3). New York: Basic Books.

Jones, E. E. (1996). Introduction to the special section on attachment and psychopathology: Part I. *Journal of Consulting and Clinical Psychology, 64*, 5-7.

Jones, E. E., Cumming, J. D., & Horowitz, M. J. (1988). Another look at the nonspecific hypothesis of therapeutic effectiveness. *Journal of Consulting and Clinical Psychology, 56*, 48-55.

Jones, H. E. (1943). *Development in adolescence.* New York: Appleton-Century.

Jones, M. C. (1924a). The elimination of children's fears. *Journal of Experimental Psychology, 7*, 382-390.

Jones, M. C. (1924b). A laboratory study of fear: The case of Peter. *Pedagogical Seminary and Journal of Genetic Psychology, 31*, 308-315.

Jones, R. R., Reid, J. B., & Patterson, G. R. (1975). Naturalistic observation in clinical assessment. In P. McReynolds (Ed.), *Advances in psychological assessment* (Vol. 3, pp. 42-95). San Francisco: Jossey-Bass.

Jones, W. H., Adams, J. A., Monroe, P. R., & Berry, J. O. (1995). A psychometric exploration of marital satisfaction and commitment. *Journal of Social Behavior and Personality, 10*, 923-932.

Jouriles, E. N., & Farris, A. M. (1992). Effects of marital conflict on subsequent parent–child interactions. *Behavior Therapy, 23*, 355-374.

Jouriles, E. N., & O'Leary, K. D. (1985). Interspousal reliability of reports of marital violence. *Journal of Consulting and Clinical Psychology, 53*, 419-421.

Kagan, J. (1989). Temperamental contributions to social behavior. *American Psychologist, 44*, 668-674.

Kahn, E. (1985). Heinz Kohut and Carl Rogers: A timely comparison. *American Psychologist, 40*, 893-904.

Kahneman, D., & Tversky, A. (1979). Intuitive prediction: Biases and corrective procedures. *TIMS Studies in the Management Sciences, 12*, 313-327.

Kalichman, S. C., Rompa, D., & Coley, B. (1996). Experimental component analysis of a behavioral HIV-AIDS prevention for inner-city women. *Journal of Consulting and Clinical Psychology, 64*, 687-693.

Kandel, E. P., Schwartz, J. H., & Jessell, T. M. (1991). *Principles of neural science.* Norwalk, CT: Appleton & Lange.

Kane, E. W., & Macauley, L. J. (1993). Interviewer gender and gender attitudes. *Public Opinion Quarterly, 57*, 1-28.

Kanfer, F. H. (1968). Verbal conditioning: A review of its current status. In T. R. Dixon & D. L. Horton (Eds.), *Verbal behavior and general behavior theory* (pp. 245-290). Englewood Cliffs, NJ: Prentice-Hall.

Kanfer, F. H., & Gaelick, L. (1986). Self-management methods. In F. H. Kanfer & A. P. Goldstein (Eds.), *Helping people change: A textbook of methods* (3rd ed., pp. 283-345). New York: Pergamon Press.

Kanfer, F. H., & McBrearty, J. F. (1962). Minimal social reinforcement and interview content. *Journal of Clinical Psychology, 18*, 210-215.

Kanfer, F. H., & Saslow, G. (1969). Behavioral diagnosis. In C. M. Franks (Ed.), *Behavior therapy: Appraisal and status* (pp. 210–215). New York: McGraw-Hill.

Kanner, A. D., Coyne, J. C., Schaefer, C., & Lazarus, R. S. (1981). Comparison of two modes of stress measurement: Daily hassles and uplifts versus major life events. *Journal of Behavioral Medicine, 14,* 1–39.

Kanner, L. (1943). Autistic disturbances of affective contact. *Nervous Child, 2,* 217–250.

Kaplan, A. (1964). *The conduct of inquiry.* San Francisco: Chander.

Kaplan, E. (1990). The process approach to neuropsychological assessment of psychiatric patients. *Journal of Neuropsychiatry and Clinical Neurosciences, 2,* 72–87.

Kaplan, M. (1983). A woman's view of DSM-III. *American Psychologist, 38,* 786–792.

Kaplan, R. M., & Saccuzzo, D. P. (1993). *Psychological testing* (3rd ed.). Pacific Grove, CA: Brooks/Cole.

Kaslow, N. J., & Rehm, L. P. (1985). Conceptualization, assessment, and treatment of depression in children. In P. H. Bornstein & A. E. Kazdin (Eds.), *Handbook of clinical behavior therapy with children* (pp. 599–657). Homewood, IL: Dorsey Press.

Kaslow, N. J., Rehm, L. P., & Siegel, A. W. (1984). Social and cognitive correlates of depression in children: A developmental perspective. *Journal of Abnormal Child Psychology, 12,* 605–620.

Kaufman, A. S. (1990). *Assessing adolescent and adult intelligence.* Boston: Allyn & Bacon.

Kaufman, A. S. (1994). *Intelligent testing with the WISC-III.* New York: John Wiley.

Kaufman, A. S., & Harrison, P. L. (1991). Individual intellectual assessment. In C. E. Walker (Ed.), *Clinical psychology: Historical and research foundations* (pp. 91–120). New York: Plenum Press.

Kaufman, A. S., & Kaufman, N. L. (1983). *KABC: Kaufman Assessment Battery for Children.* Circle Pines, MN: American Guidance Service.

Kaufman, A. S., & Kaufman, N. L. (1985). *Kaufman Test of Educational Achievement.* Circle Pines, MN: American Guidance Service.

Kaufman, A. S., & Kaufman, N. L. (1991). *Manual for the Kaufman Brief Intelligence Test (K-BIT).* Circle Pines, MN: American Guidance Service.

Kaufman, A. S., & Kaufman, N. L. (1993). *Manual for the Kaufman Adolescent and Adult Intelligence Test (KAIT).* Circle Pines, MN: American Guidance Service.

Kaufman, J., & Zigler, E. (1987). Do abused children become abusive parents? *American Journal of Orthopsychiatry, 57,* 186–192.

Kazdin, A. E. (1972). Response cost: The removal of conditioned reinforcers for therapeutic change. *Behavior Therapy, 3,* 533–546.

Kazdin, A. E. (1974). Self-monitoring and behavior change. In M. J. Mahoney & C. E. Thoresen (Eds.), *Self-control: Power to the person* (pp. 218–246). Monterey, CA: Brooks/Cole.

Kazdin, A. E. (1982a). *Single-case research designs: Methods for clinical and applied settings.* New York: Oxford University Press.

Kazdin, A. E. (1982b). Single-case experimental designs. In P. C. Kendall & J. N. Butcher (Eds.), *Handbook of research methods in clinical psychology* (pp. 461–490). New York: John Wiley.

Kazdin, A. E. (1985). *Treatment of antisocial behavior in children and adolescents.* Homewood, IL: Dorsey Press.

Kazdin, A. E. (1989). Developmental psychopathology: Current research, issues, and directions. *American Psychologist, 44,* 180–187.

Kazdin, A. E. (1993). Evaluation in clinical practice: Clinically sensitive and systematic methods of treatment delivery. *Behavior Therapy, 24,* 11-45.

Kazdin, A. E. (1994). Methodology, design, and evaluation in psychotherapy research. In A. E. Bergin & S. L. Garfield (Eds.), *Handbook of psychotherapy and behavior change* (pp. 19-71). New York: Wiley & Sons.

Kazdin, A. E., Bass, D., Siegel, T., & Thomas, C. (1989). Cognitive-behavioral therapy and relationship therapy in the treatment of children referred for antisocial behavior. *Journal of Consulting and Clinical Psychology, 57,* 522-535.

Kazdin, A. E., Esveldt-Dawson, K., French, N. H., & Unis, A. S. (1987). Problem-solving skills training and relationship therapy in the treatment of antisocial child behavior. *Journal of Consulting and Clinical Psychology, 55,* 76-85.

Kazdin, A. E., Esveldt-Dawson, K., & Matson, J. L. (1983). The effects of instructional set on social skills performance among psychiatric inpatient children. *Behavior Therapy, 14,* 413-423.

Kazdin, A. E., Esveldt-Dawson, K., Sherick, R. B., & Colbus, D. (1985). Assessment of overt behavior and childhood depression among psychiatrically disturbed children. *Journal of Consulting and Clinical Psychology, 53,* 201-210.

Kazdin, A. E., Matson, J. L., & Esveldt-Dawson, K. (1984). The relationship of role-play assessment of children's social skills to multiple measures of social competence. *Behaviour Research and Therapy, 22,* 129-140.

Kazdin, A. E., & Wilson, G. T. (1978). *Evaluation of behavior therapy: Issues, evidence and research strategies.* Cambridge, MA: Ballinger.

Keilin, W. G., & Bloom, L. J. (1986). Child custody evaluation practices: A survey of experienced professionals. *Professional Psychology: Research and Practice, 17,* 338-346.

Keiser, R. E., & Prather, E. N. (1990). What is the TAT: A review of ten years of research. *Journal of Personality Assessment, 55,* 800-803.

Keith-Spiegel, P. C., & Koocher, G. (1985). *Ethics in psychology: Professional standards and cases.* New York: Random House.

Kellam, S. G., Rebok, G. W., Ialongo, N., & Mayer, L. S. (1994). The course and malleability of aggressive behavior from early first grade into middle school: Results of a developmental epidemiology-based preventive trial. *Journal of Child Psychology & Psychiatry & Allied Disciplines, 35,* 259-281.

Kelly, E. L. (1961). Clinical psychology—1960: A report of survey findings. *Newsletter, Division of Clinical Psychology of APA, 14,* 1-11.

Kelly, E. L., & Fiske, D. W. (1951). *The prediction of performance in clinical psychology.* Ann Arbor: University of Michigan Press.

Kelly, G. A. (1955). *The psychology of personal constructs.* New York: W. W. Norton.

Kelly, G. A. (1958). The theory and technique of assessment. *Annual review of psychology* (Vol. 9, pp. 323-352). Palo Alto, CA: Annual Review.

Kelly, J. A., & Murphy, D. A. (1992). Psychological interventions with AIDS and HIV: Prevention and treatment. *Journal of Consulting and Clinical Psychology, 60,* 576-585.

Kelly, J. A., St. Lawrence, J. S., Hood, H. V., & Brashfield, T. L. (1989). Behavioral intervention to reduce AIDS risk activities. *Journal of Consulting and Clinical Psychology, 57,* 60-67.

Kelly, J. B. (1991). Parent interaction after divorce: Comparison of medicated and adversarial divorce processes. *Behavioral Sciences and the Law, 9,* 387-398.

Kempler, W. (1973). Gestalt therapy. In R. Corsini (Ed.), *Current psychotherapies* (pp. 251–286). Itasca, IL: F. E. Peacock.

Kendall, P. C. (1984). Behavioral assessment and methodology. In G. T. Wilson, C. M. Franks, K. D. Brownell, & P. C. Kendall (Eds.), *Annual Review of Behavior Therapy* (Vol. 9, pp. 123–163). New York: Guilford Press.

Kendall, P. C. (1994). Treating anxiety disorders in children: Results of a randomized clinical trial. *Journal of Consulting and Clinical Psychology, 62,* 100–110.

Kendall, P. C., & Braswell, L. (1985). *Cognitive behavioral modification with impulsive children.* New York: Guilford Press.

Kendall, P. C., & Panichelli-Mindel, S. M. (1995). Cognitive- behavioral treatments. *Journal of Abnormal Child Psychology, 23,* 107–124.

Kendall, P. C., & Zupan, B. A. (1981). Individual versus group application of cognitive-behavioral self-control procedures with children. *Behavioral Therapy, 12,* 344–359.

Kendall-Tackett, K. A., Williams, L. M., & Finkelhor, D. (1993). Impact of sexual abuse on children: A review and synthesis of recent empirical studies. *Psychological Bulletin, 113,* 164–180.

Kendler, K. S., & Roy, M. A. (1995). Validity of a diagnosis of lifetime major depression obtained by personal interview versus family history. *American Journal of Psychiatry, 152,* 1608–1614.

Kent, R. N., & Foster, S. L. (1977). Direct observational procedures: Methodological issues in naturalistic settings. In A. R. Ciminero, K. S. Calhoun, & H. E. Adams (Eds.), *Handbook of behavioral assessment* (pp. 279–328). New York: John Wiley.

Kern, J. M. (1982). The comparative external and concurrent validity of three role-plays for assessing heterosocial performance. *Behavior Therapy, 13,* 666–680.

Kern, J. M., Cavell, T. A., & Beck, B. (1985). Predicting differential reactions to males' versus females' assertions, emphatic-assertions, and non-assertions. *Behavior Therapy, 16,* 63–75.

Kernberg, O. (1976). *Object relations, theory and clinical psychoanalysis.* New York: Jason Aronson.

Kessler, R. C., Price, R. H., & Wortman, C. B. (1985). Social factors in psychopathology: Stress, social support, and coping processes. *Annual Review of Psychology, 36,* 531–572.

Kety, S. S., Wender, P. H., Jacobsen, B., Ingraham, L. J., Jansson, L., Faber, B., & Kinney, D. K. (1994). Mental illness in the biological and adoptive relatives of schizophrenic adoptees. *Archives of General Psychiatry, 51,* 442–455.

Kiecolt-Glaser, J. K., & Glaser, R. (1992). Psychoneuroimmunology: Can psychological interventions modulate immunity? *Journal of Consulting and Clinical Psychology, 60,* 569–575.

Kiesler, C. A., & Sibulkin, A. E. (1987). *Mental hospitalization: Myths and facts about a national crisis.* Beverly Hills, CA: Sage.

Kiesler, D. J. (1983). The 1982 Interpersonal Circle: A taxonomy for complementarity in human transactions. *Psychological Review, 90,* 185–214.

Kiesler, D. J. (1986a). The 1982 interpersonal circle: An analysis of DSM-III personality disorders. In T. Millon & G. L. Klerman (Eds.), *Contemporary directions in psychopathology: Towards the DSM-IV* (pp. 571–597). New York: Guilford Press.

Kiesler, D. J. (1986b). Interpersonal methods of diagnosis and treatment. In J. O. Cavenar, Jr. (Ed.), *Psychiatry* (Vol. 1, pp. 1–23). Philadelphia: Lippincott.

Kiesler, D. J. (1987a). *Check List of Psychotherapy Transactions-Revised (CLOPT-R) and Check List of Interpersonal Transactions-Revised (CLOIT)*. Richmond: Virginia Commonwealth University.

Kiesler, D. J. (1987b). *Research manual for the Impact Message Inventory*. Palo Alto, CA: Consulting Psychologists Press.

Kiesler, D. J. (1996). *Contemporary interpersonal theory and research: Personality, psychopathology, and psychotherapy*. New York: Wiley.

Kiesler, D. J., & Van Denburg, T. F. (1993). Therapeutic impact disclosure: A last taboo in psychoanalytic theory and practice. *Clinical Psychology and Psychotherapy, 1*, 3-13.

Kimble, G. A. (1989). Psychology from the standpoint of a generalist. *American Psychologist, 44*, 491-499.

Kimura, D. (1961). Cerebral dominance and the perception of verbal stimuli. *Canadian Journal of Psychology, 15*, 166-171.

Kimura, D. (1966). Dual functional asymmetry of the brain in visual perception. *Neuropsychologia, 4*, 275-285.

Kimura, D. (1967). Functional asymmetry of the brain in dichotic listening. *Cortex, 3*, 163-178.

Kirchner, E. P., & Draguns, J. G. (1979). Assertion and aggression in adult offenders. *Behavior Therapy, 10*, 452-471.

Kirkpatrick, B., & Gellad, F. (1993). Brain morphology and schizophrenia: A magnetic resonance imaging study of limbic, prefrontal cortex, and caudate structures. *Archives of General Psychiatry, 49*, 921-926.

Kissen, D. M., & Eysenck, H. J. (1962). Personality in male lung cancer patients. *Journal of Psychosomatic Research, 6*, 123-127.

Klein, M. (1960). *The psychoanalysis of children*. New York: Grove Press.

Klein, M. (1975). *The writings of Melanie Klein* (Vol. III). London: Hogarth Press.

Klein, R. H. (1983). Group treatment approaches. In M. Hersen, A. E. Kazdin, & A. S. Bellack (Eds.), *The clinical psychology handbook* (pp. 593-610). New York: Pergamon Press.

Kleinknecht, R. A., & Bernstein, D. A. (1978). Assessment of dental fear. *Behavior Therapy, 9*, 626-634.

Kleinmuntz, B. (1963). MMPI decision rules for the identification of college maladjustment: A digital computer approach. *Psychological Monographs, 77* (14, Whole No. 477).

Kleinmuntz, B. (1969). Personality test interpretation by computer and clinician. In J. N. Butcher (Ed.), *MMPI: Research developments and clinical applications* (pp. 97-104). New York: John Wiley.

Kleinmuntz, B. (1984). The scientific study of clinical judgment in psychology and medicine. *Clinical Psychology Review, 4*, 111-126.

Klopfer, B., & Davidson, H. (1962). *The Rorschach technique: An introductory manual*. New York: Harcourt.

Klopfer, B., & Kelley, D. M. (1937). The techniques of the Rorschach performance. *Rorschach Research Exchange, 2*, 1-14.

Klopfer, B., & Kelley, D. M. (1942). *The Rorschach technique*. New York: Harcourt, Brace & World.

Klopfer, W. G. (1960). *The psychological report*. New York: Grune & Stratton.

Klopfer, W. G. (1983). Writing psychological reports. In C. E. Walker (Ed.), *The handbook of clinical psychology* (Vol. 1, pp. 501-527). Homewood, IL: Dow Jones-Irwin.

Knapp, R. (1976). *Handbook for the Personal Orientation Inventory*. San Diego, California: Edits Publishers.

Koffka, K. (1935). *Principles of Gestalt psychology*. New York: Harcourt, Brace.

Kohlenberg, R. J., & Tsai, M. (1991). *Functional analytic psychotherapy: Creating intense and curative therapeutic relationships*. New York: Plenum Press.

Kohler, W. (1925). *The mentality of apes*. New York: Harcourt, Brace.

Kohout, J., Wicherski, M., & Pion, G. (1991). *1988-89 characteristics of graduate departments of psychology*. Washington, DC: American Psychological Association.

Kohut, H. (1971). *The analysis of self*. New York: International Universities Press.

Kohut, H. (1977). *The restoration of the self*. New York: International Universities Press.

Kohut, H. (1983). Selected problems of self-psychological theory. In J. D. Lichtenberg & S. Kaplan (Eds.), *Reflections on self psychology* (pp. 387-416). Hillsdale, NJ: Lawrence Erlbaum Associates.

Kokotovic, A. M., & Tracey, T. J. (1987). Premature termination at a university counseling center. *Journal of Counseling Psychology, 34*, 80-82.

Kolb, B., & Whishaw, I. Q. (1990). *Fundamentals of neuropsychology* (3rd ed.). New York: Freeman.

Kolotkin, R. H. (1980). Situation specificity in the assessment of assertion: Considerations for the measurement of training and transfer. *Behavior Therapy, 11,* 651-661.

Koocher, G. P., Goodman, G. S., White, C. S., Friedrich, W. N., Sivan, A. B., & Reynolds, C. R. (1995). Psychological science and the use of anatomically detailed dolls in child sexual-abuse assessments. *Psychological Bulletin, 118,* 199-222.

Koppitz, E. M. (1968). *Psychological evaluation of children's human figure drawings*. New York: Grune & Stratton.

Kopta, S. M., Howard, K. I., Lowry, J. L., & Beutler, L. E. (1991). Patterns of symptomatic recovery in psychotherapy. *Journal of Consulting and Clinical Psychology, 62*, 1009-1016.

Korchin, S. J. (1976). *Modern clinical psychology: Principles of intervention in the clinic and community*. New York: Basic Books.

Korman, M. (1974). National conference on levels and patterns of professional training in psychology: The major themes. *American Psychologist, 29*, 441-449.

Korman, M. (Ed.). (1976). *Levels and patterns of professional training in psychology*. Washington, DC: American Psychological Association.

Korsch, B. M., & Negrete, V. F. (1972). Doctor-patient communication. *Scientific American, 227*, 66-74.

Koss, M. P., & Shiang, J. (1994). Research on brief psychotherapy. In A. E. Bergin & S. L. Garfield (Eds.), *Handbook of psychotherapy and behavior change* (pp. 664-700). New York: Wiley & Sons.

Kraemer, H. C., & Thiemann, S. (1989). A strategy to use soft data effectively in randomized controlled clinical trials. *Journal of Consulting and Clinical Psychology, 57*, 148-154.

Kramer, J. J., & Conoley, J. C. (Eds.) (1995). *The twelfth mental measurements yearbook*. Lincoln Nebraska: The Buros Institute of Mental Measurements.

Krantz, D. S., & Manuck, S. B. (1984). Acute psychophysiologic reactivity and risk of cardiovascular disease—a review and methodologic critique. *Psychological Bulletin, 96*, 435-464.

Krasner, L., & Ullmann, L. P. (Eds.). (1965). *Research in behavior modification: New developments and implications*. New York: Holt, Rinehart & Winston.

Krasner, L., & Ullmann, L. P. (1973). *Behavior influence and personality.* New York: Holt, Rinehart & Winston.

Kratochwill, T. R., Mott, S. E., & Dodson, C. L. (1984). Case study and single-case research in clinical and applied psychology. In A. S. Bellack & M. Hersen (Eds.), *Research methods in clinical psychology* (pp. 55-99). New York: Pergamon Press.

Krol, N., DeBruyn, E., & van den Bercken, J. (1995). Intuitive and empirical prototypes in childhood psychopathology. *Psychological Assessment, 7,* 533-537.

Krull, C. D., & Pierce, W. D. (1995). IQ testing in America: A victim of its own success. *Alberta Journal of Educational Research, 41,* 349-354.

L'Abate, L. (1969). Introduction. In L. L'Abate (Ed.), *Models of clinical psychology.* Research paper number 22. Atlanta: Georgia State College.

La Greca, A. M. (1990). Issues and perspectives on the child assessment process. In A. M. La Greca (Ed.), *Through the eyes of the child* (pp. 3-17). Boston, MA: Allyn & Bacon.

La Greca, A. M., Dandes, S. K., Wick, P., Shaw, K., & Stone, W. L. (1988). Development of the Social Anxiety Scale for Children: Reliability and concurrent validity. *Journal of Clinical Child Psychology, 17,* 84-91.

Lacher, D., & Gruber, C. P. (1993). Development of the Personality Inventory for Youth: A self-report companion to the Personality Inventory for Children. *Journal of Personality Assessment, 61,* 81-98.

Lamb, H. R. (1992). Is it time for a moratorium on deinstitutionalization? *Hospital and Community Psychiatry, 43,* 669.

Lamb, H. R., & Zusman, J. (1981). Primary prevention in perspective. *American Journal of Psychiatry, 9,* 1-26.

Lambert, D. (1985). *Political and economic determinants of mental health regulations.* Unpublished doctoral dissertation, Brandeis University.

Lambert, M. J., & Bergin, A. E. (1994). The effectiveness of psychotherapy. In A. E. Bergin & S. L. Garfield (Eds.), *Handbook of psychotherapy and behavior change* (pp. 143-189). New York: John Wiley & Sons, Inc.

Lambert, M. J., Shapiro, D. A., & Bergin, A. E. (1986). The effectiveness of psychotherapy. In S. L. Garfield & A. E. Bergin (Eds.), *Handbook of psychotherapy and behavior change* (3rd ed., pp. 157-211). New York: John Wiley.

Lambert, N. M. (1981). Psychological evidence in Larry P. v. Wilson Riles: An evaluation by a witness for the defense. *American Psychologist, 36,* 937-952.

Lambert, N. M., Cox, H. W., & Hartsough, C. S. (1970). The observability of intellectual functioning of first graders. *Psychology in the Schools,* 74-85.

Landau, S., & Milich, R. (1990). Assessment of children's social status and peer relations. In A. M. La Greca (Ed.), *Through the eyes of the child* (pp. 259-291). Boston: Allyn & Bacon.

Landman, J. T., & Dawes, R. (1982). Experimental outcome: Smith and Glass' conclusions stand up under scrutiny. *American Psychologist, 37,* 504-516.

Landrine, H., & Klonoff, E. (1992). Culture and health-related schemas: A review and proposal for interdisciplinary integration. *Health Psychology, 11,* 267-276.

Lang, A. R., Pelham, W. E., Johnston, C., & Gelernter, S. (1989). Levels of adult alcohol consumption induced by interactions with child confederates exhibiting normal versus externalizing behaviors. *Journal of Abnormal Psychology, 98,* 294-299.

Lang, P. J. (1995). The emotion probe: Studies of motivation and attention. *American Psychologist, 50,* 372–385.

Lang, P. J., & Lazovik, A. D. (1963). Experimental desensitization of a phobia. *Journal of Abnormal and Social Psychology, 66,* 519–525.

Langenbucher, J., Labouvie, E., & Morganstern, J. (1996). Measuring diagnostic agreement. *Journal of Consulting and Clinical Psychology, 64,* 1285–1289.

Lanyon, B. P., & Lanyon, R. I. (1980). *Incomplete sentences task: Manual.* Chicago: Stoelting.

Lanyon, R. I. (1984). Personality assessment. *Annual Review of Psychology, 35,* 667–701.

Laosa, L. M. (1996). Intelligence testing and social policy. *Journal of Applied Developmental Psychology, 17,* 155–173.

LaPerriere, A. R., Antoni, M. H., Schneiderman, N., Ironoson, G., Klimas, N., Caralis, P., & Fletcher, M. A. (1990). Exercise intervention attenuates emotional distress and natural killer cell decrements following notification of positive serologic status for HIV-1. *Biofeedback and Self-Regulation, 15,* 229–242.

LaPiere, R. T. (1934). Attitudes vs. actions. *Social Forces, 13,* 230–237.

Lapouse, R., & Monk, M. A. (1958). An epidemiologic study of behavior characteristics in children. *American Journal of Public Health, 48,* 1134–1140.

Last, C. G., & Francis, G. (1988). School phobia. In B. B. Lahey & A. E. Kazdin (Eds.), *Advances in clinical child psychology* (Vol. 11, pp. 193–222). New York: Plenum Press.

Lawlis, G. F. (1971). Response styles of a patient population on the Fear Survey Schedule. *Behaviour Research and Therapy, 9,* 95–102.

Lazarus, A. A. (1981). *The practice of multimodal therapy.* New York: McGraw-Hill.

Lazarus, A. A. (1995). Multimodal therapy. In R. J. Corsini & D. Wedding, D. (Eds.). *Current psychotherapies* (5th ed.). Itasca, Illinois: Peacock Publishers, Inc. (pp. 322–355).

Lazarus, R. S. (1993). From psychological stress to the emotions: A history of changing outlooks. *Annual Review of Psychology, 44,* 1–21.

Lazarus, R. S., & Folkman, S. (1984). *Stress, appraisal, and coping.* New York: Springer.

Leary, T. (1957). *Interpersonal diagnosis of personality. A functional theory and methodology for personality evaluation.* New York: Ronald Press.

Lefkowitz, M. M., & Burton, N. (1978). Childhood depression: A critique of the concept. *Psychological Bulletin, 85,* 716–726.

Lennard, H. L., & Bernstein, A. (1960). *The anatomy of psychotherapy: Systems of communication and expectation.* New York: Columbia University Press.

Levenson, R. W., & Gottman, J. M. (1983). Marital interaction: Physiological linkage and affective exchange. *Journal of Personality and Social Psychology, 45,* 587–597.

Levy, L. H. (1963). *Psychological interpretation.* New York: Holt, Rinehart & Winston.

Lewinsohn, P. M., & Shaffer, M. (1971). Use of home observations as an integral part of the treatment of depression: Preliminary report and case studies. *Journal of Consulting and Clinical Psychology, 37,* 87–94.

Lewis, G. (1991). Observer bias in the assessment of anxiety and depression. *Social Psychiatry and Psychiatric Epidemiology, 26,* 265–272.

Lewis, G., Pelosi, A. J., Araya, R., & Dunn, G. (1992). Measuring psychiatric disorder in the community: A standardized assessment for use by lay interviewers. *Psychological Medicine, 22,* 465–486.

Ley, P., Bradshaw, P. W., Eaves, D. E., & Walker, C. M. (1973). A method for increasing patient re-call of information presented to them. *Psychological Medicine, 3,* 217-220.

Lezak, M.D. (1995). *Neuropsychological assessment* (3rd ed.). New York: Oxford University Press.

Libet, J. M., & Lewinsohn, P. M. (1973). Concept of social skill with special reference to the be-havior of depressed persons. *Journal of Consulting and Clinical Psychology, 40,* 304-312.

Lidz, C., Mulvey, E., & Gardner, W. (1993). The accuracy of predictions of violence to others. *Journal of the American Medical Association, 269,* 1007-1011.

Lidz, R. W., & Lidz, T. (1949). The family environment of schizophrenic patients. *American Jour-nal of Psychiatry, 106,* 332-345.

Liebert, R. M., & Spiegler, M. D. (1990). *Personality: Strategies and issues* (6th ed.). Homewood, IL: Dorsey Press.

Lindner, R. (1954). *The fifty minute hour.* New York: Rinehart.

Lindzey, G. (1952). The thematic apperception test: Interpretive assumptions and related empirical evidence. *Psychological Bulletin, 49,* 1-25.

Lindzey, G. (1961). *Projective techniques and cross-cultural research.* New York: Appleton-Century-Crofts.

Linehan, M. (1993). *Cognitive-behavioral treatment of borderline personality disorder.* New York: Guilford Press.

Linehan, M. M., & Kehrer, C. A. (1993). Borderline Personality Disorder. In D. H. Barlow (Ed.), *Clinical Handbook of psychological disorders* (pp. 396-441). New York: Guilford Press.

Linehan, M. M., & Nielsen, S. L. (1983). Social desirability: Its relevance to the measurement of hopelessness and suicidal behavior. *Journal of Consulting and Clinical Psychology, 51,* 141-143.

Link, B., Cullen, F., & Andrews, H. (1993). Reconsidering the violent and illegal behavior of men-tal patients. *American Sociological Review, 57,* 1229-1236.

Lipinski, D. P., Black, J. L., Nelson , R. O., & Ciminero, A. R. (1975). The influence of motivational variables on the reactivity and reliability of self-recording. *Journal of Consulting and Clinical Psychology, 43,* 637-646.

Lipsey, M. W., & Wilson, D. B. (1993). The efficacy of psychological, educational, and behavioral treatment: Confirmation from meta-analysis. *American Psychologist, 48,* 1181-1209.

Lipton, D. N., McDonel, B. C., & McFall, R. M. (1987). Heterosexual perception in rapists. *Jour-nal of Consulting and Clinical Psychology, 55,* 17-21.

Little, K. B., & Shneidman, E. S. (1959). Congruences among interpretations of psychological test and amnestic data. *Psychological Monographs, 73* (Whole No. 476).

Lochman, J. E. (1992). Cognitive-behavioral intervention with aggressive boys: Three-year follow-up and preventive effects. *Journal of Consulting and Clinical Psychology, 60,* 426-432.

Loftus, E. (1993). The reality of repressed memories. *American Psychologist, 48,* 518-537.

Lopez, S. R. (1989). Patient variable biases in clinical judgment: Conceptual overview and methodological considerations. *Psychological Bulletin, 106,* 184-203.

Lopez, S. R., Smith, A., & Wolkenstein, B. H. (1993). Gender bias in clinical judgment: An assess-ment of the analogue method's transparency and social desirability. *Sex Roles, 28,* 35-45.

Loranger, A. W. (1992). Are current self-report and interview measures adequate for epidemio-logical studies of personality disorders? *Journal of Personality Disorders, 6,* 313-325.

Lorr, M., McNair, D. M., & Klett, C. J. (1966). *Inpatient Multidimensional Psychiatric Scale.* Palo Alto, CA: Consulting Psychologists Press.

Lovaas, I. (1987). Behavioral treatment and normal educational and intellectual functioning in young autistic children. *Journal of Consulting and Clinical Psychology, 55,* 3–9.

Lubin, B., Larsen, R. M., & Matarazzo, J. D. (1984). Patterns of psychological test usage in the United States: 1935–1982. *American Psychologist, 39,* 451–454.

Lubin, B., Larsen, R. M., Matarazzo, J. D., & Seever, M. (1985). Psychological test usage patterns in five professional settings. *American Psychologist, 40,* 857–861.

Lubin, B., Wallis, R. R., & Paine, C. (1971). Patterns of psychological test usage in the United States: 1935–1969. *Professional Psychology, 2,* 70–74.

Luborsky, L., Singer, B., & Luborsky, L. (1975). Comparative studies of psychotherapies: Is it true that "Everyone has won and all must have prizes"? *Archives of General Psychiatry, 32,* 995–1008.

Lutgendorf, S. K., Antoni, M. H., Ironson, G., Klimas, N., Kumar, M., Starr, K., McCabe, P., Cleven, K., Fletcher, M. A., & Schneiderman, N. (1997). Cognitive-behavioral stress management decreases dysphoric mood and herpes simplex virus-type 2 antibody titers in symptomatic HIV-seropositive gay men. *Journal of Consulting and Clinical Psychology, 65,* 31–43.

Lyman, R. D. (1984). The effect of private and public goal setting on classroom on-task behavior of emotionally disturbed children. *Behavior Therapy, 15,* 395–402.

Lyness, S. A. (1993). Predictors of differences between Type A and B individuals in heart rate and blood pressure reactivity. *Psychological Bulletin, 114,* 266–295.

Lyons, H. A. (1971). Psychiatric sequelae of the Belfast riots. *British Journal of Psychiatry, 118,* 265–273.

Lyons-Ruth, K. (1996). Attachment relationships among children with aggressive behavior problems: The role of the disorganized early attachment patterns. *Journal of Consulting and Clinical Psychology, 64,* 64–73.

MacDonald, G. (1996). Inferences in therapy: Processes and hazards. *Professional Psychology: Research and Practice, 27,* 600–603.

Machover, K. (1949). *Personality projection in the drawing of the human figure.* Springfield, IL: Charles C. Thomas.

MacLennan, R. N. (1992). *Personality research form (PRF): Annotated research bibliography.* Port Hudson, MI: Sigma Assessment Systems, Inc.

MacMillan, M. (1991). *Freud evaluated: The completed arc.* Amsterdam: North-Holland.

MacPhillamy, D. J., & Lewinsohn, P. M. (1976). *Manual for the Pleasant Events Schedule.* Eugene, OR: Authors.

Magaret, A. (1952). Clinical methods: Psychodiagnostics. *Annual Review of Psychology, 3,* 283–320.

Magrab, P., & Papadopoulou, Z. L. (1977). The effect of a token economy on dietary compliance for children on hemodialysis. *Journal of Applied Behavioral Analysis, 10,* 573–578.

Mahler, M. S., Pine, F., & Bergman, A. (1975). *The psychological birth of the human infant.* New York: Basic Books.

Mahrer, A. R. (Ed.). (1970). *New approaches to personality classification.* New York: Columbia University Press.

Mahrer, A. R., & Nadler, W. P. (1986). Good moments in psychotherapy: A preliminary review, a list, and some promising research avenues. *Journal of Consulting and Clinical Psychology, 54,* 10-15.

Maier, S. F., Watkins, L. R., & Fleshner, M. (1994). Psychoneuroimmunology: The interface between behavior, brain, and immunity. *American Psychologist, 49,* 1004-1017.

Main, M. (1996). Introduction to the special section on attachment and psychopathology: 2. Overview of the field of attachment. *Journal of Consulting and Clinical Psychology, 64,* 237-243.

Maisto, S. A., & Maisto, C. A. (1983). Institutional measures of treatment outcome. In M. J. Lambert, E. R. Christensen, & S. S. DeJulio (Eds.), *The assessment of psychotherapy outcome* (pp. 603-625). New York: John Wiley.

Malarkey, W. B., Kiecolt-Glaser, J. K., Pearl, D., & Glaser, R. (1994). Hostile behavior during marital conflict alters pituitary and adrenal hormones. *Psychosomatic Medicine, 56,* 41-51.

Malgady, R. G. (1996). The question of cultural bias in assessment and diagnosis of ethnic minority clients: Let's reject the null hypothesis. *Professional Psychology: Research and Practice, 27,* 73-77.

Malmo, R. B., Shagass, C., & Davis, F. H. (1950). Symptom specificity and bodily reactions during psychiatric interviews. *Psychosomatic Medicine, 12,* 362-376.

Maloney, M. P., & Ward, M. P. (1976). *Psychological assessment: A conceptual approach.* New York: Oxford University Press.

Mann, P. A. (1978). *Community psychology: Concepts and applications.* New York: Free Press.

Manning, W. G., Wells, K. B., & Benjamin, B. (1986). Use of outpatient mental health care: Trial of a prepaid group practice versus fee-for-service (Technical Report R-3277-NIMH). Santa Monica, California: Rand Corporation.

Manuck, S. B., Kaplan, J. R., Adams, M. R., & Clarkson, T. B. (1988). Effects of stress and the sympathetic nervous system on coronary artery atheroslerosis in the cynomolgus macaque. *American Heart Journal, 116,* 328-333.

Manuck, S. B., Kaplan, J. R., & Clarkson, T. B. (1983). Behaviorally induced heart rate reactivity and atherosderosis in cynomolgus monkeys. *Psychosomatic Medicine, 49,* 95-108.

Margolin, G., Mitchell, J., & Jacobson, N. (1988). Assessment of marital dysfunction. In A. S. Bellack & M. Hersen (Eds.), *Behavioral assessment: A practical handbook* (3rd ed., pp. 441-489). New York: Pergamon Press.

Markowitz, J. H., Matthews, K. A., Wing, R. R., Kuller, L. H., & Meilahn, E. (1991). Psychological, biological and health behavior predictors of blood pressure changes in middle-aged women. *Journal of Hypertension, 9,* 399-406.

Marlatt, G. A., & Gordon, J. R. (Eds.). (1985). *Relapse prevention maintenance strategies in the treatment of addictive behaviors.* New York: Guilford Press.

Martell, R. F. & Willis, C. E. (1993). Effects of observers' performance expectations on behavior ratings of work groups: Memory or response bias? *Organizational Behavior and Human Decision Processes, 56,* 91-109.

Martin, R. P. (1988). *Assessment of personality and behavior problems: Infancy through adolescence.* New York: Guilford Press.

Marx, J. A., Gyorky, Z. K., Royalty, G. M., & Stern, T. E. (1992). Use of self-help books in psychotherapy. *Professional Psychology: Research and Practice, 23,* 300-305.

Mash, E. J. (1989). Treatment of child and family disturbance: A behavioral systems perspective. In E. J. Mash & R. A. Barkley (Eds.), *Treatment of childhood disorders* ((pp. 3-36). New York: Guilford.

Mash, E. J., & Barkley, A. (1986). Assessment of family interaction with the Response-Class Matrix. In R. J. Prinz (Ed.), *Advances in behavioral assessment of children and families* (Vol. 2, pp. 29-67). Greenwich, CT: JAI Press.

Mash, E. J., & Dozois, D. J. A. (1996). Child psychopathology: A developmental-systems perspective. In E. J. Mash & R. A. Barkley (Eds.), *Child psychopathology* (pp. 3-60). New York: Guilford.

Mash, E. J., & McElwee, J. D. (1974). Situational effects on observer accuracy: Behavior predictability, prior experience, and complexity of coding categories. *Child Development, 45,* 367-377.

Mash, E. J., & Terdal, L. G. (Eds.). (1988). *Behavioral assessment of childhood disorders* (2nd ed.). New York: Guilford Press.

Masling, J. M. (1992). Assessment and the therapeutic narrative. *Journal of Training and Practice in Professional Psychology, 6,* 53-58.

Maslow, A. H. (1954). *Motivation and personality.* New York: Harper.

Maslow, A. H. (1962). *Toward a psychology of being.* Princeton, NJ: D. Van Nostrand.

Maslow, A. H. (1968). *Toward a psychology of being* (2nd ed.). New York: Van Nostrand Reinhold.

Maslow, A. H. (1971). *The farther reaches of human nature.* New York: Viking Press.

Masterpasqua, F. (1989). A competence paradigm for psychological practice. *American Psychologist, 44,* 1366-1371.

Masters, J. C., Burish, T. G., Hollon, S. D., & Rimm, D. C. (1987). *Behavior therapy: Techniques and empirical findings* (3rd ed.). San Diego, CA: Harcourt, Brace, Jovanovich.

Masur, F. T. (1981). Adherence to health care regimens. In C. K. Prokop & L. A. Bradley (Eds.), *Medical psychology: Contributions to behavioral medicine* (pp. 442-470). New York: Academic Press.

Matarazzo, J. D. (1965). The interview. In B. B. Wolman (Ed.), *Handbook of clinical psychology* (pp. 403-450). New York: McGraw-Hill.

Matarazzo, J. D. (1983). Computerized psychological testing. *Science, 221,* 323.

Matarazzo, J. D. (1986). Computerized clinical psychological test interpretations: Unvalidated plus all mean and no sigma. *American Psychologist, 41,* 14-24.

Matarazzo, J. D. (1987). There is only one psychology, no specialties, but many applications. *American Psychologist, 42,* 893-903.

Matarazzo, J. D. (1992). Psychological testing and assessment in the 21st century. *American Psychologist, 47,* 1007-1018.

Matarazzo, J. D., & Carmody, T. P. (1983). Health psychology. In M. Hersen, A. J. Kazdin, & A. S. Bellack (Eds). *The clinical-psychology handbook* (pp. 657-682). New York: Pergamon Press.

Matarazzo, J. D, Weins, A. N., Matarzzo, R. G., & Saslow, G. (1968). Speech and silence behavior in clinical psychotherapy and its laboratory correlates. In J. M. Shlien, H. F. Hunt, J. D. Matarazzo, & C. Savage (Eds.), *Research in psychotherapy*. Washington, D.C.: American Psychological Association.

Matarazzo, J. D., Weitman, M., Saslow, G., & Wiens, A. N. (1963). Interviewer influence on durations of interviewee speech. *Journal of Verbal Learning and Verbal Behavior, 1,* 451-458.

Matlin, M. (1993). *The psychology of women* (2nd ed). Fort Worth, TX: Harcourt, Brace, Jovanovich.

Matthews, K. A. (1982). Psychological perspectives on the Type A behavior pattern. *Psychological Bulletin, 91,* 293–323.

Matthews, K. A. (1988). Coronary heart disease and Type A behavior: Update on and alternative to the Booth-Kewley and Friedman (1987) quantitative review. *Psychological Bulletin, 104,* 373–380.

Matthews, K. A., & Haynes, S. G. (1986). Type A behavior pattern and coronary risk: Update and critical evaluation. *American Journal of Epidemiology, 123,* 923–960.

May, R. (1969). *Love and will.* New York: W. W. Norton.

May, R., Angel, E., & Ellenberger, H. F. (Eds). (1958). *Existence: A new dimension in psychiatry and psychology.* New York: Basic Books.

May, W. T., & Belsky, J. (1992). Response to "Prescription privileges: Psychology's next frontier?" or the siren call: Should psychologists medicate? *American Psychologist, 47,* 427.

Mayne, T. J., Norcross, J. C., & Sayette, M. A. (1994). Admission requirements, acceptance rates, and financial assistance in clinical psychology programs: Diversity across the practice-research continuum. *American Psychologist, 49,* 806–811.

McArthur, D. S., & Roberts, G. E. (1982). *Roberts Apperception Test for Children: Manual.* Los Angeles: Western Psychological Services.

McCartney, K., Harris, M. J., & Bernieri, F. (1990). Growing up and growing apart: A developmental meta-analysis of twin studies. *Psychological Bulletin, 107,* 226–237.

McCoy, S. A. (1976). Clinical judgments of normal childhood behavior. *Journal of Consulting and Clinical Psychology, 44,* 710–714.

McCrae, R. R., & Costa, P. T. (1983). Social desirability scales: More substance than style. *Journal of Consulting and Clinical Psychology, 51,* 882–888.

McFall, R. M. (1991). Manifesto for a science of clinical psychology. *The Clinical Psychologist, 44,* 75–88.

McFall, R. M., & Lillesand, D. B. (1971). Behavior rehearsal with modeling and coaching in assertion training. *Journal of Abnormal Psychology, 77,* 313–323.

McGue, M. (1992). When assessing twin concordance, use the probandwise not the pairwise rate. *Schizophrenia Bulletin, 18,* 171–176.

McGuire, T. G. (1989). Outpatient benefits for mental health services in medicare: Alignment with the private sector. *American Psychologist, 44,* 818–824.

McIntyre, T. J., Bornstein, P. H., Isaacs, C. D., Woody, D. J., Bornstein, M. T., Clucas, T. J., & Long, G. (1983). Naturalistic observation of conduct-disordered children: An archival analysis. *Behavior Therapy, 14,* 375–385.

McKay, S., & Golden, C. J. (1979). Empirical derivation of neuropsychological scales for the lateralization of brain damage using the Luria-Nebraska Neuropsychological Battery. *Clinical Neuropsychology, 1,* 1–5.

McLemore, C. W., & Benjamin, L. S. (1979). Whatever happened to interpersonal diagnosis: A psychosocial alternative to DSM-III. *American Psychologist, 34,* 17–34.

McLeod, J. D., & Kessler, R. C. (1990). Socioeconomic status differences in vulnerability to undesirable life events. *Journal of Health and Social Behavior, 31,* 162–172.

McReynolds, P. (1975). Historical antecedents of personality assessment. In P. McReynolds (Ed.), *Advances in psychological assessment* (Vol. 3, pp. 477–532). San Francisco: Jossey-Bass.

McReynolds, P. (1987). Lightner Witmer: Little-known founder of clinical psychology. *American Psychologist, 42,* 849–858.

Mead, M. (1928). *Coming of age in Samoa.* New York: Morrow.

Mead, M. (1939). *From the South Seas.* New York: Morrow.

Meador, B. D., & Rogers, C. R. (1973). Client-centered therapy. In R. Corsini (Ed.), *Current psychotherapies* (pp. 119–165). Itasca, IL: F. E. Peacock.

Meehl, P. E. (1954). *Clinical versus statistical prediction.* Minneapolis: University of Minnesota Press.

Meehl, P. E. (1956). Wanted—A good cookbook. *American Psychologist, 11,* 263–272.

Meehl, P. E. (1957). When shall we use our heads instead of the formula? *Journal of Consulting Psychology, 4,* 268–273.

Meehl, P. E. (1960). The cognitive activity of the clinician. *American Psychologist, 15,* 19–27.

Meehl, P. E. (1965). Seer over sign: The first good example. *Journal of Experimental Research in Personality, 1,* 27–32.

Meichenbaum, D. H. (1971). Examination of model characteristics in reducing avoidance behavior. *Journal of Personality and Social Psychology, 17,* 298–307.

Meichenbaum, D. H. (1977). *Cognitive-behavior modification.* New York: Plenum Press.

Meichenbaum, D. H., & Goodman, J. (1971). Training impulsive children to talk to themselves: A means of developing self-control. *Journal of Abnormal Psychology, 77,* 115–126.

Meier, M. J. (1981). Education for competency assurance in human neuropsychology: Antecedents, models, and directions. In S. B. Filskov & T. J. Boll (Eds.), *Handbook of clinical neuropsychology* (pp. 754–781). New York: John Wiley.

Meier, S. T., & Wick, M. T. (1991). Computer-based obstrusive measurement: Potential supplements to reactive self-reports. *Professional Psychology: Research and Practice, 22,* 410–412.

Melby, J. N., Conger, R. D., Ge, X. J., & Warner, T. D. (1995). The use of structural equation modeling in assessing the quality of marital observations. *Journal of Family Psychology, 9,* 280–293.

Melton, A. W. (Ed.). (1947). *Apparatus tests.* Washington, DC: Government Printing Office.

Melton, G. B., Petrila, J., Poythress, N. G., & Slobogin, C. (1987). *Psychological evaluations for the courts.* New York: Guilford Press.

Meltzoff, J., & Kornreich, M. (1970). *Research in psychotherapy.* New York: Atherton Press.

Menninger, K. (1958). *The theory of psychoanalytic technique.* New York: Basic Books.

Mercatoris, M., & Craighead, W. E. (1974). The effects of non-participant observation on teacher and pupil classroom behavior. *Journal of Educational Psychology, 66,* 512–519.

Mermelstein, R., Lichtenstein, E., & McIntyre, K. (1983). Partner support and relapse in smoking-cessation programs. *Journal of Consulting and Clinical Psychology, 51,* 331–337.

Merrick, R. A. (1985). The tort of outrage: Recovery for the intentional infliction of mental distress. *Behavioral Sciences and the Law, 3,* 165–175.

Messer, S. B., & Winokur, M. (1980). Some limits to the integration of psychoanalytic and behavior therapy. *American Psychologist, 35,* 818–827.

Messick, S. (1995). Validity of psychological assessment: Validation of inferences from persons' responses and performances as scientific inquiry into score meaning. *American Psychologist, 50,* 741–749.

Meyer, A. J., Nash, J. D., McAlister, A. L., Maccoby, N., & Farquhar, J. W. (1980). Skills training in cardiovascular education campaign. *Journal of Consulting and Clinical Psychology, 48,* 129-142.

Meyerowitz, B. E., Heinrich, R. L., & Schag, C. C. (1983). A competency-based approach to coping with cancer. In T. G. Burish & L. A. Bradley (Eds.), *Coping with chronic disease* (pp. 137-158). New York: Academic Press.

Meyers, J. (1975). Consultee centered consultation with a teacher as a technique in behavior management. *American Journal of Community Psychology, 3,* 111-122.

Milan, M. A., Montgomery, R. W., & Rogers, E. G. (1994). Theoretical orientation revolution in clinical psychology: Fact or fiction? *Professional Psychology: Research and Practice, 25,* 398-402.

Milich, R., & Fitzgerald, G. (1985). Validation of inattention/overactivity and aggression ratings with classroom observations. *Journal of Consulting and Clinical Psychology, 53,* 139-140.

Milich, R., & Kramer, J. (1984). Reflections on impulsivity: An empirical investigation of impulsivity as a construct. In K. D. Gadow (Ed.), *Advances in learning and behavioral disabilities: A research annual* (Vol. 3, pp. 57-94). Greenwich, CT: JAI Press.

Milich, R., Loney, J., & Landau, S. (1982). Independent dimensions of hyperactivity and aggression: Validation with playroom observation data. *Journal of Abnormal Psychology, 91,* 183-198.

Milich, R., Widiger, T. A., & Landau, S. (1987). Differential diagnosis of attention deficit and conduct disorders using conditional probabilities. *Journal of Consulting and Clinical Psychology, 55,* 762-767.

Milich, R., Wolraich, M., & Lindgren, S. (1986). Sugar and hyperactivity: A critical review of empirical findings. *Clinical Psychology Review, 6,* 493-513.

Miller, I. J. (1996). Managed care is harmful to outpatient mental health services: A call for accountability. *Professional psychology: Research and Practice, 27,* 349-363.

Miller, I. J. (1996a). Time-limited brief therapy has gone too far: The result is invisible rationing. *Professional Psychology: Research and Practice, 27,* 567-576.

Miller, K. M. (1991). Use of psychological assessment and training in testing techniques in the UK. *Evaluacion Psicologica, 7,* 85-97.

Miller, T. Q., Turner, C. W., Tindale, R. S., Posavac, E. J., & Dugoni, B. L. (1991). Reasons for the trend toward null findings in research on Type A behavior. *Psychological Bulletin, 110,* 469-485.

Miller, W. R., & DiPilato, M. (1983). Treatment of nightmares via relaxation and desensitization: A controlled evaluation. *Journal of Consulting and Clinical Psychology, 51,* 870-877.

Millon, T. (1981). *Disorders of personality: DSM-III, Axis II.* New York: John Wiley.

Millon, T. (1987a). *Millon Clinical Multiaxial Inventory-II.* Minneapolis: National Computers System.

Millon, T. (1987b). On the nature of taxonomy in psychopathology. In C. G. Last & M. Hersen (Eds), *Issues in diagnostic research* (pp. 3-85). New York: Plenum Press.

Millon, T. (1991). Classification in psychopathology: Rationale, alternatives, and standards. *Journal of Abnormal Psychology, 100,* 245-261.

Millon, T., Green, C. J., & Meagher, R. B., Jr. (1982). *Millon Adolescent Personality Inventory manual.* Minneapolis: National Computer Systems.

Millon, T., & Klerman, G. L. (Eds.). (1986). *Contemporary directions in psychopathology: Toward the DSM-IV.* New York: Guilford Press.

Milner, B. (1974). Hemispheric specialization: Scope and limits. In F. O. Schmitt & F. G. Worden (Eds.), *The neurosciences: Third study program* (pp. 75–89). Cambridge, MA: MIT Press.

Minuchin, S. (1974). *Families and family therapy.* Cambridge, MA: Harvard University Press.

Mischel, W. (1968). *Personality and assessment.* New York: John Wiley.

Mischel, W. (1971). *Introduction to personality.* New York: Holt, Rinehart & Winston.

Mischel, W. (1984). Convergences and challenges in the search for consistency. *American Psychologist, 39,* 351–364.

Mischel, W. (1986). *Introduction to personality* (4th ed.). New York: Holt, Rinehart & Winston.

Mischel, W. (1993). *Introduction to personality.* New York: Harcourt Brace.

Mishler, E. G., & Waxler, N. E. (1968). *Interaction in families: An experimental study of family process in schizophrenia.* New York: John Wiley.

Monahan, J. (1988). Risk assessment of violence among the mentally disordered: Generating useful knowledge. *International Journal of Law and Psychiatry, 11,* 249.

Monahan, J. (1992). Mental disorder and violent behavior: Perceptions and evidence. *American Psychologist, 47,* 511–521.

Monahan, J., & Walker, L. (1990). *Social sciences in law: Cases and materials* (2nd ed.). Westbury, NY: Foundation Press.

Moncher, F. J., & Prinz, R. J. (1991). Treatment fidelity in outcome studies. *Clinical Psychology Review, 11,* 247–266.

Morgan, C., & Murray, H. A. (1935). A method for investigating phantasies: The thematic apperception test. *Archives of Neurology and Psychiatry, 34,* 289–306.

Morganstern, K. P. (1988). Behavioral interviewing. In A. S. Bellack & M. Hersen (Eds.), *Behavioral assessment: A practical handbook* (3rd ed., pp. 86–108). New York: Pergamon Press.

Morganstern, K. P., & Tevlin, H. E. (1981). Behavioral interviewing. In M. Hersen & A. S. Bellack (Eds.), *Behavioral assessment: A practical handbook* (2nd ed., pp. 71–100). New York: Pergamon Press.

Morris, R. J., & Kratochwill, T. R. (1983). *Treating children's fear and phobias: A behavioral approach.* New York: Pergamon Press.

Morrison, C. S., McCusker, J., Stoddard, A. M., & Bigelow, C. (1995). The validity of behavioral data reported by injection drug users on a clinical risk assessment. *International Journal of the Addictions, 30,* 889–899.

Morse, S. J. (1978). Law and mental health professionals: The limits of expertise. *Professional Psychology, 9,* 389–399.

Morton, A. (1995). The enigma of non-attendance: A study of clients who do not turn up for their first appointment. *Therapeutic Communities: International Journal for Therapeutic and Supportive Organizations, 16,* 117–133.

Mosak, H. H., & Dreikurs, R. (1973). Adlerian psychotherapy. In R. Corsini (Ed.), *Current psychotherapies* (pp. 35–83). Itasca, IL: F. E. Peacock.

Moscarelli, M., & Capri, S. (1992). The cost of schizophrenia: Editors' introduction. *Schizophrenia Bulletin, 17,* 367–369.

Mossman, K. (1994). Assessing predictions of violence: Being accurate about accuracy. *Journal of Consulting and Clinical Psychology, 62,* 783–792.

Mouton, S. G., & Stanley, M. A. (1996). Habit reversal training for tricotillomania: A group approach. *Cognitive and Behavioral Practice, 3*, 159-182.

Mrazek, P. J., & Haggerty, R. J. (Eds.) (1994). *Reducing risks for mental disorders: Frontiers for preventive intervention research.* Washington, D.C.: National Academy Press.

MRFIT (Multiple Risk Factors Intervention Trial Research Group). (1982). Multiple risk factor intervention trial: Risk factor changes and mortality results. *Journal of the American Medical Association, 248,* 1465-1477.

Mullen, B., & Suls, J. (1982). The effectiveness of attention and rejection as coping styles. *Journal of Psychosomatic Research, 26,* 43-49.

Munroe, R. (1955). *Schools of psychoanalytic thought.* New York: Dryden Press.

Murray, B. (1996). Psychology maturing, adapting to market. *APA Monitor*, October.

Murray, B. (1996). Psychology remains top college major. *The APA Monitor*, February, pp. 1, 42.

Murray, H. A. (1938). *Explorations in personality.* Fair Lawn, NJ: Oxford University Press.

Murray, H. A. (1943). *Thematic Apperception Test.* Cambridge, MA: Harvard University Press.

Murtada, N., & Haccoun, R. R. (1996). Self-monitoring and goal setting as determinants of the transfer of applied training. *Canadian Journal of Behavioural Science, 28,* 92-101.

Mussen, P. H., & Scodel, A. (1955). The effects of sexual stimulation under varying conditions on TAT sexual responsiveness. *Journal of Consulting Psychology, 19,* 90.

Myers, I. B., & Briggs, K. C. (1943). *The Myers-Briggs type indicator.* Palo Alto, CA: Consulting Psychologists Press.

Myklebust, H. R. (1975). Nonverbal learning disabilities: Assessment and intervention. In H. R. Myklebust (Ed.), *Progress in learning disabilities* (Vol. 3, pp. 85-121). New York: Grune & Stratton.

Nathan, P. E. (1987). DSM-III-R and the behavior therapist. *Behavior Therapy, 10,* 203-205.

Neisser, U., Boodoo, G., Bouchard, T. J., Boykin, A. W., Brody, N., Ceci, S. J., Halpern, D. F., Loehlin, J. C., Perloff, R., Sternberg, R. J., & Urbina, S. (1996). Intelligence: Knowns and unknowns. *American Psychologist, 51,* 77-101.

Nelson, R. O. (1977). Assessment and therapeutic functions of self-monitoring. In M. Hersen, R. M. Eisler, & P. M. Miller (Eds.), *Progress in behavior modification* (pp. 264-308). New York: Academic Press.

Nelson, R. O., Hayes, S. C., Felton, J. L., & Jarrett, R. B. (1985). A comparison of data produced by different behavioral assessment techniques with implications for models of social-skills adequacy. *Behaviour Research and Therapy, 23,* 1-12.

Newman, D. L., Moffitt, T. E., Caspi, A., Magdol, L., Silva, P. A., & Stanton, W. R. (1996). Psychiatric disorder in a birth cohort of young adults: Prevalence, comorbidity, clinical significance, and new case incidence from ages 11 to 21. *Journal of Consulting and Clinical Psychology, 64,* 552-562.

Newman, F. L., & Tejeda, M. J. (1996). The need for research that is designed to support decisions in the delivery of mental health services. *American Psychologist, 51,* 1040-1049.

Nicholson, R. A., & Berman, J. S. (1983). Is follow-up necessary in evaluating psychotherapy? *Psychological Bulletin, 93,* 261-278.

Nicholson, R. A., Briggs, S. R., & Robertson, H. C. (1988). Instruments for assessing competency to stand trial: How do they work? *Professional Psychology: Research and Practice, 19,* 383-394.

Nicholson, R. A., & Kugler, K. E. (1991). Competent and incompetent criminal defendants: A quantitive review of comparative research. *Psychological Bulletin, 109,* 355-370.

Nicholson, R. A., Norwood, S., & Enyart, C. (1991). Characteristics and outcomes of insanity acquittees in Oklahoma. *Behavioral Sciences and the Law, 9,* 487-500.

Nickelson, D. W. (1995). The future of professional psychology in a changing health care marketplace: A conversation with Russ Newman. *Professional Psychology: Research and Practice, 26,* 366-370.

Nietzel, M. T., & Bernstein, D. A. (1976). The effects of instructionally mediated demand upon the behavioral assessment of assertiveness. *Journal of Consulting and Clinical Psychology, 44,* 500.

Nietzel, M. T., Bernstein, D. A., & Russell, R. L. (1988). Assessment of anxiety and fear. In A. S. Bellack & M. Hersen (Eds.), *Behavioral assessment: A practical handbook* (3rd ed., pp. 280-312). New York: Pergamon Press.

Nietzel, M. T., & Dillehay, R. C. (1986). *Psychological consultation in the courtroom.* New York: Pergamon Press.

Nietzel, M. T., & Fisher, S. G. (1981). Effectiveness of professional and paraprofessional helpers: A reply to Durlak. *Psychological Bulletin, 89,* 555-565.

Nietzel, M. T., Guthrie, P. R., & Susman, D. T. (1991). Utilization of community and social support services. In F. H. Kanfer & A. P. Goldstein (Eds.), *Helping people change* (4th ed., pp. 396-421). New York: Pergamon Press.

Nietzel, M. T., Russell, R. L., Hemmings, K. A., & Gretter, M. L. (1987). The clinical significance of psychotherapy for unipolar depression: A meta-analytic approach to social comparison. *Journal of Consulting and Clinical Psychology, 55,* 156-161.

Nietzel, M. T., Speltz, M. L., McCauley, E. A. & Bernstein, D. A. (1998). *Abnormal Psychology.* Boston: Allyn & Bacon.

Nietzel, M. T., & Trull, T. J. (1988). Meta-analytic approaches to social comparisons: A method for measuring clinical significance. *Behavioral Assessment, 10,* 159-169.

Nietzel, M. T., Winett, R. A., MacDonald, M. L., & Davidson, W. S. (1977). *Behavioral approaches to community psychology.* New York: Pergamon Press.

NIMH Committee on Prevention Research. (1995). *A plan for prevention research for the National Institute of Mental Health* (A report to the National Advisory Mental Health Council). Washington, D.C.: NIMH.

NIMH Prevention Research Steering Committee. (1994). *The prevention of mental disorders: A national research agenda.* Washington, D.C.: NIMH.

Norcross, J. C., Hanych, J. M., & Terranova, R. D. (1996). Graduate study in psychology: 1992-1993. *American Psychologist, 51,* 631-643.

Norcross, J. C., & Prochaska, J. O. (1983). Psychotherapists in independent practice: Some findings and issues. *Professional Psychology: Research and Practice, 14,* 869-881.

Norcross, J. C., Prochaska, J. O., & Gallagher, K. M. (1989a). Clinical psychologists in the 1980s: I. Demographics, affiliations, and satisfactions. *The Clinical Psychologist, 42,* 29-39.

Norcross, J. C., Prochaska, J. O., & Gallagher, K. M. (1989b). Clinical psychologists in the 1980s: II. Theory, research, and practice. *The Clinical Psychologist, 42,* 45-53.

Nunes, E. V., Frank, K. A., & Kornfeld, S. D. (1987). Psychologic treatment for Type A behavior pattern and for coronary heart disease: A meta-analysis of the literature. *Psychosomatic Medicine, 48,* 159-173.

O'Connor, M., Sales, B. D., & Shuman, D. (1996). Mental health professional expertise in the courtroom. In B. D. Sales & D. W. Shuman (Eds.), *Law, mental health, and mental disorder*. Pacific Grove, CA: Brooks/Cole.

Obrist, P. (1981). *Cardiovascular psychophysiology: A perspective*. New York: Plenum Press .

Obrzut, J. E. (1988). Deficient lateralization in learning-disabled children: Developmental lag or abnormal cerebral organization? In D. L. Molfese & S. J. Segalowitz (Eds.), *Brain lateralization in children: Developmental implications*. New York: Guilford Press.

Office of Program Consultation and Accreditation, American Psychological Association (1996). *Guidelines and principles for accreditation of programs in professional psychology/Accreditation operating procedures*. Washington D.C.: Author.

Office of Strategic Services Assessment Staff (1948). *Assessment of men*. New York: Rinehart.

Ogden, J. (1996). *Health Psychology: A textbook*. Philadelphia: Open University Press.

Ogloff, J. R. P. (1993). A comparison of insanity defense standards on juror decision making. *Law and Human Behavior, 15*, 509-532.

Ogloff, J. R. P., & Otto, R. (1993). Psychological autopsy: Clinical and legal perspectives. *Saint Louis University Law Journal, 37*, 607-646.

Olbrisch, M. E. (1977). Psychotherapeutic interventions in physical health: Effectiveness and economic efficiency. *American Psychologist, 32*, 761-777.

O'Leary, K. D., & Becker, W. C. (1967). Behavior modification of an adjustment class: A token reinforcement program. *Exceptional Children, 33*, 637-642.

O'Leary, K. D., & Kent, R. (1973). Behavior modification for social action: Research tactics and problems. In L. A. Hamerlynck, L. C. Handy, & E. J. Mash (Eds.), *Behavior change: Methodology, concepts, and practice* (pp. 69-96). Champaign, IL: Research Press.

O'Leary, K. D., & O'Leary, S. G. (Eds.). (1972). *Classroom management*. New York: Pergamon Press.

Olfson, M. (1990). Assetive community teatment: An evaluation of the experimental evidence. *Hospital and Community Psychiatry, 41*, 634-641.

Olfson, M., & Pincus, H. A. (1994). Outpatient psychotherapy in the United States: I. Volume, costs, and user characteristics. *American Journal of Psychiatry, 151*, 1281-1288.

Olfson, M., Pincus, H., & Sabshin, M. (1994). Pharmacotherapy in outpatient psychiatric practice. *American Journal of Psychiatry, 151*, 580-585.

Olive, H. (1972). Psychoanalysts' opinions of psychologists' reports: 1952 and 1970. *Journal of Clinical Psychology, 28*, 50-54.

Ollendick, T. H. (1996). Violence in youth: Where do we go from here? Behavior therapy's response. *Behavior Therapy, 27*, 485-514.

Ollendick, T. H., & Greene, R. (1990). Behavioral assessment of children. In G. Goldstein & M. Hersen (Eds.), *Handbook of psychological assessment* (2nd ed., pp. 403-422). New York: Pergamon Press.

Olweus, D. (1995). Bullying or peer abuse at school: Facts and intervention. *Current Directions in Psychological Science, 4*, 196-200.

O'Neill, P., & Trickett, E. J. (1982). *Community consultation*. San Francisco: Jossey-Bass.

Orlinsky, D. E. (1989). Researchers' image of psychotherapy: Their origins and influence on research. *Clinical Psychology Review, 9*, 413- 442.

Orlinsky, D. E., Grawe, K., & Parks, B. K. (1994). Process and outcome in psychotherapy—Noch Einmal. In A. E. Bergin & S. L. Garfield (Eds.) *Handbook of psychotherapy and behavior change* (pp. 270-276). New York: John Wiley.

Orlinsky, D. E., & Howard, K. I. (1986). Process and outcome in psychotherapy. In S. L. Garfield & A. E. Bergin (Eds.), *Handbook of psychotherapy and behavior change* (3rd ed., pp. 311-381). New York: John Wiley.

Orne, M. T. (1962). On the social psychology of the psychological experiment: With particular reference to demand characteristics and their implications. *American Psychologist, 17,* 776-783.

Orne, M. T., & Scheibe, K. E. (1964). The contribution of nondeprivation factors in the production of sensory deprivation effects: The psychology of the panic button. *Journal of Abnormal and Social Psychology, 68,* 3-12.

Ossip-Klein, D. J., Martin, J. E., Lomax, B. D., Prue, D. M., & Davis, C. J. (1983). Assessment of smoking topography generalization across laboratory, clinical, and naturalistic settings. *Addictive Behaviors, 8,* 11-17.

Ost, L. G., Jerremalm, A., & Johansson, J. (1981). Individual response patterns and the effects of different models in the treatment of social phobia. *Behaviour Research and Therapy, 19,* 1-16.

O'Sullivan, J. J., & Quevillon, R. P. (1992). 40 years later: Is the Boulder model still alive? *American Psychologist, 47,* 67-70.

Parker, K. C. H., Hanson, R. K., & Hunsley, J. (1988). MMPI, Rorschach, and WAIS: A meta-analytic comparison of reliability, stability, and validity. *Psychological Bulletin, 103,* 367-373.

Parnas, J., Cannon, T., Jacobsen, B., Schulsinger, H., Schulsinger, F., & Mednick, S. (1993). Lifetime DSM-III-R diagnostic outcomes in the offspring of schizophrenic mothers. *Archives of General Psychiatry, 50,* 707-714.

Pasewark, R. A., Bieber, S., Bosten, K. J., Kiser, M., & Steadman, H. J. (1982). Criminal recidivism among insanity acquittees. *International Journal of Law and Psychiatry, 5,* 365-374.

Pasewark, R. A., & Pantle, M. L. (1981). Opinions about the insanity plea. *Journal of Forensic Psychology, 8,* 63.

Patricelli, R. E., & Lee, F. C. (1996). Employer-based innovations in behavioral health benefits. *Professional Psychology: Research and Practice, 27,* 325-334.

Patterson, D. R., Everett, J. J., Burns, G. L., & Marvin, J. A. (1992). Hypnosis for the treatment of burn pain. *Journal of Consulting and Clinical Psychology, 60,* 713-717.

Patterson, G. R. (1975). *Families.* Champaign, IL: Research Press.

Patterson, G. R. (1976). The aggressive child: Victim and architect of a coercive system. In L. A. Hamerlynck, L. C. Handy, & E. J. Mash (Eds.), *Behavior modification and families: Theory and research* (Vol. 1, pp. 267-316). New York: Brunner/Mazel.

Patterson, G. R. (1982). *Coercive family process.* Eugene, OR: Castalia.

Patterson, G. R., Ray, R. S., Shaw, D. A., & Cobb, J. A. (1969). *Manual for coding of family interactions* (Document NO. 01234). Available from ASIS/NAPS, c/o Microfiche Publications, 305 East 46th St., New York, NY 10017.

Paul, G. L. (1966). *Insight versus desensitization in psychotherapy: An experiment in anxiety reduction.* Stanford, CA: Stanford University Press.

Paul, G. L. (1969a). Behavior modification research: Design and tactics. In C. M. Franks (Ed.), *Behavior therapy: Appraisal and status* (pp. 29-62). New York: McGraw-Hill.

Paul, G. L. (1969b). Outcome of systematic desensitization II. In C. M. Franks (Ed.), *Behavior therapy: Appraisal and status* (pp. 63-159). New York: McGraw-Hill.

Paul, G. L., & Lentz, R. J. (1977). *Psychosocial treatment of chronic mental patients: Milieu versus social-learning programs.* Cambridge, MA: Harvard University Press.

Paul, G. L., & Licht, M. H. (1987). *The time-sample behavioral checklist: Observational assessment instrumentation for service and research.* Champaign, Illinois: Research Press.

Pavlov, I. P. (1927). *Conditioned reflexes.* New York: Oxford University Press.

Pearlin, L. I., & Schooler, C. (1978). The structure of coping. *Journal of Health and Social Behavior, 22,* 337-356.

Peck, C. P., & Ash, E. (1964). Training in the Veterans Administration. In L. Blank & H. P. David (Eds.), *Sourcebook for training in clinical psychology* (pp. 61-81). New York: Springer.

Pedersen, P., & Ivey, A. E. (1993). *Culture-centered counseling and inteviewing skills: A practical guide.* Westport, Conn.: Praeger.

Pedro-Carroll, J. L., & Cowen, E. L. (1985). The children of divorce intervention program: An investigation of the efficacy of a school-based prevention program. *Journal of Consulting and Clinical Psychology, 53,* 603-611.

Pelham, W. E., & Bender, M. E. (1982). Peer relationships in hyperactive children: Description and treatment. In K. D. Gadow & I. Bialer (Eds.), *Advances in learning and behavioral disabilities* (Vol. 1). Greenwich, CT: JAI Press.

Pelham, W. E., & Murphy, H. A. (1986). Attention deficit and conduct disorders. In M. Hersen (Ed.), *Pharmacological and behavioral treatments: An integrative approach* (pp. 108-148). New York: John Wiley.

Pelham, W. E., Murphy, D. A., Vannatta, K., Milich, R., Licht, B. G., Gnagy, E. M., Greenslade, K. E., Grenier, A. R., & Vodde-Hamilton, M. (1992). Methylphenidate and attributions in boys with attention-deficit hyperactivity disorder. *Journal of Consulting and Clinical Psychology, 60,* 282-292.

Perecman, E. (1983). *Cognitive processing in the right hemisphere.* New York: Academic Press.

Perkins, D. D., & Zimmerman, M. A. (1995). Empowerment theory, research, and application. *American Journal of Community Psychology, 23,* 569-580.

Perls, F. S. (1947). *Ego, hunger and aggression: A revision of Freud's theory and method.* New York: Random House.

Perls, F. S. (1965). Gestalt therapy. Film no. 2. In Everett Shostrom (Ed.), *Three approaches to psychotherapy.* (Three 16 mm color motion pictures). Santa Ana, CA: Psychological Films.

Perls, F. S. (1969). *Gestalt therapy verbatim.* Lafayette, CA: Real People Press.

Perls, F. S. (1970). Four lectures. In J. Fagan & I. L. Shepherd (Eds.). *Gestalt therapy now* (pp. 14-38). Palo Alto, CA: Science and Behavior Books.

Perry, C. L., Klepp, K., & Shultz, J. M. (1988). Primary prevention of cardiovascular disease: Community-wide strategies for youth. *Journal of Consulting and Clinical Psychology, 56,* 358-364.

Persons, J. B. (1991). Psychotherapy outcome studies do not accurately represent current models of psychotherapy: A proposed remedy. *American Psychologist, 46,* 99-106.

Peterson, C., & Villanova, P. (1988). An Expanded Attributional Style Questionnaire. *Journal of Abnormal Psychology, 97,* 87-89.

Peterson, D. R. (1968). *The clinical style of social behavior.* New York: Appleton-Century-Crofts.

Peterson, D. R. (1985). Twenty years of practitioner training in psychology. *American Psychologist, 40,* 441-451.

Peterson, D. R. (1995). The reflective educator. *American Psychologist, 50,* 975-983.

Peterson, D. R., & Baron, A. (1975). Status of the University of Illinois doctor of psychology program, 1974. *Professional Psychology, 6,* 88-95.

Peterson, L. (1989). Latchkey children's preparation for self-care: Overestimated, underestimated, and unsafe. *Journal of Clinical Child Psychology, 18,* 36-43.

Peterson, L., & Roberts, M. C. (1991). Treatment of children's problems. In C. E. Walker (Ed.), *Clinical psychology: Historical and research foundations* (pp. 313-342). New York: Plenum Press.

Petraitis, J., Flay, B. R., & Miller, T. Q. (1995). Reviewing theories of adolescent substance use: Organizing pieces in the puzzle. *Psychological Bulletin, 117,* 67-86.

Pettijohn, T. F. (1991). *The encyclopedic dictionary of psychology* (4th ed.). Guilford, Connecticut: Dushkin.

Piaget, J. (1947). *The psychology of intelligence.* London: Kegan Paul.

Piaget, J. (1962). *Play, dreams, and imitation in childhood.* New York: W. W. Norton.

Pilkonis, P. A., Heape, C. L., Proietti, J. M., Clark, S. W., et al. (1995). The reliability and validity of two structured interviews for personality disorders. *Archives of General Psychiatry, 52,* 1025-1033.

Pimental, P. A., Stout, C. E., Hoover, M. C., & Kamen, G. B. (1997). Changing psychologists' opinions about prescriptive authority: A little information goes a long way. *Professional Psychology: Research and Practice, 28,* 123-127.

Pinizzotto, A. J., & Finkel, N. J. (1990). Criminal personality profiling: An outcome and process study. *Law and Human Behavior, 14,* 215-234.

Pion, G. M. (1991). A national human resources agenda for psychology: The need for a broader perspective. *Professional Psychology: Research and Practice, 22,* 449-455.

Piotrowski, C., & Keller, J. W. (1989). Psychodiagnostic testing in out-patient mental health facilities: A national study. *Professional Psychology: Research and Practice, 20,* 423-425.

Piotrowski, C., & Keller, J. W. (1992). Psychological testing in applied settings: A literature review. *Journal of Training and Practice in Professional Psychology, 6,* 74-82.

Piotrowski, Z. (1972). Psychological testing of intelligence and personality. In A. M. Freedman & H. I. Kaplan (Eds.), *Diagnosing mental illness: Evaluation in psychiatry and psychology* (pp. 41-85). New York: Atheneum.

Pirozollo, F. J., & Rayner, K. (1977). Hemispheric specialization in reading and word recognition. *Brain and Language, 4,* 248-261.

Pittenger, R. E., Hockett, C. F., & Danehy, J. J. (1960). *The first five minutes: A sample of microscopic interview analyses.* Ithaca, NY: Paul Martineau.

Plante, T. G., Goldfarb, L. P. & Wadley, V. (1993). Are stress and coping associated with aptitude and achievement testing performance among children?: A preliminary investigation. *Journal of School Psychology, 31,* 259-266.

Plous, S., & Zimbardo, P. G. (1986). Attributional biases among clinicians: A comparison of psychoanalysts and behavior therapists. *Journal of Consulting and Clinical Psychology, 54,* 568-570.

Polster, E., & Polster, M. (1973). *Gestalt therapy integrated: Contours of theory and practice.* New York: Brunner/Mazel.

Pomeranz, D. M., & Goldfried, M. R. (1970). An intake report outline for behavior modification. *Psychological Reports, 26,* 447-450.

Pope, B., Nudler, S., Vonkorff, M. R., & McGhee, J. P. (1974). The experienced professional interviewer versus the complete novice. *Journal of Consulting and Clinical Psychology, 42,* 68-690.

Pope, K. S., & Bouthousos, J. C. (1986). *Sexual intimacy between therapists and patients.* New York: Praeger.

Pope, K. S., Butcher, J. N., & Seelen, J. (1993). *The MMPI, MMPI-2, and MMPI in court.* Washington, D.C.: American Psychological Association.

Pope, K. S., & Tabachnick, B. G. (1994). Therapists as patients: A national survey of psychologists' experiences, problems, and beliefs. *Professional Psychology: Research and Practice, 25,* 247-258.

Pope, K. S., & Vasquez, M. J. T. (1991). *Ethics in psychotherapy and counseling: A practical guide for psychologists.* San Francisco, CA: Jossey-Bass.

Pope, K. S., & Vetter, V. A. (1992). Ethical dilemmas encountered by members of the American Psychological Association: A national survey. *American Psychologist, 47,* 397-411.

Porter, B. (1983). Mind hunters. *Psychology Today, 17,* 44-52.

Porter, E. H., Jr. (1943). The development and evaluation of a measure of counseling interview procedures. *Educational and Psychological Measurement, 3,* 105-126.

Post, C. G. (1963). *An introduction to the law.* Englewood Cliffs, NJ: Prentice Hall.

Potts, M. K., Burnam, M. A., & Wells, K. B. (1991). Gender differences in depression detection: A comparison of clinician diagnosis and standardized assessment. *Psychological Assessment, 3,* 609-615.

Powell, T. J. (1987). *Self-help organizations and professional practice.* Silver Springs, MD: National Association of Social Workers.

Poythress, N. G., Bonnie, R. J., Hoge, S. K., Monahan, J., & Oberlander, L. B. (1994). Client abilities to assist counsel and make decisions in criminal cases: Findings from three studies. *Law and Human Behavior, 18,* 437-452.

Price, R. H., Cowen, E. L., Lorion, R. L., & Ramos-McKay, J. (1988). *Fourteen ounces of prevention: A casebook for practitioners.* Washington, DC: American Psychological Association.

Prochaska, J. O., & DiClemente, C. C. (1984). *The transtheoretical approach: Crossing traditional boundaries of therapy.* Homewood, IL: Dow Jones-Irwin.

Prochaska, J. O., & Norcross, J. C. (1994). *Systems of psychotherapy: A transtheoretical analysis* (3rd ed.). Pacific Grove, CA: Brooks/Cole.

Psychological Association (1996). *Guidelines and principles for accreditation of programs in professional psychology/Accreditation operating procedures.* Washington DC: Author.

Purdy, J. E., Reinehr, R. C., & Swartz, J. D. (1989). Graduate admissions criteria of leading psychology departments. *American Psychologist, 44,* 960-961.

Puttalaz, M., & Gottman, J. (1983). Social relationship problems in children. In B. B. Lahey & A. E. Kazdin (Eds.), *Advances in clinical child psychology* (Vol. 6, pp. 1-39). New York: Plenum Press.

Quality Assurance Project (1985). Treatment outlines for the management of anxiety states. *Australian and New Zealand Journal of Psychiatry, 19,* 138-151.

Quay, H. (1986). A critical analysis of DSM-III as a taxonomy of psychopathology in childhood and adolescence. In T. Millon & G. L. Klerman (Eds.), *Contemporary directions in psychopathology: Toward the DSM-IV* (pp. 151-165). New York: Guilford Press.

Quereshi, M. Y., & Kuchan, A. M. (1988). The master's degree in clinical psychology: Longitudinal program evaluation. *Professional Psychology: Research and Practice, 19,* 594-599.

Rabinowitz, J. (1993). Diagnostic reasoning and reliability: A review of the literature and a model of decision-making. *Journal of Mind and Behavior, 14,* 297-315.

Rachman, S. J., & Wilson, G. T. (1980). *The effects of psychological therapy.* Oxford: Pergamon Press.

Ragland, D. R., & Brand, R. J. (1988). Type A behavior and mortality from coronary heart disease. *New England Journal of Medicine, 318,* 65-69.

Raimy, V. C. (1950). *Training in clinical psychology.* New York: Prentice-Hall.

Ramirez, S. Z., & Kratchowill, T. R. (1990). Development of the Fear Survey for Children With and Without Mental Retardation. *Behavioral Assessment, 12,* 457-470.

Rapaport, D. (1951). *Organization and pathology of thought.* New York: Columbia University Press.

Rapaport, D., Gill, M. M., & Schafer, R. (1945). *Diagnostic psychological testing* (Vol. 1). Chicago: Yearbook.

Rapaport, D., Gill, M. M., & Schafer, R. (1946). *Diagnostic psychological testing* (Vol. 2). Chicago: Yearbook.

Rappaport, J. (1977). *Community psychology: Values, research and action.* New York: Holt, Rinehart & Winston.

Rappaport, J. (1981). In praise of paradox: A social policy of empowerment over prevention. *American Journal of Community Psychology, 9,* 1-25.

Rappaport, J. (1987). Terms of empowerment/exemplars of preve ntion: Toward a theory for community psychology. *American Journal of Community Psychology, 15,* 121-148.

Rappaport, J., Seidman, E., Toro, P., McFadden, L., Reischel, T., Roberts, L., Salem, D., & Zimmerman, M. (1985). Collaborative research with a mutual help organization. *Social Policy, 15,* 12-24.

Raquepaw, J. M., & Miller, R. S. (1989). Psychotherapist burnout: A componential analysis. *Professional Psychology: Research and Practice, 20,* 33-36.

Rasmussen, T., & Milner, B. (1975). Clinical and surgical studies of the cerebral speech areas in man. In K. J. Zulch, O. Creutzfeldt, & G. C. Galbraith (Eds.), *Cerebral localization.* Berlin & New York: Springer-Verlag.

Raymond, M. J. (1956). Case of fetishism treated by aversion therapy. *British Medical Journal, 2,* 854-857.

Redd, W. H., Jacobsen, P. B., Die-Trill, M., Dermatis, H., McEvoy, M., & Holland, J. C. (1987). Cognitive/attentional distraction in the control of conditioned nausea in pediatric cancer patients receiving chemotherapy. *Journal of Consulting and Clinical Psychology, 55,* 391-395.

Reed, J. E. (1996). Fixed vs. flexible neuropsychological test batteries under the Daubert Standard for the admissibility of scientific evidence. *Behavioral Sciences and the Law, 14,* 315-322.

Reed, S. D., Katkin, E. S., & Goldband, S. (1986). Biofeedback and behavioral medicine. In F. H. Kanfer & A. P. Goldstein (Eds.), *Helping people change: A textbook of methods* (3rd ed., pp. 381-436). New York: Pergamon Press.

Rehm, L. P., Kornblith, S. J., O'Hara, M. W., Lamparski, D. J., Romano, J. M., & Volkin, J. I. (1981). An evaluation of major components in a self-control therapy program for depression. *Behavior Modification, 5,* 459-489.

Reich, W., Cottler, L., McCallum, K., & Corwin, D. (1995). Computerized interviews as a method of assessing psychopathology in children. *Comprehensive Psychiatry, 36,* 40-45.

Reid, J. B. (Ed.). (1978). *A social learning approach to family intervention: Observation in home settings* (Vol. 2). Eugene, OR: Castalia Publishing.

Reid, J. B., & Patterson, G. R. (1976). The modification of aggression and stealing behavior of boys in the home setting. In A. Bandura & E. Ribes (Eds.), *Behavior modification: Experimental analysis of aggression and delinquency* (pp. 123-146). Hillsdale, NJ: Lawrence Erlbaum Associates.

Reik, T. (1948). *Listening with the third ear.* New York: Farrar, Straus & Giroux.

Reisman, J. M. (1976). *A history of clinical psychology.* New York: Irvington.

Reiss, D., & Price, R. H. (1996). National research agenda for prevention research: The National Institute of Mental Health Report. *American Psychologist, 51,* 1109-1115.

Reitan, R. M., & Davison, L. A. (Eds.). (1974). *Clinical neuropsychology: Current status and applications.* Washington, DC: V. H. Winston.

Renshaw, P. D., & Asher, S. R. (1983). Children's goals and strategies for social interaction. *Merrill-Palmer Quarterly, 29,* 353-375.

Reschly, D. J. (1984). Aptitude tests. In G. Goldstein & M. Hersen (Eds.), *Handbook of psychological assessment* (pp. 132-156). New York: Pergamon Press.

Reschly, D. J. (1990). Aptitude tests in educational classification and placement. In G. Goldstein & M. Hersen (Eds.), *Handbook of psychological assessment* (pp. 148-172). New York: Pergamon Press.

Resnick, J. H. (1991). Finally, a definition of clinical psychology: A message from the President, Division 12. *The Clinical Psychologist, 44,* 3-11.

Resnick, R. J. (1985). The case against the Blues: The Virginia challenge. *American Psychologist, 40,* 975-983.

Ressler, R. K., & Shachtman, T. (1992). *Whoever fights monsters.* New York: St. Martin's Press.

Revenson, T. A., & Felton, B. J. (1989). Disability and coping as predictors of psychological adjustment to rheumatoid arthritis. *Journal of Consulting and Clinical Psychology, 57,* 344-348.

Rholes, W. S., Blackwell, J., Jordan, C., & Walters, C. (1980). A developmental study of learned helplessness. *Developmental Psychology, 16,* 616-624.

Rice, M. E. (1997). Violent offender research and implications for the criminal justice system. *American Psychologist, 52,* 414-423.

Rice, S. A. (1929). Contagious bias in the interview: A methodological note. *American Journal of Sociology, 35,* 420-423.

Richey, C. R. (1994). Proposals to eliminate the prejudicial effect of the use of the word "expert" under the federal rules of evidence in civil and criminal jury trials. *Federal Rules Decisions, 154,* 537-562.

Richters, J. E. (1992). Depressed mothers as informants about their children. A critical review of the evidence for distortion. *Psychological Bulletin, 112,* 485-499.

Rickert, V., & Jay, S. (1995). The concompliant adolescent. In S. Parker and B. Zuckerman (Eds.), *Behavioral and developmental pediatrics* (pp. 219-222). Boston: Little, Brown & Company.

Roberts, C. F., & Golding, S. L. (1991). The social construction of criminal responsibility and insanity. *Law and Human Behavior, 15,* 349-376.

Roberts, H. (1996). Test community responds to new statement of rights. *APA Monitor,* December, p. 26.

Roberts, L. J., Luke, D. A., Rappaport, J., & Seidman, E. (1991). Charting uncharted terrain: A behavioral observation system for mutual help groups. *American Journal of Community Psychology, 19,* 715–737.

Robertson, G. J., & Eyde, L. D. (1993). Improving test use in the United States: The development of an interdisciplinary casebook. *European Journal of Psychological Assessment, 9,* 137–146.

Robiner, W. N. (1991). How many psychologists are needed? A call for a national psychology human resource agenda. *Professional Psychology: Research and Practice, 22,* 427–440.

Robins, L. N. (1995). How to choose among riches: Selecting a diagnostic instrument. *International Journal of Methods in Psychiatric Research, 5,* 103–109.

Robins, L. N., Helzer, J. E., Croughan, J. L., Williams, J. B. W., & Ratcliff, R. L. (1981). *The NIMH Diagnostic Interview Schedule: Version III.* Washington, DC: Public Health Service. (HSS) ADM-T-42-3 (5/81, 8/81).

Robins, L. N., & Rogier, D. A. (1991). *Psychiatric disorders in America: The epidemiological catchment area study.* New York: The Free Press.

Robinson, L. A., Berman, J. S., & Neimeyer, R. A. (1990). Psychotherapy for the treatment of depression: A comprehensive review of controlled outcome rsearch. *Psychological Bulletin, 108,* 30–49.

Rock, D. L., Bransford, J. D., Maisto, S. A., & Morey, L. (1987). The study of clinical judgment: An ecological approach. *Clinical Psychology Review, 7,* 645–661.

Rodgers, D. D. (1987). Computer-aided interviewing overcomes first impressions. *Personnel Journal, 66,* 148–152.

Rodin, J., & Salovey, P. (1989). Health psychology. *Annual Review of Psychology, 40,* 533–580.

Rodriguez, R., Nietzel, M. T., & Berzins, J. I. (1980). Sex role orientation and assertiveness among female college students. *Behavior Therapy, 11,* 353–366.

Rodrique, J. R. (1996). Promoting healthier behaviors, attitudes, and beliefs toward sun exposure in parents of young children. *Journal of Consulting and Clinical Psychology, 64,* 1431–1436.

Roe, A., Gustad, J. W., Moore, B. V., Ross, S., & Skodak, M. (Eds.). (1959). *Graduate education in psychology.* Washington, DC: American Psychological Association.

Roesch, R., & Golding, S. L. (1980). *Competency to stand trial.* Urbana, ILL.: University of Illinois Press.

Rogers, C. R. (1939). *The clinical treatment of the problem child.* Boston: Houghton Mifflin.

Rogers, C. R. (1942). *Counseling and psychotherapy.* Boston: Houghton Mifflin.

Rogers, C. R. (1951). *Client-centered therapy.* Boston: Houghton Mifflin.

Rogers, C. R. (1954). *Psychotherapy and personality change.* Chicago: University of Chicago Press.

Rogers, C. R. (1959). A theory of therapy, personality, and interpersonal relationships as developed in the client-centered framework. In S. Koch (Ed.), *Psychology: A study of a science: Vol. III. Formulations of the person and the social context* (pp. 184–256). New York: McGraw-Hill.

Rogers, C. R. (1961). *On becoming a person.* Boston: Houghton Mifflin.

Rogers, C. R. (Ed.). (1967). *The therapeutic relationship and its impact: A study of psychotherapy with schizophrenics.* With E. T. Gendlin, D. J. Kiesler, & C. Louax. Madison: University of Wisconsin Press.

Rogers, C. R. (1970). *Carl Rogers on encounter groups.* New York: Harper & Row.

Rogers, C. R. (1972). *On becoming partners: Marriage and its alternatives.* New York: Delacorte.

Rogers, R. (1995). *Diagnostic and structured interviewing: A handbook for psychologists.* Odessa, Florida: Psychological Assessment Resources, Inc.

Rogers, R., & Ewing, C. P. (1989). Ultimate opinion proscriptions: A cosmetic fix and a plea for empiricism. *Law and Human Behavior, 13,* 357-374.

Rogers, R., Gillis, J. R., Dickens, S. E., & Bagby, R. M. (1991). Standardized assessment of malingering: Validation of the Structured Interview of Reported Symptoms. *Psychological Assessment: A Journal of Consulting and Clinical Psychology, 3,* 89-96.

Rogers, R., Wasyliw, O. E., & Cavanaugh, J. L. (1984). Evaluating insanity: A study of construct validity. *Law and Human Behavior, 8,* 293-304.

Romanczyk, R. G., Kent, R. N., Diament, C., & O'Leary, K. D. (1973). Measuring the reliability of observational data: A reactive process. *Journal of Applied Behavior Analysis, 6,* 175-184.

Rorschach, H. (1921/1942). *Psycho-diagnosis: A diagnostic test based on perception.* (P. Lemkau & B. Kronenburg, Trans.). Berne: Huber.

Rose, S. D., & LeCroy, C. W. (1991). Group methods. In F. H. Kanfer & A. P. Goldstein (Eds.), *Helping people change* (4th ed., pp. 422-453). New York: Pergamon Press.

Rosen, R. C., & Kopel, S. A. (1977). Penile plethysmography and biofeedback in the treatment of a transvestite-exhibitionist. *Journal of Consulting and Clinical Psychology, 45,* 908-916.

Rosenberg, S. (1996). Health maintenance organization penetration and general hospital psychiatric services: Expenditures and utilization trends. *Professional Psychology: Research and Practice, 27,* 345-348.

Rosenblatt, D. (1975). *Opening doors: What happens in Gestalt therapy.* New York: Harper & Row.

Rosenfarb, I. S., Goldstein, M. J., Mintz, J., & Nuechterlein, K. H. (1995). Expressed emotion and subclinical psychopathology observable within transaction btween schizophrenic patients and their family members. *Journal of Abnormal Psychology, 104,* 259-267.

Rosenhan, D. L. (1973). On being sane in insane places. *Science, 179,* 250-258.

Rosenhan, D. L., & Seligman, M. E. (1989). *Abnormal psychology* (2nd ed.). New York: W. W. Norton.

Rosenman, R. H. (1978). The interview method of assessment of the coronary-prone behavior pattern. In T. M. Dembroski, S. M. Weiss, J. L. Shields, S. G. Haynes, & M. Feinleib (Eds.), *Coronary-prone behavior* (pp. 55-69). New York: Springer-Verlag.

Rosenman, R. H., Brand, R. J., Jenkins, D. D., Friedman, M., Straus, R., & Wurm, M. (1975). Coronary heart disease in the Western Collaborative Group Study: Final follow-up experience after 8 ½ years. *Journal of the American Medical Association, 233,* 872-877.

Rosenstock, I. M. (1966). Why people use health services. *Milbank Memorial Fund Quarterly, 44,* 94-127.

Rosenthal, D. (1970). *Genetic theory and abnormal behavior.* New York: McGraw-Hill.

Rosenthal, M. J. (1989). Toward selective and improved performance on the mental status examination. *Acta Psychiatica Scandinavica, 80,* 207-215.

Rosenthal, R. (1966). *Experimenter effects in behavioral research.* New York: Appleton-Century-Crofts.

Rosenthal, R. (1983). Assessing the statistical and social importance of the effects of psychotherapy. *Journal of Consulting and Clinical Psychology, 51,* 4-13.

Rosenthal, R., & Rubin, D. B. (1978). Interpersonal expectancy effects: The first 345 studies. *Behavioral and Brain Sciences, 3,* 377-386.

Rosenthal, T. L., & Steffek, B. D. (1991). Modeling methods. In F. H. Kanfer & A. P. Goldstein (Eds.), *Helping people change* (4th ed., pp. 70–121). New York: Pergamon Press.

Rosenzweig, S. (1949). Apperceptive norms for the Thematic Apperception Test. I. The problem of norms in projective methods. *Journal of Personality, 17,* 475–482.

Ross, D. M., & Ross, S. A. (1982). *Hyperactivity: Current issues, research, and theory* (2nd ed.). New York: John Wiley.

Ross, M. W., Stowe, A., Wodak, A., & Gold, J. (1995). Reliability of interview responses of injecting drug users. *Journal of Addictive Diseases, 14,* 1–12.

Roth, A., & Fonagy, P. (1995). *Research on the efficacy and effectiveness of the psychotherapies*. Report to the Department of Health. London: National Health Services.

Roth, A., & Fonagy, P. (1996). *What works for whom?* New York: Guilford.

Roth, M., Tym, E. Montjoy, G. Q., Huppert, F. A., Hendrie, H, Verma, S., & Goddard, R. (1986). CAMDEX: A standardized instrument for the diagnosis of mental disorders in the elderly with special reference to the early detection of dementia. *British Journal of Psychiatry, 149,* 698–709.

Rotter, J. B. (1954). *Social learning and clinical psychology.* Englewood Cliffs, NJ: Prentice-Hall.

Rotter, J. B., & Rafferty, J. E. (1950). *The Rotter Incomplete Sentences Test.* New York: Psychological Corporation.

Rourke, B. P. (1989). *Nonverbal learning disabilities: The syndrome and the model.* New York: Guilford Press.

Routh, D. K. (1994). *Clinical psychology since 1917: Science, practice, and organization.* New York: Plenum.

Routh, D. K. (1996). Lightner Witmer and the first 100 years of clinical psychology. *American Psychologist, 51,* 244–247.

Rubin, R., Holm, S., Friberg, L., Videbech, P., Andersen, H. S., Bendsen, B. B., Stromso, N., Larsen, J. K., Lassen, N. A., & Hemmingsen, R. (1991). Altered modulation of prefrontal and subcortical brain activity in newly diagnosed schizophrenia and schizophreniform disorder: A regional cerebral blood flow study. *Archives of General Psychiatry, 48,* 987–995.

Rubinstein, E. (1948). Childhood mental disease in American: A review of the literature before 1900. *American Journal of Orthopsychiatry, 18,* 314–321.

Ruble, D. N., & Rholes, W. S. (1981). The development of children's perceptions and attributions about their social world. In J. H. Harvey, W. Ickes, & R. F. Kidd (Eds.), *New directions in attribution research* (Vol. 3, pp. 1–36). Hillsdale, NJ: Lawrence Erlbaum Associates.

Ruegg, R. G., Ekstrom, D. E., Dwight, L., & Golden, R. N. (1990). Introduction of a standardized report form improves the quality of mental status examination reports by psychiatric residents. *Academic Psychiatry, 14,* 157–163.

Rugh, J. D., Gable, R. S., & Lemke, R. R. (1986). Instrumentation for behavioral assessment. In A. R. Ciminero, C. S. Calhoun, & H. E. Adams (Eds.), *Handbook of behavioral assessment* (2nd ed., pp. 79–108). New York: John Wiley.

Rutter, M. (1981). Stress, coping, and development: Some issues and some questions. In N. Garmezy & M. Rutter (Eds.), *Stress, coping & development* (pp. 1–41). New York: McGraw-Hill.

Rutter, M. I. (1997). Nature-nurture integration: The example of antisocial behavior. *American Psychologist, 52,* 390–398.

Rutter, M., Maugham, B., Mortimore, P., Ouston, J., & Smith, A. (1979). *Fifteen thousand hours: Secondary schools and their effects on children.* London: Open Books; Cambridge, MA: Harvard University Press.

Rutter, M., & Shaffer, D. (1980). DSM-III. A step forward or a step backward in terms of the classification of child psychiatric disorders. *Journal of the American Academy of Child Psychiatry, 19,* 371-394.

Ryan, J. J. Paolo, A. M., & Smith, A. J. (1992). Wechsler Adult Intelligence Scale—Revised inter-subtest scatter in brain-damaged patients: A comparison with the standardization sample. *Psychological Assessment, 4,* 63-66.

Rychtarik, R. G., Tarnowski, K. J., & St. Lawrence, J. S. (1989). Impact of social desirability response sets on the self-report of marital adjustment in alcoholics. *Journal of Studies in Alcohol, 50,* 24-29.

Sackett, P. R., & Wilk, S. L. (1994). Within-group norming and other forms of score adjustment in preemployment testing. *American Psychologist, 49,* 929-954.

Sacks, O. (1985). *The man who mistook his wife for a hat.* New York: Summit Books.

Sacks, O. (1990). *A leg to stand on.* New York: Summit Books.

Safran, J. D., Segal, Z. V., Vallis, M. T., & Shaw, B. F. (1993). Assessing patient suitability for short-term cognitive therapy with an interpersonal focus. *Cognitive Therapy and Research, 17,* 23-38.

Sales, B. D., & Hafemeister, T. (1984). Empiricism and legal policy on the insanity defense. In L. A. Teplin (Ed.), *Mental health and criminal justice* (pp. 253-278). Newbury Park, CA: Sage.

Sales, B. D., & Shuman, D. W. (1996). *Law, mental health, and mental disorder.* Pacific Grove, CA: Brooks/Cole.

Salovey, P., & Singer, J. A. (1991). Cognitive behavior modification. In F. H. Kanfer & A. P. Goldstein (Eds.), *Helping people change* (4th ed., pp. 361-395). New York: Pergamon Press.

Salzinger, K. (1959). Experimental manipulation of verbal behavior: A review. *Journal of Genetic Psychology, 61,* 65-95.

Sammons, M. T., & Brown, A. B. (1997). The Department of Defense Psychopharmacology Demonstration Project: An evolving program for postdoctoral education in psychology. *Professional Psychology: Research and Practice, 28,* 107-112.

Samuda, R. J. (1975). *Psychological testing of American minorities: Issues and consequences.* New York: Dodd, Mead.

Sandler, I., Wolchik, S., Braver, S., & Fogas, B. (1991). Stability and quality of life events and psychological symptomatology in children of divorce. *American Journal of Community Psychology, 19,* 501-520.

Sandler, J., & Steele, H. V. (1991). Aversion methods. In F. H. Kanfer & A. P. Goldstein (Eds.), *Helping people change* (4th ed., pp. 202-247). New York: Pergamon Press.

Sanford, F. H. (1951). Annual report of the executive secretary. *American Psychologist, 6,* 664-670.

Santostefano, S. (1962). Performance testing of personality. *Merrill-Palmer Quarterly, 8,* 83-97.

Santoyo, V. C. (1996). Behavioral assessment of social interactions in natural settings. *European Journal of Psychological Assessment, 12,* 124-131.

Sarason, I. G., Johnson, J. H., & Siegel, J. M. (1978). Assessing the impact of life changes: Development of the life experiences survey. *Journal of Consulting and Clinical Psychology, 46,* 932-946.

Sarason, S. B. (1974). *The psychological sense of community: Prospects for community psychology.* San Francisco: Jossey-Bass

Sarbin, T. R., Taft, R., & Bailey, D. E. (1960). *Clinical inference and cognitive theory.* New York: Holt, Rinehart & Winston.

Sartorius, N., Kaelber, C. T., Cooper, J. E., Roper, M. T., et al. (1996). Progress toward achieving a common language in psychiatry: Results from the field trial of the clinical guidelines accompanying the WHO classification of mental and behavioral disorders in ICD-10. *Archives of General Psychiatry, 50,* 115-124.

Saslow, G., & Matarazzo, J. D. (1959). A technique for studying changes in interview behavior. In E. A. Rubinstein & M. B. Parloff (Eds.), *Research in psychotherapy* (Vol. 1, pp. 125-159). Washington, DC: American Psychological Association.

Satir, V. (1967). *Conjoint family therapy* (rev. ed.). Palo Alto, CA: Science and Behavior Books.

Satterfield, J. H., Hoppe, C. M., & Schell, A. M. (1982). A prospective study of delinquency in 110 adolescent boys with attention deficit disorder and 88 normal adolescent boys. *American Journal of Psychiatry, 139,* 795-798.

Sattler, J. M. (1988). *Assessment of children's intelligence and special abilities* (3rd ed.). Boston: Allyn & Bacon.

Satz, P., & Fletcher, J. M. (1981). Emergent trends in neuropsychology: An overview. *Journal of Consulting and Clinical Psychology, 49,* 851-865.

Satz, P., Taylor, H. G., Friel, J., & Fletcher, J. M. (1978). Some developmental and predictive precursors of reading disabilities: A six-year follow-up. In A. L. Benton & D. Pearl (Eds.), *Dyslexia: An appraisal of current knowledge.* New York: Guilford.

Sawyer, J. (1966). Measurement and prediction, clinical and statistical. *Psychological Bulletin, 66,* 178-200.

Saylor, C. F., Finch, A. J., Baskin, C. H., Furey, W., & Kelly, M. M. (1984). Construct validity for measures of childhood depression: Application of multitrait-multimethod methodology. *Journal of Consulting and Clinical Psychology, 52,* 977-985.

Saywitz, K. (1990). The child as witness: Experimental and clinical considerations. In A. La Greca (Ed.), *Through the eyes of the child: Obtaining self-reports from children and adolescents* (pp. 329-367). Boston: Allyn & Bacon.

Saywitz, K. J., & Snyder, L. (1996). Narrative elaboration: Test of a new procedure for interviewing children. *Journal of Consulting and Clinical Psychology, 64,* 1347-1357.

Schaefer, H. H., & Martin, P. L. (1975). *Behavior therapy* (2nd ed.). New York: McGraw-Hill.

Schmidt, H. O., & Fonda, C. P. (1956). The reliability of psychiatric diagnosis: A new look. *Journal of Abnormal and Social Psychology, 52,* 262-267.

Schneider, S. F. (1991). No fluoride in our future. *Professional Psychology: Research and Practice, 22,* 456-460.

Schonhaut, S., & Satz, P. (1983). Prognosis for children with learning disabilities: A review of follow-up studies. In M. Rutter (Ed.), *Developmental neuropsychiatry* (pp. 542-574). New York: Guilford.

Schradle, S. B., & Dougher, M. J. (1985). Social support as a mediator of stress. Theoretical and empirical issues. *Clinical Psychology Review, 5,* 641-662.

Schwab-Stone, M., Fallon, T., & Briggs, M. (1994). Reliability of diagnostic reporting for children aged 6-11 years: A test-retest study of the Diagnostic Interview Schedule for Children—Revised. *American Journal of Psychiatry, 151,* 1048-1054.

Schweinhart, L. J., McNair, S., Barnes, H., & Larner, M. (1993). Observing young children in action to assess their development: The High/Scope Child Observation Record study. *Educational and Psychological Measurement, 53,* 445-455.

Schweinhart, L. L., Barnes, H. V., & Weikhart, D. P. (1993). *Significant benefits. The High/Scope Perry School Study through age 27.* Ypsilanti, MI: High/Scope Press.

Schweritz, L. W., Perkins, L. L., Chesny, M. A., Hughes, G. H., & Silney, S. (1992). Hostility and health behaviors in young adults: The CARDIA study. *American Journal of Epidemiology, 136,* 136-145.

Schwitzgebel, R. K., & Kolb, D. A. (1974). *Changing human behavior.* New York: McGraw-Hill.

Scoville, W. B., & Milner, B. (1957). Loss of recent memory after bilateral hippocampal lesions. *The Journal of Neurology, Neurosurgery, & Psychiatry, 20,* 11-21.

Sechrest, L. (1992). The past future of clinical psychology: A reflection on Woodworth (1937). *Journal of Consulting and Clinical Psychology, 60,* 18-23.

Sechrest, L. B. (1963). Incremental validity: A recommendation. *Educational and Psychological Measurement, 23,* 153-158.

Sechrest, L. B., McKnight, P., & McKnight, K. (1996). Calibration of measures for psychotherapy outcome studies. *American Psychologist, 51,* 1065-1071.

Sedlacek, K., & Taub, E. Biofeedback treatment of Raynaud's disease. *Professional Psychology: Research and Practice, 27,* 548-553.

Sedlak, A. J., & Broadhurst, D. D. (1996). *Executive summary of the third national incidence study of child abuse and neglect.* Washington, D.C.: U.S. Department of Health and Human Services.

Seeman, J. A. (1949). A study of the process of nondirective therapy. *Journal of Consulting Psychology, 13,* 157-168.

Segal, D. L., Hersen, M., & Van Hasselt, V. B. (1994). Reliability of the Structured Clinical Interview for DSM-III-R: An evaluative review. *Comprehensive Psychiatry, 35,* 316-327.

Seidman, E., Allen, L., Aber, J. L., Mitchell, C., & Feinman, J. (1994). The impact of school transitions in early adolescence on the self-system and perceived social context of poor urban youth. *Child Development, 65,* 507-522.

Seligman, M. E. P. (1995). The effectiveness of psychotherapy: The *Consumer Reports* study. *American Psychologist, 50,* 965-974.

Seligman, M. E. P., Abramson, L. Y., Semmel, A., & von Baeyer, C. (1979). Depressive attributional style. *Journal of Abnormal Psychology, 88,* 242-247.

Seligman, M. E. P., Peterson, C., Kaslow, N. J., Tanenbaum, R. L., Alloy, L. B., & Abramson, L. Y. (1984). Explanatory style and depressive symptoms among school children. *Journal of Abnormal Psychology, 93,* 235-238.

Selye, H. (1956). *The stress of life.* New York: McGraw-Hill.

Serketich, W. J., & Dumas, J. E. (1996). The effectiveness of behavioral parent training to modify antisocial behavior in children: A meta-analysis. *Behavior Therapy, 27,* 171-186.

Shadish, W. R., Jr., et al. (1997). Evidence that therapy works in clinically representative conditions. *Journal of Consulting and Clinical Psychology, 65,* 355-365.

Shadish, W. R., Matt, G. E., Navarro, A. M., Liegle, G., Crits-Christoph, P., Hazelrigg, M., Jorm, A., Lyons, L. S., Nietzel, M. T., Prout, H. T., Robinson, L., Smith, M. L., Svartberg, M., & Weiss, B. (in press). The generalization of psychotherapy research to clinically representative conditions. *Journal of Consulting & Clinical Psychology.*

Shadish, W. R., Montgomery, L. M., Wilson, P. W., Wilson, M. R., Bright, I., & Okwumabua, T. (1993). Effects of family and marital psychotherapies: A meta-analysis. *Journal of Consulting and Clinical Psychology, 61,* 992-1002.

Shaffer, D., Schwab-Stone, M., Fisher, P., Cohen, P., et al. (1993). The diagnostic interview schedule for children-Revised version (DISC-R): I. Preparation, field testing, interrater reliability, and acceptability. *Journal of the American Academy of Child and Adolescent Psychiatry, 32,* 643-650.

Shaffer, G. W., & Lazarus, R. S. (1952). *Fundamental concepts in clinical psychology.* New York: McGraw-Hill.

Shakow, D. (1942). The training of the clinical psychologist. *Journal of Consulting Psychology, 6,* 277-288.

Shakow, D. (1948). Clinical psychology: An evaluation. In L. G. Lowrey & V. Sloane (Eds.), *Orthopsychiatry, 1923-1948: Retrospect and prospect* (pp. 231-247). New York: American Orthopsychiatric Association.

Shakow, D. (1965). Seventeen years later: Clinical psychology in the light of the 1947 CTCP report. *American Psychologist, 20,* 353-362.

Shakow, D. (1968). Clinical psychology. In D. L. Sills (Ed.), *International encyclopedia of the social sciences* (pp. 513-518). London: Collier Macmillan.

Shakow, D. (1978). Clinical psychology seen some 50 years later. *American Psychologist, 33,* 148-158.

Shannon, D., & Weaver, W. (1949). *The mathematical theory of communication.* Urbana: University of Illinois Press.

Shapiro, A. K. (1971). Placebo effects in medicine, psychotherapy, and psychoanalysis. In A. E. Bergin & S. L. Garfield (Eds.), *Handbook of psychotherapy and behavior change: An empirical analysis* (pp. 439-473). New York: John Wiley.

Shapiro, D. A., & Shapiro, D. (1982). Meta-analysis of comparative therapy outcome research: A critical appraisal. *Behavioral Psychotherapy, 10,* 4-25.

Shaprio, A. E., & Wiggins, J. G. (1994). A PsyD degree for every practitioner: Truth in labeling. *American Psychologist, 49,* 207-210.

Shariff, H. (1995). Mother-child HIV transmission: Prevention options for women in developing countries. *AIDcaptions,* 25-27.

Sharpley, C. F., & Pain, M. D. (1988). Psychological test use in Australia. *Australian Psychologist, 23,* 361-369.

Shaw, D. L., Martz, D. M., Lancaster, C. J., & Sade, R. M. (1995). Influence of medical school applicants' demographic and cognitive characteristics on interviewers' ratings of noncognitive traits. *Academic Medicine, 70,* 532-536.

Shaywitz, B. A., Shaywitz, S. E., Pugh, K. R., Constable, R. T., & Skudlarski, P. (1995). Sex differences in the functional organization of the brain for language. *Nature, 373,* 607-609.

Shemberg, K. M., & Leventhal, D. B. (1981). Attitudes of internship directors toward preinternship training and clinical training models. *Professional Psychology, 12,* 639-646.

Shepherd, M., Oppenheim, B., & Mitchell, S. (1971). *Childhood behavior and mental health.* London: University of London Press.

Sheridan, E. P., Matarazzo, J. D., & Nelson, P. D. (1995). Accre ditation of psychology's graduate professional education and training programs. *Professional Psychology: Research and Practice, 26,* 386-392.

Shiffman, S., Hickcox, M., Paty, J. A., Gnys, M., Kassel, J. D., & Richards, T. J. (1996). Progression from a smoking lapse to relapse: Prediction from abstinence violation effects, nicotine dependence, and lapse characteristics. *Journal of Consulting & Clinical Psychology, 64,* 993-1002.

Shiller, V. (1986). Loyalty conflicts and family relationships in latency age boys: A comparison of joint and maternal custody. *Journal of Divorce, 9,* 17-38.

Shipley, K. G., & Wood, J. M. (1996). *The elements of interviewing.* San Diego: Singular Publishing.

Shoham-Salomon, V. (1985). Are schizophrenics' behaviors schizophrenic? What medically versus psychosocially oriented therapists attribute to schizophrenic persons. *Journal of Abnormal Psychology, 94,* 443-453.

Shostrom, E. L. (1968). *Personal orientation inventory: An inventory for the measurement of self-actualization.* San Diego, CA: Educational and Industrial Testing Service.

Siassi, I. (1984). Psychiatric interviews and mental status examinations. In G. Goldstein & M. Hersen (Eds.), *Handbook of psychological assessment* (pp. 259-275). New York: Pergamon Press.

Siegel, A. M., & Elwork, A. (1990). Treating incompetence to stand trial. *Law and Human Behavior, 14,* 57-65.

Silver, E. (1995). Punishment or treatment? Comparing the lengths of confinement of successful and unsuccessful insanity defendants. *Law and Human Behavior, 19,* 375-388.

Silver, E., Cirincione, C., & Steadman, H. J. (1994). Demythologizing inaccurate perceptions of the insanity defense. *Law and Human Behavior, 18,* 63-70.

Silverman, L. H., & Weinberger, J. (1985). Mommy and I are one: Implications for psychotherapy. *American Psychologist, 40,* 1296-1308.

Sinacore-Guinn, G. A. (1995). The diagnostic window: Culture- and gender-sensitive diagnosis and training. *Counselor education and supervision, 35,* 18-31.

Singer, M., & Eder, G. S. (1989). Effects of ethnicity, accent, and job status on selection decisions. *International Journal of Psychology, 24,* 13-34.

Skinner, B. F. (1948). *Verbal behavior.* Cambridge, MA: Harvard University Press.

Skinner, B. F. (1953). *Science and human behavior.* New York: Macmillan.

Skinner, B. F. (1957). *Verbal behavior.* New York: Appleton-Century-Crofts.

Skinner, B. F. (1971). *Beyond freedom and dignity.* New York: Knopf.

Sleator, E. K., & Ullmann, R. K. (1981). Can the physician diagnose hyperactivity in the office? *Pediatrics, 67,* 13-17.

Sleek, S. (1996). Ensuring accuracy in clinical decisions. *APA Monitor,* April.

Sleek, S. (1997). Lawsuit seeks to return clinical control to providers. *APA Monitor,* January, p. 36.

Slipp, S. (Ed.). (1981). *Curative factors in psychodynamic therapy.* New York: McGraw-Hill.

Smith, D. (1982). Trends in counseling and psychotherapy. *American Psychologist, 37,* 802-809.

Smith, D., & Dumont, F. (1995). A cautionary study: Unwarranted interpretations of the Draw-A-Person test. *Professional Psychology: Research and Practice, 26,* 298-303.

Smith, M. L., & Glass, G. V. (1977). Meta-analysis of psychotherapy outcome studies. *American Psychologist, 32,* 752–777.

Smith, M. L., Glass, G. V., & Miller, T. I. (1980). *The benefits of pscyhotherapy.* Baltimore, MD: Johns Hopkins University Press.

Smith, S. R. (1996). Malpractice liability of mental health professionals and institutions. In B. D. Sales & D. W. Shuman (Eds.), *Law, mental health, and mental disorder.* (pp. 76–98). Pacific Grove, CA: Brooks/Cole.

Smith, S. (1989). Mental health expert witnesses: Of science and crystal balls. *Behavioral Sciences and the Law, 7,* 145–180.

Snepp, F. P., & Peterson, D. R. (1988). Evaluative comparison of Psy.D. and Ph.D. students by clinical internship supervisors. *Professional Psychology: Research and Practice, 19,* 180–183.

Snow, W. G. (1987). Standardization of test administration and scoring criteria: Some shortcomings of current practice with the Halstead-Reitan Test Battery. *The Clinical Neuropsychologist, 1,* 250–262.

Snyder, D. K. (1981). *Marital Satisfaction Inventory: Manual.* Los Angeles: Western Psychological Services.

Snyder, D. K., Lachar, D., & Wills, R. M. (1988). Computer-based interpretation of the Marital Satisfaction Inventory: Use in treatment planning. *Journal of Marital and Family Therapy, 14,* 397–409.

Snyder, D. K., & Wills, R. M. (1989). Behavioral versus insight-oriented marital therapy: Effects on individual and interspousal functioning. *Journal of Consulting and Clinical Psychology, 57,* 39–46.

Snyder, D. K., Wills, R. M., & Grady-Fletcher, A. (1991). Long-term effectiveness of behavioral versus insight-oriented marital therapy: A 4-year follow-up study. *Journal of Consulting and Clinical Psychology, 59,* 138–141.

Snyder, W. V. (1945). An investigation of the nature of nondirective psychotherapy. *Journal of General Psychology, 33,* 193–232.

Snyder, W. V. (Ed.). (1953). *Group report of a program of research in psychotherapy.* State College: Department of Psychology, Pennsylvania State University.

Sobell, L. C., Toneatto, T., & Sobell, M. B. (1994). Behavioral assessment and treatment planning for alcohol, tobacco, and other drug problems: Current status with an emphasis on clinical applications. *Behavior Therapy, 25,* 533–580.

Soldz, S., Budman, S., Demby, A., & Jerry, J. (1993). Representation of personality disorders in circumplex and five-factor space: Explorations with a clinical sample. *Psychological Assessment, 5,* 41–52.

Somers-Flanagan, J., & Somers-Flanagan, R. (1995). Intake interviewing with suicidal patients: A systematic approach. *Professional Psychology: Research and Practice, 26,* 41–47.

Spanos, N. (1994). Multiple identity enactments and multiple personality disorder. *Psychological Bulletin, 116,* 143–165.

Spanos, N. P. (1978). Witchcraft in histories of psychiatry: A critical analysis and an alternative conceptualization. *Psychological Bulletin, 85,* 417–439.

Sparr, L. (1995). Post-traumatic stress disorder. *Neurologic Clinics, 13,* 413–429.

Sperry, R. (1968). Hemisphere deconnection and unity in conscious awareness. *American Psychologist, 23,* 723–733.

Sperry, R. W. (1961). Cerebral organization and behavior. *Science, 133,* 1749–1757.

Sperry, R. W. (1974). Lateral specialization in the surgically separated hemispheres. In F. O. Schmitt & F. G. Worden (Eds.), *The neurosciences: Third study program* (pp. 5–20). Cambridge, MA: MIT Press.

Sperry, R. W. (1982). Some effects of disconnecting the cerebral hemispheres. *Science, 217,* 1223–1226.

Spiegel, D., & Bloom, J. R. (1983). Group therapy and hypnosis reduce metastatic breast carcinoma pain. *Psychosomatic Medicine, 45,* 333–339.

Spiegel, D., Bloom, J. R., & Yalom, I. (1981). Group support for patients with metastatic cancer: A randomized outcome study. *Archives of General Psychiatry, 38,* 527–533.

Spiegel, T. A., Wadden, T. A., & Foster, G. D. (1991). Objective measurement of eating rate during behavioral treatment of obesity. *Behavior Therapy, 22,* 61–68.

Spiegler, M. D. & Guevremont, D. C. (1993). *Contemporary behavior therapy* (2nd ed.) Pacific Grove, CA: Brooks/Cole.

Spielberger, C. D., Gorsuch, R. L., Lushene, R., Vagg, P. R., & Jacobs, G. A. (1983). *Manual for the State-Trait Anxiety Inventory.* Palo Alto, CA: Consulting Psychologists Press.

Spiers, P. A. (1980). Have they come to praise Luria or to bury him? The Lurio-Nebraska controversy. *Journal of Consulting and Clinical Psychology, 49,* 331–341.

Spitz, R. (1946). Anaclitic depression. *Psychoanalytic Study of the Child, 1,* 113–117.

Spitzer, R. L. (1991). An outsider-insider's views about revising DSMs. *Journal of Abnormal Psychology, 100,* 294–296.

Spitzer, R. L., Williams, J. B. W., Gibbon, M., & First, M. B. (1990). *Structured clinical interview for DSM-III-R (SCID).* Washington, D.C.: American Psychiatric Press.

Spivack, G., & Shure, M. B. (1974). *Social adjustment of young children: A cognitive approach to solving real-life problems.* San Francisco: Jossey-Bass.

Sroufe, L. A. (1985). Attachment classification from the perspective of infant-caregiver relationships and infant temperament. *Child Development, 56,* 1–14.

Sroufe, L. A., & Rutter, M. (1984). The domain of developmental psychopathology. *Child Development, 55,* 17–29.

St. Lawrence, J. S., Brasfield, T. L., Jefferson, K. W., Alleyne, E., & O'Bannon, R. E., III (1995). Cognitive-behavioral intervention to reduce African American adolescents' risk for HIV infection. *Journal of Consulting & Clinical Psychology, 63,* 221–237.

Staats, A. W. (1991). Unified positivism and unification psychology: Fad or new field? *American Psychologist, 46,* 899–912.

Starkstein, S. E., & Robinson, R. G. (1988). Lateralized emotional response following stroke. In M. Kinsbourne (Ed.), *Cerebral hemisphere function in depression.* Washington, DC: American Psychiatric Press.

Steadman, H. J. (1979). *Beating a rap? Defendants found incompetent to stand trial.* Chicago: University of Chicago Press.

Steadman, H. J., Keitner, L., Braff, J., Arvanites, T. M. (1983). Factors associated with a successful insantiy plea. *American Journal of Psychiatry, 140,* 401–405.

Steenbarger, B. N. (1994). Duration and outcome in therapy: An integrative review. *Professional Psychology: Research and Practice, 25,* 111–119.

Stein, D. M., & Lambert, M. J. (1984). On the relationship between therapist experience and psychotherapy outcome. *Clinical Psychology Review, 4,* 127–142.

Stein, D. M., & Lambert, M. J. (1995). Graduate training in psychotherapy: Are therapy outcomes enhanced? *Journal of Consulting and Clinical Psychology, 63,* 182-196.

Stein, R. E. K., Bauman, L. J., & Ireys, H. T. (1991). Who enrolls in prevention trials? Discordance in perception of risk by professionals and participants. *American Journal of Community Psychology, 19,* 603-618.

Steiner, J. L., Tebes, J. K., Sledge, W. H., & Walker, M. L. (1995). A comparison of the Structured Clinical Interview for DSM-III-R and clinical diagnoses. *Journal of Nervous and Mental Disease, 183,* 365-369.

Sternberg, R. J., & Detterman, D. K. (Eds.). (1986). *What is intelligence? Contemporary viewpoints on its nature and definition.* Norwood, NJ: Ablex.

Stevens, M. R., & Reilly, R. R. (1980). MMPI short forms: A literature review. *Journal of Personality Assessment, 44,* 368-376.

Stewart, D. J., & Patterson, M. L. (1973). Eliciting effects of verbal and nonverbal cues on projective test responses. *Journal of Consulting and Clinical Psychology, 41,* 74-77.

Stiles, W. A., Shapiro, D. A., & Elliot, R. (1986). "Are all psychotherapies equivalent?" *American Psychologist, 41,* 165-180.

Stokols, D. (1992). Establishing and maintaining healthy environments: Toward a social ecology of health promotion. *American Psychologist, 47,* 6-22.

Stone, A. A., & Neale, J. M. (1984). New measures of daily coping: Developments and preliminary results. *Journal of Personality and Social Psychology, 46,* 892-906.

Strayhorn, J. M. (1988). *The competent child.* New York: Guilford Press.

Stricker, G., & Trierweiler, S. (1995). The local clinical scientist: A bridge between science and practice. *American Psychologist, 50,* 995-1002.

Strickland, B. R. (1985). Over the Boulder(s) and through the Vail. *The Clinical Psychologist,* 52-56.

Strickner, G. (1992). The relationship of research to clinical practice. *American Psychologist, 47,* 543-549.

Strohmer, D. C., & Shivy, V. A. (1994). Bias in counselor hypothesis testing: Testing the robustness of counselor confirmatory bias. *Journal of Counseling and Development, 73,* 191-197.

Strother, C. R. (1956). *Psychology and mental health.* Washington, DC: American Psychological Association.

Stroul, B. (1993). *Psychiatric crisis response systems: A descriptive study.* Rockville, MD: Substance Abuse and Mental Health Services Administration.

Strupp, H. H. (1960). *Psychotherapists in action: Explorations of the therapist's contribution to the treatment process.* New York: Grune & Stratton.

Strupp, H. H. (1989). Psychotherapy: Can the practitioner learn from the researcher? *American Psychologist, 44,* 717-724.

Strupp, H. H., & Blinder, J. L. (1984). *Psychotherapy in a new key: A guide to time-limited dynamic psychotherapy.* New York: Basic Books.

Strupp, H. H., & Hadley, S. W. (1977). A tripartite model of mental health and therapeutic outcomes. *American Psychologist, 32,* 187-196.

Strupp, H. H., & Hadley, S. W. (1979). Specific vs. nonspecific factors in psychotherapy. *Archives of General Psychiatry, 36,* 1125-1137.

Stuart, R. B. (1971). Behavioral contracting within the families of delinquents. *Journal of Behavior Therapy and Experimental Psychiatry, 2,* 1-11.

Stumphauzer, J. S. (1986). *Helping delinquents change: A treatment manual of social learning approaches.* New York: Haworth Press.

Suarez-Balcazar, Y., Durlak, J., & Smith, C. (1994). Multicultural training practices in community psychology programs. *American Journal of Community Psychology, 22,* 785-798.

Sue, S., Fujino, D. C., Hu, L. T., Takeuchi, D. T., et al. (1991). Community mental health services for ethnic minority groups: A test of the cultural responsiveness hypothesis. *Journal of Consulting and Clinical Psychology, 59,* 533-540.

Suen, H. K., Ary, D., & Covalt, W. C. (1990). A decision tree approach to selecting an appropriate observation reliability index. *Journal of Psychopathology and Behavioral Assessment, 12,* 359-363.

Sullivan, H. S. (1953). *The interpersonal theory of psychiatry.* New York: W. W. Norton.

Sullivan, H. S. (1954). *The psychiatric interview.* New York: W. W. Norton.

Sulloway, F. J. (1996). *Born to rebel: Birth order, family dynamics, and creative lives.* New York: Pantheon Books.

Suls, J., & Wang, C. K. (1993). The relationship between trait hostility and cardiovascular reactivity: A quantitative review and analysis. *Psychophysiology, 30,* 1-12.

Sulzer, E. (1965). Behavior modifications in adult psychiatric patients. In L. P. Ullmann & L. Krasner (Eds.), *Case studies in behavior modification* (pp. 196-200). New York: Holt, Rinehart & Winston.

Summit, R. (1983). The child sexual abuse accommodation syndrome. *Child Abuse and Neglect, 7,* 177-193.

Sundberg, N. D. (1961). The practice of psychological testing in clinical services in the United States. *American Psychologist, 16,* 79-83.

Sundberg, N. D. (1977). *Assessment of persons.* Englewood Cliffs, NJ: Prentice-Hall.

Sundberg, N. D., Tyler, L. E., & Taplin, J. R. (1973). *Clinical psychology: Expanding horizons* (2nd ed.). Englewood Cliffs, NJ: Prentice-Hall.

Susser, E., & Lin, S. (1992). Schizophrenia after prenatal exposure to the Dutch hunger winter of 1944-1945. *Archives of General Psychiatry, 49,* 983-988.

Svartberg, M., & Stiles, T. C. (1991). Comparative effects of short-term psychotherapy: A meta-analysis. *Journal of Consulting and Clinical Psychology, 59,* 704-714.

Swain, M. A., & Steckel, S. B. (1981). Influencing adherence among hypertensives. *Research Nursing and Health, 4,* 213-218.

Sweeney, J. A., Clarkin, J. F., & Fitzgibbon, M. L. (1987). Current practice of psychological assessment. *Professional Psychology: Research and Practice, 18,* 377-380.

Sweet, A. A. (1984). The therapeutic relationship in behavior therapy. *Clinical Psychology Review, 4,* 253-272.

Szapocznik, J., Kurtines, W. M., Foote, F., Perez-Vidal, A., & Hervis, O. (1986). Conjoint versus one-person family therapy: Further evidence for the effectiveness of conducting family therapy through one person with drug-abusing adolescents. *Journal of Consulting and Clinical Psychology, 54,* 395-397.

Szapocznik, J., Kurtines, W., Santisteban, D. A., & Rio, A. T. (1990). Interplay of advances between theory, research, and application in treatment interventions aimed at behavior problem children and adolescents. *Journal of Consulting and Clinical Psychology, 58,* 696-703.

Szasz, T. S. (1960). The myth of mental illness. *American Psychologist, 15,* 113-118.

Szasz, T. S. (1987). *Insanity: The idea and its consequences.* New York: Wiley.

Tallent, N. (1976). Psychological report writing. Englewood Cliffs, NJ: Prentice-Hall.

Tallent, N. (1992). *The practice of psychological assessment.* Englewood Cliffs, NJ: Prentice-Hall.

Tallent, N., & Reiss, W. J. (1959). Multidisciplinary views on the preparation of written psychological reports. *Journal of Clinical Psychology, 15,* 444-446.

Taplin, P. S., & Reid, J. B. (1973). Effects of instructional set and experimenter influence on observer reliability. *Child Development, 44,* 547-554.

Task Force on Pediatric Aids, American Psychology Association. (1989). Pediatric AIDS and human immunodeficiency virus infection. *American Psychologist, 44,* 258-264.

Taube, C. A., Goldman, H. H., Burns, B. J., & Kessler, L. G. (1988). High users of outpatient mental health services: I. Definition and characteristics. *American Journal of Psychiatry, 145,* 19-24.

Taylor, S. (1995). *Health Psychology.* New York: McGraw-Hill.

Tellegen, A. (1982). *Brief manual for the Multidimensional Personality Questionnaire.* Unpublished manuscript, University of Minnesota.

Tellegen, A., & Ben-Porath, Y. S. (1992). The new uniform T scores for the MMPI-2: Rationale, derivation, and appraisal. *Psychological Assessment, 4,* 145-155.

Tellegen, A., Lykken, D. T., Bouchard, T. J., Jr., Wilcox, K. J., Segal, N. L., & Rich, S. (1988). Personality similarity in twins reared apart and reared together. *Journal of Personality and Social Psychology, 54,* 1031-1039.

Temerlin, M. K. (1968). Suggestion effects in psychiatric diagnosis. *Journal of Nervous and Mental Disease, 147,* 349-353.

Thelen, M. H., Farmer, J., Wonderlich, S., & Smith, M. (1991). A revision of the Bulimia Test: The BULIT-R. *Psychological Assessment, 3,* 119-124.

Thelen, M. H., Mintz, L. B., & Boman, J. S. (1996). The bulimia test—revised: Validation with DSM-IV criteria for bulimia nervosa. *Psychological Assessment, 8,* 219-221.

Thoits, P. A. (1986). Social support as coping assistance. *Journal of Consulting and Clinical Psychology, 54,* 416-423.

Thomas, A., & Chess, S. (1977). *Temperament and development.* New York: Brunner/Mazel.

Thomas, A., Chess, S., & Birch, H. G. (1968). *Temperament and behavior disorders in children.* New York: New York University Press.

Thomas, E. J. (1973). Bias of therapist influence in behavioral assessment. *Journal of Behavior Therapy and Experimental Psychiatry, 4,* 107-111.

Thoresen, C. E., & Powell, L. H. (1992). Type A behavior pattern: New perspectives on theory, assessment, and intervention. *Journal of Consulting and Clinical Psychology, 60,* 595-604.

Thorndike, R. L., Hagen, E. P., & Sattler, J. M. (1986). *What is intelligence? Contemporary viewpoints on its nature and definition.* Chicago: Riverside.

Thorne, F. C. (1967). *Integrative psychology.* Brandon, VT: Clinical Psychology Publishing Co.

Thorne, F. C. (1972). Clinical judgment. In R. H. Woody & J. D. Woody (Eds.), *Clinical assessment in counseling and psychotherapy* (pp. 30-85). Englewood Cliffs, NJ: Prentice-Hall.

Thorne, F. C. (1973). Eclectic psychotherapy. In R. Corsini (Ed.), *Current psychotherapies* (pp. 445-486). Itasca, IL: F. E. Peacock.

Thorpe, G. L., & Olson, S. L. (1997). *Behavior therapy: Concepts, procedures, and applications* (2nd ed.). Boston: Allyn & Bacon.

Tisdelle, D. A., & St. Lawrence, J. S. (1988). Adolescent interpersonal problem-solving skill training: Social validation and generalization. *Behavior Therapy, 19,* 171-182.

Todd, L. K. (1996). A computer-assisted expert system for clinical diagnosis of eating disorders: A potential learning tool for practitioners. *Professional Psychology: Research and Practice, 27,* 184–187.

Tomlinson, S. M., & Cheatham, H. E. (1989). Effects of counselor intake judgments on service to Black students using a university counseling center. *Counseling Psychology Quarterly, 2,* 105–111.

Tomlinson-Clarke, S., & Camilli, G. (1995). An exploratory study of counselor judgments in multicultural research. *Journal of Multicultural Counseling and Development, 23,* 237–245.

Tomlinson-Clarke, S., & Cheatham, H. E. (1993). Counselor and client ethnicity an counselor intake judgments. *Journal of Counseling Psychology, 40,* 267–270.

Totten, G., Lamb, D. H., & Reeder, G. D. (1990). *Tarasoff* and confidentiality in AIDS-related psychotherapy. *Professional Psychology: Research and Practice, 21,* 155–160.

Tremblay, R. E., Pagani-Kurtz, L., Masse, L. C., Vitaro, F., & Pihl, R. O. (1995). A bimodal preventive intervention for disruptive Kindergarten boys: Its impact through mid-adolescence. *Journal of Consulting and Clinical Psychology, 63,* 560–568.

Trickett, E. J., Dahiyal, C., & Selby, P. M. (1994). *Primary prevention in mental health: An annotated bibliography 1983–1991.* Rockville, MD: National Institute of Mental Health.

Tryon, G. S. (1989). A study of engagement and premature termination in a university counseling center. *Counseling Psychology Quarterly, 2,* 419–429.

Tryon, G. S. (1990). Session depth and smoothness in relation to the concept of engagement in counseling. *Journal of Counseling Psychology, 37,* 248–253.

Tulkin, S. R., & Frank, G. W. (1985). The changing role of psychologists in health maintenance organizations. *American Psychologist, 40,* 1125–1130.

Turk, D. C., & Rudy, T. E. (1990). Pain. In A. S. Bellack, M. Hersen, & A. E. Kazdin (Eds.), *International handbook of behavior modification and therapy* (2nd ed., pp. 399–413). New York: Plenum Press.

Turner, J. B., Kessler, R. C., & House, J. S. (1991). Factors facilitating adjustment to unemployment: Implcations for intervention. *American Journal of Community Psychology, 19,* 521–542.

Turner, S. M., Beidel, D. C., Dancu, C. V., & Stanley, M. A. (1989). An empirically derived inventory to measure social fears and anxiety: The Social Phobia and Anxiety Inventory. *Psychological Assessment: Journal of Consulting and Clinical Psychology, 1,* 35–40.

Turner, S. M., Beidel, D. C., & Long, P. J. (1992). Reduction of fear in social phobics: An examination of extinction patterns. *Behavior Therapy, 23,* 389–404.

Tutin, J. (1993). The persistence of initial beliefs in clinical judgment. *Journal of Social and Clinical Psychology, 12,* 319–335.

Tversky, A., & Kahneman, D. (1974). Judgment under uncertainty: Heuristics and biases. *Science, 185,* 1124–1131.

Twentyman, C. T., Rohrbeck, C. H., & Amish, P. (1984). A cognitive-behavioral model of child abuse. In Sanders (Ed.), *Violent individuals and families: A practitioner's handbook* (pp. 86–111). Springfield, IL: Charles C. Thomas.

Tyrka, A. R., Cannon, T., Haslam, N., Mednick, S., Schulsinger, F., Schulsinger, H., & Parnas, J. (1995). The latent structure of schizotypy: I. Premorbid indicators of a taxon of individuals at risk for schizophrenia spectrum disorders. *Journal of Abnormal Psychology, 104,* 173–183.

U.S. Department of Education. (1995). *Integrated postsecondary education data system (IPEDS) "completion" survey.* Washington: D.C.: National Center for Education Statistics.

Uchino, B. N., Cacioppo, J. T. & Kiecolt-Glaser, J. K. (1996). The relationship between social support and physiological processes: A review with emphasis on underlying mechanisms and implications for health. *Psychological Bulletin, 119,* 488-531.

Ullmann, L. P., & Krasner, L. (Eds.). (1965). *Case studies in behavior modification.* New York: Holt, Rinehart & Winston.

Ullmann, L. P., & Krasner, L. (1975). *A psychological approach to abnormal behavior.* Englewood Cliffs, NJ: Prentice-Hall.

Ustad, K. L., Rogers, R., Sewell, K. W., Guarnaccia, C. A. (1996). Restoration of competency to stand trial: Assessment with the Georgia Court Competency Test and the Competency Screening Test. *Law and Human Behavior, 20,* 131-146.

Vaillant, G. E. (1984). The disadvantages of DSM-II outweigh its advantages. *American Journal of Psychiatry, 141,* 542-545.

Vaillant, G. E. (1994). Behavioral medicine over the life span. In S. J. Blumenthal, K. Mathews, & S. M. Weiss (Eds.), *New research frontiers in behavioral medicine: Proceedings of the National Conference.* Washington, DC: National Institute of Health.

Vallis, T. M., & Howes, J. L. (1995). The field of clinical psychology: Arriving at a definition. *Canadian Psychology, 37,* 120-127.

Van Denburg, T. F., & Kiesler, D. J. (1996). An interpersonal communication perspective on resistance in psychotherapy. *In Session: Psychotherapy in Practice, 2,* 55-66.

VandeCreek, L., Knapp, S., & Brace, K. (1990). Mandatory continuing education for licensed psychologists: Its rationale and current implementation. *Professional Psychology: Research and Practice, 21,* 135-140.

VandenBos, G. R. (1993). U.S. mental health policy: Proactive evolution in the midst of health care reform. *American Psychologist, 48,* 283-290.

VandenBos, G. R., DeLeon, P. H., & Belar, C. D. (1991). How many psychological practitioners are needed? It's too early to know. *Professional Psychology: Research and Practice, 22,* 441-448.

VandenBos, G. R., & Stapp, J. (1983). Service providers in psychology: Results of the 1982 APA human resources survey. *American Psychologist, 38,* 1330-1352.

Vane, J. R. (1981). The Thematic Apperception Test: A review. *Clinical Psychology Review, 1,* 319-336.

Vane, J. R., & Motta, R. W. (1990). Group intelligence tests. In G. Goldstein & M. Hersen (Eds.), *Handbook of psychological assessment* (pp. 102-119). New York: Pergamon Press.

Vermande, M. M., van den Bercken, J. H., & De Bruyn, E. E. (1996). Effects of diagnostic classification systems on clinical hypothesis generation. *Journal of Psychopathology and Behavioral Assessment, 18,* 49-70.

Viken, R. J., & McFall, R. M. (1994). Paradox lost: Implications of contemporary reinforcement theory for behavior therapy. *Current Directions in Psychological Science, 3,* 121-125.

von Bertalanffy, L. (1968). *General systems theory.* New York: Braziller.

Wachtel, P. (1977). *Psychoanalysis and behavior therapy.* New York: Basic Books.

Wada, J., & Rasmussen, T. (1960). Intracarotid injection of sodium amytal for the lateralization of cerebral speech dominance. *Journal of Neurosurgery, 17,* 266-282.

Wakefield, H., & Underwager, R. (1992). Recovered memories of alleged sexual abuse: Lawsuits against parents. *Behavioral Sciences and the Law, 10*, 483-507.

Walker, C. E., Hedberg, A., Clement, P. W., & Wright, L. (1981). *Clinical procedures for behavior therapy.* Englewood Cliffs, NJ: Prentice-Hall.

Walker, E. F., Grimes, K. E., Davis, D. M., & Smith, A. J. (1993). Childhood precursors of schizophrenia: Facial expressions of emotion. *American Journal of Psychiatry, 150*, 1654-1660.

Wallace, C. J. (1993). Psychiatric rehabilitation. *Psychophar macology Bulletin, 29*, 537-548.

Wallace, C. J., Liberman, R. P., Mackain, S. J., Blackwell, G., & Eckman, T. A. (1992). Effectiveness and replicability of modules for teaching social and instrumental skills to the severely mentally ill. *American Journal of Psychiatry, 149*, 654-658.

Wallen, R. W. (1956). *Clinical psychology: The study of persons.* New York: McGraw-Hill.

Wallerstein, J., Corbin, S. B., & Lewis, J. M. (1988). Children of divorce: A ten-year study. In E. M. Hetherington & J. Arasteh (Eds.), *Impact of divorce, single-parenting and stepparenting on children* (pp. 198-214). Hillsdale, NJ: Lawrence Erlbaum Associates.

Walsh, K. (1987). *Neuropsychology: A clinical approach* (2nd ed.). Edinburgh: Churchill Livingstone.

Ward, J. C., & Naster, B. J. (1991). Reliability of an observational system used to monitor behavior in a mental health residential treatment unit. *Journal of Mental Health Administration, 18*, 64-68.

Watkins, L. E., Jr., Campbell, V. L., Nieberding, K., & Hallmark, R. (1995). Contemporary practice of psychological assessment by clinical psychologists. *Professional Psychology: Research and Practice, 26*, 54-60.

Watley, D. J. (1968). Feedback training and improvement of clinical forecasting. *Journal of Counseling Psychology, 15*, 167-171.

Watson, D., & Friend, R. (1969). Measurement of social-evaluative anxiety. *Journal of Consulting and Clinical Psychology, 33*, 448-457.

Watson, J. B. (1913). Psychology as the behaviorist views it. *Psychological Review, 20*, 158-177.

Watson, J. B. (1924). *Behaviorism.* New York: W. W. Norton.

Watson, J. B. (1930). *Behaviorism* (rev. ed.). New York: W. W. Norton.

Watson, J. B., & Rayner, R. (1920). Conditioned emotional reactions. *Journal of Experimental Psychology, 3*, 1-14.

Watson, R. I. (1951). *The clinical method in psychology.* New York: Harper.

Webb, E., Campbell, D. T., Schwartz, R. D., & Sechrest, L. B. (1966). *Unobtrusive measures: Nonreactive research in the social sciences.* Chicago: Rand-McNally.

Webster, C. (1996). Hispanic and Anglo interviewer and respondent ethnicity and gender: The impact on survey response quality. *Journal of Marketing Research, 33*, 62-72.

Webster-Stratton, C. (1988). Mothers' and fathers' perceptions of child deviance: Roles of parent and child behaviors and parent adjustment. *Journal of Consulting and Clinical Psychology, 56*, 909-915.

Wechsler, D. (1967). *Manual for the WPPSI.* New York: Psychological Corporation.

Wechsler, D. (1981). *Wechsler Adult Intelligence Scale-Revised.* New York: Psychological Corporation.

Wechsler, D. (1991). *WISC-III: Manual.* San Antonio, TX: Psychological Corporation.

Weick, K. E. (1968). Systematic observational methods. In G. Lindzey & E. Aronson (Eds.), *Handbook of social psychology* (Vol. 2, 2nd ed., pp. 357–451). Reading, MA: Addison-Wesley.

Weiss, G., & Hechtman, L. T. (1986). *Hyperactive children grow up.* New York: Guilford Press.

Weiss, R. D., Najavits, L. M., Muenz, L. R., & Hufford, C. (1995). Twelve-month test-retest reliability of the Structured Clinical Interview for DSM-III-R Personality Disorders in cocaine-dependent patients. *Comprehensive Psychiatry, 36,* 384–389.

Weissman, H. N. (1985). Psycholegal standards and the role of psychological assessment in personal injury litigation. *Behavioral Sciences and the Law, 3,* 135–148.

Weissman, H. N. (1991). Child custody evaluations: Fair and unfair professional practices. *Behavioral Sciences and the Law, 9,* 469–476.

Weissman, M. M., & Markowitz, J. C. (1994). Interpersonal psychotherapy: Current status. *Archives of General Psychiatry, 51,* 599–606.

Weisz, J. R., Weiss, B., Alicke, M. D., & Klotz, M. L. (1987). Effectiveness of psychotherapy with children and adolescents: A meta-analysis for clinicians. *Journal of Consulting and Clinical Psychology, 55,* 542–549.

Weisz, J. R., Weiss, B., & Donnenberg, G. R. (1992). The lab versus the clinic: Effects of child and adolescent psychotherapy. *American Psychologist, 47,* 1578–1585.

Wenar, C. (1994). *Developmental psychopathology: From infancy through adolescence* (3rd ed.). New York: McGraw-Hill.

Wernick, R. (1956). *They've got your number.* New York: W. W. Norton.

Werry, J. S., & Quay, H. C. (1971). The prevalence of behavior symptoms of younger elementary school children. *American Journal of Orthopsychiatry, 41,* 136–143.

West, M., Bondy, E., & Hutchinson, S. (1991). Interviewing institutionalized elders: Threats to validity. *Journal of Nursing Scholarship, 23,* 171–176.

Wexler, B. E., & Cicchetti, D. V. (1992). The outpatient treatment of depression. Implications of outcome research for clinical practice. *Journal of Nervous and Mental Diseases, 180,* 277–286.

Wexler, D. B. (Ed). (1992). *Therapeutic jurisprudence: The law as a therapeutic agent.* Durham, NC: Carolina Academic Press.

Whalen, C. K., Henker, B., & Dotemoto, S. (1980). Methylphenidate and hyperactivity: Effects on teacher behaviors. *Science, 208,* 1280–1282.

Whalen, C. K., Henker, B., & Hinshaw, S. P. (1985). Cognitive-behavior therapies for hyperactive children: Premises, problems, and prospects. *Journal of Abnormal Child Psychology, 13,* 391–410.

Whitehead, W. E. (1992). Behavioral medicine approaches to gastrointestinal disorders. *Journal of Consulting and Clinical Psychology, 60,* 605–612.

Wicherski, M., Woerheide, K., & Kohout, J. (1996). *Preliminary report: 1995 salaries in psychology.* Washington, D.C.: American Psychological Association Research Office.

Wickrama, K., Conger, R. D., & Lorenz, F. O. (1995). Work, marriage, lifestyle, and changes in men's physical health. *Journal of Behavioral Medicine, 18,* 97–112.

Wicks-Nelson, R., & Israel, A. C. (1991). *Behavior disorders of childhood* (2nd ed.). Englewood Cliffs, NJ: Prentice Hall.

Widiger, T. A., & Frances, A. (1985). The DSM-III personality disorders: Perspectives from psychology. *Archives of General Psychiatry, 42,* 615–623.

Widiger, T. A., Frances, A. J., Pincus, H. A., Davis, W. W., & First, M. B. (1991). Toward an empirical classification for the DSM-IV. *Journal of Abnormal Psychology, 100,* 280–288.

Widiger, T. A., Mangine, S., Corbitt, E. M., Ellis, C. G., & Thomas, G. V. (1995). *Personality Disorder Interview-IV: A semistructured interview for the assessment of personality disorders.* Odessa, Florida: Psychological Assessment Resources.

Widiger, T. A., Trull, T. J., Hurt, S. W., Clarkin, J., & Frances, A. (1987). A multidimensional scaling of the DSM-III personality disorders. *Archives of General Psychiatry, 44,* 557–563.

Wiggins, J. G. (1994). Would you want your child to be a psychologist? *American Psychologist, 49,* 485–492.

Wiggins, J. S. (1973). *Personality and prediction: Principles of personality assessment.* Reading, MA: Addison-Wesley.

Wiggins, J. S. (1981). Clinical and statistical prediction: Where are we and where do we go from here? *Clinical Psychology Review, 1,* 3–18.

Wiggins, J. S. (1982). Circumplex models of interpersonal behavior in clinical psychology. In P. C. Kendall & J. N. Butcher (Eds.), *Handbook of research methods in clinical psychology* (pp. 183–221). New York: John Wiley.

Wiggins, J. S., & Pincus, A. L. (1989). Conceptions of personality disorders and dimensions of personality. *Psychological Assessment: A Journal of Consulting and Clinical Psychology, 1,* 305–316.

Wilkinson, G. S. (1993). *WRAT-3: Wide range achievement test administration manual.* Wilmington, Delaware: Wide Range, Inc.

Williams, C. (1988). The relationship of ethnic group membership on levels of responding skills to Black and White clients. *College Student Journal, 22,* 401–403.

Williams, C. L., Arnold, C. B., & Wynder, E. L. (1977). Primary prevention of chronic disease beginning in childhood: The Know Your Body Program: Design of study. *Preventive Medicine, 6,* 344–357.

Williams, C. L., & Heikes, E. J. (1993). The importance of researcher's gender in the in-depth interview: Evidence from two case studies of male nurses. *Gender and Society, 7,* 280–291.

Williams, J. M., Voelker, S., & Ricciardi, P. W. (1995). Predictive validity of the K-ABC for exceptional preschoolers. *Psychology in the Schools, 32,* 178–185.

Williams, L. (1994). Recall of childhood trauma: A prospective study of women's memories of child sexual abuse. *Journal of Consulting and Clinical Psychology, 62,* 1167–1176.

Williams, R. B., Jr., & Barefoot, J. C. (1988). Coronary-prone behavior: The emerging role of the hostility complex. In B. K. Houston & C. R. Snyder (Eds.), *Type A behavior pattern: Research, theory and intervention* (pp. 189–211). New York: John Wiley and Sons.

Williams, T. R. (1967). *Field methods in the study of culture.* New York: Holt, Rinehart, & Winston.

Wills, R. M., Faitler, S. L., & Snyder, D. K. (1987). Distinctiveness of behavioral versus insight-oriented marital therapy: An empirical analysis. *Journal of Consulting and Clinical Psychology, 55,* 685–690.

Wilson, G. T. (1985). Limitations of meta-analysis in the evaluation of the effects of psychological therapy. *Clinical Psychology Review, 5,* 35–47.

Wilson, G. T. (1995). Behavior therapy. In R. J. Corsini & D. Wedding, D. (Eds.), *Current psychotherapies* (5th ed.). Itasca, Illinois: Peacock Publishers, Inc. (pp. 197–228).

Wilson, G. T., & Rachman, S. J. (1983). Meta-analysis and the evaluation of psychotherapy outcome: Limitations and liabilities. *Journal of Consulting and Clinical Psychology, 51,* 54–64.

Winnicott, D. W. (1965). *The maturational processes and the facilitating environment.* New York: International Universities Press.

Wirt, R. D., Lachar, D., Klinedinst, J. K., & Seat, P. D. (1984). *Multidimensional description of child personality: A manual for the Personality Inventory of Children.* Los Angeles: Western Psychological Services.

Wittchen, H. U. (1994). Reliability and validity studies of the WHO-Composite International Diagnostic Interview (CIDI): A critical review. *Journal of Psychiatric Research, 28,* 57–84.

Wittchen, H. U., Kessler, R. C., Zhao, S., & Abelson, J. (1995). Reliability and clinical validity of UM-CIDI DSM-III-R generalized anxiety disorder. *Journal of Psychiatric Research, 29,* 95–110.

Wolchik, S., Braver, S., & Sandler, I. (1985). Maternal versus joint custody: Children's post-separation experiences and adjustment. *Journal of Child Clinical Psychology, 14,* 5–10.

Wolfe, D. A. (1987). *Child abuse: Implications for child development and psychopathology.* Newbury Park, CA: Sage.

Wolpe, J. (1958). *Psychotherapy by reciprocal inhibition.* Stanford, CA: Stanford University Press.

Wolpe, J. (1982). *The practice of behavior therapy* (3rd ed.). New York: Pergamon Press.

Wolpe, J., & Lang, P. J. (1969). *Fear Survey Schedule.* San Diego, CA: Educational and Industrial Testing Service.

Wolpe, J., & Lazarus, A. A. (1966). *Behavior therapy techniques: A guide to the treatment of neuroses.* New York: Pergamon Press.

Wong, B. Y. L. (1986). Problems and issues in the definition of learning disabilities. In J. K. Torgesen & B. Y. L. Wong (Eds.), *Psychological and educational perspectives on learning disabilities* (pp. 3–26). New York: Academic Press.

Wood, J. M., Nezworski, M. T., & Stejskal, W. J. (1996). *The comprehensive system for the Rorschach: A critical examination. Psychological Science, 7,* 3–10.

Wood, L. F., & Jacobson, N. S. (1985). Marital distress. In D. Barlow (Ed.), *Clinical handbook of psychological disorders* (pp. 344–416). New York: Guilford Press.

Woodcock, R., & Johnson, M. (1977). *Woodcock-Johnson Psycho-educational Battery.* Allen, TX: DLM/Teaching Resources.

Woodcock, R. W., & Johnson, M. B. (1989). *Woodcock-Johnson Psycho-educational Battery-Revised.* Allen, TX: DLM/Teaching Resources.

Woodworth, R. S. (1920). *Personal data sheet.* Chicago: Stoelting.

World Health Organization (1994). *Schedules for clinical assessment in neuropsychiatry: Manual.* Geneva: WHO.

Wortman, C. B., & Lehman, D. R. (1985). Reactions to victims of life crises: Support attempts that fail. In I. G. Sarason & B. R. Sarason (Eds.), *Social support: Theory, research, and applications* (pp. 463–489). Dordrecht, The Netherlands: Martinus Nijhoff.

Wrightsman, L., Nietzel, M. T., & Fortune, W. (1998). *Psychology and the legal system* (4th ed.). Pacific Grove, CA: Brooks/Cole.

Wulfert, E., Greenway, D. E., & Dougher, M. J. (1996). A logical functional analysis of reinforcement-based disorders: Alcoholism and pedophilia. *Journal of Consulting and Clinical Psychology, 64,* 1140–1151.

Wyatt, F. (1968). What is clinical psychology? In A. Z. Guiora & M. A. Brandwin (Eds.), *Perspectives in clinical psychology* (pp. 222–238). Princeton, NJ: D. Van Nostrand.

Yalom, I. D. (1985). *The theory and practice of group psychotherapy* (3rd ed.). New York: Basic Books.

Ying, Y. (1989). Nonresponse on the Center for Epidemiological Studies depression scale in Chinese Americans. *International Journal of Social Psychiatry, 35,* 156-163.

Yoshikawa, H. (1994). Prevention as cumulative protection: Effects of early family support and education on chronic delinquency and its risks. *Psychological Bulletin, 115,* 28-54.

Young, A. W., & De Haan, E. H. F. (1992). Face recognition and awareness after brain injury. In A. D. Milner & M. D. Rugg (Eds.), *The neuropsychology of consciousness.* San Diego, CA: Academic Press.

Young, L. D. (1992). Psychological factors in rheumatoid arthritis. *Journal of Consulting and Clinical Psychology, 60,* 619-627.

Yutrzenka, B. A. (1995). Making a case for training in ethnic and cultural diversity in increasing treatment efficacy. *Journal of Consulting and Clinical Psychology, 63,* 197-206.

Zabow, T., & Cohen, A. (1993). South African psychiatrists' criteria for predicting dangerousness. *Medicine & Law, 12,* 417-430.

Zax, M., & Specter, G. A. (1974). *An introduction to community psychology.* New York: John Wiley.

Zeanah, C. H. (1996). Beyond insecurity: A reconceptualization of attachment disorders of infancy. *Journal of Consulting and Clinical Psychology, 64,* 42-51.

Zegiob, L. E., Arnold, S., & Forehand, R. (1975). An examination of observer effects in parent-child interactions. *Child Development, 46,* 509-512.

Zigler, E., Taussig, C., & Black, K. (1992). Early childhood intervention: A promising preventative for juvenile delinquency. *American Psychologist, 47,* 997-1006.

Zilboorg, G., & Henry, G. W. (1941). *A history of medical psychology.* New York: W. W. Norton.

Zimet, C. N., & Throne, F. M. (1965). *Preconference materials.* Conference on the Professional Preparation of Clinical Psychologists. Washington, DC: American Psychological Association.

Zimmerman, M. (1983). Methodological issues in the assessment of life events: A review of issues and research. *Clinical Psychology Review, 3,* 339-370.

Ziskin, J., & Faust, D. (1988). *Coping with psychiatric and psychological testimony* (4th ed., Vols. 1-3). Marina del Rey, CA: Law & Psychology Press.

Zook A., II, & Walton, J. M. (1989). Theoretical orientations and work settings of clinical and counseling psychologists: A current perspective. *Professional Psychology: Research and Practice, 20,* 23-31.

Zuardi, A. W., Loureiro, S. R., & Rodrigues, C. R. C. (1995). Reliability, validity, and factorial dimensions of the Interactive Observation Scale for Psychiatric Inpatients. *Acta Psychiatrica Scandinavica, 91,* 247-251.

Zubin, J., & Spring, B. (1977). Vulnerability—A new view of schizophrenia. *Journal of Abnormal Psychology, 86,* 103-126.

Zubin, J. (1969). The role of models in clinical psychology. In L. L'Abate (Ed.), *Models of clinical psychology* (pp. 5-12). Atlanta: Georgia State College.

Zubin, J., Eron, L. D., & Schumer, F. (1965). *An experimental approach to projective techniques.* New York: John Wiley.

Zuckerman, M., & Lubin, B. (1965). *Manual for the multiple affect adjective checklist.* San Diego, CA: Educational and Industrial Testing Service.

Zytowski, D. G. (1985). *Kuder Occupational Interest Survey manual supplement.* Chicago: Science Research Associates.

Index

Table X   Significant Dates and Events in the History of Clinical Psychology

1879 Wilhelm Wundt establishes first formal psychology laboratory at the University of Leipzig.

1885 Sir Francis Galton establishes first mental testing center at the South Kensington Museum, London.

1890 James McKeen Cattell coins term *mental test.*

1892 American Psychological Association (APA) founded.

1895 Breuer and Freud publish *Studies in Hysteria.*

1896 Lightner Witmer founds first psychological clinic, University of Pennsylvania.

1905 Binet-Simon intelligence scale published in France.

1907 Witmer founds first clinical journal, *The Psychological Clinic.*

1908 First clinical internship offered at Vineland Training School.

1909 William Healy founds first child-guidance center, the Juvenile Psychopathic Institute, Chicago. Freud lectures at Clark University.

1910 Goddard's English translation of the 1908 revision of the Binet-Simon intelligence scale published.

1912 J.B. Watson publishes *Psychology as a Behaviorist Views It.*

1916 Terman's Stanford-Binet intelligence test published.

1917 Clinicians break away from APA to form American Association of Clincal Psychology (AACP).

1919 AACP rejoins APA as its clinical section.

1920 Watson and Rayner demonstrate that a child's fear can be learned.

1921 James McKeen Cattell forms Psychological Corporation.

1924 David Levy introduces Rorschach Inkblot Test to America. Mary Cover Jones employs learning principles to remove children's fears.

1931 Clinical section of APA appoints committee on training standards.

1935 Thematic Apperception Test (TAT) published.

1936 First clinical textbook, *Clincial Psychology,* published by Louttit.

1937 Clinical section of APA breaks away to form American Association for Applied Psychology (AAAP).

1938 First Buros *Mental Measurement Yearbook* published.

1939 Wechsler-Bellevue Intelligence Test published.

1942 Carl Rogers publishes *Counseling and Psychotherapy,* outlining an alternative to psychodynamic therapy.

1943 Minnesota Multiphasic Personality Inventory (MMPI) published.

1945 AAAP rejoins APA.

Journal of Clinical Psychology published.

Connecticut State Board of Examiners in Psychology issues first certificate to practice psychology.

1946 Veterans Administration and National Institute of Mental Health begin support for training of clinical psychologists.

1947 American Board of Examiners in Professional Psychology organized.

APA begins to evaluate graduate programs in clinical psychology.

Shakow Report recommends clinical training standards to APA.

Certification Committee of Canadian Psychological Association recommends standards for clinical psychologists in Canada.

1949 Colorado conference on training in clinical psychology convenes, recommends "Boulder Model."

Sixteen P–F personality test pulished.

1950 APA publishes first standards for approved internships in clinical psychology.

1952 American Psychiatric Association's *Diagnostic and Statistical Manual (DSM-I)* published.

1953 APA *Ethical Standards for Psychologists* published.

1955 Wechsler Adult Intelligence Test published.